1988 TAX GUIDE FOR COLLEGE TEACHERS

AND OTHER COLLEGE PERSONNEL

For filing 1987 tax returns

Allen Bernstein, Ph.D.

Academic Information Service, Inc.

Washington, D.C. • College Park, MD

© *1987 by Academic Information Service, Inc.*
ISBN 0-916018-36-9

All rights reserved. No part of this publication may be reproduced, stored in a retrieval system, or transmitted, in any form or by any means, electronic, mechanical, photocopying, recording, or otherwise, without permission in writing from the Publisher. Printed in the United States of America.

This publication is designed to provide accurate and authoritative information in regard to the subject matter covered. It is sold with the understanding that the publisher is not engaged in rendering legal, accounting, or other professional service. If legal advice or other expert assistance is required, the services of a competent professional person should be sought.

From a Declaration of Principles jointly adopted by a Committee of the American Bar Association and a Committee of Publishers

Academic Information Service, Inc.
Post Office Box 1718
College Park, MD 20740

"The art of taxation consists in so plucking the goose as to obtain the largest amount of feathers with the least amount of hissing."

—Jean-Baptiste Colbert
Finance Minister to Louis XIV

PREFACE

This 1988 edition of the *Tax Guide for College Teachers* is designed to keep College Teachers informed about the latest tax laws and rulings that apply to them. The publication of this edition has been made possible by the continuing interest and support shown by College Teachers all across the nation.

As you're no doubt aware, Congress enacted a Tax Reform Act in the middle of 1986, phasing in changes in most every area of the tax law affecting College Teachers. Over the next few years, the most sweeping overhaul of the tax system in 40 years will be taking full effect.

Many of the changes in the 1986 Tax Reform Act first take effect on 1987 tax returns, as discussed in this year's edition of the *Tax Guide for College Teachers*. Other changes will be instituted starting with 1988 tax returns. And still others will be phased in over a period of years. For example, interest on consumer loans is only partly deductible on 1987 tax returns, with the deduction first disappearing altogether on 1991 tax returns.

Chapter 0 of this year's Tax Guide gives a brief outline of the major provisions of the 1986 Tax Reform Act. More detailed information affecting your 1987 tax return is incorporated into the main body of the book.

Ironically, the initial goal of the 1986 Tax Reform Act was to produce a simplification of the tax law. Instead, the exact opposite has taken place.

For example, instead of all interest being deductible, there are now 5 different categories of interest, each treated differently. Instead of all wage-earners being able to deduct up to $2,000 to an IRA, only some will be entitled to a full deduction with others entitled to make partly-deductible or non-deductible contributions instead. And now, if your children have sufficient income of their own from savings, you may even have to apply the rates on *your* tax return to compute the tax on *their* returns.

Because of the extent and complex nature of the new rules, the IRS has not yet issued the necessary regulations to clarify various aspects of the new law. However, they have issued a number of less official "Notices", mostly in question and answer form, which gives interim guidance as reported in this year's edition of the *Tax Guide for College Teachers*.

Meanwhile, Congress is considering further changes in the tax law. Some of these changes are considered to be "technical corrections" to the 1986 Tax Reform Act. Others are to close some loopholes that were discovered in the new law. And many others are to correct some unintended injustices in the new law as well as to raise new revenues to combat the excessive budgetary deficit.

Next year's edition of the *Tax Guide for College Teachers* will cover all the new regulations, law changes, court cases, and new interpretations expected during the upcoming year.

More than ever before, it is those who understand how to use the new law that will enjoy a tax benefit when compared with their less-knowledgeable colleagues.

Remember that saving on taxes is worth more than a raise in salary. The extra salary gets ravaged by Federal and State taxes at the highest bracket your taxes reach. It may also be reduced by social security or retirement takeouts — usually without any increase in benefits. But the money you save by knowing the tax laws goes right into your pocket; nothing is taken out before it reaches you.

TABLE OF CONTENTS

Chapter 0:   The 1986 Tax Reform Act 9

Chapter 1:   Basic Rules 15

    Section 1:   Basic Steps in Computing Your Tax 15
    Section 2:   Basic Rules for Deducting Business Expenses 21
    Section 3:   Common Mistakes 22
    Section 4:   Claiming the Standard Deduction 24
    Section 5:   Tax Returns of Dependent Children 25
    Section 6:   Single, Separate, and Joint Returns 27
    Section 7:   Recordkeeping 29
    Section 8:   Yearend Strategies for Lowering Taxes 30
    Section 9:   Free or Low-Rent Housing 33

Chapter 2:   Books, Supplies, and Equipment 34

Chapter 3:   Home Office 45

    Section 1:   When Can You Deduct for a Home Office? 45
    Section 2:   Computation of Home Office Expenses 57

Chapter 4:   Expensing and Depreciation 63

    Section 1:   Introduction 63
    Section 2:   Expensing Method 65
    Section 3:   Depreciation 67

Chapter 5:   Interest 78

Chapter 6:   Medical Expenses 84

Chapter 7:   Charitable Contributions 93

Chapter 8:   Household Services and Child Care 101

Chapter 9:   Tax Deductions for Homeowners 109

    Section 1:   Interest 109
    Section 2:   Taxes 118
    Section 3:   Capital Gains on Sale of a House 121
    Section 4:   Renting a Home to Others 126

Chapter 10:   Automobile Expenses 133

Chapter 11:   State and Local Taxes 146

Chapter 12:   Moving Expenses 151

Chapter 13:	**Divorce and Separation**	**156**
Chapter 14:	**Investing Your Money**	**162**
Section 1:	Capital Gains Tax	162
Section 2:	Passive Loss Rules	166
Section 3:	Municipal Bonds	168
Section 4:	Mutual Funds	170
Section 5:	Special Types of Mutual Funds	176
Section 6:	Money-Market Accounts	178
Chapter 15:	**Income Shifting**	**183**
Chapter 16:	**Tax-Sheltered Plans**	**189**
Section 1:	Benefit of Tax-Deferral	189
Section 2:	Individual Retirement Accounts	190
Section 3:	Keogh Plans	209
Section 4:	Tax-Sheltered Annuities	215
Section 5:	Deferred Compensation Plans	225
Chapter 17:	**Miscellaneous Deductions**	**227**
Section 1:	Basic Rules	227
Section 2:	Employment-Related Expenses	231
Section 3:	Other Miscellaneous Deductions	232
Chapter 18:	**Expenses of Attending School**	**235**
Section 1:	Basic Rules for Deducting Educational Expenses	235
Section 2:	When Do Educational Expenses Qualify for Deduction?	236
Section 3:	When Are Deductions Disallowed Under Rule A?	239
Section 4:	When Are Deductions Disallowed Under Rule B?	244
Section 5:	Temporary vs. Indefinite Absence from Profession	246
Section 6:	Which Expenses Are Deductible?	249
Chapter 19:	**Retirement Plans**	**253**
Section 1:	Introduction	253
Section 2:	Payments from Retirement Plans	253
Section 3:	Contributions to Retirement Plans	256
Section 4:	Social Security	263
Chapter 20:	**Entertainment Expenses**	**265**
Chapter 21:	**Withholding**	**271**
Chapter 22:	**Travel**	**275**
Section 1:	Basic Rules on Deducting Travel Expenses	275
Section 2:	More Than One Job Location	285

Section 3:	Temporary Job Away from Home	.288
Section 4:	Travel to Look for Employment	.301
Section 5:	Travel to Professional Conventions	.302
Section 6:	Travel Which Combines Business With Pleasure	.302
A:	Travel Within the United States	.302
B:	Travel Outside the United States	.303
Section 7:	Educational Travel	.308
Section 8:	Discount Rates for Teachers	.308

Chapter 23:	**Estate and Gift Tax**	**.310**
Section 1:	Introduction	.310
Section 2:	Gift Tax	.310
Section 3:	Estate Tax	.311

Chapter 24:	**Will Your Tax Return Be Audited?**	**.317**
Section 1:	Audits	.317
Section 2:	Private IRS Rulings	.330

Chapter 25:	**Casualty Losses**	**.334**

Chapter 26:	**Outside Business Activity**	**.341**
Section 1:	Basic Rules	.341
Section 2:	Tax Benefits	.349
Section 3:	Paying Family Members for Assistance	.353
Section 4:	Outside Activities Producing a Loss	.356

Chapter 27:	**Foreign Income**	**.360**

Chapter 28:	**Tax-Free Grants**	**.366**
Section 1:	Basic Rules	.366
Section 2:	New Rules for Grants Awarded on or After August 17, 1986	.367
Section 3:	Grants Awarded Before August 17, 1986	.370
Section 4:	How to Claim the Income Tax Deduction	.389
Section 5:	Exemption from Social Security Tax	.390

Chapter 29:	**Research Expenses of College Teachers**	**.393**
Section 1:	Deduction for Research Expenses	.393
Section 2:	Research Tax Credit	.397

Chapter 30:	**Alternative Minimum Tax**	**.399**

Chapter 0

The 1986 Tax Reform Act

The 1986 Tax Reform Act has made a basic overhaul of the tax system, taking full effect over the next few years. This chapter contains a brief outline of the major changes that affect your 1987 tax return. (Other changes, to be discussed fully in next year's edition, will affect your 1988 tax return.)

It should be cautioned that the IRS has not yet issued final regulations interpreting various provisions of the law. A more complete understanding of how to negotiate the best path through the new law awaits this guidance. Further details will be contained in next year's edition of this Tax Guide.

Highlights of the 1986 Tax Reform Act

New Tax Brackets

A major thrust of the 1986 Tax Reform Act is to lower the tax bracket rates for most individuals, starting with 1987 tax returns. However, the tax rate reductions do not actually take full effect until 1988. For 1987, there is a transitional tax rate structure, intermediate between the 1986 rates and the 1988 rates. The following table gives the new rate schedules based on *taxable income*. (*Taxable income* is equal to *adjusted gross income* less *personal exemptions* and *deductions*.)

1987
Taxable Income Brackets

Tax Rate	Joint Returns	Heads of Household	Singles
11%	0 – $3,000	0 – $2,500	0 – $1,800
15%	3,001 – 28,000	2,501 – 23,000	1,801 – 16,800
28%	28,001 – 45,000	23,001 – 38,000	16,801 – 27,000
35%	45,001 – 90,000	38,001 – 80,000	27,001 – 54,000
38.5%	Above 90,000	Above 80,000	Above 54,000

1988
Taxable Income Brackets

Tax Rate	Joint Returns	Heads of Household	Singles
15%	0 – $29,750	0 – $25,300	0 – $17,850
28%	Above $29,750	Above $25,300	Above $17,850

The above 1988 table is somewhat misleading. The benefit of the 15% bracket will be phased out for higher income individuals. This phase-out will occur between

$71,900 and $149,250 for joint filers; between $61,650 and $123,790 for heads of household; and between $43,150 and $89,560 for singles. The phase-out is accomplished by levying a 5% surtax on income falling into the above phase-out ranges. This is the equivalent of a third tax bracket of 33% (28% + 5% surtax) in these income ranges. For example, joint filers will pay tax for 1988 as though the above table had a third tax bracket of 33% applying to taxable income between $71,900 and $149,250.

For marrieds filing separately, all the dollar figures given above for joint returns are halved.

Standard Deduction

On 1988 tax returns, the standard deduction will be $5,000 for joint filers; $4,400 for heads of household; $3,000 for singles; and $2,500 for marrieds filing separately.

For 1987 tax returns, the 1987 standard deduction amounts are the same as the 1986 amounts, adjusted for inflation [cf. Chapter 1, Section 1].

Personal Exemptions

Personal exemptions are increased to $1,900 in 1987, $1,950 in 1988, and $2,000 in 1989. However, starting in 1988, personal exemptions will be phased out for higher income individuals in a manner similar to the phase-out of the 15% rate discussed right after the above tax tables. Each personal exemption adds $10,920 to the phase-out range discussed there.

For example, the extra phase-out range for a married couple with 2 children (a total of 4 personal exemptions) would be 4 × $10,920 = $43,680. This means that the 1988 effective 33% tax bracket would extend from $71,900 to $192,930 ($149,250 + $43,680). Above $192,930, the effective tax bracket reverts to 28%.

Marriage Deduction for Two-Earner Couples

The prior-law marriage deduction of up to $3,000 has been eliminated, starting with 1987 tax returns. This repeal combined with other features in the new law will make it advantageous for many married couples to file separately rather than jointly, starting with 1988 tax returns.

Income Averaging

The regular 4-year income averaging method has been repealed, starting with 1987 tax returns.

There has also been a change in the special 10-year income averaging method that applies to lump-sum distributions from retirement plans [cf. the *Retirement* chapter].

Deduction for State and Local Sales Tax

The itemized deduction for State and local sales tax has been repealed, starting with 1987 tax returns. The itemized deductions for State and local income taxes, real estate taxes, and personal property taxes have been retained [cf. the *State and Local Taxes* chapter].

Charitable Deduction for Nonitemizers

Starting with 1987 tax returns, only those who itemize their deductions can claim a charitable deduction. The prior-law charity deduction for nonitemizers has been repealed.

Medical Expenses

The floor under the medical expense deduction has been raised from 5% to 7.5%, starting with 1987 tax returns [cf. the *Medical Expenses* chapter].

Social Security Numbers Required for Children Over Age 4

You are supposed to have social security numbers for children over age 4 in order to claim them as dependents on your 1987 tax return. You list these numbers on line 6c of your 1987 Form 1040. Call your local social security office to get application forms [cf. Section 4 of the *Retirement Plans* chapter].

Employee Business Expenses and Miscellaneous Itemized Deductions

Unreimbursed travel expenses (including meals and lodging while away from home), formerly claimed as an *adjustment to income*, have been changed to a *miscellaneous deduction* on Schedule A [cf. the *Travel* chapter]. And the total of miscellaneous itemized deductions is now subject to a floor of 2% of a taxpayer's adjusted gross income [cf. the *Miscellaneous Deductions* chapter].

Mutual Fund Management Fees

Formerly, management fees on mutual funds (including money-market funds) were subtracted from income, with the net result being your investment income. But starting with the 1987 tax year, mutual funds will report as taxable income to you the investment income before management fees have been subtracted [cf. Section 4 of the *Investing Your Money* chapter]. You then have to claim management fees as an itemized miscellaneous deduction which, together with other miscellaneous itemized deductions, is now subject to a 2% of adjusted gross income floor [cf. the *Miscellaneous Deductions* chapter].

Business Meals and Entertainment

The deduction for business meals (including meals while traveling away from home) and entertainment is now generally equal to 80% of the expenses an individual incurs [cf. the *Travel* and *Entertainment* chapters].

Political Contributions Tax Credit

The former tax credit of as much as $100 for political contributions has been eliminated, starting with 1987 tax returns.

Scholarships, Fellowships, & Tax-Free Grants

Starting with amounts received for 1987 expenses or services, the income tax exclusion for scholarship and fellowship grants is limited to degree candidates and to amounts for tuition and course-required fees, books, supplies, and equipment. Additional amounts for room, board, or incidental expenses are not excludable. The $300 per month income tax exemption that applied under prior law for grants received by non-degree candidates has been eliminated. However, the total exemption from social security tax has survived.

Grants awarded before August 17, 1986 are *grandfathered*. That is, amounts received from such grants enjoy the same tax-free treatment as under the old rules, even if such amounts are received in 1987 or later.

Books, Supplies, Equipment, Furniture, Autos, etc.

New depreciation tables apply to these items. Under these tables, items are written off over a 5-year or 7-year period. Also, the basic expensing limitation has been raised from $5,000 to $10,000 [cf. the *Expensing* and *Depreciation* chapter]. For job-related auto travel, the standard mileage rate has been raised from 21 cents to 22½ cents per mile [cf. the *Automobile Expenses* chapter].

Rental Property

Residential rental property, first placed into business service after December 31, 1986, must be depreciated over a 27.5-year period using the straight-line method. For non-residential real estate the depreciation period is 31.5 years [cf. the *Expensing* and *Depreciation* chapter].

Also, special *passive-loss* rules will, in certain cases, prevent losses produced by rental property from being deducted. (These rules will not apply to the first $25,000 of losses for individuals who both participate actively in the management of their rental property and have adjusted gross income of less than $100,000, ignoring rental losses.) This provision will be phased in over a 5-year period. Amounts disallowed may be deducted in a later year when the property is disposed of or when there is net income from a similar activity to offset the carried-over losses [cf. Section 2 of the *Investing Your Money* chapter].

Capital Gains

The 60% exclusion for long-term capital gains has been eliminated for items sold after December 31, 1986. On 1988 tax returns, capital gains will be taxed at the same rate as wages or other ordinary income. On 1987 tax returns, the same is true except that a maximum rate of 28% is applied to long-term capital gains [cf. Section 1 of the *Investing Your Money* chapter].

Dividend Exclusion

The $100 dividend exclusion ($200 on joint returns) has been repealed, starting with 1987 tax returns.

Interest Deductions

The deduction for personal interest (e.g. interest on car loans, student loans, credit card balances, etc.) will be phased out over a 5-year period.

Interest on debt secured by a principal or second residence will remain fully deductible if the total debt does not exceed the purchase price of the residence plus the cost of improvements and amounts borrowed for educational or medical purposes. (There is a grandfathering provision if the debt on August 16, 1986 exceeded this amount.) Interest deductions on debt exceeding this amount will be phased out over a 5-year period. Under the 5-year phase-out rule, only 65% of affected interest will be deductible on 1987 tax returns with the deduction for such interest eliminated entirely starting with 1991 tax returns [cf. the *Homeowners* chapter].

A similar phase-out rule will apply to investment interest (e.g. margin interest on brokerage accounts) in excess of investment income (e.g. dividends) received. Also subject to phase-out will be losses from certain passive activities (e.g. investments in limited partnerships) in excess of passive income [cf. the *Interest* chapter].

IRAs

Starting with contributions based on 1987 earnings, the rules for IRAs are changed for singles with adjusted gross income more than $35,000 and joint filers with income more than $50,000. If such individuals are participants in an employer-sponsored retirement plan or tax-sheltered annuity, then they get no deduction for IRA contributions based on 1987 earnings. (This applies to both spouses filing a joint return even if only one spouse participates in a retirement plan.) However, they will be able to make non-deductible contributions of up to $2,000 to an IRA, with all earnings exempt from tax until taken out of the IRA account.

Singles with income less than $25,000 and joint filers with income less than $40,000 will be unaffected by the new rules. They will be able to make fully-deductible IRA contributions under the same rules applying to 1986 tax returns. Singles with income in the $25,000 – $35,000 range and joint filers with income in the $40,000 – $50,000 range will have their IRA deduction phased out if they participate in another retirement plan. Further details are contained in Section 2 of the *Tax-Sheltered Plans* chapter.

Retirement Annuities

Under prior law, most retirees who had contributed to their own pension plans were able to apply the *3-year rule*. Under this rule, retirement payouts were initially exempt from tax until all employee contributions were returned, provided a total return occurred during the first 3 years after retirement. This rule has been eliminated. Only a portion of each annuity payment will be tax-free based on the percentage of total annuity payments due to employee contributions [cf. the *Retirement Plans* chapter].

Tax-Sheltered Annuities

A new upper limit of $9,500 now applies, starting in 1987, to the annual contributions an individual can elect to contribute to tax-sheltered annuities under reduction-in-salary agreements. The $9,500 limit is reduced by any deductible contributions made to an IRA. The $9,500 limit is raised to as much as $12,500 for individuals who have worked for their current employer for at least 15 years, provided their previous contributions to tax-sheltered annuities with their current employer averaged less than $5,000 per year.

There is now an extra 10% penalty tax on withdrawals made from a tax-sheltered annuity prior to the date an individual reaches age $59^1/_2$, dies, or becomes disabled. This is the same penalty tax that applies to early withdrawals from an IRA. The 10% penalty tax will be waived if the withdrawal is used to pay medical expenses, if the individual has reached age 55 and has retired from his job, or if the distribution is part of a suitable series of periodic annuity payments. After 1988, further restrictions apply which generally prevent withdrawals from a tax-sheltered annuity before age 59¹/2 (except upon leaving your job) with or without a penalty [cf. Section 4 of the *Tax-Sheltered Plans* chapter].

Deferred Compensation Plans

A new annual limitation of $7,000 per year now applies to contributions made to a 401(k) deferred compensation plan, starting in 1987. The $7,000 limit is generally reduced by the amount of any deductible IRA contributions made for the same year [cf. Section 5 of the *Tax-Sheltered Plans* chapter].

Income-Shifting

Restrictions have been placed on the ability to shift income to a young child's lower tax bracket. Starting with 1987 tax returns, unearned income (e.g. dividends, interest, etc.), to the extend it exceeds $1,000, received by a dependent child under age 14 will be taxed at the parent's highest tax bracket. No such restriction will apply to children or other dependents who are age 14 or older. Also, children who can be claimed as a dependent on a parent's tax return are not entitled to a personal exemption on their own return [cf. Section 5 of Chapter 1].

There is also a change which restricts the tax-shifting opportunity offered by certain *reversionary trusts* such as *Clifford trusts* or *spousal remainder trusts*. Income earned on amounts which an individual contributes to such a trust is now taxed to that individual, not to the beneficiary or the trust itself. Existing trusts to which no funds were contributed after March 1, 1986 are not affected by this provision [cf. the *Income-Shifting* chapter].

Chapter 1

Basic Rules

SECTION 1:
BASIC STEPS IN COMPUTING YOUR TAX

The following basic procedure is used to compute your 1987 income tax:

(1) Compute your **total income** subject to tax. This consists of wages, interest, dividends, etc.

(2) Compute your **adjustments to income.** This includes (i) alimony, (ii) contributions to tax-sheltered IRA and Keogh plans, and (iii) reimbursements for job-related business expenses which were included in income under (1) above.

(3) Subtract (2) from (1). This is your **Adjusted Gross Income.**

(4) Compute your **deductions.** by either:

(a) Taking the standard deduction. This is a fixed amount depending on your Adjusted Gross Income in (3);

or

(b) Itemizing your deductions. This is done on Schedule A where you list such things as medical expenses, interest, taxes, casualty losses, charitable contributions, moving expenses, and miscellaneous deductions. Under *miscellaneous deductions* you include job-related expenses such as travel, books, supplies, professional dues, home office, etc., to the extent you receive no reimbursement from your employer. Certain deductions only apply after a minimum floor has been surpassed—7.5% of Adjusted Gross Income for medical expenses, 10% for casualty losses, and 2% for the sum total of miscellaneous deductions.

(5) You get a **personal exemption** for each dependent you claim, including yourself, your children, and your spouse. Multiply the number of exemptions by $1,900 (up from $1,080 on last year's tax return).

(6) Subtract (4) and (5) from (3). The net result is your **taxable income.**

(7) Compute your **tax** by looking up your taxable income in the appropriate tax table.

(8) Subtract **tax credits.** This includes the household services and child care tax credit, the credit for excess social security withheld by more than one employer, and the credit for the elderly not fully covered by social security. Observe that tax credits are much more favorable than deductions since they are subtracted directly from your tax instead of from your income.

Note that on 1986 tax returns, only the excess of itemized deductions over the standard deduction was included in (4) above, because the tax tables had the standard deduction amount already built in. But the 1987 tax tables no longer have the standard deduction built in, so the full amount of deductions is subtracted in (4). If you follow last year's procedure of first subtracting the standard deduction, it will probably cost you about $1,000 in extra taxes.

For 1987 tax returns, the following table shows the amount of the standard deduction for different categories of individuals:

Single (including Head of Household)	$2,540
Married filing jointly	$3,760
Married filing separately	$1,880

Individuals who are at least age 65 or are blind are entitled to a larger standard deduction than given above. The tax form instruction booklet contains a worksheet for computing the standard deduction for such individuals.

Example

A married couple with 2 dependent children has income of $45,000 and files a joint return. They each make a $1,000 contribution to an IRA, producing a $2,000 adjustment to income. Their itemized deductions total $4,200, which exceeds their standard deduction amount of $3,760. The tax computation proceeds as follows:

(1) Total Income	$45,000
(2) Less: Adjustments to Income	−2,000
(3) Adjusted Gross Income	$43,000
(4) Less: Itemized Deductions	−4,200
(5) Less Personal Exemptions: 4 × $1,900 =	−7,600
(6) Taxable Income	$31,200

The tax is then computed by looking up $31,200 in the appropriate tax table. Finally, the tax credits for child care, excess social security withheld, etc. are subtracted.

Note the two places where expenses are deducted — as *adjustments to income* and as *itemized deductions*. The main advantage in deducting expenses as an adjustment to income is that you can still use the standard deduction if it proves beneficial. (Self-employed persons may deduct all their business expenses on Schedule C. Thus, they are eligible to use the standard deduction and still deduct all their business expenses.)

Another advantage occurs in connection with the floors on various itemized deductions—7.5% of Adjusted Gross Income for medical expenses, 10% for casualty losses, and 2% for miscellaneous deductions. Claiming an *adjustment to income* reduces your Adjusted Gross Income, thereby lowering these floors. This in turn can raise the amounts you're entitled to deduct in the medical, casualty, or miscellaneous sections of Schedule A [cf. the *Medical Expenses, Casualty,* and *Miscellaneous Deductions* chapters].

Dependents

You get a $1,900 exemption for each dependent, including yourself, which you claim on your tax return. You are required to list the social security numbers of all dependents who are age 5 or older. Be sure to apply for these numbers as soon as possible so you'll have them in time to file your tax return.

The instruction booklet that comes with your tax forms lists the precise rules for who qualifies as your dependent. Basically, you must furnish more than 50% of the support of a dependent and the dependent must have gross income of less than $1,900 for the year. However, the $1,900 limitation on earnings does not apply to a child of yours who is under age 19 at the close of the year or is a full-time student during some part of each of 5 months during the year.

In determining whether a dependent has gross income over $1,900, tax-free scholarships or fellowships, social security payments, tax-free interest, disability payments, and other tax-free income are not counted. However, these items are taken into account when determining if an individual has provided more than 50% of another person's support. There is an exception for scholarship or fellowship payments received by a child of yours who is a full-time student in at least 5 months of the year. These payments are disregarded for purposes of the 50% requirement. This is the case even if part of the scholarship or fellowship payments is subject to tax.

In determining whether you have met the 50% support requirement, it is not necessary for the dependent to have used his earnings or savings for his own support. For example, suppose your child earns $3,000 during the year. You provide support (including food, lodging, clothing, etc.) of $2,500. If the child saves $600 and uses the remaining $2,400 towards his own support, then you will have met the 50% support requirement.

A student loan taken out by a child to use for his support counts as support provided by the child. In some cases, it may be better for the parent to borrow money in his own name and give it to his child, in order to preserve the dependency deduction.

A 1980 court case makes it easier to claim an exemption for an elderly parent. This case decided that Medicaid payments as well as benefits from Medicare and private insurance are not counted as support. This makes it easier for a relative to show he furnished over half the parent's support. [Archer, 73 TC #78]

If a parent could be claimed as a dependent by his grown children except that no child individually provides over 50% of support, they can agree among themselves which one is entitled to the dependency exemption. The child claiming the exemption must have furnished more than 10% of support. The children each fill out Form 2120 which is attached to the tax return of the one claiming the exemption.

A non-relative must be a member of your household for the entire year in order to qualify as a dependent. But a difficulty arises with friendly, but unmarried taxpayers. If the arrangement violates a state anti-cohabitation law, then one partner cannot claim the other as a dependent. This requires some delicate decision-making when the matter is raised in court.

For example, a court recently ruled against a North Carolina unmarried couple. According to North Carolina law, *"If any man and woman, not being married to each other, shall lewdly and lasciviously associate, bed and cohabit together, they shall be guilty of a misdemeanor."* The court found their friendly cohabitation to violate this statute, thereby ruling out a dependency claim. [Ensminger, 45 AFTR 2nd 80-373]

But a Missouri judge came to a different conclusion. Missouri law forbids *"grossly lewd or lascivious behavior."* And an 1855 court case had declared *"What act can be more grossly lewd or lascivious than for a man and woman, not married to each other, to be publically living together and cohabitating with each other."* But the judge in this case ruled that times had changed. He declared unmarried cohabitation not to be grossly lewd or lascivious conduct according to today's standards. [Shackelford, 80-1 USTC 99276]

Mailing in Your Tax Return

If you have a refund coming, mail your tax return in the envelope which is enclosed with the tax return package mailed to you by the IRS. This will speed up the processing of your tax return.

Of course, if you are mailing in a check and can use extra float time before your check is cashed, you can do the opposite, using your own envelope. An extra-large envelope will especially slow down processing, because the IRS uses automatic envelope-opening machines which work only on normal-sized envelopes. Oversized envelopes will be rejected and set aside to be opened by hand, a process that takes extra time.

When sending in your tax return, you should arrange the forms in their numerical order. Form 1040 goes on top, followed by related schedules. The remaining forms follow the *attachment sequence number* on the upper right-hand corner of the forms. You attach any supplementary information you are providing at the end.

Amending Tax Returns of Previous Years

You are permitted to amend tax returns which you filed in previous years. However, you are limited to going back three years if you wish to obtain a refund of back taxes. For example, you may amend your 1984, 1985 and 1986 tax returns if you file on or before April 15, 1988. When you amend your Federal tax return, you should amend your State tax return also.

There is a special form, 1040X, which you use for filing an amended return. You also include any applicable schedules or forms. For example, if you want to retroactively claim the child care tax credit, you would submit a Form 2441 along with your Form 1040X.

If you have overlooked a deduction or tax credit in a previous year, you must file an amended return to rectify the situation. You cannot claim the deduction or credit in a later year to compensate for its omission in the appropriate year.

It should be cautioned that amended returns are more likely to be audited than original returns. If there are questionable items on your original return, you are better off waiting until just before the 3-year limit is about to expire before amending your tax return. Requesting a refund on an amended return does not extend the

Basic Rules

3-year period for auditing your original return. Thus, the amended return will not trigger an audit of other items on your original return. The IRS will pay you 3-years interest on the amount refunded to you.

Getting Copies of Tax Returns

If you need a copy of an old tax return including attachments, you can get it from the IRS. (The IRS keeps tax returns for at least 6 years.) Send in Form 4506 along with a check for $4.25 to the IRS Service Center where you filed your return. Allow 6 weeks for delivery. Also, you can get free of charge just an information printout of 6 basic items on your tax return including adjusted gross income and the tax due. This is obtained by calling or writing your local IRS office. You can also request that information be sent to a third party. This can be handy for verifying financial information to a potential lender.

If you need a current last-minute blank tax form in order to complete your tax return, try a local library. Many libraries now make available a portfolio of tax forms which can be photocopied and used in filing your tax return.

IRS Ombudsmen

The IRS has a policy of having an ombudsman, called a *Problems Resolution Officer,* in each of its district offices. The ombudsman is not there to give tax advice but rather to cut through red tape in case you're having trouble getting your refund check or straightening out some other mixup.

If you're expecting a refund, give the IRS ten weeks before making an inquiry. After that time, phone your local IRS office. They can run a computer check to determine what happened and tell you when your refund check will be mailed. If you can't get things straightened out within a reasonable period of time, ask to speak to the Problems Resolution Officer.

Roundoff

The IRS allows you to round off all figures to the nearest dollar. Note that the detailed tax tables are broken down into bracket intervals of $50, with the same tax applying to everyone in the same bracket. Thus, a difference of 1 cent in income or deductions could, in the worst possible case, throw someone into a higher bracket and increase taxes by as much as $19. If your initial tax computation puts you just over the edge into a new bracket, changing your roundoff decision might throw you back into the next lowest bracket.

Extension of Time to File

You can get an automatic extension of 4 months to file your return. To receive this extension, you file Form 4868 with the IRS by April 15. Then file your return by August 15, accompanied by a copy of your Form 4868. However, you have to pay what you estimate your tax will be by April 15. Otherwise, you risk a penalty on the underpayment unless the underpayment is less than 10%. In addition, an interest charge will be assessed on all late payments. If you need more than 4 extra months, you can file Form 2688 explaining the reason you need more time. The IRS will accept this form if it approves of your reasons.

According to a recent IRS ruling, even if you have a refund coming, it is possible you could be assessed a penalty for filing an income tax return after the due date (with extensions). In this ruling, a taxpayer was hit with a negligence penalty equal to 5% of the total tax shown on his late-filed return, despite the fact he had a refund coming. [IRS Private Letter Ruling 8527012]

Reporting Interest and Dividends on Your Tax Return

You report interest and dividend payments you receive on Schedule B. The IRS computer will compare the amounts you report with its own records. A mismatch may cause the IRS to seek an additional tax assessment or even conduct an audit of your tax return.

To prevent this from happening, you should report interest and dividend payments separately according to the information slips you receive from the paying institutions; otherwise the IRS computer will get confused. For example, separate accounts with the same bank should be listed separately. Dividends on stocks held in street name with a broker and reported to the IRS as a total sum received from the broker should be reported that way on your tax return; they should not be reported under the issuing corporations' names unless they were reported to the IRS that way. Dividends on money market funds should be reported as dividends rather than interest. (But income from money market accounts in a bank or savings & loan is reported as interest.) And deductible fees (not including non-deductible check-writing fees) on interest-paying accounts with a bank should be claimed as a miscellaneous deduction, not subtracted from the amount of interest you report on Schedule B.

Whose Name Goes First If Wife Keeps Maiden Name?

A question arising out of the modern era is which name to put first on a joint return when the wife retains her maiden name. It doesn't matter which name comes first as long as the first name matches the first social security number. But once a return is filed using separate names, the same order of names should generally be used on subsequent returns. Switching the order could cause the IRS computer to become confused and result in delinquent notices being sent. Whichever order is chosen, the two names should be listed on Form 1040 joined by "and," e.g. *Mary Brown and John Smith.*

Negative Income Tax for Low-Income Individuals

You may know students or other low-income individuals who are supporting a child. They might qualify for the *earned-income credit* which in some cases yields a negative income tax. That is, if subtracting the earned-income credit from their tax produces a negative result, the difference is actually paid out to them by the government.

To qualify for the earned-income credit for 1987, an individual must be either (1) a married individual filing a joint return who is entitled to a dependency deduction for a child or stepchild; (2) an unmarried individual who maintains a household for a dependent child or stepchild; or (3) a custodial parent, even if he agrees to let the noncustodial parent claim a dependency exemption for a child [cf. the *Divorce & Separation* chapter].

Basic Rules 21

The credit for 1987 is equal to 14% of earned income up to a maximum of $6,080 of income. If earned income is over $6,080, the credit is $851 minus 10% of the excess of adjusted gross income or earned income (whichever is larger) over $6,920. The credit is completely eliminated for those with income over $15,432. Married couples must file a joint return in order to qualify for the credit.

Note that the credit can produce a refund to the individual even if no tax was withheld from his salary. But a tax return must be filed in order to get this benefit. Many students and other low-income workers lose out on a refund because they are unaware that the earned-income credit exists.

Persons eligible for the credit can now arrange to have their employer make advance payments of the credit. Thus, the law now provides for a negative withholding rate to go along with the negative income tax.

Section 2:
Basic Rules for Deducting Business Expenses

You can claim a deduction for expenses which you incur in connection with your profession. These fall under the category of **business expenses.** The basic rule is that such expenses in order to be deductible, must be both **ordinary and necessary** expenses directly connected with or related to your profession.

On the other hand, not all business expenditures are deductible even though they may be ordinary and necessary. For example, commuting costs to and from work are in most cases not deductible.

What Is an "Ordinary" Expense?

The word "ordinary" refers to an expense connected with a common and accepted practice in your profession. Thus, attending a professional convention would be an ordinary expense. But buying a new suit for your boss would probably not be considered an ordinary expense since it is not the accepted practice to do so.

What Is a "Necessary" Expense?

The word "necessary" is not used here in its usual meaning of "indispensable." The best definition of a "necessary expense" is one that is **appropriate and helpful** in developing or maintaining your profession.

Fortunately, you do not generally have to interpret principles like the ordinary and necessary rule. There are specific rules and examples that apply to most of the particular business deductions you might have. These are described in the following chapters.

There is one other general restriction on deducting business expenses. You are not allowed to deduct certain expenses if they are considered to be lavish or extravagant. However, it is unlikely you would have to worry about this restriction.

Reimbursable Expenses Are Non-Deductible

If you incur expenses in connection with your employment for which you could have received a reimbursement, then these expenses are non-deductible. It makes no difference that you did not apply for the reimbursement and paid the expenses out of your own pocket. For example, a teacher in a recent court case tried to deduct expenses associated with field trips she took with her students. But the court ruled that since she could have been reimbursed by her employer, her expenses were non-deductible. [Patterson, TC Memo 1977-107]

Special Form for Deducting Business Expenses
There is a special form, Form 2106, which you use for deducting employee business expenses. You can obtain this form by calling your local IRS office. Self-employed persons deduct their business expenses on Schedule C.

SECTION 3: COMMON MISTAKES

Here's a list of the more common mistakes that are made on tax returns.

(1) Failure to Sign Tax Return
Don't forget that two signatures are needed on a joint tax return.

(2) Failure to Use Peel-Off Label
The IRS has issued a special request to all taxpayers to use the pre-addressed label that comes with the tax return package sent to you in the mail. This will not only save the government a little money, but it will speed up the processing of your return.

Perhaps even more important are key-punching errors that might occur. Using the pre-addressed label allows the IRS keypuncher to make 13 keystrokes instead of 85, substantially reducing the chance of error. Anyone who has tried to correct a credit card computer mistake will shudder to think of the mess that could ensue if the IRS misplaces your return due to a keypunching error. (The IRS states emphatically that the label contains no special audit codes and its use will not affect your odds of being audited.)

(3) Use of Incorrect Tax Table
Double-check to make sure you are using the correct tax table. A common error is the failure of qualified single individuals who maintain a household for a child or dependent to use the special head-of-household table. The head-of-household rate is lower than the single rate but higher than the rate for joint returns. Note that your household needs to be the child's or dependent's *principal place of abode* only for more than half the year, instead of for the entire year as once was required. Don't overlook the fact that the head-of-household rate can apply if you supply 50% or more of the support of a dependent parent, even if the parent does not live with you. Consult the instruction booklet accompanying your tax forms for the basic rules for using the head-of-household rate.

(4) Failure to Write Information on Check
You should write your social security number on your check and note what the

Common Mistakes 23

check is for, e.g., 1987 Form 1040 tax. That way, if your check is separated from your tax return, it will still be possible for the IRS to credit it to the appropriate account.

(5) Making Check Out to IRS

Make your check out to the Internal Revenue Service, not just to the IRS. A check made out to the IRS can be easily altered by changing IRS to MRS and writing a surname after it. Or, IRS can easily be changed to I. R. Stone or a similar name.

(6) Not Deducting Medical and Charity Travel

You can deduct travel to doctors, dentists, pharmacies, etc. as well as travel connected with charitable activities. A deduction of 12 cents per mile is allowed for autos used for charitable travel and 9 cents per mile for medical-related auto travel.

(7) Failure to Deduct Late Payment Charges

You might be assessed an extra charge for paying a mortgage or utility bill late. This charge is actually a form of interest and can be deducted as such. A survey undertaken by a New York consumer affairs office underlines the fact that this deduction is often overlooked. The office asked eleven tax preparers to fill out a tax return based on financial data which they worked up for a fictitious couple. The data submitted to the tax preparers included a charge for the late payment of a mortgage. The result was unanimous. All eleven of the tax preparers failed to claim the late charge as a tax deduction.

(8) Leaving Off Social Security Number of Spouse

If you file a joint return, you must include the social security number of yourself and your spouse. Many taxpayers believe that they do not have to include their spouse's social security number if their spouse does not earn any income. This is not the case.

(9) Filing a Joint State Tax Return

In many states, filing a joint return can be a mistake because the same rate schedule is used for joint returns as for single returns. For a married couple each having income, the only effect of filing a joint return is to shift income from a lower bracket to a higher bracket and increase your tax. To illustrate, consider the following example:

> *Example*
>
> A and B, a married couple, have taxable incomes of $30,000 and $20,000 respectively. On a joint return, their taxable income would be $50,000. They live in a state with the following tax rates which are used both for separate returns and for joint returns.
>
> | | |
> |---|---|
> | on first $2000 | 2% |
> | on next $4000 | 3% |
> | on next $4000 | 4% |
> | on next $4000 | 5% |
> | on next $4000 | 6% |

```
on next $4000  .................................................  7%
on next $4000  .................................................  8%
on next $4000  .................................................  9%
on next $4000  ................................................. 10%
on next $4000  ................................................. 11%
on next $4000  ................................................. 12%
on next $4000  ................................................. 13%
on next $4000  ................................................. 14%
remainder      ................................................. 15%
```

   If A and B file a joint return, their state tax is $4120. The upper $20,000 of their joint taxable income is taxed at rates from 10% to 14%.
   However, if they file separate returns, the outcome is quite different. The $20,000, which was taxed at the higher brackets in the joint return, is shifted to a separate person and is taxed at the lower range brackets of 2% to 7%. A pays the tax of $1720 on $30,000 and B pays tax of $900 on $20,000. The total $2620 is a net savings of $1500 over the tax on a joint return.

If you and your spouse both have incomes, be sure to check if the joint return rate is the same as the separate return rate in your state. If so, you could save taxes by **not** filing a joint return.

SECTION 4:
CLAIMING THE STANDARD DEDUCTION

   As explained in Section 1, the standard deduction is a fixed amount depending only upon a person's marital category. The standard deduction is now equal to $3,760 for joint returns, $2,540 for single returns, and $1,880 for returns of married individuals filing separately. (There is an exception, discussed in the next section, for those who can be claimed as a dependent on the tax return of a parent or other individual.) If your deductions total a greater amount than the standard deduction, you should itemize your deductions.
   Note that many of the chapters in this book contain information that still applies even if you claim the standard deduction.
   First of all, this chapter contains general information which applies to all taxpayers, whether they use the standard deduction or itemize their deductions. Also of general applicability are the *Divorce, Withholding, Retirement, Foreign Income, Audit, Income-Shifting, Estate Tax,* and *Investing* chapters.
   Second, several items can be claimed as an *adjustment to income* or *tax credit* even if the standard deduction is used. This includes alimony, job-related expenses reimbursed by an employer, IRA contributions, and Keogh plan contributions [cf. the *Divorce & Separation, Miscellaneous Deductions,* and *Tax-Sheltered Plans* chapters]. It also includes the tax credit for child care and household services.
   Third, many items ordinarily claimed as an itemized deduction can instead be claimed as a business expense on Schedule C by those who have some self-employ-

ment income [cf. the *Miscellaneous Deductions* and *Outside Business Activities* chapters]. This would include books, supplies, equipment, home office, auto expenses, entertainment expenses, etc.

Finally, those claiming the standard deduction should also note all the other techniques for reducing tax besides just deducting expenses. For example, they may still be able to participate in a tax-sheltered annuity, deferred compensation, IRA, or Keogh plan. Or, they may be able to claim tax exemption for a grant, make tax-favored investments, shift income to a lower-bracket child, etc. [cf. the *Tax-Free Grants, Investing,* and *Income Shifting* chapters].

SECTION 5:
TAX RETURNS OF DEPENDENT CHILDREN

You may have a dependent child with income of his own. If so, he may have to file his own tax return. The following special rules apply in this situation.

First, a child (or other individual) who is eligible to be claimed as a dependent on the tax return of a parent or other person (whether or not actually claimed) cannot use the personal exemption of $1,900 on his own tax return. This ends the situation under previous law whereby a child and parent could both claim a personal exemption for the child.

Second, a dependent child's income is divided into 2 categories for tax purposes—*earned income* and *unearned income*. *Earned income* is income produced by the child's own labor such as a summer or after-school job. The remainder is *unearned income*, including such items as interest, dividends, etc. Gifts and inheritances are in neither category since they are not subject to income tax. Scholarships and fellowships, to the extent subject to tax under the new law, are considered to be earned income.

A dependent child with only *earned income* computes his tax in the usual way. His standard deduction as a single taxpayer is $2,540. Since a dependent child can no longer claim a personal exemption on his own tax return, amounts earned over $2,540 will be subject to tax.

Unearned income is treated differently. At most $500 of the standard deduction can be used to offset unearned income. Thus, tax will be due whenever a dependent child's unearned income exceeds $500.

If a dependent child has both earned and unearned income, then the following basic rule is applied:

The standard deduction on the 1987 tax return of a single individual who can be claimed as a dependent by another taxpayer is $2,540 except that it cannot exceed $500 or the individual's earned income, whichever is greater. (Another way to view this is that the standard deduction equals earned income, except that it cannot be less than $500 nor more than $2,540.)

To illustrate, the following would be the standard deduction and taxable income (assuming no personal exemptions) of a dependent child in various situations:

Tax Returns of Children

Earned Income	Unearned Income	Dependent's Standard Deduction	Taxable Income
$ 300	$ 700	$ 500	$ 500
700	300	700	300
2,400	1,200	2,400	1,200
3,000	200	2,540	660
0	400	500	0
0	1,000	500	500

If an individual's total income is less than or equal to $500, then he owes no tax and is not required to not file a tax return.

Example 1

A dependent child has $600 earned income and $1,000 unearned income during 1987—a total of $1,600. According to the rules discussed above, his standard deduction is equal to $600. Thus, his taxable income is $1,600 − $600 = $1,000. This is taxed at the child's 11% tax bracket—11% × $1,000 = $110.

The above discussion assumes that the dependent child does not have itemized deductions exceeding $500. If in fact his itemized deductions do exceed $500, the tax forms will lead you through a different computation procedure, taking these deductions into account.

Children Under Age 14 with Unearned Income Exceeding $1,000

A special rule applies to a child who has not reached age 14 by the last day of the year and has unearned income exceeding $1,000. Namely, this excess is not taxed at the child's tax bracket, but rather at the parent's tax bracket, if higher. (If the parents are married filing separate returns, the tax bracket of the spouse with the higher taxable income is used. In the case of unmarried parents, it is the tax bracket applying on the return of the custodial parent that counts.)

This proviso was enacted into law to curb the practice of transferring assets to a young child in order that income earned on these assets be taxed at the child's lower rate rather than at the parent's. However, it applies to all unearned income of the child, whether or not due to assets given to the child by his parents.

The IRS has devised Form 8615 to be used on behalf of a child under age 14 who has unearned income in excess of $1,000. The tax on this excess amount is computed as though it had been earned by the parent on top of the income reported on the parent's tax return. The child's remaining income (i.e. earned income plus the first $1,000 of unearned income) is taxed at the child's tax rate.

Since the first $500 of income is offset by the standard deduction, the following would be the tax treatment of a child under age 14 with only unearned income:

Unearned Income	Tax Treatment
$0-$500	Exempt from Tax
$500-$1,000	Taxed at child's rate
Over $1,000	Taxed at parent's rate if higher than child's rate

Basic Rules

Form 8615 is attached to the *child's* personal tax return, not the parent's. Form 8615 makes a *what if* calculation. It determines how much extra tax the parent would have to pay if the child's unearned income over $1,000 had been earned by the parent. However, after this computation is made, it is the child who actually owes the taxes, not the parent. If there is more than one child with unearned income over $1,000, Form 8615 calculates tax as if all the excess income were earned by the parent and it distributes the tax among the personal returns of the children.

> **Example 2**
> A child has $600 in earned income and $1,300 in unearned income. His parents' highest tax bracket is 38.5%.
> The excess of unearned income over $1,000, $1,300 − $1,000 = $300 is taxed at the parents' tax rate—$300 × 38.5% = $116. The remainder, $600 of earned income and $1,000 of unearned income, is subject to tax of $110 as shown in the preceeding example. (One way to view this is that the $600 of earned income is offset by the standard deduction, with the remaining $1,000 of unearned income taxed at the child's 11% tax bracket—$1,000 × 11% = $110.) Thus the child's total tax would be $116 + $110 = $226. Observe that the parent's tax return must be completed first in order to have the appropriate information to use for the child's Form 8615 computation.

Unearned income of children who are age 14 or older as of the last day of the year is not taxed at the parent's tax bracket even if it exceeds $1,000. Instead, it is taxed along with earned income at the child's tax bracket in the usual way as discussed earlier.

When part of a child's income is taxed at a parent's tax rate, the parent's tax return is not affected. For example, the 7.5% and 2% floors on medical and miscellaneous deductions are not changed.

Section 6:
Single, Separate and Joint Returns

As you no doubt know, there are several different tax rates depending upon your marital status. Single people may use either the ordinary single taxpayer rate or the lower head-of-household rate if they maintain a household for a child, grandchild, or other dependent and satisfy the rules as stated in the instruction booklet accompanying the tax forms.

Married people may file a joint return on which they list all their combined income. Alternatively, each of them may file his or her own return subject to a special tax rate for married people filing separate returns which is higher than the rate for single taxpayers. This special rate is designed so that a married couple, each with X dollars of taxable income, pays the same tax by filing separate returns as by combining their income in a joint return with 2X dollars of taxable income. The graduated feature of the income tax rates then guarantees that people with unequal amounts of taxable income pay at least as much by filing separate returns with X and

Y dollars of taxable income respectively as they would by filing a joint return with X + Y dollars of taxable income.

In filing separate returns, a married couple must either both claim the standard deduction or both itemize their deductions. If they itemize, they must split the deductions between the two of them. And the limits on various deductions and tax credits are generally half that on single returns. This means that their taxable income on a joint return will generally be equal to the sum of the taxable incomes which would appear in separate returns, making the filing of separate returns unprofitable. However, due to the intricacies of the income tax laws, there are exceptions when the taxable income on a joint return is more than the combined taxable incomes on separate returns. In these cases, it may be better to file separate returns than to file a joint return, depending on how different the incomes are. If your incomes vary widely, the averaging effect of filing a joint return will usually make a joint return advantageous no matter what other circumstances prevail.

If you fall under any of the following exceptions, you might be better off filing separate returns. (This is especially true in 1987, because of the elimination of the marriage deduction, which in prior years could be claimed on joint returns of working couples.) You should compute your taxes both ways to see which is better.

Exceptions When Separate Returns Might Be Better

(1) If both of you have capital gains or losses produced by property owned individually.

(2) If one spouse sustains substantial medical expenses. The reason for this is that only medical expenses in excess of 7.5% of adjusted gross income are deductible.

For example, suppose a married couple each has an adjusted gross income of $25,000. He has $3,400 worth of medical expenses while she has none. On a joint return showing $50,000 adjusted gross income, they would have to subtract 7.5% × $50,000 = $3,750 from the amount of medical expenses, i.e. they would get no deduction. But on a separate return, he would only have to subtract 7.5% × $25,000 (his adjusted gross income) from his medical expenses. He would then have a medical expense deduction of $3,400 − (7.5% × $25,000) = $1,525.

However, if you live in a community property state, you might be required to split all medical expenses on separate returns. This could destroy any benefit that might be obtained by separate returns.

(3) If one spouse has substantial miscellaneous deductions while the other does not. The reason for this is that only miscellaneous deductions in excess of 2% of adjusted gross income are deductible.

For example, suppose a married couple each has an adjusted gross income of $30,000. She has miscellaneous deductions of $1,000 while he has none. On a joint return showing $60,000 adjusted gross income, they would have to subtract 2% × $60,000 = $1,200 from their total of miscellaneous deductions, i.e. they would get no deduction. But on a separate return, she would only have to subtract 2% × $30,000 = $600. This would leave her with a net miscellaneous deduction of $1,000 − $600 = $400.

(4) If one person sustains a substantial casualty loss. Since only casualty losses in excess of 10% of adjusted gross income can be deducted, separate returns might be advantageous for the same reason as illustrated in (2) for medical expenses or (3) for miscellaneous deductions.

Planning for 1988

For the 1988 tax year, many more couples will benefit by filing separate returns than before. The reason for this is the flatness of the 1988 tax bracket structure [cf. Chapter 0].

Married couples in which each spouse has income exceeding $15,000 and which have a combined income of less than $75,000 will be especially likely to benefit by filing separate returns. Such couples should choose one spouse [preferably the one with lower income] in whose name to concentrate medical payments and miscellaneous deduction payments.

As discussed above, this can serve to lower taxes when separate returns are used. Further information will be contained in next year's edition of this Tax Guide.

SECTION 7:
RECORDKEEPING

In order to substantiate your deductions, you are required to keep records of what you spend. Generally, you should retain any cancelled checks or receipts that verify expenditures. In addition, there are special recordkeeping rules which apply to certain specific types of deductions, e.g. travel expenses. These special rules are discussed in later chapters.

Except for an overall listing of your expenditures broken down into appropriate categories, you do not include your records with the income tax return which you file. It is only if your return is chosen for audit that you will be asked to produce these records.

What If You Didn't Keep Records?

You may still be able to deduct your expenses even if your return is audited. If you can establish that you are entitled to a certain business deduction, then you may be allowed to estimate your actual expenses in the absence of records. However, you can be sure that the auditor of your tax return will agree to a low estimate at best. If you should end up in Tax Court, then the court may make its own estimate of your expenses under what is called the **Cohan Rule** which permits such estimates. Once again the estimate will probably be on the low side. So you should do yourself a favor and keep records in the future if you have not done so in the past.

Exception: The Cohan Rule does not apply to travel or entertainment expenses nor to the deduction for *listed property* [cf. the *Depreciation* chapter] such as certain home computers. Charitable expenses are also now required to be substantiated. If you do not have the required substantiation, then the law permits the IRS to disallow your deduction. Even the Tax Court does not have the power to overcome this disallowance.

Loss of Records Beyond Your Control

If you lose your records due to circumstances beyond your control such as a fire or earthquake, then you will get a break. In this case, you probably will be allowed a reasonable estimate of your expenses.

Records of Home Expenses

You should be especially careful to keep records concerning the purchase and improvements of your home. These figure into computing depreciation of your home if you use a home office and also figure into any taxable gain you might receive as a result of selling your home. These now also figure into computing the maximum interest deductions you're allowed to claim for loans taken on your home [cf. the *Homeowners* chapter].

How Long to Keep Records

You should keep records associated with your tax return for at least three years. Records which show how much you paid for property and the cost of improvements should be kept indefinitely.

Don't make the mistake of throwing away your records too early just because the IRS sends you a refund check. That's what Robert Wells, a college biology teacher in Florida, did as reported in the following Tax Court case. He claimed a deduction for an automobile he used to gather specimens and perform other tasks connected with his job. As the Court explained it,

> *"After Robert filed his tax return . . . on which he asked a refund, further information was requested by the Internal Revenue Service about the claimed automobile depreciation. Before this matter was straightened out between Robert and the Internal Revenue Service, Robert was sent a refund check. Assuming that that was the end of the matter, Robert just disposed of all [his] literature on it and . . . was grateful that I.R.S. had recommended in the favor of a legitimate taxpayer and had gone on to other matters."*

But the refund check just reflected the ordinary processing procedure. It did not signify that the IRS official checking his return had accepted it as filed. Since Robert no longer had the required records, his deduction was not allowed. [Wells, T.C. Memo 1976-52]

SECTION 8:
YEAREND STRATEGIES FOR LOWERING TAXES

The end of the year often presents special opportunities to adjust one's financial affairs in order to reduce taxes.

Medical Expenses

Only medical expenses exceeding 7.5% of your adjusted gross income are deductible. If your medical bills will not exceed this amount, then they do you no good this year. Instead, you should shift the expenses to the following year by delaying payment until after the first of the year. You can also delay getting optional items like new eyeglasses, etc. In this way, you will get a deduction in case your medical expenses exceed the 7.5% limitation the next year.

If your medical expenses exceeded the 7.5% limitation this year, but you are not sure they will do so the next, the opposite strategy is called for. You will want to pay all your medical bills before the end of the year to avoid losing a deduction for them the following year because of the 7.5% floor.

Miscellaneous Deductions

A 2% of Adjusted Gross Income (AGI) floor now applies to the total of miscellaneous deductions claimed on your tax return [cf. the *Miscellaneous Deductions* chapter]. The same expense-shifting maneuver discussed above with regard to the 7.5% of AGI floor on medical expenses applies with respect to the 2% floor on miscellaneous deductions.

To illustrate with a simple example, suppose you have AGI of $50,000. In this case, the floor on the total miscellaneous deductions is 2% × $50,000 = $1,000. If you have $1,000 of miscellaneous deductions both this year and next, you lose out on any deduction in either year. However, if you can shift, say, $300 from one year to the other, you will wind up with miscellaneous deductions totalling $1,300 in one year and $700 in the other. Applying the 2% of AGI floor, this will yield a net deduction of $300 in the year to which the expenses are shifted.

In line with the above discussion, if it looks as though you might exceed the 2% of AGI floor this year but probably not the next, then you will want to shift expenses from next year to this. On the other hand, if you will not exceed the 2% floor this year, a shift to next year when the floor might be exceeded can possibly save the deduction.

For example, you can time the purchase of job-related items such as books, supplies, equipment, journals, professional dues, etc. so they occur in the year producing the best tax result. The same for investment-related expenses like safe deposit rentals, subscriptions to financial publications, etc.

(Those able to shift deductions from 1988 to 1987, as described in last year's edition of this Tax Guide, have benefited by another factor, namely the lower tax rate for 1988 than for 1987. By shifting deductions for charity, job-related items, interest, taxes, etc. to 1987, the higher tax-rate year, these deductions have a bigger tax-reducing impact.)

Using the Standard Deduction

Deduction-shifting may be advantageous when your deductions total near the standard deduction. For example, suppose the standard deduction to which you are entitled is $3,000. As of November 30, your deductions total $2,500 and you estimate another $400 of deductible expenses for the remainder of the year. These anticipated expenses will do you no good on this year's tax return because your total deduction of $2,900 would still be less than the standard deduction. It would be better to shift these deductions to the following year when your total deductions might exceed the standard deduction. This is accomplished by delaying payments until after the first of the year.

Conversely, if your deductions are exceeding the standard deduction one year but might not the next, transferring deductions to the earlier year might prevent their loss as a tax benefit. This is accomplished by paying early before the year's end.

When Are Payments Considered Made?

Generally, you make a payment when you write a check and place it in the mail (or deliver it in person). It does not matter that it isn't received until the next year. The deduction will be allowed for the year appearing on the date of the check unless there is some strong indication it was mailed in a different year.

Expenses charged on some credit cards are deductible in the year they're charged, not in the year the charge is paid. This applies to cards issued by third parties e.g. VISA, MasterCard, American Express, etc. Other charge arrangements are deductible in the year paid.

Sometimes, payments are made under a "pay-by-phone" arrangement whereby a bank or savings institution pays bills upon receiving telephone instructions from depositors. In the following month, the depositor receives a statement of bills paid on his account. The payment dates shown on the statement determine when payments can be deducted by the depositor. [Rev Rul 80-335]

Tax-Sheltered Plans

If you plan to take advantage of the tax-sheltered plans for which you're eligible, be sure to observe the appropriate deadlines. [cf. the *The Tax-Sheltered Plans* chapter]. Note in particular that you must actually establish your Keogh Plan before December 31 even though payment does not have to be made until April 15 or extended filing date. Note also that payments to a Tax-Sheltered Annuity are only deductible in the current year if made by December 31.

Pay Interest on Personal Loans

If you have outstanding personal debt (e.g. auto loans, credit card balances, etc.), you're better off paying any outstanding interest charges before the end of the year. Over the next few years, the deduction for personal interest is being phased out [cf. the *Interest* chapter]. Thus, interest paid at the end of a given year will yield a larger deduction than if paid the next year. The same situation might apply to deductions of interest on other types of loans that are also being phased out, as discussed in the *Interest* chapter.

Capital Gains and Losses

If you own stocks or bonds, then tax considerations may call for a sale of some of these assets prior to December 31. [Cf. the *Investing Your Money* chapter for the basic rules.] For example, you may wish to sell stocks that have decreased in value in order to offset capital gains or produce a deductible loss on your tax return.

SECTION 9:
FREE OR LOW-RENT HOUSING

Some colleges and universities provide housing to faculty members or administrators either rent-free or at a reduced rent. Where the housing is a condition of employment and is used in a substantial way for college-related functions, this does not generate taxable income. This tax-free fringe benefit typically applies only to Chancellors, Presidents, or other head administrators. [IRS Private Letter Rulings 7823005, 7823007]

In other cases, the rental value of a university-supplied house is considered to be equal to 5% of its appraised value (as appraised by an independent qualified appraiser). To the extent a faculty member pays less than this amount in rent, such shortfall becomes a taxable fringe benefit. However, if the rent paid is equal to or greater than 5% of value, no extra tax is due.

Members of Religious Orders

Ordained ministers are entitled to a special tax break if they receive housing allowances provided as part of their pay. Such allowances are tax-free to the extent they are actually used for housing costs, e.g. rent or ownership costs including down payments, mortgage payments, utilities, interest, taxes, and repairs.

A 1984 court case illustrates how this can apply to faculty members who qualify. Sixteen teachers at a Christian college in the South were also ministers within the Church of Christ. The teachers owned or rented their own homes and reported their housing costs to the college. The college then designated part of their pay to cover these costs as housing allowances. The Court ruled that they could exclude from tax housing allowances equal to their expenses. However, they could not deduct larger amounts equal to the "fair rental value" of their homes—only their actual out-of-pocket housing expenses. [Reed, 82 TC No. 19]

A member of a religious order under a vow of poverty may have taxable income even if he immediately turns over his salary to his religious order. This is the conclusion of a 1986 court decision concerning a priest who taught religious studies at a publicly supported institution. His contract with the university was entered into on an "individual basis" not as a priest. The fact that payments for his services were deposited in a church-related account did not alter its status as salary.

The situation would have been different had the priest been considered an employee of the religious order rather than an outside institution. This would be the case if the school were run by the religious order or possibly if the religious order had entered into the basic contract for providing services to the outside institution.
[IRS Private Letter Ruling 7917007; Rev Rul 83-127; Fogarty, 86-1 USTC ¶9139]

Chapter 2

Books, Supplies, and Equipment

You are entitled to a deduction for the cost of books, periodicals, supplies, equipment, home computers, and other items which you use in your profession or for other business purposes. Those items which have a definite short life span such as paper or pencils are deducted in the year they are purchased. For items which will be used for a number of years, such as a typewriter or desk, there are two options, the **expensing option** and the **depreciation option.**

Under the *expensing option,* you deduct the cost of the items, up to a total deduction of $10,000, in the year they are placed into service. Under the *depreciation option,* a specified percentage of the cost is deducted in each year of the depreciation period. The depreciation period for books, equipment, and furniture is 5 years or 7 years. For most individuals, the expensing option is preferable to depreciation for items purchased during 1987. A complete discussion of the two options for deducting business items is contained in the *Depreciation* chapter. As explained there, both options require the use of Form 4562 which you attach to your tax return. (You do not use Form 4562 for short-lived items such as periodicals, paper, or other supplies.)

Special Rules for Computers and Entertainment Items

In 1984, Congress instituted a new category of items, called *Listed Property* to which special depreciation and recordkeeping rules apply. *Listed Property* includes the following items:

Listed Property

1. Automobiles and other passenger vehicles.

2. Home Computers (except for employer-owned computers used exclusively at a regular business establishment or computers used exclusively in a home office qualifying for deduction as described in the *Home Office* chapter).

3. Property of a type generally used for entertainment, recreation, or amusement, e.g. video recorders, cameras, etc., except for such property used either (i) exclusively at your regular job location or deductible home office, or (ii) in connection with your principal job or business.

Special Depreciation Rules for Listed Property

Special rules apply for depreciation of listed property. These special depreciation rules apply to such items only if they were purchased after June 18, 1984. Under these special rules, such items must be *required by the employer* in order for an

34

employee to obtain any deduction. Also, if such items are used 50% or less for business purposes, a special stretched-out depreciation table must be used instead of the regular depreciation table or expensing option. Details are contained in the *Expensing and Depreciation* chapter.

Recordkeeping Rules for Listed Property

There are special recordkeeping regulations that apply to listed property. These regulations apply to all listed property for which a deduction is claimed, whether purchased before June 18, 1984 or after.

Formerly, listed property was subject only to the same basic rules applying to any other deduction. That is, the better your records, the more likely your deduction would stand up to IRS scrutiny. But no explicit standards applied. In fact, even in the absence of any records, taxpayers could often qualify for a deduction by making a reasonable estimate of business use.

However, now an estimate is no longer sufficient to support a deduction for an item of listed property. Instead, there must be adequate records to support your deduction. This means you must maintain a diary or similar written record which, for each job or business use of the item, contains the following information:

1. Date;

2. Business purpose (unless this is evident from the surrounding facts and circumstances);

and

3. Length of time the item was used.

Your records do not have to conform to any specific format. You can keep a diary, log book, journal, etc. Or, you can use a calendar on which you write down all the required data.

If you use an item of listed property both for personal and business purposes, you must keep track of the total amount of time the item was in use. This will enable you to substantiate the percentage of time the item was used for business purposes.

Your records should be maintained in a *timely* manner. According to the IRS, this means you write down each entry soon enough that you have *"full present knowledge"* of all the details. You are not required to make daily entries; IRS regulations state that it is all right to record your usage at the end of each week. However, even if your records are updated weekly, they should still give a daily breakdown of each separate period of use.

You do not need to maintain your records by hand. IRS regulations specifically allow you to use a home computer to keep a log of business and personal use.

If your business use percentage is relatively constant during the year, IRS regulations provide that a suitable sampling technique can be used instead of keeping records for the entire year. The following 2 examples are adapted from these regulations. [IRS Reg. #1.274-5T].

Example 1
You use a home computer during the year both for personal and business

purposes. You keep adequate records for the first 3 months of the year which show that 60% of the time your computer is used, it is used for business purposes. Assuming you can establish that your business usage continues at approximately the same rate for the remainder of the year, your records support a deduction based on 60% of the cost of the computer.

Example 2

Same as Example 1 except that you keep adequate records during the first week of each month. As long as it is established that these are "representative" weeks, you can base your deduction on the business use percentage determined for the sample weeks.

Questions on Tax Return

On your 1987 tax return, the following 2 questions must be answered on Form 4562, Part III, Section A concerning your deduction for listed property:

1. Do you have evidence to support the business use percentage claimed?

2. Is the evidence written?

Observe that it is possible to answer *yes* to the above questions yet not satisfy the recordkeeping requirements of the law. For example, you might create a written record at the end of the year. This would enable you to answer *yes* to the above questions so your tax return would not be spotlighted for audit. But such a record would fail the *timely* requirement described earlier. If your deduction actually were audited, it would likely be disallowed for failure to keep adequate records.

Deductible Items

The following is a list of items which are legitimate professional expenses. You may be able to think of others. Bear in mind that whether any particular item is an acceptable deduction depends on whether you use it in your professional capacity.

Books

You may deduct for the cost of books used in connection with professional duties. Those books which are only useful for a year or less are deducted in full when purchased. Books of more lasting value are either expensed in the year of purchase or depreciated over a 7-year period [cf. the *Expensing and Depreciation* chapter].

Supplies

You may deduct the cost of pens, pencils, paper, tape, maps, records, slides, film, sheet music, staples, desk blotters, briefcases, record books, etc. These items fall into the short lifetime category and are deducted in the year of purchase.

Periodicals

You may deduct subscriptions to journals, periodicals, etc. connected with your job.

However, if you pay in advance for a subscription that extends for more than one year, the IRS states that you should spread out your deductions accordingly. For example, suppose that in December, 1987, you paid $300 for a 3-year subscription to a job-related journal to begin in 1988. Only $100 of this amount would be deductible on your 1987 tax return. The remainder would be deducted in future years—$100 on your 1988 return and $100 on your 1989 return.

On the other hand, suppose the $300 subscription prepaid in December 1987 is not a new subscription, but rather is an extension of a subscription due to expire at the end of March, 1988. Then only $75 of the prepayment—covering the 3/4 of the year from April to December, 1988—will be deductible for 1987. The remaining $225 will be deductible in portions for 1988 ($100), 1989 ($100), and 1990 ($25), reflecting the termination of the subscription at the end of March, 1990). [IRS News Release IR-86-169]

The above prorating of multi-year subscriptions was proclaimed by the IRS to prevent the shifting of deductions to 1986 or 1987 in order to take into account the lowering of tax rates provided by the 1986 Tax Reform Act. As a practical matter, it is doubtful the IRS will single out such a deduction for examination unless the amount is substantially out-of-line.

Newspapers and Magazines

Newspapers and magazines can be deductible if they are sufficiently connected with your job. This is illustrated by a recent court case involving a public relations executive. He usually bought at least two newspapers daily and magazines such as *Time* and *Newsweek*. He also purchased local newspapers and magazines when he traveled.

These magazines and newspapers were needed by him in connection with his work. No record was kept of his purchases but he estimated he spent one dollar per day for a total of $360 for the year. The Court allowed the deduction but reduced the amount to $250 because of a lack of records. [Conley, TC Memo 1977-406]

As the above case shows, a deduction for general circulation magazines can stand up in court if there is sufficient business reason to subscribe. In fact, the IRS is not likely to challenge your deduction. According to a book published by a former IRS official, *"a lot of people worry about [the deduction for professional journals] and waste time deciding what's really professional and what's just for fun. Take whatever you think can possibly qualify. The IRS doesn't much care because the amounts are relatively small."* [P.N. Strassels with R. Wool, *All You Need to Know about the IRS*, Random House]

The above advice is underscored by a 1980 court case involving a consultant who claimed a deduction for books and journals connected with his profession. The IRS allowed him a $200 deduction even though he presented no documentation to back up his deduction. [Kannas, TC Memo 1980-127]

Teachers, in particular, should take note of the above. Many teachers use current information from newspapers and magazines in their teaching. And other teachers use such information in connection with their professional research. In such cases, a deduction for these items might be justified.

In addition to job-related publications, you can deduct the cost of magazines and newspapers connected with your investment activities. This would include subscriptions to the *Wall Street Journal, Forbes Magazine,* etc.

Special Clothing

The cost of uniforms or other clothing, including their cleaning, laundering, repair, etc., is deductible if the clothing is (1) required in your job and (2) not adaptable to general wear. Such items might include athletic wear, laboratory coats and safety equipment, aprons, caps and gowns, etc. However, you cannot deduct ordinary street clothes even if you wear them only at your job.

Telephone Expenses

You can deduct your professional telephone expenses (including installation charges, repair costs, equipment fees, etc.) if you need to make business-related calls from your home. However, the use of your home telephone must be a true necessity, not just a personal convenience. In such a situation, you are supposed to keep records so that a proper allocation can be made between personal and business use of your telephone. However, if you didn't keep detailed records, you can probably at least pick up your business-related long distance calls from the itemization of phone numbers listed on your telephone bills.

In the absence of any documentation, you may still want to make a best estimate of the business use of your telephone. If your return is examined, it is always possible your deduction will be disallowed for lack of records. But if a reasonable case can be made, you may still be allowed a deduction for a portion of your expenses. This is illustrated by a number of court cases on this issue.

In one case, the IRS allowed a teacher to deduct about $80 per year for teaching-related phone calls even though the teacher had presented no documentary evidence at all. She claimed she had to call parents at home, mainly to discuss problems she was having with their children. She had to make the calls from home at night or on weekends because she had insufficient opportunity to do so during her busy day at school. The calls were a necessity of the job because she needed to maintain proper discipline in her classroom. [Lingham, TC Docket No. 2860-74]

In another recent case, an individual worked in a number of different locations and also owned a few rental apartments. The IRS wanted to allow only $14 of her $362 total phone bills for the year. This was the toll call portion of her bills that could be identified as calls to business-related locations. But the Court was more generous. Because of her interest in rental apartments and employment at diverse locations, it allowed her a deduction of $132 for the year. [Yee, TC Memo 1985-379]

Rather than go through your entire year's telephone bills, you might be able to use a sampling technique if you make substantial business usage of your phone. This is illustrated by a 1986 court case involving an engineer who designed and supervised rehabilitation projects of industrial offices. He made extensive use of his home telephone to call prospective employers, headhunters, and job shops throughout the U.S. and the world, chiefly in order to find work. Instead of plowing through the entire year's telephone bills, the Court agreed to use just the January bill as a representative sample of the business use percentage of his telephone. The Court estimated that 40% of the telephone calls during January were for business purposes. Since his total telephone bills for the year came to $4,216, he was allowed a deduction of 40% × $4,216 = $1,686 for the year. [Payne, TC Memo 1986-93]

Note that your telephone calls can be deductible even if you are not permitted a home office deduction for failure to satisfy the stringent rules described in the *Home*

Office chapter.

Equipment and Furnishings

You may be able to deduct for the cost of tape recorders, cameras, projectors, home computers, typewriters, calculators, etc., which you use in connection with your job either at work or at home. In one case, the IRS even allowed a teacher to deduct for a radio used for job-related purposes [Reilly, TC Memo 1979-253]. You have to prorate the expenses if these items are also used for personal activities. You may also deduct for office furnishings such as desks, chairs, lamps, etc., which are used in a home office for which you're entitled to a deduction. [Cf. the *Expensing and Depreciation* chapter for details on how to deduct for equipment and furnishings.]

A 1984 court case shows how camera equipment can qualify for deduction. A Professor of Management spent $1731 on a Canon A-1 camera, tripod, auto bellows, and lenses. He testified that he used the equipment only in connection with his teaching duties — to take pictures and make slides to show during his lectures. He presented slides showing computer equipment and programs for use in his course in computer programming, slides of Mexico for use in his course on tourism development, and slides of Austrian coins, a passport, an international driving permit, and Austrian mountain ranges for use in connection with the tourism course.

The Court allowed full depreciation deductions for the cost of the camera equipment. It believed the Professor that he made no personal use of the equipment, noting that he also owned a different camera, a 10-year old Mamyia Sekor, for use in taking personal or family photographs. [TC memo 1984-97]

In the above case, the ownership of a second camera was probably an important factor. In another recent case, the Tax Court denied a deduction to an elementary school teacher for the purchase of a Minolta 35-millimeter camera with wide angle lens. He used the camera to take pictures of students, to take photographs for the school yearbook, and to teach darkroom techniques to his science class. There was no evidence that the teacher owned a second "personal" camera. In this case, the Court felt that the camera was basically a personal item used only occasionally for job-related activities. Therefore, no deduction was allowed. [TC Memo 1982-453]

Home Computers

Home computers, including peripheral equipment, can be expensed or depreciated to the extent the computer is used for business rather than personal purposes. In addition, the cost of electricity to operate the computer is deductible.

Software which is bundled together with your original purchase of the computer is considered part of the original cost. Software which is itemized separately or purchased at a different time can generally be deducted in the year of purchase. Although the official IRS position is that software is an intangible item which should be amortized over a period of years, most experts disagree. And the IRS is not expected to enforce its position for the relatively small purchases of home computer software.

Home computers (purchased by an employee after June 18, 1984) fall under the special rules for *listed property* described in the *Expensing and Depreciation* chapter. Unless used only in a deductible home office, the use of such a computer must be *"for the convenience of the employer and required as a condition of employment."*

As discussed in the *Expensing and Depreciation* chapter, IRS regulations state that in order to satisfy this requirement, the use of the computer *"must be required in order for the employee to perform the duties of his or her employment properly."* The following example illustrates a case where this requirement is not met.

> **Example 3**
>
> D is employed as an engineer with Z, an engineering contracting firm. D occasionally takes work home at night rather than working late in the office. D owns and uses a computer which is virtually identical to the one she uses at the office to complete her work at home. D's use of the computer is not for the convenience of her employer and is not required as a condition of employment.
> [IRS Reg. #1.280F-6T]

The above example taken from IRS regulations would suggest, at least implicitly, that the regular use of a home computer for valid work-related duties qualifies for deduction, provided adequate facilities are not available at work. However, in several IRS Private Letter Rulings issued after these regulations were published, the IRS took a much more extreme stance. It denied deductions to several individuals despite the fact that essential job-related use was made of a computer.

For example, one ruling concerned an individual called "B" who accepted a position as an Assistant Professor of Nursing at a State University. According to the ruling,

> "In compliance with the University's implied requirements for faculty appointment in regard to independent research and the development of external grant support, B purchased a personal computer. . . . The Faculty Handbook and Standards for Achievement refer to 'scholarly productivity' and, since B's appointment was only for nine months, she had to work extensively on the solicitation of grant support to continue her present employment. Grant development, by its nature, requires substantial documentation and assembly. Manual typing would allow neither the speed nor the correction capability that the word processing function of the personal computer provides. B worked nightly on the formation of grant support and on technical research and publication in the field. A contemporaneous log was kept of the computer usage. . . .
>
> "The position of Assistant Professor requires a substantial workload in terms of classes and support activities. The additional required functions of research and grant development had to be accomplished after working hours due to workload considerations and the relative unavailability of word-processing services for B's use. Only limited support staff was available to B. In consideration of B's grant development work and to facilitate her use of her personal computer, the University purchased her a modem so that she could communicate at night with the University's computer system."

It would seem that B might well fall within the IRS guidelines. That is, it would appear that she genuinely needed the home computer to perform the duties of her employment properly. And the facilities at school were less than adequate for the task.

However, the IRS denied her deduction, stating,

> "The facts suggest that computer use, although work-related, is not inextricably related to proper performance of the employee's job. Further, there appears no evidence in the facts that those employees who did not purchase a computer were professionally disadvantaged.
>
> "Accordingly, B's use of the personal computer does not meet the 'convenience of the employer' and 'condition of employment' tests under section 280F(d)(3) of the Code." [IRS Private Letter Ruling 8615024]

The above ruling seems to require a herculean task to justify a home computer deduction. Exactly how one could show that his home computer was *"inextricably related"* to proper performance of his job is unclear. And the requirement to provide evidence that similar employees who did not purchase a computer were *"professionally disadvantaged"* would appear to be a nearly impossible task—involving the submission of evidence not just of one's own employment activities but also other employees' performances of their jobs as well.

In the view of many experts, the above private letter ruling goes beyond the intent of Congress and even beyond the spirit of IRS regulations themselves. In fact, the IRS issued a formal revenue ruling on this issue near the beginning of 1987. (Unlike private letter rulings, revenue rulings can be relied upon by any taxpayer in the same circumstances.) Although the result of this revenue ruling was negative, it nevertheless appears to represent a more liberal position than indicated in the private letter ruling above.

This revenue ruling concerned an individual with a doctorate in aerospace engineering who had a research position with a private corporation. His job description, like the job descriptions of all engineers and scientists who worked for the corporation, provided that he seek to accomplish the research objectives by whatever means he and the corporation determined were necessary.

He purchased a computer and kept it at home. He purchased it because the computers at work were often used by other employees during working hours and he often performed job-related work at home. He did not use the computer for any other purpose than his job-related work.

The IRS denied a deduction because of failure to satisfy the *condition of employment* test. However, the reason given for the denial was that adequate computer facilities existed at work. In the words of the IRS,

> "In order to satisfy the requirement that a home computer is required as a condition of employment there must be a clear showing that the employee cannot perform properly the duties of employment without it. That clear showing is lacking in this situation because there is no evidence that the computers supplied [at work] are insufficient to enable him properly to perform the duties of his employment."

[Rev. Rul. 86-129, I.R.B. 1986-45,4]

The important thing to note is that the IRS based its denial of a deduction just on the fact that adequate computing facilities were at work. This was the situation the IRS chose to make public in an official revenue ruling. It did not choose to officially publicize the situation in the private letter rulings it had issued which required that the computer be *inextricably related* to the job and that similar employees who did not purchase a computer be *professionally disadvantaged*.

As the above discussion indicates, there is still considerable uncertainty as to what exactly is needed to justify a deduction for a home computer. It will take a court case or two to resolve the matter. In the meantime, an individual who requires a home computer for the proper performance of his job should not be overly deterred from claiming a deduction, in particular if similar computing facilities at work are not adequate. Even if an individual is audited, the law is not yet settled enough to predict how any particular auditor will react in a given situation.

Further details on this issue will be contained in future editions of this Tax Guide when the courts have had a chance to clarify the situation.

Of course, the above discussion only applies to computers which are **not** used in a deductible home office. If you are eligible to deduct for a home office in which you use a computer, the computer does not need to satisfy the listed property requirement that it be for the *convenience of the employer and required as a condition of employment*.

Also note that in such a case, the computer is not considered to be a fixture of the home office. Thus it can be deducted, even if the deduction exceeds the income received from the activity for which the home office is used [cf. the *Home Office* chapter].

If you can claim a deduction for your computer (purchased after June 18, 1984), *Condition 2* described in Section 1 of the *Expensing and Depreciation* chapter applies. Namely, if business use does not exceed personal use, a special stretched-out depreciation table must be used. Of course, in any event, you're only entitled to a deduction for that percentage of cost equal to the percentage of time the computer is used for business rather than personal purposes. For example, if a $2,000 computer is used 60% for business purposes and 40% for personal purposes, your deduction would be based on the cost attributable to business use — 60% × $2,000 = $1,200. However, you can still deduct the full cost of software for business or investment applications, even if the computer itself is used partly for personal purposes.

As discussed near the beginning of this chapter, new recordkeeping rules apply to use of a home computer. However, no matter what the nature of your records, the IRS may question whether your claimed business use is legitimate. Here are a number of steps you can take to safeguard your deduction:

1. Establish a clear business purpose.

To deduct a home computer, you should use it for specific business purposes — either connected with (i) your regular job, (ii) an outside business activity, or (iii) managing your investments. Of these 3 activities, the latter 2 are the safest justifications to use. As illustrated by the IRS private letter ruling described above, the IRS can be tougher about expenses incurred by an employee than it is about expenses incurred by a business owner or active investor.

It's a good idea to purchase specific business-related software in the same year you purchase your computer. Purchase of such programs as word-processing, portfolio analysis, spread sheet analysis, etc. will give credence to your claim that the computer is being used for business-related purposes. Similarly, subscriptions to data banks like the Dow Jones Information Service would point to an investment business use.

2. **Don't have personal software listed on the same invoice as your computer or business software.**

Of course, you should not be deducting that fraction of the cost of the computer corresponding to your use for personal purposes such as game playing. But you don't have to stir up doubts by having game software intimately connected with your computer. If your computer deduction is questioned, you would want to be able to present invoices which point to your business use of the computer, not your personal use.

3. **Buy a bigger rather than a smaller computer.**

Popular inexpensive computers are more questionable than higher-power, more expensive computers. The inexpensive computers are typically used for game playing while the more expensive computers are typically purchased with a business purpose in mind. There may even be a difference in image among competing brands in the same price class. Some IRS agents may be more likely to question the deduction for a computer they've seen advertised on TV by popular entertainers than they are for a less advertised brand considered more serious in purpose.

4. **Buy a different computer than the one available at work.**

The type of home computer most easy to deduct is one which is different than any computer available at work. This is illustrated by Example 3 discussed earlier in this chapter.

5. **Save your output.**

If you have a printer, save as much output as you can which illustrates your business usage. This is concrete proof that you're making substantial business use of your computer.

Insurance

You can deduct the cost of extra insurance you purchase to cover items you own. Ordinary homeowners' insurance policies usually exclude or have a special limitation on items used for business purposes. You must purchase extra insurance if you wish to cover these items. There is even special insurance you can take out on home computers to cover the extra calamities that occur such as power surges which damage equipment or software.

Where Do You Deduct These Expenses?

Items used in your professional capacity as an employee, whether deducted immediately or depreciated over their useful life, are deducted under the *Miscellaneous Deductions* section of Schedule A. These items, when aggregated with your other miscellaneous deductions, are subjected to a 2% of Adjusted Gross Income floor [cf. Section 1 of the *Miscellaneous Deductions* chapter].

Items used in connection with a self-employment activity are deducted as a business expense on Schedule C. In this case, the items escape the purview of the 2% of Adjusted Gross Income floor and can be claimed even by those who use the standard deduction. In any event, if items are used partly for personal purposes, you must prorate the expenses accordingly.

Form 4562 is used to list items with a useful life of more than one year which are being expensed or depreciated. There is a special Part III on the 1987 Form 4562 for computing your depreciation or expensing deduction for *listed property*. This Part III is used for all listed property no matter if purchased before or after June 18, 1984. [See the *Expensing and Depreciation* chapter for further details.]

Miscellaneous Materials

The deduction for miscellaneous materials used in connection with your teaching duties might yield a sizable deduction. This is illustrated by the following recent court case.

Court Case

Gardner was a Professor of Education at a university in the South. The university did not provide all the supplies and educational materials which she used in her classes. As is typical with many teachers, she dug into her own pocket to pay for certain materials she felt were needed in her classroom teaching. According to the Court, *"The furnishing of supplies and materials to supplement those provided by a school may constitute an ordinary and necessary business expense."* In Gardner's case, the Court allowed a deduction of $856 for the cost of supplies and course materials purchased during the year.

Furthermore, this was not the only miscellaneous deduction allowed in connection with her duties as professor. She was allowed a deduction of $695 for depreciation, $78 for typewriter repair, and $300 for secretarial assistance. The sum of these job-related items which could be claimed as *miscellaneous deductions* was *$1,929.* [Gardner, TC Memo 1983-541]

If you are like most people, you haven't kept complete records of all the miscellaneous supplies you purchased for use in connection with your job. Although the keeping of records is preferred, the following court case, decided about 10 years ago, shows that the lack of such records does not necessarily rule out a deduction.

Court Case

A public school teacher claimed a deduction of $125 for miscellaneous educational materials. The IRS objected to this deduction (as well as others on his tax return) because he kept no records or receipts to back up his deduction. However, the Court believed the teacher, allowing the full $125 as a reasonable deduction for his educational materials.

Interestingly, the Court was uncertain whether the educational materials were used in the classes the teacher was teaching or in a course the teacher was taking to improve his professional skills. But, no matter. The deduction was justified whichever of the two alternatives held. [TC Memo 1978-299]

Chapter 3

Home Office

SECTION 1:
WHEN CAN YOU DEDUCT FOR A HOME OFFICE?

Teachers often find it necessary to do a substantial amount of work at home. At one time, most of these teachers were able to claim a deduction on their tax returns for this use of a "home office." But a number of years ago, Congress passed tough legislation severely restricting the home office deduction. An employee must satisfy the following rules in order to claim a deduction for a portion of his home used as an office during 1987:

Rule (1). The portion of his home must be used **exclusively on a regular basis** for business purposes;

Rule (2). The home office must be the **taxpayer's principal place of business;**
and

Rule (3). The use of the home office must be for the **convenience of the employer.**

Exceptions to Rule (2). If the home office is a *"separate structure which is not attached to the dwelling unit,"* then Rule (2) does not need to be satisfied. However Rules (1) and (3) still apply. Another exception when Rule (2) does not apply is when the office is used *"by patients, clients, or customers in meeting or dealing with the taxpayer in the normal course of his trade or business."*

Let us examine the above rules separately.

Exclusive Use of Home Office on a Regular Basis

The *exclusive use* requirement of Rule (1) means that there must be a specific part of the home used solely for business or professional purposes. No deduction is allowed for a den or other area which is used both for business and personal purposes. The area set aside must be *regularly* used for business purposes. No deduction is allowed for incidental or occasional business use, even if the area is used for no other purpose.

It is not necessary for the home office to be a separate room or partitioned-off area. This is illustrated by the following court case.

Example 1.
 A college professor used a portion of his bedroom as a home office. This portion was

> *"furnished with a desk, a chair, two file cabinets, and three bookcases. In the other portion or area of the bedroom petitioner had his bed and a dresser. He insisted that although the two areas were located within a single room, they were separate and discrete areas. However, the two areas of the room were not separated by any wall, partition, curtain, or other physical demarcation."*
>
> The IRS claimed he had not met the *exclusive use* rule because the home office was not an entire room or an area physically separated from the rest of the bedroom. But the Court found nothing in law which supported this requirement. If the home office occupied a specific area of the home and this area was not used for other purposes, the exclusive use requirement [Rule (1)] was met, even if the area was not physically separated from the rest of the home. (The Court disallowed the home office deduction for other reasons discussed below but carefully pointed out that the *exclusive use* requirement was met in this case.) [TC Memo 1981-301]

A separate court case shows that a home office need not be located in an ordinary "room." In this case, the Court ruled that a large walk-in closet would qualify as a home office, if all the other requirements for deduction were met. [TC Memo 1981-140]

Home Office as Principal Place of Business

Rule (2) which requires that a home office be the principal place of business will be the most difficult for teachers to satisfy. The Tax Court has defined the principal place of business to be the **focal point** of a taxpayer's activities. And for an employee, the Tax Court has in turn defined this focal point to be the principal place of business of his *employer* [cf. Examples 2 and 3]. Were this definition to stick, it would appear to rule out a teacher's deduction for a home office used in connection with his academic duties because his school, not his home office, would become the *focal point*.

However, 3 recent Court of Appeals decisions [Examples 4-6] have overruled the strict application of the focal point test as put forward by the Tax Court. In each case, an employee was allowed to deduct his home office even though it was not the principal place of his employer's business. In particular, take note of Example 5, in which a college teacher was able to deduct his home office because he made substantial use of it for his academic research. (Another way teachers can satisfy Rule (2) is to use a home office solely in connection with a secondary business activity—writing a book, consulting, reviewing, tutoring, etc. This situation is discussed later in this section. Also, teachers who do not teach during the summer might be able to claim their home office as a principal place of business for this period of time. Similarly, the use of a home office during a sabbatical or other extended leave of absence might also qualify. So far, the courts have not ruled on this type of situation.)

> **Example 2.**
> Mr. and Mrs. Chauls were music instructors, he at Valley College and she at a different nearby school. They converted 2 bedrooms in their home into offices, one

for each of them. These offices were used for the preparation of classes and related duties.

The Tax Court disallowed both their home office deductions because these offices failed the *principal place of business* requirement. In disallowing Mr. Chauls' claim, it considered it immaterial that he may have spent more time working in his home office than at school. As the Court explained its decision,

> "In our view the record is clear that the principal place of business of Mr. Chauls was Valley College. Petitioner was an instructor and he taught his classes at Valley College. He was furnished an office at Valley College and a rehearsal room at Valley College. Petitioner contends that he spent more hours working at home than he spent working at Valley College. However, in our view, the number of hours petitioner spent working at home as compared to the number of hours spent on the business premises of his employer is not the criteria for determining where his principal place of business is located. . . . We take it that what Congress had in mind was the focal point of a taxpayer's activities. . . . It was petitioner's teaching of classes that generated his income and, even though some or even most of his preparation for those classes was done in his home, his principal place of business was at the school where he taught." [Chauls, TC Memo 1980-471]

Example 3.

Bilenas was an engineer at an aerospace firm in New York. He also was employed as an Adjunct Professor in the Department of Mechanical Engineering at a nearby college.

The college did not provide Bilenas with an office. Rather, he set up one room of his home which he used exclusively in connection with his teaching duties. The home office was used to prepare classes, grade papers, etc. More time was spent working in his home office than was spent at the school where he taught.

The Tax Court did not allow a home office deduction. The fact that the school provided no office at work was irrelevant. So was the fact that more time was spent in the home office than at school. The school was the *'focal point'* of his activities as an Adjunct Professor. Consequently, the school rather than the home office was the *principal place of business*, ruling out a deduction. [Bilenas, TC Memo 1983-661]

Example 4.

Drucker was a concert violinist employed by the Metropolitan Opera. During the New York opera season, he spent about 26 hours per week at Lincoln Center performing and rehearsing. However, the Metropolitan Opera provided no individual practice facilities. In order for Drucker to perfect his skills and master the music to be performed, he had to maintain a studio at home. During a typical week, he spent 30 hours per week working in his home studio.

The Tax Court, following its usual line of reasoning, denied Drucker a home office deduction for his studio. It held that the focal point of his activities was not his home studio, but rather, his employer's principal place of business where he performed. This meant his home studio was not his principal place of business, violating Rule (2).

However, the Court of Appeals overturned the Tax Court decision. Drucker spent more time in his home studio than at the Metropolitan Opera. Because he was not provided practice facilities at work, it was necessary for him to maintain a studio at home where he could practice. Furthermore, his practice was essential to the performance of his job. The work he performed at Lincoln Center, i.e. rehearsals and performances, was made possible only by his solo practice at home.

Consequently, the Court of Appeals found that his home studio was indeed the focal point of his activities as a concert violinist. This meant his home office satisfied the *principal place of business* requirement, entitling him to a home office deduction. [Drucker, 52 AFTR 2d 83-5804]

Example 5.

Weissman was an Associate Professor of Philosophy at a well known University in a large northeastern city. He spent about 15 hours per week at the University, teaching his courses, meeting with students, preparing lectures, and grading examination papers.

In addition to his teaching duties, he was expected to do *"an unspecified amount of research and writing in his field in order to retain his teaching position."* Under the University bylaws, a candidate for promotion must possess a record of significant scholarly achievement in his field. *"As in other university communities, scholarly achievement is usually measured by research, writing and publication in one's field."*

Weissman lived with his family in a large 10-room apartment in the city. He used 2 rooms of the apartment, plus the bathroom between them, exclusively for research and writing. The 2 rooms were furnished with a desk, typewriter, chairs, filing cabinets and books. Weissman spent 50 to 60 hours per week in this space, doing research and writing on a book which he planned to have published.

Although the University provided Weissman with an office on campus, he was obliged to share his office with several other professors. It contained several desks, chairs and filing cabinets, but no typewriter. However, it was *"not a safe place to leave teaching, writing, or researching materials and equipment."*

When Weissman claimed a deduction for his home office, he wound up in Tax Court. As it had done in about a dozen other cases involving educators, the Tax Court threw out his deduction with little hesitation. Because his job was that of a teacher, the Tax Court considered the focal point of his duties to be the school where he taught, not the home office where he spent the majority of his time working on his research and writing.

However, when Weissman appealed his case to the Appeals Court in his district, he won a victory. The Appeals Court overruled the Tax Court, allowing a home office deduction.

The Appeals Court ruled that the *focal point* test had been misapplied in this case because Weissman's job consisted of 2 separate activities—teaching and research. In the Court's words,

"... *when a taxpayer's occupation involves two very distinct yet related activi-*

ties, such as practice and performance, see Drucker v. Commissioner [cf. Example 4] or writing and teaching, the 'focal point' approach creates a risk of shifting attention to the place where a taxpayer's work is more visible, instead of the place where the dominant portion of his work is accomplished.

"In the case of educators, the focal point approach does not always adequately distinguish between individuals with very different employment activities. No doubt many college professors spend most of their working hours teaching or engaging in teaching-related activities such as preparing for classes, meeting with students, and grading examinations and papers. Some college professors, however, spend the major share of their working hours researching and writing. Both types of employee have earned the designation 'professor,' but the title should not obscure the differences between them. In this case, the Tax Court focused too much on Professor Weissman's title and too little on his activities. . . . To the extent that the Tax Court found [the] College to be the focal point of Professor Weissman's employment activities simply because he taught courses there, it erred as a matter of law by failing to consider all aspects of his activities.

"A college professor's principal place of business is not necessarily the college at which he teaches any more than a musician's principal place of business is necessarily the concert hall at which he performs. . . . Here the taxpayer is a college professor who spends the majority of his employment-related time—80% of it—researching and writing. He needs a place to read, think, and write without interruption, and it is necessary for him to work at home because his shared, unsafe office does not provide the privacy needed to undertake sustained scholarly research and writing. Though the College library is available for research, it affords Professor Weissman no working space in which his research materials may be set aside or where he may use his typewriter. The lack of a private on-campus office makes Professor Weissman's home office a practical necessity."

Not only had Weissman's home office satisfied the *principal place of business* test but also the *convenience-of-the-employer* test as well. In the Court's words,

"The cost of maintaining his home office was almost entirely additional to nondeductible personal living expenses because it was used exclusively for employment-related activities and because such use was necessary as a practical matter if Professor Weissman was faithfully to perform his employment duties. This practical necessity negates any claim that the office was used as a matter of personal convenience rather than for the convenience of the employer. . . . Although [the] College has provided some space to Professor Weissman, it has not provided space in which he can effectively carry out his employment duties. The maintenance of a home office was not a personal preference of the employee: it spared the employer the cost of providing a suitable private office and thereby served the convenience of the employer." [Weissman, CA-2, 85-1 USTC 9106]

Note the 2 requirements Weissman satisfied in order to be able to deduct his home office expenses in the above case. First of all, the research and writing performed in his home office were the most substantial part of Weissman's professional activities—he devoted more time to these activities than to his teaching duties.

Second, the office facilities at school were inadequate. It was necessary for him to do his research and writing in his home office. This meant his home office satisfied the **convenience of the employer** requirement. Weissman's office at school was inadequate because of lack of safety and lack of privacy. Other factors that make a school office inadequate might include lack of availability at night or weekends, inadequate space to store research materials, lack of air conditioning in the summer months, noise in the surrounding halls or nearby offices, etc.

The IRS has decided not to appeal the above case to the next highest court, the Supreme Court. Strictly speaking, the decision only has legal force in the area covered by the Second Circuit Court of Appeals which decided the case. (This area includes only the states of New York, Vermont, and Connecticut.) However, professors in situations similar to Professor Weissman's, now for the first time since the restrictive home office rules were instituted over 10 years ago, have a legal precedent under which to claim their home office deductions.

Much of the home office controversy concerning college faculty is due to the widespread misunderstanding of the nature of duties of faculty members at research-oriented Colleges and Universities. While the Second Court of Appeals in the above case has shown it understands the central role research and publishing play in such duties, other court opinions have not shown such perception. For example, in one footnote to another professor's home office case, a Tax Court judge indicated his opinion of why the research and publishing of scholarly articles were required as follows: *"Petitioner's research and publishing activities were required not only so that petitioner could retain his job and eventually achieve tenure (a personal reason), but also to enhance the prestige of [the] College so it could continue to attract high caliber students"* [Storzer, TC Memo 1982-328]. The fact that the 5 articles which the professor published that year might have inherent value to society which the College considered its duty to support (even if they didn't "attract" any more students) apparently did not cross the mind of the judge.

The next 1986 court decision opened the door even further for claiming home office deductions. In this case, decided by the Seventh Circuit Court of Appeals (with jurisdiction over northern midwest states), the relative length of time spent in the home office was the most important factor. Here, the *focal point* test of the Tax Court was cast aside altogether. Even though the home office was used only 2 hours per day, this constituted a majority of time spent on business. As a result, the Court found the home office to be the *principal place of business*, qualifying for deduction.

Example 6.

John and Sally Meiers were employees of a corporation they owned, managing a laundromat in a Midwestern city. In the Court's words,

> *"Sally Meiers managed the laundromat and retained five part-time employees to assist the customers, make change, sell laundry products, launder customers' clothes, and clean the laundromat. Mrs. Meiers' duties as manager included drafting the work schedule for employees, collecting money from the machines and filling the coin changer, assisting customers, performing bookkeeping, and other*

managerial tasks. On average, Mrs. Meiers spent an hour a day at the laundromat and two hours a day in an office in her home drafting work schedules for employees and doing the laundromat's bookkeeping. The 'home office' consisted of a separate room in the taxpayers' home and contained a desk, filing cabinet, safe, change counter and sofa. It is undisputed that this separate room was used exclusively for administrative work on behalf of the laundry."

When Mrs. Meiers claimed a home office deduction on her tax return, the IRS objected. And when the case wound up in Tax Court, the objection was initially upheld. As it had in other cases, the Tax Court invoked its own *focal point* test. Since the laundromat was the *focal point* of the business, the Tax Court ruled that the laundromat was the principal place of business, not the home office where she did most of her work.

After rebuff from the Tax Court, Mrs. Meiers took her case to the Seventh Court of Appeals which had jurisdiction over the midwestern region where she lived. This Court, as did the Court in the Weissman case [Example 5], did not think the focal point test to be the controlling factor. Most relevant were the length of time and importance of work done in the home office. In the Court's words,

"We, like the Second Circuit, question the usefulness of the focal point test. As Weissman points out, at least where a taxpayer's occupation involves distinct activities, the 'focal point' approach shifts attention to the place where the taxpayer's work is more visible, instead of the place where the dominant portion of his work is accomplished. Here, it is undisputed that Sally Meiers' 'principal place of business' in terms both of hours worked and probably of functions performed, was the home office, not the laundromat. The focal point test as applied by the Tax Court places undue emphasis upon the location where goods or services are provided to customers and income is generated, not necessarily where work is predominantly performed. The focal point test is concededly easy to apply and is less subjective than [previous] standards. Yet we do not believe this approach is fair to taxpayers or carries out in the most appropriate way the apparent intent of Congress.

"In determining the taxpayer's principal place of business, we think a major consideration ought to be the length of time the taxpayer spends in the home office as opposed to other locations. But time spent is not necessarily the only consideration. There are other factors, which may from time to time weigh in the balance, such as the importance of the business functions performed by the taxpayer in the home office; the business necessity of maintaining a home office; and the expenditures of the taxpayer to establish a home office....

"In applying these standards to the present case, we conclude that the Tax Court erred in denying taxpayers a deduction for a home office.... Accordingly, we reverse the decision of the Tax Court...." [Meiers, 57 AFTR 2d 86-642]

Shared Use of Home Office

A common situation that arises is this. A married couple sets aside one room which they both use as a home office. One spouse uses the office in connection with his regular job. This usage does not qualify because it fails the *principal place of business* test. The other spouse uses the office in connection with a separate business activity. This usage meets with all the requirements of the home office deduction.

The question becomes whether and to what extent a deduction is allowed. The following 1984 court case answers this question in the best possible way. The couple can deduct for the home office based just on the qualifying spouse's usage. The use of the office by the other spouse in connection with his regular job is simply disregarded. Furthermore, no allocation is required; in this case the full deduction for the home office was allowed just as if the non-qualifying spouse had not existed.

Example 7.

Max and Tobia Frankel set aside one room in their house which was used solely as a home office. The room was equipped for use by both of them, with two desks, filing cabinets, etc.

Max used the office in connection with his job as a newspaper editor. He needed the office to be in touch with his newspaper during off hours regarding changes that had to be made in the late edition which went to press at 11:30 p.m. each evening. He also used the office for reading and research connected with his editorial duties and for extensive telephone conversations with politicians and other community leaders who wanted their point of view represented in the editorial writing. His use of the office was found to fail the tests for a home office deduction because it was not his principal place of business. His extensive contact via the telephone did not fall under the *meeting or dealing with clients or customers* exception to Rule 2 [cf. the first page of this chapter] because there was no *personal* contact, just contact by telephone.

Tobia Frankel used the home office for her work as a free-lance consultant. She spent most of the year working on a report she had contracted with the government to prepare on a study of centrally planned economies in other countries. The home office qualified as the principal place of business of her consulting activity.

The Court allowed the Frankels a home office deduction based only on Tobia's use of the office. Even though Max's business use of the office would not qualify it for deduction, this did not violate the *exclusively for business purposes* requirement. The office was still used exclusively for business rather than personal purposes. In fact, the IRS did not even object to the deduction on this point. Their only objection was a technical one, overruled by the Court, relating to the length of time she used the office.

As discussed in the next section, the home office deduction cannot exceed the income produced by use of the home office. Here, Tobia's consulting income was $5000 and her home office expenses only $1600 so there was no problem. Had her expenses exceeded her income, this limitation would have come into force. She could not have used Max's income to justify the expenses, since his usage of the office did not itself qualify for the home office deduction. [Frankel, 82 TC No. 26]

Home Office Used for Secondary Business Activity

For most people, except as described in Examples 4-6, the *principal place of business* requirement rules out a deduction for a home office used in connection with their main job. But the use of a home office connected with a secondary business activity can be deducted, as long as the home office is the principal location of that activity. It does not matter that an individual's main job is located elsewhere. For example, the use of a home office for writing a book, consulting, tutoring, running a side business, etc. would qualify. However, as discussed in Section 2, the deduction for a home office used as the principal place of business for a secondary business activity cannot exceed the gross income from that activity.

> **Example 8.**
> Samuel was a full-time education teacher, working on a master's degree at a nearby University. His wife was a former teacher and was also working on a master's degree at the same University. Together, they decided to develop and manage a sales business in order to earn extra money. They operated this business solely out of an office in their home and claimed a $2,500 deduction on their tax return. In the Court's words,
>
> > "Samuel testified that within petitioner's three-bedroom apartment, two children slept in one room, an infant child slept in petitioner's bedroom, and the third bedroom was used as an office. They also testified that there was a desk and a telephone in the third bedroom and that the closets were used to store the sales products. Samuel testified that he did not use the room to prepare for his teaching job or his university studies."
>
> The IRS objected that the room was not used exclusively as the principal place of their sales business. But the Court did not agree with this objection, stating,
>
> > "In our opinion, the evidence is sufficient to establish that petitioners exclusively used the office in their home on a regular basis as the principal place of their sales business. The room was not used for recreational purposes, and petitioners used local libraries and university facilities to study for their courses at the university. [The IRS] has presented no evidence to the contrary. Therefore, we hold that petitioners may deduct expenses incurred in maintaining the office in their home."
>
> That was the good news. Had the sales business produced a reasonable amount of income, they would have obtained substantial benefit from their home office deduction. But the bad news was that they only had $46.50 in sales for the year. Not only was this a business disappointment, but under the rules described in Section 2, this meant their home office deduction could not exceed $46.50. [TC Memo 1985-49]

You cannot get around the home office limitation by renting your home office to your employer or to an entity for which you are providing services as an independent contractor. This was ruled out by a provision in the 1986 Tax Reform Act. This loophole was eliminated in response to an accountant who, under prior law, rented his home office to the accounting firm for which he worked, converting a home office that was secondary to his job into a primary place of business of his "rental business."

Also, a home office deduction cannot be claimed for purely investment activities—reading financial periodicals, clipping bond coupons, etc. because these do not qualify as *trade or business* activities. (In order to be in the *trade or business* of investing, one must be a short-term active *trader* rather than a long-term *investor*.) But this restriction does not apply to overseeing rental properties if it involves active management duties. This is illustrated by the following court case.

> **Example 9.**
> Curphey was a dermatologist, employed 40 hours per week by a hospital in Hawaii. He owned 6 single-family residential properties which he managed himself. He lived in a two bedroom condominium and
>> "used one bedroom exclusively as an office for bookkeeping and other activities related to management of his rental properties. That room was furnished with a desk, a bookcase, a filing cabinet, calculators, and a 'code-a-phone answering service'. There was no television, sofa, or bed in that room and petitioner did not allow guests to stay there. The closet of that room was used only to store items related to the rental properties such as lamps, carpets, and other furnishings, signs which petitioner used to advertise the units for rent, cleaning materials which he needed to prepare a rental unit for a new tenant, and a tool box."
>
> Since Curphey was actively involved in the management of his properties, his efforts constituted a *trade or business* activity rather than just an *investment activity*. And since his home office was used regularly as the principal business location for this activity, it qualified for deduction. [Curphey 73 TC No. 61]

Home Office For Convenience of the Employer

Rule (3) requires that the home office be for the *convenience of the employer.* This requirement does not apply to self-employment activities since there is no *employer* involved. For employees, this requirement means that there must be a genuine need for you to have a home office. If you have an office at work, you will be required to show why the facilities there are inadequate.

Vacation Office Ruled Deductible

The following 1984 court case shows how a vacation home office can qualify for deduction, even when used only a small portion of the year.

> **Example 10.**
> Heineman was the chief executive officer of a large corporation in Chicago. He spent his summers in Wisconsin where he owned property overlooking Lake Michigan. The property contained a vacation residence plus a separate structure which was furnished as an office. The office was used by Heineman each August for long-range corporate planning. The rest of the year, the office was unused.
> The Wisconsin office was more suitable than his Chicago office because he could avoid the interruptions of daily business that would occur in Chicago. By using his Wisconsin office during August, he could find the isolation he wanted for concentrating on long-range planning.
> The IRS objected to Heineman's home office deduction. It claimed that the office was simply a personal convenience, not a necessity of the job; he could have

> just stayed in Chicago and worked in his regular office.
> The Court did not buy this objection. It found that *"there was a business reason for performing the review of the long-term plans away from the Chicago office, and the expenses of the office for performing that work are not made nondeductible because the petitioner chose to perform the work in an environment more suitable to him."*
> The IRS also objected that Heineman had not asked his employer to reimburse him for the cost of constructing his home office. But the Court overruled this objection too. There was no evidence that he could have been reimbursed. And, even if he could have been reimbursed, he did not want his company to have a claim on any of his Wisconsin property.
> Consequently, the Court allowed Heineman a home office deduction. This included a full year's depreciation on the cost of constructing the office, even though it was used only one month a year. [Heineman 82 TC No. 41]

The above case opens the door for individuals with summer property who perform work-related duties there. Note however that in the above case, the home office was in a separate structure not attached to the residence. This exempted it from the *principal place of business* test as described earlier in this section. Home offices which are not located in detached structures fall under the *principal place of business* requirement.

Items Used in a Home Office

As discussed in the next section, the home office deduction includes the basic cost of providing office space (including depreciation, furniture, utilities, etc.) plus the cost of auxiliary items such as equipment and telephone service. But even if you don't qualify for the home office deduction, a deduction for the auxiliary items used in the home office may still be permitted.

The cost of providing telephone service is an example of this [cf. the *Books, Supplies, & Equipment* chapter]. In several court cases, a deduction for business use of a home telephone was permitted at the same time the basic deduction for home office was ruled out. [Shepherd, TC Memo 1976-48; Barry, TC Memo 1978-250]

Supplies and equipment such as a typewriter or calculator would also qualify for deduction independent of the basic home office deduction. For example, in one court case a deduction for the rental of a typewriter and calculator was permitted, even though these items were used in the person's residence at night and there was no deduction allowed for the basic cost of providing these residential facilities. [Hicks, TC Memo 1960-48]

Office Decorating

The cost of cleaning, decorating, and furnishing your home office is deductible, as long as the home office meets the requirements described above.

Pictures and other works of art do not qualify for a deduction because they do not wear out. However, in a recent court case, deductions of $445 were allowed for the cost of framing pictures which were then hung in a home office. [Fanning, TC Memo 1980-462]

But beautifying your regular office at work might not qualify for deduction. A recent court case disallowed a deduction to a government worker for a live plant and framed print she purchased for her office at work. Her employer had provided all the furnishings considered necessary to do her job. The cost of beautifying her office was ruled to be a personal rather than a business expense. [Henderson, TC Memo 1983-372]

Travel from a Home Office to Another Business Location

If you have a home office which is the principal location of a business activity, then you can deduct the cost of traveling from your home office to another location in connection with that business activity. This is illustrated by the following 1986 court case.

Example 11.
Wickler was an anesthetist at a small hospital in the South. She was not considered an employee of the hospital, but rather was an independent contractor. The hospital billed patients for her fees and deducted an agreed percentage of the fees and remitted the balance to the anesthetist. In the Court's words,

"So far as this record discloses, petitioner was the only full time anesthetist practicing at the hospital. That institution, however, would not provide any office space for petitioner's use, and accordingly she maintained an office in the basement of her home, which she used exclusively for the practice of her profession. In that office, inter alia, she maintained professional books such as books and manuals on anesthesia. She also maintained a ledger of the cases in which she had served, including the patients' name[s], copies of the charges which she made with respect to each patient, medical notes related to patients which she was handling, a schedule of her appointments for operations, records of other anesthetists secured by her to perform services at the hospital, and the like. . . .

"In addition to the various records and educational materials prepared and kept by petitioner in her home office, she also conferred by telephone there with doctors at the hospital, both with regard to scheduling of appointments as well as with respect to the condition of patients, and used her office telephone to arrange for the services of other anesthetists.

"Petitioner's office in her home was the only office which she had. She traveled between her home office and the hospital in her own automobile, and frequently made several round trips a day in connection with her duties."

The Court found her home office to be her principal place of business in which a substantial part of her work was performed. In such a case, travel between her home office and another business location (in this case the hospital where she worked) is deductible. Since 90% of her automobile mileage was incurred traveling between her home and the hospital, she was permitted to deduct 90% of her automobile operating expenses and depreciation for the year. [Wickler, TC Memo 1986-1]

Section 2:
Computation of
Home Office Expenses

If you have an allowable home office deduction, then you may deduct a pro rata portion of the expenses incurred in the general maintenance of the home. The list of allowable home expenses includes:

1. rent (if residence is rented).

2. depreciation (if residence is owned).

3. cost of heat and light.

4. cleaning expenses (including salary for cleaning person).

5. painting the outside of the house.

6. premiums on home insurance.

7. general house repairs (e.g. repairing the gutters).

8. extermination and termite inspections.

9. mortgage interest.

10. property taxes.

Note that if you claim a portion of your mortgage interest and property taxes as a home office deduction, you cannot claim these same amounts again as itemized deductions elsewhere on Schedule A.

Be on the alert for any expenses which you think are relevant. For example, in one case a taxpayer was allowed to depreciate a pro rata portion of the cost of a vacuum cleaner since it was used in cleaning his home office.

Expenses relating solely to the use of your office may be deducted in full, such as the cost of painting only the office or the cost of furniture used in the office. You may not deduct expenses relating only to portions of the house excluding the office such as painting the living room.

How Is the Pro Rata Proportion Computed?

Suppose that you have a room set aside for use as a home office. There are two methods to determine what proportion of home expenses can be attributed to your home office. The first method is to divide the area occupied by the home office by the total area of the entire home. Thus, if the office occupies 140 square feet and your home has a total area of 2,500 square feet, then you can deduct 140/2,500 = 5.6% of the allowable home expenses.

The second method is to divide the number of rooms used for your home office by the total number of rooms in the home. For example, if you use one room of a five room house as your office and the rooms are about the same size, you may deduct $1/5$ of the allowable home expenses [IRS Publication 587]. In general, this method will give the higher deduction. (A recent court case indicates you don't have to count every area as a full room; in this case, a kitchen in a house was counted only as ½ of a room, resulting in a deduction equal to 1/5.5 of the home expenses. [Moretti, TC Memo 1982-552])

Example

You use one room of a 6 room house you own as a home office for which you are entitled to a deduction. You can deduct ⅙ of the following expenses:

Depreciation on house	$2,000
Electricity for light and air conditioning	490
Gas for heating	250
Repair of the roof	300
Fire insurance	100
Cleaning person	390
Mortgage interest	2,500
Property taxes	800
TOTAL	$6,830

Thus, your home office deduction is ⅙ × $6,830 = $1,138. In addition, you can deduct for the cost of furnishings or equipment used in the home office [cf. the *Expensing and Depreciation* chapter].

Home Office Can Be More Than One Room

A recent court case illustrates that the home office deduction need not be limited to a single room or even two rooms.

Court Case

Greenway was a professor of anthropology, specializing in ethnomusicology. He was also an author, having written several published books and numerous articles.

He set aside 3 rooms of his house as a home office. He used 3 rooms in order to keep separate projects on which he was working simultaneously and did not use those rooms for any other purpose. Under the rules in effect at the time, he was entitled to a deduction for the use of his home office.

The IRS allowed him a deduction for the full use of all 3 rooms. The only home office question among the issues that came up at the trial was a secondary one concerning the amount of depreciation that should be allowed. [Greenway, TC Memo 1980-97]

Home Office Deduction Cannot Produce a Loss

Under the new law, if a home office deduction would result in a loss on your tax return, you cannot deduct this loss. The way to proceed in such a case is as follows:

Start with the gross income produced by the business activity for which you are using the home office. From this, subtract expenses other than home office—supplies, salaries, travel, etc. Next, subtract home office expenses in the following order:

(1) Interest and Taxes

(2) Operating Expenses such as repairs, utilities, insurance, cleaning, etc.

(3) Depreciation

If a loss results at any step, you must stop; in such case the business activity produces a net result of $0 for the year. (However, under a new provision in the law, any unused losses can be carried over to future years as described later in this chapter.)

Of course, in the above list you only subtract that pro rata portion of interest and taxes, etc. corresponding to the percentage of the home used as an office. The remainder of interest and taxes is deducted on Schedule A in the usual way. The following illustration is adapted from an example published by the IRS. [Prop. Reg. 1.280A-2(i) (7)]

Example

X operates a consulting business out of his home office for which he is entitled to a deduction. X has a special telephone line for the office and occasionally employs secretarial assistance. X determines that his home office occupies 20% of his home. On the basis of the following figures, X determines that the sum of the allowable business deductions for the use of the office is $1,050.

Income from consulting services		$4,000
Expenses for secretary	$ 500	
Business telephone	250	
Supplies	350	
	$1,100	
Total expenses other than home office		−1,100
Net income derived from use of home office		$2,900

1. Interest and Taxes:

	Total	Allocable to Office
Mortgage interest	$6,000	$1,200
Real estate taxes	2,000	400
	$8,000	$1,600

Amount allowable	−1,600
Limit on further deductions	$1,300

2. Operating expenses:

	Total	Allocable to Office
Insurance	$ 250	$ 50
Utilities	2,500	500
Repairs	250	50
Cleaning	500	100
		$700

Amount allowable... −700

Limit on further deductions.. $ 600

3. Depreciation:

	Total	Allocable to Office
Depreciation on house	$5,500	$1,100

Amount allowable in current year................................. $ 600

Remainder (carried over to future years as described below)......... $ 500

X may claim the remaining $6,400 ($8,000 − $1,600) paid for mortgage interest and real estate taxes as itemized deductions on Schedule A.

Home Office Losses Carried Over to Future Years

As illustrated above, a home office deduction is not allowed to the extent it creates a net loss from the business activity to which it belongs. However, such a disallowed amount can be carried over to the following year to the extent it does not produce a net loss for the business activity in that year. There is no time limit on the carryover. Any amounts disallowed can continue to be carried over until there is a net profit from the business activity they can be deducted against.

Example

Smith operates a consulting business from his home office which generated gross income of $6,000 in 1987. Business expenses that are not attributable to home office itself (e.g. secretarial services, telephone, supplies, etc.) total $4,000. Home office expenses (interest, taxes, utilities, depreciation, etc.) total $3,000. Thus, Smith has a net loss of $1,000 ($6,000 − $4,000 − $3,000) for 1987. This $1,000 loss cannot be deducted in 1987 but must be carried over to the following year.

In 1988, Smith has gross income from his consulting business of $9,000, home office expenses of $2,500, and other expenses of $3,500. The result, as reported on his 1988 Schedule C, would be as follows:

A. Gross income:	$9,000
B. Expenses other than home office:	-3,500
C. A − B:	5,500
D. Home office expenses for 1988:	-2,500
E. C − D:	3,000
F. Carryover from 1987:	-1,000
G. Net profit reported on Schedule C:	$2,000

In the above example, E ($3,000) exceeded the $1,000 carryover from 1987. Had it not, any excess would continue to be carried over until there was a year in which the consulting business had a profit. For example, suppose that in the above, E equaled $600 instead of $3,000. In this case, $600 of the $1,000 carryover would be applied to reduce the net profit to $0. The remaining $400 would continue to be carried over into the future.

Telephone Expenses

You may be able to deduct a portion of your telephone expenses (including installation charges, repair costs, equipment fees, etc.) on your 1987 tax return. You do not need to satisfy the home office rules to deduct these expenses. A further discussion of deducting telephone expenses is contained in the *Books, Supplies, & Equipment* chapter.

Moving Your Home Office

If you move from one residence to another, then you may deduct the cost of moving the furnishings, books, etc. in your home office. You are not restricted by the mileage limitation which applies to general moving expenses.

Where Do You Deduct Home Office Expenses?

Employees may claim a deduction for home office expenses only if they itemized their deductions. This deduction is taken under *Miscellaneous Deductions* on Schedule A. Thus it, when aggregated with other miscellaneous deductions, is subject to a 2% of Adjusted Gross Income floor [cf. the *Miscellaneous Deduction* chapter].

You should attach an explanation which shows the amounts in each category of home expenses such as rent, cleaning, etc. It should also show your method of prorating these expenses to determine the amount attributable to your home office.

Home office expenses connected with a self-employment activity can be deducted even if you claim the standard deduction. And there is no 2% of Adjusted Gross Income floor. The net result of your self-employment income is reported on line 13, *Business Income*. You should attach a statement which gives a breakdown of your income and expenses.

Schedule C can be used for this purpose. However, you should be aware that Schedule C contains a specific question, *"Did you claim a deduction for expenses of an office in your home?"* If you check the "Yes" box and your return is audited, you can be almost certain that your home office deduction will be questioned.

How to Avoid Capital Gains Tax If You Sell Your Home

Ordinarily, when you sell an item that has appreciated in value, you must pay a capital gains tax on the profit. However, as discussed in the *Homeowners* chapter, there is an exception to this rule. You do not pay capital gains tax upon sale of your principal residence, provided you reinvest in another principal residence of the same or greater value. But the exception does not apply to that portion of your house used as a home office. For example, if part of your house is being used as a home office, then capital gains tax would be due on an appropriate fraction of the profit at the time of sale plus any depreciation you had claimed in prior years.

However, a 1982 IRS ruling has provided a way to avoid this situation. According to this ruling, the IRS will look only at how the residence is being used at the time of sale. Thus, if your home office no longer qualifies for deduction so it is being used 100% as your principal residence, then the reinvestment rule in the preceding paragraph applies to your entire residence. As long as you invest in a principal residence of the same or greater value and no portion of the new residence qualifies for a home office deduction, then under the rules described in the *Homeowners* chapter, no capital gains tax will be due. [IRS Revenue Ruling 82-26, IRB-6 p. 5, reversing IRS Private Letter Ruling #7935003]

This ruling is especially useful because it is so easy to satisfy the required conditions. Just make some personal use of your home office during the year you sell your old home. This will disqualify you from a home office deduction that year and thereby satisfy the condition of the ruling. Then, in a later year, you can convert a room in your new residence into a deductible home office with no capital gains tax having been paid.

Chapter 4

Expensing and Depreciation

SECTION 1:
INTRODUCTION

There are new rules for deducting non-trivial job-related, business, or investment items, first placed into service in 1987, which will be used for more than one year. Such items now generally fall into one of 3 classes.

The **real estate class** consists of houses, apartments, and other buildings. Land is not included because it generates no deduction based on its "wearing out"

The **5-year recovery class** consists of (i) automobiles and trucks, (ii) computers and peripheral equipment, calculators, typewriters, and copiers, and (iii) items used for research and experimentation.

The **7-year recovery class** includes books, furniture, and office equipment not included in the 5-year class.

For items in the real estate class, you are not allowed to deduct the cost all at once. Instead, you must apportion the cost over a period of years. This is called **depreciation.**

For items in the 5-year or 7-year recovery class (e.g. books, equipment, furniture, etc.), you can **expense** the item, that is, deduct the entire cost in the year it is first used. This option is limited to $10,000 worth of items purchased in 1987. This *expensing method* is discussed in Section 2.

You can also *depreciate* books, equipment, furniture, etc. over either 5 years or 7 years, depending upon the recovery class to which the item belongs [cf. Section 3].

Expensing is almost always preferable to depreciation because, other things being equal, a tax writeoff is more valuable the earlier it is used because of the time value of money. In fact, expensing is all the more attractive in 1987 because the entire deduction occurs in 1987 when the tax rates are higher, rather than spreading the cost over the next few years when the basic tax rates will generally be reduced.

However, there are certain cases when the depreciation method should be used for 5-year or 7-year recovery class items. First, an item must be used more than 50% for business purposes throughout the entire recovery class period. Otherwise, the item should be *depreciated* rather than *expensed*. If the expensing method is used for an item purchased in 1987 and then in a later year within the recovery class period, business use falls below 50%, the IRS can *recapture* a portion of the expensing deduction that was claimed [cf. Section 2].

Second, the expensing method should not be used on automobiles which cost more than $12,800. Because of special rules that apply, depreciation is superior to expensing for such automobiles [cf. the *Automobile Expenses* chapter].

Third, depreciation might be preferable to expensing in some cases where your business use percentage is expected to increase in future years.

Fourth, items used for investment purposes (e.g. a computer used just for tracking stocks) cannot be expensed, but must be depreciated.

Finally, there are special rules which apply to certain home computers, photo and video items, and automobiles which are considered *listed property*. As discussed below, sometimes depreciation is the only allowable writeoff method for these items.

Form 4562 is the basic form on which the items being depreciated or expensed are listed. For employees, their total job-related depreciation or expensing deductions are included under *Miscellaneous Deductions* on Schedule A. (As discussed in Section 1 of the *Miscellaneous Deductions* chapter, a 2% of Adjusted Gross Income floor applies to the sum total of all miscellaneous deductions claimed on Schedule A.) Self-employed individuals claim these deductions on Schedule C, escaping the 2% of Adjusted Gross Income floor.

Special Rules for Autos, Computers, and Entertainment Items

There are 2 special conditions that apply to *Listed Property* bought after June 18, 1984. Items bought prior to this time are not subject to these conditions. Listed Property includes the following items:

Listed Property

1. Automobiles and other passenger vehicles.

2. Home Computers (including peripherals), except for employer-owned computers used exclusively at a regular business establishment or computers used exclusively in a home office qualifying for deduction as described in the *Home Office* chapter.

3. Property of a type generally used for purposes of entertainment, recreation, or amusement (e.g. video recorders, cameras, etc.), except if used either (i) exclusively at your regular job location or deductible home office, or (ii) in connection with your principal job or business.

Condition 1: Listed Property Purchased by an Employee after June 18, 1984 Must Be Required by His Employer

In order for listed property purchased by an employee after June 18, 1984 in connection with his job to be deductible, the law states that its use must be *"for the convenience of the employer and required as a condition of employment."* According to IRS regulations, the phrase *"condition of employment"* refers to the proper performance of an employee's duties. Quoting from these regulations,

> *"In order to satisfy the 'condition of employment' requirement, the use of the property must be required in order for the employee to perform the duties of his or her employment properly. Whether the use of the property is so required depends on all the facts and circumstances. Thus, the employer need not explicitly require the employee to use the property. Similarly, a mere statement by the employer that the use of the property is a condition of employment is not sufficient."* [IRS Reg. #1.280F-6T]

The IRS has not yet similarly interpreted the phrase *"for the convenience of the employer."* However, this phrase would appear to be superfluous in this context. It is hard to produce an example where the *condition of employment* requirement would be satisfied without the *convenience of the employer* requirement being satisfied also.

The IRS regulations give 3 examples which apply to the use of automobiles or other personal transportation vehicles. In 2 cases where the employer did not provide a vehicle but the employee had to travel to various jobsites, the *condition of employment* requirement was satisfied. But in the third case the *condition of employment* standard was not satisfied where the employer made a car available to the employee, but the employee chose to use her own car and receive reimbursement instead.

The IRS regulations also contain an example concerning the use of a home computer. This example is discussed in the *Books, Supplies, and Equipment* chapter.

Condition 2: Listed Property Purchased after June 18, 1984 Must Be Used More than 50% for Business Purposes—Otherwise a Special Depreciation Table Applies

Listed property purchased after June 18, 1984 which is used 50% or less for business purposes cannot be expensed. Instead, a special *listed property depreciation table* [cf. Section 3] must be used to determine the annual writeoffs. This special table stretches out the deductions over a longer period of time than under the regular depreciation table.

Listed property which is used more than 50% for business purposes is not subject to this restriction. The expensing method (or regular depreciation table) applies to these items.

However, no matter what the percentage of business use, Condition 1 above must still be satisfied. Otherwise, no expensing or depreciation deductions can be claimed.

Maximum Limitations on Autos

There are extra limitations on the amounts that can be deducted for expensing or depreciation on an automobile. These are described in the *Automobile Expenses* chapter.

SECTION 2:
EXPENSING METHOD

On your 1987 tax return, you can deduct in full, instead of depreciating, up to $10,000 worth of items in the 5-year or 7-year recovery classes which you placed into service during 1987. These categories include automobiles, calculators, equipment, furniture, etc. but not buildings or other real estate. However, this option does not apply to certain *listed property* as discussed in Section 1.

The $10,000 limit applies to single or joint tax returns. For married persons filing separately, the $10,000 limit is allocated equally between the 2 separate returns unless a different allocation is elected.

The procedure of deducting the cost in the first year of use instead of depreciating is called *expensing*. To qualify for expensing, the items must be used in connection with your job or self-employment activity. Items which are used just for investment-related activities do not qualify for the expensing option but must be depreciated as discussed in Section 3.

> *Example 1.*
>
> You bought a $300 typewriter in 1987 which is used only for job-related purposes. Under the expensing option, you deduct the full $300 on your 1987 tax return. There are no further deductions for the typewriter in future years.

If more than $10,000 worth of items was purchased in 1987, the expensing option is limited to $10,000, with the remainder depreciated as discussed in Section 3.

> *Example 2.*
>
> You purchased a $200 typewriter and $11,000 worth of computer equipment during 1987, all of which are used in an outside business activity. You can use the expensing option on up to $10,000 worth of purchases, say the entire $200 typewriter and $9,800 of the computer. The remaining $1,200 of the computer is depreciated over the 6-year period 1987-1992, as described in Section 3. The total deductions in each year are as follows:
>
> | Year | Deduction | | |
> |---|---|---|---|
> | 1987 .... $10,000 (expensing limit) + | 20% × $1,200 = | $10,240 |
> | 1988 .... | 32% × 1,200 = | 384 |
> | 1989 .... | 19.2% × 1,200 = | 230 |
> | 1990 .... | 11.5% × 1,200 = | 138 |
> | 1991 .... | 11.5% × 1,200 = | 138 |
> | 1992 .... | 5.8% × 1,200 = | 70 |
> | | | $11,200 |

If an item is used partly for business purposes and partly for personal purposes, then the expensing option is applied to the appropriate fraction of the item's cost.

> *Example 3.*
>
> You purchased a $100 calculator in 1987 which is used 90% for job-related purposes and 10% for personal purposes. You can deduct 90% × $100 = $90 of the cost on your 1987 tax return.

Election to Use Expensing Option

Technically speaking, depreciation is considered to be the "regular" method with the expensing option a secondary method which you can elect to use instead of depreciation. To elect this option, you fill out Section A on Form 4562. If you do not make the appropriate *election to expense,* the IRS could require you to use the depreciation option. This form should be included with the original tax return you file, not an amended return.

Items Converted to Personal Use

Suppose you purchase an item which is used for business purposes the first year, but is used primarily for personal purposes thereafter. Under the expensing option, you would deduct the full cost in the first year, thereby giving you a total writeoff for an item which is used overall only partly for business purposes. To prevent this "distortion," Congress enacted into law a special recapture provision affecting the expensing option.

This provision applies if the item is *not used predominantly in a trade or business* at anytime within the period of the recovery class to which the item belongs. Under this provision, the IRS is authorized to *recapture* a portion of the expensing deduction which was claimed. That is, you would be required to report as taxable income in a later year a part of the expensing deduction you claimed in the year of purchase.

SECTION 3: DEPRECIATION

This section describes the depreciation rules that apply to items placed into service in 1987. For items placed into service prior to 1987, the tables described here do not generally apply. Instead, you would use the table applying to that year. For example, a typewriter purchased (and placed into service) in 1985 would be depreciated according to the percentages (15%, 22%, 21%, 21%, 21%) given by the 5-year table for the years 1985-1989 [cf. last year's edition of this Tax Guide].

Depreciation Methods for 5-Year and 7-Year Property

As discussed in Section 1, items other than real estate generally fall into either the 5-year recovery class (e.g. autos, computers, typewriters, research items, etc.) or the 7-year recovery class (e.g. books, furniture, etc.). For both of these categories there are 2 choices of depreciation methods — the **accelerated** method and the **straight-line** method. (The accelerated method is sometimes referred to as the *prescribed* method, abbreviated PRE, or the *double-declining balance* method, abbreviated DDB, in IRS forms.) For either of these categories, you must use the same method for all items purchased during a given year. However, you may use the straight-line method for all items in one category and the accelerated method for all items in the other. You will be able to make a different choice of methods for items purchased in future years.

For items purchased in 1987, the following table shows the percentage that would be deducted each year under the accelerated and straight-line methods. The percentages are applied to full cost of an item (including sales tax, delivery charges, etc.), assuming it is used entirely for business-related purposes. Observe that the accelerated method will be the best choice for most people because it yields the most rapid write-off. (As discussed later in this section, a different table applies to certain *listed property* purchased after June 18, 1984.)

REGULAR DEPRECIATION TABLE

5-Year Property

Year	Accelerated Method	Straight-Line Method
1987	20 %	10%
1988	32 %	20%
1989	19.2%	20%
1990	11.5%	20%
1991	11.5%	20%
1992	5.8%	10%
	100%	100%

7-Year Property

Year	Accelerated Method	Straight-Line Method
1987	14.3%	7.1%
1988	24.5%	14.3%
1989	17.5%	14.3%
1990	12.5%	14.3%
1991	8.9%	14.3%
1992	8.9%	14.3%
1993	8.9%	14.3%
1994	4.5%	7.1%
	100%	100%

Observe that in the above table, it makes no difference when during the year the item was placed into service. Thus, for example, the same deductions are produced by an item purchased in January as by one purchased in December. The tables are constructed on the basis of an item being placed into service at the midpoint of 1987 and being used, say in the case of 5-year property, until the midpoint of 1992—a total of 5 full years. That is why, for example, it takes an extra 6th year to fully depreciate an item in the 5-year recovery class.

Example

You purchased a typewriter in 1987 for $300. Using the first column in the table for items in the 5-year category, the following would be the annual depreciation deductions:

Year	Deduction
1987	20% × $300 = $ 60
1988	32% × 300 = 96
1989	19.2% × 300 = 58
1990	11.5% × 300 = 34
1991	11.5% × 300 = 34
1992	5.8% × 300 = 18
	$300

Depreciation

In the above example, it is assumed the typewriter was used 100% for business purposes. If used partly for personal purposes, the above deductions would be reduced accordingly. For example, if the typewriter were used 60% for business purposes and 40% for personal purposes, the basic depreciation percentages would be applied to 60% × $300 = $180. In this case, the deductions for each of the 6 years in the table would be 20% × $180 = $36, 32% × $180 = $58, etc.

Listed Property

As discussed in Section 1, special rules apply to automobiles and certain home computers or entertainment items purchased after June 18, 1984 which fall into the *Listed Property* category. If such items qualify for deduction but are used 50% or less for business purposes, neither the expensing method nor the regular depreciation table applies. Instead a special *listed property depreciation table* must be used.

The listed property depreciation table below applies to items purchased in 1987. For items purchased before 1987, different tables apply [cf. previous editions of this Tax Guide].

Depreciation begins in the year an item starts being used by you for business purposes and is based on its original cost (or market value at the time of initial business use, if lower). The percentages in the table are applied to the fraction of the cost of an item attributable to business use.

LISTED PROPERTY DEPRECIATION TABLE
(Applies to Listed Property purchased in 1987 used 50% or less for business purposes)

Year	Autos	Computers	Entertainment Equipment
1987	10%	10%	4%
1988	20%	20%	9%
1989	20%	20%	9%
1990	20%	20%	9%
1991	20%	20%	9%
1992	10%	10%	8%
1993			8%
1994			8%
1995			8%
1996			8%
1997			8%
1998			8%
1999			4%
	100%	100%	100%

You report depreciation for Listed Property in Part III of Form 4562. Even if an item was purchased on or before June 18, 1984, you still report the depreciation in Part III of Form 4562 if the item falls into the *Listed Property* classification.

Example

A home computer was purchased for $3000 in 1987 and is used 30% of the time for job-related research required by an employer. The computer is used at home, but not in a deductible home office. Since the computer is used 30% for business purposes, the preceeding Listed Property Depreciation Table is applied to 30% × $3000 = $900. Thus, the annual depreciation deductions are as follows:

Year	Deduction
1987	10% × $900 = $ 90
1988	20% × 900 = 180
1989	20% × 900 = 180
1990	20% × 900 = 180
1991	20% × 900 = 180
1992	10% × 900 = 90
	$900

Varying Percentage of Business Use

The business use of an employer-required *listed item* purchased in 1987 may vary from year to year. In such a case, the regular depreciation table applies, provided business use exceeds personal use in each year of the write-off period indicated in the *listed property depreciation table*, i.e. 6 years for autos, 6 years for computers, and 13 years for entertainment equipment.

Example

An automobile was purchased for $10,000 in 1987. It is used for employer-required business purposes as follows: 60% during 1987, 70% during 1988, 80% during 1989 and later years until sold. The following would be the depreciation deductions according to the regular depreciation table for 5-year property described earlier in this section.

Year	Deduction
1987	20% × 60% × $10,000 = $1,200
1988	32% × 70% × 10,000 = 2,240
1989	19.2% × 80% × 10,000 = 1,536
1990	11.5% × 80% × 10,000 = 920
1991	11.5% × 80% × 10,000 = 920
1992	5.8% × 80% × 10,000 = 464

For automobiles which cost more than $12,800, there are special limitations which might alter the above computation procedure. Details are contained in the *Automobile Expenses* chapter.

If listed property purchased after June 18, 1984 is not used more than 50% for business purposes in each year of use during the time period indicated in the listed

Depreciation

property depreciation table, then the special listed property depreciation table must be used throughout the entire depreciation period.

Example

An automobile was purchased in 1987 for $10,000. It is used 60% for business purposes each year except that in 1990, it is used only 40% for business purposes. The 40% usage in one year of the 6-year period in the listed property depreciation table disqualifies it from the regular depreciation table. Thus, the special *listed property depreciation table* must be used as follows:

Year	Deduction
1987	10% × 60% × $10,000 = $ 600
1988	20% × 60% × $10,000 = 1200
1989	20% × 60% × $10,000 = 1200
1990	20% × 40% × $10,000 = 800
1991	20% × 60% × $10,000 = 1200
1992	10% × 60% × $10,000 = 600

As discussed above, the depreciation method to be used depends upon the business usage percentage not just in the current year but in future years as well. This means you have to predict in advance what this percentage will be in order to determine which table to use. If you use the regular table because you think your business use will remain above 50% but it turns out this is not the case, a *recapture* provision will come into play. Under this provision, you are supposed to pay back the difference between the deductions yielded by the regular table and the listed property table by including this difference in taxable income. (You may always use the listed property table for a given class of items instead of the regular table if you choose. No adjustments are made if it turns out you qualified to use the regular table because the business use percentage remained above 50%.)

Items Used for Investment Purposes

As discussed in Section 1, there is a special rule (Condition 2) which requires business use to exceed 50% in order to qualify listed property purchased after June 18, 1984 for depreciation under the regular table. In deciding if this condition is satisfied, business use does not include use in connection with investment activities. However, once the correct depreciation table is determined, investment use can be taken into account. The following example illustrates this situation.

Example

A home computer is purchased in 1987 for $3000. The computer is used at home, but not in a deductible home office. The computer is used 40% of the time for job-related research and 30% of the time for managing investments.

Not counting investment use, business use does not exceed 50%. Therefore, the *listed property depreciation table* must be used. However, the investment use is taken into account when applying the table. That is, the percentages in the table are *applied to the cost attributable to business plus investment use, 70% × $3000 = $2100. Thus, the depreciation deductions are as follows:*

Year	Deduction
1987	10% × $2100 = $210
1988	20% × 2100 = 420
1989	20% × 2100 = 420
1990	20% × 2100 = 420
1991	20% × 2100 = 420
1992	10% × 2100 = 210
	$2100

Special Recordkeeping Rules for Listed Property

There are special recordkeeping rules which apply to *listed property*. Note that for this recordkeeping requirement, such items bought on or before June 18, 1984 are included as well as items bought after this date. Details of these recordkeeping rules are contained in the *Automobile Expenses* and *Books, Equipment, & Supplies* chapters.

Items Purchased Late in the Year

The preceding depreciation tables provide the same deduction no matter what date during the year an item was purchased. This is because the tables treat all items as though they were purchased at the midpoint of the first year of use. For example, the 5-year regular depreciation table would yield a 20% of cost first year deduction for an auto placed into service on December 31 even if driven for only a few miles. To prevent such a "distortion," Congress has provided a special *40%-rule* when too much is purchased in the last 3 months of a given year.

The 40%-Rule

Suppose you buy one or more items during the year (other than buildings or other real estate) for which you claim depreciation. If 40% or more of the total cost is attributable to items purchased in the last 3 months of the year, the usual depreciation tables given earlier in this section cannot be used. Instead, the 40%-rule states that each item must be depreciated according to the quarter (i.e. 3-month period) during which the item was placed into service. The 40%-rule does not apply when you use the expensing option described in Section 2 instead of depreciation.

The following table gives the first year regular or listed property depreciation percentages under this 40%-rule according to the quarter in 1987 during which an item is placed into service. (These tables cannot be used unless the 40%-rule applies.)

1987 DEPRECIATION WHEN 40%-RULE APPLIES

(Use column according to quarter of the year during which item was first placed into service.)

	Quarter 1	Quarter 2	Quarter 3	Quarter 4
Regular (i.e. Non-Listed Property)				
5-year property				
accelerated depreciation	35%	25%	15%	5%
straight-line depreciation	17.5%	12.5%	7.5%	2.5%
7-year property				
accelerated depreciation	25%	17.9%	10.7%	3.6%
straight-line depreciation	12.5%	8.9%	5.4%	1.8%
Listed Property				
Autos or Computers	17.5%	12.5%	7.5%	2.5%
Entertainment Equipment	8.8%	6.3%	3.8%	1.3%

Example

An individual depreciates a computer purchased for $1,200 on March 25, 1987 and peripheral equipment purchased for $900 on December 20, 1987. These items fall into the *listed property* category. Over 40% of the total cost is due to purchases made in the last 3 months as is verified by the following computation:

Quarter Purchased	Item	Cost
1	Computer	$1,200
4	Peripherals	900
		$2,100

$900/$2100 = 43%

Thus, the special 40%-rule tables are used—the 1st quarter column for the computer and the 4th quarter column for the peripherals.

1987 Deduction

Computer	17.5% × $1,200 = $210
Peripherals	2.5% × 1,200 = 30
	$240

Observe that if the 40%-rule had not applied, the deduction for 1987 obtained by using the listed property depreciation table would have been 10% × $2,100 = $210 instead of $240. Thus, the 40%-rule in this case yields a higher deduction than under the ordinary rules.

Houses and Other Real Estate

The *real estate class* is divided into 2 categories—the *residential rental category* and the *non-residential category*. The residential rental category consists of houses, apartments, etc. which are rented out as a personal residence. The non-residential category consists of other real estate such as office buildings, home offices, retail stores, etc. Land is not included because it cannot be depreciated, since it doesn't "wear out".

There are 2 depreciation tables—one for residential rental real estate and the other for non-residential real estate. These tables, given below, provide far less generous depreciation deductions than under prior law. These tables only apply to real estate which you first placed into business service in 1987. For items placed into business service prior to 1987 that you are continuing to so use, you would just continue with the same depreciation method you have been using under the old rules [cf. earlier editions of this Tax Guide]. (There is a transition rule which may allow you to apply the old rules to real estate you first contracted to buy or construct under a written contract signed on or before March 1, 1986, even if first placed into service in 1987 or later.)

RESIDENTIAL RENTAL PROPERTY
(Use column for the first month in the year the property is used for business purposes.)

Year	Jan	Feb	Mar	Apl	May	Jun	Jly	Aug	Sep	Oct	Nov	Dec
1987	3.48	3.18	2.88	2.58	2.27	1.97	1.67	1.36	1.06	.76	.45	.15
1988–2013	3.64	3.64	3.64	3.64	3.64	3.64	3.64	3.64	3.64	3.64	3.64	3.64
2014	1.88	2.18	2.48	2.78	3.09	3.39	3.64	3.64	3.64	3.64	3.64	3.64
2015	-0-	-0-	-0-	-0-	-0-	-0-	.05	.36	.66	.96	1.27	1.57

NON-RESIDENTIAL REAL ESTATE

Year	Jan	Feb	Mar	Apl	May	Jun	Jly	Aug	Sep	Oct	Nov	Dec
1987	3.04	2.78	2.51	2.25	1.98	1.72	1.46	1.19	.93	.66	.40	.13
1988–2013	3.17	3.17	3.17	3.17	3.17	3.17	3.17	3.17	3.17	3.17	3.17	3.17
2014	1.86	2.12	2.39	2.65	2.92	3.17	3.17	3.17	3.17	3.17	3.17	3.17
2015	-0-	-0-	-0-	-0-	-0-	.01	.27	.54	.80	1.07	1.33	1.60

Example. Residential Property

In April, 1987, you purchased a house for $100,000 (not including the price of the land) which you rent out at a fair market price. To determine the depreciation deduction each year, you use the April column in the above table. Thus, the annual depreciation deductions would be as follows:

Year	Deduction
1987	2.58% × $100,000 = $2,580
1988	3.64% × $100,000 = $3,640
1989	3.64% × $100,000 = $3,640
etc.	

If you stop using the item for business purposes before the end of a given year, then you claim depreciation for that year based on the number of months the item is

Depreciation

used, applying a mid-month convention (i.e. the month of disposition is counted as $1/2$ of a month). For example, in the above calculation if you withdrew the house from the rental market on March 2, 1989, the deduction for 1989 would be $2.5/12 \times \$3,640 = \$758$.

If you claim a deduction for an office in a home you own [cf. the *Home Office* chapter], then along with your other expenses, you deduct a pro rata proportion of the depreciation of your home. Similarly, you deduct depreciation for a home you rent out to others with a profit-making intent [cf. the *Homeowners* chapter]. You begin the depreciation calculation at the time you first start using the home for business purposes.

Example. Non-Residential Property

In 1984, you purchased a house for $100,000 (not including the price of the land). In March, 1987, you convert a room into a home office qualifying for deduction [cf. the *Home Office* chapter]. The home office constitutes 1/7 of the home, so $1/7 \times \$100,000 = \$14,286$ is the cost eligible for depreciation. Since the room was first placed into business service in 1987, the above tables apply. You must use the table for non-residential property since you are using that particular room as a business office rather than as a residence. Since the March column applies, the following would be the annual depreciation deductions:

Year	Depreciation
1987	2.51% × $14,286 = $359
1988	3.17% × $14,286 = $453
1989	3.17% × $14,286 = $453
etc.	

As in the preceding example, if you sell the house or otherwise stop using the room as a home office, then you claim depreciation based on the number of months the item is used, applying a *mid-month* convention. For example, if you sell the house in September, 1989, the deduction for 1989 would be $9.5/12 \times \$453 = \$359$.

Basis

When you compute depreciation on a used home or other building, you actually use a figure called the **basis** as the starting cost. It is used in place of "original cost" in the above examples illustrating the depreciation methods. If you start using a home for business purposes as soon as you purchase the home, then the basis is just the original price you paid for the home (including legal fees and other settlement costs that can't be deducted). However, if you start using it for business purposes in a later year than the one in which you purchased the home, then the basis is the lesser of

(1) Your original purchase price plus the cost of any improvements,

or

(2) The fair market value of the home at the time you started using it for business purposes.

The purchase price in (1) refers to the original purchase price when you bought the home. It is not dependent upon your down payment or your monthly mortgage payments.

You cannot depreciate the value of the land on which your home is situated since land doesn't wear out. Thus (1) and (2) above refer to the price of the home only, excluding the value of the land on which it is situated. You must estimate what cost was due to the home and what cost was due to the land and depreciate only the cost due to the home. Don't use a round number for estimating the cost of the house alone. Tax auditors use this as a tipoff that you haven't reduced the price by the estimated percentage attributable to the value of the land.

The same rules described above for computing the basis of a home apply to other items as well. For example, if you start using an automobile for business purposes which you purchased at an earlier date, you would use the lesser of (i) original cost, or (ii) market value as the starting cost figure. In this case, the market value would presumably be the required lesser figure.

Improvements

An improvement is a repair or addition which adds to the value or prolongs the life of the home. Ordinary maintenance or repair expenses are not improvements and cannot be depreciated. Of course, if you incur these maintenance expenses at a time when the home is being used for business purposes, then you get an appropriate deduction for these expenses.

For example, adding central air-conditioning, replacing the roof, panelling the den, installing permanent storm windows, landscaping, new plumbing, installing new shelving, etc. are improvements. But the cost of painting, cleaning, fixing a broken air-conditioner, etc. are ordinary maintenance expenses.

Importance of Recordkeeping

The following court cases illustrate the effect of inadequate recordkeeping on your home office depreciation deduction.

> **Example 1.**
> Mrs. Anderson used the family room in her home as a home office. She kept no records concerning her operating expenses for utilities, insurance, etc. nor did she present any data which could be used for computing depreciation. Instead, she just deducted $500 which she felt was a "reasonable amount."
> The IRS and the Court both felt she was entitled to a home office deduction. They were both willing to allow her a pro rata share of the estimated expenses of operating her home, e.g. utilities, cleaning, insurance, etc. The IRS allowed $112 which was 7.7% of the estimated operating expenses. This percentage represented the portion of her house occupied by an average size room. But the Court recognized that the room she used as her office was bigger than average. It computed that her office occupied 15.4% of her home. Since the IRS used a percentage figure exactly one-half the correct amount, the Court simply doubled the $112 allowed by the IRS and granted Mrs. Anderson a $224 deduction for her operating expenses.

However, the Court refused to estimate her depreciation deduction. While the cost of utilities, cleaning, etc. can be approximated reasonably well by an educated guess, the same is not true for depreciation. There was no way to know what she paid for the home and what she spent on improvements. In the absence of any documentation on these questions, the Court simply declined to make an estimate and allowed her no depreciation deduction whatever. [Anderson, TC Memo 1974-49]

Example 2.

This case is similar to the previous one. A doctor used part of his house as a home office but presented no financial records. Instead, he claimed a deduction of $1200 which represented the rental value of the rooms he used as an office.

However, the Court denied this "rental value" approach to calculating home office deductions. After all, even if he could be regarded as paying rent to himself, he would then have to report the rent paid as income, offsetting the deduction. As in the preceding example, the Court allowed a pro rata share of his estimated home operating costs. But it allowed no deduction for depreciation since it had no data with which to determine the cost of the house. [Tomsykoski, TC Memo 1974-105]

Chapter 5

Interest

Under the law prior to 1987, the basic tax rule for interest paid was simple—namely, all interest payments were equally deductible on your tax return. (The only major exception was for debts used to purchase tax-free investments such as municipal bonds.)

Those were the good old days. Under the new law, some interest is better than others. Depending upon the use of the debt on which interest is paid, the interest might be non-deductible, partly deductible, fully deductible, or deductible in the future.

There are now 5 separate categories of interest—(1) *interest on your home*, (2) *personal interest*, (3) *passive interest*, (4) *trade or business interest*, and (5) *investment interest*. The basic tax treatment for each type of interest is described below.

Except for interest on a personal residence, the categorization depends upon how the proceeds of the underlying loan are *used* rather than *secured*. For example, suppose you take out a loan, secured by stocks you own, which you use to purchase an automobile. The interest you pay on the loan falls into the *personal interest* category because the loan was used for the personal purpose of buying an automobile. The fact that it was secured by stocks does not place it into the *investment interest* category.

(1) Interest on Your Home

This is one category of interest that survives tax reform—within limits. In particular, you can deduct interest you pay on a loan secured by your primary home or a second home. The loan can be a traditional first or second mortgage. Or, it can be a home-equity loan taken out to purchase a car or other personal item. As long as the loan is *secured* by your home, it falls into this category. The *second home* need not be an ordinary house, condominium, or cooperative, but can be a mobile home, boat, or other property as long as it contains basic living accommodations, including sleeping space, toilet, and cooking facilities. (However at presstime, the use of a mobile home or boat as a *second home* was being reconsidered by Congress.)

There are limits on how much interest you can deduct on loans taken out or refinanced after August 16, 1986. Generally speaking, you are limited by the original price you paid for the home plus improvements. However, if the debt on your home on August 16, 1986 exceeded this amount, a higher limit applies. Also, you can deduct interest on loans exceeding the basic limit if the proceeds of the loan are used to pay certain medical or educational expenses of yourself, your spouse, or dependent. Details on the rules for loans secured by your home are contained in Section 1 of the *Homeowners* chapter.

Because of the new law, home-equity loans have become the debt of choice for many persons. With a typical home-equity loan arrangement, you can set up a line of credit with a bank or savings institution, secured by your equity in your house. You can then draw upon this line of credit anytime you choose. For example, if you need financing to purchase an auto, you can use a fully deductible home equity loan. This will

However, the Court refused to estimate her depreciation deduction. While the cost of utilities, cleaning, etc. can be approximated reasonably well by an educated guess, the same is not true for depreciation. There was no way to know what she paid for the home and what she spent on improvements. In the absence of any documentation on these questions, the Court simply declined to make an estimate and allowed her no depreciation deduction whatever. [Anderson, TC Memo 1974-49]

Example 2.

This case is similar to the previous one. A doctor used part of his house as a home office but presented no financial records. Instead, he claimed a deduction of $1200 which represented the rental value of the rooms he used as an office.

However, the Court denied this "rental value" approach to calculating home office deductions. After all, even if he could be regarded as paying rent to himself, he would then have to report the rent paid as income, offsetting the deduction. As in the preceding example, the Court allowed a pro rata share of his estimated home operating costs. But it allowed no deduction for depreciation since it had no data with which to determine the cost of the house. [Tomsykoski, TC Memo 1974-105]

Chapter 5

Interest

Under the law prior to 1987, the basic tax rule for interest paid was simple—namely, all interest payments were equally deductible on your tax return. (The only major exception was for debts used to purchase tax-free investments such as municipal bonds.)

Those were the good old days. Under the new law, some interest is better than others. Depending upon the use of the debt on which interest is paid, the interest might be non-deductible, partly deductible, fully deductible, or deductible in the future.

There are now 5 separate categories of interest—(1) *interest on your home*, (2) *personal interest*, (3) *passive interest*, (4) *trade or business interest*, and (5) *investment interest*. The basic tax treatment for each type of interest is described below.

Except for interest on a personal residence, the categorization depends upon how the proceeds of the underlying loan are *used* rather than *secured*. For example, suppose you take out a loan, secured by stocks you own, which you use to purchase an automobile. The interest you pay on the loan falls into the *personal interest* category because the loan was used for the personal purpose of buying an automobile. The fact that it was secured by stocks does not place it into the *investment interest* category.

(1) Interest on Your Home

This is one category of interest that survives tax reform—within limits. In particular, you can deduct interest you pay on a loan secured by your primary home or a second home. The loan can be a traditional first or second mortgage. Or, it can be a home-equity loan taken out to purchase a car or other personal item. As long as the loan is *secured* by your home, it falls into this category. The *second home* need not be an ordinary house, condominium, or cooperative, but can be a mobile home, boat, or other property as long as it contains basic living accommodations, including sleeping space, toilet, and cooking facilities. (However at presstime, the use of a mobile home or boat as a *second home* was being reconsidered by Congress.)

There are limits on how much interest you can deduct on loans taken out or refinanced after August 16, 1986. Generally speaking, you are limited by the original price you paid for the home plus improvements. However, if the debt on your home on August 16, 1986 exceeded this amount, a higher limit applies. Also, you can deduct interest on loans exceeding the basic limit if the proceeds of the loan are used to pay certain medical or educational expenses of yourself, your spouse, or dependent. Details on the rules for loans secured by your home are contained in Section 1 of the *Homeowners* chapter.

Because of the new law, home-equity loans have become the debt of choice for many persons. With a typical home-equity loan arrangement, you can set up a line of credit with a bank or savings institution, secured by your equity in your house. You can then draw upon this line of credit anytime you choose. For example, if you need financing to purchase an auto, you can use a fully deductible home equity loan. This will be better than a loan taken against the value of the auto, which would generate personal interest, not qualifying for full deduction as discussed below.

Because home-equity loans are better secured, they offer lower interest rates than most any other type of loan—typically 1½% or 2% above the prime lending rate. However, the flip side of this for the borrower is the danger that ownership of his home could be jeopardized if he defaults on the loan. Also, the origination fees for a home-equity loan may offset the savings in taxes and additional interest, especially when the loan amount is on the low side.

(2) Personal Interest

The *personal interest* category includes all interest not falling into any of the 4 other categories discussed in this chapter. Thus, for example, it includes interest on credit cards, auto loans, student loans, late utility or tax payments, etc.

On your 1987 tax return, you may deduct 65% of your total personal interest. The remaining 35% is non-deductible. The 65% figure will fall to 40% on 1988 tax returns, and continue to be lowered until it drops to zero on 1991 tax returns. The total of your personal interest is reported on line 12a on Schedule A. You then multiply by 65% to obtain the deduction amount which you enter on line 12b.

Personal interest includes not just the obvious items like interest charges on bank loans and credit card purchases, but also any other payments for the "use" of money. For example, charges for the late payment of a utility bill are a form of personal interest and can be claimed as such. This deduction was missed by eleven out of eleven tax preparers in a survey taken by a New York consumer agency. However, the annual fee which most banks are now charging for credit cards is not deductible because it is considered a service charge rather than a form of interest.

Interest paid on past due Federal or State income taxes is considered *personal interest*, even if there is investment or business income reported on the tax return. However, underpayment *penalties,* such as the penalty for late filing of a tax return or underpayment of estimated tax, are not considered to be interest and yield no deductions. If the Federal or State government assesses an interest charge, it will usually be listed as such on the notice it sends to you requesting payment.

Note that in order to claim any deduction for interest payments, you must be legally obligated to make the payments. For example, if your child took out a student loan on which you made payments, you get no interest deduction unless you also signed as a co-maker or had a similar legal obligation. This is illustrated by a recent court case. A father made payments totaling about $600 for interest due on his son's student loan and deducted this amount on his own income tax return. But because he was under no legal obligation to repay either the principal or interest on the debt, the Court threw out his deduction. [Prendergast, TC Memo 1984-419] Similarly, if you agreed to make payments on an automobile which your child purchased, then you will not get any interest deduction unless you had liability to pay the loan.

If an interest payment is due on a loan, you can't borrow more money from the original lender to cover the payment. Otherwise, you lose out on the interest deduction. The IRS has stated that it *"will disallow any deduction claimed for interest paid on a loan if the payment was made with funds obtained from the original creditor through a second loan, an advance, or any other financial arrangement similar to a loan."* (IR-83-93). In such a case, no actual payment is considered made—just a renewed promise to pay the original lender. However, if money is borrowed from a different lender to pay the interest due on the original loan, then a deduction is allowed. While common sense may point to this as an irrelevant distinction, the courts have upheld this distinction as a matter of law.

If you borrowed money from a relative, you can claim interest you paid on the loan. However, the loan should be as structured as possible; otherwise the IRS may challenge whether or not a bona fide loan really existed. That's what happened to a taxpayer in a 1984 court case. He borrowed money from his mother and sought to deduct interest payments he made to her on the loan. But there was no note or other documentation proving that a legitimate loan existed. Since he could not prove he had made interest payments on a valid loan, no deduction was allowed. [Schiffgens, TC Memo 1984-137]. For further information on loans between relatives see the *Income-Shifting* chapter.

(3) Interest on Passive Activities

There is a new category of human financial endeavor invented by the drafters of the 1986 Tax Reform Act, called *passive activities*. The *passive activities* category includes investments in limited partnerships or other business enterprises in which neither you nor your spouse participates on a regular, continuous, and substantial basis. It also includes investments in real estate, no matter what the extent or nature of your participation.

There is a limit on the deductibility of *passive interest*, i.e. interest connected with passive activities in which you have invested. This interest (along with other expenses) is fully deductible only against the total income produced by your passive activities.

If a net loss is produced because interest plus other expenses exceeds income, then only 65% of this loss can be deducted on your 1987 tax return. The remainder can be carried over to be deducted in future years when either there are passive profits, or your ownership of the passive activity is disposed of.

There is an exception that applies to rental real estate owned by individuals with Adjusted Gross Income not exceeding $100,000. Losses arising from such activities can be fully deducted up to $25,000, provided the individual is involved in basic decision-making connected with the rental activity. The $25,000 limit is phased out for those with income between $100,000 and $150,000.

Details on these passive activity rules are contained in Section 2 of the *Investing Your Money* chapter.

(4) Trade or Business Interest

You may deduct in full any interest you pay in connection with a trade or business activity (other than as an employee) in which you are a *material participant*. To be a *material participant*, you must perform services on a regular, continuous, and substantial basis.

For example, suppose you have a self-employment consulting practice. You would be able to deduct any interest payments you make in connection with this consulting business. This would include interest on loans for operating capital, mortgage payments on office facilities, etc. You would deduct your interest payments in the usual way as an expense item on Schedule C.

(5) Investment Interest

Income from investments that do not fall into either the *passive activity or trade or business* activity categories discussed above are considered to be *investment income*. This would include stock dividends, bond interest, savings account interest, etc. It would also include capital gains on the sale of stocks or bonds.

If you incur debt in order to purchase stocks, bonds, or other investments designed to provide investment income, then the interest you pay on this debt falls into the category of *investment interest* (sometimes called *portfolio interest*). Starting with 1987 tax returns, investment interest is fully deductible only against investment income, not against earnings or passive income. The way this restriction works is this.

You first determine your *net investment income* by subtracting investment losses from investment income. You can get the appropriate income and loss figures from Schedule B, Schedule D, etc. of your tax return.

Next, you total up the interest paid on any loans which were taken out to make purchases designed to produce investment income. If the total investment interest for the year is less than or equal to the total investment income, then you deduct the entire amount of interest you paid on Line 11, *Deductible Investment Interest*, of Schedule A.

If the total investment interest you paid in 1987 exceeds your total investment income, then the difference is your *excess investment interest*. In this case, you add 65% of this excess investment interest plus your total investment income. The resulting sum is deducted on Line 11 of Schedule A. The remaining 35% of excess investment interest is nondeductible on your 1987 tax return, but can be carried over to future years when there is investment income against which it can be deducted. (On 1988 tax returns, the 65% figure is scheduled to fall to 40%.)

Example

Cooke has a margin account with his stockbroker which he uses to purchase stocks and bonds. His 1987 investment income (including dividends, interest, etc.) totals $6,000 and he has a net capital loss for the year of $2,000. He pays $5,000 in interest during 1987 on his margin account.

Cooke's *excess investment interest* is computed as follows:

A.	Investment Interest	$5,000
B.	Investment Income	$6,000
C.	Less: Investment Losses	−2,000
D.	Net Investment Income (B − C):	$4,000
E.	Excess Investment Interest (A − D):	$1,000

Cooke may claim D plus 65% of E, i.e. $4,000 + (65% × $1,000) = $4,650, as an itemized deduction on line 11 of Schedule A. The remaining $350 is carried over to a future year in which there is investment income.

There are several exceptions to the basic rules for larger-scale investors. First, if you are able to deduct passive losses under the phase-in rule described in (3) above, then you must subtract the same amount from your investment income in the computation of your excess investment interest. Second, your deduction for investment interest in 1987 cannot exceed your investment income plus $6,500 ($3,250 for marrieds filing separately).

Allocation of Interest

As discussed above, the tax treatment of interest you paid during the year depends upon which of the 5 categories the interest falls into. According to the IRS, it is the *use* of the loan proceeds that determines into which category the interest is placed.

For example, suppose you borrow $10,000 from a bank, putting up stocks you own as collateral. You use the $10,000 to purchase an automobile for personal purposes. In this case, the interest paid on the loan falls into the *personal interest* category. Putting up your stocks as security did not cause the interest to fall into the investment interest category. The *use* of the funds you borrowed, not the *security* for the loan, is what counts.

Exception

Interest on loans secured by your primary home or a second home is fully deductible within certain basic limits. In this case, the use to which the loan is put does not matter. Also, interest on certain amounts exceeding the basic limits are still fully deductible to the extent the loans are used for qualified tuition or medical payments. This is discussed more fully in Section 1 of the *Homeowners* chapter.

Tracing the Proceeds of the Loan

As described above, the category to which interest belongs depends on the use to which the borrowed money is put. This involves "tracing" the loan from the time it is received by you until the time it is put to use. In simple cases, this will offer no difficulty.

For example, suppose you receive the loan in a check which you endorse over to another party from whom you are buying an interest in a passive activity. Or, suppose you open up a bank account into which only the loan proceeds are deposited and later, you write a check on this account to buy into a passive activity. In either case, you have a direct tracing of funds from the time of the loan to the time of purchase. Any interest on the loan belongs to the *passive interest* category.

The 15-Day Rule

You do not need to have a direct trace like the ones in the preceding paragraph. Under the *15-day rule*, if you deposit the loan proceeds in your regular bank account and, within 15 days, make a purchase with a check on this account, you can make a direct connection between these 2 events, if you wish.

Example

You borrow $5,000 from a bank on September 3, which you deposit into your regular checking account. On September 16, you write a $5,000 check on this account to purchase U.S. Savings Bonds. In the meantime, you have made a number of deposits into and withdrawals from the account.

Under the *15-day rule*, you are allowed to make a direct connection between the loan and the investment in Savings Bonds. Thus, interest on the loan can be placed into the *investment interest* category.

Example

Same as in the preceding example, except that only $4,000 is used to purchase Savings Bonds. The remaining $1,000 is spent on personal items.

In this case, only $4,000 of the $5,000 loan is linked to the investment. Thus, 4/5 ($4,000/$5,000) of interest payments on the loan falls into the *investment interest* category. The remainder is *personal interest*.

If the 15-day rule is not applied, then loan proceeds deposited in your bank account are considered to be spent in the order you write checks.

Example

There is $3,000 in your checking account. On September 3, you borrow $5,000 and deposit the funds into this checking account. On September 10, you purchase $2,000 worth of furniture. On September 25, you purchase $4,000 in U.S. Savings Bonds. These are the only transactions in your checking account during this period.

The 15-day rule does not apply to the September 25 purchase. Therefore, the $5,000 loan is considered spent $2,000 for furniture, with the remaining $3,000 spent towards the Savings Bond purchase. Thus, 2/5 ($2,000/$5,000) of interest payments on the loan constitute *personal interest*, with the remaining 3/5 *investment interest* toward the purchase of the Savings Bonds.

Under the 15-day rule discussed above, the date on a check is considered to be the date of purchase, as long as an unreasonable amount of time has not elapsed between the date on the check and the date the checked cleared. Also, under a special transition rule, the 15-day period is extended to 90 days for loans used to make purchases before August 4, 1987.

How Should You Handle Future Loans?

As follows from the preceding discussion, there are 3 basic ways you can control the linkage between a loan and an expenditure for purposes of placing interest into the category you want. First, you can make the purchase with the loan check, appropriately endorsed. Second, you can set up a new account into which only the loan is deposited. And third, you can spend the proceeds of the loan for its intended purpose within 15 days of receipt.

The interest tracing rules were issued in July, 1987, but are effective retroactively to January 1, 1987. In addition to covering the cases illustrated earlier, there are rules which handle more complicated situations when there is more intermingling of funds from various sources. In this situation, you should seek accounting assistance to make the proper allocations.

Also, the IRS has yet to issue final rules covering the deductions for interest. The rules discussed here are only preliminary rules to give interim guidance and are subject to likely revisions and additions. Further details will be contained in next year's edition of this Tax Guide.

Chapter 6

Medical Expenses

Schedule A includes a deduction for medical expenses of yourself, your spouse (if filing a joint return), and your dependents. This includes doctor bills, transportation, medical insurance, medical devices, etc., plus the cost of prescription medicine and insulin. You no longer can deduct non-prescription medicine such as aspirin, laxatives, etc.

From your total of medical expenses, you subtract 7.5% (up from 5% in 1986) of your Adjusted Gross Income (AGI) to arrive at your medical deduction for 1987. Schedule A leads you through the appropriate computation.

Getting Around the 7.5% of AGI Limitation

For most taxpayers, the 7.5% of AGI limitation severely restricts their medical deduction.

Here are some strategies for coping with this limitation:

1. Bunch your medical expenses into a single year.

To take a simple example, say your Adjusted Gross Income is $40,000 in each of 2 successive years, and that your family's medical expenses over this 2-year period amount to $6,000. If these expenses are spread evenly, $3,000 in each year, you lose out on any medical deduction. The medical deduction floor (7.5% × $40,000 = $3,000) wipes out the deduction in each year.

However, if expenses are shifted from one year to the other, you get a deduction. For example, if the $6,000 expenses are split up with $3,600 in the first year and $2,400 in the second, you wind up with a $600 medical deduction in the first year.

Certain elective procedures can be timed so they bunch up in one year. For example, if your family members go to the eye doctor every other year and typically need new eyeglasses, synchronize the appointments so they all occur in the same year. Similarly, non-critical elective surgery can be timed appropriately. This may be especially beneficial in the case of elective dental procedures, e.g. the pulling of wisdom teeth, because the typical medical insurance policy does not cover dental expenses.

You may also be able to arrange for a doctor or dentist to bill you all at once for work done over a period of time. For example, if your child needs $2,500 worth of orthodontia work over a 2 or 3 year period, you might be better off if you're billed for the entire amount up front rather than spreading it out over the period the work is done. However, you can't simply voluntarily pay in advance. To get a deduction, you must actually incur the financial obligation by the year you make the payment. In this example, the orthodontist would be only too happy to send you a bill showing the entire amount due in advance, and may even give you a discount for early payment.

2. Set up a medical plan under which all expenses become deductible.

This is the best idea of all because the 7.5% of AGI subtraction is totally eliminated. However, this works only if you or your spouse has income from a self-employment activity (e.g. writing, consulting, editing, reviewing, tutoring, etc.). A full deduction can be achieved by incorporating the self-employment activity and setting up a corporate medical plan to pay all expenses. Or, more simply, an individual can "employ his spouse in the business" and set up a plan which pays all the medical expenses of his spouse's family (including himself). Under either arrangement, a business deduction is obtained for the full amount of the family's medical expenses with no initial 7.5% of AGI subtraction. Also, under new 1987 rules, a self-employed person might be able to set up a medical plan, without employing his spouse, which covers 25% of the cost of medical insurance for his family. [Cf. Section 2 of the *Outside Business Activity* chapter for further details.]

3. Claim medical items as a business expense.

If you can't claim a medical deduction because of the 7.5% of AGI limitation, perhaps you can claim a medical item as a business expense. For example, suppose you need special eyeglasses which you use only at work. You might be able to claim the cost of such an item as a job-related *miscellaneous deduction* rather than as a *medical deduction*.

4. Pay attention to the rules covering divorced couples.

Divorced couples should take note of the new rule concerning the deduction for their children's medical expenses. Now, either spouse may claim medical expenses which he actually pays for his children. It makes no difference that the other ex-spouse may have custody of the children or that the ex-spouse is claiming dependency exemptions for them.

Because of this rule, it may be better to give an ex-spouse money to pay for your children's medical expenses rather than pay the expenses directly. This situation can occur when your total expenses do not exceed the 7.5% of AGI floor. Further details are given in the *Divorce and Separation* chapter.

Deductible Medical Expenses

(A) Doctors, Dentists, etc.

You can deduct for doctors, dentists, optometrists, chiropractors, osteopaths, podiatrists, psychiatrists, psychologists, physical therapists, and acupuncturists. The medical expense deduction also includes nursing services for a sick or disabled individual, but not for a healthy baby. The services need not be rendered by a professional nurse in order to be deductible.

(B) Medical Insurance

Deductible medical insurance includes hospital and health insurance whether paid directly by you or withheld from your paychecks. It does not include life insurance or disability insurance except for those portions specifically designated as covering medical expenses.

(C) Medical Aids and Devices

Hearing aids, dentures, eyeglasses, crutches, wheelchairs, orthopedic shoes, elastic stockings, etc. are deductible medical expenses. The IRS has also ruled that if one foot is smaller than the other because of a medical condition, the extra cost of buying 2 pairs of shoes instead of one is deductible. [IRS Private Letter Ruling 8221118]

(D) Birth Control Pills, Abortions, and Vasectomies

The IRS has ruled that these items are deductible medical expenses. A deduction is also generally allowed for other birth control items when prescribed by a doctor.

(E) Medical Charge Portion of School Tuition, Retirement Home Fees, etc.

Many colleges and private schools include a charge for medical expenses as part of their tuition or fees. This is deductible, provided that the tuition bill or other statement from the school indicates the amount which is attributable to such medical fees. You should ask the school to provide you with such a statement if they do not do it automatically.

Similarly, payments to a retirement home might include a fee for health care. This fee is deductible in the year paid, even if payment is made in advance for lifetime health care. If a refund is received in a later year, say because the individual leaves the retirement home, such a refund would then be includable in taxable income. [Rev. Rul. 75-302]

The IRS recently took a liberal position on how to figure the amount to be considered a health care fee in a ruling issued to a representative of a retirement community. The retirement community provided life care to its residents in return for a one-time admission fee plus a monthly service charge. This life care included access to a 31-bed medical center that was part of the facility.

The IRS ruled that the portion of the fees allocable to medically-related expenses was deductible at the time the fees were paid. In this connection, medical-related expenses included not only salaries of medical personnel and the cost of medicine plus supplies, but also *"expenses allocable to the medical facility such as housekeeping, maintenance and utilities, a proportionate share of interest on indebtedness, real estate taxes, insurance, and depreciation."* The IRS also stated that it would be appropriate to make the allocation of fees by using the financial history of a comparable facility. [IRS Private Letter Ruling 8630005].

On the other hand, the *entire cost* of nursing home or other institutional care for an individual who requires continual medical care is a deductible medical expense. IRS regulations specify, as an example, that *"medical care includes the entire cost of institutional care for a person who is mentally ill and unsafe when left alone"* [IRS Reg 1.213-1(e)(1)(v)(a)]. Presumably, the same would apply to nursing home care for a victim of, say, Alzheimer's disease who requires continual medical care for the treatment of this disease. A doctor's statement that the nursing home care is required for the person to receive proper medical care would be helpful in protecting the deduction from challenge.

(F) Drugs and Medicine

You **can deduct** the cost of prescription medicine and insulin which you purchased during 1987. You **cannot deduct** the cost of non-prescription medicines such as aspirin, laxatives, etc. as you were once permitted to do. Even if your doctor recommends an over-the-counter drug, it is not deductible if it does not actually require a prescription to obtain.

(G) Medical Expenses of Non-Dependents

If you satisfy all the requirements of claiming a dependency for a qualifying relative, except that the relative earned more than $1,900, you may still claim a deduction for medical expenses. For example, if you furnish more than 1/2 the support for a parent, then you can deduct medical expenses which you pay on his or her behalf. This is the case even though your parent's earnings may disqualify him or her from being your dependent.

To obtain the deduction, payments must be made out of your own funds. However, it is permissible for, say, a parent to give money to a child who then pays medical expenses for the parent, thereby obtaining the deduction. This is illustrated by a recent court case in which an individual paid the medical bills of his mother out of funds she had given to him. A Court of Appeals ruled that he was entitled to the deduction because the payments were made from funds which belonged to him at the time. However, it should be clear that funds are actually given to the one making the medical payments. In this case, it was necessary to go all the way to a Court of Appeals to win the deduction. The mother had just given her son a power of attorney over her funds instead of an outright gift. The Court had to sift through State law to determine that this constituted a valid no-strings-attached gift of the funds to her son. [Ruch, 52 AFTR 2d 83-6207]

When you pay the medical expenses of a parent or other individual, be sure to make the payments directly. If you just give money to a parent who uses it to pay medical expenses, you lose the deduction.

(H) Travel

You can deduct your transportation expenses incurred in connection with obtaining medical services. Thus, you can deduct your transportation costs to and from the doctor, dentist, optician, etc. You can also deduct transportation costs to and from the drug store if you are going there in order to pick up medicine. If you use your automobile, you may deduct your actual operating expenses (such as gas, oil, and parking but not depreciation or insurance) or deduct 9 cents per mile. Medical travel can include more than just the usual trips to the doctor, dentist, or drug store. For example, the following have been ruled deductible: trips to attend meetings of Alcoholics Anonymous and trips to a swimming pool by a boy suffering from rheumatoid arthritis.

According to two IRS rulings, transportation costs for relatives of the person receiving medical treatment are deductible when these are necessary. One ruling allowed a wife to deduct her costs in accompanying her wheelchair-confined husband to an out-of-town location to receive treatment [IRS Private Letter Ruling 7928088]. Another ruling permitted parents to deduct the cost of attending consultations at a psychiatric hospital concerning their son who was a patient there [IRS Private Letter Ruling 7931059]. However the cost of ordinary family visits to a patient in a hospital is not deductible.

If an individual travels out of town to obtain outpatient medical care at a licensed hospital or similar institution, up to $50 per day of lodging expenses (but not meals) are deductible. A separate $50 limit applies to someone who is needed to accompany the patient. For example, a parent accompanying a child could deduct up to an additional $50 per day for his lodging expenses. To obtain this deduction, there can be no significant element of personal pleasure, recreation, or vacation in the away-from-home travel.

(I) Childbirth Classes

Many couples now take "natural childbirth" classes prior to the birth of a child. The cost of such classes is neither specifically allowed nor disallowed by any current tax law or ruling. However, it is advised to deduct the cost of these classes, including transportation to and from. In practice, the IRS has not been known to question such deductions.

(J) Special Diet

If your doctor orders you to go on a special diet, then you can deduct the excess of what the special food costs over what regular food would cost. For example, the extra cost of special food for an individual on an ulcer diet can be deducted. Also, whiskey taken for the relief of angina pains can be deducted when recommended by a doctor's prescription. [Rev. Rul. 55-261]

Two court cases illustrate the deduction for special foods. In the first case, a couple had to eat organic food because they were allergic to regular chemically-treated food. They were permitted to deduct half the cost of their food as a medical deduction. The couple used Labor Department statistics for their area to establish the extra cost of food purchased in health stores. [Randolf, 67 TC No. 35]

The second case involved an individual who was placed on a high protein diet by her doctor. She kept records of what she spent for food, compared the total with that spent by a friend, and deducted the difference. The Court allowed her a deduction for 30% of her total grocery bill as the excess amount due to her special diet. [Von Kalb, TC Memo 1978-366]

(K) Special Equipment (Including Air Conditioning)

Under doctor's orders, you might need special equipment in your house to take care of an existing medical condition or disease. This equipment can qualify for a medical deduction. For example, the IRS has ruled that the cost of a special mattress and plywood bed boards was deductible when recommended for the relief of an arthritic condition. Another IRS ruling was issued to a family with a son suffering from allergies. Upon prescription from the son's allergist, the following items were all ruled deductible: air conditioning for the home and automobile, electrostatic air cleaner, and humidifier [IRS Private Letter Ruling 8009080]. And in a 1981 case, the Tax Court allowed a deduction for health spa equipment added to the home of a Las Vegas casino dealer as a result of a doctor's advice that it would help relieve the pain of severe arthritis suffered by his wife [Keen, TC Memo 1981-313]. However, in another ruling, the IRS stated that exercise equipment could not be deducted when prescribed in order to prevent possible future heart disease, rather than to treat an existing medical condition. [IRS Private Letter Ruling 8019025]

Under special circumstances, the cost of installing a swimming pool can qualify as a medical deduction. For example, the IRS ruled in 1983 that an individual with severe osteoarthritis could deduct the cost of constructing an indoor pool in his house when his doctor prescribed a treatment of swimming several times a day [Rev Rul 83-83]. Of course, the IRS will be quite skeptical when it is claimed that the construction of a pool is primarily for medical purposes rather than for personal purposes. In the above ruling, the IRS was influenced by the fact that the pool was only 8 feet wide by 36 feet long and no deeper than 5 feet—designed for lap swimming rather than general recreational use. However, the pool need not be specially designed to warrant a deduction if all the facts and circumstances point to medical rather than personal reasons for use of the pool. [Cherry, TC Memo 1983-470]

When deducting medical equipment, you must first subtract any increase in value which the equipment adds to your house. For example, if you purchase central air conditioning for $3,000 and this adds $2,000 to the value of your house, then you can only deduct the difference, $3,000 − $2,000 = $1,000. This $1,000 is deducted in the year of purchase, not depreciated over its useful life. However, you are entitled to a full deduction for equipment added to a rented house or for portable equipment such as a room air conditioner. In any event, you can deduct the full cost of servicing and operating the equipment, e.g. electricity, repairs, service contract, etc. Note that the IRS can be tough about allowing deductions for medical equipment. You may need an appraiser's report on how much the equipment added to the value of your house. In the absence of such a report, the IRS can throw out the deduction altogether. For example, in one case, a court disallowed the full $4,000 cost of air conditioning because of the failure to get an appraiser's report. [Wallace v. U.S., 309 F. Supp. 748]

(L) Medical Portion of Auto Insurance

A portion of your automobile insurance premium is usually designated as covering medical expenses in case of accident. The IRS has issued conflicting opinions as to whether this portion is deductible as medical insurance. In 1972, they issued a ruling which essentially disallowed such a deduction for a very technical reason. The IRS reasoned that since you can only deduct medical expenses for yourself and your dependents and since the auto insurance covers other persons as well, no deduction could be claimed unless the insurance policy lists the charges separately for dependents and non-dependents (which is highly unlikely). [Rev Rul 73-483 CB 1972-2, 75]

However, in the IRS Freedom of Information Reading Room in Washington D.C., we uncovered advice to the contrary. In a newsletter to its agents, dated February 15, 1977, the following appeared:

> *"if the charge for the medical care portion of a life or car insurance policy is reasonable and is stated separately in the contract or furnished to you in a separate statement you may include the payment for this charge in medical expenses."* [Answers for Troublesome Questions, Taxpayer Service, Ch. 19]

Because the authority for this deduction is obscure, you should bring along the exact reference above if your tax return is audited. This is highlighted by a letter we received from a reader of the '78 Tax Guide. According to this letter,

> *"The tax agent led off today with questions about my medical insurance deductions on my 1976 tax year return. When I told him I had included my auto medical insurance premiums, he turned to the appropriate page in his IRS*

Publication 17 to show me where that was specifically not permitted."

But then the reader took out his copy of the '78 Tax Guide and showed him the exact reference above. The tax agent then *"went out to get the actual volume to check it and said, 'Hmmm, you're right, they really need to change that section (referring to Pub. 17).' Even though the date of that newsletter (Ch. 19) is Feb., 1977, he did not give me a hard time and allowed the deduction for 1976."*

(M) Special Schooling

According to IRS Regulations, medical expenses include

"the cost of attending a special school for a mentally or physically handicapped individual, if his condition is such that the resources of the institution for alleviating such mental or physical handicap are a principal reason for his presence there. In such a case, the cost of attending such a special school will include the cost of meals and lodging, if supplied, and the cost of ordinary education furnished which is incidental to the special services furnished by the school. Thus, the cost of medical care includes the cost of attending a special school designed to compensate for or overcome a physical handicap, in order to qualify the individual for future normal education or for normal living, such as a school for the teaching of braille or lip reading. Similarly, the cost of care and supervision, or of treatment and training, of a mentally retarded or physically handicapped individual at an institution is within the meaning of the term 'medical care.'

"Where an individual is in an institution, and his condition is such that the availability of medical care in such institution is not a principal reason for his presence there, only that part of the cost of care in the institution as is attributable to medical care. . .shall be considered as a cost of medical care; meals and lodging at the institution in such a case are not considered a cost of medical care for purposes of this section."

The above regulations are illustrated by a 1984 Private IRS Ruling. This ruling allowed parents to deduct the full cost of private schooling for their daughter with a learning disability. The school was a special school attended only by children with learning disabilities. The ruling stated that the parents could deduct not only the full tuition, but also transportation to and from the school *"to the extent such transportation expenses are primarily for and essential to the medical care"* of the daughter. Presumably, this means they were allowed to deduct 9 cents per mile (or alternate actual costs as described in the *Automobile Expenses* chapter) for each day's commute to and from school. [IRS Private Letter Ruling 8401024]

In contrast, 2 other court cases have dealt with learning disabled children who attended schools which enrolled regular students, but had a separate program to aid the learning disabled. In both these cases, the extra cost of the special program was deductible, but not the regular tuition [TC Memo 1979-499, 76 TC No. 32]. But in another case, the Court allowed no deduction for the cost of a private school attended by a boy with a learning disability. The boy was sent to the school because he would benefit by the highly structured environment and the personal treatment afforded by a 4-1 student-faculty ratio. But since the school had no special program geared to the learning-disabled, the cost was non-deductible. [TC Memo 1980-572]

(N) Weight Reduction Programs and Health Spas

The IRS has ruled that a taxpayer can't deduct the cost of a weight reduction program if the purpose of the program is to improve the general health and well being of the participant. Similarly, membership in a health spa cannot be deducted (contrary to what those selling memberships may tell you) if you join just to lose weight or keep fit, rather than to combat a specific medical condition.

However, if a weight reduction program is part of the treatment of a specific medical condition or disease then it can be deducted. This was the conclusion of the IRS in a ruling issued to an individual suffering from hypertension and hearing problems. Since her doctors had recommended the weight reduction program for the alleviation of specific illnesses, the cost was deductible as a medical expense. [IRS Private Letter Ruling 8004111]

Similarly, the IRS recently allowed an individual to deduct the cost of participating in an intensive 13-day special exercise and diet program. The individual was advised to participate in the program as part of treatment for his hypertension and arteriosclerosis. [IRS Private Letter Ruling 8251045]

A recent IRS ruling permitted a deduction for the cost of swimming recommended by a doctor for a child who suffered from rheumatoid arthritis. This included the cost of a membership fee to use the pool plus the cost of transportation to and from the pool [IRS Private Letter Ruling 8326095]. However, the cost of swimming to maintain general health or fitness would not be deductible.

(O) Aids to the Handicapped

Individuals suffering from handicaps can claim medical deductions for expenses incurred in dealing with their handicap. For example, a blind child was permitted to deduct the cost of braille books in excess of the cost of regular editions. Similarly, the salary paid to an individual to accompany a blind child throughout the school day was ruled deductible. [Rev. Rul. 64-173]

Some recent private letter rulings indicate that the IRS will allow a wide variety of items if they are designed to aid the handicapped. For example, the cost of installing a liftgate in a van for an individual confined to a wheelchair is deductible [IRS Private Letter Ruling 8034084]. Similarly, the IRS ruled in 1981 that an adapter for closed captioning of television programs could be deducted by a hearing-impaired individual [IRS Private Letter Ruling 8112030]. And in a third ruling, the IRS allowed a hearing-impaired individual to deduct the cost of maintaining a cat because the cat was trained *"to respond to unusual sounds in an instantaneous and directional manner."* [IRS Private Letter Ruling 8033038]

Expenses incurred by a handicapped person for removing structural barriers in his residence are fully deductible. These are not considered to increase the fair market value of the residence. This includes constructing entrance ramps, widening doorways or hallways to accommodate a wheelchair, making bathroom modifications, lowering kitchen cabinets, adjusting electric outlets or fixtures, etc. [Senate Finance Committee report on the 1986 Tax Reform Act, Title I, E2]

(P) Cosmetic Procedures

According to a recent IRS ruling, procedures which are undertaken for cosmetic rather than medical purposes are still deductible as medical expenses if they affect the *structure or function of the body*. For example, face lifts and hair transplants performed by doctors would qualify. Similarly, hair removal through electrolysis is deductible (even when performed by a technician rather than a doctor) because the procedure affects the skin and subcutaneous layers of the skin. But, according to the IRS, ear piercing is not deductible because it is a *superficial procedure* with an *impermanent effect*. [Rev Rul 82-111, IRB 1982-22]

(Q) Alcoholics Anonymous Meetings

The cost of attending meetings of Alcoholics Anonymous, pursuant to competent medical advice, is deductible. This includes the cost of transportation to and from the meetings [Rev. Rul. 63-273]. The cost of attending meetings of other similar rehabilitative organizations would also be deductible.

(R) Disability Income

You might receive payments from your employer while sick or temporarily disabled. These payments are fully taxable even if made under a special sick pay plan. However, worker's compensation is tax exempt.

If you are permanently disabled, you may be able to exclude disability payments made from a plan to the extent you contributed to the plan. In addition there is a tax credit, computed on Form 2440, which may exclude a portion of employer-provided permanent disability payments from tax.

(S) Non-Traditional Medical Treatment

According to a 1986 court case, to be deductible, *"payments for medical care are not limited strictly to traditional medical procedures, but include payments made 'for the purpose of affecting any structure or function of the body'. . . . This broad view of medical care leads to the allowance of medical expense deductions for 'nontraditional' medical care"* [TC Memo 1986-138]. In accord with this policy, deductions have been allowed for holistic medical care, Navajo Indian healing ceremonies, acupuncture, etc.

Chapter 7

Charitable Contributions

You **can deduct** contributions you make to the following nonprofit agencies:

1. **Religious Organizations.** This includes annual dues, seat charges, and assessments as well as ordinary contributions.

2. **Charitable Organizations.** Examples include the Heart Fund, Salvation Army, YMCA, Travelers Aid Society, etc.

3. **Governmental Bodies** where the contribution is for some public purpose such as education, public works, civil defense, etc.

4. **Educational Organizations.** This includes colleges, universities, research organizations, etc.

5. **Civic Organizations** such as non-profit hospitals, veterans organizations (e.g. American Legion, VFW, DAV), youth organizations (e.g. Boy Scouts, Girl Scouts), volunteer fire departments, organizations to support the Olympic games and other athletic competitions, and societies for the prevention of cruelty to animals.

6. The cost of **benefit tickets** sold by charitable organizations. If these tickets are for some commercial production such as a play or concert, then you can deduct only the excess of the price of your tickets over the regular admission price. Similarly, you can deduct the excess cost of purchasing items from a charity (e.g. Christmas cards over value received).

7. The cost of maintaining an elementary or high school student (other than a dependent or relative) in your home under a program sponsored by a charity. This deduction is limited to $50 per month.

You **cannot deduct** as charitable contributions:

1. Contributions to foreign charities except as provided otherwise in treaties. However, contributions to domestic charities which distribute funds abroad are deductible.

2. Contributions to organizations which devote a substantial portion of their time in attempting to influence legislation.

3. Donations which give you a direct benefit such as tuition to a church-related school.

4. Contributions to civic leagues, social and sports clubs, labor unions, and chambers of commerce.

5. Contributions to fraternal groups except when the contribution is to be used only for charitable or other qualifying purpose.

6. The cost of raffle tickets, even if a majority of the proceeds goes to charity.

If in doubt, you can simply ask the organization in question whether they qualify for tax-free status. In questionable cases, they will probably already have received a ruling from the IRS.

Where Do You Deduct Charitable Expenses?

Charitable expenses are claimed as an itemized deduction on line 14 of Schedule A for donations of money or line 15 for donations of property. Only those who itemize their deductions can deduct their charitable contributions. The provision in prior law allowing those claiming the standard deduction to deduct part or all of their charitable contributions has been eliminated.

Donation of Services

You **cannot** deduct the value of services you perform for a charitable or other organization nor can you deduct for the cost or rent of property or equipment you allow a charity to use. You **can** deduct for telephone calls, materials, supplies, and the cost of operating equipment. You can also deduct the cost of ingredients or materials that go into something you donate, e.g. food cooked for a church supper. Similarly, you can deduct the cost of buying and maintaining special clothing such as choir robes or scout leader uniforms.

You can also deduct your travel costs. This includes the cost of commuting to and from the charity. It also includes expenses incurred in attending a convention of a qualified charitable organization, provided that you attend as an official delegate. (Meal expenses connected with attendance at such a convention are subject to the same 80%-rule described in Section 1 of the *Travel* chapter; that is, only 80% of the cost of such meals can be claimed as part of your charitable deduction.)

In order for travel expenses to be claimed as a charitable deduction, there must be no significant element of personal pleasure, recreation, or vacation in the travel.

The tax-writing committee of Congress described this requirement as follows:

"In determining whether travel away from home involves a significant element of personal pleasure, recreation, or vacation, the fact that a taxpayer enjoys providing services to the charitable organization will not lead to denial of the deduction. For example, a troop leader for a tax-exempt youth group who takes children belonging to the group on a camping trip may qualify for a charitable deduction with respect to his or her own travel expenses if he or she is on duty in a genuine and substantial sense throughout the trip, even if he or she enjoys the trip or enjoys supervising children. By contrast, a taxpayer who only has nominal duties relating to the performance of services for the charity, or who for significant portions of the trip is not required to render services, is not allowed any charitable deduction for travel costs."

Further examples were given in a 1987 IRS notice:

"For example, a taxpayer who sails from one Caribbean Island to another

and spends eight hours a day counting whales and other forms of marine life as part of a project sponsored by a charitable organization generally will not be permitted a charitable deduction. By way of further example, a taxpayer who works on an archaeological excavation sponsored by a charitable organization for several hours each morning, with the rest of the day free for recreation and sightseeing, will not be allowed a deduction even if the taxpayer works very hard during those few hours. In contrast, a member of a local chapter of a charitable organization who travels to New York City and spends an entire day attending the organization's regional meeting will not be subject to this provision even if he or she attends the theatre in the evening. This provision applies whether the travel expenses are paid directly by the taxpayer or by some indirect means such as by contribution to the charitable organization that pays for the taxpayer's travel expenses." [Notice 87-23, IRB 1987-9,6]

If your automobile is used, you can either deduct 12 cents per mile or compute your actual cost of operating the automobile, including gas and oil, but not insurance, depreciation, or general repairs such as tune-ups, lubrication, etc. With either method, you can deduct parking and tolls in addition.

Your travel is deductible if you are actually rendering services to a charitable organization, but not if your travel is for personal purposes. For example, travel to attend church choir rehearsals or to attend scout meetings as a troop leader is generally deductible. But travel just to attend church services or drive your children to their scout meetings is not.

Babysitting Expenses

It may be necessary to hire a babysitter in order to engage in charitable activities. The IRS does not consider this to be a deductible charitable expense. But the Tax Court ruled otherwise in a 1978 case brought before its Small Tax Case Division. The Court considered babysitting fees which enable a person to get out of the house in the same category as auto expenses incurred in driving to a charity's office. Since such auto expenses are specified by law to be deductible, the Court ruled that babysitting fees should likewise be deductible.

Based on the above decision, there is justification for claiming a deduction for charity-related babysitting expenses. However, it should be noted that because the case was tried in the informal Small Case Division, the IRS is not likely to change its official policy on this matter based on just this one decision. Until more definitive legal opinion emerges, the IRS will no doubt continue to disallow such expenses if brought to their attention at an audit.

Gifts of Appreciated Property

The best way to make a large contribution is to give property or securities which have risen in value since they were purchased. You might be able to deduct the full market value at the time the gift is made while no tax is paid by anyone on the appreciation in value that has taken place. If you were to sell the items first, you would have to pay tax on the capital gain and consequently would have less to donate to the charity.

In order to be able to deduct the full market value of appreciated property given in 1987, you must have held the property for more than 6 months. This applies to securities (stocks, bonds, etc.) or real estate. There are special rules which apply to other types of property such as furniture, art objects, jewelry, etc. In most cases, you must reduce your deduction by 40% of the appreciation of donated items, unless the items are directly related to the charitable purpose of the organization to which they were given.

High income taxpayers who make substantial donations of appreciated property may fall under certain new *minimum tax* rules [cf. the *Alternative Minimum Tax* chapter]. In such cases, professional advice should be sought.

Recordkeeping Rules

Special recordkeeping rules apply to the deduction for charitable contributions. Formerly, no specific type of recordkeeping was required. In fact, taxpayers were often permitted to deduct a reasonable estimate of their cash contributions even when no written documentation was available. But now, you must be able to back up each individual cash contribution by either

(i) a cancelled check;

(ii) a receipt (which can be a letter or other communication) from the charity showing the date of the contribution, the amount, and your name. For small amounts, an emblem, button, tag, or other evidence which indicates a donation has been made will suffice;

or

(iii) in the absence of a cancelled check or receipt from the donee organization, other reliable written records showing the name of the donee, the date of the contribution, and the amount of the contribution.

No specific recordkeeping format is required by the IRS under (iii). However, the most preferable form of record would be a diary in which the information concerning each contribution is recorded *contemporaneously* (i.e. at or soon after the contribution is made). According to IRS regulations,

"The reliability of the written records . . . is to be determined on the basis of all the facts and circumstances of a particular case. In all events, however, the burden shall be on the taxpayer to establish reliability. Factors indicating that the written records are reliable include, but are not limited to:

(A) The contemporaneous nature of the writing evidencing the contribution.

(B) The regularity of the taxpayer's recordkeeping procedures. For example, a contemporaneous diary entry stating the amount and date of the donation and the name of the donee charitable organization made by a taxpayer who regularly makes such diary entries would generally be considered reliable."

Note that the above rules require each contribution to be separately documented. For example, a written diary must list each individual contribution as it is made. A

Charitable Contributions

monthly listing, say, just of the total amounts given that month would not satisfy the above rules.

Despite the apparent severity of the documentation rules, there is a favorable side as well. Normally, a taxpayer must be able to substantiate his itemized deductions by receipts or cancelled checks. But the regulations now specifically allow charitable deductions to be backed by an appropriate written diary in the absence of cancelled checks or other receipts. This could be a boon to those who make a large number of cash donations during the year.

For example, say, a family usually places a $20 bill in the collection plate each Sunday at church and makes other miscellaneous cash donations during the year. Under the old rules, a tax auditor would ordinarily have balked when looking at such a large total of charitable contributions unsupported by receipts or cancelled checks. But under the new rules, as long as the family has kept an appropriate written diary listing each contribution, they will have satisfied the new IRS recordkeeping requirement.

Of course, it's still best to have receipts or cancelled checks whenever possible. Even though an appropriate written diary is a permissible option, the larger the total of otherwise undocumented amounts listed in the diary, the more scrutiny will be given as to the reliability of the diary.

Used Clothing or Other Property

If you donate clothing or other such property, you must keep written records of your donations. According to current IRS regulations, the records should include the following information for each such donation:

(A) The name and address of the donee organization to which the contribution was made;

(B) The date and location of the contribution;

(C) A description of the property in detail reasonable under the circumstances (including the value of the property), and, in the case of securities, the name of the issuer, the type of security, and whether or not such security is regularly traded on a stock exchange or in an over-the-counter market;

and

(D) The fair market value of the property at the time the contribution was made, the method utilized in determining the fair market value, and if the valuation was determined by appraisal, a copy of the signed report of the appraiser.

In addition to the written record of each contribution, you should also have a receipt or letter from the charity, with date and location of the contribution, which details the property contributed. However, a receipt is not required if the contribution is made in circumstances where it is impractical to obtain a receipt, e.g. where the property is deposited in a charity's unattended drop site.

If you donate an item worth more than $500, your written record should also include how you acquired it (e.g. by purchase, gift, inheritance, etc.), the approximate date you acquired it, and its cost (or other basis).

If there are unusual circumstances involved in the donation of property, these must be described in the written records you keep, e.g. if you have donated only a partial interest in the property, if there are "strings attached" to the use of the donated property, if the use of the property is unrelated to the charitable activities of the recipient, or if you held the property for a year or less and are valuing it at more than you paid for it.

If you made noncash contributions totaling more than $500 in value, you must fill out Form 8283 and attach it to your tax return. You are also required to attach a qualified appraiser's report if you donated property (other than listed securities) worth more than $5,000.

Limitations

There are a number of rules which place an upper limit on the amount of charitable contributions you can deduct in any one year. If you make contributions in excess of 20% of your Adjusted Gross Income, you should check the special rules which apply. These special rules may be found in Publication 526, obtainable at no charge from your local IRS office.

Evaluating Used Items

You are entitled to deduct the *fair market value* of used clothing or other items which you donate to the Salvation Army, Goodwill, church rummage sales, etc. Most charities will give you a receipt for the donated items, but will refuse to appraise their value. This means that you must determine the value yourself.

In practice, it is difficult to assign a value based on the current *market value* because the market for used clothing and other items is so variable. However, a 1980 court case gives some guidance. An individual gave the Salvation Army 12 pairs of trousers, 3 suits, 2 coats, 2 shirts, 1 pair of cowboy boots, and 2 pairs of shoes, all less than 3 years old. These items were purchased new at a total cost of $710. The Court ruled that the individual was entitled to a charitable deduction of $250 — about 35% of the value of the items when new.[Patch, TC Memo 1980-11]

If there is expert testimony as to the value of donated merchandise, then a larger deduction can be obtained than normally allowed. This is illustrated by a court case concerning a woman who was *"extravagant in purchasing clothing for herself and her children."* She donated much of this clothing to a local charity and claimed several thousand dollars in charitable deductions over a period of years. Ordinarily, the Court would be expected to trim the amount of deductions claimed. But the woman had worked for a period of time in the charity's clothes resale shop. Because of this, her estimate of the value of the clothing was considered expert testimony and the deduction was allowed in full. [Haseltine, TC Memo 1979-325]

Another court case, in contrast, shows that an unsubstantiated assignment of high value to used clothing can backfire. An individual claimed a deduction for 2/3 the new value for used items donated to Goodwill and the Salvation Army. The Court found the values assigned to the items to be *"clearly exaggerated to put it mildly."* Since his appraisal was so lacking in credibility, the Court simply accepted the IRS estimate and allowed him a deduction for only about 10% of what he had originally claimed. [TC Memo 1978-461]

Charitable Contributions

As the above indicates, the IRS will disagree with an unsubstantiated high valuation based on too high a percentage of the original cost of items given to charity. However, the result may be different if a valuation is based on a large number of donated items.

This is illustrated by a 1987 court case concerning a donation to the Salvation Army. The donation consisted of a large number of used items which had been stored in an individual's garage. The individual donated the items after he and his first wife were divorced.

According to the Court, *"He had not purchased the items donated, and was unable at trial to itemize the donated property or describe it, except for a stove, which he could describe only generally. The receipt from the Salvation Army showed the donor's declared value to be $3,000 . . ."*. However, the receipt did not purport to reflect the actual value of the donated property other than petitioner's valuation, nor did it list the items contributed. Additionally, the receipt bore the notation that *"a value for contributed property could not be determined by the receiving attendant."*

The Court did not allow a full $3,000 deduction. However, despite the meager documentation, the IRS had still allowed a rather generous deduction of $950 for the donated items. The Court accepted this figure as the proper charitable deduction [Goldstein, TC Memo 1987-47]. (However, note that under current law, you must document a donation of items to charity on Form 8283 if you claim a deduction for them of over $500.)

As the above discussion indicates, used clothing and other items usually generate a charitable deduction which is considerably less than their value when new. This is because these items are generally given away only after they are worn out, damaged, or seriously out of style. However, perhaps you donate items which are still in good condition. Maybe you are moving, have lost or gained weight, etc. If so, the value of the merchandise might be considerably higher.

There is a court case that illustrates this point. This case did not involve a charitable deduction, but rather a deduction for loss due to theft. But the identical question arises in determining both these deductions, namely deciding the fair market value of used items whose ownership has just changed hands.

The stolen items consisted of clothing, cash, a radio, and a camera. The total purchase price of these items was $1,512, with half of the total due to the clothing. The age of the items ranged from 2 years old to only a few months old. The Court placed a value of $1,054 on the items when stolen — a full 70% of the stated original price. [TC Memo 1978-332]

Giving Books to Charity

Several years ago, a court case was decided concerning an elementary school principal who had claimed a $400 deduction for books he donated to his school's library. The IRS did not directly object to his deducting the value of the books—after all, there was no doubt he had turned over the books to an educational institution and received nothing in return.

But the problem was that the principal had originally received these books free from publishers, in the hope they would be adopted for use in his school. In a twist of logic, the Court ruled that when he acquired the books, he was receiving taxable income equal to the value of the books. This amount of taxable income in effect cancelled out the amount of the charitable deduction, so no net tax writeoff could result. (The Court declined to address the fact that their ruling, if carried to its logical conclusion, would require anyone who used a free sample—even mailed to him without his consent—to include its value in taxable income.)

But the current explicitly stated regulations on substantiation of charitable deductions opens up a new opportunity. For example, suppose you have a number of books you no longer need which you donate to a library or other charity. Since you have owned these books for a number of years, you no longer remember exactly how the books were acquired. You might have purchased them for personal purposes, received them free from publishers, or received them as gifts. Of these 3 possibilities, only gifts from publishers, motivated by commercial considerations, would generate a receipt of taxable income offsetting the charitable deduction.

However, note carefully the recordkeeping requirements described earlier which are now required to back up deductions of property given to charity. All you need to record is information concerning the date of donation, name of the organization receiving the donation, and the value of the items when donated. You do not record how you actually acquired the items (except if you have owned the items for a year or less and they have increased in value). In the example in the preceding paragraph, you can simply record the information concerning date, recipient, and value as required. By doing so, you will have satisfied the IRS recordkeeping requirement for donation of the books to charity. If you attach a copy of these records to your tax return (and perhaps, for good measure, include a copy of a receipt from the organization to which you gave the books), your deduction is unlikely to be challenged, unless the market value you assign to the books is out of line. The question of how the books were acquired is simply not an issue raised by the new recordkeeping rules.

As noted earlier, if you donate an item worth $500 or more, then you are required to record how the item was acquired. But this $500 figure applies on an item by item basis. For example, even if you donate more than $500 worth of books to a library, you do not fall under this requirement because no single book is worth more than $500.

Chapter 8

Household Services and Child Care

You may qualify for a tax credit equal to a percentage of payments made to a babysitter, maid, housekeeper, day care center, nursery school, etc. This tax credit is one of the few tax benefits that has not been changed by the 1986 Tax Reform Act.

The exact percentage of the tax credit depends upon your adjusted gross income as explained later in this chapter. Like other tax credits, the credit for household services and child care is subtracted directly from your final tax liability instead of from taxable income. Thus, it is more valuable than a deduction of the same amount [cf. Chapter 1, Section 1].

Note that although it is required that there be dependents under 15 (or disabled dependents of any age) in the household, the tax credit still can apply when no child-watching services are performed. For example, payments to a maid or housekeeper can qualify even if no one is home the entire time services are being performed.

Qualification Rules

In order to qualify for the household services and child care tax credit, the following rules must have been satisfied.

(1) Your expenses were necessary to enable you to be gainfully employed during the period the expenses were incurred. Unpaid volunteer work or work for a nominal salary does not count. However, active search for gainful employment does qualify. If you are married and living with your husband or wife, then either (i) both of you were gainfully employed, or (ii) one of you was gainfully employed and the other was disabled or was a full-time student during 5 or more months of the year. In addition, married couples who live together must file a joint return;

(2) You maintained a household including a dependent under age 15 or a disabled spouse or disabled dependent over 14;
and
(3) Your payment for the service was not made to a child under age 19 of yours (or of your spouse) or to a person who is claimed as your dependent.

Payments to Relatives

At one time, payments to close relatives for child care generally did not qualify for the child care tax credit. However, now the only restriction is in (3) above. In particular, payments to a child's grandparent qualify for the tax credit.

Especially with the new personal exemption and standard deduction amounts [cf. Chapter 1], many retired persons over age 65 will pay little or no income tax.

The child care tax credit offers a way to transfer money to such persons and achieve a net reduction in tax. Note that there is no specific ceiling on the hourly rate that can be paid for child care, although the IRS might object if it were too far out of line. However, since this information isn't called for on the tax form, IRS objection is unlikely.

Which Expenses Qualify For the Child Care Tax Credit?

If you qualify under the preceding rules, then the following expenses qualify for the household and child care tax credit.

(1) Expenses Within the Home

The tax credit applies to expenses for ordinary and usual household services performed in and about the home. These services must be necessary to the home or the well-being of the qualifying dependent or disabled spouse. This includes the services of a housekeeper, maid, or babysitter, but not a gardener. Note that a maid or housekeeper is not required to have any direct child care responsibilities. The tax credit applies also to the cost of meals furnished to a qualifying household worker. But the cost of lodging is not deductible except to the extent you incur expenses beyond what you would have normally paid if you had not provided lodging. [Rev Rul 76-288]

(2) Expenses Outside the Home

The tax credit applies to the cost of care for children under 15 outside the home, such as in a day care center, nursery school, day camp, babysitter's home, etc. Benefits incident to the care (food, education, etc.) are, strictly speaking, not child care costs. However, if a payment covers incidental benefits inseparably as part of the care, then the entire cost will ordinarily be considered as being for child care. Thus, the credit applies to the full amount paid to a day care center or nursery school even if it includes lunch or educational activities. However, tuition for a child in the first or higher grade does not qualify, nor does the cost of transportation between your home and a child care location.

The tax credit also applies to outside-the-home care of a disabled spouse or disabled dependent over 14 who regularly spends at least 8 hours per day in the taxpayer's household. Dependent care centers which care for more than 6 persons per day must comply with all applicable local regulations to qualify for the credit.

Summer Camp and Vacation Trips

A recent Tax Court case has extended the child care tax credit to include out-of-town trips. According to this case, for example, the full cost of sending your child to summer camp can qualify for the credit. Even the cost of sending a child on an out-of-town excursion qualifies for the credit.

Court Case

Mr. and Mrs. Zoltan were both employed full-time. During a span of 2 years, they sent their 11-year-old son on 3 trips — to a summer camp in Canada for 8

Summer Camp & Vacation Trips

weeks, to Washington, D.C. on a school-related Easter Trip, and to France for 2 months to visit his older sister. The Zoltans claimed the child care tax credit for the full cost of summer camp, the cost of the trip to Washington, D.C., and for $350 in payments made to the sister in France for taking care of the boy. The Court considered the 3 trips separately.

Summer Camp

The Court ruled the summer camp to be a legitimate child care expense. It ruled that the Zoltans' principal purpose in sending their child away to camp was to *"provide for his well-being and protection."* Since the Zoltans both worked full time, it was necessary for them to provide some type of care for their 11-year-old son. And the choice of summer camp was a perfectly reasonable alternative. In fact, had they hired a full-time housekeeper to watch their son during the day, the cost would have been about the same. (Even if the camp had cost more, the outcome of the case should have been the same since there is no requirement to choose the least expensive mode of child care.)

After deciding that summer camp was a legitimate child care expense, the Court turned to the question of what portion of the expenses qualified for the credit. If there had been a significant educational component to the camp (as there would be with a computer or golf camp), then an allocation would have to be made between non-deductible educational costs and deductible child care costs. But the camp provided only incidental instruction in swimming, archery, and various other activities in an unstructured fashion. Thus, any educational activities were simply incidental to the child care aspect of the camp. Similarly, the costs of food and recreational services were *"incident to and inseparably a part of his care,"* so no allocation was necessary.

The IRS contended that only the time spent in camp which coincided with the hours the Zoltans were working could be counted toward the tax credit. But the Court disagreed, stating that once the decision was made to send their son to camp, they had no choice but to pay for 24-hour care, 7 days a week. Thus the Zoltans were permitted to deduct the full $1,100 cost of the 8-week summer camp.

Easter Trip to Washington, D.C.

The Court found that here, too, the trip to Washington, D.C. was *"primarily undertaken for the son's well-being and protection."* (It noted again that the cost of hiring a housekeeper to watch over the son would have been at least as expensive as the cost of the trip.) And, although transportation costs to a child care location do not qualify for the credit, that was not pertinent here. The child care began when they delivered their son to the tour sponsor at the bus depot in their home town. Thus, the bus trip was part of the basic child care, not auxiliary transportation.

However, the Court felt that a substantial portion of the trip was for educational purposes, not just child care. Thus, an allocation had to be made between the child care services and the educational services provided by the trip. The Court ruled that only $35 of the $116 expense could be deducted. Had the trip been to a less educational place than Washington, D.C., presumably the amount allocated to child care would have been higher.

Trip to France to Visit Sister

Under the law that applied at the time, payments to close relatives did not qualify for the child care tax credit. For this reason only, the Zoltans were not entitled to a credit for the $350 they paid to their son's sister for taking care of him in France. However, this *payment to relatives* restriction no longer applies. Presumably, the $350 would have been allowed as a child care expense had the case been decided under current law. [Zoltan, 79 TC No. 31]

In December, 1984, the IRS announced their decision not to appeal the above Zoltan case [IRB 1984-52,5]. With respect to the Easter trip, they "acquiesced" fully with the Court's decision. That is, they agreed that a portion of the bus trip from Ohio to Washington could be a legitimate child care expense.

With respect to the cost of summer camp, the IRS was more detailed in its acquiescence announcement. It backed away from its original contention that only the hours during which the parents were working counted toward the tax credit. That is, the IRS agreed that the cost of the weeknight and weekend food and lodging could be treated as a child care expense. However, with respect to the supervised activities such as swimming and archery lessons, the IRS was a bit more restrained. It stated it would not appeal the Zoltan case, given that the Court made a factual determination that the educational aspects of these activities were only incidental to the child care aspect of the camp. But if they were more than incidental, the IRS cautioned that the full summer camp cost would not qualify for the credit. Presumably, in such a case, an allocation would need to be made to determine what portion of the summer camp cost qualified as a child care cost.

As the above case shows, the cost of sending a child on an out-of-town trip can qualify for the child care tax credit. Technically, it is required that the *principal purpose* of the trip be to insure your child's *well-being and protection*. But if you need to provide child care in order to work, you could almost always claim this is your principal purpose in sending your child out of town. Since the above Court decision ruled this was the case even for an 8-week summer camp and a trip to Washington, D.C., it is hard to conjure up a situation which would not have satisfied the *principal purpose* requirement.

Private Schooling

You may feel it necessary to send a child to private school in order to allow you to be gainfully employed. The following court case supports your right to a child care tax credit for a portion of the expenses you incur.

Court Case

A woman and her 13-year old son moved from Maryland to Philadelphia where he was enrolled in the Wagner Junior High School. However, he was not able to adjust to his environment at Wagner. "Unlike his Maryland school, Wagner was fraught with classroom disorders and teacher strikes. Gang fights took place after school, and petitioner was concerned for her son's safety. . . . Petitioner felt that she *could not work while her son was attending Wagner because she had to remain constantly prepared to pick him up if problems arose at school."*

As a result, she enrolled her son in a private boarding school. She then claimed a tax credit for that portion of the cost which was not allocable to the cost of education. The IRS objected, claiming the private schooling was not necessary to enable her to work. Other mothers sent their 13-year old children to Wagner and were able to work without incurring any child care expenses.

But the Court overruled the IRS objection. "Petitioner considered herself unable to work while her son was at Wagner. However, no doubt many Wagner students did have working mothers. It was not objectively impossible to be employed while a child was at Wagner. However, we do not believe that the statute requires us to test the correctness of the parent's conclusion that child care is required to obtain employment, but only the sincerity of that conclusion. Different parents will apply different standards for what risks they are willing to put their children to. One parent may feel a 13-year old boy could be left alone at home after school hours; another would disagree. The statute requires the prescribed purpose; it does not impose a test of objective necessity."

*The IRS also objected that the dominant motive in sending her son to boarding school was not to enable her to work, but to provide for his education. But the Court tossed aside this objection also. ". . . if the parent could not have accepted the job without having sent the child to boarding school, she is deemed to have incurred the expense in order to be able to accept gainful employment . . . Since one of petitioner's reasons for sending her son to boarding school was to be able to take a job, and since she could not have taken a job without such child care arrangement, she is entitled to a child care deduction for some part of the cost of sending him to [private school]. We adopt in other words a 'but for' test. If the care was required to permit the taxpayer to work, and if **one** motive for obtaining the care was to permit gainful employment, the concurrent existence of other motives will not cause the expenditure to fail the statutory test. The employment motive must be present. It need not be exclusive or even dominant."*

Thus, the Court ruled in favor of the taxpayer. The portion of the cost of the private school which went for education, tuition, books, supplies, etc., would not qualify as a child care expense. However, "incidentals that go with providing well-being and protection such as room, board, and supervision before and after the normal school day" would qualify for the child care tax credit. [73 TC #15]

In the above case, the cost of education did not qualify because the child was in the "first or higher grade." For younger children, the full cost may be claimed as a tax credit. For example, a 1980 court case allowed a tax credit based on the entire cost of private school because the child was only 4 years old. The school was considered a nursery school so the full cost could be claimed as described earlier in this chapter. [Christre, TC Memo 1980-64]

Interestingly, while the regulations allow a tax credit for nursery school and forbid a tax credit for education in the first or higher grades, they do not spell out the situation for kindergarten. Presumably, a tax credit could be claimed for the cost of a private kindergarten which provided more nursery school type activities than formal schooling found in the first or higher grades.

Amount of Credit

The tax credit is equal to 30% of expenses on tax returns showing an adjusted gross income of up to $10,000. This percentage is decreased step by step for adjusted gross incomes exceeding $10,000 until it reaches 20% for those with adjusted gross incomes over $28,000. The following table shows the exact percentage to be used at each income level, subject to the limitations described below.

Adjusted Gross Income	Applicable Percentage
Up to $10,000	30%
$10,001–$12,000	29%
12,001– 14,000	28%
14,001– 16,000	27%
16,001– 18,000	26%
18,001– 20,000	25%
20,001– 22,000	24%
22,001– 24,000	23%
24,001– 26,000	22%
26,001– 28,000	21%
28,001 and over	20%

Limitations

1. The overall limitation

The household and child care tax credit is subject to a maximum limitation. The maximum amount of 1987 expenses to which the credit can be applied depends upon the number of *qualifying dependents* (i.e. dependents under age 15 and disabled dependents or spouse over age 14) as follows:

(a) $2,400 if there is one qualifying dependent

or

(b) $4,800 if there are 2 or more qualifying dependents.

Thus, for those with adjusted gross incomes less than $10,000, the credit cannot exceed in case (a), $720 (30% × $2,400); or in case (b), $1,440 (30% × $4,800), while for those with adjusted gross incomes greater than $28,000, the credit cannot exceed in case (a), $480 (20% × $2,400); or in case (b), $960 (20% × $4,800).

Under (b), you are entitled to the credit on up to $4,800 of expenses as long as there are at least 2 qualifying dependents, even if a majority of this amount was spent for the care of only one child. For example, if you spent $3,000 for nursery school for your 4-year old child and $300 for incidental care of your 13-year old, you would apply the credit to $3,300 of expenses. The $2,400 limit under part (a) would not apply, but rather the $4,800 limit under part (b).

2. The earned income limitation

The expenses to which the credit is applied cannot exceed your earned income. For married couples filing a joint return, the expenses to which the credit is applied cannot exceed either your earned income or your spouse's earned income, whichever is lower. Earned income includes income produced by

Household Services & Child Care

an individual's own work, whether it be as an employee or as a self-employed person. It does not include income from investments, such as stocks, bonds, rental property, savings accounts, etc.

In some cases, it pays to "put a spouse on the payroll" in order to boost the earned income of the lower-earning spouse and obtain a larger tax credit. For example, this might be possible for an individual with an outside business activity in which the spouse can be of assistance. This is discussed more fully in Section 3 of the *Outside Business Activity* chapter.

Special Rule for Students

The preceding earned income limitation would permit no tax credit if one spouse were a student with no earned income. But since Congress wanted to make the tax credit available to married couples in which one spouse is a student, they included the following special rule:

A spouse who is a student is treated for purposes of the earned income limitation as though

(1) He earned $200 per month for each month he was a full-time student during 1987, if there was one qualifying dependent

or

(2) He earned $400 per month for each month he was a full-time student during 1987, if there were 2 or more qualifying dependents.

The above amounts only serve to raise the limit on the amount of expenses to which the household services and child care tax credit is applied. They don't affect the adjusted gross income on which the table showing what percentage to use is based.

> **Example**
>
> A married couple has two children under age 14 for which they incur $5,000 in child care expenses. One spouse earns $25,000 for the year, while the other has no earnings but is a full-time student for 10 months during the year. They file a joint return showing an adjusted gross income of $25,000. Thus, as determined by the table given earlier, the applicable tax credit rate is 22% of expenses. The student is deemed to have earned $400 for each of the 10 months in school, or a total of $4,000 earned income for the year. Since the amount of expenses to which the credit is applied cannot exceed this amount, their credit for the year is equal to 22% × $4,000 = $880.

Social Security Taxes

If you employ a babysitter, maid, etc. inside your home, then these are employees of yours governed by the social security laws. This means that you are supposed to pay social security tax if any of these employees earned $50 or more during any one quarter in 1987. In 1987, the social security tax rate was equal to 7.15% for the employer and for the employee. (For 1988, the 7.15% rises to 7.51%.) You could withhold the employee's 7.15% from his paycheck or you could pay both portions yourself. Social security taxes are paid quarterly by filing Form 942 with the IRS. You do not have to pay social security for an outside contractor such as a day care center, outside babysitting service, etc.

You only pay social security tax on actual wages. Food, clothing, and lodging given to household workers aren't subject to social security tax even though the extra cost of these items qualifies for the household services and child care tax credit.

Note that any social security taxes you pay are considered to be part of your costs. That is, these taxes are included in the total expense figure on which you compute the tax credit.

If you claim the household and child care tax credit then you will probably want to pay any social security tax that is due. The IRS has a program for checking that those who claimed the household and child care tax credit also filed appropriate Forms 942. Note, however, that payments made by a married individual to his parent for watching the individual's child are exempt from social security tax.

When you file your first Form 942, write *"None"* in the space provided for *employer identification number.* The IRS will assign you a number and send you each quarter a new Form 942 with your name, address, and employer identification number preprinted on it.

What If You Are Separated or Divorced?

Special provisions are made for couples who are divorced or separated under a written agreement. In this case, the household and child care tax credit can be claimed only by that parent who has custody of a qualifying child for a longer period of time than the other parent. The child must be in the custody of one or both parents for half of the year and must receive over half of his support from his parents.

Ordinarily, married couples must file a joint return in order to claim the household and child care tax credit. However, there are the following exceptions to this rule for separated couples.

An individual who is legally separated from his spouse under a decree of divorce or of separate maintenance can claim the credit on a separate tax return. An individual who simply does not live with a spouse for the last 6 months of the year can also claim the household and child care tax credit on a separate tax return. In this case, the qualifying child's principal home must have been with the individual for more than half of the year and the individual must have furnished over half the cost of maintaining the home.

Where is the Tax Credit Claimed?

You use Form 2441 to claim your Household Services and Child Care expenses. This form will lead you through a step by step computation of the appropriate tax credit.

Note: At presstime, Congress was considering a change in the law that would exclude the cost of overnight camp from the tax credit for child care, starting with the 1988 tax year. Next year's edition of this Tax Guide will contain further details on this issue.

Chapter 9

Tax Deductions for Homeowners

We have discussed in a separate chapter how to deduct expenses connected with using a home office. The purpose of this chapter is to discuss the other deductions to which a homeowner is entitled simply through the use of a house as a personal residence. Throughout this chapter, the word *house* or the word *home* refers not just to a free-standing structure, but includes cooperative apartments, condominiums, etc. which you own.

In order to deduct interest or taxes on a home, you must actually **own** the home. Otherwise, the deduction is lost. For example, suppose you live in a home owned by your parents and you make the mortgage payments which include interest and taxes. Then neither you nor your parents can claim a deduction. If you had paid your parents rent and they had made the payments, then they would have been entitled to the deductions.

SECTION 1:
INTEREST

As described in the *Interest* chapter, the 1986 Tax Reform Act has chiseled away at the deduction for interest which you pay. For example, interest on consumer purchases is only 65%-deductible on your 1987 tax return and scheduled to disappear by 1991.

However, the deduction for interest on loans secured by your home remains fully deductible—within certain basic limits described below. This is the case even if the proceeds of the loan are used for consumer purchases or any other purpose. This special treatment applies to loans on your primary home and on a second home. The loans can be first or second mortgages, home-equity loans, or any other loans secured by your primary or second home. Also, late payment charges on such loans are considered to be interest on the loans since they are payments for the "use" of money.

The second home need not be an ordinary home, condominium, or cooperative, but can be a mobile home, boat, or other property as long as it contains basic living accommodations, including sleeping space, toilet, and cooking facilities. If you rented out the second home during part of the year and also made personal use of it, the home will qualify if your personal use of it is both (i) more than 14 days and (ii) more than 10 percent of the number of days during the year that the home was rented out at a fair rental. (If the home was not rented out at all, it can qualify as a second home no matter what personal use you made of it.)

If you have more than one possible second home, you can choose any one you wish to be your *second home* for the year under the new interest rules. Next year, you can make a different choice of *second home*.

(At presstime, Congress was already considering some revisions in the new rules for borrowing on your home. In particular, the deductibility of large home-equity loans was being reconsidered. Also in jeopardy was the use of a boat or mobile home as a second home under the interest rules. The proposed revisions would take effect on tax returns for the 1988 tax year. Next year's edition of this Tax Guide will contain details of any new developments on this issue.)

In most cases, a portion of your monthly mortgage payment goes toward paying interest on a home loan while another portion goes toward paying off the principal. Only the interest portion can qualify for deduction. You cannot deduct the portion which goes toward paying off the principal. Most lenders provide an annual statement which shows what portion of your payments is attributable to interest costs.

If an interest payment is due on a loan, you can't borrow more money from the original lender to cover the payment. Otherwise, you lose out on the interest deduction [IR-83-93]. In such a case, no actual payment is considered made—just a renewed promise to pay the original lender. However, if money is borrowed from a different lender to pay the interest due on the original loan, then a deduction is allowed. While common sense may point to this as an irrelevant distinction, the courts have upheld this distinction as a matter of law.

Cost-Plus Amount of Home

The **cost-plus amount** of a home is the original price you paid for the home (building and land but not furnishings) plus the cost of any improvements you made to the home. [See Section 3 for an explanation of what constitutes an improvement.] The *original price* is the full purchase price (including closing costs such as appraisal fees, recordation fees, etc.) when you bought the home, not just the amount of your down payment.

Form 8598, Home Mortgage Interest

There is a new Form 8598 that you may have to fill out to compute the amount of interest you can deduct on loans secured by a given primary or second home.

First, the good news. You do **not** have to fill out Form 8598 if either

(1) At no time during 1987 did the total debt on your home exceed its cost-plus amount. (In particular, this will normally be the case if the only home loan was the initial mortgage you took out when you purchased the home.);

or

(2) You did not take out a new home loan or borrow additional amounts on an existing mortgage after August 16, 1986.

If either of the above 2 conditions is satisfied, you ignore Form 8598 and proceed as in prior years. That is, you deduct the full amount of interest on your home mortgage as an itemized deduction on Line 9 of Schedule A.

Now the bad news. If you do not satisfy either of the above 2 conditions, then you must fill out Form 8598 and include it with your tax return. [You fill out a separate Form 8598 for a second home which does not satisfy either of the above 2 conditions.] You are required to file Form 8598 even if it turns out that all your mortgage interest is fully deductible.

Interest on Your Home

Debt-Ceiling Amount

The basic purpose of Form 8598 is to compute a *debt-ceiling* on the total amount of debt that qualifies under the new rules. If the total debt on a particular home does not exceed this debt-ceiling, then the interest on the debt is fully deductible. Interest on debt exceeding this ceiling may be only 65%-deductible on your 1987 tax returns, depending on how the debt proceeds are used. For example, this will be the case if the debt proceeds are used to make a consumer purchase [cf. the *Interest* chapter].

In general, the *debt-ceiling amount* will equal the *cost-plus amount* of the home. However, under a grandfathering provision, the debt-ceiling is equal to the debt amount on loans existing on August 16, 1986 (the date the new law was enacted), if higher than the cost-plus amount. In practice, it is not the outstanding loan balance on August 16, 1986 that is used. Rather, it is the average balance during 1987 of the loan that existed on August 16, 1986 (as continued or refinanced) that is used. However, as discussed more precisely below, if the loan has been refinanced for a larger amount, the figure used is what the balance of the old loan was or "should have-been" on December 31, 1986.

Part 1 of Form 8598 contains the basic 4-line calculation of the debt ceiling. The following explains how to determine the amount to enter on each of the 4 lines.

On **Line 1**, you report the *1987 average balance* of the debt on your home. If there is more than one loan secured by the home, you enter the total of the 1987 average balances on these loans (This is the "current" home debt figure that will be compared with the debt ceiling.)

You can choose among 5 basic methods to determine the *1987 average balance* on a particular loan. Which method is easiest to use depends upon the information provided to you by your mortgage-lender. You can either:

(i) Add the loan balance as of 12/31/86 plus the loan balance as of 12/31/87 and divide by 2. (You should be able to find these balances on the yearend statements which the mortgage-holder sends to you.) This method can be used if (1) the debt was owed during all of 1987 that the home was yours, (2) the loan balance did not increase in 1987, and (3) you made level payments during the year, unless adjusted because of a change in interest rate;

(ii) If you receive a statement from your mortgage-lender which shows the monthly loan balances during the year, you can add these balances and divide by 12. (This method assumes you owned the home during all of 1987.) In most cases, this will yield a slightly less favorable figure than method (i).

(iii) Divide the total interest paid during 1987 by the interest rate. For example, if you paid $6,000 on a 10% loan, the average balance would be $6,000 ÷ .10 = $60,000. This method can be used only if you paid all accrued interest at least monthly [This method is suitable for home-equity loans where the loan balance changes significantly during the year. It is also useful if you took out a new loan during 1987 and do not have the monthly figures needed for method (ii)];

(iv) Use the 1987 *average balance* figure provided by the lender if he reports this amount to you, say, on a yearend statement;

or

(v) Use the highest principal balance that existed on the mortgage during 1987. (This may be the simplest method to use, but is likely to yield the least favorable result.)

On **Line 2** of Form 8598, you enter the *cost-plus amount* discussed earlier.

On **Line 3**, you enter what the IRS (rather confusingly) calls the *Pre-August 17 Amount* of the loan. We will refer to it here as the *Line 3 Amount* of the loan instead. If there is more than one loan on the home, you enter the total Line 3 Amounts on all the loans. [**Note:** You fill out Line 3 only if you took out at least one loan on your home before August 17, 1986, other than the original mortgage when you purchased the home. Otherwise, enter zero on Line 3 and proceed to Line 4.]

Two cases are simple to compute. First, for a loan that was not refinanced after August 16, 1986, the Line 3 Amount is defined to be the same as the 1987 average balance computed for Line 1 above. And second, for a new loan taken out after August 16, 1986, the Line 3 Amount of that loan is zero.

For old loans existing on August 16, 1986 that were refinanced after this date, the computation is divided into 2 cases.

Case 1. Refinancing After August 16, 1986 for the Same Amount

If the refinancing was for the same amount as the old debt (disregarding the cost of refinancing including points), you let the new debt "take over" where the old debt left off. That is, if the refinancing took place in 1986, then the Line 3 Amount is taken to be the 1987 average balance of the new loan.

On the other hand, if the refinancing occurred in 1987, the Form 8598 instructions tell you to take the sum of the 1987 average balances of the old and new loans.

Case 2. Refinancing After August 16, 1986 for a Larger Amount

If you refinanced a loan for a larger amount than the balance outstanding on the old loan, then the Case 1 computation generally would yield a larger amount (more beneficial to the taxpayer) than if the old loan were allowed to continue to the end of 1987. To prevent this, the IRS has special rules for this situation.

If such an increased refinancing occurred in 1986, then the Line 3 Amount is equal to the old loan balance just before the refinancing, reduced by any principal payments paid on the new loan in 1986. (Essentially, you are taking the December 31, 1986 balance, letting the new loan "take the place" of the old loan for the remainder of 1986.)

If the increased refinancing took place in 1987, then you use the balance of the old debt on December 31, 1986 if that produces a lower amount than computed under the procedure in Case 1. (Otherwise use the Case 1 procedure.)

Example 1. *Refinancing in 1987 for Same Amount*

There was a mortgage on your home which had a remaining balance of $40,000 on 4/1/87. On this date, you refinanced by taking out a new loan for $40,000 (probably to get a lower interest rate). Assume that the 1987 average balance of the old loan was $10,200 and of the new loan, $29,300.

Since you refinanced for the same amount as the old debt, you fall into Case 1. This means you add these 2 figures ($10,200 + $29,300) to get the Line 3 Amount. Thus, the Line 3 Amount is $39,500.

Example 2. Refinancing in 1987 for a Larger Amount

Same as in Example 1, except that the new loan was for $60,000 (instead of $40,000), with a remaining balance of $57,000 on 12/31/87. Since you refinanced for more than the old loan, you use the instructions given in Case 2, i.e. you use the balance of the old loan on 12/31/86, namely $41,000. This is less than the amount that would be computed using the Case 1 method.

Thus, the Line 3 Amount is $41,000.

Example 3. Refinancing in 1986 for Same Amount

There was a mortgage on your home which had a remaining balance of $50,000 on September 1, 1986. On this date, you refinanced by taking out a new loan for $50,000. The remaining balance of the new loan was $49,000 on 12/31/86 and $47,000 on 12/31/87.

Since you refinanced for the same amount as the old debt, you fall into Case 1. This means you take the 1987 average balance of the new loan:

$$($49,000 + $47,000) \div 2 = $48,000.$$

Thus, the Line 3 Amount is $48,000.

Example 4. Refinancing in 1986 for a Larger Amount

Same as Example 3, except that the new loan was for $80,000 instead of $50,000, with a remaining balance on 12/31/86 of $77,000. Thus by 12/31/86, you have made principal payments on the new loan of $80,000 − $77,000 = $3,000.

Since you refinanced for more than the old loan, you fall into Case 2. This means that you take the old loan balance just before refinancing, less the principal payments you made on the new loan in 1986:

$$($50,000 - $3,000) = $47,000.$$

Thus, the Line 3 Amount is $47,000.

Believe it or not, the IRS Form 8598 instructions for computing Line 3 are much more complicated than the description given above. You will have to follow the IRS instructions in more unusual situations—in particular for a mortgage with negative amortization (i.e. loan balance increasing with time rather than decreasing), if only a minority portion (less than 50%) of a given old debt was refinanced in 1987, if the debt on your home ever exceeded the market value of your home, or if a mortgage refinanced after August 16, 1986 for a larger amount was paid down so swiftly that the new mortgage balance on 12/31/87 was less than the old mortgage balance just before the refinancing.

On **Line 4** of 8598 you enter the Line 2 amount or the Line 3 amount, whichever is larger. This is your basic *debt-ceiling amount* on the loan.

The above discussion assumed there was only one loan on your home. If there were more than one loan, you make the above computations for each loan separately and enter the corresponding line totals on Line 1—Line 4, except for Line 2 which is

Interest on Your Home

the *cost-plus amount* of your home. (Also, we assume throughout this section that the total debt on your home never exceeds its market value.)

After computing Lines 1-4 on Form 8598, you compare Line 1, the total 1987 average balances on your home loans, with Line 4, the total *debt-ceiling* amount.

If **Line 1 is less than or equal to Line 4**, then you're done with Form 8598. This means that the loan amounts on your home do not exceed the basic debt ceiling. In this case, all the interest you paid on home loans during 1987 can be claimed on Line 9 of Schedule A as an itemized deduction. You file Form 8598 with your tax return, which verifies to the IRS that all your interest is deductible.

If **Line 1 is more than Line 4**, then you're not done. Part of the interest on your home debt may be non-deductible. In this situation, you move on to either Part II or to the more complicated Part III of Form 8598, as you choose.

(First read the first few sentences in the instructions for Part III of Form 8598. As described there, if all proceeds from all mortgages on your home were used before the end of 1987 either to purchase the home, pay for improvements, or pay for qualified medical or educational expenses, then all of your mortgage interest is deductible and you do not have to fill out Part II or Part III. Instead, you list the amount of medical or educational expenses on the dotted line to the left of the entry space on line 2, Part I of Form 8598, and also write "QEM" on the dotted line.)

Part II of Form 8598 contains the regular method for figuring your home interest deduction. Under this method, you must treat as personal interest a percentage of your total home interest corresponding to the percentage by which your loan balance on Line 1 exceeds the debt-ceiling on Line 4.

To illustrate, suppose you have computed Line 1 to be $50,000 and Line 4 to be $40,000. You first divide Line 4 by Line 1, $40,000 ÷ $50,000 = 4/5 = 80%. You would claim 80% of your home mortgage interest as an itemized deduction on line 9 of Schedule A. The remaining 20% is considered to be *personal interest,* claimed on line 12a of Schedule A. This *personal interest* gets reduced by 35% on Schedule A before being added to the total of your itemized deductions.

You should use Part III instead of Part II if you used any of the borrowings on your home to pay for **medical or educational expenses.** In Part III, the basic debt-ceiling amount is raised by the total of these expenses. To qualify, medical expenses must generally be incurred for medical care [as described in the *Medical Expenses* chapter] of yourself, your spouse, or your dependent and not reimbursed by insurance or otherwise.

Educational expenses that qualify include required expenses for yourself, your spouse, or your dependent for tuition, fees, books, supplies and equipment. Also included are *any reasonable living expenses* while away from home attending school. In general, you have used the proceeds of a debt to pay for medical or educational expenses if you paid for these expenses within 90 days before or 90 days after you incurred the debt.

In Part III the new debt ceiling, raised by the medical or educational expenses, is used to compute your deduction in the same manner as described above for Part II.

You should also use Part III if any portion of the debt on your home was used to pay for either:

Interest on Your Home 115

(i) trade or business expenses;

(ii) any investment property or expenses;

or

(iii) any passive activity property or expenses

In this case, your home interest deduction will be the same as computed under the Part II computation method. However the remainder, instead of being *personal interest* (only 65% deductible), might be fully deductible as *business interest, investment interest*, or *passive interest* [cf. the *Interest* chapter].

Example 5

You purchased your home in 1970 for $50,000 and have not added any improvements. At the time of purchase you took out a first mortgage. The remaining balance on this loan is $30,000 on 12/31/86 and $28,000 on 12/31/87, with interest paid during 1987 of $6,000. In 1985, you took out a "balloon" second mortgage for $40,000 on which you pay only interest, not principal, for the first 5 years.

On July 1, 1987, you refinanced the $40,000 second mortgage for $52,000, placing the extra $12,000 in your bank account. On September 15, 1987, you paid tuition and other expenses totalling $5,000 for your child in college, with the remaining $7,000 used for consumer purchases. Both before and after refinancing, the interest rate on the second mortgage was 10%, with total payments during 1987 of $4,600.

First, you make the following calculations for Part 1 of Form 8598:

Line 1:
1987 Average balance of first mortgage:
($30,000 + $28,000) ÷ 2 = ... $29,000
1987 Average balance of second mortgage:
$4,600 ÷ 10 (method iii) = ... $46,000

Total **$75,000**

Line 2: Cost-Plus Amount of home **$50,000**

Line 3:
First mortgage $29,000
Second Mortgage
Old loan balance on 12/31/86 [e.g. see Example 2] $40,000

Total **$69,000**

Line 4:
Larger of Line 2 or Line 3 .... **$69,000**

Since Line 4 is less than Line 1 and you used the proceeds from a loan on your home to pay educational expenses, you fill out Part III of Form 8598. In Part III, the basic Line 4 debt-ceiling of $69,000 is raised by the $5,000 of educational expenses: $69,000 + $5,000 = $74,000. Comparing this with the Line 1 total 1987 average balance of $75,000, $74/75$ of the total interest paid during the year on your home is fully deductible as home interest, with the remaining $1/75$ reported as personal interest (and therefore only 65%-deductible). Since the total home interest for 1987 is $6,000 (first mortgage) + $4,600 (second mortgage) = $10,600, the resulting deductions are:

Home interest: $74/75 \times \$10,600$ = $10,459 (claimed on line 9 of Schedule A)
Personal interest: $1/75 \times \$10,600$ = $141 (claimed on line 12a of Schedule A)

Points

When you buy a house, you might have to pay "points" in order to be able to obtain the loan. Since these points represent money you are paying to a lender in order to borrow money, they are really a form of interest and are deductible as such. An exception occurs in the case of VA points or any portion of FHA points which represent a service charge to these agencies. When you obtain your mortgage loan, the lender can tell you about the tax status of any points being charged. Only points which are paid to purchase your *principal* residence and which do not exceed what is generally paid in your area can be deducted immediately. Other points must be deducted over the period of the loan.

If a loan was taken out in connection with improving your principal residence, then points charged on the loan are similarly deductible. However, points on a loan taken out to *refinance* your home are not deductible when paid, but must be deducted ratably over the period of the loan. For example, if you pay $2,400 in points on a 20-year loan involving 240 monthly payments, then you deduct $10 for each payment that was due during the tax year. [Rev. Rul. 87-22] (At presstime, Congress was considering a change to allow refinancing points to be deductible when paid.)

To be deducted immediately when a home is purchased, you must actually *pay* the points to the lender. If the lender *withholds* the points from the mortgage loan, the points are not deductible but must be prorated over the life of the loan. This distinction is illustrated by a recent court case in which an individual borrowed $55,000 from a bank to finance a house. The bank subtracted 2 points, $1,100, from the $55,000 and disbursed the remaining $53,900 (less an origination fee which we will ignore for purposes of this illustration).

The Court ruled that the individual could not deduct the $1,100, but must prorate it over the life of the loan. Essentially, they required the transaction to be treated, partially, as a discount loan of $53,900 with $55,000 to be paid at maturity as described in the next subsection.

Instead of structuring the transaction in the above manner, the bank should have turned over the full $55,000 to the title attorney. With a separate check, the individual would have paid the bank $1,100. Then he could have obtained an immediate deduction of $1,100 on his tax return. While common sense may indicate that this is no different than having the bank withhold the $1,100 from the loan, the Tax Court has ruled that the two situations are treated differently under the law. [Schubel, 77 TC No. 51]

Discount Loans

Sometimes, loans are issued under a discount arrangement under which you receive less than the face amount of the loan, with the difference representing the interest. FHA mortgage loans and home improvement loans are common examples of this. The following example shows how to treat this type of loan.

> **Example**
>
> You borrow money from a bank in order to make a home improvement. The face amount of the loan is $10,000. However, you receive only $8,000 and are required to pay back the face amount of $10,000 in 40 equal monthly installments of $250 each. The interest on the loan is the difference between the $10,000 you pay back and the $8,000 you received, namely $2,000. This is prorated evenly over the 40 monthly payments. Thus, $2,000/40 = $50 of each monthly payment is deductible as interest. If you made 12 such payments during the year, you would have a $50 × 12 = $600 interest deduction for the year.

In the above example, the $10,000 which you paid back all went to the lender as payment for the loan. However, often the loan will include mandatory insurance payments. These insurance payments are not deductible except in connection with home office or other business expenses. In the above example, if each of the 40 monthly payments had included $5 for insurance, then you would really be paying $200 in insurance and only $9,800 back to the lender. Thus, your interest deduction would be $9,800 − $8,000 prorated over the 40 month period. Your loan agreement will state any insurance charges that are included in your monthly payments.

Graduated Payment and Adjustable Rate Mortgages

Some mortgages are structured so that payments in early years are artificially low, increasing during later years. That is, the early payments do not cover all the interest due on the mortgage; the principal due on the loan increases by an amount equal to the unpaid interest. A similar situation can arise on certain adjustable rate mortgages when the interest rate is adjusted upward but mortgage payments remain fixed below the amount required to cover the total interest due.

In such cases, you can only deduct the amount of interest actually paid. You cannot deduct the unpaid interest which was added to your mortgage balance. (The statement received from the bank or mortgage company holding your mortgage will generally show the amount actually paid.)

However, a recent IRS ruling contains a little-known fact. If you pay off or refinance the loan with another institution, you can then deduct the deferred interest which increased the principal balance on your mortgage. In this ruling, an individual borrowed $55,400 on his home under a graduated payment mortgage. Since his payments for the first few years did not cover the amount of interest on the loan, his principal balance had grown by $3,300 to $58,700 after two years. He then refinanced his house with another lending institution, paying off the $58,700 balance with the original lender. The IRS ruled that he could deduct the $3,300 at the time he refinanced the loan as a payment of deferred interest on the original loan.

The IRS noted that had he refinanced with the same institution, the $3,300 could not have been deducted at that time. In such a case, he has made no actual payment but just promised to pay again. While this may seem a distinction without a real difference, the courts have upheld this distinction. [IRS Private Letter Ruling 8347015]

Seller Financing Restricted

Often, when a house or other real estate property is sold, the seller will help the buyer finance the purchase by lending at a below-market rate. The seller must charge an annual interest rate of at least 9% (assuming compounding semiannually) unless the going rate for U.S. Treasury securities of comparable maturity is less than 9%, in which case this lesser rate may be charged. (For land sales to family members which do not total more than $500,000 during a given year, the 9% requirement is reduced to 6%.) If the required minimum interest rate is not charged, the IRS will tax part of the principal as interest income to the seller.

Similar restrictions apply to most other types of loans, whether or not used to finance a house. Extra restrictions apply to loans in excess of $2.8 million. There is a special exception to the minimum interest requirement for certain up-front payments of $90,000 or less made to certain *continuing-care facilities* by a taxpayer age 65 or older, or on behalf of a spouse who is age 65 or older.

Penalty Payments for Prepayment of Mortgages

Many mortgage contracts provide for a penalty payment if you prepay part or all of your mortgage. These payments are deductible as interest.

Where Do You Deduct Interest Payments?

Interest payments on a primary or second home are deducted on line 9 of Schedule A. You cannot deduct interest payments on a personal residence if you claim the standard deduction.

If you make interest payments on a home mortgage to an individual rather than a bank or other lending institution, Schedule A requires you to list that individual's name and address. In theory, this can be used to check that the individual receiving the payments reports them on his tax return. However, in practice, this is more in the nature of a reminder that such payments must be reported. Without requiring the social security number of the recipient, the IRS has no way of making a general crosscheck.

SECTION 2:
TAXES

The real estate taxes which you pay on your home are deductible, the same as under prior law. Often, you do not pay these directly to the local government, but instead pay them as part of your monthly mortgage payment. What usually happens to these tax payments is this. The mortgage company accumulates these payments during the year in an escrow account. Then, when a year's worth of payments has been accumulated, the mortgage company pays your real estate taxes for the next year to the local government.

You can deduct the real estate taxes only when they are actually paid to the local government. The mortgage company which places your payments into escrow is considered to be acting as your agent. Thus, the IRS does not consider that you have paid your taxes by sending money to the mortgage company. They must actually be delivered to the taxing agency.

> ### *Example*
> Your local tax year begins on July 1 and runs through June 30. From July, 1986 through June, 1987, you pay $100 per month for local property tax as part of your mortgage payment to your bank. The bank accumulates these payments into an escrow account and pays your real estate tax bill of $1,200 on July 1, 1987. You can deduct this $1,200 on your 1987 tax return. The tax portion of your mortgage payments from July through December, 1987 is not deductible on your 1987 return. These amounts are being placed in escrow and will become deductible on your 1988 return when the bank pays your July 1, 1988 tax bill.

In its yearly statement to you, the institution holding your mortgage will state how much real estate tax it paid on your account the previous year. This is the figure you use in deducting your taxes. Do not simply multiply your current tax payments by 12 because the tax rate might have been changed recently.

Your taxes are deducted on Schedule A along with the rest of your itemized deductions. You cannot claim a deduction for taxes on your personal residence if you claim the standard deduction.

Special Assessments

If an assessment is paid for the purpose of building or improving some facility then it is a non-deductible item. For example, assessments for sewers, street paving, etc. are non-deductible. The law regards such items as capital expenditures, that is, expenditures which tend to increase the value of your property. Even if you could show that no increase in value actually took place, it would do you no good. It would not change the non-deductible category into which the IRS places these expenditures.

If a portion of an assessment represents a maintenance charge or interest expense associated with an improvement, then this portion is deductible if it is levied *against an interest in real property,* as opposed to being a *user charge* for some service or benefit. While this distinction is not always easy to make, an IRS ruling has described 3 situations which illustrate the difference. In situation 1, the city assesses a front-foot benefit charge against abutting property that is benefited by the construction of a water system. In situation 2, a city water authority imposes a 2-part charge upon its customers, one part being a metered per-gallon fee and the other a flat uniform charge for maintenance and interest on the water system facilities. And in situation 3, a sewer authority imposes a flat charge per unit for each year on all residential customers. In situations 2 and 3, no deduction is permitted because the charges are considered to be merely fees paid for receipt of water and sewer services. But in situation 1, the charge is considered to be an assessment *"imposed because of and measured by some benefit inuring directly to the property against which the assessment is levied."* Thus it is an assessment *"against the property"* and the portion representing interest and maintenance is deductible. [Rev Rul 79-201]

Observe that in situation 3, had the sewer services been paid from revenue derived from a general local tax such as a property tax, the entire tax would still be deductible. It is only when the charges are singled out as user fees for services that they become non-deductible.

You will have to check with your local government to determine if any percentage of your water or sewer bill is attributable to deductible assessments. Sometimes this information will be distributed to all city residents. However, in surprisingly many cases, the local government is unfamiliar with the tax law and cannot give this breakdown. All you can do in such a case is to refer the appropriate government official to the above cited revenue ruling and pressure for this information to be provided.

How Do You Apportion Taxes When a House Is Sold?

When a house is sold, the real estate taxes are considered apportioned according to the date the property is transferred to the new owner. The following example illustrates how this is done.

> **Example**
>
> You buy a house and sign the final settlement papers on February 1, 1988. The real estate tax year in your locality runs from July 1 through the following June 30.
>
> The settlement sheet includes real estate taxes in two places. First of all, the previous owner had paid one year's taxes in advance on July 1, 1987. (This payment was actually paid by the mortgage company from money placed into escrow taken from monthly payments from July, 1986 through June, 1987.) Since you are occupying the house from February 1, 1988 through June 30, 1988, you must reimburse the previous owner for this 5-month portion of the tax bill which he already paid for.
>
> The second place where real estate taxes appear is in compensating the previous owner for the tax portion of his mortgage payments which was placed into escrow from July, 1987 through January, 1988. In effect, you are purchasing this escrow account from the previous owner. The tax portion of your mortgage payments from February, 1988 through June, 1988 will then be added to this escrow account so that by July 1, 1988, a full year's taxes will have been accumulated. This will be used to pay your taxes for the next year, July 1, 1988—June 30, 1989.
>
> The taxes for the period July 1, 1987 through January 31, 1988 belong to the seller of the house. Since he paid these taxes in advance on July 1, 1987, his deduction is claimed on his 1987 tax return. The purchaser of the house deducts on his 1988 return, the taxes from February 1, 1988 through June 30, 1988 which he paid at settlement plus the full next year's taxes paid on July 1, 1988 by the mortgage company out of the escrow account.

The preceding example shows how taxes are divided for the purpose of determining how much tax deduction goes to the seller and how much to the buyer. The actual settlement sheet may not reflect this division correctly. For example, the seller may have paid part of the taxes attributable to the period after transfer. However, this does not count. The IRS considers this as a disguised way of reducing the price of the house. The seller can only deduct the taxes for the period when he owned the house.

The buyer deducts the taxes for his period of ownership, even if he did not actually pay them.

Transfer Taxes

When you buy a house or other real estate, the settlement charges include various transfer and recordation taxes. These taxes can add up to several thousand dollars in some localities. These taxes are **not** deductible. Only those local taxes which are specifically designated in the tax code can be deducted. And this does not include real estate transfer or recordation taxes.

Under the 1986 Tax Reform Act, transfer and recordation taxes are considered to be part of the cost of the property. If the property is used for business or investment purposes (e.g. rental real estate, home office, etc.), then those taxes will be written off over a period of years as part of the depreciation on the property [cf. the *Expensing and Depreciation* chapter].

SECTION 3:
CAPITAL GAINS ON SALE OF A HOUSE

If you sell your house for a higher price than the one at which it was purchased, then you may have a capital gain. This capital gain is computed by subtracting the original purchase price of the house and the cost of any improvements from the amount realized by the sale. You also add back any deductions you have claimed for casualty losses.

The **amount realized by the sale** means the actual sales price less the cost of expenses directly connected with making the sale. Such expenses include the cost of advertising, commissions, legal fees, transfer taxes, and points or loan placement fees charged to the seller.

You do not include the cost of furnishings such as rugs, drapes, washing machine, etc. in the price of the house. You are supposed to pay capital gains tax in the unlikely event you receive more for these items than you paid. However, you cannot claim a capital loss if you sell these items at a lower price.

The **purchase price** of a house includes not only the cost of the house itself, but also expenses connected with buying the house such as legal fees, title fees, transfer and deed-recording fees, etc.

An **improvement** is a replacement or addition which adds to the value or prolongs the life of your house. This is distinguished from an ordinary maintenance or repair expense. For example, adding central air-conditioning, replacing the roof, panelling the den, new plumbing, new furnace, installing permanent storm windows, landscaping, assessments for capital items, etc. are improvements. But the cost of painting, cleaning, fixing a broken air-conditioner, etc. are ordinary maintenance expenses.

Sometimes a repair can be converted into an improvement by working it into a major remodeling project. This can provide a tax advantage because improvements reduce the capital gains tax that might become due when the house is sold. For example, the cost of wallpapering and painting can be included as part of an overall improvement plan of remodeling or renovation. But independent of such a plan, wallpapering and painting do not constitute improvements. [Bayly, TC Memo 1981-549]

The above capital gain is subject to tax according to the usual rules for taxing capital gains (cf. the *Investing Your Money* chapter) unless you reinvest the proceeds in a new personal residence as described in the following paragraphs. If you wind up with a capital loss on the sale of a house used strictly as a personal residence, you cannot deduct the loss.

Exemption from Capital Gains Tax When a New House is Purchased

If you sell your personal residence and buy a new personal residence, then you do not have to pay capital gains tax, providing you satisfy all of the following three rules.

Rule 1. Both houses must be your principal residence. Vacation houses, second homes, etc. do not qualify.

Rule 2. The purchase price of the new house must be at least as much as the adjusted sales price of your old house.

Rule 3. You must occupy the new house within 2 years before or after the sale of your old house.

If you move into your new house before actually selling your old house, you might temporarily rent out your old house while continuing your efforts to find a buyer. This does not violate Rule 1. Your old house is still considered to be your principal residence during a reasonable period you are trying to sell it.

Furthermore, if the rental activity produces a loss, you may be able to deduct this loss on your tax return [cf. Section 4]. This was the conclusion in a recent Court of Appeals decision, reversing a previous Tax Court opinion. In this case, a couple moved out of their old residence into a new home that had just been constructed. They put their old residence up for sale, but it took about a year to find a qualified buyer. During most of this period, they found a tenant to rent the old residence. They charged the going rate for such a rental property even though the rental payments did not entirely cover the mortgage payments the couple was making on the old house.

The Court of Appeals ruled that since they had abandoned the old house as a residence and were charging a fair market rental rate, their rental activity was a legitimate business activity with a profit motive. This meant they could deduct the loss produced by the rental activity according to the rules discussed in Section 4. [Bolaris, 56 AFTR 2d 85-6472]

Note however, that if a profit motive is lacking, no rental loss can be claimed. This was the conclusion of a 1986 Court case in which a prospective tenant was allowed to occupy a house rent-free, rather than being charged market rent. [Madan, TC Memo 1986-7]

Adjusted Sales Price

To determine the adjusted sales price in Rule 2 above, you subtract expenses directly connected with the sale from the actual sales price. This includes broker fees, advertising costs, legal fees, etc. You also subtract any expenses incurred for fixing up the house to make it more salable, provided the work is done within 90 days before you sign the contract to sell. You should pay the bill for this work no later than 30 days after the sale.

Fix-up costs include such things as painting, cleaning, and repairs. They do not include capital improvements such as buying a new furnace, replacing the roof, etc.

Note the peculiar treatment of fix-up costs. You take them into consideration when determining if you satisfy the rules for avoiding current payment of capital gains tax. But you do not deduct these fix-up costs when determining the actual amount of the capital gain.

Observe that Rule 2 does not state that you must invest as much cash in the new house as you had equity in the old house. It only compares the two selling prices. Thus, you could take out a larger mortgage on the new house and wind up with an excess of cash. This would make no difference as long as the cost of the new house were larger than the adjusted sales price of the old one.

You can use the above capital gains avoidance rule only once in any 2-year period. However, this restriction does not apply if you move because of a change of employment and your move qualifies for the moving expense deduction [cf. the *Moving Expenses* chapter].

Tax Deferred — Not Eliminated

Suppose you incur a capital gain which is not taxed because you purchase a new residence in accord with the provisions of the preceding subsections. Actually, the tax on this gain is not eliminated, just deferred. Eventually, if you sell a personal residence without purchasing a new personal residence, you may have to pay tax on the gain.

The way it works is this. You subtract the capital gains on your first house from the purchase price of your second house to obtain a figure called the **basis** of your second house. If you then sell the second house and purchase a third house, the basis of the third house is equal to the purchase price of the third less the difference between the selling price of the second house and the basis of the second house. After the sale of your final house, you are liable for capital gains tax on the difference between the sales price and the basis of the final house. In effect, this computation produces a tax on the sum of all the capital gains realized on the purchase and sale of each of the houses you have owned.

If you suffer a capital loss on the sale of a house, you do not subtract the loss in making the preceding calculation. However, you get credit for any capital gains tax you paid on any of the sales because of failure to satisfy Rule 2.

The above tax regulations lead to an incredible conclusion. If you never purchase a cheaper house than the one in which you previously lived, then the law requires you to have a complete record of all your purchases, sales, selling and purchasing costs, and improvements for all the houses you have owned. It is not clear how the IRS intends to enforce this regulation in the probable situation where complete records have not been kept. In the past, the IRS has not had an effective way of even knowing during which periods people were renting residences and which periods people owned houses. Ordinarily, they do not even keep records of old tax returns beyond 7 years.

What If You Don't Satisfy Rule 2?

If the purchase price of your new house is less than the adjusted sales price of your old house, then the difference between these amounts is not protected from capital gains tax. If you have a capital gain on your old residence exceeding this difference then you pay tax on the difference. Otherwise, you pay tax on the entire capital gain if there is one.

> **Example**
>
> You sell your old house and purchase a less expensive new house. The following computation illustrates the capital gains computation.
>
> | | | |
> |---|---|---|
> | A | Sales price of old house (less selling costs) | $80,000 |
> | B | less Purchase price | −60,000 |
> | C | less Improvements | − 3,000 |
> | D | Capital gain on old house | 17,000 |
> | E | Purchase price of new house | 75,000 |
> | F | Capital gains on which tax is due (A-E) | 5,000 |
> | G | Amount of capital gains not taxed (D-F) | 12,000 |
> | H | Basis of new house (E-G) | $63,000 |

The best way to compute your tax situation upon sale and purchase of a personal residence is to file Form 2119 with your tax return. This form will carry you through the correct computation even if you don't quite understand what is going on. You are supposed to file this form even if you do not have to pay any capital gains tax.

If, by the time you file your return, you have not yet purchased a new house, but plan to do so and thereby qualify to avoid capital gains tax, you should attach a statement to that effect showing the computation of the gain on your old house. You do not have to pay any capital gains tax at the time you file. Later, when you do purchase your new house, you should notify in writing the Internal Revenue Service Center where you filed your return that you have replaced your old residence, giving the dates of purchase and occupancy of the new residence and its cost. If your plans change and it turns out you should have paid a capital gains tax, then you should file an amended return.

Special Break for Those Age 55 or Older

If you sell your home after you reach age 55 (or your spouse reaches age 55 if the home is owned in joint tenancy), then up to $125,000 of profit realized from the sale is exempt from capital gains tax. The home must have been your principal residence for at least 3 out of the 5 years preceding the sale. This break is available on only one sale in your lifetime after July 26, 1978, even if less than $125,000 of profit on the sale is exempted.

Joint Tenancy vs. Individual Ownership

Most married couples own their homes (or other property) in joint tenancy, each spouse effectively being a ½ owner. Under this type of ownership, when one of the co-owners dies, the property passes automatically to the other co-owner. It cannot be willed to another individual.

There is a special type of joint tenancy available only to husband and wife, called *tenancy-by-the-entireties*. Under ordinary joint tenancy, one party alone can demand to dissolve the tenancy and retrieve his share. But under tenancy-by-the-entireties, generally, both parties must agree on any dissolution of the ownership. As far as tax laws are concerned, ordinary joint tenancy and tenancy-by-the-entireties are treated identically.

Joint tenancy is the prevalent form of ownership among married couples mostly for personal reasons — the sense of partnership and family unity that it suggests. Also, joint tenancy provides a simple way for property to be passed on to an heir. Ownership is automatically transferred to the surviving spouse without having to go through probate proceedings. However, there are tax aspects to owning property in joint tenancy which bear upon the choice of ownership for many married couples. In fact, it is wise for a married couple to periodically review the manner in which property is owned.

For married couples filing a joint return, it makes no current tax difference whether a house (or other assets) are owned jointly or individually by one of the spouses. It is only when property is transferred after the death of one spouse that a tax difference arises.

There are two separate taxes to consider. First, there is an estate tax which is levied, when an individual dies, against the total value of his assets which are passed on to his heirs by will or automatic transfer under joint tenancy. Under current law, any amount of property which one spouse inherits from the other is totally exempt from estate tax. Also, one spouse can give any amount of property to the other without incurring any gift tax. This means that for married couples who remain together until death do them part, the estate and gift taxes do not directly bear upon the form of ownership chosen. Furthermore, married couples can change the type of ownership from joint to individual or conversely, without any gift tax complications as there were under prior law. (However, more well-to-do individuals should seek professional advice on how various forms of ownership affect the estate tax that becomes due when the longer-living spouse dies.)

The second type of tax, namely income tax on capital gains, is affected by what form of ownership is chosen. The basic rule is this. When property is inherited by one individual from another, it is given a *fresh start* basis. That is, for purposes of future capital gains computations, it is treated as though it were purchased at its market value at the time of inheritance. When the property is later sold, tax is due only on the appreciation in value since the time it was inherited. No tax is ever paid on the increase in value that took place when the property belonged to the previous owner.

From this point of view, it is better for the spouse who dies first to own the property in his name only. That way any pre-death increase in value escapes capital gains tax. If the property is owned jointly, then only $1/2$ the property gets the fresh start basis.

> **Example**
>
> John and Mary purchased a house for $50,000. John dies and the house is inherited by Mary who sells it later for $125,000. At the time of John's death, the house was worth $100,000.
>
> **Case 1. John owned the house in his name only.**
>
> The house gets a stepped-up basis of $100,000 when it is inherited by Mary. When she sells it, her capital gain is $125,000 − $100,000 = $25,000.
>
> **Case 2. Mary owned the house in her name only.**
>
> Mary's capital gain is simply the selling price minus the purchase price, $125,000 − $50,000 = $75,000.
>
> **Case 3. John and Mary owned the house in joint tenancy.**
>
> The house is treated as though it were owned 1/2 by each of them. John's half gets a stepped-up basis of $50,000 (1/2 the market value at his death) and is sold for $62,500 (1/2 × $125,000), a capital gain of $62,500 − $50,000 = $12,500. Mary's half was purchased for $25,000 (1/2 × $50,000) and sold for $62,500 (1/2 × $125,000), a capital gain of $62,500 − $25,000 = $37,500. The total capital gain is $12,500 + $37,500 = $50,000.

The above example shows that capital gains are lowest when the spouse who dies first owned the property in his name only and highest when the surviving spouse was the sole owner. This difference may not lead to a tax difference because of the exemptions from capital gains tax described earlier in this Section. But for those who will not qualify under these exemptions or wish to conserve their once-in-a-lifetime $125,000 exemption for those age 55 or over, the difference can be substantial. In such a case it might be advisable to shift jointly-owned property to the spouse most likely to die first, the husband in most cases. This will benefit the wife by lowering her tax upon sale after her husband's death. (However, shifts made within the one year period prior to the husband's death do not count.) If the wife does not wish to give up the security of her ownership position, a local attorney may be able to find a solution under the law such as her retention of the right to live in the house.

The above only touches upon the basic considerations involved in choosing the proper form of ownership. A qualified attorney should be consulted before making any major decisions. This is especially true in common law states where the rules governing ownership transfers between spouses are more complicated.

SECTION 4:
RENTING A HOME TO OTHERS

If you rent out a home you own, then you report the rent as income and you take the expenses associated with the rental as a deduction against the income. Special rules cover the situation when expenses exceed income. As discussed later in this section, these rules may prevent you from claiming a loss in this situation.

There are also special *passive loss* rules that can restrict the ability to deduct losses on rental activities. However, these passive loss rules do not apply to losses up to $25,000 incurred by persons with income under $100,000, provided they sufficiently participate in managing the rental. This $25,000 limit is phased out for those with income in the $100,000 − $150,000 range. [cf. Section 2 of the *Investing Your Money* chapter for details on these new *passive loss* rules.] In the remainder of this section, we assume that these passive loss rules do **not** affect your total deduction because of this $25,000 exemption or the existence of offsetting passive profits.

Deductible expenses include advertising costs, legal fees, utility bills you pay, homeowner's insurance, management fees, interest, and taxes. You can also deduct depreciation according to the rules described in the *Depreciation* chapter. You compute your depreciation starting from the point you first rent your home as described in the *Depreciation* chapter. That is, your depreciation is based on the original purchase price of the house plus the cost of improvements (less any casualty losses you have claimed) or else on the fair market value of the house when you start renting it out, whichever is lower.

Depreciating Your Furniture

If you rent out your home furnished, then you can deduct depreciation on the furnishings and appliances. Since used furniture and appliances are usually worth less than their original purchase price, you will have to estimate their current fair market value and use this as the basis for depreciation. You can use either the straight-line or accelerated depreciation method for 7-year property as described in the *Depreciation* chapter.

How are Rental Income and Expenses Reported?

You report your rental income and expenses on Schedule E. Note that expenses connected with renting a home are not considered itemized deductions. Thus, they may be deducted even if the standard deduction is claimed.

Example

Jones rents out a house from September 1, 1987 until December 31, 1988, a total of 16 months.

Depreciation Calculation on House

Jones originally paid $80,000 for the house when he purchased it in 1981 and later added central airconditioning at a cost of $4,000. Since the sum of these two amounts, $84,000, is less than the current fair market value, this sum is used as the basis for depreciation.

The following depreciation calculation is made according to the procedure explained in the *Depreciation* chapter.

(1) Depreciation for 4 months from
    9/1/87 to 12/31/87 .... 1.06% × $84,000 = $ 890
(2) Depreciation for year from
    1/1/88 to 12/31/88 .... 3.64% × $84,000 = $3,058

Depreciation Calculation on Furniture

Jones estimates that the furnishings and appliances in the house have a current value of $6,000. Since $6,000 is less than his original cost, it is used as the basis for depreciation. He uses the accelerated method for 7-year property, as described in the *Depreciation* chapter.

(1) Depreciation for 1987 .... 14.3% × $6,000 = $ 858
(2) Depreciation for 1988 .... 24.5% × $6,000 = $1,470

Total Expenses

Jones pays $500 per month in mortgage interest. He also pays $1,200 per year in property taxes and $120 per year in insurance. In order to make the appropriate allocations to 1987, these latter two amounts are prorated on a monthly basis—$100 per month for taxes and $10 per month for insurance.

Expense Summary

	1987		1988
Depreciation on house:	$ 890		$3,058
Depreciation on furniture:	858		1,470
Interest: $500 × 4 mo. =	2,000	$500 × 12 mo. =	6,000
Taxes: $100 × 4 mo. =	400	$100 × 12 mo. =	1,200
Insurance: $ 10 × 4 mo. =	40	$10 × 12 mo. =	120
Advertising:	25		0
Legal expenses:	40		137
Totals:	$4,253		$11,985

Rent

Jones rents out his house for $625 per month. The tenants pay the cost of utilities. Thus Jones receives rent of $625 × 4 months = $2,500 in 1987 and $625 × 12 months = $7,500 in 1988.

Net Result

For 1987, Jones has rental income of $2,500 and expenses of $4,253, a net loss of $1,753 for 1987.

For 1988, Jones has rental income of $7,500 and expenses of $11,985, a net loss of $4,485 for 1988.

The depreciation deductions illustrated in the above example apply to houses placed into rental service in 1987 or 1988. Houses placed into rental service in 1986 or earlier, come under more generous rules [cf. last year's edition of this Tax Guide], even if the rental period extends into 1987 or beyond.

Profit Motive Needed to Establish Loss

As in the above example, it may turn out that your expenses exceed the rental income, producing a net loss. In order to deduct the loss on your tax return, you should have a profit motive when you rent out the house. To begin with, you must charge the going rate for rent in your locality. But even if you charge this "fair market rate," the IRS may still question your profit motive.

This is confirmed by an IRS Private Letter Ruling [#7826006] concerning a College Professor who rented out his house when he went away on leave of absence. The Professor had listed his house with a rental agency and charged the fair market value for rent in his area. A local IRS office had apparently sought advice from the National Office on what additional factors should be considered in deciding whether a loss should be allowed.

The IRS ruling stressed that the Professor must have a profit motive. If he was just renting out his house to lessen the loss that would occur if the house were left unrented, this would not suffice. He must have actually intended to make a profit on the transaction. Beyond this, the IRS ruling did not give much further guidance, telling the local IRS office that, *"The question of whether the taxpayer had a profit-making objective is a determination to be made by you based upon all the surrounding facts and circumstances."*

According to letters we have received from readers of prior editions, the IRS has in fact been challenging the profit motive of individuals when they rent out their personal residences while temporarily located away from home. Since there is often no chance that the rental income will exceed the taxes, interest, and other expenses, the IRS simply claims that there could be no profit motive. The taxpayer is often stymied as to how to counter this logically simple objection.

However, there is a strong argument that can be made by the taxpayer in this situation. Namely, the profit motive in owning a rental house comes from the appreciation in the value of the house that will occur over the period of time the house is rented out. In fact, investors who buy houses for the sole purpose of renting them out are often in precisely this situation. Their expenses exceed the rental income but they look to the profit that will come eventually when the house is sold for more than its purchase price.

There is a Tax Court case that supports this position. An individual owned some property which he rented out at substantial annual losses. The IRS challenged the deduction of his losses, claiming that these large losses showed there could be no profit motive present.

But the Tax Court permitted the losses to be deducted. It ruled that considering the anticipated appreciation of value of the property, a profit motive was present. In permitting the eventual increase in property value to be considered, it quoted the Income Tax Regulations as follows:

> *"The term 'income' for [these purposes] includes not merely income of the taxable year but also income which the taxpayer has realized in a prior taxable year or may realize in subsequent taxable years; and is not confined to recurring income but applies as well to gains from the disposition of property. For example, if defaulted bonds, the interest from which if received would be includable in income, are purchased with the expectation of realizing capital gain on their resale, even though no current yield thereon is anticipated, ordinary and necessary expenses thereafter paid or incurred in connection with such bonds are deductible. Similarly, ordinary and necessary expenses paid or incurred in the management, conservation, or maintenance of a building devoted to rental*

purposes are deductible notwithstanding that there is actually no income therefrom in the taxable year, and regardless of the manner in which or the purpose for which the property in question was acquired." [TC Memo 1978-85]

Home Rented Out for Part of the Year

If you rent out a home for less than 15 days during the year, then it is considered that no business transaction took place. In this case, you neither report the rental income nor deduct any expenses. You deduct your taxes and interest on Schedule A as though no rental had taken place.

If you rent out your home for at least 15 days during the year, and use it for personal purposes part of the year, then you cannot deduct a rental loss if the following condition is satisfied:

The home was used for personal purposes both:

(i) more than 14 days

and

(ii) more than 10% of the number of days during the year on which the home is rented out.

However, if the above condition applies, then the home qualifies as a *primary* or *second home* under the rules discussed in Section 1. This means that all interest attributed to your personal use of the home can be deducted as *home interest* on line 9 of Schedule A.

However, if you do not satisfy the above condition, then you have not used the home enough to qualify it as your *primary* or *second* home. This means that the interest attributed to your personal use of the home is considered *personal interest*, only 65%-deductible as described in the *Interest* chapter. However in this case, because of your minimal personal use, you would qualify to deduct a loss from the rental activity.

Exception

For a home which is rented out for part of the year and used as your principal residence the remainder of the year, the above restriction on deducting rental losses does not apply if either:

(1) The rental period consisted of at least 12 consecutive months (not necessarily all in the same calendar year)

or

(2) The rental period was a consecutive period of less than 12 months ending in the sale of the residence.

For example, if you rent out your home from June 1, 1988 through May 31, 1989 and use it as your principal residence the remainder of 1988 and 1989, then the consecutive 12-month rental period satisfies the above exception.

If you are planning to be out of town for an extended period of time, you should take careful note of the above exception. By making sure you rent out your house for at least 12 consecutive months, you might become eligible to deduct a rental loss on your tax return. As shown by the preceding example, this could make a significant

difference in your taxes. (This exception permitting losses on rental houses to be deducted can be used on a *primary or second home* [cf. Section 1] even if the passive loss rules, as discussed in Section 2 of the *Investing Your Money* chapter, would otherwise apply. More specifically, any interest disallowed under the passive loss rules can be claimed as primary or second home interest on line 9 of Schedule A. To qualify, you must use the home for personal purposes both (i) more than 14 days, and (ii) more than 10% of the number of days during the year for which the home is rented out.)

What Happens If a Loss Cannot Be Deducted?

If you are prevented from deducting a loss on a rental house for the reasons above, you must use the following procedure for offsetting your rental income with your expenses: Start with the *gross rental income*. This equals the rent you receive from tenants less the costs of obtaining these tenants (advertising, rental agency fees, etc.). From this amount, (a) first subtract taxes and interest, (b) second, subtract rental expenses such as maintenance, insurance, utilities, etc., and (c) third, subtract depreciation. If a loss results, you cannot deduct the loss. The rental simply produces no tax result — neither a gain nor a loss. Of course in (a), (b), (c), you deduct only that proportion of the annual expense which corresponds to the proportion of time the house is rented out.

Note that the above order of deducting expenses forces you to deduct taxes and interest first. This prevents you from using the other expenses in (b) and (c) first to offset the rental income and then claiming the full amount of taxes and interest as an ordinary itemized deduction on Schedule A. However, if the allowable tax and interest expenses should exceed your rental income, then the excess is deductible in the usual place on Schedule A. In any event, you still deduct on Schedule A that proportion of interest and taxes corresponding to the percentage of time the home is used for personal purposes.

Example Revisited

In the preceding example, net losses resulted both in 1987 and 1988. Since the home was not used for personal purposes in 1988, the full loss of $4,485 is reported on the 1988 tax return. According to the 12-month exception described above, the $1,753 loss is also deductible on the 1987 tax return, provided the home is used as a principal residence for the period preceding the rental.

However, let us now suppose that the home was rented out only for the 4-month period Sept. 1, 1987 — Dec. 31, 1987 and used for personal purposes the remainder of 1987. In such a case, the restriction on deducting losses would apply. The rental would produce neither a net gain nor a net loss on the 1987 tax return. However, since the $2,000 interest and $400 taxes attributable to the rental period total less than the $2,475 gross rental income ($2,500 rent less $25 advertising cost), these amounts are used up in offsetting the rental income according to the (a), (b), (c) priority described above. Thus, these amounts cannot be deducted in the Interest or Taxes Sections on Schedule A. However, the interest and taxes attributable to the period the house was used for personal purposes can be deducted as itemized deductions on Schedule A.

Note: The above discussion is meant to give general guidance on the proper treatment of homes that are used both for personal and rental purposes. Because of pending IRS regulations and pending legislation in Congress, there is currently a lack of certainty as to the exact treatment that applies in every case. Especially if the passive loss rules come into play [cf. Section 2 of the *Investing Your Money* chapter], professional assistance should be sought to handle your writeoffs in the proper way. Next year's edition of this Tax Guide will contain further information on this issue.

Renting to Relatives

At one time, rental of a residence to a spouse or other family member was considered to be "personal use," thereby restricting the ability to deduct rental losses that would otherwise be allowable. But now, rental by an individual to a family member can be treated the same as rental to any other individual provided a fair market value is charged and the dwelling is the principal residence of the person to whom it is rented.

The *fair market rental* means the amount generally being charged in your locality for similar accommodations. However, a recent court case shows that it is all right to give a suitable discount to a family member. In this case, an individual rented a house he owned to his parents. The fair market rent that could have been charged a stranger was $450. But the Court ruled that this could be reduced by 20% to $360 because a management fee was avoided and the parents were trustworthy tenants. [Bindsell, TC Memo 1983-411].

Subletting a Rented Residence

If you are renting a residence which you sublet to someone else for a fair price, then you are engaged in a business activity. You must report the rent you receive as income but can deduct the rent you pay plus any other expenses you incur in connection with the rental. These deductions are taken on Schedule E and can be taken whether or not you claim the standard deduction.

Chapter 10

Automobile Expenses

Many types of auto travel can be deducted as described in the *Travel* chapter — convention trips, travel to and at a temporary job, travel between two jobs, travel to obtain education, etc. In addition, you can deduct for miscellaneous automobile travel connected with your employment such as travel from your office to libraries to do research, travel to pick up official visitors at an airport, etc.

There are two basic methods to deduct for business use of an automobile which you own. The first method is to deduct a *standard rate* per mile plus parking and tolls. The second method is to compute your *actual expenses*. As discussed below, the second method can prove superior because it includes a writeoff for the cost of the automobile in addition to operating costs.

There are special rules for automobiles purchased after June 18, 1984. Under these rules [cf. the *Depreciation* chapter] illustrated later in this chapter, a special depreciation table applies if business use does not exceed 50%. And an employee must use the standard mileage rate unless the use of his auto is required by his employer.

Where on the Income Tax Form Do You Deduct Auto Expenses?

The 1986 Tax Reform Act has changed the way automobile (and other travel) expenses are treated on 1987 tax returns. As in prior years, an employee still uses Part II of Form 2106, *Employee Business Expenses,* on which to list his automobile expenses. However, the total of automobile expenses is now entered as a *miscellaneous deduction* on Schedule A of the 1987 tax return. (In prior years, employee travel expenses were treated as an *adjustment to income* rather than as an *itemized deduction*.) And, as discussed in the *Miscellaneous Deductions* chapter, the sum total of travel expenses plus other miscellaneous deductions is subjected to a 2% of Adjusted Gross Income floor.

Exception. If an employee is reimbursed by his employer for part or all of his auto expenses, the situation is different. If such reimbursement is included as taxable income on his W-2 Form, then the employee can generally claim the reimbursed amount as an *adjustment to income* on line 23 of Form 1040 rather than as an *itemized deduction* on Schedule A. An adjustment to income is not subject to the 2% of Adjusted Gross Income floor that applies to miscellaneous itemized deductions and can be claimed by any individual, whether he uses the standard deduction or itemizes his deductions. Further details on the treatment of auto (and other job-related) expenses for which an employee is reimbursed are discussed in Section 1 of the *Miscellaneous Deductions* chapter.

Self-employed persons claim auto expenses on Schedule C the same as any other business expense related to their self-employment activity. Thus, these expenses escape the 2% of Adjusted Gross Income floor that applies to miscellaneous deductions; also, non-itemizers as well as itemizers get to deduct their auto expenses on Schedule C.

If, as discussed later, expensing or depreciation is claimed for an auto, then Form 4562 must be filled out also. Also, if a person claims auto expenses in connection with a self-employment activity, then Part III of Form 4562 must be filled out whether or not expensing or depreciation is claimed.

Recordkeeping Rules

The recordkeeping rules for auto travel were changed in 1986. Now, *local* auto travel is subject to the same general recordkeeping requirement as *away-from-home* travel as described in Section 1 of the *Travel* chapter.

Under the old rules prior to 1986, *local* travel was subject only to the same basic rules applying to any other type of business deduction. That is, the more convincing the records, the more likely your deduction would stand up to IRS scrutiny. But no explicit standards were specified. In fact, even in the absence of any records, taxpayers sometimes could qualify for a deduction just by making a reasonable estimate of their travel at the end of the year.

But now, an end-of-the-year estimate is no longer sufficient. Instead, there must be adequate records to support your deduction. In general, this means you must maintain a diary or similar written record which, for each job or business use of your auto, contains the following information:

1. Date;

2. Business purpose of trip;
 and
3. Business mileage traveled.

You should also keep track of the total mileage your auto was driven during the year by, say, writing down the odometer readings at the beginning and end of each year.

If you are deducting your actual expenses rather than using the standard mileage rate, you must also record the date and amount of each expenditure for gasoline, repairs, etc. You can take the sum of such expenses and prorate this sum based on the percentage your auto was driven for business purposes. For example, if your auto was used 60% for business purposes and you spent $1,000 for gasoline during the year, you would be entitled to a deduction of 60% × $1,000 = $600 for gasoline (assuming you are deducting your actual expenses rather than using the standard mileage rate).

Your records should be maintained in a *timely* manner. This means you write down each entry soon enough that you have full recall of all the details. However, it is no longer required that your records be contemporaneous with business use. According to the IRS, it is acceptable to record your usage or expenses at the end of each week. However, even if your records are kept weekly, they should still give a daily breakdown of each separate period of business use.

Automobile Expenses

It is not necessary to write down information in a diary (or other record) which duplicates information reflected on a receipt as long as your diary and receipts complement each other in an orderly manner. And you do not have to write down the business purpose of your travel if it is evident from the surrounding facts and circumstances.

Below is a suggested recordkeeping format for an auto for which you use the standard mileage rate. You can use a different format as long as the requisite information is recorded.

AUTO MILEAGE & EXPENSE RECORD

Date	Destination/Business Purpose	Odometer Start	Odometer End	(Round Trip) Mileage Bus	Invest	Med	Char	Parking/Tolls
1/1	Beginning Odometer Reading	7168						
1/5	Dr. Jones—appointment	7216	7237			21		
1/6	Drop off Goodwill donation	7237	7259				22	
1/10	Seminar at State Univ.	7342	7371	29				3.00
1/12	Pick up Dr. Smith (Visiting Consultant) at Airport	7410	7462	52				
1/16	Church Choir Rehearsal	7531	7543				12	
1/18	Pick up Medicine at Drug Store	7571	7579			8		
1/20	Consult with Stockbroker	7612	7632		20			
12/31	Ending Odometer Reading		15,641					
	TOTALS			1,264	124	212	314	$146
	CENTS/MILE ALLOWED			21	21	9	12	
	TOTAL DEDUCTIONS			$265	$26	$19	$38	$146

Sampling Rule for Local Auto Travel

The type of detailed records normally expected for out-of-town travel do not have to be kept for local auto travel of a recurring nature. According to a 1986 IRS regulation, it is permissible to use a "sampling technique" for deducting such travel on your tax return [IRS Reg. 1.274-5T]. The following examples are adapted from this regulation.

Example 1.

You work at 2 different business locations and often drive from one location to the other on the same day. You should record the date of each trip at or near the time of each trip. However, you need to record the distance between the 2 business locations only once, not each time you drive. You also should record the total number of miles your auto is driven overall. This will satisfy the recordkeeping requirement for this travel.

Example 2.

You use your auto during the year for miscellaneous business travel, e.g. travel between job locations, to seminars, to libraries, etc. You keep adequate records for the first 3 months of the year which show that this business mileage is 15% of the total mileage put on your auto. You also record the beginning and final odometer readings for the year which show your auto was driven for 10,000 miles during the year. Assuming it is established that your business usage continues at approximately the same rate for the remainder of the year, your records support a deduction for 1,500 miles (15% × 10,000 miles) of business auto travel for the year.

Example 3.

Same as Example 2 except that you keep adequate records during the first week of each month which show your auto is used 15% for business travel. As long as it is established that these are "representative" weeks, your records support a deduction for 15% of the total mileage for the year.

Observe that in both Examples 2 and 3, the sampling period constitutes about 1/4 of the year. The IRS specifically states that this can be an adequate sampling period. However, the IRS has not stated what the shortest acceptable sampling period would be. For example, if records were kept only during 1 or 2 months of the year, there is no current guidance as to whether or not this would constitute an acceptable sampling period.

Information Required on Tax Return

You do not include your mileage or expense records when you send in your tax return. Rather, you keep these records in case your tax return is audited. However, on your 1987 tax return, the following questions (stated in slightly different words) must be answered for all auto travel (local and out-of-town) either on Form 2106 for employees or on Part III of Form 4562 for self-employment travel:

1. When was the vehicle first placed into service?
2. What was the total number of miles driven during the year?
3. Was the vehicle used for commuting? If so, what was the total commuting mileage for the year?
4. How many miles was the vehicle driven for non-commuting personal purposes?

5. Was another vehicle available for personal use?

6. Do you have evidence to support your deduction? If so, is the evidence written?

Note that the purpose of asking the above questions on tax returns is twofold. First, the existence of these questions (in particular question number 6) will discourage carelessly made estimates, rather than more careful recordkeeping. Second, if the IRS examines the answers to these questions, indication of an unjustified deduction may be spotlighted. For example, if the answer to question 3 indicates the auto was used a large percentage for non-deductible commuting, this may be inconsistent with the percentage of business use claimed. Or, if the answer to question 6 is "no," this will raise a red flag concerning the ability to justify the auto deduction claimed.

Note that a written re-creation of your business travel made at the end of the year might entitle you to answer "yes" to question 6 above, thereby avoiding spotlighting your return for audit. However, should your return actually be audited, such a re-creation would not actually satisfy the recordkeeping requirement discussed earlier in this chapter.

The Standard Mileage Rate

Under the standard rate method, you deduct $22^{1}/_{2}$ cents per mile for the first 15,000 miles during the year of business use and 11 cents per mile for additional miles above 15,000. In addition, you may deduct parking fees and tolls.

If your auto is fully depreciated or if your auto has more than 60,000 business miles on it for which you claimed the maximum permissible standard rate, then you cannot use the $22^{1}/_{2}$ cents per mile rate. Instead, you must use the 11 cents per mile rate or compute your actual expenses excluding depreciation.

The standard mileage rate is not meant to cover interest or taxes on the auto. These might be able to be deducted separately according to the rules discussed in the *Interest* and *Taxes* chapters. However, note that sales tax can no longer be claimed as an itemized deduction.

There are some restrictions which the IRS has placed on the use of the standard mileage rate [Rev. Proc. 82-61]. First of all, if you use the standard rate, it must be used right from the beginning of business use. That is, you cannot use the standard rate on an automobile for which you have deducted your actual expenses in a prior year. This restriction applies to automobiles first placed into service for business purposes in 1981 or later years. For automobiles placed into service before 1981, you cannot now use the standard rate if either the accelerated depreciation method or extra 20% first year allowance which applied before 1981 was used. Instead, you must make a computation of your actual automobile expenses and base your deduction on that amount.

Secondly, once you use the standard rate on an automobile first placed into service in 1981 or later years, you cannot use the usual depreciation method in a later year. Instead, you must continue to use the standard rate, or else compute your actual expenses using an appropriate straight-line depreciation method. This restriction does not apply to automobiles placed into service before 1981.

Extras in Addition to the Standard Rate

According to the IRS, the standard rate is used *"in lieu of all operating and fixed costs of the automobile allocable to business purposes. Such items as depreciation, maintenance and repairs, tires, gasoline (including all taxes thereon), oil, insurance, and registration fees are included in operating and fixed costs. However, parking fees and tolls attributable to use for business purposes may be deducted as separate items."* [Rev. Proc. 82-61]

According to a recent court case, the above quote is not interpreted as restricting the extras that may be deducted to the *parking fees and tolls* described in the third sentence above. Other items not covered by the first two sentences can be deducted also. In this case, an individual used his automobile 50% for business purposes for which he claimed the standard mileage rate. During the year, he incurred towing expenses of $173.25.

The Court ruled that these towing costs were not part of the operating and fixed costs covered by the standard mileage rate. It ruled,

". .under the standard rate method, petitioners are also entitled to deduct certain additional amounts actually incurred, such as parking and tolls. We believe that petitioners' towing costs which respondent has conceded were substantiated fall within this category."

Since the individual's automobile was used 50% for business purposes, the Court allowed a deduction of 50% × $173.25 = $86.62 for towing costs. The allocation was not based on the nature of auto use when the towing costs were actually incurred. [Alcorden, TC Memo 1984-334]

No indication is given as to what items besides towing costs would be allowed in addition to the standard rate covering *"operating and fixed"* costs. Clearly, garage rental fees could be considered parking fees. But other extras (e.g. auxiliary auto supplies) are neither clearly included or excluded. What the above court case suggests, for the first time, is that an individual can use the standard rate and still be entitled to deduct extras besides parking and tolls which can also be considered neither *operating* nor *fixed* costs.

Computing Your Actual Auto Expenses

Instead of the standard mileage rate, you can deduct your actual automobile expenses. This includes gas, oil, repairs, insurance, etc. — plus parking and tolls. It also includes a portion of the cost of the automobile. It is here that a substantial deduction can be claimed.

To write off the cost of the automobile, you use the appropriate expensing or depreciation procedure as described in the *Expensing and Depreciation* chapter. However, there are special maximum limitations, described below, that apply only to automobiles.

Also, as described in Section 1 of that chapter, expensing or depreciation can be claimed by an employee for job-related use of an auto purchased after June 18, 1984 only if such use is required by his employer. Otherwise, the standard mileage rate must be used.

Automobile Expenses

Interest on an auto owned by an employee is considered personal interest even if the auto is used for job-related purposes. As such, it can only be claimed as an itemized deduction on line 12a of Form 1040, subject to the 65% reduction rule for personal interest [cf. the *Interest* chapter].

Expensing and Depreciation Rules for Autos

There are special **maximum limitations** on the total of expensing plus depreciation deductions that can be claimed for a given automobile in any one year. The following table gives the maximum limits on annual deductions that can be claimed for an automobile placed into service in 1987. (For autos placed into service before 1987, different limitations apply [cf. last year's edition of this Tax Guide]. Also, after 1988, the limits will be raised according to the increase in the automobile component of the Consumer Price Index.) These limits were designed to affect only "luxury" automobiles costing more than $12,800. However, because of the expensing option, the initial first year limit can affect the deduction for any automobile costing more than $2,560.

Maximum Annual Deductions for Autos Placed into Service in 1987

Year	Maximum Deduction
1987	$2,560
1988	4,100
1989	2,450
each succeeding year	1,475

The above limitations apply to an auto used 100% for business purposes. They are reduced proportionately for autos used partly for personal purposes. For example, the upper limit on an auto used 60% for business purposes would be 60% of the above amounts.

If the maximum limitations come into play, the full value of the automobile can still be written off—the writeoff period is just extended. Examples 3 and 4 illustrate this situation.

When the expensing method is used, the remainder not expensed is depreciated according to the usual 5-year table [cf. the *Depreciation* chapter]. However, the total expensing plus depreciation deductions for a given year are subject to the maximum limitations described above. This can lead to an unexpected pitfall. [Temp. Reg. 1.280F-2T]

To illustrate, suppose that an automobile costs $9,000 and the maximum expensing deduction of $2,560 is claimed in the first year. The remainder, $9,000 − $2,560 = $6,440, would then be depreciated according to the 20%, 32%, 19.2%, 11.5%, 11.5%, 5.8% percentages provided by the 5-year depreciation table. Since the maximum $2,560 writeoff has been used up by the expensing deduction, no depreciation deduction is allowed for the first year. The depreciation deductions for the remaining years are as provided in the following table. Observe that an extra 7th year is now required to achieve the full $9,000 writeoff for the cost of the auto.

Automobile Expenses

Year	Deduction
1987	$2,560 expensing
1988	32% × $6,440 = 2,061 depreciation
1989	19.2% × $6,440 = 1,236 depreciation
1990	11.5% × $6,440 = 741 depreciation
1991	11.5% × $6,440 = 741 depreciation
1992	5.8% × $6,440 = 374 depreciation
1993	Remainder = 1,287 depreciation
	$9,000

It is possible to avoid the above pitfall of spilling over the auto writeoff into a 7th year. The key is to claim an expensing deduction of less than $2,560, with the remaining depreciation deductions filling out the normal depreciation period for 5-year items. This can generally be done for automobiles costing less than $12,800 by using the following formula to compute the optional Expensing amount E:

$$E = \frac{\$12,800 - \text{Cost of Auto}}{4}$$

For autos costing $12,800 or more, the depreciation method alone should be used, with no expensing deduction.

Example 1. Auto Costing Less than $12,800

An auto is purchased in 1987 for $9,000 and is used entirely for business purposes. According to the formula above, the following amount E should be expensed:

$$E = \frac{\$12,800 - \$9,000}{4} = \$950$$

The remainder, $9,000 − $950 = $8,050, is depreciated via the usual 5-year depreciation table.

Year	Expensing	Depreciation	Deduction
1987	$950 +	20% × $8,050 =	$2,560
1988		32% × $8,050 =	2,576
1989		19.2% × $8,050 =	1,546
1990		11.5% × $8,050 =	926
1991		11.5% × $8,050 =	926
1992		5.8% × $8,050 =	466
			$9,000

Example 2.

Same as Example 1 except that the auto is used 60% for business purposes. In this case the amount to be written off is 60% of the cost, namely 60% × $9,000 = $5,400. In the formula for E, the $12,800 is similarly multiplied by 60%: 60% × $12,800 = $7,680. Thus, the expensing deduction E in this situation is:

$$E = \frac{\$7{,}680 - \$5{,}400}{4} = \$570$$

The remainder, $5,400 − $570 = $4,830, is depreciated via the usual depreciation table for 5-year property.

Year	Expensing	Depreciation		Deduction
1987	$570 +	20% × $4,830	=	$1,536
1988		32% × $4,830	=	1,546
1989		19.2% × $4,830	=	927
1990		11.5% × $4,830	=	556
1991		11.5% × $4,830	=	556
1992		5.8% × $4,830	=	279
				$5,400

Note that the deduction for 1987 is equal to the maximum limitation that applies, namely 60% × $2,560 = $1,536.

Example 3. Auto Costing $12,800 or More

An auto is purchased in 1987 for $16,000 and is used 100% for business purposes. Because the auto costs more than $12,800, the deduction produced by the 5-year depreciation table would exceed the maximum limitations ($2,560 is less than 20% × $16,000 = $3,200; $4,100 is less than 32% × $16,000 = $5,120, etc.). Thus, the depreciation deductions for each year are equal to the maximum limitations until the final year, when the amount used is chosen to fully depreciate the $16,000 cost.

Year	Deduction
1987	$2,560
1988	4,100
1989	2,450
1990	1,475
1991	1,475
1992	1,475
1993	1,475
1994	990
	$16,000

In the above example it is presumed that the automobile continues to be owned through the end of 1994. Under any depreciation method, for items in the 5-year or 7-year category placed into service in 1987, half a year's depreciation is allowed in the year of disposition. Thus, in the above example, if the automobile were disposed of in 1992, the depreciation deduction for 1992 would be 1/2 × $1,475 = $738. The automobile would produce no further deductions after 1992, the year of disposition.

Also, in the above example, it was assumed the automobile is used 100% for business purposes. The following example illustrates a situation where business usage is less than 100%.

Example 4.

Same as the previous example, except that instead of 100%, the business use percentage is 60% for 1987 – 1990, and 55% for 1991 – 1994. In this case, the amounts in the previous example are multiplied by these percentages to arrive at the depreciation deductions for each year.

Year	Depreciation Deduction
1987	60% × $2,560 = $1,536
1988	60% × 4,100 = 2,460
1989	60% × 2,450 = 1,470
1990	60% × 1,475 = 885
1991	55% × 1,475 = 811
1992	55% × 1,475 = 811
1993	55% × 1,475 = 811
1994	55% × 990 = 545

Comparing the Actual Expenses Method with the Standard Mileage Rate

The following examples illustrate the use of the actual expenses method and compare the results with the standard mileage rate.

Example 5.

You purchased an automobile in February, 1987 for $9,000. You drive the automobile 10,000 miles per year for each of the years 1987 – 1992. Of these 10,000 miles, 6,000 (60% of the total) are for business purposes.

Actual Cost Method

Your operating expenses per year are as follows:

Repairs and parts	$650
Insurance	250
Car washing	50
Gas and oil	700
License (including driver's license)	75
Motor club membership	40
Garage rent	150
Total	$1,915

Since your auto is being used 60% for business purposes, the amount of operating expenses attributable to business use is 60% × $1,915 = $1,149.

The expensing and depreciation deductions for this situation have already been calculated in Example 2. Thus, the total deductions for each year are as follows:

Automobile Expenses

Year	Expensing/Depreciation		Operating Expenses		Total Deduction
1987	$1,536	+	$1,149	=	$2,685
1988	1,546	+	1,149	=	2,695
1989	927	+	1,149	=	2,076
1990	556	+	1,149	=	1,705
1991	556	+	1,149	=	1,705
1992	279	+	1,149	=	1,428
					$12,294

(In addition to the above amounts, parking fees and tolls incurred in business-related travel are deductible.)

On a per business mile basis, the figures above become:

1987:	$ 2,685/6,000 business miles	= 45 cents per mile
1988:	$ 2,695/6,000 business miles	= 45 cents per mile
1989:	$ 2,076/6,000 business miles	= 35 cents per mile
1990:	$ 1,705/6,000 business miles	= 28 cents per mile
1991:	$ 1,705/6,000 business miles	= 28 cents per mile
1992:	$ 1,428/6,000 business miles	= 24 cents per mile
Overall:	$12,294/36,000 business miles	= 34 cents per mile

(The above figures were based on a purchase price of $9,000 and will change according to any change in purchase price. For example, for an auto costing $12,800 or more, the overall cents per mile figure in this example for the period 1987 – 1992 would be 42 cents instead of 34 cents.)

Standard Mileage Rate

The standard mileage rate is $22\frac{1}{2}$ cents per mile. This is less than the amount computed under the actual cost method. However, when an employee uses an auto purchased after June 18, 1984 for job-related travel, such use must be required by his employer in order for the actual cost method to be used [cf. the *Depreciation* chapter]. Otherwise, the standard mileage rate must be used.

Comment. Observe that under the depreciation option, the higher the percentage of business use, the higher will be the deduction. Thus, it pays you to limit your personal use of an auto which is used for business purposes in order to increase the percentage of business use. For example, if you own two automobiles, use one of them (as much as possible) for business purposes and the other (as much as possible) for your personal activities.

As described in Section 1 of the *Depreciation* chapter, special rules apply to automobiles purchased after June 18, 1984 which are not used more than 50% for business purposes in each of the first 6 years of ownership. For such automobiles, a special *Listed Property Depreciation Table* must be used.

Example 6.

You purchased an automobile in March, 1987 for $12,000. You drive the automobile 10,000 miles during each of 1987 – 1992. Of these miles, 30% are for business purposes each year. Since the automobile is used 30% for business purposes, the cost attributable to business use is 30% × $12,000 = $3,600.

Your operating expenses (not including expensing or depreciation) total $1,200 per year. Since your auto is being used 30% for business purposes, the amount of operating expenses attributable to business use each year is 30% × $1,200 = $360.

Actual Cost Method

Since business use does not exceed 50% in each of the first 6 years, the expensing method cannot be used. And depreciation is limited to the amounts in the *Listed Property Depreciation Table* given in the *Depreciation* chapter. Thus, the annual deductions for 1987-1992 are as follows:

	Depreciation		Operating Expenses		Total Deduction
1987:	10% × $3,600	+	$360	=	$ 720
1988:	20% × 3,600	+	360	=	1,080
1989:	20% × 3,600	+	360	=	1,080
1990:	20% × 3,600	+	360	=	1,080
1991:	20% × 3,600	+	360	=	1,080
1992:	10% × 3,600	+	360	=	720
					$5,760

(In addition to the above amounts, parking fees and tolls incurred in business-related travel are deductible.)

To see how this works out on a per mile basis, the calculation is as follows:

Total mileage, 1987-1992:   60,000 miles
Business miles: 30% × 60,000 = 18,000 miles
Total expenses, 1987-1992: $5,760
Per mile deduction: $5,760/18,000 = 32 cents per mile

Standard Mileage Rate

As in the preceding example, the standard mileage rate of 22½ cents per mile can be used instead of the actual cost method. (The standard rate is mandatory if the use of the auto is not required by the employer.)

Taxes and Registration Fees

The annual fee you pay to register your automobile and receive your new license plate or sticker is deductible to the extent the automobile is used for business purposes.

For an automobile used for personal purposes, this annual fee is generally not deductible. However, in some states, part of the fee is based on the value of the automobile and constitutes a form of personal property tax. In such a case, the part of the fee that qualifies as a personal property tax is deductible under *Taxes* on Schedule A. States that qualify include Arizona, California, Colorado, Indiana, Iowa, Maine, Massachusetts, Nevada, New Hampshire, Oklahoma, Washington, and Wyoming.

Allocating Repair Expenses

A 1980 court case shows how to allocate repair expenses when an auto is used both for personal and for deductible purposes. You do not have to establish which repairs are directly attributable to your deductible travel. Instead, just multiply the total of your repair bills for the year by the fraction: deductible mileage/total mileage for the year. [Goodman, TC Memo 1980-122]

Trading In Your Old Automobile

Suppose that you trade in or sell your old automobile when you purchase a new one. If you did not claim a deduction for your old automobile, then your old automobile does not enter into the computation of depreciation for your new automobile. Thus, you use the full price of your new automobile (without subtracting the trade-in value of your old automobile) in calculating your depreciation the same way as if you had no trade-in.

If you sell or trade-in an automobile on which you have claimed depreciation, then you must take this into account in depreciating your new automobile. The following example illustrates how this is done:

Example

You owned an automobile which was used two-thirds for business and one-third for pleasure. It originally cost $7,200, which had been allocated $4,800 to business use and $2,400 to personal use. $2,700 of depreciation (and/or expensing) had been claimed and allowed in prior years. You trade it in on a new one that sells for $12,000, and were given a trade-in allowance of $2,400. The new automobile is also to be used two-thirds for business. The depreciable portion of the basis of the new automobile is computed as follows:

1. Cost of old car allocable to business use, 2/3 of $7,200 ....$4,800
2. Less:
   (a) Trade-in allowance applicable to business
       portion, 2/3 of $2,400............................1,600
   (b) Total depreciation allowed on old car............... 2,700   4,300
3. Unrecognized loss applicable to business portion...................(500)
4. Purchase price of new car.......................................12,000
5. Portion of new car allocable to business use, 2/3 of $12,000.........8,000
6. Plus: Unrecognized loss on trade-in (from line 3) 500
7. Depreciable portion of basis of new car $8,500

If the amount on line 3 were a gain instead of a loss, you would subtract it on line 6 rather than add it.

Chapter 11

State and Local Taxes

The 1986 Tax Reform Act made only one significant change in the deduction for State and local taxes. Namely, the deduction for sales tax and transfer tax has been eliminated, starting with 1987 tax returns. The deduction for other State and local taxes remains the same.

More specifically, you **can deduct** the following taxes on your 1987 tax return, imposed by a State or local government:

Property tax [cf. the *Homeowners* chapter]

Income tax

Personal property tax

You **cannot** deduct:

Sales tax

Beverage tax

Cigarette tax

Admission tax

Gasoline tax

Driver's license fee

Dog license

Fishing or hunting license

Also, you cannot deduct a passport fee unless qualifying as a legitimate business expense. (For example, a passport fee for a business-related trip would be deductible, but not for a pleasure trip.) Automobile registration fees are deductible only to the extent the auto is used for business purposes or the fees are based on the value of the automobile and, therefore, qualify as a personal property tax [cf. the *Automobile Expenses* chapter].

Generally, the deduction for State and local taxes is only available to the taxpayer who incurs the taxes. For example, a child may have a State tax liability on income he receives. Even if the parents pay the tax, they get no deduction on their Federal tax return. Such a payment is considered to be a gift to the child followed by payment of the tax by the child. Thus the child, not the parents, gets the deduction for State taxes paid.

In most cases, the child will not be able to use the deduction for State and local taxes paid. Under the new law, a dependent child is entitled to a 1987 standard deduction of at least $500, even if he has only unearned income. (Formerly, dependent children with only unearned income received no standard deduction at all.) Thus, unless a child has at least $500 in deductions, including the deduction for State and local taxes, he will use the standard deduction instead of itemizing—thus the deduction for State and local taxes will not be usable [cf. Section 5 of Chapter 1].

Payroll Taxes

In some places, contributions to unemployment or disability funds are deducted from employees' paychecks. The IRS will allow contributions to state disability funds in New York, California, New Jersey, and Rhode Island to be deducted as a tax on Schedule A. Tax returns for the three preceding years may be amended to include this deduction. [Cf. Chapter 1 for information on filing an amended return.] Contributions to private disability funds remain nondeductible.

Transfer Taxes

When you buy stocks, bonds, real estate, etc., you may have to pay a transfer tax. Under prior law, such a transfer tax could generally be deducted when paid in the year of the purchase. But now, these taxes are no longer deductible expenses. Instead, they are considered to be part of the purchase price. As such, they reduce any capital gains (or increase losses) in the year of sale and increase annual depreciation write-offs in the case of investment real estate [cf. the *Expensing and Depreciation* chapter].

State and Local Income Taxes

Schedule A includes a deduction for State and local income taxes which you pay. These taxes are deductible in the year in which they are paid by being withheld from your paychecks or by direct payment. For example, amounts withheld during 1986 from your paychecks and credited toward your State income tax due April, 1987 were deductible on your 1986 Federal tax returns. If you made an additional direct payment toward these taxes in 1987, then this amount becomes deductible on your 1987 tax return.

On the other hand, you may have received a State or local tax refund during 1987 because of overwithholding during 1986. In this case, the full amount withheld during 1986 should have been deducted on your 1986 tax return and you report the refund as income on line 11 of your 1987 tax return. (The 1986 refund is still reported as income even if you have it credited against your current tax rather than having a refund check mailed to you.)

An exception to this has been described in an IRS ruling. You do **not** have to report a 1987 tax refund as income to the extent it was due to overwithholding during 1986 from which you derived no Federal tax benefit.

For example, suppose you claimed the standard deduction on your 1986 tax return. This means that you did not get any Federal tax benefit from the **deduction** for State taxes withheld from your paychecks. In such a case, you would not have to report a 1987 tax refund as income. This is illustrated in Example 2 below.

Example 1.

In 1986, $2,000 in State income tax was withheld from your paychecks which you deducted on your 1986 Federal tax return along with $4,000 in other deductions. When you filled out your 1986 State tax return, you computed $1,500 as the amount of State income tax for the year. Since $500 too much was withheld during 1986, the State sent you a refund check for that amount in 1987. Since you deducted the $2,000 withheld on your 1986 Federal tax return but received $500 of this amount back, you're really entitled only to a net $1,500 deduction. To compensate for the extra benefit you obtained by deducting $2,000 instead of the $1,500, you report the $500 refund as income on your 1987 Federal tax return.

In the above example, the $500 State tax refund received in 1987 was due to overwithholding in 1986. Because the overwithholding produced an extra tax benefit on your 1986 tax return—a $2,000 deduction instead of a $1,500 deduction—the $500 refund had to be included as income on your 1987 return to offset the extra benefit.

However, if a State tax refund is the result of overwithholding from which no extra benefit was obtained, then the refund check does not have to be included in income. The following example illustrates this situation.

Example 2.

In 1986, $1,000 in State tax was withheld from Smith's paychecks. His other deductions amounted to $800. Since $1,000 + $800 = $1,800 was less than the standard deduction, Smith did not itemize his deductions on his Federal tax return but used the standard deduction instead. Smith received no Federal tax benefit from the $1,000 withheld in State taxes because he didn't itemize his deductions.

Now suppose Smith received a State tax refund in 1987. This refund resulted from the fact that the $1,000 withheld in 1986 was too much. But, because he claimed the standard deduction, this overwithholding produced no Federal tax benefit on his 1986 return. Therefore, he does not have to include the refund in income on his 1987 Federal tax return.

In the above example, Smith received no Federal tax benefit from the State tax overwithheld from his paychecks because he used the standard deduction. Therefore, the State tax refund which resulted from this overwithholding did not have to be reported as income in the following year.

However, sometimes an individual receives a **partial** benefit from State tax overwithholding. This can occur only when an individual's other deductions are less than the standard deduction, but when the State tax is added in, the total exceeds the standard deduction. In this situation, you report as income on line 11 of your 1987 tax return that portion of the overwithholding during 1986 (which you received in 1987 as a refund of State tax) from which you derived a tax benefit.

In practice, you compute this amount by filling out the worksheet in the instructions to Form 1040. However, the following illustrates the basis behind this computation.

Example 3.
C and D filed joint Federal income tax returns for 1986 and 1987. For 1986, their State income tax deduction (equal to the amounts withheld from their 1986 paychecks) was $1,000 and their other itemized deductions were $2,700. On their 1986 State tax return, they computed their State tax to be $600. This meant that $400 of State tax had been overwithheld during 1986 resulting in a $400 State tax refund received in 1987. However, only a portion of this $400 overwithholding had actually produced a tax benefit on their 1986 Federal tax return. This portion is computed as follows:

(1) Total deductions actually claimed on 1986 Federal tax return: $2,700 + $1,000 = **$3,700**

(2) Total deductions that would have been claimed on 1986 Federal tax return had there been no State tax overwithholding. [The greater of (i) $2,700 + $600 = $3,300 or (ii) the Standard deduction for 1986, $3,540]: **$3,540**

(3) Tax benefit on 1986 Federal tax return resulting from State tax overwithholding, (1) − (2): **$3,700 − $3,540 = $160**

The amount computed in (3) above, $160, is the portion of the $400 refund which yielded a tax benefit the preceding year. Thus $160 is reported on line 11 of their 1987 Federal tax return.

The above examples concern refunds of State or local income taxes. However, the same principle would apply to refunds of property taxes. Thus, a 1988 refund of property taxes overpaid in 1987 would be reportable as income only to the extent it pushes deductions over the standard deduction as illustrated in the above examples. IRS instructions have been misleading on this matter.

Tax Refunds Reported on Form 1099-G

If you received a State or local income tax refund during 1987, you may receive a statement of this amount on Form 1099-G which is mailed to you by the payer of the refund. The IRS will also receive a copy of the Form 1099-G.

Don't make the mistake of automatically including the amount reported on Form 1099-G on your tax return. If this amount is exempt from tax according to the discussion above, then you do not report any of this amount on your return. If partially exempt, you only report the amount that is taxable on line 11 of Form 1040. It is allright if this amount does not agree with the amount reported on Form 1099-G.

However, it is advisable to attach a statement to your tax return explaining any discrepancy. This will protect against being questioned on this issue should the IRS matching program kick out your tax return because of the discrepancy.

Some States allow you to contribute, by means of a check-off on your State income tax return, to one or more special funds for certain public purposes. Examples include funds for veterans' benefits, food and housing aid to the poor, wildlife conservation, etc. These check-offs might reduce the amount of the State tax refund you receive. In such a case, the amount reported on Form 1099-G will probably exceed your actual refund—it will report the refund you would have received in the absence of any check-offs. You would then use the higher amount reported on Form 1099-G as the basis for reporting your tax refund on line 11. You would then deduct the amounts contributed via check-offs as a charitable contribution on your Federal tax return.

1987 Taxes Paid in 1988

Ordinarily, deductible items belong on the tax return only for the year payment is actually made. However, suppose you pay 1987 State or local taxes in early 1988. According to a recent court case, you might actually be entitled to deduct such a payment on your 1987 tax return.

In this case, an individual made a $1,000 estimated State tax payment in January. He could have deducted this $1,000 in the year it was paid. However, this $1,000 payment was for State taxes estimated to be owed for the preceding year. Therefore, he wanted to be able to claim the $1,000 payment on the Federal tax return for this preceding year.

The Court ruled that this was permissible. In essence, it allowed him to use the *accrual system* of accounting for non-business income and deductions. Under the *accrual system,* income and deductions are credited to the year in which they are produced, even if actual payment is made in a later year. Since the $1,000 payment was for a tax liability "accrued" in the preceding year, it could be deducted in that year instead of in the next year when the payment was actually made. [Flagg, 53 AFTR 2d 84-1321]

The above court case concerned the payment of State income taxes. But the same reasoning would apply to other types of taxes such as property taxes. For example, a payment made in early 1988 for property taxes incurred in 1987 could presumably be deducted on your 1987 tax return.

Since the basic tax rates will generally be lower in 1988 than in 1987 [cf. Chapter 0], the above shifting technique could prove particularly useful because a deduction will have more tax-lowering effect in 1987 than in 1988.

Chapter 12

Moving Expenses

If you moved to a new residence because you went to work for a new employer or transferred to a new place of employment, then you may deduct your moving costs, provided you meet the following two requirements:

1. The distance between your new principal place of work and your old residence must be at least 35 miles farther than the distance between your old place of work and your old residence. (The distance between two points is measured by the shortest of the more commonly traveled routes between the two points.) If you went to work for the first time or went back to full-time work after a substantial period of part-time work or unemployment, then your new principal place of work must be at least 35 miles from your old residence.

2. You must work full-time for at least 39 weeks during the first 12 months following your arrival in the general location of your new place of employment. (Self-employed persons must also work full-time for at least 78 weeks during the first 24 months after arrival in the new job location.)

The 39 weeks of employment need not be consecutive, nor do they have to be for the same employer. It is necessary only that you be employed on a full-time basis within the same general commuting area. Any week during which you work on a full-time basis counts in satisfying the 39-week test. The requirement that your work be full-time is judged by the customary practices in your job. For example, a teacher with a full schedule is working full-time even if the school day is 5 hours or less.

If the work is seasonal, then off-season weeks count as weeks of employment as long as your work agreement covers an off-season period of less than 6 months. For example, teachers are not excluded from a moving expense deduction merely because their academic year is less than 39 weeks. Also, you will be considered as working during any week that you are out through no fault of your own. This refers to a temporary absence from work because of illness, strike, shutout, layoff, natural disaster, etc.

If you paid the moving expense in 1987 but have not met the 39-week test by the time your 1987 return is due, you should take a 1987 deduction for the moving expense if it appears that you will later meet the 39-week test. However, if you later fail the test, you must report an amount equal to the 1987 moving expense deduction as 1988 taxable income. If you leave the deduction off your 1987 return and later meet the 39-week test during 1988, you will have to amend your 1987 return to get your refund.

A recent court case emphasizes the fact that you must deduct the moving expenses in the year the move takes place. A nurse, who had not yet worked the required number of weeks at her new job when filing time came along, waited until a later year, after she had worked the required amount of time, to claim the moving expense deduction. But the Court overruled her deduction. It said she should have claimed the deduction in the year of the move. The only thing she could do now is amend her original return. [Meadows, 66 TC 51]

If you are married and file a joint return and if both you and your spouse are employees, then either of you may satisfy the full-time work requirement. However, you may not add the weeks your spouse works to those you work to satisfy the 39-week requirement.

Moving expenses are deductible if paid in connection with the commencement of work at a new principal place of work. It is not necessary that you have a contract or commitment of employment prior to moving to the new location—the moving expense deduction is allowable if employment actually does occur.

Moving expenses are deductible only if reasonable under the circumstances of the particular move. Travel should be by the shortest and most direct route available from your former residence to your new residence by the conventional mode of transportation actually used and in the shortest period of time required to make the move. Additional expenses for circuitous scenic routes or sidetrip stopovers are not deductible.

Which Moving Expenses Can You Deduct?

If you qualify to deduct moving expenses as described above, you may deduct reasonable amounts for the items listed below.

Note that the cost of meals included in the items below is subject to the same 80%-Rule that applies to travel-related meals as discussed in Section 1 of the *Travel* chapter. That is, only 80% of the cost of meals can be claimed as a moving expense. However, this 80%-Rule does not apply to meals for which a reimbursement is received from one's employer. The basic treatment of reimbursed meal expenses is similar to that discussed in Section 1 of the *Miscellaneous Deductions* chapter.

1. **Travel expenses** including meals and lodging for yourself and your family while en route from your old residence to your new residence. This deduction is allowable for only one trip made by you and members of your household; however, it is not necessary that you and all members of your household travel together or at the same time. Members of your household include your spouse and your dependents for tax purposes; economically independent relatives or others are not included.

2. The cost of **moving household goods** including automobiles, personal effects, and household pets of both you and members of your family. This includes the cost of transportation from your old to your new residence, plus packing, crating, insurance, and 30 days worth of storage, as well as connecting and disconnecting utilities (but not a telephone). It does not include the cost of automobile registration, driver's license, carpet installation, or appliance installation.

Transportation of goods to your new residence from some place other than your old residence is deductible to the extent that it does not exceed the cost of transportation from your old residence. But you cannot deduct the cost of transporting goods purchased en route from your old to your new residence.

3. Provided you have already obtained employment at the new location, your travel costs (including meals and lodging) of **premove house-hunting trips** from your former residence to the area of your new employment and back.

4. The cost of **temporary quarters** (including meals and lodging) at the new location of work during any period of 30 consecutive days after obtaining work.

5. The **cost of selling your residence** or settling your lease at the old location and purchasing a residence or acquiring a lease at the new location. This includes:

- Real estate commissions
- Attorney's fees
- Title and escrow fees
- Points (to the extent not deducted elsewhere as interest)
- State transfer taxes
- Advertising expenses of selling your old residence
- Payments for release of a lease
- Expenses of obtaining a sublessee
- Excess of rent paid under a lease over that received under a sublease.

The above expenses may not then also be used in reducing any capital gains tax you might pay on the sale of either your old or new residence.

If you use your automobile to transport yourself, your family, or your goods, then you may take either of these options:

1. Deduct your actual expenses such as gasoline, oil, repairs, etc. but not depreciation. (You must keep a record of each expense in this case.)

or

2. Deduct 9 cents per mile.

Limitations

A. The move should be within 1 year from the time you first report to your new job. If the move does not take place within that time, the expenses will not be deductible unless there are extenuating circumstances the IRS finds acceptable (e.g., a child needs to finish school at the old location).

B. The deduction for the combined expenses of house-hunting trips, temporary quarters, and selling your residence is limited to $3,000 overall. No more than $1,500 of this may be used for house-hunting trips and temporary quarters.

The above dollar limitations apply to the taxable unit, regardless of whether it is a single individual or a family. Thus, husband and wife filing separate returns would each be limited to half the above amounts. No dollar limitations are placed on en route travel expenses and moving of household goods.

Exceptions

1. If, after you move to your new residence, you are farther from your new job than if you had stayed in your old residence, then your moving expense deduction may be disallowed unless you can give a suitable justification for your move, such as lower commuting time or costs.

2. The 39-week full-time employment requirement is waived if you are involuntarily discharged (other than for willful misconduct), transferred at the request of your employer, or become disabled. However, you must show that you would have satisfied the 39-week test except for being discharged, transferred, or disabled.

3. The 39-week employment requirement need not be met to the extent that you receive reimbursement by your employer for an item of moving expense. In this case, you claim a moving expense deduction to offset your employer's reimbursement included in your gross income.

Where Do You Report Moving Expenses?

Moving expenses are now claimed as an itemized deduction on line 19 of Schedule A. (Under prior law, they were an *adjustment to income* rather than an *itemized deduction*.) Thus, moving expenses cannot be claimed on a 1987 tax return if an individual uses the standard deduction.

Moving expenses are placed in a separate category on Schedule A. The 2% of Adjusted Gross Income floor that applies to miscellaneous deductions [cf. the *Miscellaneous Deductions* chapter] does *not* apply to moving expenses.

Form 3903 is used to compute the moving expense deduction to which you are entitled. It will lead you through the 80%-Rule that applies to meal expenses, as well as the treatment of reimbursements received from your employer. The total moving expense deduction is then entered on line 19 of Schedule A.

Foreign Moves

The limits are higher for moves to a foreign location. First, the cost of temporary quarters qualifies for deduction for a 90-day period after obtaining work instead of just 30 days. Second, the $3,000 and $1,500 limitations under item B given earlier are raised to $6,000 and $4,500, respectively. Finally, costs associated with the storage of furniture and other effects are eligible to be deducted.

Moving to a Temporary Job

If you move to obtain a temporary post away from home, you cannot deduct both moving costs and the travel costs described in the *Travel* chapter.

Example

A professor at a midwestern university accepted a one-year temporary appointment with a government agency in Washington, D.C. He returned to his teaching post at the end of the year. There was no quarrel with his deduction for the cost of his meals and lodging during the stay in Washington, D.C. These were legitimate deductions while at a temporary position away from home as described in the *Travel* chapter. Also, he could deduct the cost of his transportation to and from his temporary post for the same reason.

But he was not allowed to deduct, as a moving expense, the cost of transporting his family and his household goods to and from Washington. It was inconsistent with the IRS regulations to allow a moving expense deduction to a place where the taxpayer has been allowed deductions for travel, meals, and lodging while at a temporary post away from home. [Goldman, 34 AFTR 2nd 74-5046]

Chapter 13

Divorce and Separation

Filing Status

Your marital status on December 31 determines the type of tax return you can file for the year. If, on December 31, you are married and not legally separated under a decree of divorce or separate maintenance, then you may file a joint return. If you are divorced or legally separated, then you may not file a joint return. Instead, you file as a single person. In this case, you may use the lower head-of-household rate if you meet the usual requirements for using this special rate.

A separated couple must have a legal separation under a court decree in order to file as single persons. An informal separation, even under a written agreement, does not count with the following exception:

Exception

Even if you are not divorced or legally separated, you may file as a single person (including as a head-of-household) if you meet **all** of the following tests:

(1) You do not file a joint return,

(2) You paid more than half the cost to keep up your home for the year,

(3) Your spouse did not live in your home at any time during the last 6 months of the year,

and

(4) For over six months of the year, your home was the principal residence of your child or stepchild whom you are entitled to claim as a dependent (or would be entitled except that you relinquished the exemption to your spouse on Form 8332 as described later in this chapter).

Note that the above tests apply to your tax return only. Your spouse must also meet the above tests in order to file as a single person. Otherwise, he or she must file using the high rates for married individuals filing separately. Of course, you both could file a joint return together if that is preferable, provided you are not divorced or legally separated on December 31.

A couple might be better off taxwise if a joint return is used, especially if only one of them has a significant amount of income. Or, they might be better off filing as single persons. In accord with the above tax rules, this consideration may play a role in deciding whether to turn a separation agreement into a legal separation.

Alimony

When a married couple is separated or divorced, one of them may make "alimony" payments to the other. If these payments are made on an informal basis, then there is no tax consequence. The payer does not claim the payments as a tax deduction nor does the recipient treat the payments as taxable income. However, if all of the following conditions are met, then the alimony payments are deducted by the payer and reported as income to the recipient. (This often reduces the total tax bill since the payer is usually in a higher tax bracket than the recipient.)

Conditions Under Which Alimony Is Deducted by Payer and Reported as Income by Recipient

Pre-1985 Rules

Divorce or separation agreements executed prior to 1985 must satisfy the following rules in order for alimony to be deductible:

(1) Payments are required by an official agreement. This agreement could be part of a divorce, legal separation, or other court decree, or it could simply be a written agreement between the two parties without any court proceedings.

(2) The couple lives separately.

(3) The payments are periodic. They could be fixed monthly amounts, a percentage of annual income, etc. There are several additional requirements that need to be checked out to make sure this periodic condition is satisfied.

and

(4) The payments are for the general support of the recipient. Amounts designated specifically for child support do not qualify. Neither do payments to settle loans or other obligations.

Post-1984 Rules

Divorce or separation agreements executed after 1984 must satisfy the following rules in order for alimony to be deductible:

(1) Alimony payments must be required by an official agreement. This agreement could be part of a divorce, legal separation, or other court decree. Or, it could simply be a written agreement between the two parties without any court proceedings.

(2) Alimony payments must be made in cash, check, or money order and there must be no liability to make payments after the death of the recipient spouse. Payments made to a third party on behalf of the spouse (e.g. tuition, medical expenses, etc.) can count as alimony if they are made under the terms of the divorce or separation instrument. However, an individual cannot count payments he makes to maintain property he owns (e.g. mortgage payments, taxes, insurance) even if such payments are made pursuant to the terms of the divorce or separation instrument.

(3) Alimony payments cannot be scheduled to decrease upon a child marrying, leaving school, moving out of the house, getting a job, or similar contingency. For example, if the agreement provides for payments of $800 per month, de-

creasing to $600 after a child marries, only $600 per month will be considered alimony. The remaining $200 per month will be considered non-deductible child support. Similarly, payments cannot be scheduled to decrease upon a child reaching age 18, 21, or local age of majority (give or take 6 months).

(4) Alimony payments for the first 3 years must not be excessively *front-loaded*. The exact requirement is rather complicated to state. However, in all cases, if alimony payments do not decrease by more than $10,000 from either of the first 2 years to the next, this requirement will be satisfied. (This result of the 1986 Tax Act is more liberal than under previous law.) Also, for agreements executed in 1985 or 1986 only, alimony payments must generally continue for at least 6 years unless all payments are less than $10,000. However, this 6-year requirement ceases to apply upon the death of either spouse or the remarriage of the recipient spouse.

This rule (4) applies to payments made under a divorce decree or separation decree or agreement. It does not apply to payments made under only a temporary support decree. The purpose of this rule is to discourage property settlements which typically have a large initial payment from being treated as alimony.

(5) Once a divorce or separation decree is entered, the spouses cannot live in the same dwelling. Payments made while living in the same dwelling after a decree is entered do not qualify as alimony, except for a 1-month grace period allowed for the spouses to separate. This restriction does not apply to payments made under a written separation agreement, rather than a divorce or separate maintenance decree.

If payments satisfy the above rules, they can be deducted by the payer and become taxable income to the recipient. However, the spouses may designate that payments otherwise qualifying as alimony shall be nondeductible by the payer and nontaxable to the recipient by so providing in a divorce or separation instrument. An existing instrument can be legally amended to make this provision. The recipient should attach a copy of such a designation to the tax return for each year to which the designation applies.

Alimony Can Be Claimed Even If You Use the Standard Deduction

Alimony payments are claimed as an *adjustment to income* on line 28, Form 1040, rather than as an itemized deduction. This means that you can deduct alimony payments whether you claim the standard deduction or itemize your deductions.

Reporting Requirements

There is a special reporting requirement that applies. If you deduct alimony payments on your 1987 tax return, you are required to list the recipient's social security number on your return. The IRS can use this to crosscheck that the recipient reports these amounts as taxable income. This reporting requirement applies to all alimony payments, even if made under divorce or separation agreements executed before 1985.

IRA Deduction Based on Alimony Payments

Contributions to an IRA for 1987 can be based on alimony income. Individuals may be able to contribute up to $2,000 of alimony income to an IRA and deduct this amount on their 1987 tax returns [cf. Section 2 of the *Tax-Sheltered Plans* chapter].

Dependency Exemptions

When separate returns are filed, it must be determined which parent is entitled to claim a child as a dependent. The current rule is that the parent (called the *custodial spouse*) having custody of a child for the greater portion of the year is entitled to the dependency exemption. (This assumes that the parents together would have been entitled to the dependency exemption had they been married and filing a joint return.) It makes no difference that the other parent may have furnished most or all of the funds for support of the child.

However, the custodial spouse may release the right to a dependency exemption, in which case the non-custodial spouse can claim the exemption. This release is made by the custodial spouse on Form 8332 which the non-custodial spouse attaches to his return. The exemption may be released for a single year, for a number of specified years (for example, alternate years), or permanently. A copy of the release form must be attached to the tax return of the non-custodial spouse each year he claims the exemption.

Exception: The non-custodial spouse is entitled to the dependency exemption if so specified under a decree or written agreement executed before 1985. In such a case, no release form is needed. This exception only applies if the non-custodial spouse furnishes at least $600 towards the support of the child.

According to a 1986 IRS ruling, the pre-1985 agreement must **explicitly** assign the dependency exemption to the non-custodial spouse. In this ruling, a man was ordered to pay $300 per month child support in a 1973 divorce agreement. Since the divorce, he had been providing more than half the support of his 3 children and been claiming dependency exemptions for them. However, even though he had been entitled to the dependency exemptions under the law existing at the time, the divorce agreement did not explicitly specify that he was entitled to the dependency exemptions. Thus, under the new law starting with 1985, since the children lived with their mother, she was now entitled to the dependency exemptions. This could not even be changed by amending the language of the old divorce agreement. The only way he could now claim the exemptions would be for her to release her claim on Form 8332 which he would attach to his tax return each year he claimed the exemptions. [IRS Private Letter Ruling 8609034]

Altering Old Agreements

You may have a divorce or separation agreement with an ex-spouse that results in a total tax bill which is higher than necessary. This is especially true because of recent changes in the law governing divorce and alimony. If so, you should seek legal advice to straighten matters out. In many cases, you can amend a pre-1985 divorce or separation agreement so that it comes under the new rules, should that be advantageous. Sometimes, only a wording change will suffice, with no change in the underlying specifics of the agreement.

Effect of 1986 Tax Act on Divorce & Separation Agreements

Except for a few changes in the rules defining alimony, the main impact of the 1986 Tax Act on divorce and separation agreements comes from the lowering of the basic tax rates and the increase in the basic dependency exemption amount.

To illustrate, suppose a man is paying $8,000 a year in alimony to an ex-wife. The man gets an $8,000 deduction while his ex-wife has an extra $8,000 taxable income. Let's say the 1986 Tax Act lowers the tax bracket of each by 15 percentage points. This reduces the value of the man's $8,000 deduction by 15% × $8,000 = $1,200. Meanwhile, the $8,000 payment becomes more valuable to the ex-wife because she pays 15% × $8,000 = $1,200 less tax. In effect, the new law has raised the alimony settlement by an after-tax $1,200.

Many individuals may seek to have their alimony payments reduced because of the above effect. However, success will usually depend upon offering the ex-spouse sufficient incentive to make such a change.

The rise of the personal exemption amount from $1,080 to $1,900 and eventually to $2,000 [cf. Chapter O], also has an impact on divorce and separation settlements. In particular, an assignment of a child's dependency to the non-custodial spouse now becomes significantly more valuable.

One other notable change is the rise in the floor on medical expenses from 5% of adjusted gross income to 7.5% [cf. the *Medical Expenses* chapter]. This may provide an incentive for the lower-earning spouse to pay all medical expenses directly from his own checking account. As discussed below, this can lower the amount of taxes paid in some cases.

Medical Expenses

Either spouse may claim medical expenses which he actually pays for his child. It makes no difference that the other spouse may be claiming the dependency exemption. This assumes that the child receives over half of his total support from his parents.

Because of the 7.5% of income floor on deductible medical expenses [cf. the *Medical Expenses* chapter], divorced spouses should take care who actually pays the medical bills for a child. For example, suppose the ex-wife earned $20,000 and the ex-husband $50,000. For simplicity, let's say their child ran up a $3,000 bill at the orthodontist and that there are no other medical expenses involved. If the ex-husband paid the bill directly, there is no deduction because his medical expenses floor, 7.5% × $50,000 = $3,750, exceeds the $3,000 expense. But the ex-wife's medical expense floor is 7.5% × $20,000 = $1,500. If he gave his ex-wife $3,000 and let her pay the bill, she gets a deduction of $3,000 - $1,500 = $1,500 while he has lost nothing in the transaction.

Property Transfer

A house or other property such as stocks or bonds may be transferred from one spouse to another as part of a divorce settlement. At one time, the IRS could treat such a transfer as a sale subject to capital gains tax. For example, a husband who transferred a house worth $85,000, but which he purchased for $45,000, to a spouse was liable for capital gains tax on the $40,000 increase in value.

But now, divorce-related property settlements no longer trigger a capital gains tax at the time of transfer. However, the spouse who receives the property must treat it as acquired at the original purchase price. When sold, the difference between the sale price and original purchase price will be subject to capital gains tax. In the example in the preceding paragraph, if the wife were to sell the house for $95,000 in a later year, she would have a capital gain of $50,000. This $50,000 profit would be subject to capital gains tax, unless the usual exemption for purchasing a new house of greater value or the exemption for those over 55 applies [cf. the *Homeowner's* chapter].

Legal Fees

The legal fees involved in obtaining a divorce are not generally deductible. However, the portion of such fees which covered tax advice to the individual can be deducted. Also, a spouse may deduct legal costs associated with obtaining or collecting taxable alimony. In any divorce or separation proceeding, your lawyer should provide an itemization which indicates any portion of his fee that is deductible.

Chapter 14

Investing Your Money

SECTION 1:
CAPITAL GAINS TAX

Most of the income you receive, whether salary from your job, stock dividends, interest on a savings account or bond, rent from property you own, etc. is considered **ordinary income**. As such, it is taxable according to the usual tax table rate that applies to your income bracket.

But one type of income falls into a different category. If you buy an item at one price and sell it at a higher price, then the resulting profit is not considered ordinary income but falls into a special category called a **capital gain**. As such, it is governed by special tax rules described below. The item could be a bond, stock, real estate, or any other type of property or security.

The same distinction exists with respect to losses. If you lose money in a business venture, or rental property because expenses exceed income, etc., then you have an **ordinary loss**. This ordinary loss is just subtracted from your ordinary income when you compute your tax. But if you sustain a loss because you sell an investment item at a lower price than the one at which you purchased it, then you have a **capital loss**. This capital loss cannot always just be subtracted from your income, but is treated according to the special rules below.

The 1986 Tax Reform Act changed the rules that apply to capital gains and losses. As described below, capital gains on items owned more than 6 months are subject to a maximum tax rate of 28% on 1987 tax returns. (The tax brackets for ordinary income go up to 38.5% on 1987 tax returns.) On 1988 tax returns, capital gains will be treated the same as ordinary income, subject to effective tax rates of as much as 33%, a 67% rise from the maximum 20% rate in 1986 [cf. Chapter 0].

If you are undecided whether or not to sell an asset which will produce a long-term capital gain, you may be better off waiting. If the maximum tax brackets are raised in a future tax bill (a likely possibility), then the capital gains rate may well be lowered again as part of a compromise package. It is not considered as likely that the rate on capital gains will rise in the near future. Congress specifically provided that if the basic tax rates are changed in a future tax bill, the rate on long-term capital gains would not rise, but instead remain capped at the 28% or 33% rate.

Short vs. Long-Term

If you purchased an item and held it for more than 6 months, then you are considered to have owned it for a **long term**. Less than or equal to 6 months is **short term**. The capital gain or loss resulting from a sale in 1987 is then either a long-term or short-term gain or loss accordingly.

Capital Gains and Losses

Your first step is to subtract the total of your long-term losses from the total of your long-term gains for 1987. If you have more gains than losses, the result is your **net long-term gain**. On the other hand, if you have more losses than gains, the difference is your **net long-term loss** for the year.

You perform a similar operation on your short-term gains and losses. If you have more short-term gains than losses, then the difference between the two is your **net short-term gain**. If the losses exceed your gains then the difference is your **net short-term loss**.

To understand how capital gains are taxed, let us first suppose you have only one category of net gains or losses. That is, you do not have both a net long-term gain or loss and a net short-term gain or loss for 1987. For example, if you have a net short-term loss, then we are assuming you have no net long-term result, i.e., you have neither a net long-term gain nor a net long-term loss for 1987.

Special rules apply to capital gains produced by the sale of your personal residence. These are discussed in the *Homeowners* chapter.

Long-Term Gain

This is the one category that offers some tax break on 1987 tax returns. Long-term capital gains are taxed at a rate no higher than 28%, even if ordinary income falls into a higher tax bracket. (The maximum tax bracket for ordinary income on 1987 tax returns is 38.5%.)

There is a special part IV on the 1987 Schedule D which is used when taxable income is high enough that using the 28% rate for capital gains would be to your advantage. This will occur when taxable income exceeds $27,000 for singles; $45,000 for marrieds filing a joint return; $22,500 for marrieds filing separately; or $38,000 for heads of household.

Short-Term Gain

A net short-term capital gain is treated just like ordinary income. That is, you simply add it to your other income and pay tax at the usual rate. The reason for this difference between the tax treatment of short and long-term gains is that the government was interested in encouraging long-range investment, rather than short-term speculation.

Both Long and Short-Term Gains

If you have both types of net gains for 1987, you treat each separately as described above. The net short-term gain is taxed as though it were ordinary income and the net long-term gain is similarly treated, except that a maximum 28% tax rate applies. Schedule D will lead you through the appropriate computations.

Capital Losses

If you have a net capital loss (long-term and/or short-term), you deduct it from your ordinary income up to a maximum of $3,000. If your total net loss for 1987 exceeds $3,000, then you deduct $3,000 from your ordinary income on your 1987 tax return and carry over the excess into the future.

For example, if you have net capital losses of $7,000, then you deduct $3,000 on your 1987 tax return and carry over $7,000 − $3,000 = $4,000 to be deducted on future tax returns. It makes no difference if the net loss is long-term, short-term, or both. Unlike the situation in prior years, net losses of any type are now deducted on a dollar for dollar basis from ordinary income until the maximum $3,000 ceiling is reached.

Net Long-Term Gain and Net Short-Term Loss

If you have a net long-term gain combined with a net short-term loss, you subtract the smaller number from the larger. If the gain is bigger than the loss, then you treat the difference as a long-term gain as described above. If the loss is bigger than the gain, the difference is treated as a net short-term loss.

Net Short-Term Gain and Net Long-Term Loss

This case is just like the previous. You subtract the smaller number from the larger and are left with either a short-term gain or a long-term loss for the year.

> *Example*
>
> You have a net short-term gain of $3,000 and a net long-term loss of $1,000. You subtract $1,000 from $3,000 and are left with a net short-term gain of $2,000 for the year which is taxed at your ordinary income rate.

Unrealized Capital Gains and Losses

The above rules only come into force when you actually sell the item in question. Until you sell, you pay no tax on your capital gains and get no deduction for your losses.

> *Example*
>
> You buy 100 shares of common stock at $10 per share and the price doubles to $20 per share. You have a profit of $1,000, but it is an unrealized gain (sometimes called a "paper profit") and generates no tax liability. If you were to sell, then you would realize a $1,000 gain and would have to pay tax on the gain.

Where Are Capital Gains and Losses Reported on Your Tax Return?

You use Schedule D to report your capital gains and losses. This Schedule will lead you through the appropriate computations.

Reconciliation with Broker's Statements

If you sold stocks, bonds, etc. during the year, you will receive a Form 1099-B at the end of the year from your broker, mutual fund, etc. reporting the proceeds from the sales. The total of all amounts reported on Forms 1099-B you receive, other than for real estate transactions, is reported on Line 1, Schedule D. You must attach a statement to your tax return explaining any discrepancy between the amount reported on Line 1 and the total sales prices shown in the sections on Schedule D where you compute your capital gains and losses on stocks, bonds, etc.

The Form 1099-B which you receive from your stock broker reporting 1987 transactions will show the amount being reported to the IRS as the *total proceeds* from your sales of securities. It will also indicate whether these proceeds are the *gross proceeds* or the *gross proceeds less commissions* you paid on the sales.

If your broker reported the *gross proceeds* to the IRS, you list the gross amounts received on each sale before commissions are subtracted in Column d, *Sales price*, on Schedule D. You then add the commissions to the amount reported in Column e, *Cost or other basis*. Thus, the amount reported in Column e will include your purchase price plus the commissions paid both on the purchase and the sale of the security. In this way, when the amount in Column e is subtracted from the amount in Column d, your true monetary gain or loss will be calculated, including the effect of the commissions you have paid.

If your broker reported the *gross proceeds less commissions* to the IRS, then these are the amounts you report in Column d. The amount in Column e will then be your purchase price plus the commissions you paid on the purchase, but not including the commissions you paid on the sale which were already taken into account in the figure reported in Column d.

Wash Sales

Especially because of the 1987 stock market crash, many individuals currently own stocks or other securities which are selling at a lower price than when purchased. Tax considerations might call for a sale of such securities in order to create a currently deductible tax loss. However, if it is desired to still own the securities while producing a tax loss, you can't just sell securities at a loss and then buy them right back. Any purchase of the same securities within 30 days before or 30 days after selling them negates any losses. To get around this restriction, you can purchase similar but not identical securities to the ones sold. Or, in the case of bonds, you can achieve the same result by making a swap through a brokerage house. They can also advise you of more exotic methods of achieving the same result such as using appropriate short sales or options transactions.

Brokerage Fees

You cannot deduct brokerage commissions or other charges related to the purchase or sale of securities or other assets. Instead, as discussed above, these fees serve to lower the capital gain or increase the capital loss computed on Schedule D when you make a sale.

Custodian or management fees you pay on investments are deductible as a *miscellaneous deduction* on your 1987 tax return. For example, a fee charged by a bank for management of a money-market account would be deductible (unless it represented a normal check-processing fee). For management fees on mutual funds, see Section 4 for the new rules that apply.

Special Treatment for Inherited Property

Inherited property such as real estate, stocks, bonds, etc. is given a *fresh start* basis when inherited. That is, for purposes of future capital gains tax computations, it is treated as though it were purchased at its market value at the time of inheritance.

Thus, when you sell property which was acquired by inheritance, tax is due only on the appreciation in value since the time it was inherited. No tax is ever paid on the increase in value that took place when the property belonged to the previous owner.

Shifting Profits to Different Years

When you sell property on which you have a profit, you may wish to shift some or all of this profit to later years. This can be done by making an *installment sale*. That is, you agree to receive part or all of the money due you in one or more future years. Then, you would report the proportionate profit in the years you receive the various payments from the buyer. There are no restrictions on the number of payments or on the size of the initial payment.

The installment sale reporting procedure does not apply to the sales of stocks or securities that are traded in an established marketplace. Also, there are restrictions that apply to the sale of real estate for more than $150,000 when the seller owes any business-related debts. These restrictions do not generally apply to the sale of a personal home even if for more than $150,000.

If you receive delayed payments, you must charge interest. You can't simply regard all money received as part of the selling price and thereby convert what ought to be taxed as interest into capital gains taxed at a lower rate. Check with the IRS to determine the minimum acceptable interest rate to charge at the time of sale.

The law prevents tax reduction by using an installment sale to a very close relative as an intermediate step. For example, suppose you sell property on which you have a profit to your father with payments to be made in future years and he immediately resells it for the same price. You would have to include the entire profit on your tax return in the year of sale, not as you received the payments from your father.

You do not have to use the installment reporting procedure described above. If you wish, you may elect to report the entire profit in the year the sale is consummated, even if payments are to be made in future years. In such a case, you should check the appropriate box in Part VI of Schedule D.

SECTION 2:
PASSIVE LOSS RULES

In the past, many high-earning individuals sought *tax-shelter* investments that were designed to produce a current loss rather than a profit. This loss could then be used on the individual's tax return to cancel out earnings which otherwise would be taxed at a high-bracket rate of as much as 50%. Ideally, a tax-shelter investment would mostly generate "paper losses" produced by the tax law rather than an actual cash loss.

For example, the most common of these tax shelters has been investments in rental real estate. The paper losses in real estate come from the annual depreciation allowances permitted under the law. (Depreciation can be claimed as a deduction even if the property is increasing in value.)

The 1986 Tax Reform Act cracks down on tax-shelter investments by restricting losses produced by *passive activities*. The basic idea is that losses produced by a *passive activity* cannot be used to offset either *earned income* or *portfolio income* from stocks, savings accounts, etc. These losses can only be used to offset income from other passive activities. As enacted by Congress, the new rules apply not just to passive activities which produce a paper loss, but also to activities which produce cash losses as well.

What is a Passive Activity?

A *passive activity* is a limited partnership or other business activity in which neither you nor your spouse participate on a regular, continuous, and substantial basis. However, any rental activity is automatically considered to be a passive activity no matter what the level of personal participation.

In contrast to *business* activities, *investing* in stocks, bonds, savings accounts, etc. is not considered to be a *passive activity*. Also, there is a special exception for oil and gas working interests in which there is no limit on the taxpayer's liability.

Limit on Passive Losses

Losses produced by a passive activity cannot be used to offset income from active sources such as a business run by the taxpayer. And it cannot be used to offset *portfolio income* such as dividends or interest. Rather, losses from passive activities can only be used to offset income from the same or other passive activities.

The way this restriction on passive losses works is as follows. You first total up the profits and losses from all your passive activities. This includes any capital gains or losses generated by the sale of a passive activity. It also includes interest on debt used to buy into the passive activity as well as interest expenses incurred by the activity itself. It does not include any portfolio income such as dividends or interest on securities, even if connected with a passive activity.

Next, you compare the total profits with the total losses produced by the passive activities. If the total profits exceed the total losses, then you have a *net passive profit* for the year. In this case, the new passive loss rules do not apply. The profits and losses from your passive activities are treated in the same manner as before.

However, if the losses exceed the profits, then you have a *net passive loss* for the year. Under the new law, this net passive loss cannot be fully deducted on your tax return. However, losses not currently deductible may be carried over to future years, as discussed later in this section.

Exceptions

There are 2 basic exceptions to the above disallowance rule for passive losses. First, there is an exception for rental real estate losses that applies to anyone whose adjusted gross income does not exceed $100,000 (ignoring IRA contributions, taxable social security benefits, and passive activity losses). Such an individual can exempt up to $25,000 of his net losses produced by rental real estate from the passive loss disallowance rule. To qualify for this exception, the individual (together with his spouse) must own at least 10% of the rental real estate and must be an *active participant* in the rental activity. To qualify as an *active participant*, the individual need not manage the property himself. But he needs to be involved in basic decision-making activities such as choosing tenants, approving repairs, etc.

Second, there is a *phase-in* provision that applies to interests in passive activities acquired before October 23, 1986. For net losses produced by these activities, only 35% is disallowed on 1987 tax returns. The remaining 65% is deductible. For 1988, the disallowance percentage increases from 35% to 60%.

The $25,000 passive loss exemption for rental real estate is phased out at the rate of 50 cents for each dollar of income over $100,000. For example, an individual with adjusted gross income of $110,000 could exempt $20,000 of rental real estate losses. The exemption is entirely phased out for those with adjusted gross income of $150,000 or more.

For married persons filing separately, the $25,000, $100,000, and $150,000 figures above are halved, provided they lived apart for the entire year. If they did live together and are filing separately, the $25,000 exemption is eliminated altogether.

Carry-Over Provisions

There are 2 carry-over provisions which cushion the new passive loss rules. First, any passive losses which are disallowed in a given year may be carried over to be deducted against passive profits in future years. Second, in the year you sell your entire remaining interest in a passive activity to an unrelated party, any unused passive losses connected with this activity can be deducted. Thus, the passive loss rules do not really *deny* deductions, so much as *delay* these deductions until a future time.

What Should You Do If You Have Disallowed Passive Losses?

Seek help. You will need professional assistance if you are caught in the web of the passive loss rules. For one thing, you may be able to negate the effect of these rules by investing in other suitable passive activities which produce a profit. Or, you may want to sell a passive activity in order to be able to claim any unused losses under the carry-over provisions.

There is a new Form 8582 that must be filled out by anyone who has one or more passive activities with net losses. This form will carry you through the appropriate computation. In addition, there are special instructions on Schedules A, C, D, and E of Form 1040 that may apply if you have passive losses.

If you rent out a home you own for part of the year and live in for part of the year, then the passive loss rules may result in disallowance of interest expenses on your 1987 tax return. If this is the case, any interest disallowed in connection wih the passive activity may still be deductible as interest on a primary or second home [cf. Section 2 of the *Investing Your Money* chapter].

SECTION 3:
MUNICIPAL BONDS

Municipal Bonds are issued by cities, states, counties, or other local governments. The chief feature of such bonds is that the interest they pay is entirely exempt from Federal Income Tax. If the bond is issued by a governmental body in the purchaser's home state, then the interest is also exempt from State Income Tax.

A bond is simply a loan. The **purchaser** of a bond is loaning the issuer a fixed amount of money called the **principal** of the loan. In return, the issuer pays periodic interest at a fixed rate for a certain length of time. After this length of time, the bond reaches its **maturity date** and the issuer returns the principal to the purchaser. Municipal bonds are issued in denominations of $1,000.

General Obligation Bonds are fully guaranteed by the issuing municipality. That is, the full taxing authority of the municipality stands behind the bond. **Revenue Bonds** are guaranteed only by the revenue of some income-producing facility. A typical example of this is a toll road bond which is backed by the income which that toll road produces. If the toll road operates at a deficit, the bondholders will suffer because there will not be enough revenue to make the required interest payments.

Certain *private activity* municipal bonds issued after August 7, 1986 might be subjected to a *minimum tax* provision of the new law [cf. the *Alternative Minimum Tax* chapter]. An individual should seek professional advice before purchasing a sizable amount of such bonds.

How Bonds Are Purchased

When they are issued, bonds are usually sold through brokerage houses. After that, the bonds may be traded on the open market. That is, the original purchaser can sell to someone else who in turn can sell when he wishes, etc. Typically, bonds are resold through brokerage houses. That is, brokerage houses will keep an inventory of certain bonds. They will be willing to buy your bonds from you or sell bonds to you from their inventory. They make their profit by keeping a spread between the price they are willing to pay for a bond and the price at which they are willing to sell.

Due to the large number of different types of municipal bonds, they are not as liquid an investment as stocks or corporate bonds. This is particularly true for small numbers of bonds or bonds issued by obscure municipalities.

The interest rate paid by a bond depends upon the maturity date, the financial strength of the issuer, and the general level of interest rates in the economy. The current market value of a bond rises and falls as the general interest level varies. When interest rates rise, the value of a bond will fall and when interest rates fall the bond value will rise. However, this effect is muted as the maturity date draws close because a bond is worth precisely its face value on the maturity date.

There are also mutual funds which invest in municipal bonds and pass along the tax-free feature to the individual investors. These mutual funds are useful because they provide instant liquidity with no sales or redemption charges. Further discussion of these funds is contained in Section 5.

Reporting Tax-Free Income on Your Tax Return

You are now required to report tax-free interest you receive from municipal bonds on line 9 of your Form 1040. The amount you report on this line is not subject to tax. However, Congress wants data on tax-free income to use in designing future tax bills.

Section 4:
Mutual Funds

A mutual fund is an easy way to invest in securities. The fund maintains a diversified portfolio of securities and sells shares in the fund to the general public. When you purchase a share in the fund, you are simply purchasing a proportionate piece of all its securities. The securities held by the fund do not remain constant. The management of the fund will buy and sell securities as it feels such a change will be advantageous.

There are hundreds of different funds. Almost any type of investment philosophy is represented by some fund. The majority of funds maintain a portfolio of common stocks. Some of these stock funds aim at high growth, some at high current yield, and some aim in the middle. Whatever their basic objective, most invest in a wide number of different industries. But there are exceptions to this. For example, you can invest in a fund which only purchases stocks involved in the energy industry.

While mutual funds investing in common stocks have been around a long time, a number of different types of funds have been developed within the past decade. These new funds invest in tax-free municipal bonds, money-market instruments, high-yielding bonds, etc., depending upon their objective. And these new funds permit money to be withdrawn much easier than the old type funds — by telephone, telegram, or even by writing a check against the funds in one's account. Further discussion is contained in the next section.

Load vs. No-Load Funds

A *load fund* is one for which you must pay a sales commission (usually around 8 or 9 percent) in order to purchase shares. A *no-load fund* charges no sales commission. Most funds are load funds which testifies to the salesmanship ability of the investment industry. There is no reason to believe that by charging a sales commission a fund will be better able to decide what stocks to purchase. In fact, studies show that, on the average, no-load and load funds perform about the same.

No-load funds are typically sold through the mail and a number are advertised in newspapers and financial publications such as the *Wall Street Journal*. A directory of no-load mutual funds can be obtained for $2 from the *No-Load Mutual Fund Association* [address: 11 Penn Plaza, Suite 2204, NY, NY 10001].

Beware of the *"hidden-load"* funds (also known as *12b-1 funds*) now being offered by most major brokerage houses. Instead of a visible up-front charge of 8%-9%, the funds spread the charge over time by, typically, charging an extra fee of 1% of net assets each year. This extra fee is in addition to the annual fee for management and operating expenses charged by all mutual funds. Those expenses usually amount to about 1% of assets, so the hidden-load fund's annual charges can add up to 2% or more.

There may also be a redemption fee if you withdraw funds before a specified period of time. This guarantees that the commission paid to the broker who sold you the fund will be covered should you pull out before enough annual fees have been collected.

The change to hidden-load funds has been a huge marketing success for brokerage houses because investors can't spot the hidden fees like they could the up-front sales fees on regular load funds. However, a detailed description of all fees is contained in the prospectus. One place to spot the fee easily is usually a table contained in the prospectus which indicates the ratio of total annual expenses to total assets. If this is in the neighborhood of 2%, you're probably looking at a *hidden-load fund*.

Open-End Funds

Most funds are *open-end* funds. This means that you can always buy shares directly from the fund itself. The purchase price you pay is determined by evaluating the market value of all the securities and assigning a proportionate value to each share. This is called the *net asset value* of the share.

Similarly, you can redeem your shares in the fund any time you wish by selling them back to the fund at the current net asset value. When more people buy than redeem shares, the fund invests the excess cash in new securities. Conversely, when more shares are redeemed than purchased, the fund must sell some of its holdings to meet the excess redemption.

Closed-End Funds

A *closed-end* fund does not sell or redeem shares. It just invests and reinvests the money it already has, without receiving any input of new capital or experiencing any withdrawals. If you wish to buy a share of such a fund, you must find someone who will sell it to you. Similarly, to sell a share you must find a buyer. In practice these funds are sold on a stock exchange or else there are brokerage houses which make a market in them. Thus you don't have to look for a buyer or seller yourself.

The market value of a closed-end fund is determined by the law of supply and demand. It need not be the same as the net asset value (the proportionate share of the market value of the stocks in the fund). In fact, the market price of closed-end funds often differs from the net asset value. Generally, closed-end funds sell at a discount, that is at a price less than the net asset value. One partial explanation for this is that since they do not guarantee redemption at net asset value as do open-end funds, the lack of this feature makes them less attractive to investors.

One might think that this discount represents a bargain. But this bargain is in the most part illusory. Unless the discount narrows in the future for some reason, the shares in the fund will not appreciate in price any faster than the value of the securities in the fund. However, you will be receiving a greater portion of the dividends than you would receive if you bought shares of the stocks themselves instead of shares in the fund.

Over the past 2 years, over 10 billion dollars worth of new closed-end funds have been sold by stockbrokers. When issued, these funds sell at their net asset value rather than at a discount. After a while, a discount generally appears in a loss of value, even if the stocks themselves do not change in price. This loss, when combined with commissions brokers get for selling these funds, generally makes it an unwise move to be an initial purchaser of a closed-end fund.

Tax Aspects of Mutual Funds

As with the purchase of individual shares of common stock, there are two types of taxation that occur with mutual funds. First of all, the stocks in the portfolio of the fund may pay dividends (or interest in the case of bonds). Usually, the fund allows you to periodically receive your proportionate share of these dividends in cash or else it automatically reinvests these dividends in more shares of the fund. Either way, the value of these dividends is ordinary income to you and is taxed at your usual rate. The fund will provide you with an annual statement as to the amount of dividends on which you must pay tax.

The second type of taxation is the tax on capital gains. This can occur in two ways. First of all, the fund itself realizes a capital gain or loss as it sells shares of some securities in order to purchase others. If the fund sells stock at a higher price than the purchase price, then a capital gain is created. The opposite situation produces a capital loss. Once a year, the fund will make a distribution if it has realized a net capital gain on the shares it sold during the year. It may distribute this gain in cash or may automatically reinvest it for you in more shares of the fund. In either event, you must report this capital gain on your tax return.

Of course, a mutual fund may realize a net capital loss in a given year instead of a capital gain. In such a case, you are not allowed to deduct the loss on your own tax return. Instead, the mutual fund is allowed to carry over these losses up to 5 years into the future in order to cancel out future capital gains. For example, if the fund incurs a $50,000 capital loss in one year followed by a $70,000 capital gain in the next year, then the outcome would be a $20,000 capital gains distribution to be reported on shareholders' tax returns the second year.

In addition to tax paid on annual capital gains distributions, you must also pay tax on capital gains if you sell your shares in the mutual fund at a higher price than your purchase price. This is treated the same way as a capital gain arising from the purchase and sale of any other asset. Of course, if you sell at a lower price than the purchase price, then you have a capital loss which can be deducted according to the usual rules for capital losses [cf. Section 1].

If you purchased shares of the same fund on different dates, when you sell some of these shares you will be presumed to have sold the earliest purchased shares. However, there are exceptions to this rule. If you can identify certain shares as having been purchased on a particular date, then you can use the purchase price on that date as the original cost. Or, you can use the *average cost method* to determine the purchase price. Under this method your purchase price is considered to be the average price paid for all the shares you own. There is another *double-category averaging method* under which you take 2 such averages, one for purchases resulting in long-term gains and another for short-term gains. Shares sold are considered to be taken first from the long-term category unless you specify otherwise to the mutual fund at the time of sale. With either averaging method, you have to indicate on your tax return what you're doing. Consult your mutual fund for further information on electing one of these alternate methods.

If the mutual fund has been reinvesting your dividends or capital gains distributions, the following example shows how to avoid overpaying tax on capital gains when you sell your shares.

Mutual Funds

Example

You purchase $5,000 worth of shares in a mutual fund. Over a period of years, your shares are credited with $1,000 in dividends and $2,000 in capital gains distributions which are automatically reinvested to purchase more shares of the fund. You pay tax on these dividends and distributions in the years in which they are declared and reinvested. After 5 years, you sell all your shares in the fund (both the original shares and the shares obtained by reinvestment of dividends and capital gains) for $10,000. To determine your final capital gain you subtract from this $10,000 your original purchase price, $5,000, as well as all dividends and capital gains on which you have already paid tax, $3,000. Thus you must pay a tax on the capital gain of $10,000 − $5,000 − $3,000 = $2,000.

If you had sold your shares for $7,000, then this computation would yield $7,000 − $5,000 − $3,000 = − $1,000. Thus, you would have a long-term capital loss of $1,000 in the year of sale which you deduct according to the usual rules for deducting capital losses.

New 1987 Rules on Deducting Fees

Starting with the 1987 tax year, mutual funds (other than tax-free municipal bond funds) will report to the IRS the investment income you earn **before** the mutual fund's investment management fees have been subtracted.

For example, suppose you own shares in a money-market mutual fund. Your pre-expense earnings for a given year total $1,000. The investment management fees on your account amount to $70. Thus, you receive as net income for the year, $1,000 − $70 = $930.

However, the mutual fund will report the *gross earnings,* $1,000, to the IRS. You then have to report the full $1,000 as dividend income on your 1987 Schedule B, even though you only received the *net income* of $930. The $70 in fees would then have to be claimed as a miscellaneous deduction on Schedule A. Because of the 2% of adjusted gross income floor that now applies to miscellaneous deductions [cf. the *Miscellaneous Deductions* chapter], this might cause you to lose the benefit of this $70 deduction. However, if your other miscellaneous deductions will exceed the 2% floor, the net result will be the same as under prior law. The $1,000 earnings and the $70 deduction combine to increase your taxable income by $930.

The Form 1099 which the mutual fund sends you after the close of the year will include the data you need for filling out your tax return. It will list both the *gross earnings* you must include in income and the investment management *fees* you can deduct as a miscellaneous deduction.

Tax-free municipal bond funds are not subject to the new rules. Such funds will report only the net income after all expenses have been subtracted. Therefore, you do not claim any of the expenses on these funds as a miscellaneous deduction.

(At presstime, Congress was considering a repeal of the above rules requiring mutual fund management fees to be included in income, possibly retroactive to January 1, 1987. You will be able to determine the proper treatment of these fees by examining the yearend Form 1099 sent to you by the mutual fund. Further details will be reported in next year's edition of this Tax Guide.)

Tax Tricks and Traps in Buying Mutual Funds

The tax rules regarding capital gains distributions suggest a number of important considerations. First of all, you should **not** buy mutual funds shortly before a capital gains distribution is about to be declared. Otherwise, you're simply buying a tax liability.

> **Example**
>
> On November 1, you purchase shares in a mutual fund for $5.00 per share. One month later, a capital gains distribution of 50 cents per share is declared. The price of the mutual fund will automatically decline a corresponding amount so that you now have shares worth $4.50 per share plus the 50 cents per share distribution. But you must now pay tax on this 50 cents per share. Had you purchased your shares after the distribution was declared, you would not have paid any tax. Of course, in the first case, the decline from $5.00 per share to $4.50 per share produces an unrealized capital loss. But until you sell your shares in the fund, this loss gives you no tax benefit. In the meantime, you lose all the interest you could earn on the tax you paid.

Before purchasing a mutual fund, you can check to see if they have realized any capital gains so far that year. This information should be contained in their quarterly reports.

Opportunity from 1987 Stock Market Crash

The disadvantage in buying a tax liability corresponds to an advantage in the opposite situation. That is, you may be able to buy a tax credit. For example, many mutual funds incurred capital losses during the 1987 Stock Market crash. These losses can be carried over into the future to offset capital gains. Thus, if the mutual fund realizes capital gains after you purchase it, no capital gains distribution will be declared until the gains exceed the carried-over losses. In effect, you have bought into a tax credit situation. You will be delaying the payment of capital gains tax until you sell your shares of the mutual fund.

In addition, you should consider not only the *realized* capital gain or loss situation of a mutual fund, but also its *unrealized* capital gains or losses. For example, the current portfolio may have a market price which is lower than the total prices at which the stocks were purchased, so that the fund has a net unrealized loss.

It is better to purchase mutual funds with an unrealized loss than an unrealized gain. As the mutual fund changes its portfolio by selling stocks it owns, these unrealized losses become realized and produce a capital loss. Thus any capital gains the mutual fund achieves will be reduced by these losses. Conversely, if a fund has unrealized gains, then capital gains are produced when the fund sells their stocks, even if their value is no higher than when you bought into the fund. You may wind up with a capital gains distribution even though you haven't made any profit. You can find out the extent of any unrealized capital gains or losses listed in the prospectus or annual report of the mutual fund.

We have seen in the above discussion that it is better to buy mutual funds with realized or unrealized capital losses. In the case of open-end funds, the tax advantage of such funds costs nothing extra because the price of shares in the fund is simply determined by the prices of the stocks in the portfolio. The tax situation of the fund plays no part in determining the price of its shares. This is one of the rare cases of getting something for nothing that exists in the investment world.

How Do You Select a Mutual Fund?

We have already touched upon the various criteria which are important in selecting a fund in which to invest. You should purchase a no-load fund which invests in the type of securities meeting your general objective, whether it be high current income, long-term capital growth, speculation, etc. You should also look for a fund with unrealized or realized capital losses. Next, you should check to see what the expense rate of the fund is. All funds deduct a certain percentage of the net asset value to cover operating expenses, investment advice, and provide a profit to the fund operators. This percentage is generally in the 1% range. Ordinarily the larger funds will have a lower expense rate because they are more economical to run.

Note that the expense rate of a mutual fund does not include brokerage commissions. These are considered a "capital expense" and serve to reduce any capital gains or enlarge capital losses incurred as the fund changes its portfolio. Therefore, you should also check the turnover rate of the fund, that is, the percent of the portfolio which gets changed during the year. For example, a fund with a turnover rate of 20% during a given year has bought and sold stocks representing 20% of its portfolio. The other 80% has not changed. Turnover rates vary widely among funds. By selecting a fund with a low turnover rate, you will in effect be paying less brokerage costs. This could amount to an advantage of several percentage points a year.

Finally, you might want to examine the past performance of the funds in which you are interested. However, this information may be of dubious value. Frankly, there is no good evidence that funds which have performed well in the past will continue to perform well in the future.

Where Do You Find Information about Mutual Funds?

A number of services provide annual data on mutual funds, including their past performance, investment philosophy, expense rate, and turnover rate. These services can be found in the financial reference section of your library. Also, the November, 1987 issue of *Money Magazine* contains a listing of mutual funds with past performances, expense rates, and toll-free telephone numbers. And each August, *Forbes Magazine* publishes statistics on all mutual funds currently available.

The *Wall Street Journal* and major local newspapers report the prices of mutual funds each day. Strangely, they do not report the most important piece of information needed to evaluate bond funds — namely their yield. Some information can be found in *Money Magazine* which publishes each month a list of the yields paid by the larger bond funds.

One piece of information that is not likely to be found in general reference material is the extent of unrealized or realized capital gains or losses. You will probably have to get this information from the mutual fund prospectus or annual report itself.

Section 5:
Special Types of Mutual Funds

Municipal Bond Funds

These funds invest in bonds issued by State and local governments. As interest income is distributed to investors, this income is exempt from Federal income tax. Most of these funds are set up to provide maximum liquidity. Interest is credited on a daily basis from the date of investment to the date of withdrawal. Usually, this interest is automatically reinvested to purchase additional shares in the fund. If you prefer, you can have monthly interest checks mailed to you.

Investments are made by mailing in a check or having your bank wire money to the fund. A number of options are available when it comes to withdrawal. The slowest way to withdraw funds is to request the fund to mail the money to you. More speedy withdrawal methods are provided by most funds. For example, you can call a toll-free number and request that money be wired to your bank account by the next day.

The best withdrawal system, offered by a number of the funds, is a check-writing privilege. These funds have a special arrangement with a bank. The bank issues you checks which you write against the balance in your municipal bond fund. The checks must exceed a specified minimum, typically $500.

This check-writing arrangement has the extra advantage that your funds are earning interest up until the day your check clears. This can be especially useful when paying taxes. Often, governmental agencies will take a long time before they cash checks. You can be earning interest on your money in the meantime.

Opening an account with a municipal bond fund is easy. You fill out a short application form and mail in a check to open your account. Monthly statements are mailed to you showing the activity in your account. Each fund has a minimum amount which must be exceeded in order to open an account and a smaller minimum figure for additional contributions.

Below is a list of 4 major municipal bond funds and addresses where you can write for a prospectus and application form. The funds have different contribution limitations, withdrawal options, and expense charges.

T. Rowe Price Tax-Free Income Fund
100 East Pratt Street
Baltimore, MD 21202

Fidelity Municipal Bond Fund
82 Devonshire Street
Boston, MA 02109

Scudder Managed Municipal Bonds
175 Federal Street
Boston, MA 02110

Dreyfus Tax Exempt Bond Fund
600 Madison Avenue
New York, NY 10022

All of the above funds are **no-load** funds which means there is no sales charge when you move money into or out of the funds. However, the interest rate earned by bonds in the fund is reduced by expense charges and management fees. During the past few years, yields on mutual bond funds were generally in the 7%-10% range.

Of course, you should realize that the value of your investment will be subject to fluctuation. This is due to the fact that the municipal bonds in the fund rise and fall in value as the general level of interest rates changes in the economy.

Most municipal bond funds invest primarily in bonds with a high quality rating. This means there is minimal likelihood the bond will default on any interest payments. But higher quality bonds pay a lower interest rate than lesser quality bonds. Those willing to accept more risk can invest in a high-yield municipal bond fund. This type of fund invests in lower-rated bonds and therefore can pay higher interest than other bond funds. An example of such a fund is the *Fidelity High Yield Municipal Bond Fund*. A prospectus and further information can be obtained by calling their toll-free telephone number, 800-544-6666.

Actually, the chance of substantial loss due to default is quite low. For one thing, even medium quality municipal bonds have a good record of meeting their interest payments. And the portfolio diversity offers substantial protection against serious default loss.

Just as there are bond funds which offer a higher risk coupled with a higher yield, there are also lower risk-lower yield funds. In this case it is not the risk of default but the risk of falling prices that is protected against. Shorter-term bonds fall less in value when interest rates rise (and rise less in value when interest rates fall). Thus municipal bond funds investing in shorter-term bonds carry a lower risk than regular municipal bond funds.

The *Vanguard Municipal Bond Fund* provides an attractive opportunity for those who wish to shift their investment according to changes in the market and changes in their own personal circumstances. This fund maintains three separate regular portfolios — short-term, medium-term, and long-term. The shorter the term, the lesser the market risk and the lesser the yield. In addition, there is a high-yield portfolio investing in lower quality bonds. An investor can choose to have his funds apportioned among any of the portfolios he chooses. Then, at any time he chooses, a toll-free telephone call will cause funds to be switched from one of the portfolios to another. The Vanguard Municipal Bond Fund provides check-writing privileges and a lower than average management fee. Further information can be obtained by calling their toll-free telephone number, 800-523-7025.

Municipal Bond Trusts

A Municipal Bond Trust is a second type of investment which provides tax-free interest through the purchase of municipal bonds. However, in contrast to mutual funds, these trusts do not buy and sell municipal bonds as market conditions change or as more money is invested. Instead, these trusts purchase a single portfolio of bonds which are kept until maturity. Shares of the trust are sold until the full portfolio is paid for, after which no further investments or withdrawals can be made. It is possible to sell one's shares in the trust, although this is not as easily done as withdrawing funds from a Mutual Fund.

These trusts generally pay a higher interest rate than Municipal Bond Mutual Funds because they invest in somewhat lesser quality bonds and charge a lower annual expense fee. However, they are subject to an initial sales charge of about 4%. Because of the initial sales charge and relative illiquidity, these trusts are only suitable for the longer range investor. The portfolios of some Municipal Bond Trusts are insured against default by an insurance company. Municipal Bond Trusts are sold by most stockbrokers who will be pleased to give you further information upon request.

To escape state and local tax as well as Federal tax, there might be a trust investing only in bonds issued in your state. Otherwise, investments in a different state's municipal bonds are subject to your state's income tax. Such trusts are available in a number of states including NY, CA, MD, MA, MI, NJ, CT, FL, OH, OR, PA, and VA.

High-Yield Corporate Bond Funds

Mutual funds which invest in corporate bonds have been around a long time. But recently, there has been considerable interest in mutual funds which invest in lesser quality bonds because these funds make it practical for an individual to earn high interest rates on his money. Since these funds invest in a wide portfolio of bonds, the risk of significant loss due to default is much less than if only a few of these bonds were purchased individually.

Most mutual funds which specialize in higher-yielding bonds are load funds. One high-yielding no-load fund is the *Fidelity High Income Fund.* (Call 800-554-6666 for further information on this fund.) There is no fee charged upon investment or upon withdrawal.

Of course, the value of shares in a bond fund is affected by changes in the interest rate. If interest rates fall, the shares will rise in value and if interest rates rise, the share price will fall.

Money-Market Funds

Money-market funds invest in short-term debt securities offered by the nation's leading banks and corporations. These funds operate similarly to an interest-bearing checking account, except that only large-denomination checks can be written. Further details on money-market funds are contained in the next section.

SECTION 6:
MONEY-MARKET ACCOUNTS

Money-market accounts are special accounts which pay interest based on the going short-term market rate. These accounts are liquid, allowing you to withdraw your funds at any time. Since the funds pay interest on a short-term basis, there is no market risk. That is, you can't experience a loss of principal because the underlying investment goes down in value as can happen with longer-term bonds or with stocks.

The going money-market interest rate can vary widely during the course of the year depending upon conditions in the economy.

There are now four basic different types of money-market accounts. Two of these are offered by banks and savings & loans. The other two are offered by mutual funds and stockbrokers. These 4 types of money-market accounts are discussed below.

Bank and Savings and Loan Money-Market Accounts

These accounts have been in existence only about 5 years but have become enormously popular. You can make an unlimited number of deposits or withdrawals in person or by mail. You can also make up to 6 additional transactions per month including telephone transfers to another account, third party transfers, and check-writing against your account. There is no minimum amount for which checks must be written. However, no more than 3 checks per month can be written without penalty. The same $100,000 Federal insurance that applies to regular accounts applies to these accounts as well.

Each bank or savings & loan is allowed to set its own interest rate that it pays on money-market accounts. Some institutions impose various fees while others impose no fees at all. And the method of computing whether the minimum balance has been breached may vary. Only by exploring these features in addition to the stated interest rates can one account be compared with another.

Fees charged on a money-market account for investment management are deductible as a *miscellaneous deduction* on your 1987 tax return. But ordinary checking account charges are not [IRS Private Letter Ruling 8345067]. The institution running your money-market account should inform you of any deductible fees charged against your account in the yearend statement it mails to you.

NOW Accounts

These accounts, sometimes called *Super-NOW* accounts, offered by banks and savings & loans, are similar to money-market accounts as described above. However, there is no limitation upon the number of checks that can be written. And the interest rate paid by NOW accounts is lower because of government-imposed reserve requirements and the cost of check-processing.

Most NOW accounts have a minimum balance requirement, generally in the $1,000–$5,000 range. If your balance falls below the minimum, you may be hit with a monthly fee and/or checkwriting fees. If your account is likely to remain below the minimum for a period of time, you will probably be better off with an ordinary checking account instead of a NOW account.

Cash Management Accounts

A *cash management account* is basically a checking account opened with a stock brokerage house. But unlike ordinary checking accounts, your money is invested in a special money-market fund, earning daily interest on your entire balance. Unlike ordinary money-market funds, there is no minimum denomination on the amount for which the checks may be written nor is there a limitation on the number of checks that may be written each month.

One of the chief advantages of cash management accounts is that they provide instant borrowing power to those who own securities. The way it works is this. You deposit with the brokerage company a combination of securities and cash. The cash is deposited in a money-market fund and interest and dividends received on the securities in your account also go into the money-market fund automatically. As checks are written, money is withdrawn from the money-market fund to cover the checks. If that is depleted, you can continue to write checks against the borrowing power of the securities (generally 50%-70% of their value). These are considered loans and interest is charged at a rate based on the going rate for brokerage margin accounts. This rate is lower than the rate charged on typical bank loans. As cash is deposited into your account, your loan is automatically paid down and interest charges reduced.

In addition to check-writing privileges, you are issued a VISA (or other) charge card. You can use this card to charge purchases in the usual way. You can also use this card to obtain immediate cash at any of the 100,000 bank locations in the world connected with VISA. Many banks will permit you to obtain the full value of your account on the spot. Others place a $5,000 or other daily limit on how much can be withdrawn in this way. The VISA (or other) card is usually a *debit card* rather than a true *credit card*. With such cards, there is no one-month billing period on charge purchases, as is the case with ordinary credit cards. As soon as the charge slip reaches the bank, the amount is subtracted from your account. Also, there are stricter reporting requirements should your card be lost, in order for you to avoid liability for unauthorized purchases.

Merrill Lynch was the pioneer in instituting cash management accounts followed by *Dean Witter.* The plans operated by these two brokerage houses are virtually identical. Both require stiff minimum initial deposits — securities and/or cash with a combined value of at least $20,000. It is not necessary that the account value remain this high although if it falls below $10,000, there is a possibility your account will be terminated. Both plans allow you to choose a tax-exempt money-market fund as a substitute for an ordinary money-market fund. These pay interest at a lower rate than ordinary money-market funds but might still be advantageous for high bracket taxpayers.

There is an annual fee of $50–$75 for maintaining a cash management account. There are no further bank charges, check printing charges, annual credit card fees, etc. The *Dean Witter* plan also allows you to designate which checks are for tax-deductible expenses as you write them. At the end of the year, you are provided a complete computerized listing of all your tax-deductible expenditures made by check. The *Dean Witter* plan also gives you check-cashing privileges at any of 850 Sears department stores, many open until 9:30 PM.

Cash management accounts are a good deal for the consumer. The brokerage houses do not offer them in order to profit from their operation. The annual fees serve only to defray the cost of the checking services (they pay 10 cents or more to a clearing bank for each check or VISA entry) and bookkeeping expenses. And the money-market management fees are, if anything, lower than average. Rather, the chief motivation of the brokerage houses is to get your money and securities under their wing. That way, when you buy or sell securities generating lucrative commission revenues, you are likely to do it through them.

Merrill Lynch has about 65% of the cash management market. By now, most major brokerage houses have set up cash management accounts to remain competitive. And many banks offering brokerage services have set up such plans also.

Charles Schwab & Co., the nation's largest discount brokerage house, has introduced a cash management account which is of interest to those who cannot meet the minimum deposit requirements of most brokerage houses. The *Schwab* account can be opened with a minimum cash deposit of only $5,000 instead of the $20,000 required by *Merrill Lynch* or *Dean Witter.*

Money-Market Funds

Money-market funds are mutual funds which pay money-market interest rates. These funds bear a similarity to money-market accounts offered by banks and savings & loans, the principal difference being that you do not transact your business in person. Instead, you mail in your deposits or have them wired by telephone transfer. Your funds earn daily interest from date of deposit to date of withdrawal.

You can write checks against your account any time you choose. There is no limit on the number of checks that can be written nor upon the number of transactions you can make per month. However, money-market funds usually set a minimum amount for which a check can be written or a telephone transfer can be made — typically $250 or $500.

Money-market funds also have a minimum amount which you need to open an account. This varies from fund to fund but there are a number of prominent funds requiring only a $1,000 minimum deposit. Unlike most bank money-market accounts, you earn full money-market interest on your entire balance even if it falls below the minimum amount necessary to open an account.

There is no Federal deposit insurance on money-market funds. However, they are virtually risk-free because they invest only in short-term securities offered by the most financially secure institutions.

If you are seeking the highest rate, you will have to check out individual institutions to see what rates are currently being offered. A listing of the current rates paid by the major money-market funds is published once a week in the *Wall Street Journal* (on Mondays) and in other newspapers. The published interest rates are net rates after expenses have been deducted.

When comparing interest rates, be sure to take into account the difference in the way the interest rates are quoted. Banks and savings & loans may quote you the effective annual rate — the actual rate you would earn on funds left in a full year with the result of interest-compounding figured in. Money-market funds, however, generally publish a daily rate which does not include the effect of compounding.

If the daily rate is known, there is a way to approximate the effective annual yield produced by compounding the daily rate over a full year. The extra effective annual yield produced by the daily compounding is approximately equal to $i \times i/2$, where i is the quoted uncompounded interest rate. For example, 8% annual interest yields approximately $8\% + (8\% \times 8\%/2) = 8\% + .32\% = 8.32\%$ when compounded daily. (The mathematically trained may observe that this approximation works because $i \times i/2$ is the 3d term in the Taylor series expansion for $\exp(i)$ which is the end result of continuously compounding interest rate i for one year, starting with an initial investment of one dollar.) Because the extra compounding effect is proportional to the *square* of the interest rate, it becomes more significant the higher the interest rate. For example, if the 8% interest were to rise by 1/4 to 10%, the extra compounding effect would be about $10\% \times 10\%/2 = .5\%$. This is an increase of over 1/2 in the .32% extra compounding term for 8% interest.

Income received from a money-market mutual fund is technically considered a *dividend* rather than *interest* and should be reported as such on your tax return. If you report it as interest, the IRS computer may become confused and send you a dunning notice. Income from bank or S&L money-market accounts is considered *interest*.

The table below lists a number of leading money-market funds. You can obtain further information and an application blank by writing to the fund or calling the telephone number listed in the table.

Most of the organizations which run the regular money-market funds listed in the table also run 2 other types of special money-market funds — tax-exempt funds and government-securities funds. *Tax-exempt money-market funds* invest in short-term securities issued by State and local governments which are exempt from Federal income tax. These funds pay less interest than regular money-market funds and are suitable only for those in higher tax brackets. *Government securities money-market funds* invest in short-term securities issued by the Federal government.

Comparing the Different Types of Money-Market Investments

Money-market funds are convenient for those who want the ability to switch into other types of mutual funds via telephone and for those who want to write more than 3 checks per month. Bank money-market accounts, on the other hand, have several advantages of their own. There is no minimum denomination on the three checks per month that can be written, they are convenient for those who prefer in-person rather than mail transactions, and they are insured by the FDIC.

NOW accounts and cash-management accounts are the choice for those who want full checking services. Between these two, NOW accounts are generally the most convenient because of the ability to make in-person transactions and the typically lower minimum for opening an account. However, cash management accounts pay a higher rate of interest and have other features such as instant borrowing power that may make them attractive to those who meet the minimum requirements.

SELECTED MONEY-MARKET FUNDS

Fund	Minimum Initial Deposit	Minimum Subsequent Deposit	Minimum Check Redemption	Telephone Number for Information
Dreyfus Liquid Assets, Inc. 600 Madison Ave. New York, NY 10022	$2,500	$100	$500	(800) 645-6561 in NY (212) 715-5000
Fidelity Cash Reserves P.O. Box 193 Boston, MA 02101	1,000	250	500	(800) 544-6666 in Mass. (617) 523-1919
T. Rowe Price Prime Reserve Fund 100 E. Pratt St. Baltimore, MD 21202	1,000	100	500	(800) 638-5660 in Md. (301) 547-2308
Scudder Cash Investment Trust 175 Federal St. Boston, MA 02110	1,000	None	500	(800) 225-2470 in Mass. (617) 426-8300
Vanguard Money Market Trust P.O. Box 2600 Valley Forge, PA 19482	1,000	100	250	(800) 523-7025 in Penn. (800) 362-0530

Chapter 15

Income Shifting

Basic Principle

The basic principle behind income-shifting is simple. You are in a certain tax bracket and your child is in a lower (usually zero) tax bracket. If you can shift some of your income from yourself to your child, then you will have reduced or eliminated altogether the income tax due on such amounts.

Actually the beneficiary need not be your child, but could be a parent, relative, or other person to whom you desire to transfer property or money. However, you cannot use the methods described here to shift money to your spouse.

What Kind of Income Can Be Shifted?

You cannot transfer income you earn as a salary to someone else and relieve yourself of tax. You are always liable for the tax on your own *earned income*. But *unearned income* produced by investments such as stocks, bonds, savings accounts, and royalties can be shifted. However, you can't just assign the income on such investments to someone else. In order to shift the tax burden, you must also transfer the property (real estate, stocks, bonds, royalty contract, money, etc.) which produces such income.

If you wish to transfer income-producing property to someone else, you can make an outright gift of that property. However, if the recipient of your gift is a minor child, an outright gift can cause difficulty. Because your child lacks legal responsibility, it may be impossible to control the property. For example, a broker may be unwilling to sell a security and buy another, because he is concerned about the lack of legal obligation of the minor to pay.

Gifts Under the Uniform Gifts to Minors Act

This Act provides a simple way to transfer securities (or life insurance policies or money) to a minor and still retain the power to buy, sell, and reinvest these items on behalf of the minor. You buy the securities in your child's name with yourself or your spouse declared as custodian. (Your broker or banker will know how to handle such a transaction.) You then have the power to reinvest (into other securities, savings accounts, etc.) as you choose, providing you do so for the benefit of the child. When the child reaches majority age, he or she then assumes complete ownership and control over the investment and your custodianship ends. During your custodianship, the income earned on the investments is taxed to the child. (Make sure you obtain a separate social security number for your child so the income won't be taxed to you.) But there is one important exception. If the income is used to discharge your legal obligation to support the child, then you must pay the tax on the amounts so used. See the subsection later in this chapter on what constitutes support.

New Rules for 1987

New rules apply to children under the age of 14. Under these rules, discussed in Section 5 of Chapter 1, unearned income in excess of $1,000 is taxed at the parent's tax rate rather than at the child's. These rules were designed by Congress to prevent large-scale income-shifting to young children. As a result, current taxes are no longer saved to the extent property producing income in excess of $1,000 is transferred to a child under age 14.

Another change for 1987 is that a child cannot claim a personal exemption if he is eligible to be claimed on a parent's tax return. This means that lower levels of income will be subject to tax than before. In particular, only the first $500 of unearned income is now exempt from tax. Amounts between $500 and $1,000 are taxed at the child's rate (11% for 1987). The remainder of unearned income may be subject to tax at the parent's rate, depending upon whether or not the child is under age 14.

Although large-scale income shifting to young children has been eliminated, this does not mean income-shifting is dead. For one thing, the first $1,000 of unearned income each year is taxed to the child. Under the 1987 tax tables, the tax on this amount would be only $55, no doubt less than if taxed at the parent's top tax bracket.

Second, the income of a child age 14 or older is still taxed at the child's rate. Only children under age 14 are affected by the rule taxing unearned income at the parent's rate. Thus, income-shifting to an older child or other relative remains intact. Furthermore, by choosing appropriate investments, advantage can be taken of the potential for income-shifting to an older child, even if the child is currently under age 14. This is done by choosing investments which pay off in a future year in which the child will be at least age 14.

One example of such an investment would be U.S. Series EE savings bonds. The interest on these bonds need not be reported until the year in which the bonds are redeemed, which can be arranged to occur after the child has reached age 14.

A second example would be stocks chosen for growth rather than for dividends. If the stocks are sold after the child has reached age 14, the entire capital gain will be taxed at the child's tax bracket. (However a stock mutual fund would not serve the same purpose because it would declare periodic capital gains distributions.)

Further examples of investments which delay income to future years would be real estate, deeply discounted bonds, insurance policies, and gold or other precious metals.

Trusts

Another way to shift income is to set up a *trust* for the benefit of your child. You then transfer money or other assets into the trust. The trust can then accumulate the income produced by these assets.

This income earned by the trust enjoys a tax advantage. Namely, the first $5,000 in earnings during 1988 will be taxed at the lowest 15% rate. This assumes the income is accumulated by the trust rather than being distributed to a beneficiary.

The trust can be set up to distribute money to a child at some later time, e.g.

when the child goes to college. Or, arrangements can be made to delay distributions of remaining funds until the child reaches age 21 or some later age. These distributions are taxed at the child's rate as long as the child is at least age 14 and the distributions are not used to discharge your legal obligation to support the child.

In addition to allowing income-shifting on earnings up to $5,000, setting up a trust has another advantage over making an ordinary gift. Namely, a trust allows you to maintain control over the funds until your child reaches an age you regard as being sufficiently mature. In contrast, under the Uniform Gifts to Minors Act, the child gets automatic control over all the funds when he reaches the age of majority, typically age 18.

For example, suppose an individual wishes to set aside $20,000 for a child's college education. He is reluctant to make a gift under the Uniform Gifts to Minors Act because the money would come under the complete control of the child when he reaches age 18. He is not sure he can adequately predict how his child will use so large a sum of money received at a relatively young age.

Instead, the individual could set up a trust with his spouse as trustee. The money in the trust can be spent for the child's benefit, but only at the direction of his spouse, the trustee. Eventually, when the child reaches a sufficiently mature age any remaining funds in the trust can be turned over to him.

Formerly, it was possible to set up a trust under which the funds an individual contributed would be returned to him after a period of 10 years or to his spouse after a shorter period of time. (These types of trusts were called *Clifford trusts* or *spousal remainder trusts* respectively.) But these trusts will no longer work for income-shifting purposes. Earnings on funds contributed on or after March 1, 1986 to these types of trusts will be taxed to the individual making the contributions. Earnings on funds placed into such trusts before March 1, 1986 are unaffected by this new rule. However, amounts paid to a child under age 14, in excess of $1,000, will still be taxed to the child at the parent's rate, as discussed earlier in this chapter.

What Constitutes Support?

As stated above, tax shifting isn't allowed on amounts used to discharge your legal obligation to provide support. But the definition of what is included in this legal obligation depends upon the state where you live. In most states, only the necessities such as food, shelter, and clothing are considered support so that income-shifting can be used for the cost of private school, music lessons, summer camp, etc. In other states, support includes all that is commensurate with the parents' wealth and social position, possibly including a college education. However, in most states, a child reaches majority at age 18, after which there may be no support obligation.

Hiring a Child or Spouse

One of the best ways to shift income to a child (or spouse) is to hire him in connection with an outside business activity. A dependent child can earn up to $2,540 before any tax is due. Earned income above this amount is taxed at the child's tax bracket [cf. Chapter 1.].

Examples of work he might do include operating a computer, clerical work, cleaning a home office, etc. This type of arrangement is discussed more fully in Section 3 of the *Outside Business Activity* chapter.

Stock Investment Plans

A number of companies offer special *dividend reinvestment plans* under which dividends are automatically invested to purchase additional shares of stock. These plans are particularly useful for investing funds held in your child's name because the dividends are automatically reinvested without any action required on your part. Furthermore, under many of these plans, the reinvested dividends purchase additional shares at a 5% discount. Your stockbroker won't tell you about these plans because the purchases are made directly through the companies with no commission costs whatever. Many plans even permit further purchases of stock to be made still with no commission charges. Ordinarily the charge for purchasing a small number of shares of stock would be quite high.

Most of the dividend reinvestment plans have the following features. First of all, in order to participate, an individual must already be a stockholder in the Company. However, you do not have to own any specific amount of stock. Ownership of just one share entitles you to full participation in the plan.

There are two features to the plan. The first feature is that you can choose to have all or a portion of your dividends on Company stock automatically reinvested to purchase further shares of the Company. These shares are purchased with no commissions or other service charges. Also, there may be a discount of up to 5% of market price. Full reinvestment of dividends is made possible because the plan permits fractions of shares to be issued.

The other feature of the plan is that at any time, additional funds can be mailed in to purchase further shares of the Company at the full market price. Once again, no commissions are charged and the issuance of fractional shares allows the full amount to be invested. However, there is an upper limit, typically $3,000-$5,000 that can be invested in any one quarter (3-month period).

Recordkeeping is all done by the Company. Unless you request otherwise, no certificates will be issued. Instead, purchases will be credited to your account with statements mailed to you periodically. At any time, you can request to have certificates issued to you in the amount of your account.

You can get a free list of about 600 companies on the N.Y. Stock Exchange with dividend reinvestment plans by writing to: *NY Stock Exchange Marketing Group; 20 Broad St., 18th floor; New York, NY 10005*. Also, the *Value Line* advisory service, found in many libraries, can be used to check whether a given company offers a stock purchase plan. If a company does have such a plan, this fact will be noted at the bottom of the page description of that company. If a discount on reinvested dividends is offered, this will be indicated in the note. You can then write to the company itself for full details of the plan.

Dividend Reinvestment Plans should be considered especially when accounts are maintained for children or other dependents. The automatic reinvestment feature, the simplified recordkeeping, the ability to invest small amounts, and the 5% discount all combine to make these plans very attractive.

Rules for Interest-Free Loans

At one time, interest-free loans could be used as a means of income-shifting between family members. For example, a child could have received an interest-free loan from a parent and then earned interest on the money. The interest would have been taxed at the child's lower tax bracket rather than at the parent's higher bracket.

But the 1984 Tax Act eliminated this technique. Now, if an individual makes an interest-free loan to another person who invests it at a lower tax bracket, the IRS will "impute" interest to the lender at the going interest rate. For example, suppose a parent makes an interest-free loan of $5,000, payable on demand, to a child who invests the money in his name in a certificate of deposit. If the short-term U.S. Treasury interest rate is 7%, then the IRS will impute interest to the parent of 7% × $5,000 = $350. This amount will have to be included in the taxable income of the parent and is deductible by the child. Effectively, this undoes the tax-shifting of the interest-free loan.

For loans made at a below-market interest rate, a similar provision applies. In this case, the difference between the going Treasury rate and the interest actually charged will be imputed to the lender.

The above rules apply to interest-free loans made in order to shift income to a lower tax bracket. For other interest-free loans, where the avoidance of tax is not *"one of the principal purposes,"* the rules are different. In such a case, you can make up to $100,000 of loans to an individual without the imputed interest rules coming into play. (For example, parents could loan money interest-free to a child to buy a home, attend school, etc.). In this situation, if the recipient does earn some income on the money, interest can still be imputed to the lender. The amount imputed is either the going Treasury rate or the actual amount of income earned, whichever is lower. However, no interest is imputed if the recipient's net investment income (from all sources) for the year is less than $1,000. This $1,000 exemption as well as the use of actual income earned instead of the Treasury rate only applies if tax-avoidance is not one of the principal purposes of the loan.

Also, if the total balance of amounts you loaned to an individual does not exceed $10,000 and the loans are *not directly attributable to the purchase or carrying of income-producing assets,* then no income is imputed to you. This $10,000 limit and the $1,000 limit in the preceding paragraph are the same for married couples as for individuals; they are not doubled.

The above rules apply to loans made after June 6, 1984. However, for demand loans (i.e. loans without a predetermined maturity date), the above rules apply no matter when the loans were made.

Turning Your Child's Purchase of a Car, Stereo, Computer, Etc. into a "Tax Shelter"

One way to utilize the $10,000 exemption for income-shifting purposes you have a child with his own money from a part-time job or gifts from Say the child was planning to spend this money on "extras" such as home computer, jewelry, etc. Instead, you can lend your child the purchase. He keeps the money he would otherwise have spe income-producing account or investment. The first $500 exempt from tax and the next $500 is taxed at the child's tax bracket [cf. Chapter 1, Section 5]. At some later date, he returns the money you have lent him, i.e. he repays the loan. In the meantime, income earned on the money saved by the child might be taxed at his tax bracket instead of yours.

In the above manner, you can lend up to a total of $10,000 per child or other recipient, apparently without running afoul of the imputed interest rules. Technically speaking, you are making *interest-free, payable-on-demand* loans to your child which should be documented by a simple promissory note signed by the child (and custodian, if applicable). In practice, since the loan transaction does not appear on any tax form, the IRS is not likely to find out about the transaction, even in the event of an audit. This is especially true since the amounts loaned are not large.

Chapter 16

Tax-Sheltered Plans

Section 1:
Benefit of Tax-Deferral

A number of different types of tax-sheltered plans are available under the current tax laws, including IRAs, Keogh Plans, tax-sheltered annuities, and deferred compensation plans. Of particular note are the remarkable *Defined-Benefit Keogh Plans* discussed in Section 3. With such plans, those with self-employment income can often **shelter up to 100% of this income from tax.**

The principle behind the various types of tax-sheltered plans is the same. First, you place a certain amount of money which you earn this year into one of these plans. You do not generally pay any current tax on this money. That is, it is subtracted from your adjusted gross income on this year's tax return. (A major exception to this is non-deductible payments made to an IRA, as discussed in Section 2.)

Second, after the money is placed into the plan, it is invested in savings certificates, stocks, bonds, or other securities depending upon the type of plan it is. As income is earned on the investment, no tax is paid. Year after year, the interest or other investment income compounds without the interference of any amount being taken out to pay taxes. If instead of placing an amount of money into such a plan, you were to invest it yourself, you would have to pay the tax as you went along. Any amount taken out in tax would no longer be available to earn investment income for you. In effect, the tax-sheltered plan is letting you use these amounts you would have to pay in tax as an interest-free loan to invest for your benefit.

Finally, when you start withdrawing the income earned by the IRA, then you must pay tax as the money is withdrawn. Thus, you have not avoided tax but simply deferred it. But this deferral can result in a tremendous benefit because of all the extra interest, interest on interest, etc. you have earned on that amount of money not taken out in tax.

The table below illustrates the monetary advantage of a tax-sheltered plan. It examines the options of an individual with $1,000 he wishes to invest at the end of year 1. The table assumes that the individual's highest Federal tax bracket remains at 28% and that there is an additional effective marginal state tax rate of 9%.

Column A shows the yearly total accumulation of original investment plus all income earned, assuming that the individual first pays the tax due on $1,000 ($370) and invests the remainder ($630) himself. Column B shows the yearly total, assuming the $1,000 is placed in a tax-sheltered plan. Column C shows the amount the individual would receive if distribution of the accumulated funds were subject to tax at the same rate used throughout the table. All three columns assume the funds earn 9% annual interest.

Year	Column A Invested by individual; all taxes paid	Column B Invested in tax-sheltered plan; tax not paid	Column C Invested in tax-sheltered plan; all taxes paid
1	$ 630	$ 1,000	$ 630
5	786	1,412	889
10	1,035	2,172	1,368
15	1,364	3,342	2,105
20	1,796	5,142	3,239
25	2,367	7,911	4,984
30	3,118	12,172	7,668
35	4,108	18,728	11,799
40	5,413	28,816	18,154

For some, the above table understates the advantage of tax-sheltering. If a person's income tax rate rises through the years, the Column A accumulations might decrease markedly. The Column C distribution would not be affected nearly as much because there is no compounding effect caused by the annual application of a higher tax rate. Also, the Column C distribution might be greater than indicated if the individual's tax rate drops after retirement, if he elects an annuity option which further defers tax, or if he can use the special lump sum averaging provision discussed later in this chapter.

SECTION 2:
INDIVIDUAL RETIREMENT ACCOUNTS

The 1986 Tax Reform Act has changed the basic rules governing Individual Retirement Accounts (IRAs). These are individual tax-sheltered savings plans set up with a mutual fund, savings institution, insurance company, etc.

Under prior law, any person could deduct up to $2,000 of his earned income contributed to an IRA. But under the new law, some persons will be denied a deduction and others will be allowed a deduction of less than $2,000. Only those who are not covered by another retirement plan or whose income does not exceed certain limits will qualify for the full $2,000 deduction. However, even if an individual does not qualify for an IRA **deduction**, he can still contribute up to $2,000 to an IRA on a **non-deductible** basis.

Other than the rules for deducting contributions, IRAs operate the same basic way as in prior years. That is, funds in the IRA can be invested as an individual wishes, with all investment income exempt from tax. Only upon withdrawal is tax paid on any of the income accumulated by the IRA. It is this ability to compound income over a period of time in a tax-free manner that may make contributing to an IRA desirable, even if no initial deduction is received for the contribution.

Who Can Still Deduct Contributions to an IRA?
Some persons will still be able to fully deduct their contributions to an IRA as

before. To qualify for a full deduction of $2,000 contributed to an IRA, you must satisfy **either** of the following conditions:

Condition A: Neither you nor our spouse is covered by another retirement plan.

or

Condition B: The total Adjusted Gross Income (ignoring IRA contributions) on your tax return is less than $40,000 on a joint return or $25,000 on a single person's return.

To satisfy Condition A, you must not be an *active participant* at any time during the year in a *retirement plan*. Here, the term *retirement plan* includes tax-favored plans run by your employer such as a pension, profit-sharing, deferred compensation, or stock bonus plan. It also includes tax-sheltered annuities [sometimes called 403(b) plans] and Keogh plans. However, it does not include social security, nor does it include unfunded deferred compensation plans established by a government or tax-exempt organization.

Your employer will determine whether or not you are an *active participant* in a retirement plan which it sponsors. In some cases, this determination can rest upon certain technical factors. However, in general, you are an *active participant* in a plan if any contributions were made to the plan on your behalf during the year. However, if you are covered by a retirement plan with a specific defined benefit (e.g. an amount based on salary and length of service), then you are automatically considered to be an *active participant*, even if no contributions were made on your behalf that year. Furthermore, you can be an *active participant* even if you have not been in the plan long enough to be vested. Your employer is required to inform you on your yearend W-2 Form, by placing a checkmark in Box 5, if you were an *active participant* in one of its plans during the year.

Also, Condition A requires that your spouse not be an active participant in any retirement plan either. This is colorfully called the *tainted spouse* rule. Even if you are not an active participant in any plan, you still fail Condition A because of the taint of your spouse's participation. Although not yet settled, it appears that under a pending technical amendment to the 1986 Tax Reform Act, the tainted spouse rule will still apply if you and your spouse file separate returns, unless the two of you live apart during the entire year. If affected, you should check with the IRS to find out the status of this provision at the time you are filling out your tax return.

If you satisfy either Condition A or Condition B (and so does your spouse), then you can deduct any IRA contributions totalling up to $2,000 for the year, provided the total does not exceed your own *earned income*. In this situation, your spouse can also deduct up to $2,000 of his or her earned income contributed to a separate IRA, for a total of $4,000.

Earned Income means income produced by your own work, whether as an employee or as a self-employed person. It does not include income earned from investments such as stocks, bonds, savings accounts, rental property, etc., nor does it include income which is exempt from tax.

Spousal IRAs

If your spouse has no earned income, then you can deduct contributions totalling up to $2,250 to IRAs in each of your names, provided Condition A or Condition B is satisfied. (A spouse with earnings of less than $250 can be treated here as though he had no earned income.) You set up two separate accounts, one in each name, and divide the total between these accounts any way you choose, as long as the contribution credited to any one individual for the year does not exceed $2,000.

For example, you can contribute $2,000 to your IRA and $250 to your spouse's IRA, or vice versa. Or, you can divide the total in another manner, e.g. $1,125 to each IRA. However, the working spouse should open at least a token account in his name, even if he wishes to put the maximum possible into his spouse's account. Also, a joint return should be filed.

The decision on how to divide up the $2,250 each year could be an important one. From a tax-saving point of view, it is best to put the most funds into the account of the younger spouse. That way, the funds will have a longer period of time to accumulate tax-free interest before distribution is required to begin at age $70^{1/2}$.

For example, suppose a 60-year-old husband has a non-working wife age 50. If he contributes $2,000 to his wife's account, then this $2,000 can accumulate tax-free income for as long as 20 years before distribution begins, instead of the 10 years if placed into the husband's account. (On the other hand, if earlier withdrawal of IRA funds is desired, the opposite strategy might be called for. That is, the maximum level of funds might be placed into the older spouse's account.)

Phase-Out Range

The $2,000 individual limit for deductible IRA contributions is phased out if Adjusted Gross Income (ignoring IRA contributions) falls into the *phase-out range*. The phase-out range is $40,000-$50,000 for joint filers and $25,000-$35,000 for singles.

For joint filers in the $40,000-$50,000 phase-out range, the maximum amount that can be deducted is given by the formula: 20% × ($50,000 − AGI). As can be seen from the formula, the maximum IRA deduction for joint filers is $2,000 if AGI (Adjusted Gross Income) is $40,000, and $0 if AGI is $50,000, with an intermediate amount between the phase-out endpoints of $40,000 and $50,000.

Analogous formulas apply to singles and marrieds filing separately. The following table gives the formulas and phase-out ranges for these formulas:

PHASE-OUT TABLE

COLUMN I Type of Tax Return	COLUMN II Maximum Deduction for IRA Contributions	COLUMN III Phase-Out Range for which Column II Applies
Joint	20% × ($50,000 − AGI)	$40,000-$50,000
Single	20% × ($35,000 − AGI)	$25,000-$35,000
Married filing separately	20% × ($10,000 − AGI)	$0-$10,000

You can round up to a multiple of $10 after using Column B to determine the maximum IRA deduction that applies. For example, if you compute $1,488 using Column B, you can round this up to $1,490. Also, if you compute a deduction limit of less than $200 but more than $0, you are allowed to use $200 as the deduction limit.

As discussed earlier, the $2,000 individual IRA deduction limit is raised to $2,250—an increased of 12 1/2 %—when you also contribute to a separate *spousal IRA* for a non-working spouse. In the phase-out range ($40,000-$50,000 for joint filers), the maximum deduction computed using the Phase-Out Table is similarly increased by 12 1/2 %, when contributions are made to a spousal IRA. This is illustrated by Example 5.

Example 1

Morgan files a joint tax return showing AGI of $70,000. Neither he nor his wife is covered by a retirement plan.

In this case, Condition A applies. Morgan can deduct a contribution to his IRA of any amount of his earned income up to $2,000. His spouse can also deduct a contribution to a separate IRA of any amount of the spouse's earned income up to $2,000.

Example 2

Scott files a joint tax return showing AGI of $70,000. He is covered by a retirement plan provided by his employer.

Scott can get no deduction for contributing to an IRA. Neither Condition A nor Condition B applies. Furthermore, his AGI is above the $40,000-$50,000 phase-out range given in the preceding Phase-Out Table.

Example 3

Farley files a single tax return showing AGI (ignoring IRA contributions) of $28,560.

Case 1. Farley is covered by his employer's retirement plan. Using the appropriate formula in Column B of the Phase-Out Table, Farley's IRA deduction cannot exceed 20% × ($35,000 − $28,560) = $1,288, which can be rounded up to $1,290.

Case 2. Farley is not covered by any retirement plan. In this case, Condition A applies. This means that Farley can deduct any amount up to $2,000, when contributed to an IRA.

Example 4

John and Mary file a joint tax return with AGI of $42,000 (ignoring IRA contributions). Mary is covered by her employer's retirement plan.

Case 1. John and Mary each earn $21,000. To compute the maximum IRA deduction for each spouse, the Column B formula for joint returns is applied:

$$20\% \times (\$50,000 - \$42,000 = \$1,600.$$

Thus, each spouse can deduct an IRA contribution of up to $1,600—a total of $3,200 for the couple.

> **Case 2. John earned $1,500 and Mary earned $40,500.** In this case, Mary can deduct an IRA contribution of up to $1,600, the same as in Case 1. But John's deductible IRA contribution is limited to $1,500, the amount of his earned income.

> **Example 5**
> You and your spouse file a joint tax return with AGI (ignoring IRA contributions) of $42,000. Your spouse has no earned income.
> You use the Phase-Out Table to compute your own deduction limit:
>
> $$20\% \times (\$50,000 - \$42,000) = \$1,600.$$
>
> If there is a spousal IRA, an additional deduction of $12\frac{1}{2}\% \times \$1,600 = \$200$ is permitted—a total deduction of $1,600 + $200 = $1,800. You can divide the $1,800 between your IRA and your spouse's IRA any way you choose, as long as each IRA is allocated a deduction no less than $200 and no more than $1,600.

Where Is the Deduction for IRA Contributions Claimed?

The deduction for IRA contributions is claimed as an adjustment to income on line 24 of Form 1040. Because it is an *adjustment to income* rather than an *itemized deduction*, it can be claimed by those who use the standard deduction as well as by those who itemize.

Non-Deductible Contributions

If you do not qualify for the full $2,000 IRA deduction, you can make *non-deductible contributions* to your IRA for the 1987 tax year. Although these IRA contributions are not deductible, all *earnings* on these funds compound entirely free from tax until distributions are made.

The total of all your IRA contributions (deductible and non-deductible) for the year cannot exceed $2,000 ($2,250 if there is a spousal IRA), nor can it exceed earned income. If, for example, you were allowed no deductible IRA contribution, you can make a $2,000 non-deductible contribution.

On the other hand, if you make a $2,000 *deductible* contribution to your IRA, you cannot make any *non-deductible* contribution for the year to the same or different IRA in your name. (However, if you wanted to designate part or all of the $2,000 contribution as being non-deductible, this would be allowed. You might wish to do this, say, if your tax rate in a given year was unusually low and you intended to make distributions in the near future.)

You make non-deductible contributions to an IRA in exactly the same way you make deductible contributions—i.e. you just deposit funds into the IRA account. You can mingle deductible and non-deductible contributions in the same IRA. No purpose is served by segregating these 2 different types of contributions into different IRAs.

At the time you contribute to an IRA, you do not need to specify to the institution running your IRA what the tax-nature of the contribution is. Only when you fill out your tax return, do you need to specify what percentage of your total contribution for the year is deductible and what percentage is non-deductible.

For example, you can make a $2,000 contribution to your IRA at the beginning of the year, even if you don't know what your tax situation will be for the year. You will determine what percentage is deductible when you fill out your tax return after the end of the year. And, as discussed later, you can even undo any contributions for the year you wish to retract by making withdrawals before the tax-filing deadline.

To illustrate the rules for making non-deductible contributions, let us revisit the previous examples in this section. In Example 1, if Morgan makes the maximum deductible IRA contribution of $2,000, then no non-deductible contribution can be made to an IRA in his name. On the other hand, in Example 2, since no deductible contribution is allowed, a $2,000 non-deductible contribution could be made.

In Case 1 of Example 4, if each spouse makes the permitted $1,600 deductible contribution to his own IRA, then each spouse could make an additional $400 non-deductible contribution; in Case 2, only the higher-earning spouse could make a $400 non-deductible contribution.

And in Example 5, if $1,800 in deductible contributions were divided between your IRA and a spousal IRA for your non-working spouse, then an additional $450 ($2,250 − $1,800) in non-deductible contributions could be made. The division must be made so that the total contribution for the year made to each of these IRAs is between $250 and $2,000.

If you make a non-deductible contribution to an IRA for 1987, you must fill out Form 8606 and include it as part of your tax return. Only a few lines on this form need to be filled out. Basically, you list the value of all your IRAs on December 31, 1987 (as reported to you by the institutions running your IRAs), and the amount of non-deductible contributions you made for the 1987 tax year.

Your spouse must file a separate Form 8606 if any non-deductible contributions were made to an IRA in her name.

You should keep copies of any Form 8606 which you file, as long as you have any IRAs in your name. These can be used to verify all the non-deductible contributions you make over the years. When you withdraw funds from your IRA(s), the more non-deductible contributions you have made, the larger the portion of the withdrawal that is exempt from tax [cf. Example 6].

You may have to report the total of non-deductible IRA contributions on all future tax returns until your IRAs have been depleted. Whether or not this will require filing Form 8606 in future years remains to be decided. Next year's edition of this Tax Guide will contain further information after the IRS issues regulations on this matter.

When Are Your IRA Contributions Due?

You can choose any schedule you want for making contributions. You can make periodic contributions or make one big contribution. You are under no obligation as to the amount you contribute in any given year, as long as your contributions do not exceed the maximum allowable amount. You have until the filing date of your tax return to establish or make contributions to an IRA. Thus, contributions for 1987 can be made up until April 15, 1988. You don't need to have made your contribution when you file your tax return as long as the contribution is made by April 15.

However, the April 15 deadline applies even if you have an extension to file after this date.

According to a 1986 IRS ruling, if you mail in your IRA contribution, the postmark date is what counts. In this ruling, a person mailed a $2,000 contribution on April 11 which the bank did not receive until April 16, one day after the deadline. The IRS ruled that since the envelope was postmarked April 12, three days before the April 15 deadline, the $2,000 payment could be deducted as an IRA contribution. [IRS Private Letter Ruling 8611090]

If you make an IRA contribution and later change your mind, you can withdraw the contribution before the due date of your tax return, with no penalty. You should also withdraw any investment income earned by the withdrawn funds while in the IRA.

Contributing After Age 59$^{1}/_{2}$

Suppose you don't want to contribute to an IRA because you want to have the funds readily available to spend if you need them. However, if you are age 59$^{1}/_{2}$ or older, an IRA is generally a no-lose proposition, because you can withdraw funds at any time with no IRS penalty. You can use the IRA simply as a tax-free savings account in which you want to keep readily available emergency funds.

Can IRA Contributions Be Made After Age 70$^{1}/_{2}$?

The general rule is that you cannot contribute to an IRA for the year you reach age 70$^{1}/_{2}$ or any year thereafter. However, if you have reached age 70$^{1}/_{2}$ and are still working, you may contribute to an IRA for your non-working spouse as long as your spouse is less than age 70$^{1}/_{2}$ at the end of the tax year. Also, you can roll over a lump sum distribution from a pension plan (see below), even though you have reached age 70$^{1}/_{2}$, provided you begin distributions as required.

When Is Money Withdrawn from an IRA?

You may start withdrawing money from your IRA anytime after the age of 59$^{1}/_{2}$. However, you must begin the distribution of money by April 1 of the year following the year in which you reach age 70$^{1}/_{2}$. You don't have to retire from your ordinary job in order to receive payments. You can choose to receive the entire account in one lump sum or receive the amount in periodic payments spread out over a number of years.

It is permissible for you to withdraw money from an IRA before reaching age 59$^{1}/_{2}$. However, as discussed later in this section, an extra 10% penalty tax may apply to such early withdrawals.

How Are IRA Distributions Taxed?

If you have never made any non-deductible contributions to an IRA, then the taxation rules for distributions are simple. Namely, any withdrawal of funds from the IRA is taxed at your ordinary income tax rate along with your other income. Thus, you will probably want to spread out payments over a number of years instead of receiving a lump-sum distribution. Note that lump sum distributions do not qualify for the special averaging rule that applies to regular retirement plans or to Keogh Plans [cf. the *Retirement Plans* chapter].

Distributions of Non-Deductible Contributions

If you have made non-deductible contributions to an IRA, then a portion of any distributions you later make from the same or a different IRA in your name is not taxed. (You have already paid tax when you earned the money to make the non-deductible contribution.) Also, the 10% penalty tax on early withdrawals before age $59^{1}/_{2}$, discussed later, does not apply to a return of non-deductible contributions. Thus, the portion of a distribution attributed to non-deductible contributions escapes not only the ordinary tax, but the additional 10% penalty tax as well.

To determine the non-taxable percentage of a distribution, you divide the total non-deductible contributions you have made over the years by the *value* of your IRA at the end of the year of distribution. The *value* of your IRA is the yearend account balance, adding back any distributions made during the year. If you have more than one IRA in your name, you group them together and treat them as if they were all part of one big IRA.

Example 6

You make the following contributions to an IRA:

	Deductible	Non-Deductible
1985	$2,000	
1986	1,500	
1987	1,000	$1,000
1988	1,000	1,000
	$5,500	$2,000

On October 31, 1989, you make a withdrawal of $3,000. Let's say that at the end of 1989, the total in the IRA account is $7,000.

The percentage of your account that is due to non-deductible contributions is:

$$\frac{\$2,000}{\$3,000 + \$7,000} = 20\%.$$

Thus, 20% of the $3,000 distribution is tax-free: 20% × $3,000 = $600. The remaining $2,400 ($3,000 − $600) is included in taxable income on your 1989 tax return.

As can be seen from the above example, the tax treatment of a distribution depends upon the percentage of your IRA due to non-deductible contributions—the higher the percentage, the larger the portion of the distribution that is exempt from tax.

If you have a choice, you are better off concentrating non-deductible contributions in one spouse's IRA and deductible contributions in the other's. That way, if you want to make a withdrawal, you can do so from the IRA in which the non-deductible contributions are concentrated. Since amounts attributable to non-deductible contributions are not taxed upon withdrawal, this will maximize the amount of the withdrawal that is exempt from tax.

> **Example 7**
>
> You have one IRA in your name, and your spouse, who also works, has none. The account balance in your IRA at the end of the year (due to contributions in previous years plus interest) is $10,500. You wish to make a $1,500 non-deductible contribution on this date and intend to make a $1,000 distribution one year later. We will assume an interest rate of 10% for this one-year period.
>
> **Case 1. You make a $1,500 non-deductible contribution to your own IRA.**
>
> This brings your account balance to $10,500 + $1,500 = $12,000. Under the 10% interest assumption, this rises to $13,200 by the end of the next year when you make the $1,000 distribution. Under the rules illustrated in Example 6, the percentage of the distribution that is untaxed (as a partial return of non-deductible contributions) is $1,500 ÷ $13,200 = 11%. Thus 11% × $1,000 = $110 is untaxed, with the remaining $890 subject to tax in the year of distribution.
>
> **Case 2. You make the $1,500 non-deductible contribution into an IRA set up in your spouse's name.**
>
> Under the 10% interest assumption, the account balance of $1,500 rises to $1,650 by the end of the next year when the $1,000 distribution is made. Following the method illustrated in Example 6, the percentage of the distribution that is untaxed is $1,500 ÷ $1,650 = 91%. Thus 91% × $1,000 = $910 is untaxed, with only $90 remaining to be taxed in the year of distribution. When compared with Case 1, this is a decrease in current taxable income of $890 − $90 = $800.

In the preceding example, each spouse had earned income of his own, so they could choose into whose IRA the $1,500 would be placed. The same situation occurs when there is a non-working spouse. Under the *Spousal IRA* rules discussed earlier, among your choices are to contribute $2,000 to your IRA and $250 to your spouse's, or the reverse—$250 to your IRA and $2,000 to your spouse's.

As in the preceding example, you are better off placing the $2,000 non-deductible contribution into your spouse's IRA if your existing IRA balance is greater than your spouse's. This will generally minimize tax if a partial distribution is made in the future. Conversely, if your spouse's existing IRA is greater than yours, you would be better off contributing the $2,000 to your IRA.

Are Non-Deductible Contributions Worthwhile?

Before making non-deductible contributions to an IRA, you should exhaust all the tax-deductible plans for which you are eligible—Keogh plans, tax-sheltered annuities, and deferred compensation plans [cf. the remaining sections in this chapter]. If you still have money left that you wish to invest on a long-term basis, then non-deductible contributions to an IRA make sense. The ability of the IRA to compound earnings without paying current tax is valuable, especially over a long period of time.

However, if you expect to make withdrawals from your IRA before many years have passed, you should be careful about making non-deductible IRA contributions when you already have an existing IRA.

The reason for this is illustrated in Case 1 of the preceding example. In that case, a non-deductible contribution of $1,500 was followed the next year by a $1,000 withdrawal—leaving a net $500 addition to the IRA. Because there was a substantial amount already in an IRA, a tax was triggered on $890 of the withdrawal. If we assume the tax on this $890 amounts to $300, the withdrawal would yield $700 in after-tax money.

However, instead of making the full $1,500 contribution, it would have been better to hold on to $700 and contribute the remaining $800 to the IRA. This leaves you with the same in-pocket $700, but the IRA winds up with an extra $800—$300 more than the net $500 addition in the preceding paragraph. (Investment income was ignored in the preceding analysis because its inclusion would not affect the basic comparison.)

Can Money Be Withdrawn Before Age 59$^{1}/_{2}$?

Yes. However, the purpose of the legislation creating the IRAs was to provide a retirement vehicle. Thus, there is a penalty for early withdrawals. If you do withdraw money before age 59$^{1}/_{2}$, and you have never made any non-deductible contributions to an IRA, then there is a 10% penalty tax on the amount of the distribution. This is in addition to the ordinary income tax that applies.

If you have ever made a non-deductible contribution to an IRA, then as discussed above, only a portion of any distribution is subject to ordinary income tax. The 10% penalty tax only applies to this taxable portion. The remaining portion of the distribution attributed to non-deductible contributions is not subject to ordinary income tax nor to the 10% penalty tax.

Note that the 10% penalty is not so severe as to absolutely limit the use of an IRA to those seeking a retirement vehicle. You still might be better off setting up an IRA and making a premature withdrawal than you would had you invested the money outside an IRA.

For example, suppose you could make a $1,000 deductible contribution to an IRA or invest without tax protection. If you were in the 28% tax bracket, then investing the funds yourself would mean you could put $720 to work earning interest or other income. But the IRA would have an extra $280. It would not take many years before the extra income earned on the $280 would be sufficient to compensate for the 10% penalty. In addition, the fact that your money is compounding entirely tax-free in an IRA instead of being taxed each year provides a further advantage.

Assuming no non-deductible contributions have been made, the breakeven point is generally around 7 years, depending upon the interest rate and your tax bracket. That is, you are generally better off with an IRA if the money is left in for about 7 years or more and then withdrawn prematurely (with 10% penalty) than you would have been with a comparable investment outside the IRA.

In the case of non-deductible contributions, the breakeven point is longer—up to as much as 15 years, depending upon the details of your tax situation. For this reason, it is not usually advisable to make non-deductible contributions to an IRA if you plan to withdraw funds before reaching age 59½.

Under a new provision in the law, you can start annuity distributions from your IRA, prorated over your lifetime, at anytime you wish. In such a case, the 10% penalty does not apply, even if you are under age 59½. If you wish, the annuity payments can be stopped after 5 years, provided you are at least age 59½ at that time. You can also make penalty-free early withdrawals in the event of permanent disability.

IRA Contribution Based on Alimony Payments

A special rule applies to alimony payments. As long as these payments qualify as alimony [cf. the *Divorce & Separation* chapter], taxable to the recipient, they can be considered the same as *earned income* for purposes of the IRA rules. The person paying the alimony still gets to make his normal IRA contribution based on his earned income.

Custodial Fees

Many institutions charge a set-up fee or an annual maintenance fee. If these fees are separately billed, they can be deducted in addition to the maximum allowable IRA contribution which you make. For example, suppose you are eligible to make a $2,000 IRA contribution with an institution charging a $25 custodial fee. You could pay the institution $2,000 for the IRA contribution which you deduct on line 24, plus the $25 fee which you deduct as a Miscellaneous Deduction on Schedule A. You should pay the fee with a separate check so you're not accidentally credited with an excess contribution.

However, you can't separately deduct brokerage commissions connected with the purchase and sale of securities in your IRA.

Hidden IRA Bonus

When contemplating how much to contribute to your IRA, take note of the extra bonus you get if you also are claiming a medical deduction. Only medical expenses in excess of 7.5% of your Adjusted Gross Income (AGI) are deductible on your 1987 tax return. But your IRA contribution is an "above the line" *adjustment to income* which reduces your AGI, thereby raising your medical deduction.

For example, if you make a deductible contribution of $2,000 to an IRA, your AGI is reduced by $2,000 which in turn raises your medical deduction by 7.5% × $2,000 = $150—a 7.5% bonus.

A similar situation occurs with the 2% of AGI floor discussed in the *Miscellaneous Deductions* chapter. A $2,000 deduction for an IRA contribution would raise the deductions for miscellaneous expenses by $40.

What Kinds of IRA Plans Are Available?

Most financial institutions have set up IRA plans in which you can invest your money. The following is a general discussion of the types of plans being offered by different institutions.

Banks and Savings & Loans

Generally, IRAs run by *banks* or *savings & loans* place your money into a certificate of deposit. Most of these institutions give you a choice of several types of certificates. For example, the choice will often include an 18-month fixed-rate certificate and an 18-month variable-rate certificate. In addition, many institutions offer certificates with a longer term, typically 30-months, which allow you to lock up existing interest rates for a longer period of time.

The interest rate paid on certificates of deposit will usually be pegged to the rate paid by 6-month Treasury bills or other similar standard. The rate on a *fixed-rate certificate* is set at the time of purchase and remains the same during the entire certificate period. The rate on a *variable-rate certificate* is adjusted periodically, usually once a month, based on a formula tied to the going rate on Treasury bills or other standard. Some institutions set a floor below which the interest on a variable-rate certificate cannot fall. This can be a valuable feature if short-term interest rates drop a significant amount.

Each institution is free to set its own interest rate according to any method it chooses and to select which kinds of certificates it will offer. This means that you will have to shop among your local banks and savings institutions if you want to get the best deal. When you inquire about the interest rate being offered, be sure to ask for the **ffective annual yield**. This takes into account the effect of the compounding method used by the institution, e.g. daily, monthly, etc., and therefore is an accurate standard of comparison. Also, be sure to inquire whether money can be added to an existing account and whether there are any fees for opening or maintaining an account.

Many institutions allow you to add funds to an existing IRA account, with the maturity date remaining the same. This is a particularly useful feature because it avoids the unwieldy situation of having numerous different IRA accounts, each with a separate maturity date.

A number of institutions allow additional funds to be added at the original interest rate, regardless of rates being paid on new IRA accounts. This can be a valuable feature if interest rates fall. For example, those who opened an account several years ago when the prevailing rate was 15% could have continued to get this rate on newly deposited funds until the original maturity date. This was much higher than the average rate prevailing during succeeding years.

IRA accounts with a bank or Federal savings & loan are backed by the same Federal Deposit Insurance applying to regular accounts. The minimum amount which can be invested varies among institutions from as little as $1 to as much as $1000 or more. Most banks and savings & loans do not charge a fee to open or maintain an IRA account.

Like regular certificates of deposit, there is generally an interest penalty if funds are withdrawn prior to maturity. However, an institution may waive the penalty if funds are withdrawn early from a certificate of deposit at age $59^{1/2}$ or thereafter or upon death or disability. A majority of institutions (but not all) will make such a waiver as a general policy.

Money-Market and Other Mutual Funds

Nearly every money-market or other mutual fund can be used as an IRA by filling out the appropriate form with the fund's sponsor. You make all investment and other transactions through the mail. The typical minimum investment to open an IRA account with a mutual fund is $500, although some have lower minimums.

There are mutual funds which concentrate in virtually any type of investment, e.g. long-term bonds, growth stocks, money-market instruments, etc.

The following is a list of 4 major primarily no-load mutual fund organizations. Each organization runs a money-market fund, corporate bond fund, stock fund, and other types of funds. There is no sales charge for investing in a *no-load* fund. In contrast, *load-funds* offered by stockbrokers typically assess an initial sales charge of around 8%. You can obtain complete information by writing to the addresses or calling the toll-free telephone numbers listed below.

T. Rowe Price Funds
100 East Pratt Street
Baltimore, MD 21202
800-638-5660
(In MD: 301-547-2308)

Vanguard Investment Group
1300 Morris Drive
Wayne, PA 19087
800-662-7447
(In PA: 800-362-0530)

Fidelity Group
82 Devonshire St.
Boston, MA 02109
800-544-6666
(In MA: 617-523-1919)

Scudder Funds
175 Federal St.
Boston, MA 02110
800-225-2470
(In MA: 617-439-4640)

An annual custodial fee may be charged by a mutual fund for running your IRA. *T. Rowe Price, Vanguard* and *Fidelity* charge $10 per fund per year. *Scudder,* on the other hand, has no custodial fee. However, *Scudder* has a smaller variety of choices of mutual funds.

Each of the above organizations generally allows you to switch all or part of your IRA account from one of their funds into another at any time with no charge. If you choose, you can make the switch by calling a toll-free telephone number which each organization has established for this purpose.

The yields on money-market funds are published each week (on Mondays) in the *Wall Street Journal* and in other newspapers. Curiously, there is no such listing of the current yields on other types of mutual funds. You will have to call the mutual fund's toll-free telephone number to obtain this information.

Stockbrokers

Most stockbrokers offer *self-directed IRA accounts*. These are used like ordinary brokerage accounts to buy stocks, bonds, etc. You can also make more esoteric purchases such as limited partnerships in real estate or oil drilling ventures. You instruct your broker which securities to buy and sell with the money in your account. There are usually fees connected with self-directed IRA accounts. These vary widely from one brokerage house to another, but a typical fee structure might be a one-time

$25 set-up charge plus an annual $25 maintenance charge. (However, at least one discount brokerage house, the nation's largest, charges no set-up or maintenance fees: Charles Schwab & Co.; One Second Street; San Francisco, CA 94105.) In addition, the usual brokerage commissions would apply.

Because of the custodial fees and commission charges, self-directed plans are not suitable for most individuals with less than $5000 in an IRA. Unless they have a particular investment strategy in mind, they are better off with an IRA run by a bank, savings institution, or a no-load mutual fund.

When long-term capital gains were taxed at a lower rate, investing IRA funds in common stock (or other securities) with the aim of producing capital gains was generally not advisable. All stock profits were taxed at the ordinary tax rate, not the lower capital gains rate, when withdrawn from the IRA. But starting in 1988, long-term capital gains are taxed at the same rate as ordinary income. This means that common stock is now a more suitable investment for IRAs.

However, if you plan on holding your stock investments for an extended period of time, the tax-sheltering ability of an IRA is wasted. No tax on capital gains would be due on stock held outside the IRA until the stock is actually sold [cf. Section 1 of the *Investing Your Money* chapter].

In addition to self-directed accounts, many stockbrokers offer IRAs which place money into mutual funds. The custodial fees may be lower for this type of account than for a self-directed account. However, most of the mutual funds used by stock-brokers are *load funds* which impose a sales charge of around 8%. If you want to invest in a mutual fund, you would be better off with a no-load fund offered directly by the sponsoring organization, with no sales fee imposed.

Insurance Companies

Insurance companies offer annuity plans into which you can place your IRA money. Many of these plans offer a choice of several investments including money-market or other mutual funds. Other plans may guarantee a certain rate of return for a short period of time but after that, the rate could drop substantially.

Insurance company IRAs usually have significant fees associated with their use. These fees can include an "up-front" sales charge or a "back-loaded" fee for withdrawing money within 7-10 years after investment. Or, the "fee" could take the form of a lower interest rate or lower payout calculation than would be justified by market conditions or actuarial calculations. Because of the fees which are charged by insurance company IRAs, most individuals will be better off with an IRA run by a bank, savings & loan, or mutual fund.

Gold and Silver Coins

Under prior law, IRA contributions could not be invested in *collectibles* such as art, coins, antiques, stamps, etc. But now, there is one exception for U.S. minted gold and silver coins. These coins can be purchased for an IRA, provided they are held for you by a trustee such as a broker, banker, etc.

If you are planning on holding coins over a long period of time, it may not be worthwhile to hold them as part of your IRA portfolio. Since coins yield no income until they are sold, there is no need to hold them in a tax-deferred plan. On the other hand, if you think you will buy and sell your coins over time, the ability to keep capital gains tax-deferred will be of value.

Switching Funds from One IRA to Another

The IRS allows you to switch your funds from one IRA into another. There are two ways to make such a switch — by direct transfer or by rollover.

A *direct transfer* is accomplished by having the institutions running the IRAs transfer the funds between them. You do not take possession of the funds at any time. There is no limit on the number of direct transfers that can be made during any period of time.

A *rollover* is an investment switch which you make yourself. You withdraw the funds out of your existing IRA account which you then invest in your new IRA. As long as the reinvestment is made within 60 days after receipt of the funds, no tax is paid. (Be sure to properly notify the institution from which you are withdrawing funds that you're planning to make a rollover.) You are limited to one such rollover of an existing IRA account during any 12-month period. You keep and pay tax on any income earned on funds during the period the funds have been removed from the first IRA and not yet rolled into the second IRA.

Partial rollovers of amounts withdrawn from an IRA are permitted. This enables you to defer tax on that portion which is rolled over. The portion withdrawn which is not rolled over is includible in your ordinary income.

Most (but not all) institutions will permit you to switch out of their IRAs at any time. If you want the switch made with dispatch, a rollover may be better than a direct transfer. Institutions often take several months to complete a direct transfer because of delays in processing the paperwork.

There may or may not be a small switchover fee, depending upon the institution. And if your money is invested with a bank in a certificate of deposit, there will usually be a penalty (typically 3 or 6 months loss of interest) if a switch is made before the certificate matures.

You can avoid the bother of making a direct transfer or rollover by investing with a large no-load family of funds. Typically, you will then be allowed to switch between funds just by making a toll-free telephone call whenever you wish. You can also divide up your IRA among several different funds as you choose.

Borrowing from Your IRA

You might need to borrow money for a short time to meet an unexpected emergency. Your IRA can come in handy for this purpose. Even though your IRA cannot make a formal loan to you, the same effect can be obtained by using the rollover privilege.

Under the rollover privilege described above, you can withdraw funds from your IRA anytime you choose. You then have 60 days in which to deposit the funds in a new IRA. This gives you 60 days use of the money to cover a temporary emergency. Of course, the money should be redeposited in an IRA within the 60-day period, otherwise tax (plus 10% penalty if under age $59^{1/2}$) will be triggered on the withdrawn amount. You should deposit the money in a different IRA than the one from which it was withdrawn so it becomes a legitimate rollover. As mentioned above, these funds cannot be rolled out again until 12 months have elapsed since the previous rollout.

What If You're Short of Cash to Fund Your IRA?

You may want to contribute to an IRA for 1987 but are temporarily short of cash to contribute as much as you wish. Here are some ways to get around this difficulty.

1. Borrow from a bank or savings institution

You are permitted to borrow funds to make your IRA contribution. You get a deduction for the IRA contribution and can still deduct part or all of the interest as *investment interest* under the rules described in the *Interest* chapter. Ordinarily, you can't deduct interest on any loan if the proceeds are used directly to make a tax-exempt investment. But the IRS recently ruled that this restriction does not apply to IRAs because the income earned by IRA funds is not strictly *exempt* from tax as with, say, municipal bonds. Eventually, tax does have to be paid on IRA earnings when money is withdrawn at some later date [IRS Private Letter Ruling 8527082]. It is best to borrow from a different institution than the one with which your account is established so the IRS can't construe that you're using your IRA as collateral for the loan.

2. "Borrow" from an existing IRA

As discussed in the previous subsection, you can "borrow" from an existing IRA for a period of 60 days or less. If you are short of funds, you can use this 60-day turnover period to pay this year's IRA contribution out of an existing IRA account from a previous year. For example, suppose you file a tax return on March 15, 1988 showing that you're due a refund of $1,000. Let's say you listed a $1,000 IRA deduction on the tax return but didn't have the money to make the contribution (which is due by April 15).

On April 10, you roll $1,000 out of an existing IRA and deposit it in your checking account. You then write a $1,000 check to open a new IRA for the 1987 tax year. When you receive your $1,000 tax refund, you can write a $1,000 check to your new IRA which is regarded as completing the rollover started on April 10.

The period from March 15 to 60 days after April 10 (when the rollover must be completed) is sufficient time to receive your refund unless there is a foul-up. However, since the rollover needs to be completed within 60 days, you might want to have a backup source of emergency funds to avoid the situation of making a premature withdrawal should your refund be inordinately delayed.

3. Contribute your tax refund to your IRA

You must make your IRA contribution by April 15, 1988 in order for it to be deductible on your 1987 tax return. However, you may take the deduction on your 1987 tax return even if you have not yet contributed to or even opened your IRA account. As long as your contribution is eventually made by the April 15 deadline, you're allright.

For example, suppose you want to make a $2,000 deductible contribution to your 1987 IRA but only have $1,200 on hand. Let's say you fill out your tax return by February 10, 1988 which shows a large refund due to you. In this situation, you can do the following:

Contribute the $1,200 to your IRA, but claim a $2,000 IRA deduction on your tax return. Then mail in your tax return promptly. Since the IRS usually sends refunds within 6-8 weeks, you should receive your refund before April 15, 1988. You then contribute the remaining $800 to your IRA out of the refund money you receive from the IRS.

This procedure has been officially approved by the IRS. Your IRA account does not even have to be opened at the time you mail in your tax return. As long as you eventually contribute by April 15, 1988 the amount claimed on your 1987 tax return, your deduction is proper. [Rev. Rul. 84-18]

However, if April 15, 1988 rolls around and you don't have enough money to make the contribution claimed on your 1987 tax return, you'll have to file an amended tax return. This is done by filling out Form 1040X [cf. Chapter 1, Section 1] on which you report the actual IRA contribution made and recompute your taxes with this new lower figure as your IRA deduction instead of the old one. You should enclose a check for the extra tax due when you mail in your Form 1040X to the IRS.

Why Two IRAs Can Be Better than One

There are several reasons why an individual might want to have his money split into two (or more) IRAs instead of one.

One consideration is the ability to use your IRA as a short-term source of money as described earlier in this Section. With one IRA, you can borrow money in this manner only once in any 12-month period. But, under regulations proposed by the IRS, each IRA is considered separately for purposes of this 12-month rule. For example, suppose you have two IRAs, IRA 1 and IRA 2. If you roll over IRA 1 into a new IRA 3, you cannot withdraw this money until 12 months have elapsed. But this does not restrict withdrawals from IRA 2. You can use the rollover privilege to withdraw funds from IRA 2 without regard to the rollover of funds from IRA 1. In effect, you have had the use of IRA money for two 60-day periods instead of one.

If you contemplate an IRA as a backup source of emergency cash, you might want to have 2 IRAs for a different reason. You would want one IRA in a liquid investment such as a mutual fund required to disburse funds upon request with no penalty. The remainder of your money could be placed in a less liquid investment such as a bank C.D. requiring an interest penalty on premature withdrawals.

Finally, of course, is investment diversification. Spreading money out in different investments is typically recommended to lessen market risk. This benefit alone, however, may not be sufficient to outweigh the extra bother of maintaining more than one account, especially if the amounts are small relative to your overall financial picture.

Placing a Spouse on the Payroll

In some cases, it pays to "put a spouse on the payroll" in order to obtain the maximum $4,000 IRA deduction for married couples. This might be possible, for example, for those with an outside business activity in which the spouse could be of assistance. This is discussed more fully in the *Outside Business Activity* chapter.

Choosing a Beneficiary

When you set up your IRA, you will be asked to choose a beneficiary in case you die before all funds are distributed to you. Several years ago, Congress altered the tax consequences of such a choice. Formerly, only if the beneficiary were a spouse could the funds remain in a tax-sheltered IRA. Other beneficiaries had to draw out all the funds within 5 years, paying tax upon withdrawal.

But now, tax-sheltering can continue over the life of a non-spouse beneficiary. In fact, some individuals will want to change their beneficiary from a spouse to a child to take advantage of the new rules. The rules are as follows:

(1) Starting within one year of death, annual payments can begin to the beneficiary based on his life expectancy. For example, a beneficiary with a life expectancy of 60 years would receive at least 1/60 of the value of the IRA the first year, 1/59 (approximately) the second, etc. The remaining funds continue to earn tax-free income in the IRA.

(2) If payments do not begin within one year, the entire balance must be distributed to the beneficiary within 5 years after death. However, if the beneficiary is a spouse, payments do not have to begin until April 1 of the year following the year in which the deceased would have reached age $70^{1}/_{2}$ and they can be spread out over the life of the spouse.

(3) In any event, income tax is due on any payments received by beneficiaries from the IRA.

According to (1) above, naming a young child as beneficiary allows the IRA to continue sheltering funds from tax for a long period of time. But under (2) above, naming a spouse as beneficiary means distributions need not begin until a later time. Which option has a stronger tax-savings effect depends upon the ages of the various people involved.

The above only refers to the *income tax* consequence of inherited IRAs, not to the *estate tax* consequence. If your estate will be large enough to fall under the estate tax rules [cf. the *Estate Tax* chapter], professional estate planning should be sought to minimize that tax also.

Rolling Over a Pension Plan Distribution into an IRA

Let us say you leave your current job at which you have been working for a number of years. If you have been participating in a retirement plan, then a certain portion, perhaps all, of your employer's contributions to this plan will have become **vested**. This means that these amounts now belong to you and do not revert back to your employer when you change jobs. If you elect to receive these amounts plus investment income thereon when you leave the job, then you must pay tax on such amounts at that time. The special averaging rule and capital gains treatment [cf. Section 2 of the *Retirement Plans* chapter] lessen this tax burden substantially but your money is no longer sheltered. Any future investment income is subject to tax.

The *rollover* provision of the IRA legislation allows you to avoid the above situation. If a lump-sum distribution [cf. Section 2 of the *Retirement Plans* chapter] of the money in your retirement plan is received after leaving your job (including death or disability) or after reaching age $59^{1}/_{2}$, then this sum or a portion of this sum can be transferred into an IRA. (Employee contributions on which you have paid tax are excluded as are *minimum distribution amounts* that must be made if you are over age 70 1/2 when the distribution is made.) You should complete the rollover within 60 days and should inform the institution with which you set up the IRA that you're making a lump-sum rollover.

You can divide the rolled over funds among 2 or more IRAs if you choose. The money and all investment income on this money then continues to be exempt from tax until withdrawn from the IRA according to the regular rules. However, the averaging rule and capital gains treatment will no longer apply. If you roll over only part of the distribution into an IRA, the remainder (less employee contributions on which you have already paid tax) is taxed in the year of receipt and is not eligible for the averaging rule and capital gains treatment.

If you receive a lump-sum distribution from a tax-sheltered annuity after leaving your job or after you are age 59 1/2, then you can similarly roll over all or a portion of this distribution into an IRA [cf. Section 3 for further details].

If you have rolled over a retirement distribution into an IRA, you can place part or all of this IRA into the retirement plan of a new employer, if he permits it. If this is done, the special averaging rule and capital gains treatment will become applicable again. Similarly, tax-sheltered annuity distributions rolled over into an IRA can be rolled back into a tax-sheltered annuity plan provided by a new employer.

At one time, the rollover privilege applied only if a 100% distribution was received either of all the vested amounts in your pension plan or of the amounts in your tax-sheltered annuities. You need not have placed the entire distribution into an IRA, but you must have received a complete distribution to begin with. But now, distributions of 50% or more made on account of an employee's separation from service or because of the employee's death or disability generally qualify for the rollover privilege. However, if all amounts are not distributed, future distributions from the same plan (or similar plans maintained by the same employer) are disqualified from the special averaging rule or capital gains treatment. Also, amounts from a partial distribution which are rolled over into an IRA cannot be rolled tax-free back into a new retirement plan or tax-sheltered annuity.

The rules for partial distributions are more strict than total distributions. A partial distribution qualifies for tax-free rollover only if it is paid on account of the employee's leaving his job (including death or disability). In contrast, total distributions can qualify for tax-free rollover if the employee is over age 59 1/2, even if he does not leave his job. Also note that if an employer maintains several retirement plans of similar type, these may have to be aggregated (i.e. considered to be one plan) when determining if the 50% requirement in the previous paragraph is satisfied.

Lump-sum distributions are subject to withholding unless you elect otherwise by filling out an appropriate form your employer will provide. If you are planning to roll over a distribution into an IRA, you should elect to avoid this withholding.

You should place rolled-over funds into separate IRAs distinct from any other IRAs which you may use. Otherwise, you may lose the right to roll back the funds into a new employer's retirement plan. Tax-free rollovers of lump-sum distributions are made by receiving funds and placing them into an IRA within 60 days of receipt.

Spouses of employees may also benefit from rollover IRAs. If an employee dies and his spouse receives a lump-sum retirement fund distribution, all or part of this distribution can be placed into an IRA and continue to grow tax-sheltered.

Note that the contribution limits do not apply to IRA rollover contributions nor do the active participant or earnings tests (Condition A and B) discussed at the beginning of this section. Any amount may be rolled over without paying tax. However, you cannot include your own non-deductible contributions which you made to your retirement plan. These amounts must be subtracted from the total distribution before being transferred to the IRA. Of course, no tax is due on the return of your own contributions to you since you have already paid tax on these amounts when they were earned [cf. the *Retirement Plans* chapter].

Before deciding to use the rollover feature of an IRA, be sure to examine whether or not the loss of the special averaging rule and capital gains treatment will make such use unwise. However, the ability to continue a tax-free shelter for a number of years often outweighs the loss of the averaging rule and capital gains treatment.

Of course, if a new employer will accept the distribution into his retirement plan, then the rollover feature probably should be used. Or, if you are eligible to set up a Keogh Plan [cf. Section 3], then you may be able to transfer the lump-sum distribution to your Keogh Plan. This would continue the tax-sheltering of the distribution and preserve your ability to use the special averaging rule and capital gains treatment [IRS Private Letter Ruling 8547075]. Similarly, if your original employer allows you to leave your money in his plan even though you terminate employment, then this may be the best arrangement of all. This is especially true because your own contributions to the plan remain tax-sheltered.

However, there are cases when people will prefer to have their money in an IRA rather than a regular retirement plan. The flexibility of being able to make premature withdrawals (although subject to a 10% penalty tax), the ability to choose your own investment vehicle, and the ability to precisely determine the payout rate during retirement may create such cases.

Due to the complexity of the rules, professional advice should be sought before making any lump-sum distribution decisions.

SECTION 3:
KEOGH PLANS

A Keogh Plan (named after a congressman) is a tax-sheltered retirement plan which can be used to shelter self-employment income from tax. Self-employment income includes earnings resulting from personal services which are not employee wages (i.e. the type from which social security is withheld).

This might include income from consulting, royalties from writing a book, fees for editing or reviewing, sales from an invention, income from tutoring, honorariums for lecturing, commissions from real estate sales, director's fees, or any other income earned from a side business or as a private contractor. Sometimes an employee can rearrange his agreement with a current employer so as to become a self-employed private contractor. Self-employment income does not include investment income such as interest and dividends.

Each year, you can contribute a certain portion of your self-employment income into your Keogh Plan. These contributed amounts are not taxed in the year of contribution. You get this benefit even if you claim the standard deduction. Furthermore, no tax is paid on the investment income as it is earned by the amounts you contribute. Only when money is withdrawn from the Keogh Plan is any tax paid.

Note that you do not have to specifically withhold your contributions from the earnings you receive. You can contribute any funds you have to a Keogh Plan within the maximum limitations described below. For example, you can make a contribution by taking money out of a savings account and placing it in your Keogh Plan. You still get a tax deduction for the amount shifted to the Keogh Plan and furthermore, your savings are now shielded by the umbrella of a tax-sheltered plan.

The same types of plans can be set up for a Keogh Plan as for an IRA as discussed in Section 2. The chief differences between Keogh Plans and IRAs are the eligibility requirements and contribution limitations. In addition, there is a special averaging rule that applies to lower the tax on lump-sum distributions from Keogh Plans, but not from IRAs. Also, if your self-employment activity requires you to hire other employees who work either more hours than you or at least one thousand hours per year, you may have to make contributions to your Keogh Plan on their behalf.

How Much Can Be Contributed?

You can contribute up to 20% of your earned self-employment income up to a maximum contribution of $30,000. For example, if your 1987 self-employment income is $10,000, you can contribute 20% × $10,000 = $2,000. The 20% figure applies to your **net** self-employment earnings. That is, you must subtract business expenses from income before multiplying by 20%.

The above limits apply to regular Keogh Plans. There is a special type of plan, called a *Defined-Benefit Keogh Plan*, to which far more can be contributed—in many cases, **up to 100% of a person's net self-employment earnings.** This type of plan is discussed later in this section.

The above limitations are maximum levels of contribution. You may contribute any amount not exceeding these maximums. Furthermore, you do not have to be consistent from year to year. You might contribute the maximum one year and nothing the next. If your Keogh Plan has been established by December 31, you have until April 15 of the following year to make contributions. If you obtain an extension of time to file your tax return [cf. Chapter 1], you have until the extended due date to make a contribution. Of course, the earlier you make a contribution, the sooner your funds are put to work earning tax-free income.

Those with incomes in 1987 from both a regular job and an outside business activity should apportion their expenses judiciously if they want to make full use of the Keogh Plan limitations. Swing items, such as professional books, may best be taken as a miscellaneous employee deduction connected with the regular job rather than as a business expense against self-employment income. (This assumes that the 2% of AGI floor discussed in the *Miscellaneous Deductions* chapter has already been exceeded.) This will keep net self-employment income as high as possible, maximizing the contributions that can be made to a Keogh Plan. (However, if extra social security tax is triggered by an increase in self-employment income, this may not be the best strategy. This would happen if total earnings do not exceed the social security wage base, $43,800 in 1987.)

What if You Missed the December 31 Deadline?

If you missed the December 31, 1987 deadline for opening a Keogh Plan to shelter your 1987 earnings, all is not lost. There is another type of plan, called a SEP (Simplified Employee Pension) which is similar to a Keogh Plan but which can be opened up until April 15, 1988. SEPs were designed to be simplified pension systems for small businesses with more than one employee but can be used by individual self-employed persons as well. Ordinarily, a Keogh Plan is preferable to a SEP because the contribution limitations are more generous and the lump-sum averaging privilege applies. However, in the case where the Keogh Plan deadline is missed, a SEP can be the remedy. Most banks, mutual funds, etc. can set up a SEP for you upon request.

How Is a Regular Keogh Plan Established?

The simplest procedure is to choose a mutual fund, bank, or savings institution of your choice. They will have the appropriate forms you need to establish your plan. All investment income will then be automatically reinvested in the mutual fund, savings account, etc. Insurance companies also sell plans which combine investment features with insurance features.

When you set up your Keogh Plan, you will probably be asked to specify what percentage of self-employment income you wish to contribute. If in a later year, you wish to change the percentage, you can make a simple "amendment," specifying the new percentage. However, if you do not want to contribute more than 13% of your self-employment income, you can set up your Keogh Plan as a *profit-sharing* plan. Profit-sharing plans let you contribute any amount you wish each year within the legal limits, without specifying a particular percentage.

Keogh Plans set up with banks or savings institutions generally invest money in higher-paying certificates of deposit rather than in passbook accounts. With most institutions, the waiting period before such certificates can be cashed in does not apply when money is withdrawn after an individual is age 59 1/2 or over.

Individuals should shop around before choosing a Keogh Plan. There are even differences between plans set up with savings institutions or banks. Some require an annual service charge while others do not. And the top interest rate can vary depending upon the manner in which the interest is compounded. According to the IRS, you can have your Keogh Plan funds transferred from one institution to another without incurring any tax penalty.

It is also possible to set up a Keogh Plan in such a way that you control the investment of the funds. One way to maintain indirect control is to set up a *self-directed* Keogh Plan with a bank or stock broker. The bank or stock broker acts as custodian and agrees to invest the funds as you direct. You can deduct any custodial fees you pay as a separate business expense in addition to the actual contributions to the plan which you make.

You must file a special report form each year with the IRS giving information on your Keogh Plan. This form must be filed by July 31, 1988 for the calendar year 1987. (A 2½ month extension may be filed if needed.) For one-person plans, Form 5500-EZ is generally the one you will use. The institution running your Keogh Plan can give you the appropriate information for filing the right form for the calendar year 1987.

Defined-Benefit Keogh Plans

Because of a change in the law a few years ago, a tremendous new opportunity has become available to those with self-employment income. Instead of being bound by the limitations on a regular Keogh Plan as described above, they can set up a more generous *Defined-Benefit Keogh Plan*.

Defined-Benefit Keogh Plans, in their present form, came into being in 1984 after a new "pension parity" law went into effect. Congress decided that persons with self-employment income should be placed on a par with individuals operating under the shell of a corporation (e.g. physicians who list the initials P.A. or P.C. after their name). Because the laws for corporations allow for the funding of such generous pensions, those with even a modest amount of self-employment income have now been handed this big tax break.

Defined-Benefit Keogh Plans work like other tax-sheltered plans, e.g. IRAs, tax-sheltered annuities, or regular Keogh Plans. You get a full deduction on your tax return for any contributions made to your Plan. And the money in your Plan is invested, with all interest, dividends, etc. compounding entirely exempt from tax until withdrawn from the Plan. Also, the same special averaging break that applies to lump sum distributions from regular Keogh Plans applies to Defined-Benefit Keogh Plans as well.

The chief advantage of Defined-Benefit Keogh Plans is that far more can be contributed (and deducted) than to a regular Keogh Plan. The exact amount is based on a person's age, sex, marital status, and self-employment earnings. (As with regular Keogh Plans, *self-employment earnings* here means *net self-employment earnings* after related business expenses have been subtracted.) As an illustration, here's a rough estimate of the maximum contribution range for a married man if the plan is set up the right way:

Age	Maximum Deductible Contributions as a Percentage of Self-Employment Earnings
40	40% - 70%
45	50% - 75%
50	55% - 100%
55	55% - 100%

A history of prior self-employment earnings will place the maximum allowable contribution in the upper end of the range in the table above, in many cases 100% of self-employment earnings. For example, suppose a 50-year old married man anticipates self-employment earnings during 1988 of $10,000. Let's say he had self-employment earnings during each of 1985-1987 which averaged $4,000 or more. In such a case, he could generally contribute (and deduct) any amount up to 100% of these earnings, namely $10,000.

Note that under a regular Keogh Plan, the above individual would be limited to a contribution of only 20% × $10,000 = $2,000. Thus, the Defined-Benefit Keogh Plan in this case permits a deduction of 5 times as much as a regular Keogh Plan.

A person with no self-employment earnings prior to 1988 might be restricted to the lower percentage figure in the table for his age. However, this percentage can be boosted—perhaps up to 100%—if the person "employs his spouse" in the business activity. Any legitimate employee activity will do, e.g. clerical work, typing, answering business calls, etc., as long as wages are actually paid to the spouse. Because of a special provision in the law for employees, even a small wage paid to a spouse can dramatically increase the percentage of earnings that can be contributed to the Plan.

Employing a spouse to perform some business activities can have another beneficial effect. This might enable you to set up a plan to pay all medical and dental expenses of your employee-spouse and family (including yourself). In this way, you get a full medical deduction for your family's medical expenses, with no initial 7.5% of adjusted gross income subtraction. [Cf. the *Outside Business Activity* chapter for further details.]

The figures in the above table represent the **maximum amounts** that can be contributed. With a properly structured plan, you have the option of making any contribution amount you choose as long as it doesn't exceed the maximum allowable. Each succeeding year, you can contribute any portion of your self-employment income you choose that year, as long as the maximum contribution level is not exceeded. If there are contributions to a tax-sheltered annuity or other Keogh Plan, these may, in certain circumstances, lower the contributions you are permitted to make to your Defined-Benefit Keogh Plan.

An important extra benefit is that you can serve as manager of your Defined-Benefit Keogh Plan, in complete charge of all the money in your Plan. You directly control the investments in and disbursements from the Plan. On the other hand, you may prefer to delegate investment responsibility to a professional investment advisor, stock broker, etc. The choice depends upon you.

To take advantage of a Defined-Benefit Keogh Plan to shelter 1988 earnings, you must set up your Plan before the end of 1988. (However, the earlier in the year you set up such a Plan, the better.) These Plans are more complicated to set up and run than regular Keogh Plans because an actuary must be involved in making the appropriate calculations and sending in the appropriate certification forms each year to the IRS. Fees for such services are tax deductible as a business expense.

How Do You Set Up a Defined-Benefit Keogh Plan?

To get further information on how to set up a Defined-Benefit Keogh Plan, write to *Academic Information Service, Inc.* at the address on the back cover of this book with the envelope marked *Attention: David Harry*. This information will include the name of an actuarial firm to whom we have referred many readers of previous editions of this Tax Guide with favorable results. If you wish, this firm can handle all the details of setting up and maintaining your Plan.

When May Funds Be Withdrawn?

You may start withdrawing money from your Keogh Plan anytime after the age of $59^{1}/_{2}$. However, you must begin withdrawing money by April 1 of the year following the year in which you reach age $70^{1}/_{2}$. It is possible to contribute to a Keogh Plan after age $70^{1}/_{2}$ even though, as required, you are withdrawing funds at the same time.

If you withdraw any funds prior to age $59^{1}/_{2}$, then such funds are taxed along with your other income that year. In addition, an extra 10% tax is imposed on the amount of the early withdrawal, except in the case of death or disability. The 10% penalty tax will be waived if either (i) the withdrawal is used to pay medical expenses in excess of 7.5% of your adjusted gross income, (ii) the distribution is made after you stopped working and is part of a series of substantially equal periodic payments intended to extend over your lifetime or the joint lives of you and your spouse, or (iii) you have retired after reaching age 55 under an early retirement provision in your plan. As a general rule of thumb, even if you have to pay the extra 10% tax prior to age $59^{1}/_{2}$, the tax advantage of sheltering your savings under a Keogh Plan puts you ahead if the funds withdrawn were in the Plan for 7 years or more.

How Are the Proceeds of Your Keogh Plan Taxed?

You can take your money out of a Keogh Plan in the form of a lump-sum distribution. Lump-sum settlements can receive favorable tax treatment provided that you have been a plan participant for at least 5 tax years before the tax year of the distribution.

This favorable tax treatment is provided by a special averaging rule that applies to most or all of the lump-sum distribution. For example, this rule applied to $100,000 of distribution yields a tax rate of about 15%. Furthermore, the tax rate is totally independent of your other taxable income. This averaging rule is described in Section 2 of the *Retirement Plans* chapter.

Except in the case of death or disability, you can use the averaging rule for a Keogh Plan you maintain only after reaching age $59^{1}/_{2}$ and then can use it only once. If you withdraw any money from your Keogh Plan prior to age $59^{1}/_{2}$, this might destroy your right to use averaging at a later time when you otherwise would qualify [IRS Private Letter Ruling 7726047]. Also, if you have made contributions to a Keogh Plan prior to 1974, special capital gains rules may apply when the amounts are included in a lump-sum distribution [cf. the *Retirement Plans* chapter].

You do not need to take a lump-sum settlement. It is often advantageous to elect to receive the distribution over one of the following periods:

(a) your lifetime
(b) the joint lifetime of you and your spouse
(c) a period not extending beyond your life expectancy

or

(d) a period not extending beyond the joint life expectancies of you and your spouse.

The advantage of receiving the distribution over an extended period of time, say the joint life expectancy of you and your spouse, is that the balance of the funds

remains in the Plan, compounding investment income entirely free from tax. The distributions you take out from the Plan this way are taxed as ordinary income.

Can You Combine a Keogh Plan with Other Plans?

Yes. You can contribute to a Keogh Plan even if you participate in some other type of retirement plan, IRA, or tax-sheltered annuity. Of course, your contributions to the Keogh Plan are based only on your self-employment income. And your combined contributions to an IRA and a Keogh Plan cannot exceed your earned income.

Comparing Keogh Plans with IRAs

If an individual with self-employment income does not wish to contribute the maximum amounts to both a regular individual Keogh Plan and an IRA, he will have to make a choice. Which is better? Operationally, there is little difference—the usual investment choices can be made with either type of plan. And the requirement to begin distributions between age $59\frac{1}{2}$ and $70\frac{1}{2}$ applies to both types of plans. However, there is one distinguishing feature, namely the special lump-sum averaging rule described above. This feature applies to Keogh Plans but not to IRAs. Because of this, a Keogh Plan is generally preferable to an IRA. (Of course, a Keogh Plan is much preferable to an IRA if contributors to the IRA are non-deductible, as discussed in Section 2.)

Where Do You Deduct Payments to Your Keogh Plan?

Payments on your behalf to your Keogh Plan are deducted on line 26 as an *Adjustment to Income*. Contributions made on behalf of any employees covered under your Keogh Plan are deducted on line 21 of Schedule C.

SECTION 4:
TAX-SHELTERED ANNUITIES

A *Tax-Sheltered Annuity* is a special type of plan available only to employees of educational institutions and certain other non-profit organizations. Most of these institutions maintain a list of one or more of these plans which are available to their employees. All employees are eligible to participate including principals, librarians, clerical help, etc.

Employees of State or local departments of education are also eligible unless they are holding a public office such as a trustee or board of education member. For example, the IRS recently ruled that an electrical engineer qualified for a tax-sheltered annuity because he worked for a State Department of Education. [IRS Private Letter Ruling 8137067]

The actual rule is that only an employer's contribution to such a plan is not taxable. However, the usual policy is to permit an employee to reduce his current or next year's salary by an amount equal to that being contributed to the annuity plan. Thus the employer incurs no cost but the employee may still take advantage of the tax-saving feature of the plan.

For example, suppose a teacher's annual salary is $30,000 and he wishes to contribute $1,000 toward the purchase of an annuity. He would agree with his school to take a reduction of $1,000 in his salary. His annual salary would then officially be $29,000 and his school would contribute $1,000 toward the purchase of an annuity. The teacher would pay tax based on his $29,000 salary but not on the amount contributed to his annuity until he retired and started receiving annuity payments.

Note that an institution may have a regular retirement plan and still provide their employees the opportunity to participate in tax-sheltered annuities.

In order to get a tax break for contributions to a tax-sheltered annuity, the appropriate *reduction-in-salary* agreement must be signed in advance. Failure to sign the appropriate form can ruin the entire arrangement. This was learned the hard way by a New Jersey teacher in a recent court case.

The teacher authorized her employer to withhold part of her salary and place it into a tax-sheltered annuity. But she failed to sign the appropriate reduction-in-salary agreement. This meant that the contributions to the annuity plan were not technically made from her employer's funds, but rather from her funds. The court was sympathetic but ruled against the teacher as a matter of law. As the written court opinion stated,

> *"The Court recognizes that the myriad of statutory and administrative provisions may be confusing. Nevertheless, plaintiff did not comply with the base provision that the contributions be made 'by' the employer."* [Bollotin vs U.S., 38 AFTR 2nd 76-5712]

Withdrawals from Tax-Sheltered Annuities

Previous law did not require there to be any restrictions on when you were first allowed to withdraw funds from a tax-sheltered annuity. However, starting in 1987, an extra 10% penalty tax applies to withdrawals made from a tax-sheltered annuity prior to the date an individual reaches age 59 1/2, dies, or becomes disabled. The 10% penalty tax will be waived if either (i) the withdrawal is used to pay medical expenses in excess of 7.5% of adjusted gross income, (ii) the individual has retired from his job after reaching age 55, or (iii) the distribution is part of a series of substantially equal period payments intended to extend over the life of the employee or the joint lives of the employee and a beneficiary.

The exception in (iii) can be used to withdraw amounts before age 59 1/2 and escape the 10% penalty tax. For example, an individual could begin receiving his annuity payments at age 50. As long as the distribution method provides for substantially equal lifetime payments as described in (iii), the 10% penalty tax does not apply.

Furthermore, the individual can alter the distribution agreement after reaching age 59 1/2 as long as no change is made in the first 5 years other than by reason of death or disability. For example, an individual can start receiving payments at age 50 and alter or stop the payments after reaching age 59 1/2. Or, he could start receiving payments at age 57, continuing for 5 years until he reached 62. In either case, the 10% penalty tax is waived. (However, observe the rules below for years after 1988 under which the ability to receive distributions prior to age 59 1/2 is restricted.)

Also exempted from the extra 10% penalty tax are cashouts not requiring the employee's consent of amounts up to $3,500. And there is another exception from the 10% penalty tax for individuals who, as of March 1, 1986, had separated from service and elected to start receiving a scheduled series of specified benefit payments.

There is also a mandatory distribution rule that applies to benefits accruing in 1987 or later years. Distribution of such benefits must start by April 1 of the year following the year in which you reach age 70$^1/_2$. (However, those who reach age 70$^1/_2$ before 1988 may continue to defer the receipt of benefits until actual retirement, if they wish.) This mandatory distribution rule does not apply to benefits accrued before 1987. (However, there may be a mandatory distribution requirement imposed by the tax-sheltered annuity plan to which you have contributed.)

Starting in 1989, there will be a new restriction on the ability to withdraw funds from a tax-sheltered annuity, with or without the 10% penalty. Specifically, starting in 1989, withdrawals from tax-sheltered annuities of amounts attributable to contributions made under a reduction-in-salary agreement can be made only after an employee leaves his job, attains age 59$^1/_2$, becomes disabled, dies, or encounters *financial hardship*. Hardship withdrawals will be restricted to contributions invested in the annuity under a reduction-in-salary agreement, excluding any earnings earned by the investments. An employee will be considered to encounter a *financial hardship* only to the extent he has *"an immediate and heavy bona fide financial need and does not have other resources reasonably available to satisfy the need."*

1988 is Last Chance to Withdraw Funds Early from Tax-Sheltered Annuities

Observe carefully the impact of the rule change described in the preceding paragraph. If you wish to withdraw funds from a tax-sheltered annuity prior to age 59$^1/_2$, in most cases you will have to do so by December 31, 1988. Starting in 1989, such early withdrawals will be forbidden, except in the case of separation from service, financial hardship, death, or disability. Of course as described above, a 10% penalty tax can apply to early withdrawals made in 1987 or 1988. But this penalty tax may be worth paying for some individuals who wish to avoid having their tax-sheltered annuity funds locked up until age 59$^1/_2$.

What Types of Tax-Sheltered Annuity Plans Are Available?

Many different types of plans exist. Most eligible non-profit institutions select several different plans which they make available to their employees. Some of them provide investment in fixed income securities such as bonds, and others provide investment in common stocks as well. Some plans require that you wait until retirement whereupon the amount accumulated in your account is used to purchase an annuity. Others allow you to withdraw the cash value of your account at any time you wish. This latter feature is attractive for those who wish to put aside money to be received in an otherwise low income year.

To get further information on the plans available to you, contact the personnel office where you work. They will have a list of those plans in which you can participate and either provide you with descriptive brochures or give you the addresses of where to write for these brochures. Be sure to obtain and read these brochures carefully. Different plans have different combinations of features. You will want to select the plan which best meets your own personal objectives.

Some institutions allow their employees to choose any commercially available plan. In this case, a way to get a sampling of available plans would be to contact a few of the large mutual fund organizations [cf. Section 2 for addresses and toll-free telephone numbers], write to TIAA/CREF [cf. the discussion later in this section], and check with some major insurance companies.

When selecting which tax-sheltered annuity plan to invest in, be sure to examine the options available for the withdrawal of funds. Some plans allow more withdrawal opportunities than others. And some plans provide for a fixed annuity payout after retirement while others gear the payout to the performance of stocks or other securities in their portfolio. Also, different options may be offered governing the period during which payments are made, as well as different survivorship options under which payments continue to a beneficiary after the death of the individual.

It is possible to have your funds in one tax-sheltered annuity plan shifted to another plan with no tax consequence, provided the two plans permit such a shift. The IRS prefers you *"immediately surrender the proceeds of the first plan pursuant to a binding agreement you have previously signed to turn over the funds to the second plan."* [Rev. Rul. 73-124, 1973-1 C.B. 200; IRS Private Letter Rulings 8322101, 8628053, 8628058]

However, according to a recent court case, it may not be mandatory to make a binding agreement in advance to purchase the second annuity. In this case, a teacher received a check closing out her existing annuity and, a few days later, filled out the application for the new annuity accompanied by the close-out check which she endorsed over to the new annuity company. Despite IRS objection, the Court ruled this to be a valid tax-free shift even though she had previously not made a binding agreement. [Greene, 85 TC #9]

Choosing a Beneficiary

When you set up a tax-sheltered annuity, you will be asked to name a beneficiary in case you die before funds are distributed to you. The tax rules are the same as for beneficiaries of an IRA. Under existing rules, naming a child rather than a spouse as a beneficiary can save on taxes in some situations [cf. Section 2 of this chapter].

Rolling Over Your Tax-Sheltered Annuity into an IRA

There is one further option which some plans may provide, namely the right to receive the funds credited to an individual's account in a lump sum payment. Due to a little known provision in the law, this could be the most beneficial option of all. Here's why.

Lump-sum distributions from tax-sheltered annuities can now be rolled over into an Individual Retirement Account (IRA). This is a special type of account set up with a mutual fund, savings institution, or brokerage house. The funds placed into an IRA continue to earn income entirely free from tax. Only when funds are withdrawn is income tax paid.

The rollover privilege for tax-sheltered annuities is basically the same as for pension plans discussed in Section 2 of this chapter. It applies to lump-sum distributions received after leaving your current employer, or after you are age $59 1/2$. It also generally applies to a partial distribution, received upon leaving your job, of at least 50% of the total amounts credited to your account in tax-sheltered annuities with your employer.

There are several requirements that must be met for a lump-sum distribution from a tax-sheltered annuity to qualify for rollover into an IRA. Check with your employer for the exact rules that apply. [Also see Section 2 of this chapter.] Note that in particular, the payouts constituting the distribution must be made within the same calendar year and the rollover made within 60 days after the final payout.

The advantage of an IRA over an annuity is in the flexibility and individual control it provides. Your funds can be placed into virtually any type of investment you choose. Often, funds can earn a higher interest rate than would be credited to your account under a fixed annuity arrangement. And you can switch your funds from one type of investment to another as your goals change.

Finally, you can control the payout of funds from an IRA. Each year, you can withdraw any portion of the funds you choose. Or, you can leave the funds alone and let the tax-free income build up, subject to the following restrictions: (i) Funds withdrawn prior to age $59 1/2$ are subject to a 10% penalty tax in addition to the regular income tax, and (ii) You must start withdrawing funds no later than April 1 of the year following the year in which you reach age $70 1/2$, with the rate of withdrawal high enough that the funds would be entirely paid out based on life expectancies. [Cf. Section 2 for further information on IRAs.]

TIAA/CREF Supplemental Retirement Annuities

A Supplemental Retirement Annuity (abbreviated SRA) is a type of tax-sheltered annuity run by TIAA/CREF (Teachers Insurance and Annuity Association/College Retirement Equities Fund, a pair of non-profit foundations; address: 730 Third Avenue, New York, NY 10017). SRAs are attractive because of the relatively low fees charged by TIAA/CREF and because of the liberal provisions which allow money to be withdrawn. Note that your institution does **not** have to be part of the TIAA/CREF regular retirement program in order for you to purchase an SRA.

Funds placed into an SRA are invested the same way as funds under the regular TIAA/CREF retirement programs as described in the *Retirement Plans* chapter. That is, you choose which fraction of your contributions are to be invested with TIAA and which fraction with CREF. TIAA funds are invested primarily in fixed-income securities such as bonds while CREF funds are invested in the stock market. SRAs are offered as Tax-Sheltered Annuities by many colleges, universities and non-profit organizations, even if the regular retirement program is not run by TIAA/CREF.

The difference between money placed into an SRA and money placed into the regular TIAA/CREF retirement program is that funds may be withdrawn from an SRA before retirement. (However, as discussed earlier, a 10% penalty tax now general applies to withdrawals from tax-sheltered annuities made before reaching age $59 1/2$. Also, starting in 1989, new withdrawal restrictions will generally prohibit withdrawals before reaching age $59 1/2$ or leaving your job.) At any time you choose (before 1989), you may withdraw all the funds, with accumulated interest, that are in your SRA. You do not have to terminate your employment to make such a withdrawal. The amount may be received in a lump-sum payment or used to purchase an annuity from which you receive periodic payments. There are a number of options concerning how you wish periodic payments to be made. For example, payments can run through your lifetime, or you may have payments continue to a spouse after your death. Or, payments may continue for only a fixed number (between 2 and 10) of years. You pay ordinary income tax on any amounts received if the original contributions were made under a reduction-in-salary or other tax-free basis.

You may make a partial withdrawal as long as the amount withdrawn is at least $1,000 and no other partial withdrawal has been made from the same contract in the preceding six months.

At any time before annuity income begins, you can make a full or partial transfer of funds accumulated in your CREF account into TIAA, but not conversely. The transfer to TIAA is of particular interest to those nearing retirement because annuity payments will be regular, not dependent upon the ups and downs of the stock market as would be the case with funds left in CREF.

A one-time 1.5% fee is levied against amounts placed into an SRA. In addition, an annual amount of about $1/4$ of 1% of total assets is taken out to cover operating expenses.

In addition to SRAs, TIAA/CREF permits tax-sheltered annuity payments to be made under the regular retirement plan rules. This would result in lower fees, but early withdrawal privileges would be sacrificed.

The above discussion applies to TIAA/CREF plans as they have been run in the past. At presstime, TIAA/CREF was seriously studying possible changes in its rules. Any new developments will be claimed in next year's edition of this Tax Guide.

Switch to Unisex Mortality Tables

Because of a recent Court decision, TIAA/CREF will use a unisex mortality table to compute pensions for individuals retiring after May 1, 1980. This decision decreases benefits for men in some cases with a corresponding increase for women [cf. the discussion in the *Retirement Plans* chapter]. However, only those annuity payments which are an integral part of the plan are affected. If you receive the benefits in a lump sum which you then use to purchase a commercial annuity, then the Court ruling does not apply. Unless the law is changed, the commercial annuity can generally be based on mortality tables which are differentiated by sex.

Women, on the other hand, benefit from plans based on unisex mortality tables if they are planning to select a single-life annuity at retirement [cf. the *Retirement Plans* chapter]. For example, TIAA/CREF, which will pay the same annuities to men and women per dollar invested, becomes more attractive than a plan which lets the individual select only a commercial annuity paying less to women than to men. For women, unisex annuities can also be more attractive than the do-it-yourself withdrawals provided by rolling over a tax-sheltered annuity into an IRA. This is because they are based on a life-expectancy assumption which is shorter than that expected by the average woman.

Tax-Sheltered Annuities

Social Security Tax

Amounts contributed to a tax-sheltered annuity under a reduction-in-salary agreement are subject to Social Security tax. The Social Security tax is withheld from the employee and matched by an employer's contribution.

Contribution Limits for Tax-Sheltered Annuities

There are 3 basic limitations on how much can be contributed to a tax-sheltered annuity, the *elective deferral limitation*, the *annual limitation*, and the *overall limitation*.

The **elective deferral limitation** requires that the total voluntary contributions made by an individual to tax-sheltered annuities under a reduction in salary agreement cannot exceed $9,500 per year. This is a new limitation enacted by the 1986 Tax Reform Act. The $9,500 limit is reduced by deductible contributions made to an IRA and by amounts deferred under a 401(k) deferred compensation plan.

The $9,500 limit will be raised to as much as $12,500 for individuals who have worked for their current employer for at least 15 years, provided their previous contributions to tax-sheltered annuities with their current employer averaged less than $5,000 per year. Precisely, for such long-term employees, the $9,500 limit is raised by the lesser of (i) $3,000, or (ii) the excess of $5,000 multiplied by the number of years of service with the current employer over the total voluntary contributions made in prior years to tax-sheltered annuities with that employer.

The extra amounts provided by this rule cannot total more than $15,000 over a lifetime. Thus, if a person voluntarily contributes $12,500 under this rule for each of 5 years, his lifetime maximum of $15,000 would be used up. His voluntary contributions for future years could then not exceed $9,500 per year.

Example

Smith has worked for his current employer for 20 years. During each of the first 10 of these years, he made voluntary contributions of $3,000 to his tax-sheltered annuity, and during the last 10, $6,000 per year. HIs total voluntary contributions for these 20 years add up to (10 × $3,000) + (10 × $6,000) = $90,000. This is subtracted from 20 × $5,000 = $100,000 as required in (ii) in the above discussion: $100,000 − $90,000 = $10,000. Since this exceeds the $3,000 figure in (i), the maximum allowable voluntary contribution under the elective deferral limitation is $9,500 + $3,000 = $12,500.

The above $9,500 (or $12,500) limit applies only to *voluntary* contributions that you elect to have made to your tax-sheltered annuities. It does not apply, for example, to contributions which are a fixed percentage of compensation that are required to be made as a condition of employment.

In contrast, the next 2 limitations, the *annual limitation* and the *overall limitation*, apply to the *total* contributions made during any one year, whether the contributions are voluntary or required. Thus, contributions which are required to be made to a pension plan set up under the tax-sheltered annuity rules (and thereby exempted from current tax) are included in computing the *annual limitation* and the *overall limitation*, but not included in the *elective deferral limitation*.

The **annual limitation** states that contributions in any given year cannot exceed 25% of your reduced salary. Your reduced salary is the amount you are paid after the annuity contribution is deducted from your original salary.

Example

Your annual salary is $40,000 before any contributions to tax-sheltered annuities are made. The annual limitation in this case would be $8,000. This yields a reduced salary of $40,000 − $8,000 = $32,000. Then $8,000 = 25% × $32,000, verifying that $8,000 is the annual limitation. (Observe that $8,000 is equal to 20% of the unreduced salary of $40,000; this same 20% percentage would apply in general no matter what the actual salary figure.)

To determine if this year's contributions to your tax-sheltered annuity satisfy the **overall limitation** you perform the following steps:

(1) Subtract this year's contributions (voluntary and required) to your tax-sheltered annuities from your salary to obtain your reduced salary.

(2) Take 20% of your reduced salary and multiply this by the number of years you have worked for your current employer. (Count part-time work in proportion to the fraction of the full-time load you worked.)

(3) Under your current employer, add up the total of all amounts that have been contributed to your tax-sheltered annuity plus the amounts contributed by your employer to your regular retirement plan, including this year's contribution. Also, add in salary which your employer deferred under a Governmental deferred compensation plan.

(4) If (3) does not exceed (2), you have satisfied the overall limitation.

Example

You have worked for your current employer for 5 years. Your initial salary was $30,000 and you received a $2,000 raise in each of the succeeding years. In each of these years, your employer contributed 6% of your salary to your regular retirement plan. In addition, you arranged to have $4,000 of your salary contributed to a tax-sheltered annuity in each of the first 4 years. For the 5th year, the overall limitation restricts your tax-sheltered contribution to $5,900. This is verified according to the following computation.

Year	Salary	Employer's Contribution to Retirement Plan	Contribution to Tax-Sheltered Annuity	Reduced Salary
1	30,000	1,800	4,000	26,000
2	32,000	1,920	4,000	28,000
3	34,000	2,040	4,000	30,000
4	36,000	2,160	4,000	32,000
5	38,000	2,280	5,900	32,100
		10,200	21,900	

To verify that the $5,900 contribution in year 5 falls within the overall limit, note that $10,200 (Retirement Plan Contributions) + $21,900 (Annuity Contributions) = $32,100 does not exceed 20% × $32,100 (reduced salary) × 5 (number of years on job) = $32,100.

We have presented the above rules for your information in planning for the future. In actual practice, your employer will, at your request, compute for you the maximum amount that can be placed tax-free into your tax-sheltered annuity for any given year.

Reduction of the Annual Limitation

This reduction rule only applies if you are covered by a "defined contribution" pension plan with the same employer under which you are having contributions made to your tax-sheltered annuity. A **defined contribution** plan is one that computes your retirement benefit strictly on the basis of how much was contributed to your account. If your retirement plan provides a pension based on a percentage of your salary during a certain period of time, then it is **not** a defined contribution plan. Most governmental and private pension plans are not defined contribution plans. However, pension plans run by TIAA/CREF are defined contribution plans so the reduction rule would apply.

The reduction rule states that in computing the 25% annual limitation, you must add in your employer's contribution to your retirement plan plus certain other amounts such as forfeitures credited to your account. If you are covered by a defined contribution plan, you'll have to check with your employer to determine the precise limitation in your case.

Options Which Permit an Increase in the Annual or Overall Limitations

Believe it or not, the above are only basic rules which apply. The law provides several options you are permitted to adopt which may increase the contributions that can be made to your tax-sheltered annuity. (If you don't wish to contribute more than the regular rules allow, you don't have to concern yourself with these options.) These options provide alternatives to either the annual limitation or the overall limitation. They do not affect the elective deferral limitation. In all cases, your annual voluntary contributions to a tax-sheltered annuity cannot exceed $9,500 (or $12,500 for certain 15-year employees as described earlier).

Each of the following three options may serve to increase the amount you can have contributed to your tax-sheltered annuity with the tax-exempt educational, charitable, or religious organization for which you work. Once you utilize one of these options, you cannot use any of the other options in a later year.

Option #1. You can choose to forget entirely about the overall limitation. You would still be restricted by the annual limitation which provides a 25% ceiling on contributions as well as by the $9,500 (or $12,500) elective deferral limitation.

Option #2. You can raise the annual limitation by $4,000. If you adopt this option, your annual contributions are still subject to the overall limitation plus a third limitation of $15,000. Also, the elective deferral limitation would still apply.

Option #3. For your final year of your employment, you can disregard the annual limitation altogether and be restricted by the overall limitation where you take into account only the last ten years. However, the $9,500 (or $12,500) elective deferral limitation would still apply.

Discussion of the Options

Option #1 is of little use to the average individual. It would only come into use if someone wishes to make consistently high contributions to a tax-sheltered annuity during his entire employment period. Most people would not be able to afford such contributions in their earlier years so that the overall limitation does not come into force. However, those switching to a new job late in their careers might be benefited by this option.

Example

Jones obtains a new position three years from retirement age. He wishes to contribute the maximum possible amount to a tax-sheltered annuity. Jones adopts Option 1. He can then have 25% of his reduced salary contributed each year (provided the elective deferral limitation is satisifed). Under the basic rules or the other options he would be restricted to 20%. However, note that Option 3 provides a limitation based on 20% of the **final** year's salary. Thus, if his salary were to go up substantially, this could turn out to be the best choice.

Option #2 might be chosen if you wish to make large contributions now but have made low contributions in the past.

Example

Stirling has 5 years left until retirement and will earn $25,000 in each of these years. He has held his current job for the past 15 years and has not participated in a tax-sheltered annuity to date. During these 15 years, his total salary has added up to $200,000. By selecting Option 2, he could have $8,200 per year contributed to a tax-sheltered annuity for his remaining 5 years with the remainder, $25,000 − $8,200 = $16,800 being his reduced salary. Since he is in no danger of exceeding

Deferred Compensation Plans

> the overall limitation, the 25% + $4,000 limitation of Option 2 applies: $8,200 = $4,200 + $4,000 where $4,200 is 25% of the reduced salary of $16,800.

Option #3 represents an opportunity for anyone who wishes to defer tax on a substantial portion of his final salary and spread it out via an annuity over his lower-bracket retirement years.

> ### Example
> Rodgers has been working for the same employer for 20 years and decides to quit. His employer has annually contributed $1,000 to his regular retirement plan. In addition, during the last 10 years, he had a total of $14,000 contributed to a tax-sheltered annuity. His final salary was $30,000. Under Option 3, Rodgers can have $12,000 contributed to a tax-sheltered annuity in his final year (assuming the elective deferral limitation is satisfied). This is verified as follows:
>
> | | |
> |---|---:|
> | Salary in final year | $30,000 |
> | Contribution to tax-sheltered annuity | $12,000 |
> | Reduced Salary | $18,000 |
> | Allowable total contributions: | |
> | $18,000 × 20% × 10 years = | $36,000 |
>
> The total contributions made by his employer to the regular retirement plan plus the total of all contributions to a tax-sheltered annuity do not exceed this allowance as is verified by the following computation:
>
> | | |
> |---|---:|
> | Employer's contribution to retirement plan: | |
> | $1,000 × 10 = | $10,000 |
> | Previous contributions to tax-sheltered annuity | $14,000 |
> | Final year contribution to tax-sheltered annuity | $12,000 |
> | Total | $36,000 |

There is no special form to file with the IRS to elect one of the above options. You just arrange with your employer to withhold the appropriate amount. You are considered to have elected an option when it is needed to justify the extra amounts being contributed to your tax-sheltered annuity. In following years you can elect the same option or apply the regular limitations, but not elect a different option.

If you contribute to a regular Keogh plan or participate in another pension plan of a company you own, then there is a $30,000 upper limit on the total annual contributions to tax-sheltered plans made on your behalf.

Section 5:
Deferred Compensation Plans

Some employers permit deferral of income under a *Deferred Compensation Plan*. Under such a plan, typically, salary is set aside instead of being paid out currently. The money set aside is invested on behalf of the employee, with the accumulated funds paid out after retirement, usually in the form of an annuity.

Deferred compensation plans may not have the same legal status as regular retirement plans or tax-sheltered annuities. In particular, they may be *unfunded* instead of *funded* plans. This means that the employee's claim to the funds owed him has the same status as any other creditor's claim instead of having the preferred status that applies to regular retirement plans.

Deferred compensation plans offered by private companies vary from organization to organization. Each organization sets its own limits (within IRS guidelines) on how much pay can be deferred. Many private companies will match part of their employees' contributions, making these plans particularly attractive. The special lump-sum averaging rule [cf. the *Retirement Plans* chapter] can apply to plans run by private companies. Details should be available from the personnel office where you work.

Note that the 1986 Tax Reform Act has placed a new $7,000 limit on contributions to deferred compensation plans known as 401(k) plans run by private companies, starting in 1987. This $7,000 limit is reduced by deductible contributions to an IRA and by an individual's contributions to a tax-sheltered annuity made under a salary reduction agreement.

Different rules apply to deferred compensation plans run by tax-exempt organizations. The basic rule for such plans is as follows:

> *During any given year, the amount of salary set aside cannot exceed either $7,500 or 25% of an individual's full salary before reduction. If the employee participates in a tax-sheltered annuity, then this limitation applies to the total amount contributed to both plans.*

There is an exception to the above limitation which allows catch-up contributions to be made. During each of the 3 years prior to normal retirement age, an employee may defer up to $15,000 per year. However, this catch-up provision only applies to the extent that full utilization was not made of the full limitations in prior years going back to 1979. In other words, the total amounts set aside over the life of the plan still cannot exceed the total amounts that would have been set aside had the individual made full use of the $7,500 or 25% of salary contribution each year starting in 1979.

Chapter 17

Miscellaneous Deductions

SECTION 1:
BASIC RULES

This chapter describes the items that can be claimed under the category of *miscellaneous deductions* on Schedule A. As discussed in Section 2, this now includes all deductible job-related expenses for which an employee is not reimbursed by his employer. (In particular, travel expenses, which under prior law were claimed as an *adjustment to income* on Page 1 of Form 1040, now become a *miscellaneous deduction* on Schedule A.) As discussed in Section 3, *miscellaneous deductions* also include investment-related expenses and expenses connected with tax computation (e.g. the cost of this book).

New 2% of Adjusted Gross Income (AGI) Floor
The 1986 Tax Reform Act has instituted a new 2% of Adjusted Gross Income floor, starting with 1987 tax returns. That is, to determine your deduction for *miscellaneous expenses* on Schedule A, you must subtract 2% of your Adjusted Gross Income (AGI) from the total of your allowable expenses. The new Schedule A builds in this subtraction (on line 23) in the computation procedure for determining your total itemized deductions.

> **Example 1**
> Johnson computes Adjusted Gross Income of $50,000 on his tax return. He has allowable miscellaneous expenses of $1,500. His miscellaneous deduction is computed as follows:
>
> | | |
> |---|---|
> | Total Expenses: | $1,500 |
> | less 2% of AGI (2% × $50,000): | −1,000 |
> | Deduction: | $ 500 (entered on line 24 of Schedule A) |

There are some miscellaneous deductions which escape the application of the 2% floor. As discussed below, this includes job-related expenses for which you received a reimbursement from your employer. It also includes a few specialized items such as gambling losses up to gambling winnings, certain expenses for handicapped workers, etc. [cf. the end of Section 3].

227

Where Do You Claim Job-Related Expenses?

Form 2106, *Employee Business Expenses*, is used for reporting your job-related expenses. This form is separated into 2 columns, one for meals and entertainment and the other for the remainder of your expenses. This separation is made so that the 80%-Rule for meals and entertainment [cf. the *Travel* or *Entertainment* chapter] can be factored into the computation.

Page 1 of Form 2106 is divided into 4 sections, called "Steps." In Step 1, you report the amounts of your job-related expenses, broken down into several categories as listed on the form.

If your employer **did not reimburse** you for any of your job-related expenses, then you skip Steps 2 and 3, proceeding directly to Step 4. In Step 4, your total of job-related expenses is computed. The total is then entered as a miscellaneous deduction on line 20 of Schedule A.

Reimbursed Expenses

You may have included expenses in Step 1 for which you received a reimbursement from your employer. If so, then you do not skip from Step 1 to Step 4, but must proceed to Steps 2 and 3 as well. (On the other hand, reimbursements for expenses that you did not claim in Step 1 are ignored.)

If your yearend W-2 Form **does not include** the reimbursement as part of your income (the usual case), then you use Step 2. On line 7 of Step 2, you list the amount of expenses you reported in Step 1 which were covered by this reimbursement. The excess of expenses over this reimbursement is computed on line 10, with the instructions on Form 2106 later directing you to report the appropriate excess as a miscellaneous deduction on line 20 of Schedule A.)

On the other hand, if your yearend W-2 Form **does include** the reimbursement as part of your income, then you report this reimbursement on line 11 of Step 3. (The new W-2 Form contains a separate box in which your employer reports the total reimbursement that has been included in your income.) In this case, be sure you have claimed the reimbursed expenses in Step 1. As directed on Form 2106, this reimbursement is then claimed as an *adjustment to income* on line 23 of Form 1040. This same amount is then subtracted in Step 4 from the total Step 1 expenses, with the remainder carried over to line 20 of Schedule A as a miscellaneous deduction.

Claiming the reported reimbursement amount in Step 3 as an *adjustment to income* can be a distinct advantage. As an *adjustment to income*, it can be claimed by those who use the standard deduction as well as by those who itemize [cf. Chapter 1, Section 1]. And, it is not subjected to the 2% AGI floor that applies to *miscellaneous deductions*.

Meal and Entertainment Expenses

An extra complication arises from the *80%-Rule* on meal and entertainment expenses. Under this rule, only 80% of these expenses can be claimed as a deduction [cf. the *Travel* and the *Entertainment* chapters].

The IRS handles this by dividing Form 2106 into 2 columns. Column B is used for meal and entertainment expenses, while Column A is used for all other employee business expenses.

Miscellaneous Deductions

The computation procedure given by Steps 1-4, as discussed above, is applied to each column separately. Thus, any reimbursements for meal and entertainment expenses are subtracted from the total expenses given in Column B while other reimbursements are subtracted from the total expenses given in Column A. The resulting 2 remainders, one for Column B expenses and one for Column A expenses, appear separately on the next to last line of Form 2106.

The bottom line is obtained by adding the Column A result plus 80% of the Column B result. This is the amount you carry over to line 20 of Schedule A as a miscellaneous deduction.

Example 2

Smith has deductible employee business expenses totaling $3,000 — $900 for meals and entertainment plus $2,100 of other expenses. His employer has a policy of reimbursing employees for 2/3 of their expenses. Under this policy, Smith receives a reimbursement of $2,000 (2/3 × $900 = $600 for meals and entertainment, plus 2/3 × $2,100 = $1,400 for other expenses). His employer does not include the reimbursement in income reported on Smith's yearend W-2 Form.

The computation of Smith's employee business expense deduction proceeds as follows:

	Column A Other than Meals and Entertainment	Column B Meals and Entertainment
Step 1. Expenses:	$2,100	$900
Step 2. Reimbursements not reported on W-2 Form:	−1,400	−600
Remainder (reported on line 10):	$ 700	$ 300
Step 3. Reimbursements reported on W-2 Form:	0	0
Step 4.	$ 700	$300

Deduction: $700 + (80% × $300) = $940.

Smith transfers the $940 deduction computed above to line 20 of Schedule A. (On Schedule A, this $940, when combined with other miscellaneous deductions, is subjected to the 2% of AGI floor that applies.)

Example 3

Parker takes a 4-day business-related trip, incurring meal expenses of $300 and other expenses of $700. His employer reimburses Parker for meals at the rate of $50 per day (a total of $200 for the 4 days), plus the full amount ($700) of his other travel expenses. Thus, the total reimbursement is $200 + $700 = $900. Parker's employer includes this $900 in taxable income, identified as a reimbursement on Parker's yearend W-2 Form. In addition to the travel expenses, Parker has other non-reimbursed job-related expenses of $800, none of which is for meals or entertainment. The computation proceeds as follows:

230   **Miscellaneous Deductions**

	Column A Other than Meals and Entertainment	Column B Meals and Entertainment
Step 1. Travel Expenses:	$ 700	$300
Additional Expenses:	+800	
Total Expenses:	$1,500	$300
Step 2. Reimbursements not reported on W-2 Form:	0	0
Step 3. Reimbursements reported on W-2 Form:	−$ 700	−$200
Step 4.	$ 800	$100

Deduction: $800 + (80% × $100) = $880

The $880 computed above is carried over to line 20 of Schedule A as a miscellaneous deduction. (On Schedule A, this $880, when aggregated with other miscellaneous deductions, is subjected to the 2% of AGI floor.)

In addition to the $880 deduction, Parker reports the total amount of reimbursements shown in Step 3, $700 + $200 = $900, as an adjustment to income on line 23 of Form 1040. The effect of this adjustment to income is to cancel out the $900 reimbursement which was included in the income reported on Smith's W-2 Form. Because it is an adjustment to income, the $900 can be claimed by those who use the standard deduction as well as those who itemize. Furthermore it escapes the purview of the 2% of AGI floor.

The above 2 examples represent a somewhat simplified version of the basic computation procedure on Form 2106. The actual Form 2106 leads you through a longer computation than illustrated in these examples. The main reason for the extra computation is to cover the possibility that the total amounts you received as reimbursements exceeded your allowable expenses. (This situation could arise, say, if your employer reimbursed you for some meals while you were traveling, but not away from home overnight.) Essentially, Form 2106 will direct you to report any excess reimbursement as income on line 7 of Form 1040.

Escaping the 2% of AGI Floor

The 2% of AGI floor only affects items claimed as *Miscellaneous Deductions* on Schedule A. It does not apply to items connected with a self-employment activity which can be claimed on Schedule C, *Profit (or Loss) from Business or Profession*. You might be able to claim an item on Schedule C as a *Business Expense* rather than on Schedule A as a *Miscellaneous Deduction*. This might "save" all or part of the deduction from being hit by the 2% floor on miscellaneous deductions.

For example, suppose an employee earns extra income from his own consulting business. Certain items such as books, periodicals, professional dues, etc. may be reasonably attributed to either his regular job or his consulting business. By claiming these items as a business expense on Schedule C instead of as a job-related expense on

Miscellaneous Deductions

Schedule A, the 2% of AGI floor may be sidesteppped. This will lower taxes unless the total of other miscellaneous deductions already exceeds the 2% of AGI floor. (In that case, further miscellaneous deductions will have the same tax-lowering effect as any other deduction.)

For example, suppose an individual's Adjusted Gross Income is $50,000 and he has miscellaneous deductions totaling $1,500. After subtracting 2% of Adjusted Gross Income (2% × $50,000 = $1,000), his deduction on Schedule A is $1,500 − $1,000 = $500. If he has an additional expense of $100 for, say, dues to a professional society, then his miscellaneous expenses would total $1,600 instead of $1,500 and his deduction would be equal to $1,600 − $1,000 = $600. Thus, the extra $100 expense would lower taxable income by an extra $100 ($600 -$500), the same as any other deduction.

However, if he had no other miscellaneous deductions, then claiming the $100 as a miscellanous deduction would do him no good. The 2% of AGI floor would just reduce the amount to $0. In such a case, claiming the $100 on Schedule C rather than on Schedule A would save the deduction.

SECTION 2:
EMPLOYMENT-RELATED EXPENSES

The following employment-related expenses are deductible as *miscellaneous deductions*:

Travel Expenses [cf. Chapter 22]

Auto Expenses [cf. Chapter 10]

Educational Expenses [cf. Chapter 18]

Entertainment Expenses [cf. Chapter 20]

Home Office [cf. Chapter 3]

Research Expenses [cf. Chapter 29]

Books, Supplies, & Equipment [cf. Chapter 2]

Job-Hunting Expenses. These expenses are deductible whether or not you are successful in obtaining a job. However, you must be looking for a job in your same profession, not a different one. An IRS ruling indicates that a part-time teaching position is sufficient to establish membership in a profession. The ruling permitted an attorney who lectured part-time at a law school to deduct the cost of looking for a full-time teaching position. [Rev Rul 78-93]

Deductible expenses include employment agency fees, travel expenses, resume typing costs, job counseling fees, newspapers to check want ads, etc. Also, don't overlook entertainment expenses incurred in your hunt for a job. For example, taking a friend to lunch for the purpose of getting him to help you obtain a job where he works would be deductible, subject to the 80% rule described in the *Entertainment Expenses* chapter.

Required Physical. You may deduct the cost of a physical examination or TB test which was required by your school. These may be deducted as a business expense if you wish to avoid subjecting them to the 7.5% floor on medical deductions [cf. the *Medical Expenses* chapter].

Payment of Substitute. If your school requires you to pay a substitute teacher when you are absent, then you may deduct this expense. This is covered by an IRS ruling issued to a faculty member at a school with a sabbatical program under which he received full salary during the period of absence. However, the faculty member had to contribute to a fund out of which payments to a substitute were made. The IRS ruled that he could not simply reduce his salary by his payments to the fund and report the difference as income. Instead, he had to report his salary as income and deduct his payments to the substitute fund as a miscellaneous deduction. If he claimed the standard deduction, he would lose out on the deduction for payments to the substitute fund. (The same situation applies if a teacher is required to pay for a bond when taking a sabbatical.) [Rev. Rul 76-286]

Dues to Professional Organizations or Teachers' Unions. Agency shop fees required of a nonmember in lieu of union dues are also deductible.

Extracurricular Activities. Do you travel on school business, coach a school athletic team, sponsor a school organization, visit students' homes, lead student tours, etc.? You can deduct expenses connected with these activities if they are a legitimate part of your profession.

Preparing Master's Thesis or Doctoral Dissertation. You may deduct expenses for such things as typing, research, clerical help, etc., which are connected with writing a thesis or dissertation. However, you must qualify under the rules described in the *Expenses of Attending School* chapter.

Employment or Certificate Fees. You may have to pay a fee to obtain or renew your credentials to teach. Such a fee is deductible.

Telephone Expenses. You can deduct the cost of business-related long distance calls made from your home telephone. You may also be able to deduct a portion of your monthly bill for basic telephone service [cf. the *Books, Supplies, & Equipment* chapter].

SECTION 3:
OTHER MISCELLANEOUS DEDUCTIONS

In addition to the employment-related expenses discussed in the preceding section, the following items can be claimed as miscellaneous deductions:

Investment Expenses. You can deduct the costs associated with managing your investments. These include safe deposit boxes to store investments, burglar alarms to protect investment items, telephone calls, miscellaneous supplies, investment fees (but not bank fees charged for the privilege of writing checks even on interest-bearing accounts), etc. It also includes travel associated with managing your investments—e.g. to stock brokers for advice, to manage rental property, to place items in your safe deposit box, etc.

Postage. Don't forget to put down a few dollars for the cost of postage connected with your job, investment activities, tax form filing, etc. Even Jimmy Carter didn't overlook this deduction when he was President. His tax return included a $15.53 deduction for the cost of mailing tax records between Georgia and the White House.

Tax Guide. You may deduct the cost of this book and any other book or professional service which aids you in the preparation of your tax return or in tax planning for the future.

Mutual Fund Fees. All mutual funds (including money market funds) have built-in management fees. Typically, these fees on an annual basis range from about $1/2\%$ to $1 1/2\%$ of net assets and are automatically subtracted before earnings are credited to your account [cf. Section 4 of the *Investing Your Money* chapter].

For example, suppose you invested $10,000 in a money-market fund. Say the annual pre-expense earnings on this $10,000 are $700 and that the management fees on this amount are (as reported to you by the mutual fund) are $70. Thus, you receive net income for the year of $700 − $70 = $630.

In prior years, the mutual fund would simply have reported the amount you received (or had credited to your account), $630, to the IRS as your income from the fund for the year. But for 1987 and later years, the mutual fund would report the gross earnings, $700, to the IRS. You would then have to report the full $700 as dividend income on your 1988 Schedule B, even though you only received $630. The $70 in fees would then be claimed as a *miscellaneous deduction* on line 21 of Schedule A to offset the $70 of *phantom income* included in your taxable income.

As discussed in Section 1, this $70 miscellaneous deduction comes under the purview of the 2% of Adjusted Gross Income floor. If the total miscellaneous deductions do not exceed this floor, then no net deduction will be obtained. This means that in this case you would receive only $630 in income, but would wind up paying tax on $700. [Cf. Section 4 of the *Investing Your Money* chapter for a further discussion.]

(At presstime, Congress was considering a repeal of the above *phantom income* tax rules, possibly retroactive to January 1, 1987. You should be able to determine the proper treatment of management fees by examining the yearend Form 1099 sent to you by the mutual fund. Further details will be contained in next year's edition of this Tax Guide.)

Legal Expenses are deductible to the extent they are connected with income-producing investment activities or tax advice. Your lawyer should show a breakdown on his bill indicating the amount of his fees that can be properly claimed as a miscellaneous deduction. (Legal expenses connected with a self-employment business activity are deducted on Schedule C.)

Periodicals. You may deduct magazines, newspapers, etc. connected with your income-producing investment activities. Such publications might include the *Wall*

Street Journal, Barrons, Forbes Magazine, etc. For information on how to handle subscription fees for periods longer than one year, see the *Books, Supplies & Equipment* chapter.

IRA & Keogh Fees. You may have an IRA or Keogh Plan which levies a set-up fee or annual maintenance fee. Such a fee can be claimed as a miscellaneous deduction if separately itemized and paid from your personal bank account (rather than paid out of the IRA or Keogh account). On the other hand, brokerage fees for buying and selling securities in the IRA or Keogh Plan are not deductible.

Appraisal fees to value a deductible charitable donation or casualty loss.

Items Exempted from 2% of AGI Floor

There are a few special-purpose items which the law specifies to be miscellaneous deductions **not** subject to the 2% of AGI subtraction. These include:

Impairment-related work expenses incurred by a handicapped individual in order to be able to work. This would include such items as special tools and attendant care services at work.

Deductible gambling losses up to the amount of gambling winnings that are included in taxable income.

Deductions connected with certain specialized investment activities—namely, the expenses of short sales, deductions for amortizable premiums on bonds you own, deductions for an unrecovered investment in a terminated annuity, and deductions that arise under the *"claim of right"* doctrine when you return funds that were received erroneously in a prior year.

Chapter 18

Expenses of Attending School

SECTION 1:
BASIC RULES FOR DEDUCTING EDUCATIONAL EXPENSES

The expenses of attending school are deductible provided that certain conditions are satisfied. These conditions are designed to permit an individual to deduct schooling which aids him in his **current** occupation but to rule out schooling which prepares him for a **new** career. For example, a teacher can deduct the cost of a summer refresher course but a college student cannot deduct the cost of education preparing himself for a new career.

When Are the Expenses of Attending School Deductible?

You may deduct the cost of attending school if your attendance is for any one of the following purposes:

(1) Maintaining or improving skills required in your present employment;

(2) Keeping your current employment, status, or salary;

or

(3) Meeting the express requirements of your current employer.

However there are two exceptions. Your expenses **cannot** be deducted if either:

Rule A. The courses were required in order to meet the minimum educational requirements for your employment;

or

Rule B. The education would qualify you for a new trade or business. A change of duties is not considered as being a new trade or business if the new duties involve the same general work that you did previously.

You may have several purposes for attending school. If Rule A or B listed immediately above is among your reasons, then you may not deduct your educational expenses.

There is one further requirement. You must be considered a current member of your profession at the time you incur the educational expenses. This does not mean you must actually be employed at the time. If you were employed prior to the education and intend to resume employment in the same general profession, then your expenses may still be deductible. This is discussed further in Section 5.

Educational Reimbursements Received from Employer

Some employers have a plan under which employees are reimbursed for the cost of courses which they take. For 1987, as long as the plan meets certain non-discrimination rules, reimbursements for educational expenses are tax-free, whether or not the education is job-related. There is a ceiling of $5,250 per year on the amount of tax-free educational benefits an employee can receive. This ceiling does not apply to educational expenses which the employee could have deducted (according to the rules described in this chapter) had he paid the expenses himself. Also, this ceiling does not generally apply to graduate assistants who receive tax-free aid under a qualified educational reimbursement plan, nor does it apply to non-discriminatory tuition remission plans for faculty dependents. (At presstime, Congress was reconsidering the rules for educational expenses incurred in 1988. Details will be contained in next year's edition of this Tax Guide.)

Tuition Remission Plans

Many universities and colleges have plans under which faculty family members receive free college tuition. The value of this fringe benefit is exempt from tax if it is generally made available to all employees on a non-discriminatory basis—not restricted just to faculty members. Otherwise, the value of the free tuition will be included in taxable income.

Also, tuition remission will be considered a tax-free fringe benefit only for education below the graduate level. However, tuition remission at the graduate level can still qualify for tax-free treatment if it falls under the usual fellowship or scholarship rules [cf. the *Tax-Free Grants* chapter].

Tax-free treatment does not apply to *cash reimbursements* made to children of faculty members to enable them to attend colleges of their choice. According to a recent IRS Private Letter Ruling, such reimbursements generally constitute taxable income to the faculty member. Such a situation is distinguished from *tuition remission* plans where a college or a group of colleges agrees to *waive* tuition for children of any of the colleges' qualified employees. [IRS Private Letter Ruling 8541002]

Section 2:
When Do Educational Expenses Qualify for Deduction?

Education Which Maintains or Improves Skills

If you incur expenses for education which maintains or improves your professional skills, these expenses are deductible provided they are not disqualified under either the *minimum requirements* of Rule A or the *new trade or business* of Rule B. To qualify, the education must be in subject matter related to your teaching, research, or other professional duties. For example, a German teacher would be allowed to deduct expenses for taking a course in German literature. The education in question may be day courses, refresher courses, vocational courses, research on a dissertation, or any other educational activity. In the following example, 2 physical education teachers were recently permitted to deduct a portion of their membership fees in racquetball clubs, because the facilities were used to improve their teaching skills.

> **Example**
> A married couple were both physical education teachers at different schools in neighboring cities. They each taught a variety of courses covering different athletic

> *activities, including racquetball and handball.*
>
> *During the year in question, they paid for memberships in 4 different facilities with racquetball courts. She learned to play racquetball at one of the facilities to which she belonged; she also attended some clinics which taught her how to play racquetball so she could teach the activity to her students.*
>
> *He already knew how to play racquetball and handball, but he observed clinics in these sports and, from time to time, gave some instruction to students of his who also belonged to the facilities. The clinics were conducted by a professional and he picked up some teaching techniques for use in his classroom. He also played racquetball against handball and vice versa; he used this mixed-sport for a special education class he taught where he matched children with impaired vision (who used a racquet) against those without impaired vision (who used their hands).*
>
> *The Court ruled that the above activities involved the "maintenance or improvement of skills required in petitioners' employments as physical education teachers. We believe that the business aspect of the foregoing activities predominates over the personal pleasure or general fitness aspect of petitioners' activities at the Facilities."*
>
> *However, the Court complained that it did "not have any information as to how much of their time at the Facilities was essentially for pleasure or for general physical or mental well-being, rather than being specially connected with their job-related activities." As a result, it allowed a deduction of only $200, 17% of the total cost of the memberships. Had the couple presented better information on which a more favorable allocation could have been made, their deduction would have been higher.* [Cohn, TC Memo 1985-480]

Education which contributes to your general education but is not directly related to your professional duties does not qualify for deduction. For example, a mathematics teacher would not ordinarily be allowed a deduction for taking a course in political science. However, if there is an employment-related reason for you to take courses outside your area of expertise, then your expenses can be deductible. This is illustrated by the following IRS ruling.

> **Example**
>
> *Because of shifting enrollments, a college encouraged its faculty members to take courses in the business economics area. In response to this encouragement, a Professor of American History took courses in the Labor and Industrial Relations Program at another institution. The IRS noted that "surveys have shown that many colleges. . .have been experiencing a decline in the number of History Majors and an increase in the number of Business-Economics Majors." Thus, his education was sufficiently related to his professional duties to qualify for deduction.* [IRS Private Letter Ruling 8030093]

Education Which Maintains Your Current Employment, Status, or Salary

You may deduct expenses for education which meets the express requirements for maintaining your employment, status, or rate of compensation, provided the education does not fall under the *minimum requirements* of Rule A or the *new trade or business* of Rule B. For example, suppose a teacher has already met the minimum requirements for employment but the school board requires that periodic refresher courses or other education be taken to retain employment. Then these expenses are deductible. Similarly, educational expenses are deductible if the education is required in order to avoid demotion or other loss of status. Thus, a teacher can deduct required courses if the requirement is imposed not on the teacher's right to enter the profession (disqualified by Rule A) but on his right to continue in it.

A teacher may be required to obtain further education in order to participate in the normal increases provided by a set salary schedule or by, for example, an across-the-board cost of living increase. As illustrated by Example 5, expenses incurred in meeting this type of requirement are deductible.

Education Which Meets the Express Requirements of Your Employer

You may deduct expenses which meet the express requirements of your employer as long as the requirements have been imposed for a bona fide purpose. Again, the education must not fall under the *minimum requirements* of Rule A or the *new trade or business* of Rule B. The requirements must be identifiable. General encouragement alone will not constitute an express requirement. Even if your employer fails to enforce the rule, you can still normally take the deduction.

Example 1.

From 1953 to 1958, Robertson was an Assistant Professor in the Department of Economics at the University of Nebraska. He had received an M.A. in 1948 and had all the requirements for a Ph.D. except for his doctoral dissertation. At the time he was first appointed, there was no requirement that a staff member have a Ph.D. as a requirement to the granting of tenure. However, in 1958 there was such a policy so Robertson was told that his employment would be terminated unless he obtained a Ph.D. He took a one-year leave of absence in 1958 in order to complete his dissertation.

Ruling: *Robertson's costs incurred in returning to school to finish his dissertation were deductible. He had met the minimum requirements which were in effect at the time he was appointed and his schooling was for the purpose of maintaining his current employment.* [37 TC 1153]

Example 2.

Dawson is required by his employer, every two years, to either read a list of books or take certain courses that give 6 hours credit in order to retain his teaching position. If Dawson takes courses in order to satisfy this requirement to maintain his job, his expenses for education are deductible.

Example 3.

Same as above but due to a teacher shortage, Dawson's employer does not enforce the educational requirements. Dawson's expenses are nevertheless deductible.

Example 4.

Mr. Barker is a 7th grade teacher at an elementary school that has K-8 grades. The system is reorganized so that 7th to 9th grades become "junior high" years. To continue teaching 7th graders, Mr. Barker must get a secondary certificate. His educational expenses are deductible because he is merely meeting increased educational requirements imposed by his employer for the same position.

Example 5.

Truxall was a high school English teacher in Mt. Vernon, Ohio. She had tenure and was not required to take any further education in order to retain her teaching job. However, the Mt. Vernon City Board of Education required that all teachers in its employment had to gain additional training within a designated 3-year period, and each succeeding 3-year period, in order to be eligible to participate in salary increases. If the requirement as to additional training was not met, the only consequence was that the teacher so failing to meet the requirement would not be advanced in salary.

In order to satisfy the requirement, Truxall took a trip to Mexico which was sponsored by the School of Education of Indiana University. She received 2½ semester hours of credit by taking the trip and keeping a diary.

Ruling: Truxall could deduct her expenses. The Tax Court ruled:

"We think it fairly appears from the record presented that the additional education was required of all teachers, and that failure to secure additional education would result in loss of salary rights. The salary for a teaching job was not a constant sum. It was an adopted regulation of the school board providing for a schedule for annual advancements in salary. Withholding of such an advancement in salary was more in the nature of a sanction against a teacher who failed to satisfy the additional training requirement. Under the circumstances, we feel it would be correct to say the additional training was undertaken to preserve petitioner's existing salary rights which included rights to annual advancements which would be lost if she did not comply with the additional training requirements." [TC Memo 1962-137]

SECTION 3:
WHEN ARE DEDUCTIONS DISALLOWED UNDER RULE A?

You cannot deduct education which is required in order to meet the minimum requirements for employment in a new job. You may accept a job for which you do not meet the minimum educational qualifications, but you are hired temporarily or provisionally pending fulfillment of those requirements. If you then take courses in order to meet these qualifications (even though you may also qualify under (1), (2), or (3) of Section 1), then you may not deduct your expenses. However, if you meet the minimum educational requirements that are in effect when you are first employed in a job, and those qualifications are raised later, then you may deduct expenses for courses taken to satisfy the new minimum qualifications.

What Are Minimum Educational Requirements?

The IRS has issued the following regulation defining what is meant by minimum educational requirements for teachers.

"The minimum educational requirements for qualification of a particular individual in a position in an educational institution is the minimum level of education (in terms of aggregate college hours or degree) which under the applicable laws or regulations in effect at the time this individual is first employed in such position, is normally required of an individual initially being employed in such a position. If there are no normal requirements as to the minimum level of education required for a position in an educational institution, then an individual in such a position shall be considered to have met the minimum educational requirements for qualification in that position when he becomes a member of the faculty of the educational institution. The determination of whether an individual is a member of the faculty of an educational institution must be made on the basis of the particular practices of the institution. However an individual will ordinarily be considered to be a member of the faculty of an institution if (a) he has tenure or his years of service are being counted toward obtaining tenure; (b) the institution is making contributions to a retirement plan (other than Social Security or a similar program) in respect of his employment; or (c) he has a vote in faculty affairs."
[Reg. Sec. 1.162-5(b) (2)]

Note the words *"in terms of aggregate college hours or degree"* in the first sentence of the IRS regulation. According to this, if you have the degree and the specified number of total hours required, then you are considered to have the minimum qualifications (even if you lack some other requirement such as a specific course or courses). This is illustrated by Example 3 below.

Example 1.
A state requires its elementary school teachers to possess a bachelor's degree at an accredited institution. However, if a school district cannot obtain enough teachers meeting this requirement, they may hire applicants who have completed their junior year of college under the provision that they obtain their bachelor's degree within 3 years or else their employment will be terminated. An applicant who is hired under these circumstances may not deduct expenses for courses leading to his bachelor's degree, since they are taken to meet the minimum requirements of his current position.

Example 2.
A state requires its secondary school teachers to have a bachelor's degree plus 6 hours of graduate school credits. However, if a school district cannot obtain enough teachers meeting these requirements, they may hire applicants with bachelor's degrees who have 3 hours of graduate school credits. These applicants are hired on a provisional basis and must complete the additional 3 hours of graduate credits within one year or their employment will be terminated. An applicant hired under these circumstances may not deduct expenses for a course taken to meet the 6-credit requirement. The additional course which the applicant must take is used to satisfy the minimum requirements of the employee's current position.

Example 3.
A state requires secondary school teachers to have a bachelor's degree, 6 hours of graduate school credits, and at least 3 hours of graduate education courses (which may

also be used in satisfying the other requirements). If a school district cannot get enough teachers meeting these requirements, it may hire an applicant with a bachelor's degree provisionally, under the condition that the applicant complete the requirements within 2 years or his employment will be terminated.

Smith has a bachelor's degree and 6 hours of graduate courses, but none of these are in education. He is hired by the school district and he attends night school to obtain the remaining 3 hours of education courses. Since he has the required degree and the required total number of hours of education, he is considered for tax purposes to have satisfied the minimal educational requirements for this employment. He may deduct the expenses for taking the 3 additional hours of education courses that he needs to retain his job.

Example 4.

At the time Brown starts his employment as a secondary school teacher, the only requirement for employment is the possession of a valid bachelor's degree. Two years after he begins working, the school board raises the qualifications by requiring 9 graduate credit hours for all applicants. Those who are already employed are given 3 years to obtain the credits or their employment will be terminated. Brown takes one semester's leave of absence to obtain the 9 credit hours, and he then returns to his job.

Since Brown satisfied the minimum educational requirements in effect when he started employment, his educational expenses are for the purpose of maintaining his current employment. Hence they are deductible. If he attends school away from home, he may deduct his travel expenses (including meals and lodging while away from home overnight) as well as the cost of tuition, books, supplies, etc.

Example 5.

Michaelson had a provisional certificate from the State of Washington and was employed as a teacher by the Spokane School Board. According to the Washington Board of Education, a person is qualified to obtain a provisional certificate upon completion of 4 years of education. The provisional certificate is valid for 1 year and is renewable for not longer than 5 years. The fifth year of education at the graduate level is required in order to obtain a standard general certificate. During the time Michaelson was teaching under his provisional certificate, he attended night school. He took courses to satisfy the fifth year of education required for obtaining a standard certificate.

The Tax Court allowed Michaelson to deduct the expenses of his education. It ruled as follows:

> "Here the state, by its provisional certification, had licensed taxpayer to enter upon his teaching livelihood. It did not withhold judgment as to taxpayer's qualifications. It did not require any appraisal of the manner in which he had provisionally taught. It certified him as presently qualified to teach — not to serve a period of apprenticeship or internship or of professional learning or tutelage but to teach professionally as a teacher.
>
> "The standard certificate when issued granted him no new authority or capacity. He continued to do precisely what he had already been doing and what he had already been certified as qualified to do. The conditions imposed upon his right to a standard certificate

were not then, conditions upon taxpayer's entrance into his profession but upon his continuing it." [313 F2nd 668]

Example 6.

Toner was a fifth grade parochial school teacher in Philadelphia. At the time of her initial employment, she had completed 2 years of a 4-year college degree program. The school only required its teachers to have a high school diploma as long as they were taking at least 6 college credits per year towards a bachelor's degree. A teacher without a bachelor's degree earned less than one with a degree, but in all other respects had full faculty status.

An appeals court allowed Toner to deduct the cost of education leading to her bachelor's degree. Since she already had full faculty status, she had met the minimum requirements for her current employment. This case represents the rare situation of an individual qualifying to deduct the cost of obtaining an initial bachelor's degree. [Toner, 46 AFTR 2nd 80-5156]

Example 7.

An individual obtained employment in August 1981 as a Professor of Physical Education. At the time, he was enrolled in a doctorate program at a university in a different location. He completed his dissertation about a year later, obtaining his Ph.D. degree in December, 1982. A contingency clause was written into his second year contract to complete the doctorate. However when he was employed, he had already met the minimum requirements for his position as a regular faculty member.

The IRS ruled that he could deduct all his expenses in working toward his doctorate after he became employed. This included tuition as well as *"the reasonable expenses of editing, typing, photocopying, telephone, photography, graphics, mailing, supplies and any reasonable expenses that were incurred as incident to the preparation of [his] doctoral dissertation to obtain [his] graduate doctoral degree."* He was also permitted to deduct his travel expenses, including meals and lodging, for a 2½ month trip back to the institution where he was enrolled in the doctorate program. The trip was needed to enable him to finish some experimental animal work and to use some specialized equipment which was located there. [IRS Private Letter Ruling 8340025]

Example 8.

Wilkins, who holds a master's degree, obtains temporary employment as an instructor at a university. He undertakes graduate courses as a candidate for a doctoral degree. He may become a regular faculty member only if he obtains a doctoral degree. He can continue his position as instructor only as long as he shows satisfactory progress towards obtaining that degree.

The graduate courses Wilkins takes are necessary to meet the minimum educational requirements for qualification in his trade or business. Thus the expenditures for these courses are not deductible.

Example 9.

Jungreis worked for the University of Minnesota on a part-time basis as a graduate teaching assistant in the zoology department. Since he then had only a Bachelor of Science degree, he was not qualified for a position as a regular faculty member of the University. He was enrolled as a student in the graduate school and was a candidate for a Doctor of Philosophy degree in zoology which was required to qualify him as a regular full-time faculty member. The University required Jungreis to be enrolled as a graduate student before he could be eligible for an appointment as a graduate teaching assistant.

While serving under an appointment as a graduate teaching assistant, he was required to be making satisfactory progress toward a graduate degree to maintain his appointment. The employment as a graduate teaching assistant was a temporary position which terminated upon receipt of the Ph.D.

Jungreis claimed he was entitled to deduct expenses relating to his graduate school education since they were required for him in order to maintain his position as a teaching assistant. He claimed he had already met the minimum requirements, i.e., a bachelor's degree, which were required of him in his current position.

The Tax Court disallowed his deduction. It ruled that the position at an educational institution for which an individual must meet the minimum educational requirements before he can get a deduction is a **permanent position** on the faculty of the institution. In this case, the minimum education required for permanent employment in the University's zoology department is a Ph.D. Jungreis was enrolled in a program to meet those minimum requirements and hence his expenses were not deductible. [55 TC 581]

Example 10.

Damm, after working as a registered civil engineer for 5 years, enrolled in graduate school at a leading California university. He obtained his master's degree and continued as a student in the Ph.D. program for an additional year. He then left school and obtained a job as a lecturer in Engineering at a State college. After several years of full-time teaching, he returned to the university for 2 years and completed his Ph.D. studies. He then returned to teaching, first at the State college for a year and then at a university in the midwest.

When Damm deducted his education expenses for the period he was completing his Ph.D. studies, the IRS objected. It referred back to the Jungreis decision [Example 9], claiming that Damm had not met the minimum requirements for the position of permanent college faculty member, namely the Ph.D. degree.

But the Court did not agree with the IRS, permitting the deduction to stand. It contrasted Damm's situation with that of Jungreis as follows:

"Jungreis was a teaching assistant, he taught part time, his salary was less than that of the regular faculty members, his work was different from that of regular faculty members, his service did not count toward tenure, and from the outset he could not hold his job for any period unless for that period he was enrolled as a student and making satisfactory progress toward a graduate degree. We concluded that Jungreis was essentially an apprentice, rather than a teacher. Damm, by contrast, was a full-time teacher doing what regular faculty members did in the classroom, he was paid the same as regular faculty members, up to two years of his service could count toward tenure, and his job did not depend on a condition precedent."

> The Court also pointed out that the State college
>
> *"did not normally require a doctorate degree as a minimum level of education for lecturers or for faculty members in general. We concluded that Damm, who had already been awarded the baccalaureate degree and the master's degree, met the minimum educational requirements for lecturers and for faculty members in general at [the State college].*
> *"From the foregoing, we concluded that Damm's educational expenses are not rendered nondeductible by the minimum educational expenses test."* [Damm, TC Memo 1981-203]

SECTION 4:
WHEN ARE DEDUCTIONS DISALLOWED UNDER RULE B?

Rule B states that you may not deduct expenses for education which will qualify you for a new trade or business. In the case of an employee, a change of duties does not constitute a new trade or business if the new duties involve the same type of work that he was formerly doing. Furthermore, all teaching and related duties are considered to involve the same general type of work. For example, none of the following changes are considered to constitute a new trade or business:

a. *change from elementary to secondary classroom teacher*
b. *change from teaching one subject to teaching another*
c. *change from teaching to guidance counselor*
d. *change from teacher to principal*

Note that the above does not explicitly state that you can deduct the expenses for education required to make the above changes. It only states that these education expenses are not automatically excluded from being deductible. However, the following examples taken from government rulings and regulations indicate that expenses undertaken to meet the requirements for such changes are generally deductible.

> **Example 1.**
>
> Green, who had a master's degree, was an Education Professor at a college. He became eligible for appointment as President of a junior college within the same educational system. The next year, the requirement for this position was raised from a master's degree to a doctorate. In order to be retained on the eligibility list, Green earned a doctorate in education. Note that prior to getting the additional education, Green had met the minimum educational requirements. His appointment as President of a junior college would not be a new trade or business, but merely a change of duties in his accustomed type of work. Hence his expenses in obtaining a doctorate were deductible.
> [Rev. Rul. 68-580]

> **Example 2.**
>
> A high school mathematics teacher is told by his employer that he must transfer to the science department to fill a vacancy. The transfer requires his taking two science courses.

Again, this transfer is considered only a change of duties and is not a new position. So the expenses for the two courses are deductible. They would also be deductible if the transfer had been initiated at the teacher's request.

Example 3.
Miss Delano, a first-grade teacher, wished to become a 6th grade teacher in the same school district. To do so, she had to take 3 additional specified courses. Since the employer and basic duties of the old and new jobs were the same, the cost of the courses is deductible.

Example 4.
Mrs. Dodd taught secondary school in Ohio where she had a permanent teaching certificate. She moved to Missouri because her husband was transferred by his employer. In Missouri she got a temporary teaching certificate and took courses to meet the qualifications for a permanent certificate.
The IRS ruled that Mrs. Dodd's expenditures were not made for education required of her in order to meet the minimum qualifications in her business. She met those requirements in Ohio and was merely changing employers but not acquiring a new trade or business. Thus, her expenses were deductible. [Rev. Rul. 71-58]

Example 5.
Laurano, a Canadian citizen, was certified to teach elementary school in Toronto, Canada. In order to obtain certification to teach in New Jersey, she took several education courses at a college in New Jersey. The Court ruled her education to be deductible. Her switch from teaching in Canada to teaching in New Jersey was considered simply a change of duties. [Laurano ¶ 69.90 P-HTC]

Example 6.
Schwerm was employed as a discussion leader in a local college's adult education program. Discussion topics included family relationships, self-awareness, and coping with problems such as stress, retirement, etc. She enrolled in a graduate program for a master's degree in Educational Psychology. She thought this course of study would aid her in becoming a better discussion leader. After obtaining her master's degree, she entered an internship program to train her to become a school counselor.
The Court ruled she could deduct the expenses of both the master's degree program and the internship program. Even though the internship program was qualifying her for the new position of school counselor, the Court ruled that her positions as discussion leader and school counselor were part of the same trade or business. (In fact, she would perform similar guidance services in both these positions.) [Schwerm, TC Memo 1986-16]

Note the above examples all show situations in which Rule B did not apply. For teachers, the only case where Rule B is likely to apply is if courses taken were in a completely different field.

Law School Expenses

Rule B eliminates a deduction for education which **qualifies** you for a new trade or profession. It does not matter if you actually make the switch into the new trade or profession. As long as the education enables you to make the switch, a deduction is ruled out. This is best illustrated by a number of cases involving individuals attempting to deduct the expenses of attending law school. In several of these cases, the individual involved did not intend to become a lawyer, but rather to use the law school education in his current profession. But since the education **qualified** him for the new profession of being a lawyer, Rule B prevented a deduction.

One case involved an insurance adjuster who intended to use the legal training in his same line of work [TC Memo 1977-236]. Another case involved a college teacher of mathematics who intended to switch to teaching law, a change of duties which usually qualifies for deduction [Bouchard, TC Memo 1977-273]. A third case involved someone who performed quasi-legal activities for a corporation prior to and after law school [McDermott, 36TCM144]. A fourth case concerned a contracts manager who never took the bar examination and used his law school only to aid in legal negotiations connected with his job [Rehe, TC Memo 1980-316]. And a fifth case concerned an Associate Professor of Communication who was studying law because his primary teaching responsibility was a course on the legal aspects of mass communication [IRS Private Letter Ruling 8432028].

In all of the above cases, it was ruled that the profession of being a lawyer was different than the employment they had before. Since their law degree *qualified* them for this new profession, they were not permitted to deduct their educational expenses whether or not they actually entered the new profession.

There was the one lawyer who succeeded in deducting his educational expenses. But he already held a law degree and was a member of the bar. His education consisted of a one-year advanced graduate program in law in the area of his specialty [IRS Private Letter Ruling 7801002].

SECTION 5:
TEMPORARY VS. INDEFINITE ABSENCE
FROM PROFESSION

An additional requirement for deductibility is that the education be undertaken when you are a current member of your profession. If you are actively teaching, on vacation, or on a temporary leave of absence, then you are considered to be a current member of the teaching profession. But if you leave your profession for an **indefinite period** of time, then you may not deduct expenses related to that profession. This holds even if you return to the profession at a later date.

If you temporarily leave your profession for a **fixed period** of time to take courses that maintain or improve your skills, then these expenses are eligible for deduction. It is not necessary that you be on official leave of absence or even that you plan to return to the same job. However, you must plan to resume employment in the same field you left.

The IRS had been following the general policy of considering any period exceeding one year, as an indefinite period of time. Thus, education requiring an absence from work for more than a year was considered non-deductible. But the Tax Court has thrown out this one-year policy as being arbitrary and unjustified. In several court cases, they have permitted a deduction for full-time study lasting 3 years or more. These cases are discussed below.

Deduction for Graduate School Education

The court cases permitting a deduction for extended periods of education all involved graduate students returning to school after a period of employment. The key to qualifying for deduction was that their education was sufficiently related to their profession. The extended length of time required to complete the education was no barrier.

> **Example 1.**
> Mrs. H. held a master's degree in the field of nursing education. She held positions first as an Assistant Professor at a community college and then as a consultant to an educational organization. Mrs. H. left her employment to undertake a 3-year doctoral program in nursing education. When she left her job, she did not have any specific intent to return. However, after receiving her doctoral degree, she did in fact return to work for the same educational organization that she had worked for before.
> The IRS did not dispute that the education was for the purpose of improving her skills as a nursing educator. However, it maintained that her 3-year absence from the profession ruled out a deduction.
> The Court did not agree with the IRS. It found nothing in the law which placed "an arbitrary limitation on the self-improvement process." Rather, "the 3-year period of study was an appropriate period in which to accomplish her educational objective."
> [Hitt, TC Memo 1978-66]

> **Example 2.**
> Over a period of 10 years, Mr. P. was employed by various public school systems in New England. He served as school teacher, curriculum coordinator, and finally principal of an elementary school.
> Mr. P. resigned his position as principal and undertook full-time graduate studies in the field of educational administration. He received his Ph.D. three years later. Upon graduation, he wrote letters to various universities, colleges, and school systems seeking employment in a teaching or administrative capacity. However, he met with little success. In spite of continuing his job-seeking efforts for a number of years, he was unable to secure employment except for a few minor part-time positions. In fact, at the time his case came to trial, he was still unemployed.
> Mr. P. claimed a deduction for the cost of his schooling. However, the IRS challenged the deduction, reasoning that his extended absence from work meant he was not a member of his profession at the time of his education.
> But the Court upheld the deduction. His graduate studies were of definite as opposed to indefinite duration. Moreover, they were directly related to his profession as an educator and educational administrator. The fact that he was unable to obtain a regular job upon graduation was not held against him. To establish that he continued being a member of his profession, it sufficed that he actively **pursue** employment in that profession, not that he actually **obtain** employment. [TC Memo 1977-321]

> **Example 3.**
> For several years, Wyatt was a teacher of secretarial skills in a secondary

> school in Kansas. From 1963 to 1967 she was employed as a secretary, working for various employers. In March 1967 she accepted an offer to begin teaching again in August 1967. Even though she still had a valid teaching certificate, she took graduate school courses in education in the spring and summer of 1967 preparatory to her resumption of teaching.
>
> **Ruling:** Wyatt left the teaching profession in 1963 for an indefinite period. At the time she incurred the expenses for her education, she was not engaged in the profession of teaching even though she had accepted a teaching position to begin later. Her expenses were not deductible because they did not improve her skills in the profession she was engaged in at the time she took the courses. [56 TC 517]

If you leave your profession temporarily, you should still list that profession on the *Occupation* line on your tax form. A recent court decision denied an education deduction to a registered nurse who went back to school after a long period of time during which she was unemployed. The denial was based on the Court's conclusion that she was no longer in the nursing profession when she undertook the education. It stated that the fact she did not consider herself a nurse at the time was *"demonstrated by the fact that she listed her occupation on her Federal income tax returns for those years to be that of a student and housewife."* [Cannon, TC Memo 1980-224]

However, you should take care how you fill out the *occupation* line at the top of Form 2106 so that it is clear that you are claiming an *educational deduction* rather than a *job-related travel deduction* [cf. Example 12 in Section 3 of the *Travel* chapter for details].

Court Gives Green Light to Deducting MBA Expenses

A 1977 court case will bring cheer to those pursuing advanced degrees in business schools. Often these students have returned to school after a stint in the working world. As the following court case shows, the expenses of obtaining education in these circumstances will generally be deductible.

> **Example 4.**
> Sherman was a civilian employee with the military. He held a managerial job, being in charge of a regional "Plans and Programs Office." He left this employment after two years to attend Harvard University as a candidate for a Master's Degree in Business Administration (MBA). After a two-year period, he received his degree and became Director of Planning and Research in a private corporation.
>
> As in the previous two examples, the IRS asserted first that he had not established any "trade or business" in which he was improving his skills by attending school. And second, his absence from employment beyond one year automatically excluded his deduction in any event.
>
> Once again, the Court sided with the taxpayer against the IRS. Sherman had established himself in a trade or business, namely *"the business of being an employee who was an administrator and planner."* And the MBA program improved his skills in this "business." As in Examples 1 and 2, the Court rejected the one-year

> *limitation placed by the IRS on deductible education. The 2-year program was of fixed duration and entirely reasonable for the purpose of obtaining an MBA degree.*
> [Sherman, TC Memo 1977-301]

Despite the above court cases, the IRS has still not thrown in the towel on the *one-year limitation* question. A recent IRS Private Letter Ruling concerned an individual in the same situation as Schwerm, discussed in Example 6 of Section 4. This individual held a managerial job, left this job for 2 years to enter an MBA program, and got a new job in a similar field after receiving his degree. But the IRS denied a deduction for his educational expenses because his absence from work exceeded one year. The IRS simply stated that it was going to stick by its one-year limitation despite the Tax Court opinion to the contrary. [IRS Private Letter Ruling 8538068]

While the IRS almost always abides by the opinions of the Court, legally speaking it can refuse to do so in future cases, unless the Court issuing the opinion is the Supreme Court. Thus, an individual who stops working for more than one year to go back to school may encounter IRS resistance to his educational deduction. If challenged, he should appeal to the next level up in the IRS and if rebuffed there, at least threaten to go to Tax Court. Because the IRS would expect to lose in Tax Court, they will likely drop the matter unless they intend to make a test case to appeal to a higher court.

SECTION 6:
WHICH EXPENSES ARE DEDUCTIBLE?

If your education qualifies for deduction, you may deduct tuition, fees, books, supplies, photocopying, and other related costs (e.g., required physical examination, tutor's fees, etc.). If your education includes writing a thesis or dissertation, then you may deduct associated costs such as typing, research expenses, etc.

Transportation Expenses To and From School
You may deduct transportation expenses for qualified educational activities that you incur in going between:

1. the general area of your principal place of employment and a school located **beyond the general area;**

or

2. your place of employment and a school **within the same general area.** However, if you return home before going to school, you may deduct the expense in going from home to school only to the extent it does not exceed the transportation expense you would have incurred had you gone from work to school.

> **Example 1.**
> You live and work in Newark, New Jersey, and go to New York City three

times a week to attend night classes at a university there. If your educational expenses are deductible, you may deduct your round trip transportation expenses, including tolls and parking fees.

Example 2.
You attend night classes at a college located in the same city as your job. (Assume that you can deduct your educational expenses.) You go directly to the college after work. You may deduct the cost of going from your job to the college.

You may not deduct the cost of local transportation between your residence and school on a non-working day. This expense is in the nature of a personal commuting expense.

You cannot deduct transportation between your residence and school during a period of unemployment. This is illustrated by the following court case.

Court Case.
An unemployed teacher took college courses, using local transportation to travel the 30 miles between her home and the college. She deducted $1,178 for educational expenses, including $564 for transportation. The IRS allowed the deduction to the extent it covered tuition, fees, and books, but disallowed the $564 travel costs on the grounds they were personal commuting costs.

The Tax Court agreed with the IRS. Since she was unemployed, her travel did not fall into the deductible category described in the preceding example. Also, her schooling was not temporary employment so that the examples in Section 3 of the *Travel* chapter were inapplicable. The Court simply considered her expenses to serve her personal convenience by allowing her to reside at some distance from her school. Note also that since her education did not require her to be away from home overnight, the provisions of the next subsection do not apply. [Zimmerman 71 TC §34]

Travel Expenses While Away from Home Overnight

Perhaps you attend school out of town to obtain education that qualifies for deduction. In this case, you are governed by the rules for deducting travel expenses as described in the *Travel* chapter. The IRS describes as follows the general situation concerning travel away from home overnight to obtain education:

"If you travel away from home primarily to obtain education the expenses of which are deductible, you may deduct your expenditures for travel, meals [subject to the 80%-rule described in Section 1 of the *Travel* chapter], and lodging while away from home. However, if you engage in incidental personal activities, such as sightseeing, social visiting, or entertaining, the portion of your expenses attributable to those personal activities are nondeductible.

"If your travel away from home is primarily personal, your expenditures for travel, meals and lodging (other than meals and lodging during the time spent on deductible educational pursuits) are not deductible.

"An important factor in determining whether a particular trip is primarily personal or primarily to obtain qualifying education is the relative amount of time devoted to personal, as compared with educational activities." [Reg. Sec. 1.162-5(e)]

Example 1.

You work in Newark, New Jersey. You went to Chicago to take a 1-week course, the cost of which is deductible, and while there, you took a sightseeing trip, entertained some personal friends, and took a sidetrip to Pleasantville for a day. Your transportation expenses to Chicago and back are deductible, but your transportation expenses to Pleasantville are not. You may deduct only the meals [subject to the 80%-rule described in Section 1 of the *Travel* chapter] and lodging allocable to your educational activities. [IRS Pub. 17]

Example 2.

You work in Newark and you went to a university in California to take a course, the cost of which is deductible. The course was one-fourth of a full program of study and you spent the rest of your time on personal activities. Your trip is considered to have been primarily personal unless you can show otherwise. You may not deduct the cost of your transportation to California but you may deduct one-fourth the cost of your meals [reduced further by the 80%-rule] and lodging while attending the university. [Reg. Sec. 1.162-5(e)2]

If your travel was outside of the United States, see Section 7b of the *Travel* chapter.

Where Do You Deduct Educational Expenses?

Educational expenses incurred by an employee in connection with his job are claimed on Form 2106, *Employee Business Expenses*. The total of expenses computed on Form 2106 is claimed on line 20 of Schedule A as a *miscellaneous deduction*, and when aggregated with other miscellaneous deductions, subjected to a 2% of Adjusted Gross Income floor.

Educational expenses connected with a self-employment activity are claimed on Schedule C. This has the advantage of escaping the 2% floor and being available to those who claim the standard deduction as well as to those who itemize.

Section 1 of the *Miscellaneous Deductions* chapter discusses this in more complete detail. It also shows how to handle the situation where a full or partial reimbursement is received from an employer. Note that as discussed there, certain reimbursements received from your employer are claimed as an *adjustment to income* on line 23 of Form 1040 rather than as a *miscellaneous deduction*.

You cannot deduct your educational expenses to the extent you receive a tax-exempt scholarship to defray such expenses. For example, if your educational expenses are $1,500, toward which you receive a $500 scholarship, then your deduction would be $1,500 − $500 = $1,000. [Rev Rul 83-3].

You should attach a statement to your tax return including the nature of your occupation and the amount of expenses that constitute deductible educational expenses (broken down into such broad categories as tuition, fees, transportation, meals, and lodging while away from home, etc.). You should also keep records and supporting evidence to substantiate each element of expenditure, in case your return is audited.

Further information on the requirements for deducting and keeping records of travel expenses is contained in the *Travel* chapter.

Chapter 19

Retirement Plans

Section 1:
Introduction

The chances are good that you participate in some sort of retirement plan other than Social Security. This plan may be entirely funded by contributions from your employer or it may be funded by both employer contributions and employee contributions. In almost all cases, contributions required of employees are simply withheld from their paychecks.

In addition to simply providing a savings vehicle for later years, retirement plans are a significant tax-shelter. As explained in Section 3, tax might be avoided on the contributions paid into the plan. And no tax is paid on the annual income earned by funds in the retirement plan. Thus, these funds earn income compounding at a higher effective rate than they could earn in the hands of a taxpaying individual.

To illustrate, compare placing $1,000 into a retirement plan with placing $1,000 into the hands of an individual in the 30% tax bracket (Federal plus State). Let's suppose each $1,000 is invested at 8% interest compounded annually. The retirement plan earns interest at the full 8% rate. But the individual earns a net interest rate of only 5.6% after paying taxes. The $1,000 in the individual's hands would grow to $3,905 after 25 years. But the $1,000 in the retirement plan would grow to $6,848, an increase of 75%.

Section 2:
Payments from Retirement Plans

When you receive annuity payments from your retirement plan, your employer will furnish information concerning the tax status of these payments. A portion of each payment reflecting your own contributions on which you have already paid tax is not subject to further taxation. The remaining portion is taxable. Thus you are taxed when you receive amounts reflecting contributions made by your employer, as well as investment income.

The former *3-year rule* under which initial payments from an annuity, up to the total amount of your contributions, could be tax-free has been abolished.

Lump-Sum Distributions

If benefits from a retirement plan are paid out in one lump sum after you reach age 59$^{1}/_{2}$ (or upon your death or disability), then you can choose to apply a special 5-year averaging rule. Essentially, this rule allows you to treat the lump-sum distribution as though it were spread out over a 5-year period and taxes it entirely independent of any other income. The tax on your other income is computed as though you never received any retirement payment.

For example, a $100,000 lump-sum distribution would be taxed at a rate of about 15%. The 5-year averaging rule also applies to lump-sum distributions from Keogh Plans but not from IRAs or Tax-Sheltered Annuities [cf. the *Tax-Sheltered Plans* chapter].

The 5-year averaging rule generally applies only to employees who were plan participants for at least 5 full years prior to the year of distribution. Also, the 5-year averaging rule can be used only once in a lifetime.

In case of death, many retirement plans provide a benefit payment to a beneficiary which also qualifies for the 5-year averaging rule. In such a case, the employee need not have been a plan participant for 5 years.

A distribution cannot qualify for the lump-sum treatment described above unless it constitutes the entire balance to the credit of the employee. The entire distribution need not be made at one time as long as the entire balance is distributed within the same tax year. Ordinarily, inclusion of an annuity does not bar lump-sum distribution treatment. If an employer maintains several retirement plans of similar type, these may have to be aggregated (i.e. considered to be one plan) when determining if a total distribution has been made.

There is also a special transfer provision of the law which applies to a lump-sum distribution from your retirement plan. A lump-sum distribution received after you leave your job or after you reach age 59 1/2 can be rolled over, in whole or in part, to another tax-sheltered plan you set up called an Individual Retirement Account (IRA). No tax will be paid until money is paid out from the IRA. Partial distributions of 50% or more of a given pension plan or tax-sheltered annuity received upon leaving your job can generally still qualify for rollover treatment but not for 5-year averaging. You also might be able to transfer the distribution to your new employer's retirement plan if he permits it. Details are discussed in Section 2 of the *Tax-Sheltered Plans* chapter.

Special Transition Rule for Individuals Born Before 1936

There is a special transition rule for individuals born before 1936. They can choose to apply the prior law 10-year averaging rule using 1986 tax rates if they wish. The 10-year averaging rule works like the 5-year rule, except that the distribution is taxed as though it were spread out over a 10-year instead of a 5-year period. Except for very large distributions, this 10-year averaging produces a somewhat smaller tax than 5-year averaging.

More specifically, individuals born after 1936 who receive a lump-sum distribution after 1986 may elect either to apply the 10-year averaging rule using 1986 tax rates or the 5-year averaging rule using current tax rates. And either of these rules can be applied to a distribution received upon separation from service, even if the individual is younger than age 59 1/2.

However, the once-in-a-lifetime rule still applies. That is, if either the 5-year or 10-year averaging rule is used on a lump-sum distribution received after 1986, then no use of a special averaging rule is permitted for any future lump-sum distributions.

There is a special rule for those who received a lump-sum distribution between January 1, 1987 and March 15, 1987 on account of separation from service during 1986. Such individuals may elect to treat the lump-sum distribution as though it were received in 1986, if they wish [cf. last year's edition of this *Tax Guide*].

Pre-1974 Contributions

If you were a participant in your retirement plan before 1974, then you have another option that applies to the *pre-1974 portion* of a lump-sum distribution. This *pre-1974 portion* is determined by multiplying the taxable amount of the distribution by the number of pre-1974 years of participation and dividing by the total number of years of participation. (This amount will be set out in an information sheet accompanying your lump-sum distribution.) You can then choose to regard the pre-1974 portion as long-term capital gains in the year of distribution and apply 5-year (or 10-year if applicable) averaging to the remainder. Or, you can group the pre-1974 portion with the remaining portion and apply 5-year (or 10-year) averaging to the entire amount. Your choice should be made after computing the consequences of both choices and determining which is the more advantageous in your particular situation.

Starting with distributions made in 1988, only a certain *phase-out percentage* of the pre-1974 portion will qualify for the capital gains treatment described in the preceding paragraph. For 1988, this percentage is 95%.

For those who were born before 1936, an extra option is available. They can choose to apply a flat 20% rate to the entire pre-1974 portion, with no phase-out percentage for years after 1987. Either 5-year or 10-year averaging can be applied to the remaining portion of the distribution, as discussed earlier.

The special option for treating the pre-1974 portion of a lump-sum distribution falls under the same once-in-a-lifetime rule that applies to the 5-year averaging option or 10-year averaging option. That is, if any of these 3 options is used for a lump-sum distribution received after 1986, then none of these options can be used for any future lump-sum distributions.

Extra 10% Tax on Distributions before Age 59^1/$_2$

In general, an individual who receives a distribution from a pension plan prior to reaching age 59^1/$_2$ is subject to an additional "penalty tax" equal to 10% of the taxable portion of the distribution. This 10% tax is in addition to any income tax due on such distributions. However, there is no additional tax on the portion of the distribution that is a return of non-deductible employee contributions.

The 10% penalty tax is waived if either (i) you die and your beneficiaries get the money, (ii) you become disabled, (iii) you leave your job and take your pension entitlement in the form of a annuity payable in equal periodic amounts over a lifetime, (iv) you leave your job after reaching age 55, (v) you use the distribution to pay for medical bills in excess of 7.5% of your adjusted gross income, or (vi) you roll over the distribution tax-free into an IRA.

Due to the complexity of the rules, professional advice should be sought before making any lump-sum distribution decisions. Also, special rules apply if you are covered by a retirement plan of a company of which you are at least a 5% owner.

Section 3:
Contributions to Retirement Plans

Employer's Contributions

Your employer's contributions to your retirement plan are not taxable at the time the contributions are made, provided (as is usually the case) the IRS has approved the plan as qualifying for this benefit.

Employee's Contributions

An employee's contributions to his retirement plan are taxable. That is, the taxable wages figure reported on his W-2 Form includes his full salary before his contributions to the retirement plan are taken out. He must pay tax based on this full figure and can get no deduction for his contributions to the retirement plan.

This situation is inherently unfair. To illustrate this unfairness, compare the situations of the following two persons:

A earns $32,000 per year. He is required to participate in a retirement plan to which both he and his employer contribute $1,000 per year. Effectively, A's annual salary is $31,000 plus the $2,000 which is contributed to his retirement system.

B, on the other hand, earns an annual salary of $31,000. His retirement plan is entirely funded by his employer who makes a contribution of $2,000 per year. Thus, like A, B has an annual salary of $31,000 plus the $2,000 retirement contribution. The employers of both A & B have precisely the same expense — $33,000 per year.

But there is one important difference. A must pay tax based on his official $32,000 salary while B pays tax only on $31,000 — a considerable difference. For no good reason, A is required to pay more tax than B. However, when A and B retire, then B must pay tax on the full amount of his retirement pay (see Section 2). A does not have to pay tax on that amount which represents a return of his contributions to the plan. Thus, the net result is A pays tax on the additional $1,000 in the year he earns it while B defers paying tax on his amount until he receives it in the form of retirement benefits. Meanwhile, B has been able to earn interest on the difference for many years. This amount could be multiplied many times over, especially if retirement is far away. In addition, B's tax rate is likely to be lower during retirement than when he is working.

The only distinction in the two situations described above is a semantic one, namely whether contributions are **designated** as being made by the employee or the employer. But Congress has specifically made this semantic distinction the criterion for deduction. The employee must pay tax on any amounts designated as salary even if these amounts are put into a retirement plan as an employee contribution without passing through his hands. However, he does not have to pay tax on amounts put into a qualified retirement plan if these payments are designated as employer contributions.

Private employers are well aware of this distinction. They usually designate all contributions to a retirement plan to be employer contributions. This produces the best tax result for the employee without costing the employer anything extra. In fact, keeping pension plan contributions outside the employee's official salary can even benefit the employer by lowering worker's compensation premiums, social security contributions, and other payments based on salary.

Public institutions are another matter. Their pension plans are often part of a large system established by state or local law. For example, teachers in public institutions typically are covered under the same general retirement plan applying to all state employees. These plans often require contributions to be made both by employer and employee.

Exception. A number of IRS rulings have highlighted an exception to the general rule that employee contributions are included in taxable income. This exception applies when a state or local government retirement plan requires employee contributions but a school district or other subdivision agrees to "pick up" the employee contribution. The IRS uses a Congressional committee's report to describe the situation as follows:

> *"However, some state and local government plans designate certain amounts as being employee contributions even though statutes authorize or require the relevant governmental units or agencies to 'pick up' some or all of what would otherwise be the employee's contribution. In other words, the governmental unit pays all or part of the employee's contribution but does not withhold this amount from the employee's salary. In this situation, the portion of the contribution which is 'picked-up' by the government is, in substance, an employer contribution for purposes of Federal tax law, notwithstanding the fact that for certain purposes of State Law the contribution may be designated as an employee contribution. Accordingly, ... in the case of a government pick-up plan ... the portion of the contribution which is paid by the government, with no withholding from the employee's salary, will be treated as an employer contribution under the tax law."* [H. Rep. 93-807]

A number of IRS rulings have made it relatively easy to qualify under the above pick-up rule. First, the IRS issued a Revenue Ruling stating that pick-up plans need only satisfy the following two criteria:

> *"(1) the employer must specify that the contributions, although designated as employee contributions, are paid by the employer in lieu of contributions by the employee;*

and

> *(2) the employee must not be given the option of choosing to receive the contributed amounts directly instead of having them paid by the employer to the pension plan."* [Rev. Rul. 81-36]

Then, an IRS Chief Council Memorandum liberalized the interpretation of criteria (2). According to this memorandum, criteria (2)

> *"must not be interpreted to prohibit 'pick-up' of amounts that are, in substance, employer contributions. This rationale suggests that criteria (2) should only be applied to cases in which an employee is considered to have the option to choose to receive the amounts directly rather than having them contributed to a plan because the employee is in fact controlling the amounts and,*

therefore, the contributions are not, in substance, employer contributions.

"An option that would be impermissible under criteria (2) is one in which the employee will currently receive the amounts unless he must annually opt to have these amounts contributed on his behalf to the employer's pension plan. In this case the employee, not the employer, is in fact controlling the contributions."

But a one-time nonrevocable election whether or not to participate in a pension plan is all right. According to the memorandum,

"it is our opinion that the nonexercise of a one-time election to opt out of a plan or the one-time, nonrevocable election to begin early participation in a plan does not vest in the employee enough control of the employer contribution to taint the amounts contributed on the employee's behalf." [G.C.M. 38820]

For example, under this policy, the IRS issued a private ruling approving a pick-up plan which provided that an employee became a participant when first hired unless he filed a written notice of election not to participate within a 30-day period. [IRS Private Letter Ruling 8209038]

There is no restriction on how the contributions are to be picked up. According to an IRS Private Letter Ruling, *"The employer may pick up these contributions by a reduction in cash salary of the employee or by an offset against future salary increase or by a combination of reduction in salary and offset against a future salary increase."* [IRS Private Letter Ruling 8206146]

As the above discussion indicates, it has become quite easy for governmental units to establish pick-up plans. Essentially, all they need to do is pass the appropriate statute authorizing the pick-up. Practically speaking, this is just a bookkeeping change, costing the employer nothing while saving the employee many hundreds of dollars in taxes. In fact, many pick-up plans involving government employees, including teachers, have been established in States across the country the past few years. Presumably, other States will be giving this no-cost benefit to their employees in the near future.

Special Rules for School Employees

There is another alternative available to schools and certain other non-profit organizations. Instead of qualifying under the usual retirement plan rules, they can set up their retirement plan under the special tax-sheltered annuity regulations that apply only to these types of organizations. To qualify, the retirement plan must provide that all contributions to the plan are non-transferable and non-forfeitable. This means that amounts credited to the account of an employee cannot be assigned over to someone else nor can they be forfeited because the employee terminates his employment or for any other reason. (Also, starting in 1989, certain new *non-discrimination* rules will apply that require retirement plans not to overly benefit higher salaried employees when compared with lower salaried employees.)

Under the tax-sheltered annuity regulations, an employee can make an agreement with his employer to reduce his salary by an amount equal to his contribution to the retirement plan. Then, the institution contributes this amount to the retirement plan. The net result is that the employee's contribution is transformed into an employer's contribution. The employee's W2 Form shows the reduced amount as his taxable wages. Since his official salary is reduced, the employee escapes tax on the amount of his contribution to the plan.

Of course, as discussed in Section 2, tax must be paid later when this amount is received in the form of retirement benefits. But in the meantime, the tax that was not paid can be invested to earn interest for many years. In effect, the deferral of tax gives the same benefit as obtaining a long term interest-free loan from the government. Over the long run, this can amount to a substantial benefit.

Private institutions have little trouble qualifying their plans under the tax-sheltered annuity regulations. Public institutions are another matter. Often, their employees are included in the same retirement system that applies to all state employees. These state plans typically require that both the employer and employee contribute to the plan. And, as discussed earlier, amounts designated as being contributed by the employee are included in taxable wages.

However, a recent court case shows that even if the state retirement system designates amounts as *employee* contributions, this may not rule out a deduction. The administration of the educational organization may be able to *redesignate* these amounts as *employer* contributions, exempting them from tax. This case involved the retirement system applying to employees of the State of North Dakota. According to North Dakota law, both employer and employee were required to contribute 4% of the employee's salary to the state retirement system. The Court ruled that the State Board of Higher Education, under its broad administrative authority, had the power to authorize salary reduction agreements transforming employee contributions into employer contributions, despite the state statute requiring contributions from the employee. [University of North Dakota, 44 AFTR 2d 79-5392]

The TIAA/CREF Retirement System

TIAA and **CREF** (Teachers Insurance and Annuity Association/College Retirement Equities Fund) are a pair of non-profit organizations founded by the Carnegie Foundation. Their basic function is to provide a universal retirement plan which allows faculty members to transfer their retirement plan from one institution to another without losing any benefits.

Most private colleges and a number of public colleges use the TIAA/CREF system as the basic retirement system for their employees. It is also used by a number of other eligible non-profit institutions.

The TIAA/CREF system consists of two basic funds. The TIAA fund is invested primarily in fixed income securities such as bonds and mortgages. The CREF fund is invested in the stock market, primarily in a weighted portfolio which tracks the performance of the Standard and Poor 500 Stock Average (similar to the Dow Jones Industrial Average, but more representative of the stock market as a whole). The employee designates which proportion of his account is to be invested in each fund. He can have his entire account in TIAA or in CREF or he can have part in each.

An individual may withdraw up to 10% of his CREF or TIAA account upon retirement. The remainder not withdrawn is used to purchase an annuity.

Under TIAA, an annuity can be selected which essentially pays a fixed monthly amount until death, based on the size of the employee's account and his age at retirement. Or, an annuity can be chosen which starts at a lower level and increases annually to compensate, roughly, for the increase in the cost of living. A number of options are available to provide that payments continue to a spouse after the death of the employee. Of course, any options which provide payments to a spouse reduce the amount of the original annuity according to the appropriate actuarial computation.

Amounts in the CREF fund are used to purchase a variable annuity upon retirement. Monthly payments are made which vary according to the dividend payments made by the stocks and the rise and fall in market value. Options providing benefits to a beneficiary apply to these variable annuities also.

At any time before annuity income begins, you can make a full or partial transfer of funds accumulated in your CREF account into TIAA. The transfer to TIAA is of particular interest to those nearing retirement because annuity payments will be regular, not dependent upon the ups and downs of the stock market as would be the case with funds left in CREF.

Contributions to TIAA/CREF are non-transferable and non-forfeitable. Thus, TIAA/CREF satisfies the basic tax-sheltered annuity regulations described above. Most institutions which use the TIAA/CREF system permit their employees to make a reduction-of-salary agreement to shelter their contributions from tax. However, some institutions do not permit such agreements, either because local law does not allow it, because the bookkeeping requirements cannot be met, or for other reasons.

Many institutions permit employees to make tax-sheltered contributions to TIAA/CREF in addition to the regular required contributions to the basic retirement plan. This is the case even if TIAA/CREF is not used for the basic retirement plans. These additional contributions are subject to certain limitations provided for in the law. Details are discussed in Section 4 of the *Tax-Sheltered Plans* chapter.

Some institutions offer their employees a choice between the TIAA/CREF system and a second retirement plan sponsored by the institution. Often, this second plan is a state or local retirement system that applies to all government employees. In such cases, there can be substantial differences between the two plans. The TIAA/CREF system may permit reduction-of-salary agreements to defer tax on employee contributions, while the state or local retirement system may not.

However, this tax advantage could be outweighed by other advantages of the state or local system. Benefits paid by TIAA/CREF are actuarially computed to correspond precisely to the amounts that have been contributed to your account and the investment experience of the funds. But state and local systems are often not based on such actuarial computations. Especially in times of high inflation, governmental pension plans often pay out benefits far more than that which an actuarial computation would yield. This is particularly true when cost-of-living adjustments are provided for.

Often, employees who anticipate changing jobs within a few years will be better off with a plan like TIAA/CREF because it provides for no forfeiture of amounts in the employee's account. This is not the case with many other pension plans. Employees who do not anticipate changing jobs will have to make a careful evaluation of the features of each of the plans being offered to determine which is more favorable in their case. (Also note that TIAA/CREF is considering offering more flexibility— primarily by making new investment vehicles available in the future. More information will be contained in next year's edition of this Tax Guide.)

Supreme Court Unisex Ruling

In 1983, the Supreme Court issued a ruling concerning payments from *defined contribution* pension plans. These are pension plans under which each year, money is credited to an individual's account. At retirement, an annuity is purchased based solely on the amount in the individual's account, including investment income earned on the contributions. The plans run by TIAA and CREF are defined contribution plans. Pension plans which promise a certain monthly benefit based on final salary are **not** defined contribution plans.

Historically, two different life-expectancy tables were used to calculate the annuity payments which the funds in an individual's account would purchase—one table for women and the other for men. Since women, on average, live longer than men, their annuity payments would be expected to continue over a longer period of time. Therefore, the monthly payments they received were less than the payments received by men to compensate for the expectation that more payments would be made.

However, the Supreme Court ruled that this policy violated antidiscrimination requirements of the law. As of August 1, 1983, employers must use one unisex mortality table in computing the annuity payments an individual is to receive based on the value of the funds accumulated in his retirement account after this date. That is, there can be no different treatment of men and women as there had been in the past. If women as a class live longer than men, they will simply receive more total benefits than men.

The U.S. Court of Appeals for the Second Circuit extended the Supreme Court ruling to cover all individuals in the TIAA/CREF system retiring after May 1, 1980. It ruled that the pensions of such individuals should be adjusted to conform to a unisex mortality table applied to the entire value of their account. In October, 1984, the Supreme Court declined to review this Court of Appeals decision, thereby letting it stand as law. Although the Second Circuit Court of Appeals only has jurisdiction over a limited geographical area, TIAA/CREF has announced that it will apply the decision nationwide. (A separate recent court decision applies to about 50,000 ex-teachers who retired between March 24, 1972 and May 1, 1980 under the TIAA/CREF retirement system. As of January 1, 1986, the dividend portion of their retirement checks is being computed on a unisex basis.)

TIAA/CREF has computed the difference that a switch to unisex mortality tables makes. Pension payments to men generally decrease while pension payments to women generally increase. But the amount of change depends on the type of annuity which is selected.

There are two basic types of annuities—single-life and joint-life annuities. A *single-life annuity* makes payments to the individual until he dies. A *joint-life annuity* continues payments to the surviving spouse until the spouse dies.

Single-life annuities are the ones most affected by the switch to unisex tables. TIAA single-life annuities are lowered 4 1/2 % for men and raised 4 1/2 % for women. CREF annuities are lowered 8% for men and raised 8% for women.

Single-life annuities can also be chosen which guarantee that payments continue for 10 or 20 years (to a beneficiary) if the individual dies before that time. For a 10-year guaranteed period, the men's loss/women's gain is 2 1/2 % for TIAA and 6% for

CREF. For a 20-year guaranteed period, the figures are 1% for TIAA and 2½% for CREF.

Joint-life annuities which continue payments to the surviving spouse at the same rate or at a ⅔ reduction are unaffected by the switch to unisex tables. If annuity payments to the spouse are ½ the payments to the individual, the TIAA change is 2% and the CREF change is 3½%. (All of the above figures are based on an assumption that both husband and wife are 65 years old.)

Those who participate in the TIAA/CREF Retirement System should take note of the above percentage changes when making a selection of payout option. For example, men who select the single-life annuity option are hit the hardest, so from an actuarial point of view this option is the least preferable. The joint-life option is the most favorable with no reduction in benefits if the surviving spouse receives full or ⅔ benefits.

The opposite is true for women. Under the single-life option, they get an increase in benefits of as much as 8% while under the joint-life option with full or ⅔ survivor benefits there is no increase.

Of course, non-actuarial considerations may play a larger role in an individual's decision on which payout option to use. For example, a man may still want to choose a straight single-life option if he has no heirs he wishes to provide for. Also, the actuarial tables are based on average life expectancies from which a person may have reason to believe he will deviate. The health, family history, or living habits of an individual may indicate a different life expectancy than average. In such a case, this may point to a particular payout option. For example, the joint-life option is statistically preferable for a female in ill health with a healthy husband even though the single-life option benefits from the switch to unisex mortality tables.

The Supreme Court ruling applies to all defined benefit plans, so they will be affected similarly to TIAA/CREF. However, only employer-provided annuities are required to use unisex tables. If a pension plan pays a lump-sum benefit and allows the individual to purchase an annuity from a commercial insurance company of his choice, the Supreme Court ruling does not apply.

It should be pointed out that there is controversy as to why females outlive males on average. It is not known for certain to what degree this is due to biology and to what degree this is due to lifestyle factors such as smoking habits, stress levels, etc. To the extent lifestyle factors play a role, the switch to unisex mortality tables may reflect a more accurate assessment of life expectancy for working women. However, most researchers believe that women do enjoy an inherent biological advantage in life expectancy. Estelle Ramey, a prominent endocrinologist at Georgetown Medical Center, has estimated the inherent longevity difference between women and men to be between 4 and 5 years. Also to be pointed out is that some States now require unisex pricing on commercial annuities or other types of insurance.

SECTION 4:
SOCIAL SECURITY

A major new social security law was passed by Congress in 1983. This law was designed to "rescue" the social security system by increasing taxes and lowering benefits in a variety of different ways, including raising the social security tax, gradually increasing the retirement age, and restricting the cost-of-living benefit increases under certain circumstances. And under this law, the following items are included in the wage base subject to social security tax: deferred compensation, employee contributions to a State retirement plan which are "picked-up" by the employer [cf. Section 3], and amounts paid to a tax-sheltered annuity under a salary reduction plan.

Tax on Social Security Benefits

Congress also subjected social security benefits to income tax. Now, half the social security benefits an individual receives are required to be included in taxable income, provided the individual has total income which exceeds a certain trigger point—$32,000 on joint returns; $25,000 on single returns. (The trigger point for marrieds filing separately who live with their spouses anytime during the year is $0).

The exact procedure for computing how much is taxed is complex. Here's how it works. Start with Adjusted Gross Income (AGI). Add to this any untaxed interest from municipal bonds. Then add in half the social security benefits. If the total is less than the trigger point, no benefits are taxed. If the total exceeds the trigger point, half this excess is taxed except that no more than half the social security benefits can be subjected to tax in any case.

The obvious effect of this new tax on social security benefits is to lower the net benefit for those who exceed the trigger points. A less obvious but equally strong effect is that for some, an increase in other income triggers a tax on social security benefits. For example, suppose a single person has $22,000 AGI plus $6,000 social security benefits. His AGI + 1/2 of social security benefits equal $25,000. Since this places him right at the trigger point, no tax is paid on his social security benefits. He simply computes his tax on the $22,000 of Adjusted Gross Income.

But now suppose he earns an extra $3,000 in taxable income, bringing his AGI to $25,000. Now the total of his AGI + 1/2 of social security benefits equals $28,000. This exceeds the $25,000 trigger point by $3,000, so half this excess, 1/2 × $3,000 = $1,500 is subjected to tax. He must pay tax on $25,000 + $1,500 = $26,500. Thus, the extra $3,000 in earnings triggers an increase in taxable income of $4,500. In effect, his marginal tax bracket on extra earnings has been increased by 50%!

A similar effect would occur if instead of an extra $3,000 in earnings, he earned an extra $3,000 in tax-exempt income. This would trigger a tax on $1,500 of benefits just as in the preceding computation. Effectively, instead of being totally exempt from tax, half of this "tax-exempt" income is subject to tax.

The taxable amount of social security benefits is reported on line 20b of Form 1040. A worksheet is provided in the instruction booklet accompanying your tax forms for computing this taxable amount.

Note that many States which tie their State income tax computation to the Federal tax computation make an exception in the case of Social Security benefits. In these States, all Social Security benefits are completely exempt from State income tax.

Checking Your Social Security Account

The Social Security Administration allows you to check to make sure that your earnings have been properly credited. Call or write your local social security office and ask for Form 7004PC, *"Request for Statement of Earnings."* After you fill out the form and send it in, you will receive notification of the earnings credited to your account.

It is recommended that you fill out this form at least once every three years. Otherwise, even if you discover an error, it may be too late to correct it. There are any number of ways your account might have been fouled up. The prudent person will not wait until retirement, when it might be too late, to make sure the proper benefits will be received.

Over the years, the system has been unable to credit over $70 billion in wages because it couldn't figure out to whom the credits belonged.

Social Security Numbers Required for Children

You are supposed to have social security numbers for children (or other individuals) over age 4 if you wish to claim them as dependents on your 1987 tax return. You list these numbers in column (3) of line 6c on Form 1040. It is best to apply for these numbers early to avoid the backlog that will develop when many persons first discover they need these numbers to complete their 1987 tax returns. Call your local social security office to get application forms.

If you have applied for but not yet received the required social security numbers by the time you file your tax return, the IRS suggests you enter *"Applied For"* in column (3) of line 6c. This might spare you an unpleasant letter from the IRS as well as a fine.

Chapter 20

Entertainment Expenses

Many teachers entertain as part of their job. They may take a visiting educator out to lunch or dinner. Or, they may host a dinner or reception in their home in honor of such a visitor. The question then becomes whether or not the expense of such entertainment can be deducted.

There has been no direct guidance on this question in any published court case or IRS ruling. And the basic Tax Code section under which entertainment expenses are deducted offers little illumination. It states only:

"In the case of an individual, there shall be allowed as a deduction all the ordinary and necessary expenses paid or incurred during the taxable year . . . for the production or collection of income."

Thus, to qualify for deduction in 1987, entertainment must be an *ordinary and necessary* activity connected with your job. The word *ordinary* refers to an expense connected with a common and accepted practice in your job. For example, a professor could regard the expense of taking a visiting colloquium speaker out to dinner as an ordinary expense if this is typically done on his campus. On the other hand, the expense of treating a class to ice cream cones would not be an ordinary expense because it is not common practice to do so.

The term *necessary* in this context does not have its usual meaning of "compulsory." Here, a necessary expense is one that is *appropriate and helpful* in the conduct of your job.

Employees sometimes have a difficult time convincing the IRS that an entertainment expense qualifies for deduction. The IRS generally expects the employer to pick up the bill for all job-related expenses. Of course, teachers are in a special category. They often have to dig into their own pockets to pay for job-related items for which an employee in private industry would receive a reimbursement.

The IRS may not always appreciate this fact. However, assistance has come from an unexpected source. President Carter's 1978 Tax Proposal to Congress contained an entire section devoted to entertainment expenses. His exact proposals were not enacted into law, but the explanatory material is of considerable interest. As an illustration of existing law, Carter's message listed examples of entertainment deductions which were allowed in recent audits. And one of these examples is the case of a college professor who was permitted a $1,300 deduction for entertainment expenses. The exact quote is as follows:

Excerpt from the President's 1978 Tax Program

"A university professor received $30,000 in annual salary and, in addition, many of his expenses are reimbursed. His department did not reimburse him for

$1,300 spent to entertain visiting professors, but these expenses were deductible on the basis of his department chairman's statement that entertaining visiting professors was required as part of the professor's job." [PH Federal Taxes, Booklet #1252, p. 197]

Of course, President Carter offered the above example, as well as others, to show why current law should be changed. But his message clearly stated that the law permits such a deduction. Thus, a definite reference has been provided to back up the right of teachers to deduct their entertainment expenses.

Further details concerning the above example are not available since they were part of a private IRS audit. Neither the President's staff nor the IRS was permitted to give out further information on the professor's audit to us when we inquired. However, a telephone discussion with a high IRS official concerning this matter did offer one piece of further guidance.

The official stated that it was not necessary for there to be an absolute requirement to entertain. As long as the entertainment in question is a general practice in one's institution and is appropriate and helpful to the job, a deduction can be justified. Of course, a statement that such entertainment is required as part of the job would boost one's case. But it is not an absolute requirement.

The *ordinary and necessary* rule discussed above applies to the most common type of business entertaining, namely dining out in a restaurant. This includes having drinks at a bar or cocktail lounge provided there is no distracting floor show or other entertainment. It also includes the cost of *quiet business meals* served to your guests at home.

There is an additional rule that now applies under the 1986 Tax Reform Act. This rule states that entertainment (including meals and beverages except when traveling away from home) must either (1) be *directly related to the active conduct of the taxpayer's trade or business,* or (2) take place either directly before, at the same time as, or directly after a *substantial and bona fide business discussion* associated with the active conduct of the taxpayer's trade or business. Exactly how this rule will apply to teachers is unclear at this time because there have not yet been any rulings or court cases on this issue. Further details will be contained in future editions of this Tax Guide after more information becomes available.

The above discussion indicates that the cost of hosting a dinner party for an out-of-town visitor can be a deductible entertainment expense. But how about dinner parties attended only by in-town guests? The presumption is that such parties are simply personal gatherings rather than deductible business activities. But a recent court case shows how this presumption might be overcome, namely, by pointing to parties for which no deduction was claimed. A newspaper publisher held dinner parties to which he invited people from politics, business, journalism, publishing, theater, and other fields. He did not have specific business to transact with these individuals. Rather, *"the purpose of the dinners was to provide an opportunity to discuss developments and ideas with people who were prominent in their professions."* The publisher claimed a deduction for about a dozen of these dinner parties. Had these been the only parties given by the publisher, they would have been considered merely social gatherings. But he had hosted many other dinner parties for which no deduction was claimed. Because of this, the Court was able to accept the publisher's contention that the relatively few parties for which he claimed a deduction were business-related rather than being just social gatherings. [Howard, TC Memo 1981-250]

Whose Expenses Can Be Deducted?

When your entertainment activities are deductible, the letter of the law only allows you to deduct your own meal to the extent it exceeds what you would ordinarily have spent. However, in practice, the IRS almost always lets you deduct the full cost of your own meal in addition to that of the person you are entertaining. The IRS also recognizes that when entertaining an out-of-town visitor, it may be impractical to leave out his or her spouse. In such a case, the expenses of the spouse will be deductible also. Furthermore, if your spouse is included because the visitor's spouse is present, these expenses can also be deducted. However, all expenses are subject to the 80%-Rule discussed below.

To be deductible, entertainment expenses should not be reimbursable by the employer. This is illustrated by a 1983 Court case in which an engineer was denied a $122 deduction for lunches and dinners with professional colleagues. The Court agreed that such costs might qualify for deduction. But in this case, the engineer testified that his employer would have reimbursed him for the costs if he had asked. An employee cannot deduct expenses which he pays that his employer would have reimbursed him for. [Narain, TC Memo 1983-701]

80%-Rule for Entertainment Expenses

Entertainment expenses are no longer deductible in full. Instead, only 80% of the cost of entertainment (including meals and beverages) can be deducted. All expenses associated with the entertainment such as tax, tips, parking, etc. are included under this 80%-Rule. However, transportation to and from the place of entertainment is not subject to the 80%-Rule.

Exception. The 80%-Rule does not apply to expenses which are reimbursed by an employer, provided the reimbursement is not included as taxable income on the employee's W2 Form.

The 80%-Rule for entertainment expenses is exactly the same as the 80%-Rule for meal expenses described in Section 1 of the *Travel* chapter. Also see Section 1 of the *Miscellaneous Deductions* chapter which shows how the 80%-Rule is applied when expenses are reported on Form 2106.

Lunch and Dinner

Sometimes, an individual attends lunch or dinner meetings in connection with his professional duties. The cost of attending such meetings can be deductible if they are sufficiently business-related. In one 1982 court case, Example 1 below, the Court even allowed a deduction for luncheon meetings which consisted of discussions of recent journal articles. This court case opens the door for college teachers to deduct for "luncheon meetings" with colleagues organized for similar purposes.

> **Example 1**
> Beltran was an anesthesiologist at a hospital in Maryland. He periodically joined a group of other anesthesiologists in "Journal Club" luncheons held at various local restaurants. The purpose of these luncheons was for the anesthesiologists "to discuss the latest professional journals they had read."
> The Tax Court ruled that the cost of these luncheons was a legitimate professional expense. Thus, the cost could be claimed as a "business meal" deduction. The Court allowed the full amount claimed by the anesthesiologist — about $400 over a two-year period. [Beltran, TC Memo 1982-153]

> **Example 2**
> A Vocational Education Coordinator belonged to several vocational organizations which often met over lunch or dinner. The IRS ruled that these meetings were directly related to his professional duties. Therefore, he was entitled to deduct the portion of the cost of any such meal which was in excess of what he would have normally spent. Since he ordinarily simply ate a sack lunch at his school or ate dinner at home, this would cover almost the entire cost of the meals. [IRS Private Letter Ruling 8006004]
> While this ruling forced the educational coordinator to subtract what he ordinarily would have spent from the cost of the meals at those meetings, in practice the IRS is not so strict. If a business meal qualifies for deduction, the full cost (subject to the 80%-Rule) will almost always be allowed.

Each of the above examples concerned an individual deducting for lunch or dinner meetings with other persons whom he ordinarily did not work with. But what about meetings with co-workers? Can you deduct for lunch or dinner meetings attended just by those whom you regularly see at work? The following recent court case indicates that the answer is yes, as long as the meetings are not too frequent. Thus, you can't simply use the entertainment deduction to write off all your lunches even if business is always discussed. But occasional lunches with co-workers can qualify for an entertainment expense deduction.

> **Example 3**
> Moss was a partner in a law firm in Chicago. The partners and other employees met over lunch at a nearby restaurant each day to give each other advice on handling current matters and to discuss other business. This was the most convenient time to meet since the courts were in recess at this time and all the lawyers would generally be free to attend.
> When Moss attempted to deduct his share of the daily lunches, the IRS objected. The Tax Court upheld this objection. It ruled that even though the lunches served a business purpose, the frequency of these lunches meant they became a normal personal expense.
> However, 9 of the Tax Court judges signed a concurring opinion that the

deduction was only ruled out in this case because of the frequency of the lunches. As the justice who wrote the opinion noted,

"*I do not view this opinion as disallowing the cost of meals in all instances where only partners, co-workers, etc. are involved. We have here findings that the partners met at lunch because it was 'convenient' and 'convenient' 5 days a week, 52 weeks a year.*"

The concurring opinion thus indicates that occasional meetings with co-workers could qualify for the entertainment expense deduction. The line between occasional and regular is not spelled out. That would depend on the particular facts and circumstances.

While only 9 of 19 Tax Court judges signed the concurring opinion, the position of the other 10 is not indicated. Since it is likely that at least one of these 10 would join the other 9 were it necessary to rule on this issue, it is reasonable to treat this as representing the viewpoint of the Tax Court. [Moss, 80 TC No. 57]

Example 3 Continued

Moss appealed to the U.S. Court of Appeals in his district. But the Appeals Court upheld the decision denying the deduction. However, its 1985 written opinion gives additional information as to where to draw the line when deciding the deductibility of lunches with co-workers.

First of all, the purpose of the deduction is to compensate persons who "*spend more money on business meals because they are business meals than they would spend on their meals if they were not working.*" Thus, if you are planning to deduct a business lunch, you should go to a more expensive restaurant than the ones to which you ordinarily go. Of course, if you ordinarily bring your own lunch or dine cheaply at the cafeteria where you work, then going out to lunch at a restaurant automatically satisfies this criterion. In the Moss case, they always ate at the same modestly-priced cafe, so there was no evidence that their business lunches were costing them any more than personal lunches would have cost.

Second, the business purpose of lunching together is to provide, in the Court's phrase, "*social lubrication*" conducive to the transacting of business. This extra *social lubrication* would not ordinarily be needed if you are lunching with an officemate or someone else you work with closely. On the other hand, discussing business matters with someone you don't know as well might provide the helpful *social lubrication* conducive to the business-related matters being discussed. In the Moss case, the lawyers eating lunch together were part of a small 8-lawyer firm who "*did not need a daily lunch to cement relationships among them.*"

And finally, the Appeals Court agreed with the Tax Court that deducting the cost of daily meals was pushing it too far, even had there been more business justification. According to the Court, "*It is all a matter of degree and circumstance (the expense of a testimonial dinner, for example, would be deductible on a morale-building rationale); and particularly of frequency. Daily—for a full year—is too often, perhaps even for entertainment of clients.*" [Moss, CA-7 85-1 USTC ¶ 9285 CCH]

Recordkeeping Requirement

The IRS requires you to record the following information for all entertaining which you claim as a deduction:

(1) The **amount** of each separate item of entertaining, except that incidental items like taxi fares or telephone calls can be aggregated together.

(2) The **date** of the expenditure.

(3) The **place** of entertainment, including the name and location of restaurants where dining occurred.

(4) The **business purpose** of the entertainment. (A sentence or two describing the nature of your business conversation would be appropriate.)

(5) The **occupation** or other information concerning the persons being entertained, including name, title, or other designations sufficient to establish their business relationship to you.

You should record the above information in a timely manner. That is, you should write it down soon after the entertainment occurred, not reconstruct it from memory at a later date.

You must also keep a receipt, cancelled check, or other documentary evidence substantiating any expenditure of $25 or more.

Where Do You Deduct Entertainment Expenses?

Unreimbursed entertainment expenses are claimed by employees as a an *employee business expense* in column B of Form 2106. The total computed on Form 2106 is carried over to Schedule A where it is claimed as a miscellaneous deduction. The total of miscellaneous deductions is then subjected to the 2% of Adjusted Gross Income floor [cf. Section 1 of the *Miscellaneous Deductions* chapter for information on how to report your expenses on Form 2106]. Self-employed persons claim entertainment expenses on line 26b of Schedule C. (This has the advantage of escaping the 2% floor and being available to those who claim the standard deduction as well as those who itemize.)

An employee who receives a reimbursement that is not included as taxable income on his W-2 Form can simply ignore the reimbursement and expenses for tax purposes, provided the appropriate records are maintained. For situations where a partial or taxable reimbursement is received, see Section 1 of the *Miscellaneous Deductions* chapter.

Chapter 21

Withholding

Withholding from Salary
The amount withheld from your paychecks is determined by your salary and the number of *allowances* claimed on the most recent W-4 (or W-4A) Form which you filed with your employer. In the past, many employees remained governed by the original W-4 Form they filled out when they first started work for their current employer. However, as you probably know, all employees were required this past year to fill out a new W-4 (or W-4A) Form before October 1, 1987. (Failure to file by this date resulted in the employer withholding as though there were no children or deductions.)

One allowance is claimed for each dependent and for deductions, business losses, tax credits, etc. which have the same tax lowering effect as claiming an additional dependent. In other words, the "value" of each allowance is the same as the personal exemption amount for dependents. For example, the withholding for an individual who claimed 6 allowances on his W-4 Form would be about the same as the taxes paid by an individual with 6 personal exemptions and no itemized deductions, tax credits, etc.

The reason employees were required to fill out a new W-4 (or W-4A) Form in 1987 was that the personal exemption amount was raised sharply from $1,080 on 1986 tax returns to $1,900 on 1987 tax returns. Thus, $10,000 worth of deductions, for example, would produce 9 allowances in 1986, but only 5 allowances in 1987. An old W-4 Form which generated 9 allowances for this amount of deductions would produce too little withholding in 1987. (Recall each extra allowance *reduces* the amount of withholding.)

In fact, many employees who waited until well into 1987 before filing a new W-4 will have had too little withheld from these paychecks. If you are in this category, be prepared to owe more taxes than usual or receive less refund. Also in such a case, don't automatically conclude that your W-4 needs adjustment. Because the W-4 was in effect only during part of 1987, the amount of tax due on your 1987 tax return is not a good indicator for future years, when your new W-4 will be in full effect.

In fact, if you filed your new W-4 on the late side and still owed little tax or received a refund, this may be a tipoff that you claimed too few allowances. You should review your Form W-4 or W-4A to see if more allowances should be claimed to avoid overwithholding in the future.

The Form W-4 issued by the IRS for 1987 takes into account all taxable income, deductions, tax credits, etc. that are estimated for the year. Also available was a simplified version, Form W-4A, which could be used instead of Form W-4, at the option of the employee. Form W-4A is simpler and shorter because it does not take into account such items as tax credits (other than the child care tax credit) or nonwage income from interest, dividends, capital gains, etc. Form W-4A also requires $2,000 of deductions to generate one allowance instead of the more accurate $1,900 required on Form W-4. Thus, Form W-4 is generally more accurate than Form W-4A in predicting the amount of tax that will actually be due.

Form W-4A generally results in overwithholding except when there is nonwage income from interest, dividends, etc. Since this type of income is not included on Form W-4A, underwithholding can be the result when such income is present.

Form W-4 (or Form W-4A) has 2 basic components—a worksheet for computing the number of withholding allowances you are entitled to claim, and the shorter actual W-4 (or W-4A) itself, which is what you actually file with your employer. You do not file the worksheet, but rather keep it for your own records.

Married couples should use only one worksheet based on their combined exemptions, deductions, etc. The total number of allowances computed on this worksheet is then divided between the husband and wife who file individual W-4 (or W-4A) Forms with their respective employers. The IRS recommends that the higher-earning spouse claim all the withholding allowances on his W-4 Form, while the other spouse claims 0. Married couples who choose a different allocation method will usually experience overwithholding.

Similarly, if you work for more than one employer during the year, you cannot claim the same allowance twice. You must allocate the allowances among the W-4's filed with each of your employers.

Individuals whose tax picture is expected to materially change for 1988 are supposed to file a new withholding form with their employer. (As discussed below, a penalty applies unless the total withholding plus estimated taxes paid during 1988 is at least either (i) 90% of the actual 1988 tax liability, or (ii) 100% of the 1987 tax liability.) At presstime, it was undecided whether the IRS would offer one or two forms for taxpayers wishing to change their withholding for 1988.

If you claim 10 or more withholding allowances, your employer is required to report this fact to the IRS. In such a case, the IRS may write you, asking for your computation of the allowances to which you claim you're entitled.

Students with summer jobs may be able to avoid any withholding on their wages. Any student (or other individual) who owed no tax the previous year and expects to owe no tax for the current year qualifies. The exemption from withholding is claimed by writing *"exempt"* on the appropriate line of Form W-4. However, under the new law, exempt status cannot be claimed by any person who (1) can be claimed as a dependent by a parent or someone else; (2) expects his total income to be more than $500; and (3) has some interest, dividends, or other nonwage income. A person satisfying all 3 of these conditions will generally owe tax on 1987 income. For example, a dependent student who earns $1,500 on a summer job and has $400 in interest income in 1987 would owe $44 tax. (However, he could *earn* up to $2,540 in wage income in 1987 without owing any tax, as long as he had no additional *nonwage* income.)

Backup Withholding on Interest and Dividends

If you fail to furnish a correct social security number to a bank, savings & loan, stock broker, or other financial institution, this could subject you to backup withholding. This backup withholding consists of 20% of the interest, dividends, etc. paid to you. Upon your furnishing of a correct social security account number, the withholding ceases. This is not a penalty, just extra withholding. You get credit for this withholding when you file your tax return, the same as for amounts withheld from your paychecks.

Estimated Tax Payments

If you have taxable income which is not subject to withholding, then you may be required to make quarterly estimated tax payments throughout the year. Generally, you are required to prepay (through withholding and/or estimated tax payments) the lesser of

(i) 90% of your total tax liability for the year
or
(ii) 100% of the tax shown on the preceding year's tax return.

If salary withholding equals either (i) or (ii), then no estimated tax payments are required. Also, no estimated tax payments are required if the total amounts due for the year are $500 or less.

You don't have to verify on your tax return that you have paid the appropriate amount of estimated tax; the IRS computers will check this automatically. If you have not, you will be sent a bill for amount of penalty due. (At presstime, Congress was considering lowering the 90% figure to 80% for the 1987 tax year only. The 80% figure is the one that applied prior to 1987.)

Your estimated tax is paid in four installments, the first one being due April 15. You use Form 1040-ES to make your estimated tax payments. This form contains a worksheet for computing the amount due plus four vouchers which you send in with your payments. You do not send in your computation worksheet — only the vouchers indicating the amounts you are paying.

There is an exception which applies if your income is irregular, with more being earned toward the end of the year than toward the beginning. You will escape penalty if your estimated taxes at each quarterly payment date meet the 90% test for your income through the end of the corresponding quarter—i.e. your estimated taxes are computed as though your income would continue to be earned at the same rate for the rest of the year. To use this exception, you file Form 2210 with your tax return for the year. The IRS can also waive the penalty for an underpayment due to an unexpected calamity such as loss of records in a fire or serious illness.

If your 1987 tax return shows a refund due, you can indicate on the tax form to have part or all of this refund treated as an estimated tax payment made on April 15, 1988, rather than being paid out to you.

There is a penalty for underpayment of estimated tax. This penalty is adjusted periodically, based on the prime interest rate. This penalty is not deductible.

There is an exception that applies to estimated payments made for the 1987 tax year. Many individuals had too little withheld from their paychecks during the first part of 1987 before they filed their new W-4 or W-4A Form. The IRS will waive the penalty attributable to this underwithholding, as long as new W-4 or W-4A forms were filed with employers by June 1, 1987 (unless filed in *bad faith*). This exception only applies to wage income, not to other income such as self-employment income, investment income, etc.

Don't overlook the following remedy if you discover towards the end of the year that you did not make sufficient estimated tax payments. You can request your employer to withhold extra amounts from your yearend paychecks. Form W-4 is used to make this request. This enables you to move the total prepayment (withholding plus estimated tax) towards the required amount. Under IRS regulations, your employer is *required* to honor your request. He must withhold any extra amounts you request after being given reasonable advance notice to make the adjustment. [Reg. section 31.3402(1)-2]

Having extra amounts withheld from your yearend paychecks is better than making an extra estimated tax payment near yearend. Your estimated tax payments are generally supposed to be made evenly throughout the year. Even if the total is sufficient to cover your liability, you could be penalized because the early payments were less than the later payments.

But withholding can be considered spread out evenly no matter when it occurs. This means that amounts withheld late in the year are treated exactly the same as if they were withheld earlier. There is no penalty unless the total for the year is insufficient.

Withholding on Pension and Annuity Payments

Under current law, income tax will be withheld on payments from pension plans, annuities, IRAs and Keogh plans. However, any individual can exempt himself from this withholding (for any reason) by filing an appropriate form with the payer. Payers are required to notify you in advance of your right to elect out of the withholding rules. In any event, even if no election is made, nothing will be withheld from payments which do not exceed a certain minimum amount.

Chapter 22

Travel

SECTION 1:
BASIC RULES ON DEDUCTING TRAVEL EXPENSES

You can deduct the cost of travel connected with your job or other income-producing activity. This includes travel between two or more job locations the same day, travel to professional or union meetings, travel related to a temporary job away from home, travel to obtain education, travel in connection with an outside business activity, etc. An exception is ordinary commuting expenses which cannot be deducted except as discussed in Sections 2 and 3.

There are special rules which apply to various types of deductible travel. These are discussed in later sections. The remainder of this introductory section concerns those general rules which apply to all types of travel.

Where on the Income Tax Form Do You Claim Travel Expense Deductions?
The 1986 Tax Reform Act has changed the way travel expenses are treated on 1987 tax returns. As in prior years, an employee still uses Form 2106, *Employee Business Expenses*, on which to list his travel expenses. However, the total of travel expenses is now entered as a *miscellaneous deduction* on Schedule A of the 1987 tax return. (In prior years, employee travel expenses were treated as an *adjustment to income* rather than as an *itemized deduction*.) And, as discussed in the *Miscellaneous Deductions* chapter, the sum total of travel expenses plus other miscellaneous deductions is subjected to a 2% of Adjusted Gross Income floor. However, an exception is discussed there under which expenses which were reported on your W-2 Form as having been reimbursed by your employer are still claimed as an *adjustment to income* rather than as a *miscellaneous deduction*.

Self-employed persons claim travel expenses on Schedule C, the same as any other business expense related to their self-employment activity. Thus, these expenses escape the 2% of Adjusted Gross Income floor that applies to miscellaneous deductions; also, non-itemizers as well as itemizers get to deduct their travel expenses.

An employee with an outside business activity should take note of the more favorable treatment accorded self-employed persons when deciding how to treat his travel expenses. For example, suppose a college professor incurs unreimbursed travel expenses in attending a convention in his field of expertise. If the professor has self-employment income from consulting or writing, then he may have a choice. Instead of treating travel expenses as a miscellaneous deduction connected with his college duties, he may be able to treat these expenses as a Schedule C writeoff connected with his self-employment activity. [cf. Section 1 of the *Miscellaneous Deductions* chapter for further discussion.]

Which Expenses Are Deductible?

The first point to note is the distinction between travel and transportation expenses. **Transportation** refers to the task of getting from one place to another. But **travel** expenses may include, in addition to transportation expenses, certain living costs.

Let's assume that your travel meets the requirements for deductibility. Then if you are **away from home overnight,** the following are deductible travel expenses:

- Air, rail, or bus fares both en route and at your destination
- Lodging both en route and at your destination
- Meals both en route and at your destination (subject to the 80%-Rule discussed
  later in this section)
- Transportation costs to and from your destination
- Baggage charges
- Reasonable cleaning and laundry expenses
- Transportation between the airport and your hotel
- Transportation between where you obtain meals and lodging and a temporary work assignment
- Telephone and telegraph expenses (non-personal)
- Reasonable tips connected with the above expenses

If, on the other hand, you are not away from home overnight, then only your transportation costs are deductible. You cannot deduct the cost of meals, lodging, or laundry. For example, if you drove from Washington, D.C. to New York and back all in one day, you would not be permitted any deduction for meals. Several courts felt this rule was unreasonable until the Supreme Court upheld it as a fair and workable administrative approach.

What Does "Away From Home" Mean?

"Home" has a special meaning to the IRS. It means the general area of your principal place of employment, regardless of where you maintain your family residence. For example, if your family residence is in Chicago but you work in Milwaukee, then your *"tax home"* is the Milwaukee area. If you stay overnight in Milwaukee, then you are not considered to be away from home overnight. Of course, you probably live and work in the same general area. Then this general area is considered to be your tax home.

Exactly how much territory the "general area" includes is not well specified. Distinct cities at a distance of 50 miles apart would probably be considered in different areas. However, two points in the same metropolitan area would be consid-

ered in the same general area, even if those points were considerably far apart.
[Harris, TC Memo 1980-56]

What About Commuting Costs?

In general, the cost of commuting between your residence and your work is not deductible. However, there are two exceptions relating to temporary assignments away from your home.

(1) If you are on a business trip out of town or if you are on a temporary assignment out of town, you may deduct all your transportation costs between your temporary lodgings and your business destination. You may also deduct all transportation costs from one business destination to another.

(2) If you are required to work at a temporary location outside the general area of your home city, you may deduct transportation expenses for daily round trips from your home to the temporary business location. For example, if your home is in Baltimore and you are required to work in Washington, D.C. for a month, then you can deduct your commuting expenses.

See Sections 2 and 3 for further details.

80%-Rule for Meal Expenses

Meal expenses are no longer deductible in full. Instead, only 80% of meal (and beverage) expenses can be deducted. All expenses of the meal such as tax, tips, parking, etc. are included under this 80%-Rule. However, transportation to and from a meal is not subject to the reduction.

Example 1

While attending an out-of-town professional meeting, you incur the following unreimbursed expenses for dinner: $40 for meals and beverages, $3 for tax, $1 for coat check, and $6 for tip—a total of $50. The cost of taxi fare (including tip) to and from the restaurant is $7.

The $50 total is subject to the 80%-Rule, but not the taxi fare. Thus, the meal yields a deduction of 80% × $50 = $40 plus the entire $7 taxi fare—a total of $47.

The 80%-Rule is used before application of the 2% of Adjusted Gross Income floor that applies to the total of miscellaneous deductions [cf. the *Miscellaneous Deductions* chapter]. This illustrated by the following example:

Example 2

An individual's Adjusted Gross Income is $50,000 and his miscellaneous deductions other than travel expenses total $700. In addition, he incurs the following unreimbursed deductible travel expenses during the year:

Transportation:	$620
Lodging:	300
Laundry:	50
	$970
Meals:	$200

In computing his travel expenses, he first applies the 80%-Rule to the meal expenses: 80% × $200 = $160. Thus, the total deductible travel expenses come to $970 + $160 = $1,130. His total of all miscellaneous deductions is then $700 + $1,130 = $1,830. However, this is reduced by 2% of Adjusted Gross Income: × $50,000 = $1,000. This produces a net deduction of $1,830 − $1,000 = $830.

The above 2 examples illustrate the principles involved in deducting meal expenses, combined with travel and other job-related expenses. In practice, Form 2106 separates these expenses into 2 columns, Column B for meal and entertainment expenses and Column A for other employee business expenses. At the bottom of the form, the total deduction for employee business expenses is obtained by adding the final Column A total plus 80% of the Column B total. In the body of the form, any reimbursements received from your employer are credited against either Column A or Column B expenses and subtracted from the total *expenses* accordingly. Further details, including examples on how to handle expenses on Form 2106, are contained in Section 1 of the *Miscellaneous Deductions* chapter.

Exception to the 80%-Rule

The full cost of certain *banquet meals* can be included in travel expenses, with no 80% reduction. To qualify, the banquet must be part of a convention, seminar, meeting, or similar business program attended by at least 40 individuals, with more than 50% of the participants being away from home. The meal must include a speaker and the expense of the meal must be included as part of the "package cost," rather than being separately stated. (It is surely a coincidence that members of Congress are so often speakers at just these types of banquets.)

Expenses of Spouse or Other Family Member

When you travel for professional reasons and are accompanied by your spouse or other family members, their expenses are not deductible unless it can be definitely established that their travel has a bona fide business purpose. The performance of incidental services does not satisfy this business purpose requirement. However, if your spouse accompanies you on a business trip, you do not have to split your expenses down the middle. Instead, you can deduct what it would have cost had you traveled alone. For example, if you and your spouse occupy a double room at a hotel which charges $65 for a single room and $80 for a double room, then you may deduct $65 as your lodging cost.

Travel

Recordkeeping

You should keep two kinds of records of your travel expenses—receipts and an expense diary. You do not include these records with the tax return you file. Rather, they are kept in case your return is audited.

Expense Diary

Your diary should contain the following:

1. The place or places of your travel
2. The dates of your departure and return home
3. The business reason for your travel
4. A daily list of your deductible expenses

You should list the amount of each separate expenditure (such as the cost of your transportation or lodging). However, each day the cost of your breakfast, lunch, dinner, and other expenses may be grouped together if they are set forth in reasonable categories such as meals, gasoline and oil, cab fares, telephone calls, etc. Tips may be grouped with the cost of the conncted service.

You are not required to record amounts your employer pays directly for any ticket or other travel item. However, if you charge these items to your employer (through a credit card or otherwise), then you must make a record of the expenditures.

A receipt, paid bill, or similar evidence is required to support any expenditure of $25 or more and any expenditure for lodging, even if less than $25. The receipt should show the amount, date, place, and type of expenditure and should be sufficiently detailed to show the different elements of the expenditure. For example, a hotel bill should show as separate items, the cost for lodging, telephone calls, meals, etc. A cancelled check together with an appropriate bill will be sufficient. However, a cancelled check alone is inadequate.

If you cannot establish the portion of an expenditure attributable to each person participating in the travel but you have established the amount of the expenditure, it will ordinarily be allocated to each participant on a pro rata basis.

Your records should be timely. You should write down your expenses in your expense diary at or near the time they are incurred. If the record entries are made later when there is a lack of accurate recall, they will not comply with this rule.

The following is a sample of how a diary should look for attending a 2-day professional convention. The format is copied from an official IRS publication.

Date	Item	Place	Amount	Business Purpose
April 1	Airplace fare (round trip Chicago-Dallas)	Dallas	$260.20	Attend Convention of XYZ Assn.
	Meals and tips		35.10	
	Lodging		62.50	

April 2	Meals and tips	28.50
	Automobile Rental (2 days)	62.00
	Tips	3.50

Remark: Pay careful attention to the recordkeeping requirements as illustrated in the above example. Note the **5 different pieces of information required — date, item, place, amount, and business purpose.** If you leave any of these pieces out, your travel expenses could be ruled nondeductible. That's what happened to the taxpayer in the following court case.

> *Example*
>
> Mr. Coursey was a manufacturer's representative and traveled extensively for his job. He kept a diary and produced cancelled checks for his lodging expenses. But his expenses were ruled nondeductible because his diaries were not adequate. They did not show the location or the business purpose of his away from home business expenses. Even though the cancelled checks might have established the location of his lodging expenses, the Court said that still would not be good enough. Coursey had presented no evidence indicating the business purpose of his trips. Coursey's failure to write down a few extra words in his diary turned out to be a very expensive mistake. [TC Memo 1974-43]

Reimbursed Expenses

You may receive a reimbursement from your employer for travel expenses which you incur. Usually, you are required to give an expense accounting to your employer. If this accounting satisfies the recordkeeping requirements described above, then you do not have to provide any further accounting to the IRS. They will check your employer's records if they wish to see verification of these expenses. If you did not make an adequate accounting to your employer for reimbursed travel expenses or if your expenses exceeded the reimbursement, then you must retain your expense diary and receipts yourself.

Your employer may reimburse you for your travel expenses by allowing a fixed mileage rate for automobile transportation or a per diem rate for subsistence while away from home overnight. (Subsistence includes meals and lodging, laundry, cleaning, and tips but does not include transportation, taxi fares, or the cost of telegrams or telephone calls.) If the automobile mileage rate does not exceed $22\frac{1}{2}$ cents per mile and the per diem subsistence rate does not exceed $44 per day, then this will be accepted by the IRS provided the other elements of time, place, and business purpose of travel are substantiated. In most major and mid-sized cities, a substantially higher per diem rate will be accepted, depending upon the price level in the particular city. You can check with the IRS to find out what the current allowable per diem rate is for the city to which you are traveling.

The $44 per diem allowance only applies if you are reimbursed by your employer. If you pay expenses out of your pocket, you cannot use the $44 per diem rate.

What If You Are Missing Records or Receipts?

You are supposed to keep a contemporaneous diary and receipts, as described at the beginning of this section. But, legally speaking, this is not a strict necessity. You are entitled to offer other evidence in support of your deduction, as long as the 5 basic pieces of information (date, item, place, amount, and business purpose) are attested to. For example, the Congressional tax-writing committee specifically noted that *"testimony from a disinterested, unrelated party describing the taxpayer's activities, may be of sufficient probative value that it should not be automatically excluded from consideration."* It also noted that records created at a later date might have some value, but would have far less *"probative value"* than *"written evidence arising at or near the time of the expenditure."*

As a matter of fact, the courts have not been impressed with travel records in which entries were not made in a timely fashion. Four cases illustrate this situation. In the first case, a salesman presented a spiral notebook in which, he claimed, he had made entries on a day to day basis concerning his travel expenses. But the Court took a look at the notebook and promptly threw the case out. The pages were too clean and there was too little wear at the wire ring bindings for a notebook handled frequently. And the ink was suspiciously uniform in color and intensity. [79,002 PH Memo TC]

The second case centered upon the adequacy of a travel diary. In this case, the Court was convinced that the diary was *"an accurate, contemporaneous record of the date and amounts of expenditures."* But, the Court stated, *"we believe that, in certain instances, the place and business purpose of petitioner's travel were recorded in later years. In such instances, petitioner's diary does not satisfy the adequate records requirement with respect to those elements."* Because of this inadequacy, about 60% of the claimed travel deduction was disallowed. [Benke, TC Memo 1979-195]

The third case illustrates the pitfall of recording suspiciously uniform numbers in the diary. An individual who traveled quite a bit on business presented a diary of his expenses, as required. But for each day he was away during the year, his diary listed meal expenses of exactly $20. The Court found *"it hard to believe that petitioner's expenses remained so perfectly consistent throughout that year."* The Court concluded that the diary simply represented an after-the-fact estimate of expenses rather than a contemporaneous diary of actual expenses incurred. Because of this, it disallowed his meal expenses altogether. [TC Memo 1979-432]

And the fourth case makes it clear your diary should be handwritten, not typed. The only record which was presented to the court was a neatly-typed statement listing mileage, motel costs, and meal costs. This indicated the entries were not made in a timely fashion and no deduction was allowed. [Johnston, 51 AFTR 2d 83-313]

When some receipts are missing, the matter is not so serious. In the past, IRS agents have been known to disallow a deduction whenever a required receipt is missing. But in recent instructions to its agents, the IRS suggested going a bit easier on this requirement. According to these instructions,

"If a taxpayer cannot document precisely the amounts spent for expenses while away from home for a business purpose, examiners may establish that reasonable amounts were spent for such items if the taxpayer can clearly establish the following.

(a) Time — Dates of departure and return for each trip away from home, and number of days away from home.

(b) Place — Destinations or locality of travel, e.g. name of city or town.

(c) Business Purpose — Business reason for travel or nature of business benefit derived or expected to be derived, and

(d) Proof that Expenditures were Actually Incurred — A reasonable showing based upon secondary evidence, including oral testimony that out-of-pocket expenses were paid." [Internal Revenue Manual, Section 4244]

However, despite the liberal wording of item (d), this should not be taken as a go-ahead to ignore the receipt-keeping requirement. IRS agents are only permitted, not required, to allow deductions without the required receipts. And this is only suggested when not too much is missing. If there is substantial disregard of the receipt-keeping rule, the IRS will probably disallow any deductions and perhaps even assess a negligence penalty in flagrant cases. Furthermore, even if an IRS agent allows a deduction for undocumented expenses, he is instructed that such an allowance

"should be kept to a minimum consistent with an appraisal of the facts in each case in order to ensure that a taxpayer does not profit from his/her failure to keep required records of all elements of travel expenses."

In deciding how far to go in permitting estimates to be made of expenses, IRS agents are instructed to take a look at the overall credibility and accuracy of the entire tax return. According to the IRS,

"Due consideration should be given to the reasonableness of the taxpayer's stated expenditures for the claimed purposes in relation to his/her reported income, to the reliability and accuracy of his/her records in connection with other items more readily lending themselves to detailed recordkeeping, and to the general credibility of his/her statements in the light of the entire record in the case." [IRM 4244]

Standard Per Diem Meal Allowance

There is a standard per diem meal allowance you can use while traveling away from home. You have the option of using this per diem rate or keeping track of your actual expenses. This per diem rate only applies to the cost of meals, not to other travel expenses such as lodging, transportation, etc.

The standard meal allowance is $14 per day for travel requiring a stay of less than 30 days in one general locality and $9 per day for travel that requires a stay of 30 days or more in one general locality. This rate can be adjusted by the IRS from time to time.

On the day that travel begins or ends, the allowance is prorated on the basis of 6-hour periods. For each 6-hour period or portion thereof, you are allowed 1/4 of the daily allowance. For example, if you start your trip at 5 a.m. you get the full daily allowance, but if you start at 7 a.m. you get only 3/4 of the daily allowance for that day.

For a given year, you must either use the standard meal allowance for all travel during the year or else deduct your actual meal expenses throughout the year.

On days for which you receive a travel reimbursement from your employer which is designed to include meal expenses, you cannot use the standard meal allowance. However, such reimbursements do not prevent you from using the standard meal allowance on days for which you are not reimbursed. If you receive a specific per-diem meal reimbursement from your employer which falls short of the IRS allowance, you can deduct the difference between the IRS allowance and your employer's allowance. This only applies if the employer allowance is a straight per diem rate not based on an accounting of your actual expenses.

If you use the per diem rate, you still must substantiate the other basic elements for deductible travel — namely time, place, and business purpose. Observe that if you keep a diary as described above, the $14 and $9 rates are low enough that they will not be useful in the majority of cases. On a typical convention trip, for example, most people spend far more than this amount for meals. However, if you neglected to keep a diary, then the per diem amounts might be useful.

Example

You attended a 3-day professional convention at which you presented a paper. You did not create any diary of your expenses. However, you have receipts for your airplane ticket and your hotel bill. Technically, you have not met the precise recordkeeping requirements for deducting your travel expenses because you have no diary of your expenses. However, you have enough secondary evidence (see the preceding subsection) to establish the time, place and business purpose of your travel. Since you have no record of your meal expenses, you could use the standard allowance of $14 per day for meals if you wish.

Another case where the per diem rate might be useful is if you are at a temporary job out of town where you eat your meals at home. In such a case, the $9 per day might exceed your actual cost. However, even sporadic dining at restaurants could push your actual total above this amount. And all you need in such a case is a diary in which the proper entries have been made.

The standard meal allowances are subjected to the same 80%-Rule, described earlier in this section, that applies to meal expenses in general. For example, suppose an individual travels away from home for 10 days, with the standard meal allowance yielding: 10 × $14 = $140. Under the 80%-Rule, the amount actually claimed as a miscellaneous deduction for these meals would be 80% × $140 = $112.

Miscellaneous Travel

The following sections describe special rules that apply to various types of job-related travel. However, don't overlook miscellaneous travel not covered by any of these specific situations. As long as the travel is a non-reimbursable "ordinary and necessary" expense connected with your job, it is deductible [cf. Chapter 1, Section 2].

This is emphasized by several recent court cases. The first concerned a teacher of the handicapped who deducted transportation costs for taking his students on trips to various activities in the community. He was not required to take the students on these trips but that did not matter. According to the Court,

> "Although there is no proof that Mr. Gudmundsson was obligated by his employer to take the students on these trips, we know of no requirement that there must be an underlying legal obligation to make an expenditure before it can qualify as an 'ordinary and necessary' business expense. . . The arrangement of such activities for his students is in accord with what a teacher of the handicapped might do and the expenses incurred therein are clearly business expenses [and therefore deductible]." [Gudmundsson, TC Memo 1978-299]

The second case concerned an assistant principal at a high school who was responsible for student discipline and attendance, computer scheduling and grading, student transportation, and other duties. He was expected, although not required, to attend job-related meetings and seminars and to serve on school and civic committees.

During the year, he attended many meetings at different locations at which he discussed the problems which his school and other schools in the county were experiencing. The IRS and the Court both agreed that he was entitled to deduct his transportation costs in attending these meetings. The Court allowed him a $600 deduction, indicating it would have been higher had his recordkeeping been better. [Wilhelm, TC Memo 1978-327]

And a third case involved a Professor of Management and Marketing at a university in the South. During the course of a year, he made about 100 trips by automobile in connection with his professional duties. These included 31 trips to a library 100 miles away which had extensive materials not available in his home town, 44 trips in connection with seminars he ran at a local hotel, 13 trips to the airport to pick up visiting speakers, 2 trips to attend a Board of Regents meeting, and 8 trips to conduct surveys on grocery prices. The Court ruled that all of these trips could be deducted. His total deduction for auto travel during the year amounted to $1,939. [Stearns, TC Memo 1984-97]

Travel to Libraries

Traveling to a library for employment-related purposes is a common occurrence. If the library is located within your general home area, then the rules discussed in Section 2 apply. That is, you will be entitled to a deduction if you visit more than one business location during the day. But if you go on an otherwise nonworking day, travel to and from the library will generally be considered nondeductible commuting.

On the other hand, if the library (or other business destination) is located outside your general home area, the rules allow you to deduct your transportation costs even if it is the only business activity that day. Such travel falls under the *temporary job away from home* category discussed in Section 3.

However, a recent court case shows that to be deductible, you must be able to point to a business reason for traveling to the out-of-town library. A community college English teacher took courses at a college 160 miles from home. The IRS did not challenge the deduction for traveling to and from the college for days on which he attended class. This was a legitimate educational expense [see the *Expenses of Attending School* chapter].

But he also traveled to the distant college on days he had no class in order to do research in the library. The Court did not allow a deduction for this travel. The only reason the teacher gave for using this particular library was that he was familiar with the layout and it was near his parents' home. According to the Court, there *"were other libraries closer to petitioner's home, that were more extensive in their collection of books and periodicals pertaining to subject matter useful for petitioner's job."* Thus, travel to the library was for *"personal convenience"* rather than for a valid business purpose. [Ginkel, TC Memo 1980-424]

This case offers an important tip to those who travel to a library distant from home. They should have a solid reason why the library was chosen over one closer to home, especially if the closer one has a more extensive collection. For example, the smaller library might have certain materials not found in the larger one. Or, materials in the larger library's collection might typically be off the shelf due to heavy use by faculty and students.

SECTION 2:
MORE THAN ONE JOB LOCATION

If you work in more than one location during a given day, you can deduct the cost of transportation from one location to another. This applies whether or not you are working for the same employer at both locations or for different employers. You cannot deduct the cost of traveling from your home to the day's first place of employment nor from the final place of employment back home.

Example 1.

Atkins is employed at the State University where he is a Professor of Poultry Science. On Monday and Wednesday nights, he goes from the University to the local office of the CROA (Chicken Raisers of America) where he is employed to teach a course in Chicken Management to interested farmers. Along the way, he stops off at a restaurant for dinner. He may deduct the cost of his transportation from the University to the CROA. However, he cannot deduct the cost of dinner because he is not away from home overnight.

Example 2.

Baker is a Professor of Computer Science and teaches primarily at the main campus of a State University. However on Tuesday and Thursday, she teaches in the morning at the main campus and in the afternoon she teaches a programming course at a second campus in a different location. She may deduct the cost of transportation from one location to the other. If she stops off at an intermediate point, she deducts what the transportation cost would have been had she traveled directly.

Example 3.
Mrs. Chu teaches Chemistry in a high school five days a week. On Saturdays she works at a chemical firm. She cannot deduct any transportation costs since she did not visit two different locations during the same day.

Example 4.
Beards was an associate professor at a Community College in a large northeastern city. The College had 5 buildings located in various parts of the city and she found it necessary to travel from one building to another, usually by taxi, during the course of a day.
Beards was permitted to deduct the cost of traveling from one College building to another the same day. This constituted deductible travel between job locations the same day. [Beards, TC Memo 1984-438]

The above case concerned traveling from one college building to another the same day. Although these buildings were not located on the same "campus," the following case would indicate that travel in such a situation would still be deductible. This case involved travel between different locations on the same Air Force base. But this is the same type of situation as occurs when a college teacher uses his auto to get from one building to another located on the same campus.

Example 5.
Brandt was a flight engineer assigned to work at an Air Force base for a period of 44 days. He needed to transport himself from one part of the base to another in connection with the duties he was expected to perform. However, after 2 days, he found the motor pool transportation to be unreliable and rented an automobile for the remainder of his stay.
Brandt was permitted to deduct the cost of his rental automobile. He used the auto to travel from one business location to another. Even though the locations were on the same Air Force base, this made no difference. Because the existing motor pool transportation was inadequate and the Air Force would not reimburse him for his transportation, the Court allowed the deduction. [Brandt, TC Memo 1982-180].

Example 6.
Smith drives to his office on the campus of a large University. Later in the morning, he drives several miles to and from a library on the other side of town. In the afternoon, he drives to the airport and back to pick up a visiting faculty member at the airport. None of his travel expenses is reimbursable by the school.
The cost of these side trips is a deductible business expense. If, instead of returning to his office after a side trip, he goes straight home, his deduction is limited to the mileage in excess of what he would have traveled in commuting back and forth directly between home and office.

Example 7.
Kutchinski was a teacher at an Air Force base. Since she had no office at the Air Force base, she set up an office in her home for the preparation of classes and related duties. She was not permitted to deduct the cost of driving between her home and the classroom. The Court ruled her travel to be a non-deductible commuting expense. [Kutchinski, ¶ 65,043 P-H Memo TC]

Example 8.
Lacy was a physician who worked at a medical clinic during the day. He also maintained an office at home which he used for storage of records, bookkeeping, and transcription of medical records in connection with his own medical practice. Lacy attempted to deduct the cost of traveling between his office at home and the clinic where he worked.

The Court denied his deduction. The clinic was the *principal place of business* for his medical practice. His home office was a *secondary* location for this medical practice. When an individual maintains a secondary office at home, travel between his home and his principal place of business is not deductible. [Lacy 55AFTR 2d 85-1273]

Example 9.
Davis was employed as a minister for a newly-founded church in a northeastern state. The congregation rented a parsonage adjacent to the church building in which Davis resided. Because the church could not provide Davis with sufficient compensation, he obtained a job teaching at a Bible College in another town. He claimed a deduction for the cost of commuting between his two jobs, one at the church where he lived and the other at the college where he taught.

The Court denied his deduction. His principal place of business was the college where he earned the vast majority of his livelihood. When an individual's residence is located at a minor place of business (in this case the church), the transportation between his residence and his principal place of employment is considered a non-deductible commuting expense. [Davis, TC Memo 1984-302]

As the above 2 examples show, travel between one's home and principal place of business is not deductible, even if some business activity is carried out at home. But, as the next example shows, if one's home is the *principal place of business,* then travel to a secondary business location is deductible.

Example 10.
Curphey owned and managed a number of residential rental properties as a side business. His management activities were conducted out of a home office from which he periodically traveled to the various rental properties. Because his home office was *the principal place of business* for his rental activities, this was considered to be deductible business travel rather than personal commuting. [Curphey, 73 TC No. 61]

If, instead of traveling from one job location to another, you go home first, then you cannot deduct any of your transportation expenses. Each trip between home and a job location is considered nondeductible commuting. An exception occurs if you travel to a job location outside the general area of your principal place of work.

Example 11.
Parker makes several trips during the day between his home and his office at school. His expenses are not deductible — he is commuting each time.

Example 12.
Jones works regularly at two different locations in the same city. He drives from home to one of the locations and then back home again. Later, he drives to and from the second location. None of his expenses is deductible. This was spelled out in a recent case involving a doctor who drove to and from his office and later drove to and from his hospital. Both of his trips were ruled to be nondeductible commuting. [Shea, TC Memo 1979-303]

Example 13.
Chandler was the principal of a high school in the Massachusetts town where he lived. Two nights a week, after returning home for dinner, he drove 37 miles to Boston where he taught a college accounting course. Since Boston was outside the *general location* of his home, he could deduct the entire cost of driving from his home to Boston and back. [Chandler, 226 F 2nd 467]

Example 14.
A professor taught in a large Texas city during the week. On weekends, he often traveled 150 miles to an out-of-town location in order to oversee a launderette business which he owned. He was permitted to deduct travel expenses connected with his secondary business out-of-town. Since he was away from home overnight, this included meals and lodging in addition to transportation expenses.

SECTION 3:
TEMPORARY JOB AWAY FROM HOME

If you have a temporary job, then you may be able to deduct your travel expenses provided you satisfy these two requirements. First, your temporary job must be **located away from home.** Second, the temporary job must qualify as being **temporary** in the eyes of the law.

Job Located Away From Home

You must show that you have some fixed home base in a different location than your temporary job. In unusual circumstances this may hinge on the particular facts involved in your case. But, to take a common example, suppose you have a regular job at which you worked prior to the temporary job and to which you return after the temporary job. Suppose further that you rent your house out during the period you are away. These two conditions are generally sufficient to establish a fixed home base.

When Is a Job Temporary?

A job is considered temporary if at the time you start, it can be *foreseen to end within a fixed and reasonably short time.* A period of less than one year is considered by the IRS to be a short time for this purpose. For time periods of one year or longer, the matter is not so clear. Prior to 1983, the IRS considered any time periods of this length to be a strong indication that the job was not temporary. Basically, they pretty much held to a one-year cut off policy for deciding whether a job was temporary or not.

But the courts never accepted this one-year principle, stating that only by looking at the facts and circumstances in each case could it be decided whether a job was temporary or not. And in practice, they allowed deductions in a number of cases where the absence exceeded a year in length. In a few cases, they even allowed deductions for temporary stays exceeding 2 years. [Otness, TC Memo 1978-481; Miller, TC Memo 1979-87; Williams, 52 AFTR 2d 83-5929]

In response to these court decisions, the IRS issued a new ruling in 1983 governing temporary jobs away from home [Rev Rul 83-82]. As before, an absence of less than one year qualifies as a short period of time. Absences of 1 year or longer are still *"presumed"* to be too long to be temporary. However, this 1-year presumption may be *"rebutted"* by the taxpayer where the temporary employment lasts for 1 year or more but less than 2 years.

For stays between 1 and 2 years, the following 3 tests are applied:

1. Did you live in and work near your permanent home immediately prior to your temporary job and did you continue to maintain bona fide work contacts (job seeking, leave of absence, on-going business, etc.) back home during your temporary employment?
2. Did you incur duplicate living expenses because you maintained a residence back home?
3. Did a family member (marital or lineal only) live in your permanent home while you were away or did you travel back home frequently to stay at your permanent home?

If you can demonstrate that you satisfy all 3 tests, then your 1-2 year stay is temporary. If you satisfy only 1 of the 3 tests, then the IRS considers your stay not to be temporary. If you satisfy 2 out of the 3 tests, no definite conclusion is reached. In such a case, the IRS would have to consider all the facts and circumstances regarding your stay to determine if you qualify for a temporary position away from home.

If you work away from home for 2 years or more, then your stay is considered permanent or indefinite in length and does not qualify for the *temporary job away from home* deduction.

One other case where a stay of one year or longer qualifies for deduction is when you reasonably anticipate it will last for less than one year, but because of a change in circumstances it extends up to 2 years (but not longer). In such a case, the above 3-part test does not come into force, but rather the usual rules for stays less than one year are applicable.

Conversely, if your temporary job is scheduled to last for longer than 2 years, but is cut short due to unexpected circumstances, it would not qualify for deduction. The fact you *anticipated* it would last for more than 2 years disqualifies it from deduction.

> *Example 1.*
> You work in city A and live there with your family in an apartment. You take an 18-month leave of absence to accept a temporary position in city B. Your family stays behind in city A while you rent an apartment in city B. You visit your family regularly while you are away.
> **Rule:** You have satisfied all 3 tests by (1) being on official leave of absence, (2) incurring duplicate living expenses, and (3) having your family live back home. Thus, your visiting position qualifies for the *temporary job away from home* deduction.

> *Example 2.*
> Same as Example 1 except that you give up your apartment in city A and your family lives with you in city B.
> **Rule:** You have satisfied only test 1. You did not satisfy test 2, the *duplicate living* test nor test 3, the *family back home* test. Since you have satisfied only 1 out of the 3 tests, your stay does not qualify for deduction under the above IRS guideline.

> *Example 3.*
> You work in city A and live there with your family in a home which you own. You take an 18-month leave of absence to accept a temporary position in city B. Your family moves with you to city B where you live together in a rented apartment. While away, you rent out your house in city A.
> **Rule:** You have passed test 1 because you were on official leave of absence and have failed test 3 because your family did not remain behind. What about test 2, the duplicate living expense test? The IRS ruling gives no direct guidance as to what this test requires in the way of duplicate expenses except to state that mere storage of furniture does not suffice. However, numerous court cases have discussed the concept of duplicate living expenses in connection with temporary jobs. From these cases, it appears that the maintenance of 2 residences, one back home and one at the temporary post, qualifies as duplicate living expenses. This has been the case even when, as in this example, the house back home is rented out thereby mitigating or eliminating the actual economic loss involved. [cf. Robert J. Henry, *Visiting Professor's Tax Shelter*, Saint Louis University Law Journal, Vol 25, pp 779-811.] This would mean that test 2 is satisfied, placing the temporary position in the 2 out of 3 category. That is, the temporary position is neither automatically qualified nor automatically disqualified under the above tests. Rather, the IRS reserves the right to consider all the facts and circumstances surrounding the temporary job. However, the *facts and circumstances* described above would call for a deduction in this case, even though not explicitly permitted under the ruling.

Note. The above tests for temporary jobs are guidelines issued by the IRS to express their current opinion on the travel deduction rules. They have not yet been put to the test of court review. In fact, the Tax Court has in the past rejected the idea of a mechanical test for temporariness, stating *"no single element is determinative of the ultimate factual issues of temporariness, and there are no rules of thumb, durational or otherwise"* [Norwood, 66 TC 467 (1976)]. Whether or not the Court will allow deductions going beyond the above new IRS guideline in the future as they have done in the past remains to be seen.

Which Expenses Can You Deduct?

If your temporary job is located away from home and you do not return home overnight, then you may deduct the cost of meals, lodging, cleaning and laundry, and commuting between where you obtain your meals and lodging and your temporary job. Your meal expenses are subject to the 80%-Rule discussed in Section 1. That is, you can deduct only 80% of your unreimbursed meal expenses.

In addition to expenses at the location of your temporary job, you can also deduct the initial and final transportation costs of traveling between your permanent home and your temporary residence. If, on the other hand, you commute daily between your permanent home and your temporary job, then you may deduct the cost of commuting between home and work provided your temporary job is located "away from home." If your temporary job is in your home area, you cannot deduct these commuting costs.

Temporary Academic Position

Faculty members at academic institutions commonly accept visiting positions at other institutions for a temporary period of time. The following 1979 IRS ruling issued to a college teacher spells out exactly what can be deducted and what cannot.

IRS Private Letter Ruling #7917044

"You are regularly employed as a professor in the Department of Aeronautics and Astronautics at X University. Y offered you a temporary appointment as a professor in its Aerospace Engineering Department. The appointment which you accepted is of fixed duration commencing October 15, 1978, and ending September 1, 1979. When this temporary appointment terminates, you intend to return to your tenured professorial position at X University.

"In order to discharge your appointment, you will have to travel across country and set up a temporary residence in the vicinity of Y. During the term of the appointment your permanent residence is being rented to unrelated parties.

"In light of these facts you request a ruling finding the following expenses deductible to the extent not reimbursed by your temporary employer:

1. *Travel expenses to and from the temporary work site;*
2. *Local transportation costs at the temporary work site;*
3. *Lodging at the temporary work site;*
4. *Meals at the temporary work site* [now subject to the 80%-rule described in Section 1—ed.];

5. Incidental expenses at the temporary work site;
6. Travel expenses to and from the temporary work site twice during the appointment (i.e. Christmas and Easter);
7. Costs for transportation of personal and professional articles with which to set up housekeeping at the temporary work site.

"Although your wife will be accompanying you, no deductions will be claimed for any of the above travel expenses which would be applicable to her.

". . .if your records will establish the recordkeeping and substantiation elements required by [the law], you may claim a deduction for reasonable amounts expended for meals [now subject to the 80%-Rule-ed.] and lodging plus other incidental expenses such as laundry you incur as a result of your temporary employment. In addition, your expenses for transportation are deductible to the extent they are reasonable in amount and were incurred in the pursuit of your temporary assignment in going between your place of lodging and place of temporary employment.

"In view of these holdings and. . .the regulations you will not be entitled to a deduction for moving expenses. [Cf. the end of the *Moving Expenses* chapter which explains that moving expenses cannot be claimed in connection with a temporary job.—ed.]

"The cost of any trips back and forth to the city of your residence are personal expenses and nondeductible under section 262 of the Code. Such travel expenses bear no relation to the execution of your duties at Y, nor in any way benefit your temporary employer. . . . [However, the initial cost of traveling to the location of the temporary job and the final trip back to the permanent home would be deductible.—ed.] Similarly, since you will be only temporarily away from your tax home, such expenses as you incur for transportation of personal and professional articles with which to set up housekeeping at Y, are nondeductible personal or living expenses."

Example 1.

Professor Jones teaches History at a well-known university in Princeton, New Jersey. He takes a leave of absence in order to accept a position as visiting professor at a minor university in New Haven, Connecticut. In September, he drives with his family from Princeton to New Haven to assume his duties there. He returns to Princeton in June. He rents his house in Princeton to a faculty member who was visiting there for the school year. While in New Haven, he and his family live in a rented house five miles from the university he is visiting. He commutes daily by automobile.

Rule: Professor Jones has taken a temporary position away from home. He can deduct the cost of his transportation between Princeton and New Haven and the cost of his daily commuting between the rented house and his office in New Haven. While in New Haven, he may also deduct his lodging, laundry, and 80% of the cost of his meals. The expenses of his wife and children are non-deductible.

Example 2.

Mr. Black teaches at a special education elementary school in New York City and lives in a nearby suburb. He takes a 10-month leave of absence in order to accept an offer of organizing and setting up a new special education school in New Haven, Connecticut during one school year. He commutes daily from his home in the New York suburbs to his office in New Haven.

Rule: Mr. Black has a temporary position in a different general location than that of his tax home. He deducts his daily commuting costs to and from New Haven. He cannot deduct the cost of meals or other living expenses since he is not away from home overnight.

Example 3. Several Temporary Positions

Professor Brown teaches Physics at a university in Pennsylvania. He accepts a position as a Visiting Professor of Physics at a west coast university in the San Francisco area. He teaches for the academic year plus summer school, his appointment lasting from October 1 through August 30 of the following year. He vacations in Canada during the month of September, after which he travels to a New Mexico university where he has a visiting position in connection with a government funded special semester in his field of expertise. He returns back to his original university to resume his duties for the spring semester.

Professor Brown claims that his tax home is Pennsylvania and that both of his visiting positions qualify as temporary positions. He claims that he is entitled to his transportation costs from Pennsylvania to San Francisco, from New Mexico to Pennsylvania, and what it would have cost him to travel from San Francisco to New Mexico had he traveled directly. In addition, he claims as deductions his cost of lodging, commuting expenses between his temporary homes and temporary jobs, and 80% of the cost of his meals. He does not claim any deduction for expenses incurred while vacationing in Canada.

Rule: Brown's positions in California and New Mexico were both temporary positions away from home. In similar cases (not involving academic personnel), the courts have allowed such deductions.

Example 4. Temporary Position Plus Trip Back Home on Weekends

Professor Dodd's regular job is in Chicago. He takes a 5-month leave of absence to accept a temporary position in St. Louis. His family remains in Chicago. On weekends, he travels back to Chicago to visit his family.

Rule: He is entitled to deduct his living expenses (lodging, commuting, laundry, and 80% of the cost of his meals) while in St. Louis. He cannot deduct his living costs while he is back home in Chicago. However, he may deduct the cost of transportation of returning home for the weekend, provided this cost does not exceed what it would have cost him for food and lodging had he stayed in St. Louis. If the cost of transportation is in excess of this, he may deduct only what he could have deducted for food and lodging in St. Louis.

Example 5.

Cass was a Professor of Economics at a university in the East. He accepted an appointment under a "distinguished scholar" program to spend the academic year at a well-known university in Southern California. His stipend qualified as a fellowship grant under the rules that applied at the time.

Cass took a leave of absence from his regular position, rented out his house, and moved—together with his wife, 17-year old son, 11-year old daughter, and dog—out west for the academic year. He was permitted to deduct his living expenses during this stay in California. The issue that arose at trial was how much was spent on food for Professor Cass.

Cass proved by production of receipts that the total food expenses for his family amounted to $4,390. Of this amount, it was agreed that $173 was clearly deductible for lunches Professor Cass ate on campus. Of the remaining $4217, $3307 was for food purchased at the supermarket and $910 for restaurant meals. It was in allocating what part of this $4217 worth of food was consumed by Professor Cass that the dispute arose.

Cass claimed that about 1/3 of this $4217 was allocable to food that he ate. He testified that making this type of allocation was right up his alley as an economist. His methodology for making the allocation here was to apportion the cost of food for each family member according to their body weight.

However, the court did not buy this method. It ruled, *"Petitioner's allocation is, to say the least, creative. However, if it proposes to approach a scientific approximation of the amount of food consumed by each member of the household, it is flawed, e.g., it ignores factors such as the relative metabolic rate of each person. Any parent having a teenage child can attest to the fact that a teenager eats as much as, or more than, the parent regardless of weight.*

"Of course the best proof would be to have receipts directly related to petitioner's own food consumption. Understandably, in a situation such as the one before us now, such a requirement would be onerous. Thus, we will make an estimation which we deem best reflects or approximates the true costs involved. In the absence of proof of a more precise method, we deem it best to employ the simplest approach available. Accordingly, we allocate one-fourth of the total contested food expenses ($4,217) to petitioner, discounting the grocery expenses ($3,307) by 5% to account for dog food. Thus, petitioners may deduct $1,185.91 of the $4,390 food costs as a food expense." (Note that under current law, only 80% of the cost of meals would be deductible.) [Cass, 86TC No. 75]

Example 6. Married People Living Apart

Professor and Professor Lighthouse, a married couple, both have regular teaching positions in cities 400 miles apart. They live in the cities where they work on weekdays but one of them visits the other on weekends. Since neither of their positions is temporary, they are not entitled to deduct any transportation or living expenses. Each person's tax home is considered to be the city where that person works. A weekend trip to visit a spouse is a personal non-deductible activity.

> However, if one of their positions were temporary and in a different location than the person's permanent home, then expenses as described in Example 4 would be deductible.

Example 7.

Mr. and Mrs. Felton moved to a midwestern city where he enrolled as a student at the State university located there. After obtaining his degree, he obtained a position on the faculty of the same university.

Mrs. Felton also enrolled at the university and obtained a master's degree in economics. After teaching part-time for several years in the same locality, she obtained a temporary appointment as a Visiting Lecturer at a university 100 miles away. After 2 years as a Visiting Lecturer, she was promoted to a full-time position on the faculty, as a Lecturer for half a year and then as Assistant Professor upon attainment of her Ph.D. degree.

Mrs. Felton did not move her personal residence. She arranged her schedule so she could spend 5 nights a week back home with her husband, making 2 round trips per week between where she worked and her permanent residence. She rented a room the 2 nights a week she stayed near her job.

Mrs. Felton was permitted to deduct her travel expenses during the 2 years she held a *temporary* position as a Visiting Lecturer. But once she obtained a *permanent* position, her travel expenses were no longer deductible. This was the case even though she prepared classes and did research in the library back home. The Court ruled that the primary reason for her traveling back and forth was for personal rather than business purposes. [Felton, TC Memo 1982-11]

Example 8.

An individual sought a ruling from the IRS in the following situation. He was currently doing research and writing from his home. Apparently, he had no other source of employment at the time. He received an appointment as a Visiting Professor for one academic year at a college in a different location. Following his appointment, he expected to return back home.

The IRS ruled that his permanent tax home was where he was currently doing his research and writing. His position as a Visiting Professor constituted a temporary job away from home. Thus, he could deduct his travel expenses, including the cost of commuting, meals [now subject to the 80%-Rule], lodging, and laundry while at his temporary teaching position. [IRS Private Letter Ruling 8449013]

Example 9. Student Working at Summer Job

Hantzsis was a student at a major law school in the Boston area. During the summer of her second year of law school, she accepted a 10-week job as a legal assistant at a New York law firm. While in New York, she rented a small apartment in which she lived. Her husband, a faculty member at a Boston-area university, remained in Boston.

Mrs. Hantzsis viewed her employment in New York as a temporary job away from home. Thus, she claimed a deduction for her transportation between Boston and New York and for meals and lodging while living in New York. The Tax Court allowed the deduction. The amount allowed was surprisingly large — $3,080 just for meals and the rental of a small apartment for the 10 weeks spent in New York.

However, an Appeals Court overruled the Tax Court, disallowing the deduction. It ruled that Boston was not her tax home because she did not work there. Thus she was not entitled to an away-from-home travel deduction while in New York. In order for her to be allowed a deduction, she would need to *"establish the existence of some sort of business relation both to the location she claims as 'home' and to the location of her temporary employment sufficient to support a finding that her duplicative expenses are necessitated by business exigencies."* Presumably, had she held even a part-time job in Boston, her deduction for living expenses in New York would have been allowed. [Hantzsis, 47 AFTR 2d 81-721]

Temporary vs. Indefinite Job

An issue that often arises is whether a job away from home is *temporary* or *indefinite* in length. A *temporary* job is one that is expected to last for a short period of time. An *indefinite* job is one whose expected duration is indeterminate or else a long period of time. Only away-from-home expenses connected with a *temporary* job, not an indefinite job, can qualify for deduction.

Sometimes, a job starts out being temporary, but later becomes indefinite. For example, suppose you accept a position for a temporary period. At the end of this period, an unexpected permanent slot opens up and you accept the position. At that point, your job changes from being temporary to indefinite. If you are *"away-from-home,"* you can deduct your living expenses during the temporary period, but not thereafter. This is illustrated by a revealing recent court case.

Example 10.

Kaster was a certified welder who worked at various jobs in the northeastern quarter of Ohio and a small portion of northwestern Pennsylvania. He and his family lived in Titusville, 120 miles east of Cleveland, from which he commuted to his various jobsites. He and his family had lived in Titusville their entire lives.

In July, 1981, Kaster obtained work at a nuclear power plant in Perry, Ohio. He expected he would work only two months at the power plant. This was based on his previous work record which showed a large number of short-term jobs during the previous several years. However, the power plant did not advise him of the expected duration of this particular job and Kaster could not know exactly how long his job would last.

Kaster was subject to immediate layoff at any time. Welders were not generally notified that they were to be laid off until the day that the layoff occurred. However, under the *"last hired, first fired"* method of determining layoffs, the longer he worked at that job, the less likely he was to be edged out by a fellow employee in the event of a layoff. In fact, his job lasted for 27 months until November, 1983 before he was laid off.

The IRS agreed that Titusville was Kaster's tax home and that the job at Perry to which he commuted was *away-from-home*. The only question that remained was determining for which period of time the job was temporary and for which period indefinite.

Kaster claimed a deduction on his 1982 tax return for an entire year of commuting between his Titusville home and his job at Perry. His total commuting mileage for the year was 50,000 miles for which he claimed a deduction of $7,178. In order for this claim to be allowed, it would be necessary to determine that his job at Perry was temporary rather than indefinite during the entire 1982 year.

When the IRS audited Kaster's tax return, it allowed a deduction for only part of the year. The IRS said that Kaster's job at Perry was temporary for the first 12 months from July, 1981 to July, 1982. After that, the job became indefinite, ruling out a deduction. But how did the IRS auditor, George Lubic, decide that this was the appropriate cutoff? Most interestingly, it was simply a general policy of Lubic's office to use a one-year standard. According to the Court's written opinion,

> *"Lubic worked in respondent's Erie, Pennsylvania office. This office follows a 'one-year rule' in making determinations as to temporary versus indefinite employment. That is, employment up to one year is considered temporary; if a single employment lasts longer than one year, then the expenses incurred after the end of one year are treated as nondeductible 'commuting' expenses. Lubic's audit report, which followed this one-year rule, was forwarded to respondent's Appeals Office in Pittsburgh, Pennsylvania. This Appeals Office followed the same one-year rule in preparing the notice of deficiency in the instant case. In the notice of deficiency, respondent allowed $4,886.59 of petitioners' claimed deduction and disallowed the remaining $2,291.41."*

The IRS lawyer who prepared the case for trial backed away from the Pennsylvania office's one-year policy. He argued for a denial of any deduction whatsoever for the 1982 tax year. But the judge did not agree. Clearly, the job was temporary for the beginning months because of the expectation it would end shortly. It was reasonable that this expectation would have continued for about a year. After that, the job simply became indefinite in length because its imminent end could no longer be reasonably expected. Thus, the Court accepted the original auditor's determination and allowed a deduction of $4,886.59 for the period through July, 1982. [Kaster, TC Memo 1985-580]

The above case is interesting because of the glimpse it gives of the workings of one particular IRS office. Because of the inherent difficulty of determining whether an impermanent job is *temporary* or *indefinite*, this office apparently adopted a one-year rule in all questionable cases. That is, as long as a permanent tax home was established, a job in a different area would be considered temporary for a period of up to one year, but not thereafter.

As noted above, this one-year policy is not an official position of the IRS. But those in a similar situation should take note of the above case. The fact that one IRS office adopted a one-year policy as a basic test would support the reasonability of considering a similarly impermanent job to be temporary for up to one year, even when no definite end is known in advance.

Duplicate Expenses Test

When in doubt, the Tax Court in recent decisions has referred back to the original justification in allowing deductions for living expenses while at a temporary job away from home, namely to provide relief to those who incur extra *"duplicate living expenses"* because of their situation. When no extra expenses are incurred, the Court is sometimes reluctant to permit a deduction. Another factor the Court has been looking for is secondary evidence such as auto registration, voter registration, bank accounts, etc. which point to where a person considers his permanent home to be. The following recent court case illustrates both of these considerations.

> ### Example 11.
>
> For 5 years, Thomas Crain and his wife lived with his parents in a house in Hot Springs, Arkansas. During this time, he worked as an electrician in various places near Hot Springs, obtaining his job assignments through his union. Then he received an assignment near Baton Rouge, Louisiana which lasted for about 10 months. Despite the impermanence of his job in Louisiana, the Court denied a temporary job-away-from-home deduction.
>
> The Court pointed to the absence of any extra living expenses beyond what would have been normal had they stayed in Hot Springs. During their absence, the Court noted,
>
> > "Petitioners did not pay any rent to Thomas' parents, nor did they contribute any money to them for the purchase of groceries, the payment of utility bills, or the payment of other expenses associated with the upkeep of a home. . . .
> >
> > "The purpose of allowing the deduction of living expenses while a taxpayer is 'away from home' is 'to mitigate the burden of the taxpayer who, because of exigencies of his trade or business, must maintain two places of abode and thereby incur additional and duplicate living expenses. . . .
> >
> > "There is no evidence in the record which supports petitioners' contention that they have incurred the requisite increased or duplicate living expenses by maintaining the house [in] Hot Springs, Arkansas."
>
> The Court also noted the extent to which they settled into their new location, stating
>
> > "We think it pertinent that in Baton Rouge, Mr. and Mrs. Crain rented and lived in an apartment and maintained an account in a local bank. Mrs. Crain held a Louisiana driver's license, registered to vote in that state, and held a job there during at least part of their stay. Mr. Crain also registered to vote in Louisiana and served as a reserve deputy sheriff in Baton Rouge." [Crain, TC Memo 1985-498]

Travel Expenses While Under a Fellowship Grant

A person at a temporary position away from home might have been paid under a grant qualifying for the $300 per month tax-free treatment described in the *Tax-Free Grants* chapter. Sometimes, the IRS will contend there is no temporary job in such a case. Rather, it claims the taxpayer is simply studying or doing research under a fellowship grant. It makes no difference that tax is paid on that portion of the grant exceeding $300 per month. Since there is no temporary job, the IRS claims there can be no deduction for expenses incurred at a temporary job away from home.

One can counter such an objection by the IRS by claiming that the expenses were incurred as an *educational expense while on temporary leave of absence from one's regular job* (see the *Expenses of Attending School* chapter). Usually, in the process of denying that a job exists, the IRS contends that the grant is provided simply for the educational benefit of the recipient. Thus, the same travel and living expenses that were denied as a *temporary job* deduction can become an *educational expense* deduction. In fact, there is an IRS ruling concerning teachers' sabbaticals which supports this viewpoint [Rev Rul 64-176]. But don't expect the IRS to point this out to you if your deduction is challenged in an audit. You must be prepared to point this out to them.

Exactly how you list your claimed deduction on your tax return could be an important factor. This is underscored by the following 1985 court case.

Example 12.

A teacher received a $10,000 grant from the small liberal arts College in the Midwest where he taught. Such grants were awarded after 7 years of employment. The teacher pursued a Ph.D. program at a major University with the grant. During the period he attended the University, he was not employed at the College which provided the grant, nor was he under any obligation to return to the College after he completed his Ph.D. work.

While at the University, he claimed a deduction of $2,006 for his living expenses. The issue arose at trial as to the category under which this deduction was being claimed. Was the deduction being claimed as a *business expense* or an *educational expense*?

The IRS asserted that the teacher was claiming the $2,006 deduction as a *business expense*. If so, it could object to the deduction because the teacher was not actually employed when the expenses were incurred. To support its assertion, the IRS pointed to the fact that the expenses were claimed on the part of Form 2106, labeled "*Employee Business Expenses.*"

But the teacher asserted that the deduction was being claimed as an *educational expense*. As discussed in Section 5 of the *Expenses of Attending School* chapter, one can deduct educational expenses even while not currently employed, as long as one is considered to be *temporarily* on leave of absence from his profession. The teacher claimed that the only reason he listed the expenses under the "*Employee Business Expenses*" section of Form 2106 was that there was no special place for the listing of *Educational Expenses* on Form 2106.

The judge ruled in favor of the teacher, allowing him to deduct the $2,006 as an

> educational expense. It agreed that the teacher's claim for a refund hinged on how he had claimed these expenses, i.e. as business expenses or educational expenses. But the teacher had placed the IRS on notice that his deduction was claimed in connection with his education because under the *occupation line* on Form 2106 he had listed "*Scholarship Grant.*" He had not listed his occupation as "*teacher*" nor linked the expenses to his job by naming the college where he taught. Since there was no special place for the listing of *educational expenses* on Form 2106, the teacher had acted sufficiently to identify that the amounts were being deducted as *educational expenses* connected with his studies rather than as *business expenses* connected with a job. [Pelowski, DC Ohio, 1985 CCH ¶ 9217]

Sabbaticals

A sabbatical leave of absence is governed by the same basic rules that apply to temporary jobs as discussed above. Thus, the costs of travel, meals, lodging, commuting, cleaning, and laundry while away from home are generally deductible. This provides a tremendous opportunity for teachers to obtain a substantial travel deduction.

This was confirmed by the IRS in the following ruling issued to a University Professor.

IRS Private Letter Ruling #7828042

"This is in reply to your letter with enclosures of January 12, 1978, which concerns the treatment, for federal income tax purposes of certain expenses incurred while away from your permanent place of employment on a temporary employment assignment.

"You are regularly employed as a Professor of Industrial Systems Engineering at X University. During your sabbatical you are working for the Federal Government as a Visiting Mathematical Scientist at Y Agency which is located in the metropolitan Washington, D.C., area. This assignment is of fixed duration commencing October 1, 1977, and ending September 29, 1978. Your Department Chairman at X University attests that you are a university employee on temporary government assignment for which you are paid by the University. The government agency where you are temporarily employed then reimburses the University for that part of your salary designated in your Assignment Agreement which is not covered by sabbatical pay and certain sponsored research which you continue to carry out. This latter research is separately funded under a federal grant program and although you will be working on the project during your temporary employment at Y Agency, the University continues to administer the grant project.

"You have rented out your condominium apartment for part of the time you will be away. During this temporary employment assignment, you are incurring certain expenses which you believe may be deductible for federal income tax purposes. Specifically, you ask whether you may deduct the cost of meals, rental of a temporary apartment, and the cost of commuting between where you obtain your meals, your temporary apartment and Y Agency. Y Agency has paid your

round-trip travel expenses between the city of your permanent employment and your temporary post.

"*...Assuming that your appointment with Y Agency is temporary for the term described and that upon expiration of the appointment you will return to your permanent employment at X University, we conclude that while temporarily employed in the metropolitan Washington, D.C. area, you will be traveling away from home for purposes of section 162 of the Code.*

"*Accordingly, if your records will establish the recordkeeping and substantiation elements required . . ., you may claim a deduction for reasonable amounts expended for meals* [now subject to the 80%-Rule] *and lodging plus other incidental expenses such as laundry you incur as a result of your temporary employment. In addition, your expenses for transportation are deductible to the extent they are reasonable in amount and were incurred in the pursuit of your temporary assignment in going between your place of lodging and place of temporary employment.*"

The above letter ruling concerns a sabbatical during which a teacher studies or does research at a distant location. In such a case, the usual rules for deducting business travel expenses apply. Another type of sabbatical occurs when a teacher travels extensively and claims the travel itself is a form of education. This type of travel is no longer deductible as discussed in Section 7 of this chapter.

The expenses of renting out a home while on sabbatical or other leave of absence are deductible. This is discussed further in Section 4 of the *Homeowners* chapter.

SECTION 4:
TRAVEL TO LOOK FOR EMPLOYMENT

You can deduct expenses connected with looking for a new job, whether or not you are successful. However, you can only deduct job-hunting costs if you are looking for work in your current profession. You cannot deduct the expenses of looking for work in a new profession even if you are successful.

If you take a trip to look for a new job in your own profession, then you can deduct all your travel expenses. If the trip combines the search for a job with sightseeing or other personal activity, then you can deduct your travel expenses provided that the **primary purpose** of your trip was to look for a job. Of course, any expense directly connected with your sightseeing activity is not deductible.

> *Example*
> Whitman takes a 2-day trip to New York to interview for a new job. While in New York he rides the Staten Island ferry and does some other incidental sightseeing. He can deduct the entire cost of his trip including transportation, meals, and lodging. He can't deduct the fare for the Staten Island ferry or other direct sightseeing expenses.

SECTION 5:
TRAVEL TO PROFESSIONAL CONVENTIONS

If you attend a convention which is directly connected with your profession, then you may deduct the cost of travel including meals and lodging if you are away from home overnight. This includes professional conventions, conventions of learned societies, union conventions, etc. but not conventions of fraternal organizations. Also excluded now are conventions which provide investment information rather than relate directly to an individual's job or business.

If your spouse accompanies you (and your spouse has no business purpose for being there), you may deduct what it would have cost had you gone alone. Thus, if the hotel rate is $80 for a double and $65 for a single room, you may deduct $65 as the cost of the room. Likewise, you may deduct $22^{1/2}$ cents per mile (for the first 15,000 miles of business use) for your automobile expenses whether or not your spouse travels with you.

For conventions held outside the North American area, it must be "reasonable" for the convention to be held abroad. For example, a foreign convention of an international professional society would qualify, but a convention, say, of the Iowa Engineering Association held in France would not.

Many convention trips include some sightseeing or other personal activity. Section 6 discusses how to treat travel which combines business with personal activities.

SECTION 6:
TRAVEL WHICH COMBINES BUSINESS WITH PLEASURE

A. Travel Within the United States

If your trip was entirely for business, your ordinary and necessary travel expenses may be deducted. If your trip was solely personal, no part of your travel expenses are deductible, even if you engaged in some business activity at your destination.

You may travel to a business destination, and extend your stay for nonbusiness reasons, make a nonbusiness side trip, or engage in other nonbusiness activities. In this case, your travel expenses are deductible only if the trip was related **primarily** to your profession.

Regardless of whether the primary purpose of your trip was business or pleasure, an expense that is properly attributable to a business purpose, such as a registration fee at a professional convention, is deductible.

Whether a trip is primarily for business or is primarily personal in nature depends on the facts and circumstances in each case. However, the length of time spent in business or personal activities is an important factor in determining the primary purpose of the trip.

Example 1.

Jones is a Professor of Chemistry at a university in Iowa. He attends the annual convention of the American Chemical Society in San Francisco. The convention consists primarily of papers presented by various members of the society on research in chemistry. Jones attends the convention for five days and spends most of his time during the day attending sessions of the convention. He rides a few cable cars for fun and does some other incidental sightseeing.

Rule: The travel is primarily for business. He may deduct the cost of transportation between Iowa and San Francisco, lodging, and 80% of the cost of meals both while in transit and at the convention. His sightseeing costs are not deductible.

Example 2.

Same as in Example 1, except that instead of returning directly from San Francisco to Iowa, Dr. Jones flies to Los Angeles for a day to visit his brother. He then returns to Iowa from Los Angeles.

Rule: Jones can claim that his was primarily a business trip to attend the convention. The side trip to Los Angeles was not his primary purpose in taking the trip. Jones may deduct his lodging and 80% of the cost of meals in San Francisco, plus what the cost of transportation would have been had he traveled directly between Iowa and San Francisco instead of stopping over in Los Angeles. He cannot deduct expenses incurred while in Los Angeles.

Example 3.

Mr. Burns teaches high school in Atlanta and travels to St. Louis to attend the convention of the teacher's union to which he belongs. He does little or no sightseeing.

Rule: Travel to union conventions is a legitimate business expense. Therefore his transportation, lodging, and 80% of the cost of his meals while in St. Louis are deductible.

Example 4.

Cooper teaches Psychology at a New Mexico high school. After the school term is over, he and his family take a month-long camping trip in California. He leaves his family at Yosemite National Park for two days to attend a meeting of the American Society for Teachers of Psychology in San Francisco.

Rule: His trip was primarily for personal activities connected with his camping trip. However, he may deduct any expenses directly connected with his attendance at the convention. Thus, his living expenses in San Francisco and the cost of transportation between Yosemite and San Francisco are deductible.

B. Travel Outside the United States

Different rules govern travel inside the U.S. and travel outside the U.S. For combined business-with-pleasure travel **inside** the U.S., you may deduct all of your travel expenses (except those specifically connected with personal activities such as sightseeing) as long as you can establish that the primary purpose of your travel was of a business or professional nature.

For combined business-with-pleasure travel **outside** the U.S. where the primary purpose of the travel is for business purposes, you must meet one of the following conditions in order to deduct all of your travel expenses:

1. **You were outside the U.S. a week or less.** In counting the days, do not count the day of departure from the U.S. but do count the day of return to the U.S.

2. **You were reimbursed** by or received a travel expense allowance from your employer (and you are not a managing executive nor related to your employer).

3. **You spent less than 25 per cent of the total time outside the U.S. on nonbusiness activities.**

4. **You had no substantial control over arranging the trip.** You are not considered to have control merely because you have control over timing the trip.

5. **You can establish that a personal vacation was not a major consideration.**

Even if you satisfy one of the above conditions for a trip taken primarily for business, you still cannot deduct for expenses which are strictly personal in nature, such as sightseeing expenses. Similarly, if you extend your stay just to engage in some personal activity, then your living expenses during such an extension are not deductible. However, if you spend time on personal activities during the middle of a business trip, your living expenses during such a period can still be deductible.

Example

You traveled to Paris primarily for business purposes connected with your profession. You left Denver Tuesday and flew to New York. On Wednesday, you flew nonstop from New York to Paris, arriving Thursday morning. Thursday and Friday were spent on business activities and from Saturday until Tuesday you were sightseeing. You flew back to New York, arriving Wednesday afternoon. On Thursday, you flew back to Denver. Since the day of departure from the United States does not count, you were not outside the United States for more than a week. You may deduct what it would have cost you to fly from Denver to Paris, stay there Thursday and Friday, and return on Saturday. The cost of your stay in Paris from Saturday through Tuesday is not deductible since it is not attributable to a business purpose.

However, suppose that your professional activities had temporarily ceased on Friday afternoon, resuming on Monday and Tuesday. In this case, the fact that you spent Saturday and Sunday sightseeing would not disqualify your living expenses during such days from being deductible. You had to stay in Paris during the weekend for the business purpose of being able to continue your professional activities on Monday and Tuesday. Of course, you still cannot deduct your sightseeing expenses.

Allocating Expenses

If you do not meet one of the five conditions listed above for travel outside the U.S. your expenses must be allocated between business and nonbusiness activities. Generally, the amount of your travel expense outside the United States incurred in getting to and from your business destination that is not deductible is determined by multiplying the total travel expenses by the total number of nonbusiness days outside the United States, and dividing the result by the total number of days outside the United States. For this purpose you must count both the day of your departure from, and return to, the United States. The allocation to business or nonbusiness activity is generally made on a day by day basis according to the following rules.

Transportation days. If you travel a reasonably direct route without interruption to your business destination, each day en route outside the United States is considered a business day. If your travel is interrupted by a substantial nonbusiness diversion, or if you do not travel a reasonably direct route, you count as business days only the number of days you would have been outside the United States if you had traveled to your business destination by a reasonably direct route without interruption, using the same means of transportation.

Presence required. Any day that your presence is required in a particular place for a specific and bona fide business purpose is counted as a business day, even though your presence is required for only a part of the day and if during the normal working hours of the day you spend more time in nonbusiness activities than in business activities.

If your principal activity during normal working hours is in pursuit of your business, the day is counted as a business day. Any day that you are prevented from engaging in the conduct of your business as a principal activity because of circumstances beyond your control is also counted as a business day.

Weekends, holidays, and other necessary standby days are counted as business days if they fall between business days. But if they are at the end of your business activity and you remain at your business destination for nonbusiness or personal reasons, they are not business days.

If the nonbusiness activity occurred between the point of departure from the United States and your business destination, you allocate what it would have cost you to travel (including meals and lodging) between the place where your travel outside the United States begins and the place of your nonbusiness activity, and return to the United States, using the same mode of travel as you actually used.

Example

You live in New York and flew to Brussels on Monday, May 31 for professional activities that began at noon Tuesday, June 1, and were over at noon Friday, June 4. That evening you flew to Dublin, Ireland, where you visited with friends until the afternoon of June 17, when you flew home to New York. The primary purpose of the trip was for business purposes. If you had not stopped in Dublin, you would have arrived home the evening of June 4. You were outside the United States more than a week, and you are unable to show that you had no substantial control over arranging the trip, or that a personal vacation was not a major consideration in making the trip. May 31 through June 4 (5 days) are business days and June 5 through June 17 (13 days) are nonbusiness days. Your expenses while in Dublin are nondeductible. In addition 13/18 of the cost of the round-trip airline fare from New York to Dublin is not deductible. You may deduct the cost of lodging and 80% of the cost of your meals while in Brussels, to the extent they are not lavish or extravagant, all other necessary travel expenses while in Brussels, and that portion of your roundtrip transportation cost (including meals) from New York to Brussels, that exceeds 13/18 of the round-trip plane fare between New York and Dublin. [IRS Pub. 463]

If the nonbusiness activity was at or beyond your business destination, you would allocate your total travel expenses (including meals and lodging en route) from the place where travel outside the United States began to the place of business activity and return to the United States.

Example

Assume the same facts as in the example above, except that instead of going to Dublin for your vacation, you fly to Venice, Italy, for a vacation, and arrive back in New York on the evening of June 17. (Note that in this example, Venice is further from New York than Brussels, whereas in the preceding example Dublin was closer to New York than Brussels.) You may not deduct any part of the cost of your trip from Brussels to Venice.

You may deduct 5/18 of the round-trip plane fare from New York to Brussels (including 80% of the cost of meals en route), plus lodging and 80% of the cost of your meals while in Brussels to the extent they are not lavish or extravagant, and any other ordinary and necessary business expenses incurred while you were in Brussels. [IRS Pub. 463]

Other allocation method. You may use a different allocation method if it more clearly reflects the proportion of your time spent on business activity.

Converting a Personal Trip Into a Deductible Business Trip

Sometimes, it is possible to convert a trip originally motivated by personal considerations into a deductible business trip. The following court case should prove an inspiration to those who attempt to accomplish this objective.

Example

Habeeb was an assistant professor at a Medical School in the South. For six years in a row, he made an annual trip to Egypt where he visited his mother and other relatives who lived there. The court case involves one of these years when

Habeeb claimed that his trip qualified for a tax-deduction because it was made primarily for business purposes. The court opinion describes his trip as follows:

"The trip lasted 45 days and travel was by a chartered flight because it was cheaper. During his stay in Egypt petitioner delivered 5 lectures at the University of Alexandria and 2 lectures at the University of Cairo. These lectures involved subjects within petitioner's expertise, such as 'Antigenicity of Proteins' and 'Chemistry of Antibodies.' The lecture dates span the 14-day period from July 4 to July 18. Petitioner testified that he was invited to give these lectures, but also admitted on cross-examination that he had volunteered his services. He received no compensation or expense reimbursement for such lectures. Petitioner testified that he had numerous discussions with students, professors, and other lecturers while in Egypt for the purpose of exchanging ideas, keeping abreast, reviewing articles, and generally to avoid the isolation which one would experience if one did not travel. Petitioner's testimony on this score was general and nonspecific."

Habeeb had three strikes against him. First, he had volunteered to give the lectures and received no pay or expense reimbursement from the universities he visited. Second, the trip had a strong personal component since he was visiting his mother and other relatives. And third, he spent less than 1/3 of his time, 14 out of 45 days, for business purposes.

In spite of these three negative points, the Court decided that his trip was undertaken primarily for business purposes and therefore a portion of his expenses could be deducted. The written opinion of the Court shows how it reached this conclusion.

"Even though petitioner may have solicited the invitations to lecture, there is no question that he did give the lectures; and additionally, it has been established that petitioner is well-respected for his specialized learning, his writings, and his lectures, and that his lectures helped to maintain that reputation.

"The first question to be answered is whether the trip to Egypt was primarily personal in nature. If so, [IRS regulations] would require disallowance of the travel deduction even though some business activities took place during the trip. Two weeks of the approximate 6-week trip were spent delivering a series of lectures, for which petitioner devoted substantial time and effort in preparation. Even though petitioner might have chosen some other country for some of his lectures had it not been for his mother and father in Egypt, the trip does not, for that reason become 'primarily personal.' It is true that the presence of close relatives at the place of destination may raise a question of disguised personal motive for a trip or series of trips. Cf. William R. Kenney [Dec. 33, 778], 66 T.C. 122 (1976). But if an adequate business justification exists, the fact that trips are repeated to the same destination, where the taxpayer has relatives or friends does not, ipso facto, obliterate the business character of the trip.

"As to the overall time spent on the trip, it is to be noted that petitioner took a 45-day charter flight because it was cheaper. [Although IRS regulations state] that the amount of time spent on personal versus business activities is 'an important factor' in determining primary purpose, it is believed that under the totality of facts and circumstances here present, the trip was taken primarily for the business

> *purpose of maintaining petitioner's reputation in the field of his specialty."* [Habeeb, 35 TCM]

SECTION 7:
EDUCATIONAL TRAVEL

There are two basic types of travel for educational purposes. The first is travel to one or more locations in order to obtain education there. In this case, travel expenses are deductible providing the education qualifies as described in the *Expenses of Attending School* chapter.

The second is travel of a type that the travel itself is of educational value. Travel of this type is no longer deductible, as of January 1, 1987.

> **Example 1.**
> A scholar of French literature travels to Paris to take courses that are offered only at the Sorbonne or to study, doing specific library research that cannot be done elsewhere. Assuming that the cost of his studies is deductible as educational expenses, his associated travel costs are deductible [cf. the *Expenses of Attending School* chapter. Also see Section 3 of this chapter for other examples where travel expenses connected with research can be deducted as an *employee business expense*.]

> **Example 2.**
> A French language teacher travels to France in order to improve his general knowledge of the French language and customs. He doesn't spend any significant amount of time doing specific scholarly research or taking classes. His travel is considered to be for personal purposes. As of January 1, 1987, expenses for this type of travel are no longer deductible.

SECTION 8:
DISCOUNT RATES FOR TEACHERS

Some hotels and motels offer discounts to teachers who present a faculty ID upon registration. The *Sheraton* chain, in particular, offers an attractive arrangement. At most of its hotels and motels, it offers, subject to availability, a discount of 25% to educators presenting an ID card, pay stub, or other proof of faculty status.

Other hotels give discounts on an individual basis. For example, in New York City, the *Roosevelt Hotel* gives discounts to educators of up to 50%, depending upon the time of year and day of the week involved. Some *Hilton Hotels* also offer discounts that range to over 30% off for both teachers and students. And some *Howard Johnsons* and *Quality Inns* offer discounts to teachers or to "government employees" which include teachers who work for public schools or colleges.

Discount Rates for Teachers

Even if a hotel doesn't have a standard discount policy toward teachers, the management often has authority to give a discount. Sometimes, they'll give a teacher their standard corporate discount rate when asked.

Also, most motel and hotel chains give discounts to members of certain "senior citizen" organizations. For example, most *Holiday Inns, Howard Johnsons, Quality Inns, Scottish Inns, Ramada Inns, Travelodges,* and *Econolodges* will give a discount to members of the *National Retired Teachers Association* (NRTA) or *American Association of Retired Persons* (AARP). And some *Marriotts* have a limited number of rooms at a 40-50% discount for NRTA or AARP members. Also, some of these motels offer a discount to members of the *National Council of Senior Citizens,* or to people who can simply show any ID to prove their age is over 55, 60, or 65, depending upon their policy.

Despite their names, memberships in the National Retired Teachers Association and the American Association of Retired Persons are open to those age 50 or over, whether or not they are retired. And the National Council of Senior Citizens is open to anyone who wants to join, irrespective of age. These organizations charge a nominal fee of $10 or less for an annual membership. [*Addresses: NRTA, 1909 K St., N.W., Washington, D.C. 20049; National Council of Senior Citizens, 925 15th St., N.W., Washington, D.C. 20005; AARP, 1909 K St., N.W., Washington, D.C. 20049*]

All of the above discount arrangements are subject to "space availability." This means that during extra busy periods, discount privileges may be suspended. You should check ahead of time to determine the precise discount arrangement that is in effect at the time you are planning to travel.

If you are renting a car during your trip, ask about discounts there, too. Thrifty and Avis Rent-A-Car give discounts to members of AARP. Similarly, some Budget Rent-A-Cars give AARP discounts and discounts to federal and state government employees. And Hertz gives discounts to members of NEA and AARP.

Chapter 23

Estate and Gift Tax

Section 1: Introduction

Basic Gift and Estate Tax Law

Prior to 1977, there were two separate taxes, one on estates and one on gifts. The estate tax was levied on property passing from one individual to another upon death of the first individual. And to prevent an individual from escaping estate tax simply by giving away his property before death, a separate gift tax applied to the **giver** of substantial amounts.

The 1976 Tax Reform Act combined these two taxes into a new Unified Estate and Gift Tax. The way it works is this.

To determine the amount of gift tax due, a cumulative total of all gifts made by an individual during his lifetime is kept. When this total exceeds a certain minimum amount, then gift tax becomes due. Excluded from this cumulative total are gifts totalling less than $10,000 per year per recipient and gifts made in any amount to a spouse.

The tax rate is graduated with the rate determined by the cumulative lifetime total of gifts. For example, if a person has made gifts worth X amount in prior years and gives Y amount of gifts this year, then the gift tax rate that applies is the one in the X to X + Y bracket.

To determine the amount of estate tax due, the deceased's taxable estate is first computed by subtracting certain adjustments (as explained in Section 3) from the sum total of all property passing to his heirs. The tax on this estate is then obtained by using the same tax schedule that applies to gifts. And the cumulative total of all gifts made during the individual's lifetime determines which tax bracket applies. For example, if a person has made gifts worth G during his lifetime and his taxable estate is worth E, then the tax rate used is the one that applies to the bracket G to G + E.

In summary then, the Unified Estate and Gift Tax applies to the sum total of all taxable gifts made during one's lifetime plus the value of the taxable estate. However, no tax is due unless this total exceeds $600,000.

Section 2: Gift Tax

If one person makes a substantial gift to another, then the giver may have to pay a gift tax. The recipient pays no tax. The gift tax is computed by adding up the cumulative total of all gifts made during an individual's lifetime to other individuals.

There are two exemptions which are excluded from this cumulative total.

(1) Each year you may exempt gifts totalling $10,000 to any one person. You get a separate $10,000 exemption for each person to whom you make a gift. If your spouse consents, you can regard a gift to a third person as being 1/2 from each of you and give $20,000 tax-free to each person.

(2) In addition to (1), you may exempt any gifts made during your lifetime to your spouse. Also, you can exempt any amounts paid on behalf of any donee directly to a school for tuition or to a health care provider for medical services.

The following is a sampling of the 1987 tax rates that would apply to different amounts of lifetime gifts:

Lifetime Total of Taxable Gifts	Tax
$ 600,000	$ 0
$ 750,000	$ 55,500
$1,000,000	$153,000
$2,000,000	$588,000

The above schedule is not applied separately to each year's gifts, but instead is applied to the sum total of all gifts you have made in your lifetime. For example, suppose that (after subtracting exclusions) you have made taxable gifts totalling $200,000 in previous years and have paid gift tax (under prior law) totalling $7,800. If you now make a taxable gift of $550,000, this will bring your lifetime total of gifts up to $750,000. Since the tax on $750,000 is $55,500 and you have already paid $7,800 tax in previous years, you must now pay the difference, $55,500 − $7,800 = $47,700.

Section 3: Estate Tax

The Gross Estate

The first step in computing the estate tax of a deceased person is to determine the gross estate. The gross estate includes the value of the following items:

- Home and other owned real estate
- Cash and debts owed to the deceased
- Stocks and bonds
- Personal belongings and household furnishings (including automobiles)
- Life insurance
- Annuities and death benefits

In order for you to estimate the size of your estate, let us consider the above items separately.

Your Home and Real Estate

Include the value of all your real estate holdings, including your own home and real estate in other countries. If you have a mortgage on your property, then the amount of the unpaid balance will be subtracted from the value of the property. If you own property jointly, see the subsection on jointly-held property.

Cash and Amounts Owed to You

Include money you have in banks and savings accounts as well as currency on hand. Also include any amounts which others owe to you via a note, mortgage, etc. which you hold.

Stocks and Bonds

All stocks and bonds you own are subject to estate tax. This includes U.S. savings bonds, income-tax-free municipal bonds, stocks in foreign countries, etc. These are valued at their current market value. If you own a piece of a small business, then the IRS will, at your death, evaluate your shares more or less according to what it thinks a willing buyer would pay for it.

Life Insurance

If you own a life insurance policy on your life, then the face amount of the insurance is included in your estate. However, there is a way to avoid having this insurance included in your estate. If the insurance goes to a beneficiary and if that beneficiary or other individual owns the policy, then the insurance is not included in your estate. However, that person must have complete control of the policy. You must not possess any "incident of ownership" in the policy such as the right to borrow on the policy, to surrender it for cash, or change the beneficiary. There is also a problem if the policy was transferred to the beneficiary within 3 years prior to the death of the insured.

There is another restriction which forbids you having a "reversionary interest" in the policy. Roughly speaking, this restriction states that you should have less than a 5% chance of getting back the policy or its proceeds because of your beneficiary dying before you. This restriction can be satisfied by having your beneficiary name someone other than yourself to inherit the policy in the event the beneficiary dies before you.

Jointly-Owned Property

There are two basic ways in which property can be jointly owned. The first way, called tenancy-in-common, means that each of the owners has a share of the property and can dispose of that share as he chooses. Upon death, his share passes to whomever is named in his will. If there is no will, it, together with his other property, passes according to the inheritance laws of the state.

Under tenancy-in-common, your share of the ownership would be included in your estate. For example, if you own an equal share of a house under tenancy-in-common with another person, then your estate would include $1/2$ the value of the house. It would make no difference who had contributed the funds to buy the house.

The second and more prevalent type of co-ownership is called joint tenancy. Under this type, when one of the co-owners dies, the property passes automatically to the other co-owner. It cannot be willed to another individual.

Your estate includes 1/2 the value of any property held in joint tenancy with your spouse. For property held in joint tenancy with a non-spouse, your estate includes that portion of the joint property which represents the fraction you paid for.

There is a special type of joint tenancy available only to husband and wife, called **tenancy-by-the-entireties.** Under ordinary joint tenancy, one party alone can demand to dissolve the tenancy and retrieve his share. But under tenancy-by-the-entireties, generally, husband and wife must agree on any dissolution of the ownership. In most states, tenancy-by-the-entireties is available only in joint ownership of real estate. There is no difference between ordinary joint tenancy and tenancy-by-the-entireties as far as estate tax is concerned.

Annuities and Death Benefits

Many annuities and pension plans have a survivorship feature which pays a beneficiary either a lump sum or periodic payments upon the death of the original participant. Also, tax-sheltered annuities, Keogh plans, and IRAs may make payments to survivors. The value of such payments is generally included in the estate.

Deductions from the Gross Estate

To compute the taxable estate, the following deductions are subtracted from the gross estate:

(1) The marital deduction

The full value of all property left to a spouse is deductible from the estate. Thus, if the entire estate is left to a spouse, no estate tax is due.

(2) Funeral expenses, administration expenses, and debts

This includes undertaker charges, cost of burial plot and tombstone, and any personal debts that must be settled by the estate. Also deductible are the costs of settling the estate—attorney fees, court costs, executor fees, and appraiser fees.

(3) Charitable contributions

The full market value of any bequest made to charity is deductible. Sometimes, bequests are made in a form other than an outright donation. For example, income-producing property might be left in trust with the provision that the income from such property be paid to a child, upon whose death the property is given to charity. In such a case, an actuarial computation is made to determine how to allocate the benefits between the child and the charity. The estate would get a deduction for the value allocated to charity.

Computation of the Estate Tax

The estate tax is computed as follows: First, the taxable estate is computed by subtracting allowable deductions from the gross estate. Then, the total of lifetime taxable gifts is added in and the tax computed on this amount. Next, any gift taxes that have already been paid are subtracted from the tax bill. Last, there are several tax credits which are subtracted to reduce the tax bill further.

Tax Credits
(1) State death tax credit
You can subtract state death taxes up to a certain maximum amount. There is also a credit for death taxes paid to a foreign country on property in that country.

(2) Credit for prior Federal estate tax
Suppose one person inherits part of an estate on which estate tax was paid and then dies soon after the inheritance. The estate of the second person to die might then be hit by a second estate tax. To reduce the effect of this double taxation, a credit is allowed on the estate tax of the second person to die if death occurs within ten years of the first death — the longer the time, the less credit allowed.

State Inheritance Taxes
Virtually all states have some type of inheritance tax. These taxes differ widely from state to state both in the size of the tax and the manner in which they are applied. Many states vary the rates according to the relationship between the deceased and the beneficiary—the closer the relationship, the lower the tax.

How Is the Estate Settled?
The rules differ according to state law but the basic procedure is the same. Property which is owned in joint tenancy passes directly to the surviving owner. Property in certain types of trusts remains governed by the trust agreement. Other property is distributed to the heirs as provided in the will. If there is no will, then State law governs how the property is distributed.

A court will be responsible for supervising the distribution of the estate. In the will, an executor is named who has the responsibility of evaluating the assets, paying the appropriate taxes, and distributing the property according to the will. If there is no will, an executor will be appointed by the court. If the estate is simple, a family member or friend may be named as executor. Complicated estates are often executed by an individual or bank trust department specializing in such matters. In such cases, executor fees typically range in the neighborhood of 5% of the value of the estate governed by the will.

Making a Will
Anyone with even a modest amount of assets should have a will. In the absence of a will, your assets will be distributed according to an arbitrary formula given by State law. The distribution formula may not be what you think. For example, in some states, the estate of a married individual with no children would be distributed 50% to the individual's parents and 50% to the spouse. Elsewhere, the estate of a married individual with children might be distributed $33^{1}/_{3}$% to the spouse and $66^{2}/_{3}$% to the children. This could impose a hardship on the spouse who might actually have to go to court to get permission to use the children's share for their benefit.

If there are children, a will should be drawn up which includes the appointment of a guardian in case both the parents die. Otherwise, the court would be in charge of appointing a guardian. Even if there are no children and all property is held in joint tenancy, a will may be called for. To illustrate what can happen without a will, suppose an individual with no children owns all property in joint tenancy with a spouse. If the two of them die in a joint accident, without a will the property would pass from the first to die to the second to die and then to, say, the parents of the second party. The family of the first to die would get nothing.

Note that the cost of drawing up a will isn't deductible as such. However, if your will includes provisions designed to reduce estate tax, the cost of working out these provisions is deductible. Ask your lawyer to itemize on his bill that portion of his fee attributable to estate tax planning.

What Can Be Done to Minimize Estate Tax?

There are many strategies for reducing estate tax. If your estate will be sizable, then you should consult one of the many lawyers specializing in such matters to design a plan to minimize your estate tax. In fact, many people claim that the main effect of the estate tax is not to raise significant amounts of money for the Treasury, but to force people to arrange their affairs in such a way as to avoid or minimize the tax.

Here are just three of the basic techniques used for reducing estate tax:

(A) Give property away before death.

The annual exemptions of $10,000 per recipient per year ($20,000 if married) can be used to transfer a substantial amount over a period of years. Gifts of income-producing property can also have the advantage of reducing income tax by shifting income to a lower-bracket taxpayer.

Sizable gifts made to minors are usually made under the Uniform Gifts to Minors Act. Under this act, a custodian is named who controls and invests the funds until the minor reaches majority age whereupon he assumes control of the funds. You or your spouse can serve as custodian. However, if you serve as custodian of funds you gave and you die before the minor reaches majority age, then the value of the funds held as custodian would be included in your estate. Thus, it might be better to name your spouse or someone else as custodian to avoid this possibility.

(B) Use trusts to avoid double estate tax.

A common device used in estate-planning for large estates is to place funds in a trust. Typically the situation is this: An individual wants to leave funds first to his spouse and, after the death of his spouse, to his children. If the funds were left outright to the spouse, these funds would escape estate tax at that time but would be subjected to estate tax at the death of the spouse. The second estate tax is usually more severe than the first because the second estate does not qualify for the marital deduction (unless the surviving spouse remarried) and is generally larger in amount.

To lessen the taxation of the spouse's estate, most planned estates leave a certain portion of the funds to a trust. For example, the trust might be directed to pay the interest earned by the funds to the spouse as long as the spouse is living. Upon death of the spouse, the funds would be transmitted to the children. The trust could also provide that in case of emergencies, the trustees are directed to pay to the spouse part of the principal in addition to the interest.

The value of the funds placed in such a trust is included in the estate. But, since the spouse never has control of the funds, there is no second estate tax upon the death of the spouse. The principal simply passes automatically over to the children without a second estate tax being paid.

(C) Make charitable gifts.

There is an estate tax deduction for any funds left to charity. However, an individual may want to benefit a charity, but is worried that an outright bequest would leave a surviving spouse or child without adequate support.

A common approach is to leave funds to a charitable trust. For example, a trust might be directed to pay all annual income earned by the funds to a spouse or child. Upon death of the spouse or child, the remaining principal is given to charity. The estate gets a charitable deduction based on an actuarial computation of the present value of the future gift to charity.

Sometimes, instead of leaving funds directly to charity, it is better to leave the funds to someone else with the express understanding that this person will donate the funds to charity. This second person will then get an income tax deduction for the charitable gift. This income tax deduction might save more taxes than the corresponding estate tax deduction if the funds were donated directly.

Caution

We have only briefly touched upon some of the basic principles involved in estate planning. The only proper way to plan an estate is to consult with a lawyer who specializes in such matters and is familiar with the intricacies of Federal and State law.

Chapter 24

Will Your Tax Return Be Audited?

SECTION 1:
AUDITS

At one time, IRS procedures for checking tax returns were kept top secret. But now, a number of documents give a considerable amount of insight into the inner workings of the IRS. Most important are various IRS manuals which it issues for general guidance to its Tax Auditors. These documents were forced into public view by suits brought under the Freedom of Information Act. Another elucidating document is a report prepared several years ago by the GAO (General Accounting Office), a watchdog agency of the Congress. The GAO report provides an independent outside look into how the IRS behaves in its dealings with taxpayers.

Basic Procedures
After you fill out your tax return, you send it to one of the 10 IRS Service Centers. At the Service Center, your tax return is subjected to an initial inspection both by a human being and by a computer. One of the purposes of this initial inspection is to determine if the return contains any of a number of designated **Unallowable Items**. The GAO report contains a list of these Unallowable Items. If you have one of these items on your tax return, the IRS will send you a notice to that effect. The most pertinent of these IRS notices are given below.

Personal Legal Expenses
Your deduction of legal expenses, reported on Schedule A, has been disallowed. Deductions for personal, living, or family expenses are allowable only if expressly provided for in the law. Personal legal expenses for wills, trusts, adoption, divorce, and other items not connected with the production of income are not provided for, and are therefore not deductible.

Educational Expenses for Other Than Taxpayer or Spouse
Your deduction of educational expenses for someone other than yourself or your spouse, reported on Schedule A, has been disallowed. Deductions for personal, living or family expenses are allowable only if expressly provided for in the law. Educational expenses for someone other than yourself or your spouse are not provided for, and are therefore not deductible.

Automobile Expenses — Donated Services
Your deduction for automobile expenses incurred in donating your services to a

qualified charitable organization, reported on Schedule A, has been adjusted because you used an unallowable mileage rate to compute your automobile expenses. When using a mileage rate to determine automobile expenses for donated services, you are limited to 12 cents a mile, which is the rate we used in determining your deduction.

Contributions — Nonqualifying

Your charitable contributions deduction, reported on Schedule A, has been adjusted because contributions to individuals or to other nonqualifying recipients, such as lobbying organizations and foreign charities (except Canadian charities), are not deductible by law.

Federal Taxes

The deductions you claimed on Schedule A for Federal taxes have been disallowed. The law denies a deduction for Federal income tax; social security and railroad retirement taxes; social security tax you paid for a personal or domestic employee; Federal excise taxes on automobiles, tires, telephone service, and air transportation; customs duties; and Federal estate and gift taxes.

Utility Taxes

Your deduction for taxes, reported on Schedule A, has been adjusted. . . . Utility taxes with respect to sewers, water, phones, and garbage collection are not . . . deductible by law.

Automobile License, Registration, and Tag Fees or Taxes

Your deduction for automobile license, registration, tag fees, or taxes, reported on Schedule A, has been adjusted. The law provides that such amounts may be deductible as personal property taxes only if they are imposed by your State annually, and in an amount based on the value of your automobile. Because your State does not impose the fees and taxes in this manner, they do not qualify as personal property taxes and are therefore not deductible.

Sale or Purchase of Personal Residence

Your deduction of expenses incurred in the sale or purchase of your residence, reported on Schedule A, has been disallowed. Deductions for personal, living, or family expenses are allowable only if expressly provided for in the law. Closing expenses, settlement fees, legal fees, or realtor commissions are not provided for, and are therefore not deductible.

Matching Program

The income you report on your return is matched against the W-2, interest, and dividend forms which were sent to the IRS by your employer, bank, companies whose shares you own, etc. If the computer discovers that you did not report all your income, it will tag your return for examination.

In practice, the IRS matches your tax return against virtually all information sent to it on magnetic tape. This includes most wage information forms because the Social Security Administration now converts this data to magnetic tape and passes it on to the IRS. Also, stockbrokers and financial institutions which send out more than 50 dividend or interest information forms must now report this information to the IRS on magnetic tape. At one time, relatively few interest and dividend forms sent to the IRS on paper were fed into the matching program because of the extra cost of processing such forms. But now, the IRS expects to process about 95% of these paper forms with new optical scanning equipment.

Matching usually starts early in the year after the tax return is filed. Thus, for example, matching on 1987 tax returns which are filed in 1988 will probably begin early in 1989. The IRS has a tough new policy when the matching program turns up unreported dividend and interest income—an automatic negligence penalty will be assessed. To escape the penalty, the taxpayer will have to provide proof that he was not intentionally or carelessly omitting the income, but rather that there was justification for the omission.

After your return is checked for routine omissions, it is fed into the master computer in West Virginia. All tax returns are classified into categories, depending upon the total income reported and whether it is a *business* return or a *personal* return. For each category, the computer assigns to each return in that category a number called the DIF (Discriminate Function) number. This number indicates the likelihood that an audit of the return will result in an additional tax assessment. The higher the DIF number, the greater is the potential additional tax assessment.

The formula used by the computer program to assign the DIF number to a tax return is a highly guarded secret. It is based on the experience of the IRS in previous audits and is regularly updated.

According to a declassified IRS audit manual, it is not just the items which appear on your tax return that can produce a high DIF score. The **absence** of certain items can raise the DIF score and cause your return to be targeted for examination. [MT 41(12)0-1:310]

For example, the absence of dividend income when Schedule D shows sales of stock you've owned may be an examination trigger [IRM 41(12)0-1:330]. Or, the absence of a deduction for real estate taxes when a mortgage interest deduction is claimed may cause suspicion. If there is a suspicious inconsistency on your tax return, it would be wise to attach an explanation of the reason for such inconsistency to your tax return, in order to deflect the possibility of an audit.

The DIF program is highly effective in singling out tax returns which are filled out incorrectly. Only about 17% of audits of taxpayers in the $25,000—$50,000 income category result in no change in the amount of tax due.

Middle-Income Taxpayers Over-Audited

The GAO has criticized the IRS for auditing too many middle-income taxpayers. These individuals have shown the greatest level of compliance with the tax laws of any category of taxpayers. In contrast, the tax returns of small businesses exhibit a much lower level of compliance. Yet, the audit rate of these small business returns is about the same as the audit rate for middle-income individuals.

The reason there is little difference in the audit rates is that individual tax returns can be audited in much less time than business returns so that the yield per manhour of IRS time becomes higher. But the GAO feels that this is a shortsighted approach. The purpose of conducting audits is not just to extract money from the most vulnerable taxpayers, but also to encourage a high level of compliance from others out of a fear of audit. In fact, it has been shown that as the audit frequency increases among a given class of taxpayers, the general compliance level among all taxpayers in that class rises. Thus, the GAO recommended that more audits be directed to those taxpayers with a history of lower compliance than middle-income taxpayers. However, recent figures show that middle-income taxpayers continue to be significantly over-audited.

How to Reduce the Odds of an Audit

After the computer assigns DIF numbers to all the tax returns, the local IRS offices request from the computer those returns in each category showing the higher DIF numbers. When these returns arrive at the local office, an experienced IRS classifying officer reviews these returns to see if there is an auditable issue involved in the return. The officer may accept the return as submitted or he may send it to an IRS examiner who will contact you for the purpose of setting up an audit. Of tax returns that the computer has kicked out, about 50% are selected for audit with the remaining 50% accepted as filed.

It's here that you have a chance to lessen the odds you will be audited. Your tax return should be filled out in such a way that the examining officer is encouraged not to select it for audit.

The first thing you can do is to avoid suspiciously rounded figures. According to the GAO, this is one of the first things an examiner is trained to look for. Figures of $200, $350, $600 will arouse suspicion which $213, $371, $594 will not. If your figures represent a guess, then at least guess an odd amount. And if your return accidentally contains too many round numbers, you might even want to go back and "unround" a few of these numbers to be on the safe side.

The second thing is to avoid having identical numbers appear on a return for two different items. This is an indication you may have miscopied a number in the wrong place. According to one tax newsletter, the IRS uses a quality control procedure to kick out such returns for examination. For example, if your return shows a $2,000 IRA deduction and a $2,000 credit for estimated tax, the processing of your return is halted. At the least, you then could be sent a letter asking for an explanation. [Tax Hotline; October, 1984]

The third thing you can do is to attach documentation to your return which substantiates any large or unusual deduction that is likely to kick out your return for audit. When the classifying officer reviews your return, this attached evidence may convince him that an audit is not likely enough to produce additional revenue. If so, then you have prevented an audit.

If the problem is an unusually high deduction, you can attach copies of supporting documents such as bills or checks. An example of this kind would be unusually large medical expenses. However, in this case, you should show in your attached statement that you have substracted any amounts of insurance payments you received.

On the other hand, if the problem is mainly one of understanding the law, you might just write a short statement proving you understand the law. For example, to support a home office deduction [cf. the Home Office chapter], you might include the following statement:

"The home office is the principal place of business for the taxpayer's job or business activity of _____. It is used exclusively on a regular basis for business purposes. The home office deduction does not exceed the gross income from this activity after deducting other business expenses attributable to the activity."

The attaching of documentation to a tax return is confirmed by the GAO Report as being of great importance in influencing the examiner not to choose your return for audit. In fact, the IRS has agreed to lessen the arbitrary manner with which classifying officers choose returns for audit after the computer has kicked them out with high DIF scores. This means that appropriate documentation attached to your tax return may become virtually the only way a classifying officer will accept your return without audit. The IRS asks that supporting statements not be attached directly to their related forms. Rather, all supporting statements should be assembled in the same sequence as the forms they support and placed at the end of the tax return.

Another helpful factor is for your tax return to include some income which would not show up unless you reported it. This is an indication to the examiner that you are an honest and careful taxpayer.

You should be careful when you fill out the *occupation* lines for yourself and your spouse that appear on your tax return. This information is likely to be the first thing an examining officer looks at. An occupation of mostly salaried individuals will arouse less suspicion than an occupation of mostly self-employed individuals because there is less opportunity to hide income or exaggerate deductions. Thus, a consulting engineer should list his occupation as *engineer* rather than *consultant*. Similarly, a music teacher should list his occupation as *teacher* rather than *musician*.

Not all audited tax returns are computer-selected under the DIF program. A significant number are selected because the IRS has special reason to think they might contain errors. The most common of these special reasons is that the return was prepared by a professional tax preparer whom the IRS has on its list of preparing erroneous returns in the past.

The number of returns each IRS office requests depends upon the availability of personnel in that office to examine such returns. Thus, a return with a given DIF number might be sent to one local office for examination, while in a different locality, another return with the same DIF number might escape examination because the office in that locality is understaffed. In fact, there is a wide discrepancy in the percentage of returns audited in various districts. This variation is due partly to a geographic maldistribution of questionable returns and partly to a maldistribution of agents across the country. There is also a wide discrepancy in the extra tax collected by various IRS offices from those taxpayers that are audited.

Each year, the IRS selects a certain number of tax returns at random under its Taxpayer Compliance Measurement Program, or TCMP. The purpose of this program is to obtain a detailed statistical profile of taxpayers in various income categories. Using this profile, the IRS constructs its general DIF program for auditing tax returns with high adjustment potential. If your tax return is selected under the TCMP program, it's bad news. Your return will be subjected to an exhaustive audit, much more detailed than an ordinary audit. The entire tax return must be verified and documented, line by line. For example, if an "over 65 standard deduction" is claimed, it must be backed up by a birth certificate or other record of birth.

Safe Deductions

A declassified IRS audit manual lists a number of items which it suggests an examiner not audit because their examination is *"usually not productive"* [MT 41(12)0-1, Chapter 500]. These include:

1. Home mortgage interest.
2. Interest deduction consisting of a combination of a number of small items.
3. High medical expenses for large families or older taxpayers.
4. Auto expenses when the standard mileage computation is used and the mileage shown does not appear excessive.

What If There Is Only One Questionable Item on Your Tax Return?

Suppose your tax return contains only one questionable deduction. Is this sufficient to cause your tax return to be audited? According to a recently declassified IRS Audit Manual, the answer is generally "no." This manual advises its examiners that,

"Single issues should generally not be examined, as experience has shown that such examinations frequently result in insignificant or no tax change when other questionable items are not present on the return." [MT 41(12)0-1:510(4)(b)]

If there is one large item on your tax return which is susceptible to IRS challenge, take note of the above suggested IRS policy. Avoid including any other questionable items if they do not significantly lower your taxes. Or, if there are other unusually large deductions, attach documentation to your tax return which removes them from the questionable category. That way, the *"questionable items"* on your tax return will consist only of the one large susceptible item you're concerned about. According to the above quote, this will place your tax return in the category the IRS suggests not generally be audited.

Make Sure Your State Tax Return Agrees with Your Federal Return

The IRS has entered into a cooperative arrangement with a number of different States. Entries on Federal and State tax returns are checked against each other for consistency. In case of discrepancy, both returns could be flagged for audit. Be sure your tax returns agree with each other to avoid triggering an unnecessary audit.

Average Deductions

Although the formula used by the IRS computer to select returns for audit is a closely guarded secret, the basic principle behind the formula is not. The formula is based primarily on the amount and relationship between the deductions claimed. If a person's deductions are significantly higher than the average of those with the same income, then the computer is likely to select his return for audit. However, it is not just the total of all deductions which counts. If a person's deductions in any one category are high enough, the computer may tag his return for audit, even if the total of all deductions is in line with the average. For this reason, it is interesting to know what the average deductions in various categories are in relation to income. The table below lists the average deductions on 1985 returns claiming such deductions, as related to the adjusted gross income listed on such returns. (Data for 1986 returns won't be available until later in 1988.)

Adjusted Gross Income	Medical	Taxes	Charity	Interest	Business Expenses
$ 20,000- 25,000	$1,713	1,830	809	3,220	2,086
25,000- 30,000	1,379	2,133	800	3,591	1,947
30,000- 40,000	1,639	2,696	891	4,121	2,179
40,000- 50,000	1,727	3,483	1,105	5,243	2,153
50,000- 75,000	3,127	4,750	1,575	6,730	3,053
75,000-100,000	5,550	6,942	2,538	10,038	3,778
100,000-200,000	8,497	11,043	4,237	14,419	5,424

We caution that the average deductions listed in the table are for informative use only in assessing the likelihood you will be audited. You are not allowed to use the average amounts in these tables on your own return in place of the actual amounts to which you are entitled. In fact, the IRS computer selects a certain number of returns at random, so simply filing an "average return" will not guarantee that you won't be audited.

Types of Audits
There are 3 types of audits.

(1) Correspondence Audit. Here, the IRS will write you a letter asking for further information. All dealings are conducted through the mail. This is the most convenient type of audit because you do not have to travel to the IRS office. Furthermore, you are not faced with making on the spot reactions or decisions as you might be in a face-to-face interview.

(2) Office Audit. In this type of audit, you will be requested to pay a visit to your local IRS office and discuss your return with an IRS auditor. The letter requesting such a visit may ask you to bring documentation to support items on your return.

You may be able to avoid an office audit if it is chiefly a matter of verifying that you actually paid deductions claimed on your tax return. Contact the auditor and ask if you can send in copies of the cancelled checks or other evidence of payment. Then if he agrees, mail in the information so that it reaches him before the scheduled time of examination. If everything is in order, you will have saved yourself a trip to the IRS office.

(3) Field Audit. In this type of audit, the IRS agent comes to your home or office. Field audits will usually occur only if you operate a business or live in a remote area.

The IRS Manual lists the following deductions as suitable for examination by correspondence audit: *"interest, taxes, contributions, medical expenses, and simple miscellaneous deductions such as union dues and small tools."* More complicated issues such as travel expenses, educational expenses, etc., fall into the office audit category.

The letter informing you of an audit will specify certain items on your return in which the IRS is interested. These are usually the only items that will be questioned.

IRS Cutoff Figures Made Public

Amended returns are subjected to a special audit procedure. These returns are classified into categories depending upon the kind and amounts of the deductions being amended. All the tax returns in one category are examined while only a small percentage of returns in the other category are subject to examination.

A recent IRS Agents Manual makes a surprising revelation of just what the cutoff numbers are for placement into the must-examine category. Usually, this type of data is withheld to prevent individuals from claiming just below the cutoffs. In addition to providing data on amended returns, these cutoff numbers give insight into the audit policy on regular returns because they illustrate the relative weights that the IRS assigns when comparing the questionability of one deduction versus another.

The following IRS list shows the amount of change in various items on an amended tax return which will place it into the must-examine category.

(1) *Schedule B (Interest & Dividend Income) — Decrease of $2,000 or more.*

(2) *Schedule D (Capital Gains or Losses) — Decrease in gain or increase in loss of $10,000 or more.*

(3) *Education Expense — Increase in excess of $400.*

(4) *Travel Expense — Increase in excess of $2,000.*

(5) *Moving Expenses — Increase in excess of $5,000.*

What to Do if You Are Audited

The letter informing you of an office audit will list the items being challenged and the time and place of the audit. If the time is not convenient, you have the right to rearrange the time to fit in with your schedule although you can't make extensive delays. The best time to schedule an audit is in the time-slot before lunch or before the end of the day. The auditor will be less likely to prolong the audit to examine an extra secondary issue.

You can also request the audit be moved to a different IRS district office if you have a sufficient reason (e.g. you moved outside the original district or you work in a different district). Making such a request is a good idea. A substantial delay can occur in transferring your file from one office to another. And your file might go to

Audits

the bottom of the stack when assigned to a new agent. Meanwhile, the statute of limitations for auditing your return can expire.

You can have a lawyer, CPA, or enrolled agent (who has passed a special IRS exam) argue your case for you (in your absence if you wish). If you are presenting your own case, you can bring with you one other friend or relative. Representatives from commercial preparation firms may accompany you to the audit, but they usually can't argue your case.

Note that you are entitled to bring up deductions you overlooked in addition to defending those the IRS is challenging. About 5% of all audits result in refunds to the taxpayer for this reason.

The notification letter from the IRS will contain a checklist of the items being questioned on your tax return. Normally, these will be the only items discussed at the audit. You should bring documentation to support your deductions for these items. However, you should not bring supporting documents for other items not mentioned in the IRS notification. If the auditor's curiosity is aroused by another item, he will be deterred by the fact you haven't brought documents to examine. He will be more likely to let the matter drop and close the examination than to force you to come back with the extra documents.

There are two different types of examiners — Revenue Agents and Tax Auditors. Revenue agents usually have a college education with a major in accounting and are used to audit more complicated tax returns. Tax auditors, on the other hand, are not required to have taken any accounting or business courses, although they must take some training in accounting before advancing to the journeyman level.

How to Get the IRS to Call Off Repeat Audits

Few things are more irritating than to be audited, to convince the auditor that you're correct, and then to be audited on the very same issue the next year. To prevent this from happening, the IRS has adopted a special policy. Namely, a taxpayer is generally not supposed to be audited on any issue on which he was audited in either of the two preceding years — provided the taxpayer was cleared on that issue in the previous audit. (However, if he was cleared in one of the preceding years and had to pay tax in the other, the current audit can proceed.)

Note that the IRS does not generally check for previous audits. It is up to you to tell the IRS agent about a preceding no-change audit. He should then call off the audit after verifying your story.

The IRS Agents Manual

The manual which the IRS issues to its own agents offers some interesting glimpses into how agents are instructed to treat taxpayers. Below are some excerpts from this manual. We have added underlining for emphasis.

Office Interview Examination

A. Direct contact with a taxpayer is a more satisfactory way to determine the proper depth and scope of an audit. Thus the office interview technique should be used when selected returns contain issues which require an analytical approach and individual judgment. The following types of issues should . . . be initiated for examination by office interview.

1. Dependency exemptions unless they clearly meet the criteria for the correspondence method [e.g. the dependent is a spouse, child, or parent.]

2. Income from tips, pensions, annuities, rents, royalties, and determination of gains as capital or ordinary income.

3. Deductions for employee's business expenses.

4. Deductions for bad debts.

5. Determination of basis of property.

6. Complex miscellaneous deductions such as casualty and theft losses requiring determinations of fair market value and education expenses; and fellowships and scholarships.

7. Salaried employees whose occupations lend themselves to possible outside employment.

B. Regardless of issue, this technique will be used if needed to ensure the rights of taxpayers under the law. Aside from tax issue, other factors, such as those below, may indicate that an office interview examination is necessary:

1. Taxpayer's income is low in relation to his financial responsibilities as indicated by entries on the return (number of dependents, interest expense, etc.)

2. Taxpayer's occupation is of the type that requires only a limited formal education.

3. The appearance of the tax return (writing, grammar, neatness, etc.) indicates the taxpayer may not be able to effectively correspond with us.

Instructions For Examining Officer

Evaluation of Evidence

(a) Oral statements — The principal method of introducing evidence in a court case is through the testimony of a witness. Therefore, oral statements made by taxpayers to examining officers represent direct evidence which must be thoroughly considered. Uncontradicted statements which are not improbable or unreasonable cannot be disregarded even if made by an interested party. The degree of reliability placed by an examining officer on oral statements must be based on the credibility of the taxpayer as supported by surrounding circumstantial evidence. If the issue involves specific record-keeping required by law and regulations, . . . then of course, oral evidence alone cannot be substituted for necessary written documentation.

(b) Credibility:

1. It is the responsibility of the examining officer to establish the degree of credibility of the taxpayer. It is here that the examining officer must exercise to the fullest his skill and judgment. <u>He should take into account the demeanor of the taxpayer, his manner of making the statement and the extent of subject knowledge demonstrated.</u> These first impressions should be carefully tested by skillful questioning to bring out all pertinent surrounding circumstances. Corroborative or contradictory details will have an important bearing on determining the reasonableness and probability of the statements.

2. *If the statements of the taxpayer, although self-serving, are not improba-*

ble or unreasonable, self-contradictory, or inconsistent with surrounding facts and circumstances, they should be accepted. If the statements of the taxpayer, in the judgment of the examining officer, reveal some degree of unreliability, his findings should take this into account. Unless the taxpayer's statements have been found to be wholly unreliable, they must be given some weight in the conclusion reached.

3. In considering issues susceptible to abuse by taxpayers, the examining officer should assess the credibility of the taxpayer with caution. Since oral statements with strained constructions of fact are more likely to be encountered in these cases, the examining officer's skill and judgment in developing the surrounding circumstances are especially important, so that the taxpayer does not profit from his failure to maintain documentation substantiating his income and deductions. Some examples of such issues are personal expenses disguised as business, convention or education expenses and determination of income from tips, prizes, awards, gambling, or miscellaneous independent activities.

Soliciting Agreements

(1) Upon completion of an examination, the examining officer will explain the basis of the proposed adjustments to the taxpayer or his representative, and make an effort to obtain an agreement to the proposed tax liability. If necessary, the examining officer will cite the provisions of the law, regulations, published rulings, Tax Court and other court decisions on which he has based his conclusions. If the taxpayer indicates disagreement with any of the proposed adjustments, he should be informed of his appeal rights, as well as his right to pay any deficiency and file claim for refund. If agreement can be reached on one or more, but not all issues or years, the taxpayer should be encouraged to enter into a partial agreement by executing a waiver of restrictions covering the agreed issues or years. In attempting to reach agreement, however, Audit personnel must recognize that they are not authorized to settle cases in the same sense that a settlement may be negotiated by Appellate Division.

(2) If a taxpayer specifically requests a written record of what has been agreed to at the time a partial agreement is entered into, an appropriate letter or statement may be furnished covering such agreed issues or years. The issuance of such a letter or statement will be subject to the same review procedures as a regular report.

Will the IRS Bother with Small Amounts?

Officially, *"The primary objective in selection of tax returns will be the highest possible revenue yield from the examination manhours expended, and the examination of as many returns of all classes as is feasible for the maintenance of a high degree of voluntary taxpayer compliance."*

The average office audit results in a recommended tax increase of about $800 and takes about 90 minutes.

The IRS Manual also states,

"The Service recognizes that many accounts outstanding on the books are so

small that the expenses of collection are out of proportion to the amount to be realized from further collection effort. In the interest of efficient and economical utilization of available manpower and other resources, small balance accounts may be written off when it is determined in accordance with Manual instructions that the collection costs involved do not warrant attempting to collect."

IRS Tells Its Agents: Be Reasonable

Often, taxpayers are put into a no-win situation when challenged by the IRS. The trouble and expense of fighting the IRS in court leads the taxpayer to give in even when the law is on his side. IRS agents sometimes take advantage of this by disallowing legitimate deductions, figuring that the taxpayer will not fight back.

To lessen the incentive for government abuse, Congress passed a law under which the IRS can be forced to reimburse taxpayers for court and attorney's fees when they lose in court. Because of the danger of having to reimburse taxpayers when the IRS acts in bad faith, agents are instructed to be reasonable. Instead of trying to twist the law, IRS agents are instructed to apply the law in a reasonable way as it was intended to be applied.

> ". . . it is the responsibility of each person in the Service, charged with the duty of interpreting the law, to try to find the true meaning of the statutory provision and not to adopt a strained construction in the belief that he is 'protecting the revenue.' The revenue is properly protected only when we ascertain and apply the true meaning of the statute.
>
> "The Service also has the responsibility of applying and administering the law in a reasonable, practical manner. Issues should only be raised by examining officers when they have merit, never arbitrarily or for trading purposes. At the same time, the examining officer should never hesitate to raise a meritorious issue. It is also important that care be exercised not to raise an issue or to ask a court to adopt a position inconsistent with established Service position.
>
> "Administration should be both reasonable and vigorous. It should be conducted with as little delay as possible and with great courtesy and consideration. It should never try to overreach and should be reasonable within the bounds of law and sound administration . . . ." [Internal Revenue Manual Supplement 42G-369]

How Long Does the IRS Have to Audit Your Return?

The general rule is that the IRS has 3 years from the due date of your return in which to make an audit. There are several exceptions to this general rule. If you file late, then the IRS has 3 years from your actual filing date. If the IRS can prove that at least 25% of gross income was omitted from your tax return, the time span is 6 years. However, if the government can prove fraud, there is no time limit on auditing a return, although it generally destroys returns after 7 years. But if the government wishes to prosecute for criminal fraud, it must do so within 6 years. Criminal prosecution for fraud is a rare occurrence — about 1/50,000 of all tax returns filed.

Although the IRS has 3 years in which to conduct an audit, the IRS Manual instructs its agents to do so in a shorter period of time. Except when a return is suspected of fraud or covered under some special audit program, the examination and disposition of income tax returns will be completed within 26 months after the due date of the return (or the date filed in the case of returns filed late). The IRS ordinarily allows 6 months for the examination process. Thus, to complete the examination within 26 months, the IRS must usually initiate examination no later than 20 months after the filing date. Thus, if you haven't heard from the IRS by late 1989, your 1987 return will be safe from audit except in unusual circumstances.

Appealing Within the IRS

If you feel an auditor is taking an unreasonable position, you can ask to speak to his supervisor right then. The supervisor can change the auditor's mind if he agrees with you that the position is unreasonable. Otherwise, if you can't come to an agreement at the audit, you can appeal to the Appellate Division of the IRS. The auditor will explain your rights under this appeals procedure.

An IRS directive issued to the Appeals Division makes it easier to reach a settlement. Formerly, the Appeals officer was not allowed to suggest what would be acceptable as a settlement. Instead, all offers had to come from the taxpayer. But now, if you make a reasonable offer of settlement, the Appeals agent *"should give an evaluation of the case in such a manner as to enable the taxpayer to ascertain the kind of settlement that would be recommended for acceptance."* In plain English, this means that they will make a counteroffer. This negotiation policy makes settlements easier to reach, especially if the amounts involved are not large. In more than 80% of appeals cases, the taxpayer achieves a reduction or elimination of extra taxes or penalties.

One situation where an appeal is particularly effective is when the auditor imposes a negligence penalty. Such penalties are often mistakenly assessed by tax auditors in routine cases, rather than in the *"clearly erroneous"* type of case for which they are intended. The Appeals Officer will often cancel such negligence penalties.

Small Case Tax Court

There is a way to contest the IRS without having to get a lawyer or incur beyond a small charge. Disputes involving less than $10,000 may be submitted to the Small Case Tax Court. Here, cases are decided by an impartial judge who will keep the proceeding informal, explaining it as he goes along. You do not need a lawyer and the decision of the judge is final — neither you nor the IRS can appeal and the decision does not set legal precedent.

The procedure for taking a case to Small Case Tax Court is relatively simple. You file a petition asking for a hearing and pay a $60 filing fee. A free booklet describing the procedure can be obtained by writing to Clerk of the Court, U.S. Tax Court, 400 Second Street, N.W., Washington, D.C. 20217.

Note that even if you don't want to appear in court, it pays to submit the petition anyhow. The IRS does not want to send their lawyers into court to adjudicate small issues in a forum that does not involve setting legal precedent. Some time after you file a petition, the IRS will contact you to arrange a settlement. About 90% of small tax cases are settled without going to trial, with the IRS settling for about 50% of the amounts it claimed were due. And if you have a reasonably good case, you might even be able to beat this average.

Section 2:
Private IRS Rulings

You might want to learn in advance the tax consequences of an action you contemplate taking. Many times, the question of whether or not a particular activity falls under the rules for tax-free treatment becomes a matter of judgment. This is especially true when the issue involves determining whether the primary purpose of an activity is for business or personal purposes.

In order to determine how the IRS will treat a particular matter, you can solicit a *Private Letter Ruling* from the IRS. This written opinion, which you attach to your tax return, will then govern the treatment of your particular case by the IRS.

Soliciting a written opinion from the IRS is completely different from merely phoning the information number the IRS provides. It is well established that you cannot legally rely on oral advice from IRS personnel. Past surveys have found substantial error rates in such advice although some improvement has taken place since these surveys were taken. The error rate is no doubt even higher on specialized or complicated matters. After all, it is unreasonable to expect any given individual to be familiar with all the tax laws as they apply to people in all professions.

What Kind of Questions Will the IRS Rule On?

The IRS has the option of deciding whether or not to issue a ruling. Basically they will issue a ruling on most matters with the following major exceptions:

1. The IRS will not issue a ruling to specify how much a certain property is worth, to specify the building/land ratio of property for depreciation purposes, or to specify other such "numerical" issues.

2. The IRS will not rule on a hypothetical question nor on one involving several alternatives. They will not rule on a transaction to be consummated at some indefinite future time. They must be presented with a single definite course of action which is seriously being considered.

3. The IRS will not rule on a transaction or matter having as a major purpose the reduction of Federal taxes. In other words, they won't issue a ruling if they feel they are simply being presented with a tax-dodging scheme.

If the ruling request deals with a matter on which the IRS will not issue a ruling, the taxpayer will be so advised. However, the request may be forwarded to the district IRS office for association with the taxpayer's return. The IRS is also reluctant to issue rulings applying changes in the Tax Code until the IRS has had time to issue regulations interpreting the changes.

Preliminary Contact

The National Office of the IRS ordinarily won't discuss a "substantive tax issue" prior to receipt of a written ruling request. However, you can always inquire whether the IRS will rule on a particular question. Any such written inquiry must contain your name and social security number. You can also make inquiries as to procedural questions concerning the request for a ruling.

A ruling request may be withdrawn at any time before the ruling is issued. However, withdrawal won't necessarily prevent the IRS from furnishing its views to the local IRS office where your tax return is filed.

How to Request a Ruling

To request a ruling, you write a letter describing all the circumstances addressed to: Internal Revenue Service, Assistant Commissioner (Technical), Attention: CC:IND:S, Room 6545, 1111 Constitution Ave., N.W., Washington, D.C. 20224. Ordinarily, either you or your attorney, accountant, or enrolled agent will sign the letter.

The request for a ruling should include the following:

1. The names, addresses, and social security or taxpayer account numbers of all interested parties.

2. Location of the IRS district office having audit jurisdiction over the tax return in question.

3. A carefully detailed description of the transaction including a full and precise statement of the business reasons for the transaction.

4. Copies of all relevant documents. Photocopies will usually be accepted as true copies of the original documents. Originals should not be sent since they won't be returned.

5. A description of how the attached documents or exhibits bear on the issue in question.

6. A statement whether, to the best of the knowledge of the taxpayer or his representative, the identical issue is pending before any other IRS office and if so the office involved.

7. If the request pertains to only one step of a larger transaction, the facts concerning the larger transaction.

8. A statement of the taxpayer's view as to what the tax outcome should be, including reference to relevant authorities in support of this view.

9. A statement whether or not the identical issue is being or has been examined in an IRS audit of a prior tax return which has not yet been finally resolved.

10. Any regulations, rulings, etc. which are contrary to the taxpayer's position, or a statement that none are known.

11. A separate signed declaration as follows: *"Under penalties of perjury, I have examined this request, including accompanying documents, and to the best of my knowledge and belief, the facts presented in support of the requested ruling or determination letter are true, correct and complete."* This statement does not have to be notarized.

If a ruling request does not contain all the needed information, the IRS will write back and request the missing information. Only one copy of the ruling needs to be sent unless more than one issue is presented. In such a case, duplicate requests should be mailed.

Optional Statement of Controlling Facts

If you request a ruling, your request might include some information on future actions which you are not certain will take place. If you feel this information is not critical to your case, you would not want the ruling invalidated because of an irrelevant change in plans. In your ruling request you can make a statement as to what you feel are the "controlling facts." That is, you feel these controlling facts alone should determine the tax outcome. In their ruling, the IRS can then agree with your list of controlling facts or they can make their own list. Any change in facts or circumstances not on the list of controlling facts would then not invalidate the ruling.

Rulings Made Public

The IRS is required to make public all private letter rulings which it issues. Before making a ruling public, the IRS deletes the name of the taxpayer as well as any identifying details or confidential information.

If there is any confidential information which you do not want revealed, you should send a statement to this effect along with your original ruling request. Attached to the statement should be a copy of your ruling request with the material you wish to be kept private indicated by brackets. If there is no information you wish kept confidential, you must attach a separate statement to your ruling request which states that no information needs to be deleted other than your name, address, and social security number.

The release of IRS rulings is of great assistance to the taxpaying public. At one time, the only information that was made public was contained in rulings which the IRS chose to issue and in reports of cases which wound up in court. Now, it is possible to find out the IRS position on any question about which some taxpayer was concerned enough to request a ruling.

Future editions of this Tax Guide will contain reports of all pertinent rulings issued in the future. This provides new information on many issues for which there is currently no clear guidance.

Compliance with Ruling Checked

You must attach to your return a copy of any ruling you have received which is relevant to that return. The IRS wants to make sure that rulings are complied with.

Rulings on Completed Transactions

In addition to obtaining a ruling on future transactions, you can also obtain a ruling on completed transactions if you wish. If the issue concerns clearly established rules, such a request is directed to your local IRS District Director. He will issue a judgment called a determination letter. If the issue involved is novel, the ruling request should go to the address in Washington, D.C. given earlier. If the ruling request is misdirected to either Washington, D.C. or your local District Director, it will be forwarded to the appropriate office.

Ordinarily, it is not recommended that you seek a ruling on a completed transaction. Nor is it advisable to seek a ruling concerning a future course of action which you are planning to take regardless of the tax consequences. In such cases, you are usually best advised just to treat the transaction in the most favorable manner you consider reasonable.

Can You Rely on Rulings?

If you request and receive a ruling concerning your own tax situation then you can safely rely on that ruling as long as the facts you have described are correct. The IRS won't change its mind in your case. However, you cannot absolutely rely on rulings issued to other people even if the circumstances are the same. That is, the IRS can treat two taxpayers in the same situation differently. However, they do attempt to maintain a consistent policy whenever possible.

Speedy Action

The IRS has a procedure for processing ruling requests in a speedy fashion. If the subject matter of the request falls into one of the categories set up for fast processing, then the taxpayer will generally be contacted within 3 weeks by an official of the IRS. This official will inform the taxpayer if he will recommend to the IRS that the ruling be approved or disapproved or whether any additional information is needed. If he is not recommending a fully favorable ruling, the official may suggest how the situation covered in the request can be altered so as to warrant a favorable ruling.

Chapter 25

Casualty Losses

If you suffered a casualty or theft loss, then you might be entitled to a deduction. At one time, you could deduct all but $100 of each loss that occurred. But now, you must also subtract 10% of your adjusted gross income from your total losses when computing the deduction. In particular, only a large amount of losses will yield any deduction at all. The exact procedure for computing your casualty deduction is discussed later in this chapter.

What Is a Casualty?

A casualty is the complete or partial destruction or loss of property resulting from an identifiable event that is sudden, unexpected, or unusual in nature.

Examples of deductible casualty losses include:

Damage from a natural disaster, e.g. hurricane, tornado, flood, storm, fire, accident, heavy rains, landslides, extreme dry and wet spells, sudden sinking of land, etc.

Damage from an auto accident to your own automobile. This is deductible even if the accident was your own fault, provided it was not caused on purpose or by willful negligence. You do not deduct payments you make to the owner of another car you damaged in an accident.

Loss from vandalism.

Sonic boom damage.

Damage to your house from boiler explosion, water pipe break, etc.

Smog damage from an unusual, severe concentration of chemicals in the atmosphere. Progressive damage from a long term smog problem is not deductible.

Loss to personal property caused by accident. For example, one court case allowed a deduction for the loss of a diamond ring jarred loose by a car accident in the person's driveway. Another case allowed a deduction for a ring demolished by a garbage disposal.

Damage from snow, ice, and freezing. Court cases have allowed deductions for damage due to icy road, freezing of an automobile motor, garage wall collapse due to unusual freeze, collapse of eaves due to ice and snow, damage to driveway and brickwork from severe freeze, damage to a house from thawing of collected ice and snow, and damage to trees, shrubs, plants, etc. from extreme winter weather.

Casualty Losses

Loss from severe drought. Unusual droughts can cause deductible casualty losses. This is illustrated by a 1981 court case involving a married couple who lived in Marin County, California. Because of an unusually severe drought, residents were limited to using only 148 gallons of water a day. As a result, the couple could not water the trees, shrubs, and lawn they had planted on their property, resulting in the complete destruction of these items. Because the Court felt the drought to be unusually sudden and unexpected, it allowed a $2,000 deduction for the decline in property value caused by the destruction of the landscaping. In another case, decided in 1984, a homeowner claimed a deduction for $10,500 worth of damage caused by drought. The drought had caused the house to settle, producing cracks in the interior walls, ceiling, and driveway. Because the damage was caused by an identifiable event (severe drought) rather than progressive deterioration, the Court allowed the deduction. [Stevens, TC Memo 1984-365]

Note that the elements of suddenness and unexpectedness must be present to justify a deduction. For example, damage to tropical plants caused by a freeze would be deductible in an area where freezes are practically unknown. But if you live in an area where a freeze is not abnormal, the deduction would be disallowed. Similarly, if your driveway is damaged by an unusual freeze or hot spell, then this would be deductible. However, the event should be sudden. Damage caused by progressive deterioration due to an unprecedented hot summer would probably not be deductible.

Similarly, termite damage is not generally deductible because it is not considered to be a sudden misfortune. Another example occurs with diseases affecting your trees or shrubbery such as Dutch Elm disease. The Court ruled in 1981 that damage caused by a disease does not qualify for the casualty deduction [Coleman, 76 TC No. 49]. But a sudden insect invasion might cause a deductible casualty loss if the damage is caused by the insects themselves, rather than a disease they are carrying. For example, in a 1979 IRS ruling, a deduction was allowed for damage to trees caused by an invasion of pine beetles.

Further illustration of the *suddenness* requirement is given by two cases involving damage due to heavy rainfall. In one case, a deduction was allowed because the rain was concentrated in a short period of time—14.5 inches in a single week [Clapp, 321 F 2d 12]. But in another 1983 case, a deduction was denied because the damage was caused by excessive precipitation over a 4-month period. Since the damage was not caused by a *sudden event* but rather by *progressive deterioration*, a deduction was disallowed [Forrest, TC Memo 1983-177].

You cannot deduct common, ordinary household misfortunes. For example, you cannot deduct breakage of china or glassware that you drop, the loss of a pet which has run away, or the loss of a ring which has been misplaced.

You can deduct a casualty loss even if you were at fault. In one case, a court allowed a deduction for damage to a lawn due to careless use of a weed poison.

A recent court case has established that you don't necessarily have to identify the event that caused the casualty loss. In this case, a supermarket cashier noticed that the diamond was missing from a woman's ring as she went through the checkout counter. The woman was sure the diamond was still in the ring earlier that morning when she polished her nails. Apparently it had been dislodged when the woman was doing various chores that morning.

When the ring was examined after the diamond was lost, two of the prongs were missing and the claws on the opposite side of the ring were forced upward. According to expert testimony, this could only have happened if a fairly strong blow had struck the side of the ring. The Court concluded that the *"cause of such a loss was not an ordinary, common, or easily predicted occurrence"* but rather that *"there was a sudden, unexpected, destructive blow to the ring that, although unnoticed by petitioner in her rush to perform her morning's chores, caused damage to the ring's setting and the resulting loss of the diamond."* Even though the precise incident causing the loss could not be pinpointed, the Court allowed a deduction of over $10,000 for the loss of the diamond. [Kielts, TC Memo 1981-329]

Theft Losses

To claim a theft loss, you must establish that an actual robbery, burglary, embezzlement, etc. took place. The mere disappearance of money or property from your person or home is not sufficient proof. You might have misplaced the item, dropped the money, etc. Usually, you need some evidence that another person took the property in question. Of course, if you return home to find your grand piano missing, no one would dispute that a theft had occurred.

You should always report a theft to the police. The first thing the IRS will ask for if it questions a theft deduction on your return is a copy of the report you made to the police.

However, lack of a police report does not automatically rule out a deduction. In a recent court case, an individual claimed a $1,700 deduction for the value of a stereo, TV, and diamond ring stolen when his apartment was burglarized. He had not reported the burglary to the police because he did not believe they would be able to recover the property. He felt this way because the police had been unsuccessful in recovering property stolen in a previous burglary. Because the Court believed his testimony that the items were stolen, it allowed a deduction despite the lack of a corroborating police report. [Novik, TC Memo 1981-446]

How to Compute Your Loss

The amount of your casualty or theft loss is defined to be the decrease in the value of your property caused by the loss. If you incur expenses for restoring the property back to its original condition, then this will usually be accepted as being equal to the loss. However, you do not have to replace or repair the damaged property in order to deduct the loss.

The value of your property before the casualty loss would be its resale market value if there is a realistic market for the item. This would be the case for a house, automobile, jewelry, etc. But using the resale value is not always a reasonable way to set the value of items. For example, used clothing is worth quite a bit more to an individual than its value in the secondhand market.

This is illustrated by a Tax Court case involving a couple whose home and contents were destroyed by fire. The Court rejected the IRS method of evaluating the destroyed property by what it *"would have brought if hawked off by a secondhand dealer or at a forced sale."* Instead it accepted the insurance industry's general

Casualty Losses

valuation method of using the original cost of the items less a depreciation factor of 20% to 25%. [56 TC 976]

You cannot deduct the cost of repairs or replacements to the extent they represent an improvement over the condition of the property before the casualty or theft. For example, if your watch is stolen, your loss is equal to its used price value. You cannot deduct the cost of a new watch you buy to replace it. Similarly, if your furnace is ruined by a flood, you cannot deduct the cost of a new furnace—only the value of the old furnace.

If you suffer casualty damage, you can establish the amount of the loss by obtaining an appraisal from an experienced and reliable appraiser. You can then deduct the appraiser's fee as a miscellaneous deduction. You should also take photographs where appropriate before the damaged property is repaired.

Your loss cannot exceed the actual price you paid. For example, suppose you purchased your house for $30,000 a number of years ago and then it is totally destroyed by fire. At the time of destruction, the house was worth $75,000. Your casualty loss would be limited to $30,000 plus the cost of any improvements you had made.

You treat your house, land, shrubbery, and other items on your property as one unit. For example, suppose your trees sustain $2,000 worth of damage in a hurricane. You planted these trees yourself many years ago at a cost of $10. You do not have to limit your casualty loss to this $10. Since you are treating the entire property as one unit, the entire $2,000 is the amount of your casualty loss since it doesn't exceed the price you paid for the entire property.

Damage to Trees, Shrubs, and Plants

You are entitled to a casualty deduction for damage due to unexpected ice, snow storms, fire, wind, rain, vandalism, smog, or damage from vehicles. You can deduct the costs of removing damaged trees or shrubs, pruning, bracing, and replanting in order to eventually restore the property to its original state.

However, if there has been extensive damage, another computation procedure may be better. Namely, you can deduct the difference in the value of your property before and after the casualty. This computation procedure may give a larger deduction because damage to landscaping can cause a reduction in property value far greater than the cost of repairing and replanting. You will need to get a qualified appraiser's report to substantiate your claim of decrease in property value.

Casualty deductions for trees and other plant life can be substantial because of the extra value they contribute to property. For example, a recent court decision granted a Florida homeowner a $15,000 deduction for damage to landscaping caused by an unexpected freeze. [Thebaut, TC Memo 1983-699]

The Tax Court, as illustrated by several recent cases, has been quite sympathetic when trees are destroyed. In one case, a $3,500 deduction was allowed for the loss of 5 cypress trees located 90 feet away from a house after the trees were blown down during a storm. The Court indicated the deduction might have been even higher had there been better testimony as to the loss incurred. [Zardo, TC Memo 1982-84]

In another case, 12 trees were blown down by a tornado. The IRS had denied any deduction whatever because the property contained 10 acres filled with trees and it felt the loss of only 12 of them would cause no measurable decrease in the value of the property. But the Court noted that 7 of the destroyed trees were on the cleared portion of the lot near the home and therefore contributed extra value to the property as shade trees. Consequently, it allowed a deduction of over $19,000 for the loss of the trees. [Bowers, TC Memo 1981-658]

And a third case is the most striking of all. In this case, the Court allowed a deduction of $14,900 for the loss of a single prominent oak tree which was done-in by a sudden attack of woodborers. [McKean, TC Memo 1981-670]

Insurance Payments Reduce Loss

You must reduce your loss by any reimbursements you receive from your insurance company. However, you only have to subtract insurance payments which are direct compensation for the loss. Indirect payments for living expenses after a house has been damaged or for a rental car after your automobile has been stolen, for example, are not subtracted in computing your loss.

You must reduce your loss by the amount covered by your insurance policy even if you don't file a claim. This is a specific new requirement contained in the 1986 Tax Reform Act.

The $100 and 10% of Adjusted Gross Income Limitations

After computing your casualty and theft losses, you must make two subtractions in order to obtain your deduction. First, you subtract $100 from the loss caused by each individual incident and total up the remainders. Then, you subtract 10% of your adjusted gross income from the total to obtain your deduction.

Example

The adjusted gross income on your tax return is $50,000. During 1987, you had a theft loss of $4,000 of which $1,000 was covered by insurance. Also, a windstorm caused $1,600 damage to your roof, $550 to your fence, and $700 to your shrubbery, none of which was covered by insurance.

	Windstorm		**Theft**	
Roof	$1,600		$4,000	
Fence	550		−1,000	insurance
Shrubbery	700		$3,000	net loss
	$2,850		− 100	exclusion
	− 100	exclusion	$2,900	
	$2,750			

Total losses ($2,750 + $2,900) $5,650
Less 10% of Adjusted Gross Income (10% × $50,000) .... −5,000
Amount of your deduction .... $ 650

Business Casualties Fully Deductible

The $100 per event and 10% of adjusted gross income subtractions only apply to casualties involving property used for personal purposes. If you suffer a casualty to an item used for professional or business purposes, these subtractions do not apply. Instead, you can deduct the full casualty loss up to your *adjusted basis* in the item. Your *adjusted basis* is equal to the price you paid less any depreciation you were entitled to claim.

> **Example**
>
> You purchased a typewriter in 1986 for $200 which you used entirely for job-related purposes. During 1987, the typewriter was stolen. Your *adjusted basis* in the typewriter is $170 ($170 = the purchase price, $200, less the depreciation deduction of $30 that was allowable in 1986, $200 × 15% = $30).
>
> The entire $170 can be claimed as a casualty deduction. Neither the $100 per casualty subtraction nor the 10% of adjusted gross income subtraction applies since the casualty occurred to *business* property rather than *personal* property.

When to Deduct Your Casualty Losses

You deduct your loss in the year the casualty or theft actually occurred. If you anticipate that you will be reimbursed by insurance, you subtract the amount of the expected reimbursement from your loss in computing your tax. If the reimbursement does not turn out to be what you expected, then you adjust your next year's tax return accordingly. If you suffer a disaster loss in an area declared by the President as qualifying for Federal assistance, you can deduct the loss either in the year the disaster occurred or in the prior year.

Casualty and Collision Insurance

You cannot deduct premiums you pay on insurance against fire, theft, or other casualties. Only actual losses due to such casualties are deductible.

Free Inventory Book From the IRS

You can obtain a free inventory workbook from your local IRS office. This workbook is used to make an inventory of all your personal possessions, including their cost, current value, description, location, etc. The workbook has separate sheets for listing the contents of each room along with pre-printed entries of items typically found in these rooms.

If you should suffer a casualty or theft loss, this inventory workbook will be a valuable document in establishing your loss. You should keep this workbook in your office or a safe deposit box so that it will not disappear in a theft or major disaster. To request this workbook, call your local IRS office and ask for Publication 584.

To complement the workbook, the IRS suggests you keep a file of pictures of both your home and its contents. Note that the workbook and picture file are also valuable in establishing your loss for insurance purposes. It's also a good idea to take pictures immediately after a casualty. For example, photographs of a house ransacked by burglars or damaged by fire would support your claim to a deduction.

Effect on Capital Gains Tax

If you claim a casualty deduction on property you later sell at a profit, then you are supposed to add in this casualty deduction when computing capital gains tax. For example, suppose you buy a house for $50,000 and sell it later for $60,000. If you had claimed a casualty loss deduction of $2,000, then your capital gain would be $12,000 ($60,000 − $50,000 + $2,000). Of course, as described in the *Homeowner's* chapter, if you buy a new house at a higher price or if you are age 55 or over, there might be no tax due on this capital gain.

Where Do You Deduct Your Losses?

There is a special line on Schedule A for listing your total casualty losses. You also attach Form 4684 on which the amount of your deduction is computed.

Chapter 26

Outside Business Activity

SECTION 1:
BASIC RULES

In addition to your regular job, you or your spouse may have an outside "business" activity, e.g. writing, tutoring, consulting, refereeing, reviewing, art, photography, etc. If this activity produces extra income, it becomes taxable along with the rest of your income. As discussed in Sections 2 and 3, there are a number of ways to ease the tax burden on this outside income.

Of particular note are the remarkable *Defined-Benefit Keogh Plans*. With such Plans, those with self-employment income can often **shelter up to 100% of such income from tax** [cf. Section 3 of the *Tax-Sheltered Plans* chapter for details].

On the other hand, the activity might produce a loss. When a loss is produced, the question arises whether the activity qualifies as a business activity or is simply a hobby. Losses produced by a business activity are fully deductible while losses produced by a hobby are not. Section 4 discusses the rules for deducting losses in more detail.

The methods described in this chapter apply only to income which is earned as a result of your labor. Investment income, income from rents, etc. do not qualify. Furthermore, such income must be self-employment income earned when you are working for yourself or income received from a corporation which you own.

> *Example*
> Jones, in addition to his regular job, does consulting work for an industrial company in the city where he lives. He arranges it so that he is not considered an employee of the company for which he works. Rather, he is a self-employed professional contracting out his services. Alternatively, he could form the Jones Consulting Firm (whose only employee is Jones) which contracts with the company for the services of Jones. Actually, the industrial company is quite happy with this arrangement. It doesn't have to pay social security, unemployment insurance, or worker's compensation premiums as it has to do on its regular employees. In fact, Jones' remuneration as a private contractor may be higher than it would be as an employee because of these savings.

What Is an Employee?

You cannot call yourself a private contractor just because you and the party engaging your services agree. There is a definite body of law as to when a person is an employee and when he is a private contractor. The basic definition of an employee is one who performs services subject to control by an employer *"not only as to the result to be accomplished by the work, but also as to the details and means by which that result is accomplished. That is, an employee is subject to the will and control of the employer not only as to what is to be done, but also as to how and when it shall be done."* Of course, the preceding definition is not sufficiently precise to determine borderline cases. There may be specific IRS guidelines which apply in your case. If not, the particular circumstances of your situation will determine your status. You can get a ruling from the IRS in any doubtful situation by filling out a special questionnaire for that purpose.

Basic Forms of Organization

There are three basic forms of business organizations:

(1) Sole Proprietorship (i.e. Self-Employed)

(2) Partnership

(3) Corporation

(1) Sole Proprietorship (i.e. Self-Employed)

This is how most people in business for themselves operate. It just means you are self-employed. No special form of organization or legal paraphernalia is required. If you are performing services for a fee such as consulting, reviewing, etc. and are not an employee of the party for whom you perform these services, then you are automatically operating a sole proprietorship. Even your child mowing lawns for a fee is a sole proprietor.

Income and expenses due to self-employment are reported on Schedule C. In addition to income tax, self-employment income is subject to social security tax at the rate of 12.3%. However, there is no social security tax if self-employment income for the year is less than $400. The self-employment social security tax is computed on Schedule SE. However, if an individual has another job which pays at least as much as the social security wage base ($43,800 in 1987), there is no additional social security tax on his self-employment income.

(2) Partnership

A partnership is similar to a sole proprietorship except that it involves two or more people sharing a business. Each shares in the profits and each is responsible for any liabilities incurred by the business. If one of the partners absconds with all of the company's funds, the remaining partners are personally liable for the debts of the partnership.

(3) Corporation

A corporation is a distinct legal entity which is owned by one or more stockholders. The stockholders have no personal liability by virtue of their ownership. Thus, unlike a partnership, if the company gets into financial difficulties, the stockholders are not required to pay the corporation's liabilities out of their own pockets.

There are two basic types of corporations.

(a) S-Corporation. A corporation with 35 or fewer stockholders may, under certain circumstances, elect S-corporation status. Any profit or loss from the corporation passes directly through to the stockholders as though it were ordinary income from any other source. But the stockholders still benefit from the limited liability protection offered by corporate status.

(b) Regular Corporation. Profits and losses accrue to the corporation itself. The corporation pays tax on any profits. The stockholders pay tax only when they receive dividends or upon the sale or liquidation of the business.

As explained later, more tax-saving benefits are available to regular corporations than to S-corporations or any other form of business organization. However, there are two disadvantages. First, if the business consistently loses money, the stockholders are not always able to get a direct write-off of the losses against their other income. Second, there might be a double taxation involved — first the corporation tax — then the tax on dividends. However, this disadvantage need not always occur. For example, if you are able to pay out all of the profits as salary to yourself, then there is no double taxation since the corporation has no net income.

Consultants

A consultant should have a high degree of independence in his work in order to be considered *self-employed* rather than an *employee* of the firm for which he consults. An illustration of such a situation is contained in a recent IRS ruling. This ruling authorized a consultant to consider himself as self-employed rather than an employee. The IRS noted that he did not have any formal schedule of duties and consulted only on an irregular basis when matters came up in an area in which he had special competence. Also, as the IRS told the consultant, the company *"will not exercise supervision over you in the performance of your consulting duties, nor will it require compliance with detailed orders or instructions."* [IRS Private Letter Ruling 7912055]

At one time, consultants generally had to be available to work for more than one client in order to be considered self-employed. Individuals who agreed to work for only one company were usually considered to be employees of that company. However, some recent rulings have changed this policy.

In 1982, the IRS issued a ruling concerning an engineer who retired from the company where he worked. Upon retirement, he set up his own laboratory and entered into a consulting contract with the company for which he had worked. His contract precluded him from working for any other company. The IRS ruled that he was a self-employed consultant. The terms of the contract and the nature of his duties were such that he could not be considered an employee of the company. This meant his status was that of a self-employed individual, despite the fact he was not available to perform services for any other company. [Rev. Rul. 82-212, IRB 1982-49, p.34]

The policy in the above IRS ruling was upheld by a 1983 Court of Appeals decision. The Court ruled that the proper focus of an inquiry as to self-employment status is *"not upon the number of clients or customers an activity generates but upon the nature of that activity that produced those clients or customers."* In the case at hand, it ruled that an individual had self-employment income even though he was performing services for only one client. [Steffens 83-1 USTC ¶ 9425]

It should be noted that even if consulting activities cannot be considered self-employment, they might still come under the shelter of a corporation owned by the individual. This is discussed later in this chapter.

Technical Service Specialists

The IRS issued a ruling in 1987 that applies to services performed under an arrangement with a *technical service firm*. This type of firm acts as a broker between technical service specialists—engineers, designers, drafters, computer programmers, systems analysts, etc.—and companies who need their services. In the past, such technical service specialists were generally considered to be self-employed independent contractors. This meant they could benefit from Keogh Plans and other advantages accorded self-employed persons, as described in Section 2.

In general, if it is common industry practice to treat a category of workers as self-employed individual contractors instead of employees, then the IRS will go along with this classification as long as the appropriate annual tax-reporting forms have consistently been filed. This is the basis under which the technical service specialists described in the preceding paragraph could classify themselves as self-employed. However, the 1986 Tax Reform Act specifically declared this *common industry practice* principle to no longer apply to such technical service specialists.

With the *common industry practice* umbrella now being denied technical service specialists, most of them will no longer qualify for self-employed status. In general, under the basic rules governing the self-employed/employee distinctions, they will generally be considered employees of the technical service firm acting as broker [Notice 87-38,IRB 1987-23]. (At presstime, Congress was considering a repeal of the above special restriction on technical service specialists. Next year's edition of this Tax Guide will describe any further developments on this issue.)

Authors

Income which authors receive is usually considered self-employment income. This is the case even if the individual works at a regular job. For example, the IRS has ruled that income received by a college teacher from writing textbooks is self-employment income when the writing of the books is not part of the basic contract with the college. This IRS ruling, excerpted below, is instructive since it applies to the typical situation encountered by college faculty who do writing on the side.

IRS Revenue Ruling 55-385

"In the instant case, a professor, employed by a State university to perform full-time teaching services at the university, is engaged in sideline activities involving public lecturing and the writing of several books. One of his books is a college textbook which he revises from time to time under contract with the publisher; another is a laboratory manual which he has devised for the use of students at the university where he teaches and which he sells direct to them. He receives royalties from the publisher from the sale of his textbook. During the past year, the publisher made him an advance on his royalties with respect to the preparation of a current revision of the textbook. Although the books and lectures are in the general field of education, they are the result of his own *initiative and are not instigated pursuant to his employment contract with the university.*

". . . In the instant case, it is held that . . . the royalties and other income received by him from those sideline activities are to be taken into account in computing his net earnings from self-employment."

A basic question is whether an author is in the *trade or business* of writing or has just written a once-in-a-lifetime book. Being in the "trade or business" of writing qualifies the income for Keogh Plan tax-sheltering [cf. Section 3 of the *Tax-Sheltered Plans* chapter]. Income from a once-in-a-lifetime book would not qualify.

To qualify as a "trade or business," the writing of a book should be part of a *continuing and regular* activity. This is illustrated by a 1981 IRS ruling issued to a teacher who had written several books. IRS stated that,

"If an individual writes only one book as a sideline and never revises it, he would not be considered to be 'regularly engaged' in an occupation or profession and his royalties therefrom would not be considered net earnings from self-employment. However, when an individual prepares new editions of the book from time to time, and writes other books and materials, such activities reflect the conduct of a trade or business." [IRS Private Letter Ruling 8137103]

A recent court case illustrates that an author need not necessarily have written a previous book to be considered in the trade or business of writing. In this case, a lawyer who moonlighted as a photographer worked on a book of nature photographs. A lower court had agreed with the IRS that the photographer could not already be in the *trade or business* of writing because of his lack of previous work. But the Court of Appeals held that as long as he was engaged in a substantial ongoing activity with a profit making objective, this constituted a *trade or business*. [Snyder, 49 AFTR 2d 82-1061]

Royalties from writing a book are treated differently depending upon the distinction, discussed above, between the *trade or business* of writing and the writing of a *once-in-a-lifetime book*. Authors in the trade or business of writing report their income (and expenses) on Schedule C. This means they are liable for the social security tax on self-employed individuals, as computed on Schedule SE. (However, if they already have income from another job which exceeds the Social Security wage base, $43,800 in 1987, no self-employment social security tax is paid.) However, they can shelter a portion of their net self-employment income by placing it into a Keogh Plan.

Royalties from a once-in-a-lifetime book do not count as self-employment income [Rev. Rul. 68-498]. Such royalties can be entered on Schedule E, *Rents and Royalties*, with the total of such income being recorded on line 17 of Form 1040. No social security tax is paid on royalties reported on Schedule E. However, such income does not qualify for Keogh Plan tax-sheltering.

Work Done While Outside the U.S.

Authors should take particular notice of the foreign earned income exclusion. Under this exclusion, $70,000 or more per year of payments received for writing a book can be totally exempted from tax. This exclusion applies as long as the writing was done outside the U.S., even if the work is published and sold only in the U.S. However, the author must be abroad for at least a year and the payments must occur no later than the year following the year in which the work was performed. See the *Foreign Income* chapter for further details.

Deducting vs. Capitalizing Expenses

When an author works on a book, he will usually incur expenses prior to publication for such items as research, travel, typing, etc. The question arises whether such expenses can be deducted immediately, or must be amortized over the period during which the book is actually producing income for the author.

In the past, most authors have just deducted expenses in the year in which they were incurred, even if no income had yet been received. This treatment is consistent with that accorded most other types of business activities.

However, the 1986 Tax Reform Act has changed this situation. According to the staff of the tax-writing committee of Congress, the new law requires that expenses connected with writing a book now be matched with income. That is, these expenses must be amortized over the period during which the book is actually producing income for the author.

An appropriate method to use for this amortization is what is called the *income-forecast* method. This requires, first, an estimate be made of the total income to be produced by the book. Expenses are then allocated to the years during which this income is to be received, in proportion to the amounts received. (Under this method, if a book-writing project yields no income in a given year, deductions would have to be carried over into the future. If the book is never published, then all expenses are written off at the point when the publishing attempt is abandoned.)

Example

An author incurs $3,000 of expenses during 1987 for writing a book. He receives an advance of $5,000 during 1987 and estimates his total income (advances plus royalties) from the book to equal $20,000. Let's say he received royalties of $6,000 in 1988 and $4,000 in 1989. Under the income-forecast method, his Schedule C deductions for 1987-1989 generated by the $3,000 of expenses would be as follows:

Year	Deduction
1987:	$3,000 × $5,000/$20,000 = $ 750
1988:	$3,000 × $6,000/$20,000 = $ 900
1989:	$3,000 × $4,000/$20,000 = $ 600
	$2,250

The remaining $750 ($3,000 − $2,250) not yet deducted would be similarly claimed in future years as the next $5,000 of income from the book is received.

As is evident from the above example, the income-forecast method is difficult to use. Just how is one to forecast how much income a particular book will produce? If this type of income is predictable, then how come publishers lose money on so many books they produce?

One suggestion that has been made for dealing with the income-forecast method is to use only advances contracted for with the publisher in making an income forecast [Tax Angles; July, 1986, p. 54]. Such advances are concrete figures on which to base a forecast. And in fact, books often fail to produce royalties in excess of advances.

For example, suppose a contract calls for an author to be paid $1/2$ of the advance upon signing the contract and the remaining $1/2$ in a later year upon final completion of the manuscript. Then under the method suggested in the preceding paragraph, the author would deduct $1/2$ of his expenses in each of the two years in which he received payments.

Of course, sometimes an author starts working on a book, but in a later year, abandons work on the book altogether. In this later year, he would be able to deduct as an "abandonment expense" any expenses not yet claimed.

While the income-forecast method is an appropriate one to use, it is not altogether clear from reading the law whether it is the only method that will be allowed. It remains for future rulings or court cases to clairfy this issue. Also, at presstime, vigorous attempts were being made to change the law to allow authors to deduct their expenses currently, possibly retroactive to January 1, 1987. Next year's edition of this Tax Guide will contain further information on this issue as it becomes available.

(Ironically, a 1987 court opinion based on the old law specifically granted an author the right to deduct current expenses as opposed to capitalizing them over a period of years. However, the case does not apply to expenses incurred in 1987 or later years. The only applicability this case would have now is to those who may be able to amend their income tax returns for 1986 or earlier years accordingly. [Hadley, 87-1 USTC 9327]

Profit-Making Intention

One further requirement for the deductibility of expenses is that there be an *intention to make a profit*. Writing a book without expectation of profit is considered a hobby activity and expenses can only be deducted to the extent there is income. However, if there is **intent** to make a profit, expenses can be written off even if income from the book does not cover the expenses. This is discussed in Section 4.

Of course, if expenses are related to one's regular job instead of being incurred to produce a profit-making book, then there is no problem. For example, a professor who incurs research expenses in connection with his job may claim these expenses concurrently as a miscellaneous deduction. It is only when the expenses are incurred to produce a book as a separate business activity that the question of deductibility arises.

An individual whose writing activities produce substantial income might consider incorporating. In effect, the corporation contracts with the publisher to produce a book. After publication, royalties are paid to the corporation which in turn pays out the money in salary and fringe benefits to the author. As discussed later in this section, incorporation can provide certain tax benefits unavailable otherwise.

Assigning Royalties to a Child—A Tax-Reduction Technique

A recent IRS ruling shows how authors who receive royalties from books they have written can shift some of this income to a lower-bracket child, relative, etc. whom they wish to aid financially.

Ordinarily, a person must pay tax on income he earns—e.g. he cannot shift part of his salary to a child to lower his taxes. But once an author has written a book and contracted with a publisher to receive royalty payments, the contract takes on a life of its own. If the author then assigns part or all of the contract over to, say, a child, royalties can be taxed to the child. Since the child will be in a lower (perhaps zero) tax bracket than the parent, this results in a net tax savings. (However, for amounts in excess of $1,000 per year, this income-shifting technique won't work anymore for dependent children under the age of 14. In such a situation, these amounts would be taxed to the parent in any event [cf. Section 5 of Chapter 1].)

In the above ruling, an author entered into an agreement to deliver a manuscript to a publisher. Under the agreement, the publisher was granted the exclusive right to publish the work and take out a copyright in its name. The publisher agreed to publish the work at its expense and to pay royalties on all copies sold.

The author proposed to assign to his child all of his interest in the royalty contract. He asked the IRS if royalties paid under the contract would then be taxed to his child rather than himself.

The IRS ruled in the author's favor. Since he was assigning the contract itself, not simply turning over the royalty payments to his child, the income derived from the contract became taxable to the child rather than to the parent. It was the same as if he had given any other type of property such as stocks or bonds to his child. As long as the income-producing property (in this case the royalty contract) is legally turned over to the child, income from such property can be taxable to the child, not to the parent. [IRS Private Letter Ruling 8444073]

In the above ruling, the author also agreed to later revise the book at the request of the publisher. However, if the author did make such revisions, the IRS said this would be considered rendering personal services to the publisher. Since no additional compensation for the revisions was provided for, a portion of royalty payments received after such revisions were made would be considered *compensation for personal services,* taxable to the author.

Authors (or editors of compiled works of others) who wish to take advantage of the above tax-shifting arrangement should take note of the above distinction between *royalties* and *compensation* when drawing up a contract with a publisher. A contract for the publisher to purchase a manuscript from an author or editor in return for royalties can be transferred to a child, parent, etc. as a tax-shifting maneuver. But to the extent the contract calls for services to be rendered to the publisher rather than a sale of a manuscript, payment for such services is taxable to the one who renders the services.

Also, be sure a publisher you select will be amenable to transferring the contract. If the contract is assignable only with the permission of the publisher and the publisher refuses to go along, you're out of luck. [Miedaner, 81 TC No. 21]

The above income-shifting technique works not just for royalties on a book, but also for royalties from the sale of an invention, musical work, etc. Also, more complicated arrangements can be made than the simple transfer of all royalties to a child described in the above ruling. For example, partial transfers can be made. This is illustrated by a court case in which an inventor sold his invention to a company in return for royalties. He later transferred a 25% interest in the contract each to a son and to a daughter. The Court ruled that royalties from the transferred portion of the contract were taxable to the son and daughter. [Heim v. Fitzpatrick, 262 F 2d 887]

Also, a royalty contract can be transferred to a trust to provide flexibility. The trust, for example, might invest the royalty money, with investment income paid out to a child and taxed to him. The actual funds in the trust could revert at a later time to the original author, inventor, etc. [IRS Private Letter Ruling 8337055]

In the above type of arrangements, take note of the fact that tax-shifting is not generally allowed on amounts used for basic items of support for a minor child such as food, shelter, or clothing. But money spent on extras such as music lessons, summer camp, etc. does not generally fall under this restriction [cf. the *Income-Shifting* chapter for further details]. Also, starting in 1987, tax shifting is not allowed for amounts in excess of $1,000 shifted to a dependent child under age 14 [cf. Section 5 of Chapter 1].

Lecturing Fees and Honorariums

Often, an individual who gives a talk in the field of his expertise will get a small fee or honorarium. Giving an occasional talk will not produce enough income to bother with tax-sheltering. In fact, this would not even be considered a *trade or business* activity so that the income would not qualify for a Keogh Plan.

However, when there are substantial lecturing activities or when the lecturing activities are taken together with other activities such as writing or consulting, then the income becomes self-employment income. This is illustrated by an IRS ruling issued to a teacher-author-lecturer. He had received two $100 honorariums for talks and had received $1,000 from the publication of a book and various newspaper articles. The IRS ruled that the activities, taken together, constituted a *trade or business* activity and the income qualified for Keogh Plan tax-sheltering. [IRS Private Letter Ruling 7904059]

Section 2:
Tax Benefits

Let us suppose you are either self-employed (i.e. a sole proprietor) or else you are the sole stockholder in a corporation which employs you. We assume there are no other employees who work for you or the corporation. Here's a list of some of the benefits which might apply. Certain of these benefits apply only if you incorporate. Others are also available to the self-employed as well.

The importance of fringe benefits such as pension and medical plans lies in their tax-free status. Pure salary or self-employment income is always taxable. But qualifying fringe benefits are not taxed either to you or to the business which pays them. That is, these fringe benefits are not reported as income on your tax return, yet they are taken off as a deduction by the business which pays for them.

1. Tax-Deferred Pension and Profit-Sharing Plans

If you think of private pension or profit-sharing plans as just being a method of forced savings for retirement, then you are missing perhaps the most important element of such plans. In reality, they are among the most powerful tax-saving devices allowed under the current Income Tax Laws. Furthermore, funds placed into such plans do not necessarily have to remain untouched until retirement, but may in some circumstances be withdrawn earlier.

The basic idea behind such plans is described in the *Tax-Sheltered Plans* chapter. Namely, instead of being received as salary and taxed in your highest tax bracket, money can be placed into such plans with no tax paid. The investment income earned by money placed into such plans compounds entirely tax-free until the funds are later drawn out and used for your benefit.

Upon retirement at an age you have specified, money in a pension plan can be used to purchase an annuity or can be withdrawn in a lump sum. (With corporation plans, you may also be able to withdraw all your money plus investment earnings if you cease to work for the corporation or upon dissolution of the corporation.) There is a special averaging rule you can use for computing your tax when all the money in the plan is distributed to you in one lump sum. Using this rule, you can average the money received in a lump sum distribution over a 5-year or 10-year period (depending upon your age), disregarding all other income. The tax on the rest of your income is computed in the usual way without taking into account the lump sum distribution.

An example of the value of tax-deferral is contained in Section 1 of the *Tax-Sheltered Plans* chapter. This example shows how one dollar placed in a tax-deferred pension or profit sharing plan can be equal to three dollars or more outside such a plan.

Self-employed persons can set up a tax-sheltered plan called a Keogh Plan. A few years ago, corporation pension plans had more generous limitations than Keogh Plans for the self-employed. However, this disparity has been eliminated. Keogh Plans now have the same contribution limits as regular pension plans [cf. Section 3 of the *Tax-Sheltered Plans* chapter]. Thus, an individual will generally be able to contribute 20% of his 1987 self-employed earned income to a regular Keogh Plan.

Those with self-employment income can actually do much better than this by setting up a *Defined-Benefit Keogh Plan* under the remarkable rules for this special type of plan. Under these rules, they can often **shelter up to 100% of this income from tax** [cf. Section 3 of the *Tax-Sheltered Plans* chapter for further details].

2. Medical Reimbursement Plan

Suppose you set up a corporation which hires you as its employee. The corporation agrees to pay all the medical (including dental) expenses of its employees and their spouses and children. The corporation receives a deduction but you pay no tax on these amounts. Essentially, you are receiving a tax deduction of 100% of the medical expenses you pay for yourself and your family. This is better than the usual medical expense deduction because there is no initial 7.5% exclusion. (In addition to covering medical expenses, a corporation can deduct premiums paid on a disability policy which covers you, the employee.)

A self-employed individual can't be directly covered by this type of medical plan. But he can set up a plan to cover all his other employees (including relatives) and their dependents. Thus, a self-employed person can employ his spouse to help out in the business and set up a medical plan which pays for all medical expenses of his spouse and his spouse's dependents, including himself. He gets a business deduction for the medical expenses paid under the plan but there is no tax to the recipient spouse. In this way, the self-employed person receives the equivalent of a tax deduction for 100% of his family's medical expenses without the ordinary 7.5% exclusion. (The more wages paid to a spouse, the less likely the IRS will try to disallow the arrangement as a sham, should the question arise during an audit. Professional assistance should be obtained to set up such a plan in a valid legal manner.)

Starting with 1987 tax returns, a self-employed individual can deduct 25% of the cost of health insurance for himself and his family. (This applies just to health insurance, not ordinary medical expenses.) However, no deduction is allowed if he is covered on a subsidized basis by a health plan of an employer for whom either he or his spouse works. Also, the deduction cannot exceed the net earnings from the individual's self-employment. This deduction is claimed on line 25 of Form 1040.

3. Ability to Escape the 2% of Adjusted Gross Income Floor That Applies to Miscellaneous Deductions

As discussed in the *Miscellaneous Deductions* chapter, a 2% of Adjusted Gross Income floor applies to the total of itemized *miscellaneous deductions* claimed on Schedule A. The *miscellaneous deductions* category includes unreimbursed job-related expenses such as books, supplies, travel, equipment, home office, educational expenses, etc. It also includes expenses connected with tax preparation (e.g. the cost of this Tax Guide) as well as with investment activities.

Self-employed persons can escape this 2% floor to the extent they can treat items as a business deduction on Schedule C connected with their self-employment activity rather than an itemized deduction. For example, a college professor with an outside consulting business might be able to attribute the cost of journals, books, home office, travel to meetings, professional dues, etc. to this consulting business. As such, they could be claimed on Schedule C to escape the 2% of Adjusted Gross Income floor. [See the end of Section 1 of the *Miscellaneous Deductions* chapter for a more complete discussion of this matter.]

Operating in corporate form provides the same benefit as discussed above for self-employed persons. A corporation can deduct as a business expense such items as books, supplies, travel, tax preparation, etc. The 2% floor does not apply to corporation business expenses.

4. Ability to Elect the Standard Deduction and Still Deduct Business Expenses

As an employee, you may deduct expenses connected with your job only if you itemize your deductions (except for travel and moving expenses). But self-employed persons can subtract their business expenses from their gross income and still claim the standard deduction. If you are the sole owner-employee of a corporation, you still get the same effect because the corporation pays and deducts the expenses. You can still claim the standard deduction on your salary received from the corporation.

5. Benefit of Lower Tax Rate

This benefit applies only to regular corporations. Income can be retained by the corporation instead of being paid out as salary. Tax is then paid at the rate that applies to corporation profits — the first $25,000 of profit is taxed at only 15%, the next $50,000 at 25%. The full 34% corporation tax rate only applies to profits in excess of $75,000. (These are the rates that apply as of July 1, 1987.)

6. Tax-Sheltered Accumulation of Funds

Excess funds left in the corporation can benefit from a tax-shelter of their own. Corporations pay almost no tax on dividends received from investments in other corporations. Thus, corporation funds can be used to purchase shares of preferred stock yielding high dividends virtually free from tax. There are even special mutual funds geared for corporations to take advantage of this tax shelter.

There is a limit of $250,000 on the amount of funds that can be accumulated by a corporation without having to give a business justification for the accumulation. This limit is reduced to $150,000 for corporations whose principal business consists of the *performance of services in the fields of health, law, engineering, architecture, accounting, actuarial science, performing arts, or consulting.*

The ability to accumulate and tax-shelter funds only applies to corporations involved in an active business. If a corporation receives over 60% of its income from passive sources such as dividends, interest, rents, etc., then the IRS may label it a *personal holding company.* As such, it would be subject to a much higher tax rate than that applying to other corporations.

7. Ability to Delay Tax by Choosing Proper Fiscal Year

Corporations sometimes qualify to use a fiscal year different than the calendar year. This can serve to defer the payment of tax. For example, let's say the corporation qualifies for a fiscal year beginning March 1 and that your salary is paid annually on February 28. Then on February 28, 1989, you receive pay for amounts earned primarily in 1988. If you report this amount on your 1989 return, you have effectively delayed paying tax for almost a year. This enables you to earn a year's worth of interest on the delayed payment.

Disadvantages of Being in Business for Yourself

There are a number of disadvantages in being self-employed or operating under the umbrella of a corporation. Some of these are listed below.

More Forms to Fill Out

Self-employed persons must file an extra form, Schedule C, listing their business income and expenses. Corporations also must file income tax returns of their own. In addition, there are other miscellaneous forms which may have to be filed from time to time.

Legal, Accounting, and Incorporation Fees

There are fees required to incorporate as well as legal or accounting fees. There are do-it-yourself books which will enable you to carry through the incorporation yourself for under $100. However, most people will be well advised to seek professional guidance even if it requires additional fees for advice or services. In addition, you will want professional assistance in setting up medical reimbursement plans or pension and profit-sharing plans even if this assistance is no more than selecting the appropriate standard form to use.

Social Security, Unemployment Taxes, and Worker's Compensation
You may be liable for these taxes depending on your situation.

Caution. We have only briefly touched upon some of the aspects of being in business for yourself to acquaint you with the potential for tax-savings. Especially if you contemplate incorporation, you should consult a lawyer to determine how to take advantage of the tax benefits which apply in your particular case. He can also advise you of any extra conditions you must satisfy. For example, the IRS may require you to have a "business purpose" for incorporating in addition to just the tax benefits involved. Also, restrictions on *personal service corporations* might apply in your case.

However, you should not be overly intimidated by the legal complications. Businessmen, doctors, and other professionals have learned how to take advantage of the benefits which the law allows and which the general taxpayer subsidizes. If you have an outside source of income, you should explore doing the same for yourself.

SECTION 3:
PAYING FAMILY MEMBERS FOR ASSISTANCE

If you have an income-producing outside business activity, then perhaps you can place your children, spouse, or even a live-in friend on the payroll. As discussed below, this can serve to lower the overall amount of taxes that will be paid. The following discussion concerns business activities being operated as a sole proprietorship. The situation is a bit different for corporations because of extra expenses, e.g. social security taxes, that may be involved.

Payments to Children
One way to lower the taxes due on income produced by an outside business activity is to pay your children for assisting you. You get a deduction for the wages you pay them, while they might pay no tax at all on the amounts received because of the $2,540 standard deduction to which they are entitled.

The IRS has specifically ruled that a parent can deduct payments to a child for services if such services would be deductible if performed by someone else. According to this ruling, *"to do otherwise would be tantamount to penalizing the father for employing his own child, inasmuch as a deduction would be allowable if he employed someone else's child under the same circumstances."* The payments can be for any type of normal services required in a business — cleaning, telephone answering, clerical work, business errands, etc.

A number of court cases illustrate this deduction. For example, a 1984 court case permitted a medical professor a $1500 per year deduction for payments made to his teenage children. The children performed miscellaneous clerical tasks in connection with a small private practice he ran out of his home [Moriarty, TC Memo 1984-249]. In another case, an engineer paid his children for chores performed in connection with his consulting practice. The IRS objected that the wages violated child labor laws and therefore could not be deducted. But the Court found that these laws were designed to protect children from being hired out to do work in a factory or mercantile establishment where their health or welfare would be imperiled. Since this did not apply in this case, a deduction was allowed [Denman, 48 TC 439].

Not only is the salary of a minor child working for a parent deductible, but it is also exempt from social security tax and unemployment insurance. However, the salary should be in the form of actual wages. You cannot deduct the value of meals or lodging which you provide to an unemancipated minor child in return for services. [Rev Rul 73-393]

Of course, the IRS sometimes takes a skeptical view of payments made to children because of the potential for abuse. But if the payments are made in a businesslike manner, with suitable records kept, then a deduction should be upheld even if the children are young. This is illustrated by a recent court case involving a family who owned a mobile home park. The family consisted of the parents plus 3 children with the youngest child being only 7 years old. The children were paid for a variety of chores they performed in the business including cleaning, ground maintenance, answering the telephone, clerical work, and assisting in minor repairs. The Court allowed over $15,000 to be deducted over a 3-year period as being reasonable compensation to the children — including $4,000 for the services performed by the 7-year old. [Eller 77TC#66]

Payments to a Spouse

Payments made to a spouse for services in an outside business can lower the overall tax bill, although not in the same income-shifting way as payments to a child as described above. The reason income-shifting doesn't work is, of course, that payments which are deducted as salary to a spouse become taxable income to that spouse. Thus, on a joint return, there is no change in the amount of tax due.

However, the following provisions in the law can all cause payments to a spouse to lower the overall tax bill.

1. IRA & Keogh Plan Contributions

Each spouse is entitled to contribute up to the first $2,000 of earned income to an IRA [cf. Section 2 of the *Tax-Sheltered Plans* chapter]. If the spouse has no earned income, this opportunity is lost. Also, if you have a Keogh Plan, contributions can be made on behalf of your spouse, based on your spouse's salary.

2. Household Services & Child Care Tax Credit

The expenses to which the household services and child care tax credit is applied cannot exceed the earned income of the spouse with the lower earnings, except when one of the spouses is a full time student [cf. the *Household Services & Child Care* chapter]. Thus, there is generally no tax credit allowed when one spouse has no earned income. In such a situation, placing a spouse on the payroll makes the couple eligible for the tax credit.

The maximum amount of expenses to which the credit can be applied is $2,400 for one qualifying dependent or $4,800 for two or more qualifying dependents. In the latter case, say, paying a spouse $4,800 might allow the couple to claim the maximum credit. This maximum credit depends upon the couple's adjusted gross income — ranging from $1,440 for those with Adjusted Gross Income less than $10,000 to $720 for those with Adjusted Gross Income over $28,000.

3. Reduction of Social Security Tax

No social security tax is due on salary payments made by an individual to his spouse or child under age 21. Thus, if payments made by such an individual to his spouse (or child) lower his own social security tax, a net social security tax savings is accomplished. The maximum saving that can be achieved by such a reduction in social security tax depends upon the individual's income and the amount paid to the spouse. In some cases, a savings of over $1,000 can be achieved. However if, after paying his spouse, an individual's earnings still exceed the social security base ($43,800 for 1987) above which no tax is due, there is no savings. In such a case, the individual would still be paying the same maximum social security contribution for the year.

4. Obtaining a Full Medical Deduction

Ordinarily, only medical expenses in excess of 7.5% of Adjusted Gross Income are deductible. However, a sole proprietor who employs his spouse can set up a plan to pay all the medical expenses of his spouse (and other employees) and the spouse's dependents (including himself). In this way, he gets a business deduction for 100% of his family's medical expenses with no 7.5% limitation [cf. Section 2 for further details].

How Payments Should Be Made

If you want to establish that payments made to a spouse, child, or friend represent pay for services rendered, then you should make the payments in the form of wages. This is illustrated by a recent 1987 IRS Private Letter Ruling. In this ruling, the wife of a veterinarian worked for her husband, performing such duties as being a receptionist 2 days a week, purchasing office supplies, laundering blankets and towels, and reconciling business bank accounts.

The husband filed a Schedule C on his business earnings. In the years in question, the husband took a deduction for the wife's wages on his Schedule C. The amount of the wages was computed according to the number of hours worked. In each year, a W-2 form was issued to the wife and the income was reported on the couple's joint return. However, no actual payment was made to the wife for her services. Instead, the husband deposited all income from his business into a joint bank account held with the wife.

In his view, the amount representing wages to his wife would end up in the same bank account no matter what. However, this depositing of funds was not sufficient to establish that wages had been paid. The IRS ruled that *"in order for a deduction for* wages to be allowed, actual payment must be made, and a deposit into a joint account does not constitute actual payment." Thus, the husband could not deduct these payments as salary, nor was the wife able to make an IRA contribution based on these payments. [IRS Private Letter Ruling 8707004]

Payments to a Live-In Friend

Support of a live-in friend can be converted into a tax deduction if the friend performs work in a secondary business activity. That's the conclusion the Tax Court reached in a 1983 decision. In this case, a man and woman lived together in a relationship which, in the Court's delicate phrasing, was *"other than platonic."* She assisted him in the acquisition and management of various investments and rental properties which he owned. He, in turn, provided funds for food, shelter, etc. for the household which included himself, his non-platonic friend, her child, and her dog.

The Court ruled that he could deduct $2,500 for the value of the work which she performed. Of course, the $2,500 would have to be reported as taxable income to her as well as social security tax paid on her earnings. But assuming she was in a much lower tax bracket than he, a net tax savings would still be achieved. [Bruce, TC Memo 1983-121]

SECTION 4:
OUTSIDE ACTIVITIES PRODUCING A LOSS

An activity such as art, photography, music, writing, etc. might generate expenses in excess of income received. It is desirable to be able to deduct the loss on your tax return. However, to do this, the activity must qualify as a **business activity** as opposed to simply a **hobby.**

What Is a Business Activity?

A **business activity** is one engaged in with the **objective of making a profit.** This does not need to be the only objective or even the most important objective. However, it should be a basic and dominant objective. That is, the activity should be conducted in a manner aimed at making a profit.

It is important to note what the law does not require. When the law was first drafted, the House bill required that the taxpayer show a reasonable expectation of realizing a profit. But this was changed to only require that the activity be engaged in for profit, not that there be a reasonable expectation of making one. For example, the odds might be heavily stacked against a photographer earning enough income to exceed his expenses. But in his own mind he might feel he could buck the odds and earn money at it. As long as he conducted his activities with the intention and expectation of making a profit this would suffice even if others might not expect him to succeed.

The intent to make a profit need not be an immediate one. It is recognized that many business activities result in early losses until the business can become established. This is all right as long as there is an aim to make an overall profit. That is, one should expect that over the period of years the activity is engaged in, the total income will exceed the total expenses.

Note that there is no requirement that the taxpayer not enjoy what he is doing. Just because an activity such as music, art, photography, etc. might be pleasurable does not rule out a deduction.

Presumption in Favor of the Taxpayer

The law contains the following provision: If the activity has produced a profit in any 3 of the preceding 5 years, it will be presumed to be a business activity. Any losses will be deductible.

The IRS can challenge the above presumption if special circumstances are involved. For example, an activity which produced very small profits in 3 years and huge losses the other 2 could be challenged by the IRS.

If the "business" activity has been going on less than 5 years, the above test cannot be applied. Instead, you are permitted to wait until 5 years have passed to see if a profit is produced in at least 3 of the years. If so, then the activity is presumed to have been a business activity for each of the first 5 years of existence.

What Happens if a Profit Is Not Made in 3 Out of the Last 5 Years?

If the above 3 out of 5 year test is not satisfied, this does not mean a business deduction is ruled out. It just means there is no automatic presumption of a business activity. In such a case, the taxpayer must, if challenged, show that the activity is engaged in for profit. (The profit can be expected to come from earnings generated by the activity or from the appreciation in value of assets used in the activity.) The principal indicator is the manner in which the activity is carried out. In case of dispute, the IRS suggests that the following factors be examined in order to determine if an activity is a business activity. [Reg 1.183-2 (b)]:

A. Has the activity been carried out in a businesslike manner, e.g. have appropriate records, receipts, etc. been kept?

B. Does the taxpayer have enough expertise to run a profitable enterprise?

C. Has enough time and effort been expended in carrying on the activity?

D. Has the taxpayer been successful in other business endeavors?

E. What is the past history of profits or losses from the activity?

F. What is the taxpayer's financial status, e.g. does he need to earn a profit or is he looking for a tax writeoff instead?

G. Are there significant elements of recreation or pleasure involved?

Note that the above list of factors does not constitute a set of formal criteria. There do not necessarily have to be favorable answers to all or even a majority of them.

If you are trying to qualify a money-losing activity as a business, you should conduct yourself in as businesslike a manner as possible. Any of the following would be helpful:

(1) Establish a separate bank account for the activity.

(2) Advertise your services to the public.

(3) Consult financial or other experts for the purpose of setting up a profitable operation.

(4) Keep businesslike records of income and expenses.

(5) Write down a projection showing how you anticipate future profits.

(6) Operate the activity under a trade name.

(7) Have business cards and stationery printed.

Another thing you can do is time your expenses and income to show a profit for a given year. By turning a profit in 3 out of 5 years, you establish the presumption in your favor.

Activities Never Showing a Profit

As mentioned above, in order to qualify an activity as a business, it is not necessary to actually show a profit — just have the intention of making one. This was dramatically illustrated in the following court case. In spite of 20 straight losing years, a professor's wife established that her artistic activities constituted a business endeavor, enabling her to deduct her losses.

> **Court Case. *Professor's Wife Gets Deduction in Spite of 20 Straight Losing Years***
>
> Mrs. C. was the wife of a professor at a well-known university in California. For a period of twenty years, she engaged in artistic activities, mainly painting and sculpture. She devoted a substantial amount of time to these activities and held no other job except as a housewife. She exhibited her work at local galleries several times a year, sent announcements of her shows to a small mailing list, and for a short time even ran a gallery of her own. When dissatisfied with the sale of her paintings, she also began making posters and books with the hope that these items would meet with more commercial success.
>
> However, although she occasionally sold some of her work, at no time during the 20 years did the income from her artwork exceed her expenses. The IRS challenged Mrs. C.'s deduction for the losses produced by her artistic activities. No doubt, the IRS challenge was induced by her 20-year string of losses.
>
> The Court, however, felt that the 20 straight losing years did not rule out a strong profit motive. It examined the case further to see if, despite her actual losses, she had sufficient interest and expectation to show a profit. Referring to the list A-G discussed earlier in this section, the Court noted that the factors A, B, C were in her favor — the businesslike way she maintained records, the training she obtained in art school, and the considerable time and effort she expended on her activities. On the other hand, the financial factors D, E, F, and factor G all weighed against her.
>
> But the Court did not feel that her lack of financial success was determinative. After hearing her testimony, it felt she was truly attempting to establish herself as a financially successful artist. Mrs. C. went to considerable effort to sell her works

and even to change media to achieve commercial success. As for her losses, it noted that *"a history of losses is less persuasive in the art field than it might be in other fields because the archetypical 'struggling artist' must first achieve public acclaim before her serious work will command a price sufficient to provide her with profit . . . . Petitioner has a relatively large inventory, she had considerable training, she devotes substantial time to her artwork, she has sold some paintings in the past, and is attempting to sell more. It is certainly conceivable, in our view, that she may someday sell enough of her paintings to enable her to recoup the losses which have meanwhile been sustained in the intervening years."*

As a result of the above analysis, the Court found her artistic endeavors to be a business activity entitling her to deduct the losses on her tax return. [68TC 696]

Chapter 27

Foreign Income

Congress has provided the following important tax break for citizens or residents of the U.S. who work in a foreign country. Income which you earn while outside the U.S. can be excluded from U.S. income tax provided all of the following conditions are met:

(1) The income was *earned income* received for services performed;
(2) The income was for services performed while either:
   a. You were outside the U.S. for at least 330 days out of any period of 12 consecutive months

   or

   b. You were a bona fide resident of a foreign country or countries for an uninterrupted period which includes a full calendar year;
(3) Your *tax home* was in a foreign country;

   and
(4) You were not an employee of the United States government or one of its agencies, paid from U.S. government funds.

In (1) above, *earned income* means compensation derived from personal services rendered. This includes wages, salaries, professional fees, and the like. It also includes self-employment income to the extent produced by personal services rather than capital investment. Unearned income such as dividends, interest, alimony, etc. does not qualify, nor do amounts received as a pension or annuity.

To qualify for exclusion, the earned income need not be paid by a foreign institution or company. As long as it is earned while you are outside the U.S., that's all that counts. For example, a bank president was allowed an exclusion under a similar provision in prior law for management services he performed by mail and telephone for his bank while on extended leave abroad. [Rev Rul 72-423, 1972-2 CB 446]

In (2b) above, the residency requirement does not demand that you be outside the U.S. for the full term of foreign residency. Vacations or business trips to the U.S. or elsewhere do not destroy the period of foreign residency. In fact, the only time (2b) would need to be invoked instead of (2a) would be when a foreign stay is interrupted by an extended trip back to the U.S. To establish yourself as a bona fide resident of a foreign country, you should be working there for an indefinite or extended period of time and set up permanent-style quarters for yourself and your family.

In (3) above, the term *tax home* has the same meaning as in Sections 1 and 3 of the *Travel* chapter. That is, your tax home is the location of your principal permanent place of employment. The reason Congress included the tax home condition in addition to Condition (2) was to rule out claiming away-from-home travel expenses in addition to the foreign income exclusion. Since the *tax home* must be in the foreign country to qualify for the foreign income exclusion, it would be a contradiction to claim *away-from-home* expenses in addition.

As discussed in Section 3 of the *Travel* chapter, a 1983 IRS ruling [Rev Rul 83-82] addresses the question of whether a person's tax home shifts when he takes a temporary job away from his usual home. According to this ruling, *"If a taxpayer anticipates employment to last for 1 year or more and that employment does, in fact, last for 1 year or more, there is a presumption that the employment is not temporary but rather is indefinite, and that the taxpayer is not away from home during the indefinite period of employment."* (Since the taxpayer would not be *away from home*, his *tax home* would typically shift to the foreign location.)

The ruling goes on to discuss stays lasting between 1 and 2 years. In such cases, the presumption that the tax home shifts can be rebutted *"by the taxpayer"* if he can *"clearly demonstrate"* that he meets the objective factors contained in the 3 tests described in Section 3 of the *Travel* chapter. However, technically, the ruling only refers to the **taxpayer** (not the IRS) being able to **rebut** the one-year presumption. Under this ruling, therefore, any taxpayer ought to be able to use the one-year presumption that his tax home shifts when his employment abroad lasts one year or more. Thus, he could satisfy condition (3), the tax home requirement, for excluding foreign income.

This view is supported by a 1986 Private Letter Ruling. Although such rulings do not carry the force of law and cannot be cited as legal precedent, they do give the current thinking of IRS officials.

Example

A history professor took a one-year sabbatical leave from the university where he worked. He traveled to a foreign country in order to do research, the results of which he intended to publish in scholarly journals and in a book he was writing. His stay in the foreign country lasted from June 24, 1984 to June 29, 1985—a period exceeding one year. While on sabbatical, he received money both from the National Endowment for the Humanities (NEH) and from the university where he worked.

The IRS ruled that the research he performed constituted *labor* for which he was being compensated, hence the money he received from both NEH and the university while abroad constituted *earned income*. Thus, Condition (1) on the previous page was satisfied. Also, NEH regulations specified that recipients of its grants were not classified as employees of the United States so that Condition (4) was satisfied. Condition (2) was clearly satisfied because he was outside the U.S. for the required 330-day period. The only remaining question was whether Condition (3), the *tax home* requirement, was satisfied.

The IRS ruled that he did satisfy the *tax home* requirement. The ruling itself contained no detailed examination of the tax home issue other than a passing reference to Rev. Rul. 83-82 discussed above. The professor clearly intended to return back to his university after his sabbatical year was over, so in that sense he

> was going to be away only *"temporarily."* But since his actual stay abroad during which he was doing research exceeded one year, this apparently was sufficient to establish that his tax home shifted to the foreign country during the period he was away.
>
> Since he satisfied all 4 of the foreign income conditions, the IRS ruled that he could exclude from taxable income both the money he received from NEH and from his university while away. [IRS Private Letter Ruling 8619051]

In the above ruling, the professor's research sabbatical actually exceeded one year, if only by 5 days. A stay of exactly one year, however, might be cutting it too close. This is illustrated by a different ruling issued to another teacher. In this ruling, a teacher was planning to take part in an exchange program under which he would teach in the United Kingdom, being paid by his school back in the U.S. The teacher planned to stay in the United Kingdom for only one year, whereupon he would return home to his job in the U.S. The IRS ruled that this one-year stay was too short to shift the tax home from the U.S. to the United Kingdom. [IRS Private Letter Ruling 8452103]

It is also important to note that the IRS ruling concerning tax homes refers to *employment* lasting one year or more. An individual who stayed abroad for more than one year but was considered employed abroad for less than one year might fail the *tax home* test. The professor in the example above was on a research sabbatical so he had no trouble establishing that he was actually working during the entire period abroad. The teacher referred to in the preceding paragraph ran into trouble partly because, while *living* abroad for one year, he did not actually *teach* for the entire one-year period.

It is not so clear what would happen if a person stays in a number of different countries, each stay lasting less than a year, with the total time abroad exceeding one year. It is felt that Congress intended the exclusion to apply in such a case as long as, say, condition (2a) is satisfied by being outside the U.S. the required 330 days. But under the law as written, the IRS might claim that an individual did not stay in any one country long enough to establish a tax home there. Under such an interpretation, the individual would not have established a tax home in a foreign country and be disqualified under condition (3). Only after further rulings are issued will the intentions of the IRS be known.

Limitation

If you satisfy Conditions (1) — (4) above, you can exclude income earned outside the U.S. up to a maximum of $70,000 for 1987. If you are not outside the U.S. for the entire year, the $70,000 is prorated according to how many days you were actually away. A separate $70,000 allowance applies to the earned income of your spouse. If your income exceeds this amount, an extra exclusion is provided for certain housing costs.

The exclusion is computed based on when the services were performed. For example, if you receive income in 1988 for services performed outside the U.S. in 1987, you exclude this income on your 1988 tax return, even if you are not outside the U.S. when the payments are received. However, you cannot exclude amounts received two or more calendar years after the services are performed. For example, you can't exclude amounts received in 1989 for services performed in 1987.

If you are planning a stay outside the U.S., you should obtain a copy of Publication 54 from the IRS. This publication will explain the rules governing foreign income in fuller detail and illustrate how to claim the foreign income exclusion on the appropriate form.

Sabbatical Pay

College faculty members often spend their sabbatical abroad. As shown in the earlier example, if their stay in a foreign country lasts more than 1 year, the foreign income exclusion comes into play. However, in some cases, the IRS might argue that sabbatical pay received from one's school while abroad was actually earned in prior years when the individual was teaching in the U.S., thereby disqualifying it from exclusion.

To guard against such IRS challenge, college faculty should submit a proposal to their university stressing the academic work they are going to perform while abroad. Often, colleges treat such proposals as a mere formality. But such a document, when shown to the IRS, can be strong evidence that the sabbatical pay is not a reward for previously performed work, but rather is pay for academic work performed while abroad, thereby possibly qualifying for the foreign earned income exclusion.

An important distinction should be made between two types of sabbaticals. The first is a sabbatical undertaken to study or do research for your own educational development. The second is a sabbatical undertaken to work on publishable research as part of your professional responsibilities. Payments received from your school while on the first type of sabbatical are more open to challenge as having been "earned" in prior years. Payments while on the second type of sabbatical are more likely to be considered as "earned while abroad."

Of course, in real life, the distinction between the two types of sabbaticals is not so clear cut. However, an individual teacher has an opportunity to make this distinction when he applies for sabbatical leave. He should stress the *accomplishment* rather than the *study* aspect of his sabbatical in his official letter to his school requesting a sabbatical leave. This letter then becomes the leading document describing the nature of the sabbatical.

Authors Can Exclude Royalties

Royalties or other payments which an author receives for writing are considered earned income. The situation is similar for artists, composers, inventors, etc. Any payment received for work produced by the personal efforts of these individuals is considered earned income. However, if part of the income is due to capital investment, that part might not be included in earned income. This would not apply, typically, to authors, artists, or composers, but might apply to inventors with significant investment in equipment.

The above represents a terrific opportunity for authors, inventors, etc. to exclude income from tax. For example, suppose an individual plans to write a book.

He waits until he is out of the country to do his writing. (In fact, this might be an especially good time to do such writing for, say, a professor on sabbatical or other leave of absence.) If his stay abroad qualifies under the rules in this chapter, payments he receives for his work can be excluded from tax, even though these payments come from an American publisher and the book is sold only in the U.S.

However, note the requirement that to be excluded, payments for work done during a given year must be made no later than the end of the following year. This is a serious restriction, especially for authors who usually have to wait at least a year after they have completed their work before it is published and royalties commence. Hence, an author should try to obtain as much as he can in the way of pre-publication payments. For those planning to write a book while abroad, the willingness to make advance payments qualifying for the earned income exclusion could become an important factor in choosing a publisher.

However, the advance royalties should not be repayable in the event the book does not sell as well as anticipated. Otherwise, the IRS could claim the amounts paid were just loans, not payments for work performed. [IRS Private Letter Ruling 8131016]

Denial of Double Benefits

You cannot claim any deduction or tax credit to the extent attributable to foreign income which is excluded from tax. For example, you can't deduct travel expenses connected with your foreign employment. However, such items as medical expenses, charitable contributions, mortgage interest, etc. would still be deductible.

How to Claim the Foreign Income Exclusion

The foreign income exclusion is claimed on Form 2555 which you attach to your tax return. (Be sure to file a tax return even if all your income is excluded from tax.) If you submit a suitable statement to your employer that you will qualify for the foreign income exclusion, your employer should not withhold taxes on payments made to you. You can obtain a sample of a suitable statement by writing to the Foreign Operations District, Internal Revenue Service, Washington, D.C. 20225 (Form IO-673).

Note that it is entirely possible for foreign income to be exempt from U.S. income tax as described in this chapter at the same time it is exempt from a foreign country's tax under a treaty with the U.S.

Extension of Time to File

If you are abroad on April 15, you have an automatic 2-month extension both to file your income tax return and to pay any tax due. This even applies to a joint return where only one spouse is abroad. If you need an additional 2 months, you can file the usual *Extension of Time* Form 4868 by June 15, noting across the top your special taxpayer abroad status. However, you have to pay what you estimate your tax will be by June 15. Otherwise you risk a penalty on the underpayment if it exceeds 10% of the tax due.

If you have not yet met the 330-day test by the date your tax return is due but

Income Earned While Outside the U.S.

expect to do so and thereby owe no tax or receive a refund, you should file for a special extension on Form 2350. This will give you until 30 days after the date on which you meet the 330-day test to file your tax return. Further details on the Foreign Income Exclusion may be found in Publication 54, *Tax Guide for U.S. Citizens Abroad*, obtainable from the IRS.

Other Tax Breaks for Foreign Income

Extra Moving Expense Deduction

If you move to a location outside the United States which is a new *principal place of work*, then you can claim a moving expense deduction as described in the *Moving Expenses* chapter. Note that the limitations on the amounts that can be deducted for foreign moves are substantially higher than for domestic moves. However, you can't deduct moving expenses to a foreign location if your income is excluded from tax according to the rules described above. Moving expenses back to the U.S. can be deducted.

Payment of Foreign Taxes

The United States has a number of treaties with foreign countries which generally exempt you from their tax for a period of two to three years, if you are temporarily visiting their country for the purpose of teaching or research. Such countries include Australia, Austria, Belgium, Canada, Denmark, Finland, France, Federal Republic of Germany, Greece, Ireland, Italy, Japan, Luxembourg, Netherlands, New Zealand, Norway, Pakistan, Republic of South Africa, Sweden, Switzerland, and United Kingdom countries.

Credit for Foreign Income Tax

If you have to pay income tax to a foreign government, then you may be able to get a tax credit for these payments on your U.S. income tax return. However, if you claim the foreign earned income exclusion according to the rules described above, this credit does not apply. Only in unusual circumstances would it be beneficial to forgo an earned income exclusion in order to use the tax credit for taxes paid to a foreign government instead.

Chapter 28

Tax-Free Grants

SECTION 1:
BASIC RULES

The 1986 Tax Reform Act has changed the tax treatment of scholarship and fellowship grants. There are now two sets of rules, the *old rules* and the *new rules*. The old rules apply to grants *awarded* before August 17, 1986 (even if paid after this date). The new rules apply to grants awarded on or after August 17, 1986.

The **old rules** are the ones that applied prior to 1986. These old rules generally allow degree-candidate students to exempt the full amount of their grants from tax. And, non-degree candidates came under a $300 per month limitation for a lifetime maximum of 36 months on the amounts exempted from income tax [cf. Section 3 for a detailed explanation of these rules]. However, non-degree candidates, as well as degree candidates, received a total exemption from social security tax on the full amount of their scholarships or fellowships, with no $300 per month or 36 month limitation [cf. Section 5].

The **new rules** for grants awarded on or after August 17, 1986 are much more severe. **Degree-candidate** students are only able to exempt from tax amounts used for tuition and related instructional expenses such as fees, books, supplies, and equipment. Amounts that are used for room, board, or other living expenses are subject to income tax. **Non-degree candidates** get no income tax exemption at all under the new rules.

However, the rules for social security tax remain the same under the new rules as under the old. Both degree candidates and non-degree candidates are still exempt from social security tax on the full amount of their scholarship or fellowship grants, no matter when they were awarded.

Definitions

A **scholarship** generally means an amount paid to enable a student to pursue his studies at an educational institution.

An **educational institution** is defined to be a school maintaining a regular faculty and established curriculum and having an organized body of students in attendance. This includes primary and secondary schools, colleges, universities, technical schools, trade schools, and similar institutions. Not included in this definition are correspondence schools, night schools, or on-the-job training.

A **fellowship** generally means an amount paid to aid an individual in the pursuit of study or research.

The term *scholarship or fellowship* does not include money which is given by a friend or relative, motivated by philanthropic or family considerations. Such a payment, however, will probably qualify to be a tax-free gift.

Some educational institutions participate in a program whereby tuition is not charged for the child of a faculty member at one of the other participating institutions. As discussed in the *Expenses of Attending School* chapter, such tuition remission is generally exempt from tax.

Also, if a grant meets either of the following 2 conditions, it will generally **not** be considered a scholarship and will be taxable income:
(i) The grant is paid as compensation for past, present, or future services; or
(ii) the grant is paid to enable you to pursue studies or research primarily for the benefit of the grantor. (These 2 conditions are discussed in more detail in Section 3 which also describes an exception for grants awarded before August 17, 1986, when equivalent services are required of all candidates for a given degree.)

Difference Between a Gift and a Grant

Gifts which you receive are better than grants because they are entirely tax-free, while scholarship and fellowship grants are subject to the limitations described in Sections 2 and 3. But you can't simply call a grant a gift. To be regarded as a gift, you must show that the donor was motivated by family or philanthropic reasons that were directed solely to the recipient. In other words, unless a grant you receive is given by a relative or a charity, you will not be able to treat it as a gift.

Prizes and Awards

Prior to 1987, certain prizes and awards made in recognition of past achievements (e.g. the Nobel Prize, Pulitzer Prize, etc.) were exempt from tax. However, starting in 1987, this exemption is eliminated, except where the recipient assigns the prize or award to a governmental unit or tax-exempt charitable organization.

SECTION 2:
NEW RULES FOR GRANTS AWARDED ON OR AFTER AUGUST 17, 1986

Degree Candidates

Under the new rules for grants awarded on or after August 17, 1986, students who are candidates for a degree may exempt from tax amounts used for "*qualified tuition* and *related expenses*." This includes tuition and fees required by the school plus books, supplies, and equipment required for courses of instruction. It does not include amounts used for other expenses such as room and board; these amounts must be included in taxable income.

Exception. The exclusion from income tax does not apply to any portion of amounts received as a scholarship or fellowship grant representing payment for teaching, research, or other services required as a condition for receiving the grant. Such portions are included in taxable income, even if used for tuition or course-related expenses. (Note that this exception applies even if the teaching, research, or other services is required of all candidates for a particular degree. This is opposite to the situation that applies under the old rules.)

Non-Degree Candidates

Individuals who are not candidates for a degree lose all income tax exemption under the new rules. Amounts received in 1987 or later years from grants awarded on or after August 17, 1986 are fully taxable.

However the exemption from social security tax, as discussed in Section 5, still applies. As long as the grant satisfies the requirements of being a scholarship or fellowship that applies under prior law [cf. Section 3], the full amount of the grant is excluded from social security tax, no matter when the grant was awarded.

When is a Scholarship or Fellowship Granted?

As discussed above, different rules apply to scholarships or fellowships granted on or after August 17, 1986 than to ones granted before this date. Therefore, it becomes necessary to determine the exact date when a scholarship or fellowship is considered to be *granted*. Rules for making this determination, including the case of multi-year grants, were spelled out by the IRS in a published news release [IRS Notice 87-31, IRB 1987-17]. According to the IRS,

"A scholarship or fellowship is granted when the grantor of the scholarship or fellowship grant either notifies the recipient of the award or notifies an organization or institution acting on the behalf of a specified recipient of the award to be provided to such recipient. If the notification is sent by mail, notification occurs as of the date the notice is postmarked. If evidence of a postmark does not exist, the date of the award letter shall be treated as the notification date . . . A scholarship or fellowship will be considered granted before August 17, 1986, to the extent that, in a notice of award made before that date, the grantor made a firm commitment to provide the recipient with a fixed cash amount or a readily determinable amount."

Grants awarded before August 17, 1986 which cover a multi-semester or multi-year period still qualify for exemption under the old rules, provided the grant adequately specifies the amounts to be received in the future. The IRS describes this situation as follows:

"If a scholarship or fellowship was granted for a period exceeding one academic period (e.g. semester), amounts received in subsequent academic periods will be treated as granted before August 17, 1986, only if (1) the amount awarded for the first academic period is described in the original notice of award as a fixed cash amount or readily determinable amount, (2) the original notice of award contains a firm commitment by the grantor to provide the scholarship or fellowship amount for more than one academic period, and (3) the recipient is not required to reapply to the grantor in order to receive the scholarship or fellowship grant in future academic periods. A requirement that the recipient file a financial statement on an annual basis to show continuing financial need will not be treated as a requirement to reapply to the grantor.

"If a scholarship or fellowship satisfying the requirements of the preceding paragraph does not describe the amount to be received in subsequent academic periods as either a fixed cash amount or readily determinable amount, it is presumed

that the amount granted before August 17, 1986, to be received in each subsequent academic period is equal to the amount granted for the initial academic period. To the extent that any amount received in a subsequent academic period exceeds the amount received in the initial academic period, the excess amount is treated as a scholarship or fellowship granted after August 16, 1986."

The IRS illustrates these rules with the following 3 examples.

Example 1.

On May 1, 1986, A is notified of a scholarship made in the amount of $4,000 annually for four years. The total amount of the scholarship is a fixed cash amount. Thus, the total amount of the scholarship for all four years is exempt from tax under the old rules that applied prior to the 1986 Tax Reform Act.

Example 2.

On May 1, 1986, B is notified of a scholarship that will pay for B's tuition, room and board for four years. The total amount of the scholarship is readily determinable. Thus, the total amount of the scholarship for all four years is exempt from tax under the old rules that applied prior to the 1986 Tax Reform Act.

Example 3.

On May 1, 1986, C is notified that she is the recipient of a scholarship to attend University X. The notice provides that University X will provide scholarship funds for four years, and specifies that C will receive $5,000 during the first year. C is not required to reapply in order to receive scholarship funds during years 2 through 4. However, the notice does not specify the scholarship funds to be received in years 2 through 4. The $5,000 received in year 1 is treated as granted before August 17, 1986 because this amount is a fixed cash amount described in the notice of award. In addition, because University X has made a specific commitment to provide scholarship funds during years 2 through 4 without requiring C to reapply for the scholarship, an amount equal to $5,000 per year is treated as granted before August 17, 1986 during years 2 through 4. Thus, if C receives $4,000 in year 2, the entire amount is treated as granted before August 17, 1986. If, in year 3, C receives $6,000, only $5,000 of the amount received is treated as granted before August 17, 1986. The additional $1,000 received in year 3 is treated as granted after August 16, 1986.

The new rules do not apply to amounts received prior to 1987. Thus, if a grant was awarded on or after August 17, 1986, amounts received in 1986 would fall under the old rules while amounts received in 1987 and later years fall under the new rules.

The same applies to expenses billed to the recipient which are paid out of a scholarship or fellowship granted on or after August 17, 1986. Here, it is the billing date that determines which rules apply.

For example, if in December, 1986 a school billed a student for a dormitory room, then amounts paid out of scholarship funds received in 1986 to pay the bill are exempt from tax because the old rules would still apply. This would be the case even if the bill is for 1987 dormitory rent or the bill is not paid until January, 1987. However, if the billing date is in 1987, then the new rules apply even if the bill was prepaid in 1986. [IRS Notice 87-31, IRB 1987-17]

Withholding from Grants

Under the new rules, a scholarship or fellowship grant awarded to a student might be partly tax-exempt and partly taxable. However, making this partition is the duty of the recipient. Neither the grantor nor the school is required to file a form with the IRS reporting on the taxable portion of the grant. And, since such grants are not considered wages, there should be no withholding of income tax or social security on any payments under the grant. Essentially, students are being placed on the honor system with regard to reporting taxable amounts of scholarships or fellowships.

An exception to this rule occurs to the extent amounts received under the grant represent payment for teaching, research, or other services by the student required as a condition for receiving the scholarship or tuition remission. In such a case, the school is required to make the allocation between the taxable and tax-free amounts and issue an appropriate W-2 form reporting the amount regarded as wages. In making this allocation, the school is to take into account compensation paid for similar services rendered by non-recipients of scholarships or fellowships at the same or comparable educational organizations. Only amounts allocated to compensation for services by the teaching or research assistants are subject to the reporting and withholding requirements.

Note: Under the rules described above, teaching and research assistants can be taxed on the value of tuition reduction which is considered part of their compensation package for services rendered. However at presstime, Congress was considering a change in the law to exempt such tuition reductions from tax retroactive to January 1, 1987. Teaching and research assistants will be able to determine the taxable amount of their stipends for services rendered under current rules by referring to the yearend W-2 Forms furnished by their employers. Next year's edition of this Tax Guide will contain further information on this issue.

Section 3:
Grants Awarded before August 17, 1986

Scholarship and fellowship grants awarded before August 17, 1986 are subject to the same rules that applied in 1985 and earlier years. This section contains a description of these "old rules." As discussed in Section 2, these rules apply even if funds from the grant are received on or after August 17, 1986. Under the old rules, scholarship and fellowship grants are exempt from income tax and social security tax, subject to the limitations and provisions in the remainder of this section.

Limitations

If the grant meets either of the following two conditions, it will **not** be considered a scholarship or fellowship and will be taxable income.

(1) The grant is paid as compensation for past, present, or future services. If you are required, as a condition for receiving the grant, to agree to work for the grantor after completing your training, the grant is considered compensation for future services.

or

(2) The grant is paid to enable you to pursue studies or research primarily for the benefit of the grantor. However, if the primary purpose is to further your education and training in your individual capacity, and the amounts do not represent compensation for service, neither the fact that you are required to furnish progress reports to the grantor, nor that the results of your studies or research may be of some incidental benefit to the grantor shall destroy the tax-free character of the grant.

Exception

If teaching, research, or other equivalent services are required of all candidates for a particular degree (whether or not recipients of scholarship or fellowship grants), then money received for such services may still be considered a tax-free scholarship or fellowship. According to an IRS ruling [Rev Rul 75-280], a grant will be considered to have been for the primary purpose of benefiting the recipient and hence excludable from gross income if the following conditions are satisfied:

1. *The student was a candidate for a degree at an educational institution;*

2. *The student performed research, teaching, or other services for the institution that satisfied specifically stated requirements for the degree;*

3. *Equivalent services were required of all candidates for the same degree;*
and

4. *The work required is reasonably appropriate to the degree.*

However, the above conditions will **not** suffice to establish that the grant is excludable from gross income if

A. *The student performed services for a party other than the educational institution;*

or

B. *The grant is made because of past services or conditioned upon future services or other requirements.*

If a student performs services in excess of those necessary to satisfy the degree requirements, then amounts received for these excess services are subject to tax. The remainder is tax-free, provided that the student is not required to perform the excess services as a condition to receiving amounts for the regular services required of all candidates for the degree.

Note that Restriction A above only refers to work performed directly for an outside agency. If, for example, a university contracted with an outside agency to provide funds for a research project, and then hired a student to assist in the project, Restriction A would not apply.

Teaching Assistants

If a teaching assistant has met the requirements of the above ruling, then his stipend is tax-free. The IRS based the ruling on the case of a research assistant but specifically stated at the end that the ruling applied to *"amounts received for teaching or other services."*

Note that the equivalent services required of all candidates in condition 3 must actually be **equivalent.** This is illustrated by a 1977 court case in which a teaching assistant in the Classics department attempted to claim that his stipend was a tax-free fellowship because *equivalent* teaching services were required of all Ph.D. candidates in his department. But the Court pointed out that the only stated requirement was that *"a doctoral candidate have 'teaching experience' in order to qualify for the Ph.D. degree in the classics. Neither the amount nor the nature of the required teaching experience is specified in the rule. However, there is nothing in the record to indicate that the rule requires 'all candidates' for the Ph.D. degree in the classics to have the kind or the extent of teaching experience that the [teaching assistant in this case had]."* [Pelz v. U.S., Ct. Clms. No.8-74, 3/23/77]

A similar conclusion was reached in two 1984 court cases which denied tax-exemption to students who held teaching assistantships. In each case, the student's department required some teaching experience to graduate, but not necessarily the same amount required of the teaching assistants. [Tate, TC Memo 1984-206; Zimmerman; TC Memo 1984-207]

The equivalent services must actually be a **requirement**, not just a fact of life. This is illustrated by a 1984 case, affirmed by a 1986 Appeals Court decision, concerning one of 90 teaching assistants in an English Department at a large State University. The fact that all Ph.D. students (except one) were teaching assistants did not suffice because there was *"no formal requirement of the University or the English Department that all such degree candidates teach."* [Sebberson, TC Memo 1984-605; 86-1 USTC]

A teaching assistant who did not meet the *equivalent services required of all candidates* criterion is subject to tax on his grant in almost every case. He has simply received pay for services rendered. It is not sufficient that the University characterize the stipend as a tax-free stipend rather than as taxable pay for services rendered. In the case in the preceding paragraph, the University did not withhold social security tax from the assistants' stipends. Also, the assistants' supervisors testified that the primary purpose of the teaching assistantships was to train the assistants as future teachers. This was not sufficient to convince the Court that the assistants were paid to study rather than to work.

Similarly, a different court case concerned a teaching assistant in the Language Department of a large midwestern University. He received a stipend of $3,580 in return for which he taught several undergraduate Spanish courses. The University provided him with a statement, which he attached to his tax return, characterizing $1,628 of the stipend as a scholarship and the remaining $1,952 as taxable pay. The

$1,952 taxable pay figure was calculated by the University to be that amount which *"would have been expended to hire a part-time instructor to perform the teaching services rendered by the petitioner."*

However, the Court ruled that the University's statement did not control the situation. Because substantial services were rendered to the University, it ruled that the primary purpose of the grant was to benefit the grantor rather than the recipient. Therefore, the entire $3,580 stipend represented taxable pay rather than a tax-free scholarship or fellowship.

The fact that the University could have hired part-time instructors for less money than the stipend did not make any part of it tax-free. As the Court ruled,

"It may be true that the stipend from the assistantship was intended to provide petitioner with some financial assistance so that he could continue his studies. He may have been paid more than a part-time instructor would have been. It is certainly within the University's discretion to pay a premium to its own well qualified graduate students. These factors are not inconsistent with what we find to be the primary purpose of the stipend, which was to provide teaching services for the benefit of the Department." [Ellenwood, TC Memo 1982-137]

The above case contrasted with an earlier case involving a teaching assistant in a different department at the same University. In the earlier case, the assistantship was ruled to be exempt from tax. But in that case, equivalent services were required of all candidates for the same degree. Furthermore, the entire assistantship program was geared toward providing teacher training, rather than covering courses for which extra personnel would need to be hired in the absence of an assistantship program. [Steiman, 56 TC 1350]

Research Assistants

Research assistants, in most cases, fall under the above ruling since equivalent research is usually required for all candidates. As long as the requirements of the ruling were satisfied, their grants qualify for tax-free status. [IRS Private Letter Rulings 8240081, 8348045, 8430013, 8405079, 8613005; TC Memo 1980-559]

However, it is not *necessary* to satisfy the equivalent services test in order to deduct the full amount of the stipend. This is the conclusion of the Tax Court in a recent case concerning two research assistants in the Department of Economics at a large Midwestern University. One of the assistants was in the Ph.D. program while the other was pursuing a master's degree only. Both of them worked on research projects under the direction of a professor in the Economics Department. Funds for their assistantships came both from the National Science Foundation and from the general research budget of the University.

The Court reasoned that one of the objectives of graduate education at the University was to develop the research skills of its students. These skills cannot be acquired simply by completing the regular course work, but require actual participation in some sort of research project or other similar *creative component*. The Court concluded that the amounts received by the assistants *"were not intended as compensation for services, but rather were intended to facilitate their graduate education."*

The Court pointed to 6 factors which supported its conclusion. First, each assistant derived *"clear and unmistakable educational benefits"* from his research assistantship. Second, they worked longer than the 20 hours per week that was required, without additional compensation. This was *"inconsistent with a true employment relationship where one might reasonably expect to be compensated for overtime."* Third, the review of their research by their Professors was informal and irregular. In substance their Professors *"served more in the capacity of an advisor than a supervisor, and there was a distinct absence of an employer-employee relationship in the traditional sense."* Fourth, the assistants were not required to turn over the results of the research to any persons outside the Economics Department, nor was there any contractual commitment to perform specific research activities. Fifth, the assistantships were regarded by the University and the students as a means of providing financial aid so the students could complete their studies. And sixth, *"many of the trappings associated with an employment relationship"* were absent in this case. The University did not contribute to a health plan, made no Worker's Compensation or Unemployment Insurance contributions, did not withhold social security or taxes, etc.

The IRS objected that the research services provided by the assistants went beyond what was required of graduate students who were not research assistants so they did not meet the *equivalent services* test. But the Court found this objection to be groundless. Although satisfying the equivalent services test is *sufficient* to establish the deductibility of an assistantship as described earlier in this section, it is not *necessary* to satisfy this requirement. Here, the Court found that the payments received by the research assistants were only educational in nature and were *"not intended to compensate petitioners for services rendered as an employee or any other capacity."* This meant that none of the stipend was wages, but rather the entire amount was a tax-exempt scholarship or fellowship. It did not matter whether or not equivalent services were required of all candidates for the same degree. [Langley and O'Riley, TC Memo 1982-460]

Even if a research assistant did some teaching, he can still get an exemption for a stipend covering just his research activities. This is illustrated by the following IRS Private Letter Ruling issued to a Mechanical Engineering Ph.D. candidate:

IRS Private Letter Ruling 8451053

". . . The information submitted discloses that you are an instructor and a candidate for the degree of Ph.D. in the Mechanical Engineering Department at X. You have been awarded a research grant through X, by the ***** covering a period of approximately one year beginning September 15, 1983. During this time you will perform research at a ***** research center as a portion of your dissertation research for the Ph.D. degree. You have indicated that the research that you perform for X satisfies a specifically stated requirement and that equivalent services are required of all candidates for the same degree. The research will not be performed in your capacity as an instructor at X.

"Your research is to be performed under the guidance of a 'principal investigator' that has been approved by *****. The grantee is required to submit to the grantor semi-annual status reports and a final technical report during the course of the grant. The research performed is not carried out during the course of a specific

> project of the grantor and the grant is not awarded based on past or future services to be rendered by you to X or *****.
>
> "Based upon the information submitted we conclude that the stipend that you receive from under the research grant will be excludable from gross income under section 117(a) of the Code. . . ."

Typically, universities will provide statements for research or teaching assistants to attach to their income tax returns for the purpose of claiming total or partial tax-free status for their stipends. These statements should be geared toward showing that the stipend falls within the requirements of the revenue ruling described earlier. The following is an example of what such a statement might include in the case of a research assistant. This statement is tailored to the specific language of the ruling.

TO WHOM IT MAY CONCERN:

During the calendar year 19____, _____
name of student
served as a Research Assistant in the Department of _____ at _____ from _____ to _____. He was paid a stipend of $_____for his services. The funds were derived from _____.
description of grant/contract

During the above period of time,

(1) The above student was a candidate for the degree of _____;

(2) He performed research for the above institution which satisfied then existing specifically stated requirements for the degree; and

(3) Equivalent services were required of all candidates for the degree.

Also, pursuant to receiving any of the above stipend,

(1) He did not perform services in excess of those necessary to satisfy degree requirements;

(2) Services were not performed for any party other than the above named institution;

(3) The grant was not made because of past services nor was it conditioned on, or subject to an understanding with respect to future employment or other requirements, including services in excess of those necessary to satisfy degree requirements; and

(4) The degree requirements, and the nature and extent of the work that is approved as satisfying the degree requirements are reasonably appropriate to the above degree.

In accordance with Revenue Ruling 75-280 and the above facts, the stipend is excludable from gross income as a scholarship or fellowship under Section 117 of the Internal Revenue Code before amendment by the 1986 Tax Reform Act.

The statement should also include a verification that the grant was awarded before August 17, 1986 according to the criteria described in the preceding section. This is especially important because under the new rules, Revenue Ruling 75-280 no longer applies. That is, for grants awarded on or after August 17, 1986, the fact that equivalent services are required of all degree recipients will not suffice to exempt amounts received after 1986 from tax [cf. Section 2].

Note: If the university omits any of the above information, the grant recipient should attach his own statement providing the missing information.

Interns and Residents

Interns and residents are seldom able to claim that the money they receive is a scholarship or fellowship. Their stipends are considered to be pay for services rendered to the hospital where they work. This has been the case even when stipends have covered a portion of the residency program during which no clinical services were performed [Kersten, TC Memo 1984-204]. Exceptions have occurred in programs which are not strictly medical in nature (e.g. hospital administration, psychology), where the recipients performed no substantial services for the institutions where they performed their internships. [IRS Private Letter Rulings 8206079, 8238054]

Disadvantages of Fellowships

There are two possible advantages for graduate students in having their stipends labeled as taxable pay rather than tax-free fellowships. The first advantage concerns the special negative income tax feature of the law called the *earned income credit* [cf. Chapter 1]. This credit applies to those who maintain a household for a child and earn under $15,432. In particular, for those who earn under $6,080, the credit is equal to 14% of **earned income**. Thus, $6,080 received as taxable pay could generate a $851 rebate from the government. But a tax-free fellowship would not be earned income and would therefore generate no earned income credit.

The other possible advantage in having a stipend labeled as taxable pay is that a graduate student who then cannot find a job might qualify for unemployment compensation. Whether or not unemployment compensation applies to graduate students depends upon State and Federal laws applicable at the time. However, being unemployed right after being supported by tax-free fellowship money would almost certainly not qualify.

Non-Degree Candidates

If you are not a candidate for a degree, your scholarship or fellowship grant awarded before August 17, 1986 is subject to three further restrictions.

(1) A maximum of $300 per month may be excluded from taxable income. The remainder is subject to income tax (but not Social Security tax as discussed in Section 5). In addition to the $300 exclusion, you do not have to pay tax on allowances specifically designated for travel, research, equipment, etc., provided these allowances are actually used for their intended purposes.

(2) During your lifetime, you are limited to a total of 36 months (not necessarily consecutive) during which you are eligible for this tax-free treatment.

(3) The money must be received from a governmental agency or qualifying educational, religious, charitable, scientific, or literary organization. However, a grant given a teacher by his own school is generally taxable because of the employee-employer relationship between them. (This does not necessarily apply to grants which come from a qualifying organization that are merely administered by the school.)

Amounts Specifically Designated for Expenses

As indicated in (1) above, amounts specifically designated for travel, research, equipment, etc. are totally exempt from tax provided they are spent for their intended purposes. You do not apply the $300 per month limitation to these amounts.

The "specific designation" requirement does not mean that the grant itself specify the amounts to be spent for which purposes. As long as the purpose of the grant is indicated and the grant is intended to cover expenses connected with this purpose, the "specific designation" requirement is met. A good way to show that the grant is intended to cover certain expenses is to show that these expenses were itemized in your application and that the amount of the grant was based on this itemization. [Rev Rul 69-367]

What If Less Than $300 Per Month Is Excluded?

The 36-month limitation in (2) applies whenever an individual has received an amount which was either excluded or excludable from his gross income for any prior 36 months. For example, if an individual received $200 per month for three years, his exclusion period would be exhausted. Even though he did not make use of the maximum $300 exclusion, he would no longer be entitled to any further income tax exclusion.

What If You Were Eligible but Failed to Claim the Exclusion?

You lose out. If there have been 36 months during which you were eligible to exclude any scholarship or fellowship grants as a non-degree candidate, then you are ineligible for further exclusion. It makes no difference whether or not you actually claimed the exclusion. In fact, one statistics professor was denied an exclusion because he admitted that he had received some kind of grant a number of years earlier which might have qualified for the exclusion. If so, this would have put him over the 36-month limit. He did not claim the exclusion for this grant but he could not prove that he was ineligible to claim such exclusion. [Wijsman, 54 TC 1539]

What If You Receive Several Grants the Same Year?

If an individual who is not a candidate for a degree received amounts from more than one scholarship or fellowship during the year, these are totalled in computing the amount which may be excluded from gross income. If payment is received from several scholarships or fellowships during the same month, then that month is counted only once for the purpose of determining the number of months that the individual received scholarships or fellowships. Hence if someone received a fellowship grant from one source from January to June and from another source from March to December, he is considered to have received amounts for a total of 12 months, leaving him 24 more months of eligibility for exclusion.

> **Example**
> Dr. Bettner received a post-doctoral fellowship of $22,000 which lasted from July 1, 1986 to May 31, 1987. He received monthly installments of $2,000. So during the taxable year 1986, he received $12,000 for the 6 months on fellowship. Only $1,200 of this ($300 per month) was excludable from his gross income for 1986. For the year 1987, he received $10,000 and will exclude $1,500 ($300 × 5) from his gross income. In addition, he may exclude any amounts specifically designated for research, travel, etc., provided he actually used these amounts for their intended purposes.

Grants Received While Outside the U.S.

If payments from a grant were received while outside the U.S., it might be better to consider the payments as wages for services rendered, rather than as a scholarship or fellowship. Wages can qualify for **total** exemption from income tax under the rules applying to foreign earned income [cf. the *Foreign Income* chapter]. Scholarships and Fellowships, on the other hand, run the risk of being disqualified from the foreign income exemption by the IRS as not being *earned income*.

Can the Receipt of a Tax-Free Grant Rule Out a Travel Deduction?

Sometimes the following situation arises. A person receives a grant to study or do research at a location away from home. When he uses the $300 per month fellowship exclusion and claims a deduction for travel expenses while away from home, the IRS objects. Since there were no job-related *wages*, the IRS claims no job-related expenses can be deducted. This objection can be countered by asserting that the travel expenses were *educational expenses* rather than *business expenses*. This is discussed more fully at the end of Section 3 of the *Travel* chapter.

What Kinds of Grants Qualify for Tax-Free Treatment?

Whether or not a grant qualifies for tax-free treatment depends upon the **primary purpose** of the grant. In order to be tax-deductible, the primary purpose of a grant must be *to further the education and training of the recipient in his individual capacity*. On the other hand, if the primary purpose is *for the benefit of the grantor*, then the grant is taxable.

In practice, the determination of the *primary purpose* of a grant can be difficult to make. The courts have given little guidance on how to decide this question. They simply have stated that this determination must be made *"on a case by case basis by considering the particular facts and circumstances"* concerning the grant in question.

The IRS and the courts have issued a number of rulings on specific grants, deciding in each case whether or not the grant qualifies for tax-free status. Due to the individual nature of each type of grant, it is not possible to foretell with accuracy how grants will be ruled upon. The finest of differences may cause one grant to be ruled taxable and another tax-free. Furthermore, the result might be the exact opposite of what would be reasonably expected by most people.

This is illustrated by two IRS rulings concerning grants from the National Endowment for the Humanities. The first ruling concerned a grant made to junior college professors *"to increase their understanding of the subjects they teach and to improve their teaching ability."* The second ruling concerned a grant to a professor of English literature so he could *"study the interaction of the sciences and literature with a view toward writing a book on the taxpayer's conclusion."* If anything, the first grant would seem to better qualify under the tax-free criterion of furthering *the education and training of the recipient in his individual capacity.* The second grant would seem more likely to yield a concrete result that could be regarded as *benefiting the grantor.*

But the IRS ruled just the opposite. It decided that the first grant was taxable because a non-exclusive right to reproduce publishable matter arising from the grant made the grant primarily for the benefit of the grantor. The second grant did not have this feature and was ruled to qualify for tax-free treatment.

Following are excerpts from these two rulings.

IRS Ruling 1

"The taxpayer, who was not a candidate for a degree, was the recipient of a fellowship grant by the National Endowment for the Humanities, a governmental agency. The announced purpose of the grant program was to enable junior college professors, chosen on the basis of their ability as teachers and interpreters of the humanities, to increase their understanding of the subjects they teach and to improve their teaching ability. Each applicant was to specify his proposed area of study and to explain its contribution to his development as a teacher and interpreter of humanistic knowledge and to a better understanding of matters of current national concern, or of other matters of significance to humanistic knowledge and the quality of national life.

" . . . The grantor reserved a nonexclusive license to use and reproduce for government purposes, without payment, any publishable matter, including copyrighted matter, arising out of the taxpayer's activities.

" . . . Based on the above it is concluded that the grant is made primarily for the benefit of the grantor because of the right retained by the grantor, in the form of a nonexclusive license, to any materials resulting from the recipient's research.

"A further indication that the objectives of the grant program were not solely focused on the experience to be gained by the recipients is shown by the grantor's evaluation of each applicant's ability as an interpreter of the humanities, and of the contribution to be made by the proposed area of study to a better understanding of matters of current national concern, or of other matters of significance to humanistic knowledge and the quality of national life.

"Accordingly, in the instant case, the amounts received by the taxpayer from the National Endowment for Humanities grant are not excludable from the taxpayer's gross income under the provisions of section 117(a) of the Code, but are includible in his gross income under section 61 as compensation for services." [Rev. Rul. 74-95, 1974-1 CB 39]

IRS Ruling 2

". . . The taxpayer, who was not a candidate for a degree, applied for and was granted a lump-sum grant for two months from the National Endowment for the Humanities, a governmental agency. The taxpayer was a professor of English literature and proposed to spend the two-month grant period studying the interaction of the sciences and literature with a view towards writing a book on the taxpayer's conclusions.

"As a condition to receiving the grant the taxpayer was to devote two full consecutive months during the summer to the study and research for which the grant was awarded. The taxpayer was not permitted to accept a teaching assignment, undertake another major activity, or enroll in a degree program during the two-month period and was prohibited from applying the work done during that period toward any future degree. The taxpayer was not required to publish the results of the study but was free to do so without restriction. If the taxpayer chose to publish the results of the study, the grantor requested, but did not require, a copy of the publication and advance notice thereof so that it could consider issuing a public information release or cooperating in a joint release.

". . . In this case, the grant was paid to enable the taxpayer to pursue a program of independent study. The grantor reserved no publication rights. Since the grant was awarded solely to further the education of the taxpayer, it was for the taxpayer's benefit and not for the benefit of the grantor. Further, there was no employment relationship between the grantor and the taxpayer previous to or at the time of the grant, nor was there any obligation on the part of the taxpayer to accept employment or otherwise perform services after acceptance of the grant.

"Accordingly, in the instant case, the grant received from the National Endowment for the Humanities is excludable from the taxpayer's gross income as a fellowship grant.

"This case is distinguishable from [the preceding ruling] which holds that amounts received as a grant from the National Endowment for the Humanities are not excludable from the taxpayer's gross income . . . [In that ruling], the grantor reserved a nonexclusive license to use and reproduce for government purpose, without payment, any publishable matter, including copyrighted matter arising out of the taxpayer's activities, and the objectives of the program under which the grant was awarded were not solely focused on the experience to be gained by the recipients." [Rev Rul 76-351, IRB 1976-38 p. 6]

In IRS Ruling 1 above, the nonexclusive right of the grantor to use and reproduce the results of the research disqualified the grant from tax-free treatment. In fact, two 1980 private rulings show that the IRS has latched onto this seemingly minor point as a deciding criterion. Both grants were provided by governmental agencies to support independent research in the humanities. One grant was awarded to a doctoral candidate and the other to an established researcher who had already obtained his degree. But the wording of both grants contained the fatal clause granting the government a nonexclusive right to use the results of the research without paying royalties. And in both rulings, the IRS declared that this alone was enough to rule out tax-free treatment for the grants. [IRS Private Letter Rulings 8021120 and 8008056]

NSF Grants

The preceding ruling offers a good example of a common type of grant received by college professors. Namely, the grant provides funds for the professor to do research in his specialty.

For scientists, the most common grant of this type comes from the NSF (National Science Foundation). The Tax Court has, on the two occasions when the issue came to trial, denied a deduction for NSF research grants. In 1977, the Tax Court ruled against a computer scientist. In an ironic twist, the computer scientist's expertise and the fact that his work was considered valuable were used against him by the court. (A similar conclusion was reached in a different case involving a mathematics professor. In that case, the grant proposal specified that the recipient would spend 1/3 of his time during the academic year on the project funded by the grant, such services to be paid by the university. This linking of the work performed under the summer grant and his ordinary academic-year work was a decidedly negative factor. [Carroll, 60 TC 96]) But in 1978, the IRS issued a private ruling to a scientist giving him permission to deduct his NSF grant. Although the IRS ruling was devoid of detailed reasoning, it is worthwhile to take a look at the two grants in question.

1977 Court Case — Deduction for NSF Grant Denied

A Professor of Computer Science applied for and received an NSF grant to work on the development of a new kind of programming language. As is the usual case, the grant was actually awarded to the university, with the professor as principal investigator. Funds from the grant were used to pay him for a 6-month period when he was on sabbatical.

The professor claimed that he was entitled to exclude $300 per month from taxable income, a total of $1,800 for the 6 months involved. But the Court denied his claim. It appeared to be influenced by 3 major considerations.

First, it pointed out that the grant actually covered a longer period of time than the 6-month period during which direct payments were received from the grant. Over this longer period of time, the professor was to be working on the same project as part of his regular duties as a Computer Science Professor and paid his normal salary from university funds. This indicated to the Court that the payments should not be considered as a fellowship. It stated,

". . . it was not the intent of Congress that grants which were in effect continuing salary payments to the recipient while on leave from his regular job be

considered as fellowship grants. Here, part of petitioner's regular job and part of the activity he undertook during the school year while he was performing his other functions at the university was research on the project for which NSF had made a grant. When he went on sabbatical leave and pursued this research full-time instead of part-time, the nature of his research work was unchanged. He was still pursuing the research as a part of his work as a professor and in accordance with the NSF grant."

Second, the Court seemed impressed by the usefulness of the research. Ironically, this worked against the professor because it meant that NSF and the university would receive "benefit" from the research. The Court stated,

"NSF seeks to further research which it finds to be in the public interest. Because it found that the research proposal by the petitioner met that standard, NSF made funds available to support such research. The university is interested in encouraging the members of its faculty to perform research, and for that reason it undertook to administer the grant made by NSF and to make its facilities available for the performance of such research."

Finally, the Court held the professor's experience and competence against him. The fact that he was already an expert in the field was evidence the grant was not for the purpose of providing him with training or education. It stated that since he

"had so many years of work in the area with which his research dealt, it is not even shown by this record that his education was enhanced by the research he did. In any event, in this case the facts as a whole show that the funds were made available for petitioner's project because NSF wished to have it performed by him, and that the payments made to petitioner from the NSF funds were for the services he performed on the research project. Here, an essential element of having the research proposal approved was the qualifications of petitioner to perform the important research he had outlined. The grant was made to support the proposed research which NSF determined should be performed."

1978 IRS Ruling — Deduction Allowed for NSF Grant

A scientist solicited an official opinion from the IRS as to whether his NSF grant qualified for deduction. In response, the IRS issued him a private letter ruling. This private ruling does not set legal precedent, but since the IRS attempts to be consistent in its interpretation of the law, it is still of considerable interest. As is customary, the IRS ruling is published with all mention of taxpayer's name or other identifying information deleted. With this exception, the entire IRS ruling is reproduced below.

IRS Private Letter Ruling 7817011

We are writing in reply to a letter dated July 8, 1977, submitted on your behalf by ___ and prior correspondence. You request a ruling regarding the treatment for Federal income tax purposes of amounts received by you under the circumstances described below.

You received a grant from the National Science Foundation for research in your field. The grant was established for the purpose of recognizing and encouraging the work of younger scientists whose capabilities and accomplishments show exceptional promise of significant future achievements. Your grant is administered by Princeton University.

At the time you received the grant, you were on the faculty of _____. Since the beginning of the grant period, you have been on leave from your faculty position. You teach no classes and participate in no administrative duties. You have no schedule other than that which you set for yourself, and you receive no supervision from the University.

You choose your own research problems, however, when you publish the results of your work, you are required to acknowledge the support of the National Science Foundation. You must also publish a "disclaimer" that the views presented are your own and not those of the National Science Foundation. You are not required to submit any reports of the progress of your work to the University or the National Science Foundation.

You request a ruling that the amounts you receive are excludable from your gross income as a fellowship grant pursuant to section 117 of the Internal Revenue Code of 1954.

Section 61 of the Code defines gross income as all income from whatever source derived unless specifically excluded by law.

Section 117(a) of the Code provides that gross income does not include any amount received as a scholarship at an educational organization or as a fellowship grant.

Section 117(b) (2) (B) of the Code provides that in the case of an individual who is not a candidate for a degree at an educational organization, the amount of the scholarship or fellowship grant excluded in any taxable year shall be limited to an amount equal to $300 times the number of months for which the recipient received amounts under the scholarship or fellowship grant during such taxable year, except that no exclusion shall be allowed after the recipient has been entitled to exclude under this section for a period of 36 months (whether or not consecutive) amounts received as a scholarship or fellowship grant while not a candidate for a degree at an educational institution.

In *Biederdorf v. Commissioner,* 60 T.C. 114 (1973), the United States Tax Court held that a postdoctoral fellowship grant awarded to a licensed physician and funded by the National Institutes of Health was excludable from the recipient's gross income. Seventy-five to eighty percent of his time was spent performing research which was of only incidental value to the grantor, and there was no requirement for future employment services as a condition for receiving the grant. A similar result was reached in *Bailey v. Commissioner,* 60 T.C. 447 (1973).

Revenue Ruling 58-498, 1958-2 C.B. 47, provides that amounts paid as grants to high school and college teachers to attend summer institutes for science are excludable from the recipients' gross income pursuant to the limitations of section 117 of the Code. The grantees were not affiliated with the National Science Foundation (the grantor) nor did they incur any independent obligation to any educational institution by accepting the stipend.

Based upon our analysis of the authorities cited above and the information submitted by you, we conclude that you may exclude from your gross income amounts received under your grant, subject to the limitations of section 117(b) (2) (B) of the Code.

A copy of this ruling should be attached to your income tax return when it is filed.

A copy of this letter is being sent to your representative pursuant to the power of attorney on file with this office.

As the above discussion indicates, the deductibility of a research grant is often a borderline question which can be decided in either direction, depending upon who does the deciding. However, an instructive pattern has emerged from the recent cases on this issue.

First, let us compare the Court Case above in which a deduction was denied to a Computer Science Professor with IRS Ruling 2 described earlier in which tax-free treatment was approved for a Professor of English. The difference seems to lie mostly in the more specific nature of the Computer Science proposal than the English proposal. The grant to the English Professor was awarded for the purpose of *"study with a view towards writing a book."* There was no mention of any concrete results that it was hoped would be attained. The NSF grant to the Computer Science Professor, on the other hand, was made on the basis of a specific research proposal to develop a particular type of programming language. The court felt that NSF *"wished to have the research performed"* and therefore received *benefit* from the research.

It is also interesting to compare the two NSF Grants discussed above. The first grant was awarded to an established scientist by NSF in order to *"further research which it finds to be in the public interest."* Because of the existing expertise of the researcher and the desired end product of the research, the grant was considered to be for the primary purpose of *benefiting the grantor* rather than *furthering the education and training of the recipient.*

The second NSF grant, on the other hand, had the stated purpose of *"recognizing and encouraging the work of younger scientists whose capabilities and accomplishments show exceptional promise of significant future achievements."* In this case, the purpose of *furthering the education and training of the recipient in his individual capacity* predominated over the purpose of benefiting the grantor.

Two 1983 examples illustrate that when asked to rule, the IRS generally looks for some special feature of the grant which will make it fully taxable.

In the first of these rulings, the IRS denied tax-exemption for a research grant received by a professor at an unnamed college. This research grant provided not just summer support, but also provided ¼ support during the academic year so that the professor could receive a reduced teaching load to carry on his research. The ruling was devoid of detailed reasoning. However, the fact that the grant covered not just the summer months but also part of the regular academic year was clearly a negative factor—indicating the grant was more in the nature of pay for services rendered than for the educational benefit of the recipient. [IRS Private Letter Ruling 8336021]

The second ruling concerned a summer-only NSF grant to a professor for 2/9 of his academic year salary. Under this grant, however, the NSF retained the right to receive a portion of royalties from copyrights produced during the life of the grant and for 3 years thereafter. The grant also gave the NSF the rights to patentable inventions arising from work done under these grants. As discussed earlier in this section, the retention of rights by the grantor to work produced under a grant is an important indicator to the IRS that the grant is for the purpose of benefiting the grantor rather than the recipient. Hence, it ruled that this NSF grant did not qualify for tax-free treatment. [IRS Private Letter Ruling 8337049]

The above discussion indicates that the official IRS policy on tax-free grants is to be tough about allowing tax-free treatment. In fact, 4 more recent IRS Private Letter Rulings have all denied tax exemptions for various NSF grants with no obvious special features which were awarded to college faculty members. In each case, the IRS ruled that the grant was primarily for the benefit of the grantor (NSF) rather than the recipient. In 3 of these rulings, the IRS used the following same language (including reference to a 1970 court case, *Turem vs. Commissioner,* it uncovered) describing why it considered the grant to *"benefit"* the NSF:

> *"A grant in support of basic research is made because the National Science Foundation decides that the results of the research are desired and in the public interest. A grant for basic research sets forth the budget to be followed, including the allocation of the amounts to be paid as salary to the principal investigator and others working on the project. On the other hand, a fellowship grant is always made to an individual and is awarded to enhance the applicant's competence. Although a recipient of a fellowship grant may engage in research as an incident of his study and development, the objective of the grant is to further his study and not to achieve the research.*
>
> *"In Turem v. Commissioner, 54 T.C. 1494 (1970), the court found that governmental grants resulted in grantor benefit by inducing recipients to engage in educational activity beneficial to governmental agencies in the attainment of their objectives, even though the general public was expected to be the ultimate beneficiary of the petitioner's education. Thus, Turem stands for the proposition that grantor benefit need not be in the form of monetary gain or services rendered directly to the grantor."* [IRS Private Letter Rulings 8521084, 8521029, 8524071, 8528012]

The above discussion suggests that grant recipients are wise to avoid formal confrontation with the IRS, if possible. (Be sure to read Section 4 on the most inconspicuous way to claim the tax-free portion of your grant.) However, the basic legal situation remains. That is, each grant is judged separately on its merits as to whether or not it is primarily for the benefit of the grantor or the recipient.

How to Obtain Tax-Free Treatment for a Grant

As the above discussion indicates, there are no rigid rules to apply which will determine whether or not a grant is deductible. Even the Court has admitted that the tax status of a grant must be decided *"on a case by case basis by considering the facts and circumstances"* in the given situation. However, the above discussion suggests how to improve the chances of obtaining tax-free status for a grant. Namely, the **study** aspect of the research should be stressed as opposed to the **result** aspect. Funds for study tend to be regarded as benefiting the recipient while funds to obtain specific results tend to be regarded as benefiting the grantor.

Scientists, especially, should be aware of the above distinction in order to properly protect their deduction. An individual whose NSF grant is challenged may wish to present a copy of IRS Private Letter Ruling 7817011 reproduced above to support his case, even if the particulars of his situation differ somewhat from that in the ruling. A given IRS examining officer may or may not perceive a difference between two relatively similar situations.

Because the deductibility of a grant is a judgment call, most recipients of grants awarded before August 17, 1986 will probably want to go ahead and treat their grants as qualifying for tax-free treatment on their 1987 tax returns. The risk of challenge by the IRS is usually outweighed by the expected tax benefit.

Replacement Criterion

A 1975 court case outlines a criterion which can be used in your favor when establishing that a grant you have received is a tax-free fellowship rather than compensation for services rendered. The criterion is whether or not by accepting the grant, you will be replacing persons who would otherwise have been employed had there been no grant. A negative answer to this question is a mark in your favor. Since most research grants satisfy the criterion, you are likely to be able to use this point if the tax status of a grant which you have received is questioned.

> **Court Case.**
>
> Faloona received his Ph.D. in biochemistry from a prominent university in the South. A year later, he became a postdoctoral fellow at a medical school in Texas, working under a grant provided by the Public Health Service.
>
> The court ruled that Faloona's grant was a fellowship and therefore qualified for the $300 per month exclusion from taxable income. In explaining its decision, the court introduced the "replacement" criterion. It stated,
>
>> "The record shows that the postdoctoral fellows did not in fact replace persons who otherwise would have been employed by . . . the . . . Medical School." [TC Memo 1975-40]

Grants Requiring Future Services

A grant should not be conditioned upon the performance of future services. For example, if a faculty member accepted a grant which requires him to return to his school after the grant period is over, then this would disqualify the grant from tax-free status. This fact was emphasized in several recent court cases and IRS rulings.
[IRS Private Letter Rulings 7828044, 7907079, 8439055, 8439086, TC Memo 1978-449]

Sabbatical and Summer Grants

Money which a teacher received from an employer while on a sabbatical is usually not considered to be a tax-free grant. The direct employer-employee relationship that exists between the grantor and the grantee in most cases leads the IRS to consider such money to be a form of compensation for services rendered. However, if the grant is supplied by an outside organization, then the grant qualifies for the

$300 per month tax-free treatment as described in this section. The following 1986 IRS Private Letter Ruling illustrates this situation.

IRS Private Letter Ruling 8601039

"This is in reply to your letter of September 3, 1985, requesting a ruling that a stipend that you receive from X is a fellowship grant within the meaning of section 117(a) of the Internal Revenue Code.

"The information submitted discloses that during the period August 15, 1985 to August 14, 1986, you will be on sabbatical from your position as a member of the faculty of Y. The sabbatical is not a requirement for continued employment at Y. During the above-described period, you will be receiving an amount equal to one-half of your normal, annual salary from Y which you acknowledge represents taxable income for federal income tax purposes.

"During this same period, however, you will be receiving a stipend from X under a Visiting Scientist fellowship which is being treated as a postdoctoral fellowship by X.

"You were awarded this fellowship after you submitted a research proposal to X. The only responsibilities to X are to complete the project as outlined in the proposal, and to file a mid-term and final progress report to X. While you may engage in other research projects during the year, such activities are at your discretion and you are free to conduct your research as you see fit. Your sponsor at X is acting as your official contact with X and will offer advice when necessary. He is not acting in a supervisory capacity. Your only obligation to Y is to file a report on your research activities at the end of your sabbatical.

"X's description of the program provides that fellows will be selected for the importance of the work they propose—its contribution to their field, and to the fulfillment of their intellectual promise—provided such work can be undertaken successfully in X's facilities and a member of X's professional research staff is available for collaboration and assistance. X is an organization which is an instrumentality of the United States. . . .

"Rev. Rul. 58-222, 1958-1 C.B. 54, holds that the amount received from a college by a member of its teaching staff (on sabbatical leave) while engaged in research in his particular field of interest does not constitute a scholarship or fellowship grant within the meaning of section 117 of the Code. The amount so received is includible in the member's gross income as compensation.

"Rev. Rul. 58-222 further holds that the amount received by such member from a private (tax-exempt) foundation while engaged in such research is excludable from his gross income as a fellowship grant to the extent provided by section 117 of the Code. Any amount received by him which is specifically designated to cover expenses for travel (including meals and lodging while traveling and an allowance for travel of his family), research, clerical help, or equipment incident to the fellowship grant, is excludable from gross income to the extent that it is used for such purposes.

"Based upon the information submitted, and the representations made, we conclude that the stipend that you receive from X is excludable from your gross income under section 117(a) of the Code subject to the limitation of section

117(b)(2) [discussed at the beginning of Section 1—ed.].
"It is further concluded that any amount received from X designated for travel, clerical help, or equipment incident to the grant, is excludable from gross income to the extent that it is used for such purposes. . . ."

Summer Research Grants

A similar situation prevails with respect to summer grants. This is illustrated by the following IRS Ruling issued at the request of a University with a summer grant program.

IRS Private Letter Ruling 7807004

"The University awards research grants to selected faculty members so that they may pursue research in their respective fields during the summer. In order to receive a grant, a faculty member must submit a proposal for his or her project to the Committee on Research.

"Only full-time faculty members are eligible to apply for grants. Eligibility is further restrictive in that, 'only those who will remain on the . . . University faculty for the [following] academic year are free to accept an award . . . .' The amounts awarded the recipients are based upon the faculty members' rank and are limited to the amounts that could be earned by teaching six hours at visiting faculty rates.

"Since the faculty summer grants appear to be based on the employment status of the individual recipients and their obligation to render future services, the amounts paid to them are not excludable as scholarships. . ."

The above ruling contrasts with an earlier ruling [Rev Rul 62-188] which permitted a deduction for a summer research grant. In this earlier ruling, the funds came from a separate entity distinct from the University. Furthermore, faculty members were not obliged to return to the University as a precondition of receiving the grant.

Exceptions

There are exceptions when money received from an employer might qualify for tax-free treatment. The following 1985 court case shows that a grant from one's employer can qualify as a tax-free grant if there are truly no strings attached.

Court Case

Pelowski, a teacher at a small liberal arts college in the Midwest, received a $10,000 grant from the college. Such grants were awarded after 7 years of employment. Pelowski used the grant to pursue a Ph.D. program at a major University in a neighboring state.

No strings were attached to the grant. Pelowski had no obligation to return to the college where he had taught. The college did not select the curriculum for his Ph.D. thesis. While studying at the University, he was on leave of absence but not employed at the college, nor did he receive any benefits from the college. No *progress reports were given to his former employer.*

The Court ruled that based on the above facts, the $10,000 grant did not represent compensation for past, present, or future services. Nor were the studies primarily for the benefit of the college. Rather, the $10,000 was ruled to be a tax-exempt scholarship grant. [Pelowski, DC Ohio, 1985 CCH ¶9217]

SECTION 4: HOW TO CLAIM THE INCOME TAX EXEMPTION

Ideally, the W-2 form which you receive from your employer should not include any amounts received under a tax-free grant. Since the grant is not pay for services rendered, the **full amount** of the grant is supposed to be excluded from *Wages* on your W-2 form. (An exception occurs when a portion of the grant is paid for services rendered, in which case such portion should be included on your W-2 form.) You would then report any portion of the grant subject to tax as *Other Income* on line 21 of Form 1040.

However, institutions often tend to be conservative and treat all grants issued to their faculty members as wages, even though this can cost both you and the institution extra social security tax. This means the entire amount received under the grant will be included in the W-2 form which you receive at the end of the year. In this case, the official procedure calls for you to subtract the tax-free amount of the grant from the figure shown on your W-2 form and report the difference on the *Wages* line of your tax return.

However, this procedure has caused numerous grant recipients a lot of trouble because it has flagged their tax returns for audit. The IRS has a "Matching Program" to verify that the amount reported on W-2 forms matches the amount reported as *Wages* on an individual's tax return. If the figures do not match, the return will be singled out for examination. This can result not only in the tax-free status of the grant being called into question, but also other items as well.

If the W-2 form sent to you by your employer includes amounts which qualify as a tax-free grant, the following procedure is best. Report the full amount shown on your W-2 form as *Wages* on your tax return. Then list the tax-free amount of your grant as a negative amount on line 21, *Other Income*. The net tax result will be the same as if you had omitted the tax-free amount of the grant from your total wages, but you won't have stirred up the IRS computer by creating an arithmetical discrepancy. The listing of negative amounts on line 21 is a procedure suggested by the IRS in similar situations.

Note that there are two additional advantages to including tax-free grants in taxable income and then subtracting these amounts with a negative entry on line 21. First, you cannot be accused of fraud for failing to report income. Second, you have subjected the question of your grant's tax status to the statute of limitations. Otherwise, if the IRS feels you have omitted a substantial amount of income, it is not governed by the usual 3-year statute of limitations on auditing your return.

You should attach a statement to your return showing the amounts received and the letter of award to you or other description of the grant. If you received any specific allowances for travel, research expenses, etc., these should be listed separately along with a statement showing the use to which these allowances were applied.

SECTION 5:
EXEMPTION FROM SOCIAL SECURITY TAX

A grant which qualifies for exemption from income tax under the rules described in the preceding sections is also exempt from social security tax. This exemption from social security tax still applies to grants issued on or after August 17, 1986. It does not matter that the grant may be subject to income tax under the new law. The 1986 Tax Reform Act only affects the *income tax* treatment of grants, not the *social security* treatment.

This social security tax exemption applies to the **entire amount of the grant** and is unaffected by the $300 per month and 36 total-months limitations described in Section 3 for awards issued to non-degree candidates prior to August 17, 1986. For example, such a non-degree candidate who received a $2,000 per month grant for 2 months would be able to exclude $300 × 2 = $600 of this grant from income tax. But the entire $4,000 would be exempt from social security tax.

The exemption from social security tax is spelled out in a number of IRS rulings. The reasoning in these rulings goes as follows:

Under the old rules discussed in Section 3, a grant qualified for partial tax-free treatment if the *primary purpose* of the grant was to further the education and training of the recipient in his individual capacity, rather than being for the benefit of the grantor. This meant that the money received under the grant was not classified as *wages*. And social security tax is only levied against *wages*, not against any other type of income even if this income is subject to income tax. [IRS Private Letter Rulings 7929051, 7929066, and 8047019]

The exemption from social security tax on the entire amount of the grant can be worth a substantial amount of money. For example, a person earning $2,000 per month under a 12-month grant would save about $1,700 in social security taxes, a substantial tax-free benefit. (However, if a person's other income already exceeds the social security wage base, above which no additional social security tax is withheld, then there would be no social security tax savings.)

Recipients of grants qualifying for tax-free treatment should request that the institution administering the grant withhold no social security taxes. In fact, if the grant qualifies for tax-free treatment, the institution is legally required to do this.

Refund of Prior Social Security Tax

If social security (also known as FICA) was withheld on money you received from a grant which qualified for tax-free treatment, then you are entitled to a refund of the amounts withheld. This situation is covered in a recent ruling which describes the exact procedure to follow to obtain the refund. This ruling was issued to an individual who received a grant on which social security was incorrectly withheld. Since many individuals are in the same situation, we quote the relevant portion of this ruling in its entirety.

IRS Private Letter Ruling 8109026

"... We conclude that the stipend you receive is excludable from gross income to the extent of $300.00 per month for the number of months of the internship, not to exceed the 36 month limitation of Code section 117(b)(2)(B).

"Because FICA payments have been withheld on this amount, you are entitled to a recovery.

"Section 31.6402 (a)-2 (a) of the Employment Tax Regulations provides that any person who pays to the district director more than the correct amount of employee tax under section 3101 or employer tax under section 3111 of the Federal Insurance Contributions Act (FICA) may file a claim for refund of the overpayment or may claim a credit for the overpayment. The employer may file a claim for refund on Form 843 or take a credit for the overpayment on any subsequent return. Claims filed by an employer for refund, credit, or abatement of employee tax collected from an employee must include a statement by the employee that the employer has repaid him/her the amount of the overcollection or has obtained the employee's written consent to the allowance of the refund or credit. If the claim for credit or refund is for a calendar year prior to the calendar year in which the claim is made, the employer must obtain a statement that the employee has not and will not claim a refund or credit of the amount of the overcollection. This is the preferable method for recovery.

"If the employer does not correct the error, the employee may file a claim for refund or credit of an overcollection of FICA tax where: (1) the employer collects more than the correct amount of employee social security tax and pays it to the district director, and (2) the employee has not claimed reimbursement through credit against, or refund of, his income tax (or if so claimed, the claim has been rejected), and (3) the employee does not receive reimbursement in any manner from such employer and does not authorize the employer to file a claim and receive refund or credit. The employee may file a claim for refund of the overpayment on Form 843. Each employee who makes such a claim must submit along with the claim a statement setting forth (a) the extent, if any, to which the employer has reimbursed the employee in any manner for the overcollection, and (b) the amount, if any, of credit or refund of such overpayment collected by the employer. If the employee is unable to obtain the employer's statement, the employee must make the statement to the best of his knowledge and belief and include an explanation of his inability to obtain the statement from the employer.

"The statement to accompany an employer's and employee's claim for credit or refund of employee tax under section 3101 or employer tax under section 3111 made with respect to payments erroneously reported on a return as wages paid to an employee must include (1) the identification number of the employer, (2) the name and account number of the employee, (3) the period covered by the return, (4) the amount of payments actually reported as wages for the employee, and (5) the amount of wages which should have been reported for the employee. No particular form is prescribed for making such statement, but if printed forms are desired, Form 941c may be used."

Although not mentioned in the above ruling, the 3-year statute of limitations applies to the filing of a refund claim. That is, the refund claim generally should be filed within 3 years of the date the employer filed the erroneous social security withholding tax form with the government.

In addition to not taking out any social security tax, the employer should not have withheld any income tax either, even if part of the grant is subject to income tax. This can be corrected by having the employer reimburse the employee for any amounts incorrectly withheld during the same calendar year. After the end of the year, overwithholding of income tax is corrected only by filing the usual income tax return on which the appropriate refund is calculated.

Chapter 29

Research Expenses of College Teachers

SECTION 1:
DEDUCTION FOR RESEARCH EXPENSES

College teaching is one of the most misunderstood professions that exists today. Most people do not understand the difference between the job of teaching elementary or high school and that of teaching college. They do not understand that many college teachers must do more than just teach their classes, consult with students, and serve on administrative committees. College teachers are expected to keep abreast of advances in their field by reading journals, attending seminars, traveling to conventions, etc. Furthermore, in many colleges and universities, faculty members are required to be scholars in their own right. They must do original research and communicate their results by publishing articles in journals, writing books, giving colloquium and seminar talks, corresponding with colleagues, discussing topics with their fellow teachers and graduate students, etc.

College teachers often incur expenses in doing their research. They may spend money on attending meetings in their specialty, subscribing to journals, buying books, buying equipment or supplies, etc.

Fortunately, the tax regulations now specifically recognize the integral part that research plays in the duties of many professors. This was not always the case. For example, in one 1962 case, the Tax Court denied a deduction to a Professor of English at a distinguished college in California. The professor had claimed a deduction for expenses incurred doing research on *Translators and Translations into English from 1475 to 1640*. The court ruled that the purpose of his research activity was "to increase his prestige as a scholar" and not to fill a requirement of his job. Since he was already tenured, he did not have to perform this research to keep his job. For this reason, his expenses were ruled nondeductible. [Davis, 38 TC 175]

However, in 1963, the IRS issued an important ruling which is excerpted below. This ruling declared that a college professor can deduct expenses he incurs in connection with his research, provided this research is expected of him in his capacity as a professor. He does not have to show that he will be fired or suffer a salary decrease if he does not do the research.

Special IRS Ruling on Professors' Research (Revenue Ruling 63-275)

> "Advice has been requested concerning the deductibility for Federal income tax purposes of research expenses, including traveling expenses incurred by college and university professors in their capacity as educators.
>
> "The facts presented are that the duties of a professor, with or without tenure, encompass not only the usual lecture and teaching duties but also the

communication and advancement of knowledge through research and publication. Appointments are commonly made to college and university faculties with the expectation that the individuals will carry on independent research in their fields of competence and will put that research to use in advancing the body of learning in that area by teaching, lecturing, and writing. It is customary, therefore, for professors to engage in research for the above purposes. Where the research is undertaken with a view to scholarly publication, the expenses for such purposes can not usually be considered to have been incurred for the purpose of producing a specific income-producing asset.

"Based on the facts presented, it is held that research expenses, including traveling expenses properly allocable thereto, incurred by a professor for the purpose of teaching, lecturing, or writing and publishing in his area of competence, as a means of carrying out the duties expected of him in his capacity as a professor and without expectation of profit apart from salary, represent ordinary and necessary business expenses incurred in that capacity and are, therefore, deductible. The responsibility rests with each professor to show that the amounts claimed are reasonable in relation to the research performed and that the research is in his area of competence; that is, that the research directly relates to the general field in which the professor is performing services as an educator."

The above ruling applies to college faculty members whose duties include research. However, for others in a position where research is not part of their professional responsibilities, deductions may be disallowed. In one case, for example, a high school physics teacher was not permitted to deduct the cost of a trip taken to do research on solar eclipses. The Court held that he failed to show that this research was related to his job of teaching high school physics. [Feldman, TC Memo 1967-91]

If a professor's research leads to profit such as the writing of a book, then of course he may not take a double deduction for his expenses. That is, he cannot deduct his expenses under this chapter on Schedule A and also deduct the same expenses on Schedule C as business expenses incurred in the production of his book.

What Research Expenses Are Deductible?

(a) Travel. As the above ruling expressly states, you may deduct travel costs connected with your research activities. The rules governing travel expenses described in the *Travel* chapter apply here. Thus, you may deduct not only the cost of transportation, but also the cost of meals, lodging, and laundry while away from home overnight.

Example: Sabbatical to Do Research

Jones is a Professor of Art History at a major university in California. He is one of the world's leading experts on the history of Albanian lithography. Jones spends his sabbatical year at Princeton and returns home after the year is over. During his absence, he rents out his California home. While at Princeton, he does research in the history of Modern Albanian lithography and uses Princeton's spe-

> cial collection of Albanian lithographs. He also collaborates with several other scholars in his field who are on the Princeton faculty.
>
> Jones is entitled to deduct travel expenses connected with his sabbatical at Princeton. This includes not only his transportation costs between California and New Jersey, but also such living expenses as meals, lodging, laundry, and commuting costs while away from California. The same deduction and recordkeeping rules apply as for any type of travel expense. See the *Travel* chapter for details, including Section 3 which contains examples of teachers at a temporary position away from home.

(b) Home Office or Laboratory. If you use a home office or laboratory for research, or other professional duties, check the *Home Office* chapter. You might be able to deduct a portion of your house expenses such as rent, depreciation, utilities, etc.

(c) Books, Equipment, and Supplies.

(d) Publication Costs. You can deduct expenses incurred in getting material published. This is confirmed by a Tax Court case concerning a research associate. He had a number of articles published in scientific journals at no cost to himself. But he wrote one paper he couldn't get published, apparently because it criticized work by another prominent researcher. So the research associate published the work himself at a cost of $1,400 for 1,000 copies.

The IRS refused to allow a deduction for the $1,400 spent on publishing the paper. It argued that since research papers are customarily published at no expense to the author, the cost involved in publishing the paper himself was not an "ordinary and necessary" business expense.

However, the Court allowed the deduction, calling the IRS reasoning too narrow. It stated,

> "We are satisfied that petitioner's employer expected (although it did not require) its research associates to communicate the results of their research. To be sure, petitioner's employer anticipated that such communication would be accomplished through publication in scientific journals without cost to the author. However, the facts herein indicate, albeit not with crystal clarity, that with respect to the particular article in question, the normal channel of communication was not available to petitioner because the article contained critical comment of a person who was in a position to control its acceptance for publication. Such being the case, petitioner's only viable alternative to discharge his reasonably perceived responsibility to disseminate the results of his work was to finance personally the publication thereof. In this respect, he was in a position not unlike the handicapped person who, because of his handicap, is required to incur an expense which nonhandicapped persons similarly situated would not customarily incur."

However, the Court did not allow a deduction for the cost of mailing a different paper to experts in his field because he could have had his employer pay for these mailing costs. An employee is not entitled to deduct expenses for which he could have been reimbursed by his employer. [77,199 P-H Memo TC]

(e) Miscellaneous Others. Be on the alert for other deductible expenses you incur in connection with your research activities such as telephone calls, clerical help, special laboratory apparel, etc.

> *Example*
>
> Rottman is a Professor of American History at a university in Washington, D.C. He is the author of a number of books and papers on recent American history. Rottman teaches in the mornings and spends many of his afternoons doing research at the Library of Congress and the Smithsonian Institution. He also spends time tape-recording interviews with ex-government officials in connection with his research. He has an office at home which he uses for his book writing activities.
>
> Rottman can deduct the expenses he incurs in connection with his research activities. This may include travel expenses, home office expenses, and incidental costs for such things as photocopying, tapes, supplies, etc. He also may be able to claim deductions for his tape recorder, typewriter, home office furniture, etc. (cf. the *Travel*, *Home Office*, and *Depreciation* chapters).
>
> There is another item which Rottman can deduct. He can pay his children or spouse for assisting him in his research (e.g., transcribing tapes, typing, filing, etc.). This then becomes a deductible business expense as discussed in the next subsection.

Paying Your Children or Spouse for Assistance

Suppose your children assist you with your research activities. Perhaps they perform clerical work, clean laboratory equipment, help you conduct a survey, etc. If you had paid another person for these services, then you would have been able to deduct their salaries as a business expense. Under these circumstances, you can pay your children a reasonable salary and deduct this amount as a business expense. This will lower the overall tax bill since your children are in a lower (often zero) tax bracket.

Similarly, you can pay your spouse for assistance in your research activities. This will not bring the payments into a lower bracket but may still lower the overall tax due because of the effects of the IRA deduction, the child care tax credit, the social security tax, and the ability to set up a tax-deductible medical plan for your family. [Cf. Section 3 of the *Outside Business Activity* chapter.]

Where Do You Deduct Your Research Expenses?

Research expenses are treated the same as other business expenses. Employees report their unreimbursed job-related expenses on Form 2106. These expenses then become a miscellaneous deduction on Schedule A which, when combined with other miscellaneous deductions, is subject to a 2% of Adjusted Gross Income floor [cf. the *Miscellaneous Deductions* chapter]. Self-employed individuals report all their income and expenses on Schedule C. You should attach a statement to your return which reflects the amounts you spent in each category of expense, e.g., clerical help, supplies, etc. In addition, you should comply with the various requirements for reporting travel expenses, home office expenses, books, equipment, auto expenses, etc., as discussed in earlier chapters.

SECTION 2:
RESEARCH TAX CREDIT

There is a special tax credit designed to encourage research and experimentation. This credit is generally equal to 20% of the increase in research and experimentation costs for 1987 over the average expenses incurred during 1984–1986.

What Kind of Research Expenses Qualify for the Credit?

The **research tax credit** is meant to apply to research and experimentation *"performed in a field of laboratory science (such as physics or biochemistry), engineering or technology."* The research must be undertaken for the purpose of discovering information that is technological in nature. It must relate to a new or improved function, performance, reliability, or quality; research relating to style, taste, cosmetic, or seasonal design factors does not qualify.

Specifically excluded is research in connection with literary, historical, or similar projects. Also excluded is research in the social sciences (including economics, business management, and behavioral sciences), arts, or humanities.

The credit applies to costs for the development or improvement of a pilot model, product, formula, invention, or similar property. It does not apply to the cost of management or consumer surveys, routine improvements of existing products, production planning, engineering follow-through during production, or routine data collection.

The costs of developing new or significantly improved computer software can qualify for the credit. The software should relate to research or production that is technological in nature. Software for bookkeeping, payroll, personnel management, etc. does not qualify. Also, the software should be innovative, involve significant economic risk, and not be commercially available from an outside source.

The following expenses qualify for the credit: (i) wages or self-employment earned income, (ii) supplies used in the conduct of the research, and (iii) payments for computer time.

Land or property of a character subject to the allowance for depreciation does not qualify. Also excluded are the costs of activities indirectly connected with the research such as bookkeeping, quality control, market testing, routine data collection, etc., and expenses for research conducted outside the U.S.

Who Can Claim the Research Credit?

The credit can only be claimed by the taxpayer on whose behalf the research is conducted. It cannot be claimed by an individual for research activities performed for another party, whether *"funded by any grant, contract, or otherwise."* This would apparently rule out the credit for expenses incurred by an employee conducting research in connection with his job. (But if substantial rights in the research are retained by the taxpayer, expenses qualify for the credit except to the extent the taxpayer is entitled to payment for performing the research.)

However, research expenses connected with an outside activity would qualify. The activity must be an ongoing business activity undertaken with the aim of making a profit, rather than just a hobby [cf. the *Outside Business Activity* chapter]. For example, research expenses connected with inventing a new or improved product would qualify as long as the aim is to make money by bringing the product to market. The research must be performed in connection with an existing business. Expenses paid to develop a product the sale of which would constitute a new trade or business don't qualify for the credit.

A taxpayer can also deduct the cost of qualified research expenses he contracts with another party to perform on his behalf for business purposes. In this case, 35% of the cost of the contract is deemed to be overhead not qualifying for the credit.

How Is the Credit Computed?

The 20% credit is applied to the increase in qualifying research expenses for 1987 over the average annual amount of qualifying research expenses incurred during the preceding 3 years. However, in no event can the credit amount to more than 10% of the qualifying research expenses for 1987. Also, the research tax credit cannot generate a negative tax result for a given business activity. That is, the credit cannot exceed the extra tax produced by including the net income from the business activity in taxable income. The research tax credit is claimed on Form 6765.

Chapter 30

Alternative Minimum Tax

Under our basic tax system, individuals are entitled to reduce their taxable income by using various deductions, credits, exclusions, etc. which apply. A consequence of this system is that some wealthy individuals with high incomes can wind up paying little or no income tax. In fact, newspapers have periodically run stories on the number of people with income over $1,000,000 who legally pay no tax whatever.

Congress has been sensitive to this issue. Many taxpayers have been displeased with a system under which they paid sizable chunks of their earnings in taxes while some millionaires paid nothing. To remedy this situation, Congress added an extremely complex provision, the *alternative minimum tax,* as part of the 1986 Tax Reform Act.

Most people can simply ignore this provision. It is aimed only at those with an unusually large amount of tax writeoffs or shelters. In fact, individuals with less than $40,000 in deductions, exemptions, and tax losses are automatically excused from this provision.

In more detail, if you need to check that the alternative minimum tax does not apply to you, first add up your minimum tax *preferences* and *adjustments*. These include:

1. State and local taxes deducted on Schedule A.

2. Personal exemptions.

3. Miscellaneous deductions exceeding 2% of your adjusted gross income.

4. Your medical expense deduction on Schedule A (after the 7.5% subtraction) up to a maximum of 2.5% of your adjusted gross income.

5. Your deduction on Schedule A for property given to charity to the extent it exceeds what you paid for the property.

6. Tax-exempt interest on private activity bonds issued after August 7, 1986.

7. The "bargain element" of certain incentive stock options when exercised by an employee.

8. Interest you were able to deduct in computing your regular tax solely because of the phase-in rules described in the *Interest* chapter.

9. Interest on a mortgage loan on your primary or second residence which was refinanced after August 16, 1986, to the extent the new loan amount exceeds the existing mortgage, except for amounts used to acquire, construct, or substantially rehabilitate the underlying property.

10. Certain excess subtractions from taxable income produced by tax-shelter type investments in oil, gas, minerals, farming, real estate, etc.
11. A portion of your deduction for depreciation that is considered *excessively accelerated*.
12. Deferred amounts resulting from installment sales of either (i) real estate used in a trade or business, or (ii) rental real estate when the sales price exceeds $150,000.

You are exempt from the alternative minimum tax if the total of the above items on a joint tax return is both:

(1). less than $40,000 + 1/3 of your regular taxable income
and
(2). less than $77,000.

If you are not exempt from the alternative minimum tax, you need to seek professional assistance. Essentially what happens is that the sum of your regular taxable income plus the above items is subject to a flat 21% tax, replacing the income tax computed in the regular way.

However, tax computations and planning become quite complex when the alternative minimum tax is involved. The above is only a brief sketch of the actual rules designed to alert those with unusually large deductions, exclusions, etc. to the existence of the alternative minimum tax.

An individual may be ensnared by the alternative minimum tax because of an unusual situation in only one year. If so, the tax result may not be so bad. It may be possible to recapture the extra tax on later years' tax returns by use of a special tax credit that applies in this situation.

APPENDIX
Sample Tax Return

The following sample tax return is intended to illustrate the full spectrum of professional deductions. It is not meant to represent a "typical" tax return.

402

Form 1040 U.S. Individual Income Tax Return 1987
Department of the Treasury—Internal Revenue Service

For the year Jan.–Dec. 31, 1987, or other tax year beginning , 1987, ending , 19   OMB No. 1545-0074

Label (Use IRS label. Otherwise, please print or type.)

Your first name and initial (if joint return, also give spouse's name and initial): **TERRY A. & PAT B.**   Last name: **JONES**
Your social security number: **111 22 3333**

Present home address (number and street or rural route): **1234 STEEL PLACE**
Spouse's social security number: **444 55 6666**

City, town or post office, state, and ZIP code: **PITTSBURGH, PA 15219**

Presidential Election Campaign
Do you want $1 to go to this fund? Yes [ ] No [X]
If joint return, does your spouse want $1 to go to this fund? Yes [X] No [ ]

Note: Checking "Yes" will not change your tax or reduce your refund.

Filing Status (Check only one box.)
1. [ ] Single
2. [X] Married filing joint return (even if only one had income)
3. [ ] Married filing separate return. Enter spouse's social security no. above and full name here.
4. [ ] Head of household (with qualifying person). (See page 7 of Instructions.) If the qualifying person is your child but not your dependent, enter child's name here.
5. [ ] Qualifying widow(er) with dependent child (year spouse died ▶ 19). (See page 7 of Instructions.)

Exemptions (See Instructions on page 7.)
Caution: If you can be claimed as a dependent on another person's tax return (such as your parents' return), do not check box 6a. But be sure to check the box on line 32b on page 2.

6a [X] Yourself   6b [X] Spouse
No. of boxes checked on 6a and 6b ▶ **2**

c Dependents:

(1) Name (first, initial, and last name)	(2) Check if under age 5	(3) If age 5 or over, dependent's social security number	(4) Relationship	(5) No. of months lived in your home in 1987
SUSAN C. JONES		123 45 6789	DAUGHTER	12
HOWARD S. JONES		APPLIED FOR	SON	12

No. of children on 6c who lived with you ▶ **2**
No. of children on 6c who didn't live with you due to divorce or separation: **0**
No. of parents listed on 6c: **0**
No. of other dependents listed on 6c: **0**

If more than 7 dependents, see Instructions on page 7.

d If your child didn't live with you but is claimed as your dependent under a pre-1985 agreement, check here ▶ [ ]
e Total number of exemptions claimed (also complete line 35)
Add numbers entered in boxes above ▶ **4**

Income
Please attach Copy B of your Forms W-2, W-2G, and W-2P here.
If you do not have a W-2, see page 6 of Instructions.

7 Wages, salaries, tips, etc. (attach Form(s) W-2) 7 **50,120**
8 Taxable interest income (also attach Schedule B if over $400) 8 **631**
9 Tax-exempt interest income (see page 10). DON'T include on line 8 | 9 | **2,433** |
10 Dividend income (also attach Schedule B if over $400) 10 **532**
11 Taxable refunds of state and local income taxes, if any, from worksheet on page 11 of Instructions .. 11 **48**
12 Alimony received 12
13 Business income or (loss) (attach Schedule C) 13 **2417**
14 Capital gain or (loss) (attach Schedule D) .... 14 **(2681)**
15 Other gains or (losses) (attach Form 4797) 15
16a Pensions, IRA distributions, annuities, and rollovers. Total received | 16a |
  b Taxable amount (see page 11) 16b
17 Rents, royalties, partnerships, estates, trusts, etc. (attach Schedule E) .. 17
18 Farm income or (loss) (attach Schedule F) 18
19 Unemployment compensation (insurance) (see page 11) 19
20a Social security benefits (see page 12) | 20a |
  b Taxable amount, if any, from the worksheet on page 12 ...... 20b
21 Other income (list type and amount—see page 12) _____ 21
22 Add the amounts shown in the far right column for lines 7, 8, and 10–21. This is your **total income** ▶ 22 **51,067**

Please attach check or money order here.

Adjustments to Income
(See Instructions on page 12.)

23 Reimbursed employee business expenses from Form 2106 .. 23
24a Your IRA deduction, from applicable worksheet on page 13 or 14   24a **270**
  b Spouse's IRA deduction, from applicable worksheet on page 13 or 14 .. 24b
25 Self-employed health insurance deduction, from worksheet on page 14 . 25
26 Keogh retirement plan and self-employed SEP deduction **D.B.** 26 **2417**
27 Penalty on early withdrawal of savings 27
28 Alimony paid (recipient's last name _____ and social security no. _____) . 28
29 Add lines 23 through 28. These are your **total adjustments** .... ▶ 29 **2,687**

Adjusted Gross Income
30 Subtract line 29 from line 22. This is your **adjusted gross income**. If this line is less than $15,432 and a child lived with you, see "Earned Income Credit" (line 56) on page 18 of the Instructions. If you want IRS to figure your tax, see page 15 of the Instructions .. ▶ 30 **48,380**

Form 1040 (1987) — Page 2

403

Tax Computation

31	Amount from line 30 (adjusted gross income)	31	48,380
32a	Check if: ☐ You were 65 or over ☐ Blind; ☐ Spouse was 65 or over ☐ Blind. Add the number of boxes checked and enter the total here ▶	32a	
b	If you can be claimed as a dependent on another person's return, check here ▶	32b	☐
c	If you are married filing a separate return and your spouse itemizes deductions, or you are a dual-status alien, see page 15 and check here ▶	32c	☐
33a	Itemized deductions. See page 15 to see if you should itemize. If you don't itemize, enter zero. If you do itemize, attach Schedule A, enter the amount from Schedule A, line 26, AND skip line 33b	33a	21,313
b	Standard deduction. Read Caution to left. If it applies, see page 16 for the amount to enter. If Caution doesn't apply and your filing status from page 1 is: { Single or Head of household, enter $2,540; Married filing jointly or Qualifying widow(er), enter $3,760; Married filing separately, enter $1,880 }	33b	
34	Subtract line 33a or 33b, whichever applies, from line 31. Enter the result here	34	27,067
35	Multiply $1,900 by the total number of exemptions claimed on line 6e or see chart on page 16	35	7,600
36	Taxable income. Subtract line 35 from line 34. Enter the result (but not less than zero). Caution: If under age 14 and you have more than $1,000 of investment income, check here ▶ ☐ and see page 16 to see if you have to use Form 8615 to figure your tax.	36	19,467
37	Enter tax. Check if from ☒ Tax Table, ☐ Tax Rate Schedules, ☐ Schedule D, or ☐ Form 8615	37	2,801
38	Additional taxes (see page 16). Check if from ☐ Form 4970 or ☐ Form 4972	38	
39	Add lines 37 and 38. Enter the total ▶	39	2,801

Caution: If you checked any box on line 32a, b, or c and you don't itemize, see page 16 for the amount to enter on line 33b.

Credits
(See Instructions on page 17.)

40	Credit for child and dependent care expenses (attach Form 2441)	40	547	
41	Credit for the elderly or for the permanently and totally disabled (attach Schedule R)	41		
42	Add lines 40 and 41. Enter the total		42	547
43	Subtract line 42 from line 39. Enter the result (but not less than zero)		43	2,254
44	Foreign tax credit (attach Form 1116)	44		
45	General business credit. Check if from ☐ Form 3800, ☐ Form 3468, ☐ Form 5884, ☐ Form 6478, ☐ Form 6765, or ☐ Form 8586	45		
46	Add lines 44 and 45. Enter the total		46	
47	Subtract line 46 from line 43. Enter the result (but not less than zero) ▶		47	2,254

Other Taxes
(Including Advance EIC Payments)

48	Self-employment tax (attach Schedule SE)	48	
49	Alternative minimum tax (attach Form 6251)	49	
50	Tax from recapture of investment credit (attach Form 4255)	50	
51	Social security tax on tip income not reported to employer (attach Form 4137)	51	
52	Tax on an IRA or a qualified retirement plan (attach Form 5329)	52	
53	Add lines 47 through 52. This is your total tax ▶	53	

Payments
Attach Forms W-2, W-2G, and W-2P to front.

54	Federal income tax withheld (including tax shown on Form(s) 1099)	54	3161	
55	1987 estimated tax payments and amount applied from 1986 return	55		
56	Earned income credit (see page 18)	56		
57	Amount paid with Form 4868 (extension request)	57		
58	Excess social security tax and RRTA tax withheld (see page 19)	58		
59	Credit for Federal tax on gasoline and special fuels (attach Form 4136)	59		
60	Regulated investment company credit (attach Form 2439)	60		
61	Add lines 54 through 60. These are your total payments ▶		61	3,161

Refund or Amount You Owe

62	If line 61 is larger than line 53, enter amount OVERPAID ▶	62	907
63	Amount of line 62 to be REFUNDED TO YOU ▶	63	907
64	Amount of line 62 to be applied to your 1988 estimated tax ▶	64	
65	If line 53 is larger than line 61, enter AMOUNT YOU OWE. Attach check or money order for full amount payable to "Internal Revenue Service." Write your social security number, daytime phone number, and "1987 Form 1040" on it. Check ▶ ☐ if Form 2210 (2210F) is attached. See page 20. Penalty: $	65	

Please Sign Here

Under penalties of perjury, I declare that I have examined this return and accompanying schedules and statements, and to the best of my knowledge and belief, they are true, correct, and complete. Declaration of preparer (other than taxpayer) is based on all information of which preparer has any knowledge.

Your signature	Date	Your occupation
Terry A. Jones	4/9/88	TEACHER
Spouse's signature (if joint return, BOTH must sign)	Date	Spouse's occupation
Pat B. Jones	4/9/88	STUDENT

Paid Preparer's Use Only

Preparer's signature		Date	Check if self-employed ☐	Preparer's social security no.
Firm's name (or yours if self-employed) and address			E.I. No.	
			ZIP code	

SCHEDULES A&B (Form 1040)
Department of the Treasury
Internal Revenue Service

Schedule A—Itemized Deductions
(Schedule B is on back)
▶ Attach to Form 1040. ▶ See Instructions for Schedules A and B (Form 1040).

OMB No. 1545-0074
1987
Attachment Sequence No. 07

Name(s) as shown on Form 1040: TERRY A. & PAT B. JONES
Your social security number: 111 22 3333

Medical and Dental Expenses
(Do not include expenses reimbursed or paid by others.)
(See Instructions on page 21.)

- 1a Prescription medicines and drugs, insulin, doctors, dentists, nurses, hospitals, insurance premiums you paid for medical and dental care, etc. — **1a** 2942
- b Transportation and lodging — **1b** 71
- c Other (list—include hearing aids, dentures, eyeglasses, etc.) ▶ EYEGLASSES, MEDICAL PART OF TUITION, BIRTH CONTROL ITEMS, RENTAL OF HOSPITAL BED — **1c** 963
- 2 Add lines 1a through 1c, and enter the total here — **2** 3976
- 3 Multiply the amount on Form 1040, line 31, by 7.5% (.075) — **3** 3629
- 4 Subtract line 3 from line 2. If zero or less, enter -0-. Total medical and dental ▶ **4** 347

Taxes You Paid
(See Instructions on page 22.)

Note: Sales taxes are no longer deductible.
- 5 State and local income taxes — **5** 1480
- 6 Real estate taxes — **6** 938
- 7 Other taxes (list—include personal property taxes) ▶ — **7**
- 8 Add the amounts on lines 5 through 7. Enter the total here. Total taxes ▶ **8** 2418

Interest You Paid
(See Instructions on page 22.)

Note: If you borrowed any new amounts against your home after 8/16/86 and at any time in 1987 the total of all your mortgage debts was more than what you paid for your home plus improvements, attach Form 8598 and check here ▶ ☐
- 9a Deductible home mortgage interest you paid to financial institutions (report deductible points on line 10) — **9a** 6080
- b Deductible home mortgage interest you paid to individuals (show that person's name and address) ▶ — **9b**
- 10 Deductible points — **10**
- 11 Deductible investment interest — **11** 234
- 12a Personal interest you paid (see page 22) **12a** 611
- b Multiply the amount on line 12a by 65% (.65). Enter the result — **12b** 397
- 13 Add the amounts on lines 9a through 11, and 12b. Enter the total here. Total interest ▶ **13** 6711

Contributions You Made
(See Instructions on page 23.)

- 14a Cash contributions. (If you gave $3,000 or more to any one organization, report those contributions on line 14b.) — **14a** 780
- b Cash contributions totaling $3,000 or more to any one organization. (Show to whom you gave and how much you gave.) ▶ — **14b**
- 15 Other than cash. (You must attach Form 8283 if over $500.) — **15** 471
- 16 Carryover from prior year — **16**
- 17 Add the amounts on lines 14a through 16. Enter the total here. Total contributions ▶ **17** 1251

Casualty and Theft Losses
- 18 Casualty or theft loss(es) (attach Form 4684). (See page 23 of the Instructions.) ▶ **18**

Moving Expenses
- 19 Moving expenses (attach Form 3903 or 3903F). (See page 24 of the Instructions.) ▶ **19** 3788

Miscellaneous Deductions Subject to 2% AGI Limit
(See Instructions on page 24.)

- 20 Unreimbursed employee business expenses (attach Form 2106) — **20** 7453
- 21 Other expenses (list type and amount) ▶ TAX GUIDE, IRA FEE, SAFE DEP. BOX, INVESTMENT PUBLICATIONS & POSTAGE — **21** 313
- 22 Add the amounts on lines 20 and 21. Enter the total — **22** 7766
- 23 Multiply the amount on Form 1040, line 31, by 2% (.02). Enter the result — **23** 968
- 24 Subtract line 23 from line 22. Enter the result (but not less than zero) ▶ **24** 6798

Other Miscellaneous Deductions
- 25 Miscellaneous deductions not subject to 2% AGI limit (see page 24). (List type and amount.) ▶ — **25**

Total Itemized Deductions
- 26 Add the amounts on lines 4, 8, 13, 17, 18, 19, 24, and 25. Enter the total here and on Form 1040, line 33a ▶ **26** 21,313

For Paperwork Reduction Act Notice, see Form 1040 Instructions.
Schedule A (Form 1040) 1987

Schedules A&B (Form 1040) 1987 — OMB No. 1545-0074 — Page **2**

Name(s) as shown on Form 1040. (Do not enter name and social security number if shown on other side.) — Your social security number

Schedule B—Interest and Dividend Income
Attachment Sequence No. **08**

Part I — Interest Income
(See Instructions on pages 9 and 24.)

Also complete Part III.

Note: If you received a Form 1099–INT or Form 1099–OID from a brokerage firm, enter the firm's name and the total interest shown on that form.

If you received more than $400 in taxable interest income, you must complete Part I and list ALL interest received. If you received, as a nominee, interest that actually belongs to another person, or you received or paid accrued interest on securities transferred between interest payment dates, see page 24.

Interest Income		Amount
1 Interest income from seller-financed mortgages. (See Instructions and list name of payer.) ▶	1	
2 Other interest income (list name of payer) ▶		
CITIZENS S&L		315
FIRST NATIONAL BANK		12
CREDIT UNION		124
ALABAMA P.&L. BONDS	2	180
3 Add the amounts on lines 1 and 2. Enter the total here and on Form 1040, line 8. ▶	3	631

Part II — Dividend Income
(See Instructions on pages 10 and 25.)

Also complete Part III.

Note: If you received a Form 1099–DIV from a brokerage firm, enter the firm's name and the total dividends shown on that form.

If you received more than $400 in gross dividends and/or other distributions on stock, complete Part II. If you received, as a nominee, dividends that actually belong to another person, see page 25.

Dividend Income		Amount
4 Dividend income (list name of payer—include on this line capital gain distributions, nontaxable distributions, etc.) ▶		
A.T.&T.		160
VANGUARD MONEY MARKET TRUST	4	372
5 Add the amounts on line 4. Enter the total here	5	532
6 Capital gain distributions. Enter here and on line 13, Schedule D.*	6	
7 Nontaxable distributions. (See Schedule D Instructions for adjustment to basis.)	7	
8 Add the amounts on lines 6 and 7. Enter the total here	8	
9 Subtract line 8 from line 5. Enter the result here and on Form 1040, line 10 ▶	9	532

*If you received capital gain distributions but do not need Schedule D to report any other gains or losses or to figure your tax (see the **Tax Tip** under **Capital gain distributions** on page 10), enter your capital gain distributions on Form 1040, line 14. Write "CGD" on the dotted line to the left of line 14.

Part III — Foreign Accounts and Foreign Trusts
(See Instructions on page 25.)

If you received more than $400 of interest or dividends, OR if you had a foreign account or were a grantor of, or a transferor to, a foreign trust, you must answer both questions in Part III.

	Yes	No
10 At any time during the tax year, did you have an interest in or a signature or other authority over a financial account in a foreign country (such as a bank account, securities account, or other financial account)? (See page 25 of the Instructions for exceptions and filing requirements for Form TD F 90-22.1.)		X
If "Yes," enter the name of the foreign country ▶		
11 Were you the grantor of, or transferor to, a foreign trust which existed during the current tax year, whether or not you have any beneficial interest in it? If "Yes," you may have to file Forms 3520, 3520-A, or 926.		X

For Paperwork Reduction Act Notice, see Form 1040 Instructions. — Schedule B (Form 1040) 1987

SCHEDULE C (Form 1040)

Profit or (Loss) From Business or Profession
(Sole Proprietorship)
Partnerships, Joint Ventures, etc., Must File Form 1065.
▶ Attach to Form 1040, Form 1041, or Form 1041S. ▶ See Instructions for Schedule C (Form 1040).

Department of the Treasury
Internal Revenue Service

OMB No. 1545-0074

1987

Attachment Sequence No. 09

Name of proprietor	Social security number (SSN)
TERRY A. JONES	111 22 3333

A Principal business or profession, including product or service (see Instructions)
CONSULTING

B Principal business code (from Part IV) ▶

C Business name and address ▶

D Employer ID number (Not SSN)

E Method(s) used to value closing inventory:
(1) ☐ Cost (2) ☐ Lower of cost or market (3) ☐ Other (attach explanation)

F Accounting method: (1) ☒ Cash (2) ☐ Accrual (3) ☐ Other (specify) ▶

		Yes	No
G	Was there any change in determining quantities, costs, or valuations between opening and closing inventory? (If "Yes," attach explanation.)		X
H	Are you deducting expenses for an office in your home?		X
I	Did you file Form 941 for this business for any quarter in 1987?		X
J	Did you "materially participate" in the operation of this business during 1987? (If "No," see Instructions for limitations on losses.)	X	
K	Was this business in operation at the end of 1987?	X	
L	How many months was this business in operation during 1987? ▶ 12		

M If this schedule includes a loss, credit, deduction, income, or other tax benefit relating to a tax shelter required to be registered, check here. ▶ ☐
If you check this box, you MUST attach Form 8271.

Part I Income

1a	Gross receipts or sales	1a	10,540
b	Less: Returns and allowances	1b	
c	Subtract line 1b from line 1a and enter the balance here	1c	10,540
2	Cost of goods sold and/or operations (from Part III, line 8)	2	
3	Subtract line 2 from line 1c and enter the gross profit here	3	10,540
4	Other income (including windfall profit tax credit or refund received in 1987)	4	
5	Add lines 3 and 4. This is the gross income ▶	5	10,540

Part II Deductions

6 Advertising	23 Repairs	
7 Bad debts from sales or services (see Instructions)	24 Supplies (not included in Part III)	284
8 Bank service charges 41	25 Taxes	
9 Car and truck expenses	26 Travel, meals, and entertainment:	
10 Commissions	a Travel	
11 Depletion	b Total meals and entertainment 320	
12 Depreciation and section 179 deduction from Form 4562 (not included in Part III) 3,362	c Enter 20% of line 26b subject to limitations (see Instructions) 64	
13 Dues and publications 411	d Subtract line 26c from 26b	256
14 Employee benefit programs	27 Utilities and telephone	321
15 Freight (not included in Part III)	28a Wages	
16 Insurance	b Jobs credit	
17 Interest:	c Subtract line 28b from 28a	
a Mortgage (paid to financial institutions)	29 Other expenses (list type and amount):	
b Other 312	Photocopying 32	
18 Laundry and cleaning		
19 Legal and professional services 320		
20 Office expense 2,784		
21 Pension and profit-sharing plans		
22 Rent on business property		32

30	Add amounts in columns for lines 6 through 29. These are the total deductions ▶	30	8,123
31	Net profit or (loss). Subtract line 30 from line 5. If a profit, enter here and on Form 1040, line 13, and on Schedule SE, line 2 (or line 5 of Form 1041 or Form 1041S). If a loss, you MUST go on to line 32	31	2,417

32 If you have a loss, you MUST answer this question: "Do you have amounts for which you are not at risk in this business?" (See Instructions.) ☐ Yes ☐ No
If "Yes," you MUST attach Form 6198. If "No," enter the loss on Form 1040, line 13, and on Schedule SE, line 2 (or line 5 of Form 1041 or Form 1041S).

For Paperwork Reduction Act Notice, see Form 1040 Instructions.

Schedule C (Form 1040) 1987

SCHEDULE D
(Form 1040)
Department of the Treasury
Internal Revenue Service

Capital Gains and Losses and Reconciliation of Forms 1099-B
▶ Attach to Form 1040. ▶ See Instructions for Schedule D (Form 1040).
For Paperwork Reduction Act Notice, see Form 1040 Instructions.

OMB No. 1545-0074
1987
Attachment Sequence No. **12**

Name(s) as shown on Form 1040: TERRY A. & PAT B. JONES

Your social security number: 111 : 22 : 3333

1. Report here, the total sales of stocks, bonds, etc., reported for 1987 by your broker to you on Form(s) 1099-B or an equivalent substitute statement(s). If this amount differs from the total of lines 2b and 9b, column (d), attach a statement explaining the difference. See the Instructions for line 1 for examples. Do not include real estate transactions reported to you on a Form 1099-B on line 1, 2a, or 9a . . . . 1 | 24,002

Part I — Short-term Capital Gains and Losses—Assets Held Six Months or Less

(a) Description of property (Example, 100 shares 7% preferred of "Z" Co.)	(b) Date acquired (Mo., day, yr.)	(c) Date sold (Mo., day, yr.)	(d) Sales price (see Instructions)	(e) Cost or other basis (see Instructions)	(f) LOSS If (e) is more than (d), subtract (d) from (e)	(g) GAIN If (d) is more than (e), subtract (e) from (d)
2a Form 1099-B Transactions (Sales of Stocks, Bonds, etc.): (Do not report real estate transactions here. See the instructions for lines 2a and 9a.)						
100 SH. ABC	12/20/86	5/4/87	5830	4665		1165
300 SH. DEF	10/15/87	10/19/87	6132	9464	3332	

2b Total (add column (d)) . . . ▶ 11,962
2c Other Transactions:

3. Short-term gain from sale or exchange of a principal residence from Form 2119, lines 8 or 14 . . . 3
4. Short-term gain from installment sales from Form 6252, lines 23 or 31 . . . 4
5. Net short-term gain or (loss) from partnerships, S corporations, and fiduciaries . 5
6. Short-term capital loss carryover 6
7. Add all of the transactions on lines 2a and 2c and lines 3 through 6 in columns (f) and (g) . . . 7 (3332) | 1165
8. Net short-term gain or (loss), combine columns (f) and (g) of line 7 . . . . 8 (2167)

Part II — Long-term Capital Gains and Losses—Assets Held More Than Six Months

9a Form 1099-B Transactions (Sales of Stocks, Bonds, etc.): (Do not report real estate transactions here. See the instructions for lines 2a and 9a.)

| 200 SH. XYZ | 2/16/87 | 11/2/87 | 4926 | 5711 | 785 | |
| 400 SH. QRS | 3/4/82 | 10/1/87 | 7114 | 6843 | | 271 |

9b Total (add column (d)) . . . ▶ 12,040
9c Other Transactions:

10. Long-term gain from sale or exchange of a principal residence from Form 2119, lines 8, 10, or 14 . 10
11. Long-term gain from installment sales from Form 6252, lines 23 or 31 11
12. Net long-term gain or (loss) from partnerships, S corporations, and fiduciaries . 12
13. Capital gain distributions 13
14. Enter gain from Form 4797, line 7 or 9 14
15. Long-term capital loss carryover 15
16. Add all of the transactions on lines 9a and 9c and lines 10 through 15 in columns (f) and (g) . . 16 (785) | 271
17. Net long-term gain or (loss), combine columns (f) and (g) of line 16 . . . . 17 (514)

Schedule D (Form 1040) 1987

Schedule D (Form 1040) 1987 — Attachment Sequence No. 12 — Page **2**
Name(s) as shown on Form 1040. (Do not enter name and social security number if shown on other side.)
Your social security number

Part III — Summary of Parts I and II

18. Combine lines 8 and 17, and enter the net gain or (loss) here. If result is a gain, also enter the gain on Form 1040, line 14 . . . . 18 (2681)
    Note: If lines 17 and 18 are net gains and your taxable income is taxed over the 28% tax rate, see Part IV below. You may be able to reduce your tax if you qualify for the alternative tax computation.

19. If line 18 is a loss, enter here and as a loss on Form 1040, line 14, the **smaller** of:
    a The amount on line 18; or b $3,000 ($1,500 if married filing a separate return) 19 (2681)

Form **2106**	**Employee Business Expenses**	OMB No. 1545-0139
Department of the Treasury Internal Revenue Service	► See separate instructions. ► Attach to Form 1040.	**1987** Attachment Sequence No. **54**

Your name	Social security number	Occupation in which expenses were incurred
TERRY A. JONES	111 22 3333	TEACHER

Part I — Employee Business Expenses

STEP 1 Enter Your Expenses

	Column A Other than Meals and Entertainment	Column B Meals and Entertainment
1 Vehicle expense from Part II, line 15 or line 22 . . . . **1**	425	
2 Parking fees, tolls, and local transportation, including train, bus, etc. . . **2**	39	
3 Travel expense while away from home, including lodging, airplane, car rental, etc. **Do not** include meals and entertainment **3**	3465	
4 Business expenses not included in lines 1 through 3. **Do not** include meals and entertainment **4**	2391	
5 Meals and entertainment expenses. See Instructions **5**		1416
6 Add lines 1 through 5 and enter the **total expenses** here **6**	6320	1416

Note: *If you were not reimbursed for any expenses in step 1, skip lines 7 through 13 and enter the amount from line 6 on line 14.*

STEP 2 Figure Any Excess Reimbursements To Report in Income

7 Reimbursements for the expenses listed in step 1 that your employer did **not** report to you on Form W-2 or Form 1099 . . . . . . **7**		
Note: *If, in **both columns**, line 6 is more than line 7, skip lines 8 and 9 and go to line 10. You do not have excess reimbursements.*		
8 Subtract line 6 from line 7. If zero or less, enter zero **8**		
9 Add the amounts on line 8 of both columns and enter the total here. Also add this amount to any amount shown on Form 1040, line 7. This is an **excess reimbursement** reportable as income . . . . ► **9**		

STEP 3 Figure Fully Deductible Reimbursed Expenses

10 Subtract line 7 from line 6. If zero or less, enter zero **10**		
11 Reimbursements or allowances for the expenses in Step 1 that your employer identified to you, included on Form W-2 or Form 1099, and were not subject to withholding tax **11**		
Note: *The amount entered on line 11 should also have been reported as income on Form 1040.*		
12 Enter the smaller of line 10 or line 11 . . . . **12**		
13 Add the amounts on line 12 of both columns. Enter here and on Form 1040, line 23. This is your **fully deductible reimbursed expenses** . . . . ► **13**		

STEP 4 Figure Expenses To Deduct as an Itemized Deduction on Schedule A (Form 1040)

14 Subtract line 12 from line 10 . . . . **14**	6320	1416
Note: *If **both columns** of line 14 are zero, **do not complete the rest of Part I**.*		
15 Enter 20% (.20) of line 14, Column B **15**		283
16 Subtract line 15 from line 14 . . . . **16**	6320	1133
17 Add the amounts on line 16 of both columns and enter the total here. Also enter the total on Schedule A (Form 1040), line 20. (Qualified Performing Artists and handicapped employees, see instructions.) ► **17**		7453

For Paperwork Reduction Act Notice, see Instructions.   Form **2106** (1987)

Form 2106 (1987) Page 2

Part II — Vehicle Expenses (Use either your actual expenses (Section C) or the standard mileage rate (Section B).)

Section A.—General Information

		Vehicle 1	Vehicle 2
1 Enter the date vehicle was placed in service	1	4 / 3 / 85	/ /
2 Total mileage vehicle was used during 1987	2	12,603 miles	miles
3 Miles included on line 2 that vehicle was used for business	3	1,888 miles	miles
4 Percent of business use (divide line 3 by line 2)	4	15 %	%
5 Average daily round trip commuting distance	5	18 miles	miles
6 Miles included on line 2 that vehicle was used for commuting	6	4,320 miles	miles
7 Other personal mileage (subtract line 6 plus line 3 from line 2)	7	6,395 miles	miles

8 Do you (or your spouse) have another vehicle available for personal purposes? ☒ Yes ☐ No

9 If your employer provided you with a vehicle, is personal use during off duty hours permitted? ☐ Yes ☐ No ☒ Not applicable

10 Do you have evidence to support your deduction? ☒ Yes ☐ No. If yes, is the evidence written? ☒ Yes ☐ No

Section B.—Standard Mileage Rate (Do not use this section unless you own the vehicle.)

11 Enter the smaller of Part II, line 3 or 15,000 miles	11	1,888 miles
12 Subtract line 11 from Part II, line 3	12	miles
13 Multiply line 11 by 22½¢ (.225) (see instructions for a fully depreciated vehicle)	13	425
14 Multiply line 12 by 11¢ (.11)	14	
15 Add lines 13 and 14. Enter total here and on Part I, line 1	15	425

Section C.—Actual Expenses

		Vehicle 1	Vehicle 2
16 Gasoline, oil, repairs, vehicle insurance, etc.	16		
17 Vehicle rentals	17		
18 Value of employer-provided vehicle (applies only if included on Form W-2 at 100% fair rental value, see instructions)	18		
19 Add lines 16 through 18	19		
20 Multiply line 19 by the percentage on Part II, line 4	20		
21 Depreciation from Section D, column (f) (see instructions)	21		
22 Add lines 20 and 21. Enter total here and on Part I, line 1	22		

Section D.—Depreciation of Vehicles
(Depreciation can only be claimed for a vehicle you own. If a vehicle is used 50 percent or less in a trade or business, the Section 179 deduction is not allowed and depreciation must be taken using the straight line method over 5 years. For other limitations, see instructions.)

	Cost or other basis (a)	Basis for depreciation (Business use only—see instructions) (b)	Method of figuring depreciation (c)	Depreciation deduction (d)	Section 179 expense (e)	Total column (d) + column (e) (enter in Section C, line 21) (f)
Vehicle 1						
Vehicle 2						

410

Form **2441**	**Credit for Child and Dependent Care Expenses**	OMB No. 1545-0068
Department of the Treasury Internal Revenue Service	▶ Attach to Form 1040. ▶ See instructions below.	**1987** Attachment Sequence No. **23**

Name(s) as shown on Form 1040	Your social security number
TERRY A. & PAT B. JONES	111 22 3333

Note: *If you paid cash wages of $50 or more in a calendar quarter to an individual for services performed in your home, you must file an employment tax return. Get* **Form 942** *for details.*

1. Enter number of qualifying persons who were cared for in 1987. (See instructions for definition of qualifying persons.) ▶ **1** **2**

2. Enter the amount of **qualified** expenses you incurred and actually paid in 1987 for the care of the qualifying person. (See **What Are Qualified Expenses** in the instructions.) **Do not** enter more than $2,400 ($4,800 if you paid for the care of two or more qualifying persons) **2** **2,734**

3a. You **must** enter your earned income on line 3a. See line 3 instructions for definition of earned income **3a** **52,537**

  b. If you are married, filing a joint return for 1987, you must enter your spouse's earned income on line 3b. (If spouse is a full-time student or is disabled, see the line 3 instructions for amount to enter.) . . **3b** **3,600**

  c. If you are married filing a joint return, compare the amounts on lines 3a and 3b, and enter the **smaller** of the two amounts on line 3c **3c** **3,600**

4. • If you were unmarried at the end of 1987, compare the amounts on lines 2 and 3a, and enter the **smaller** of the two amounts on line 4.
   • If you are married filing a joint return, compare the amounts on lines 2 and 3c, and enter the **smaller** of the two amounts on line 4. **4** **2,734**

5. Enter percentage from table below that applies to the adjusted gross income on Form 1040, line 31. **5** × **.20**

If line 31 is:		Percentage is:	If line 31 is:		Percentage is:
Over—	But not over—		Over—	But not over—	
$0	10,000	30% (.30)	$20,000	22,000	24% (.24)
10,000	12,000	29% (.29)	22,000	24,000	23% (.23)
12,000	14,000	28% (.28)	24,000	26,000	22% (.22)
14,000	16,000	27% (.27)	26,000	28,000	21% (.21)
16,000	18,000	26% (.26)	28,000		20% (.20)
18,000	20,000	25% (.25)			

6. Multiply the amount on line 4 by the percentage shown on line 5, and enter the result **6** **547**

7. Multiply any child and dependent care expenses for 1986 that you paid in 1987 by the percentage that applies to the adjusted gross income on your 1986 Form 1040, line 33, or Form 1040A, line 15. Enter the result. (See line 7 instructions for the required statement.) **7**

8. Add amounts on lines 6 and 7. See the worksheet in the instructions for line 8 for the amount of credit you can claim **8** **547**

General Instructions

Paperwork Reduction Act Notice.—We ask for this information to carry out the Internal Revenue laws of the United States. We need it to ensure that taxpayers are complying with these laws and to allow us to figure and collect the right amount of tax. You are required to give us this information.

What Is the Child and Dependent Care Expenses Credit?

You may be able to take a tax credit for amounts you paid someone to care for your child or other qualifying person so you could work or look for work in 1987. The most the credit may be is $720 for the care of one qualifying person, or $1,440 for the care of two or more qualifying persons.

Additional information.—For more details, please get **Publication 503**, Child and Dependent Care Credit, and Employment Taxes for Household Employers.

Who Is a Qualifying Person?

A qualifying person is:
• Any person under age 15 whom you claim as a dependent (but see the rule for **Children of divorced or separated parents**).

• Your disabled spouse who is mentally or physically unable to care for himself or herself.
• Any disabled person who is mentally or physically unable to care for himself or herself and whom you claim as a dependent, or could claim as a dependent except that he or she had income of $1,900 or more.
Note: *You must have shared the same home with any person you claim as a qualifying person.*

Children of divorced or separated parents.—If you were divorced, legally separated, or lived apart from your spouse during the last 6 months of 1987, you may be able to claim the credit even if your child is not your dependent. If your child is not your dependent, he or she is a qualifying person if **all five** of the following apply:
1. You had custody of the child for the longer period during the year; and
2. The child received over half of his or her support from one or both of the parents; and
3. The child was in the custody of one or both of the parents over half of the year; and
4. The child was under age 15, or was physically or mentally unable to care for himself or herself; and
5. The child is not your dependent because—
  a. As the custodial parent, you have signed **Form 8332**, Release of Claim to Exemption for Child of Divorced or Separated Parents, or a similar statement, agreeing not to claim the child's exemption for 1987; or
  b. You were divorced or separated before 1985 and your divorce decree or written agreement states that the other parent can claim the child's exemption, and the other parent provides at least $600 in child support during the year. **Note:** *This rule does not apply if your decree or agreement was changed after 1984 to specify that the other parent cannot claim the child's exemption.*

Who May Take the Credit?

To claim the credit, **all five** of the following must apply:
1. You paid for the care so you (and your spouse if you were married) could work or look for work (but see the rules at the line 3 instructions for **Spouse who is a full-time student or is disabled**).
2. You and the qualifying person(s) lived in the same home.
3. You (and your spouse if you were married) paid over half the cost of keeping up your home. The cost includes: rent; mortgage interest; property taxes; utilities; home repairs; and food eaten at home.

(Continued on back)

Form **2441** (1987)

411

Form **3903**	**Moving Expenses**	OMB No. 1545-0062
Department of the Treasury Internal Revenue Service	▶ Attach to Form 1040. ▶ See separate Instructions.	**1987** Attachment Sequence No. **62**

Name(s) as shown on Form 1040: TERRY A. & PAT B. JONES
Your social security number: 111 22 3333

1. Enter the number of miles from your **old** residence to your **new** workplace **1** 398
2. Enter the number of miles from your **old** residence to your **old** workplace **2** 20
3. Subtract line 2 from line 1. Enter the result (but not less than zero) .... ▶ **3** 378
   If line 3 is 35 or more miles, complete the rest of this form. If line 3 is less than 35 miles, you may not take a deduction for moving expenses. This rule does not apply to members of the armed forces.

Part I — Moving Expenses

Section A.—Transportation of Household Goods
4. Transportation and storage for household goods and personal effects **4** 1091

Section B.—Expenses of Moving From Old to New Residence
5. Travel and lodging **not** including meals **5** 272
6. Total meals **6** 84
7. Reimbursements for meals on line 6 on which no income tax was withheld (see **Meal Expenses** in the Instructions). Do not enter more than the amount shown on line 6 .... **7** 0
8. Subtract line 7 from line 6 .... **8** 84
9. Multiply line 8 by 80% (.80) **9** 67
10. Add lines 5, 7, and 9 .... **10** 339

Section C.—Pre-move Househunting Expenses
11. Travel and lodging **not** including meals **11** 343
12. Total meals **12** 112
13. Reimbursements for meals on line 12 on which no income tax was withheld (see **Meal Expenses** in the Instructions). Do not enter more than the amount shown on line 12 .... **13** 0
14. Subtract line 13 from line 12 .... **14** 112
15. Multiply line 14 by 80% (.80) **15** 90
16. Add lines 11, 13, and 15 .... **16** 433

Section D.—Temporary Quarters (for any 30 days in a row after getting your job)
17. Lodging expenses **not** including meals **17** 650
18. Total meals **18** 180
19. Reimbursements for meals on line 18 on which no income tax was withheld (see **Meal Expenses** in the Instructions). Do not enter more than the amount shown on line 18 .... **19** 0
20. Subtract line 19 from line 18 .... **20** 180
21. Multiply line 20 by 80% (.80) **21** 144
22. Add lines 17, 19, and 21 .... **22** 794

Section E.—Qualified Real Estate Expenses
23. Expenses of (check one): a ☒ selling or exchanging your old residence; or
    b ☐ if renting, settling an unexpired lease **23** 520
24. Expenses of (check one): a ☒ buying your new residence; or
    b ☐ if renting, getting a new lease **24** 611

Part II — Dollar Limitations

25. Add lines 16 and 22 .... **25** 1227
26. Enter the smaller of line 25 or $1,500 ($750 if married, filing a separate return, and at the end of the tax year you lived with your spouse who also started work during the tax year) **26** 1227
27. Add lines 23, 24, and 26 .... **27** 2358
28. Enter the smaller of line 27 or $3,000 ($1,500 if married, filing a separate return, and at the end of the tax year you lived with your spouse who also started work during the tax year) **28** 2358
29. Add lines 4, 10, and 28. This is your moving expense deduction. **Enter here and on Schedule A (Form 1040), line 19.** (Note: Any payments your employer made for any part of your move (including the value of any services furnished in kind) should be included on Form W-2. Report that amount on **Form 1040, line 7.** See **Reimbursements** in the Instructions.) .... ▶ **29** 3788

For Paperwork Reduction Act Notice, see separate Instructions.

Form **3903** (1987)

Form 4562 — Depreciation and Amortization

Form 4562
Department of the Treasury
Internal Revenue Service

▶ See separate instructions.
▶ Attach this form to your return.

OMB No. 1545-0172
1987
Attachment Sequence No. 67

Name(s) as shown on return: **TERRY A. & PAT B. JONES**
Identifying number: **111-22-3333**

Business or activity to which this form relates:

Part I — Depreciation
(Do not use this part for automobiles, certain other vehicles, computers, and property used for entertainment, recreation, or amusement. Instead, use Part III.)

Section A.—Election To Expense Depreciable Assets Placed in Service During This Tax Year (Section 179)

(a) Description of property	(b) Date placed in service	(c) Cost	(d) Expense deduction
1 7-YEAR (BOOKS, CALCULATOR, TYPEWRITER)	6/3/87	705	705
5-YEAR (COMPUTER EQUIPMENT)	5/16/87	3362	3362

2 Listed property—Enter total from Part III, Section A, column (h) . . . .
3 Total (add lines 1 and 2, but do not enter more than $10,000) **4067**
4 Enter the amount, if any, by which the cost of all section 179 property placed in service during this tax year is more than $200,000
5 Subtract line 4 from line 3. If result is less than zero, enter zero. (See instructions for other limitations) . . **4067**

Section B.—Depreciation

(a) Class of property	(b) Date placed in service	(c) Basis for depreciation (Business use only—see instructions)	(d) Recovery period	(e) Method of figuring depreciation	(f) Deduction
6 Accelerated Cost Recovery System (ACRS) (see instructions): *For assets placed in service ONLY during tax year beginning in 1987*					
a 3-year property					
b 5-year property					
c 7-year property					
d 10-year property					
e 15-year property					
f 20-year property					
g Residential rental property					
h Nonresidential real property					

7 Listed property—Enter total from Part III, Section A, column (g) **92**
8 ACRS deduction for assets placed in service prior to 1987 (see instructions) **1136**

Section C.—Other Depreciation

9 Property subject to section 168(f)(1) election (see instructions) . . . .
10 Other depreciation (see instructions) . . . .

Section D.—Summary

11 Total (add deductions on lines 5 through 10). Enter here and on the Depreciation line of your return (Partnerships and S corporations—Do NOT include any amounts entered on line 5.) **5295**
12 For assets above placed in service during the current year, enter the portion of the basis attributable to additional section 263A costs. (See instructions for who must use.) . .

Part II — Amortization

(a) Description of property	(b) Date acquired	(c) Cost or other basis	(d) Code section	(e) Amortization period or percentage	(f) Amortization for this year
1 Amortization for property placed in service **only** during tax year beginning in 1987					
2 Amortization for property placed in service prior to 1987					

3 Total. Enter here and on Other Deductions or Other Expenses line of your return . . . .

See Paperwork Reduction Act Notice on page 1 of the separate instructions.

Form **4562** (1987)

413

Form 4562 (1987)   Page **2**

Part III **Automobiles, Certain Other Vehicles, Computers, and Property Used for Entertainment, Recreation, or Amusement (Listed Property).**
If you are using the standard mileage rate or deducting vehicle lease expense, complete columns (a) through (d) of Section A, all of Section B, and Section C if applicable.

Section A.—Depreciation (If automobiles and other listed property placed in service after June 18, 1984, are used 50% or less in a trade or business, the Section 179 deduction is not allowed and depreciation must be taken using the straight line method over 5 years. For other limitations, see instructions.)

Do you have evidence to support the business use claimed? ☒ Yes ☐ No   If yes, is the evidence written? ☒ Yes ☐ No

(a) Type of property (list vehicles first)	(b) Date placed in service	(c) Business use percentage (%)	(d) Cost or other basis (see instructions for leased property)	(e) Basis for depreciation (Business use only—see instructions)	(f) Depreciation method and recovery period	(g) Depreciation deduction	(h) Section 179 expense
VIDEO RECORDER	6/12/83	40%	900	342	PRE-5YR	72	
CAMERA	9/24/84	45%	483	217	S/L-12YR	20	

Total (Enter here and on line 2, page 1.) . . . .

Total (Enter here and on line 7, page 1.)   92

Section B.—Information Regarding Use of Vehicles
Complete this section as follows, if you deduct expenses for vehicles:
- *Always complete this section for vehicles used by a sole proprietor, partner, or other more than 5% owner or related person.*
- *If you provided vehicles to employees, first answer the questions in Section C to see if you meet an exception to completing this section for those items.*

	Vehicle 1	Vehicle 2	Vehicle 3	Vehicle 4	Vehicle 5	Vehicle 6
1 Total miles driven during the year . . .						
2 Total business miles driven during the year						
3 Total commuting miles driven during the year.						
4 Total other personal (noncommuting) miles driven						
	Yes No	Yes No	Yes No	Yes No	Yes No	Yes No
5 Was the vehicle available for personal use during off-duty hours?						
6 Was the vehicle used primarily by a more than 5% owner or related person? . . .						
7 Is another vehicle available for personal use?.						

Section C.—Questions for Employers Who Provide Vehicles for Use by Employees.
*(Answer these questions to determine if you meet an exception to completing Section B. **Note:** Section B must always be completed for vehicles used by sole proprietors, partners, or other more than 5% owners or related persons.)*

	Yes	No
8 Do you maintain a written policy statement that prohibits all personal use of vehicles, including commuting, by your employees?		
9 Do you maintain a written policy statement that prohibits personal use of vehicles, except commuting, by your employees? (See instructions for vehicles used by corporate officers, directors, or 1% or more owners.)		
10 Do you treat all use of vehicles by employees as personal use?		
11 Do you provide more than five vehicles to your employees and retain the information received from your employees concerning the use of the vehicles?.		
12 Do you meet the requirements concerning fleet vehicles or qualified automobile demonstration use (see instructions)?		

Note: *If your answer to 8, 9, 10, 11, or 12 is "Yes," you need not complete Section B for the covered vehicles.*

Form 8598 — Home Mortgage Interest

Form 8598
Department of the Treasury
Internal Revenue Service

▶ Attach to Form 1040.
▶ See Separate Instructions.

OMB No. 1545-1009
1987
Attachment Sequence No. **85**

Name(s) as shown on Form 1040: **TERRY A. & PAT B. JONES**
Your social security number: **111 22 3333**

Do Not File This Form If:
- Your only mortgage debt was the mortgage you took out to buy your home; OR
- The price you paid for your home plus the cost of improvements was greater than the total of all your mortgage debts at all times in 1987; OR
- You have not borrowed any new amounts against your home after August 16, 1986.

Otherwise, you must complete this form and attach it to Form 1040. If you do not have to file this form, you can deduct all of the interest as home mortgage interest.

Note: Home mortgage interest is deductible **only** on your principal home and one other home. You must determine separately for each home if you are required to file Form 8598.

Which Parts Should I Complete?
Complete Part I to see if you can deduct all interest paid on your home mortgages.

When you complete Part I, if line 4 is more than or equal to line 1, you can deduct all of your interest as home mortgage interest. If line 4 is less than line 1, you must ordinarily complete either Part II or Part III. **Note:** If you used mortgage proceeds to pay for medical or educational expenses, in some cases, you may not need to complete either Part II or Part III. See the separate instructions for Part III.

Part II and Part III are alternative methods for determining the amount of deductible home mortgage interest. Part II is a simplified method, which anyone may use. You may instead use Part III, which is an exact method.

In general, it will be to your advantage to use Part III if you used mortgage proceeds to pay for medical or educational expenses or to pay for trade or business, investment, or passive activity expenses.

See the separate instructions for this form that explain:
- How to figure the average balance of each mortgage (line 1).
- What is meant by purchase price plus improvements (line 2).
- What is meant by pre-August 17 amount if you had a mortgage on your home before August 17, 1986 (line 3).

Part I — Complete To See If You Can Deduct All Home Mortgage Interest

Note: *Complete a separate Form 8598 if you have two qualified homes. See separate instructions.*

1	Figure the average balance for 1987 of **each** mortgage on your home using one of the methods provided on page 2 of the separate instructions. Then add the average balance of each mortgage and enter the total	1	78,111
2	Enter the purchase price of the home plus the cost of any improvements	2	74,630
3	If you took out a mortgage on your home before August 17, 1986, **other** than to buy your home, enter the pre-August 17 amount as determined in the separate instructions. Otherwise, enter zero	3	0
4	Enter the **larger of** the amount on line 2, or the amount on line 3	4	74,630

- If line 4 is **more than or equal to** line 1, **STOP HERE.** Enter on Schedule A (Form 1040), line 9a or 9b, as applicable, ALL interest paid on the mortgages included on line 1.
- If line 4 is **less than** line 1, read the instructions above to see if you must complete Part II or Part III.

Part II — Simplified Method To Figure Deductible Home Mortgage Interest

5	Enter the total interest paid for 1987 on the mortgages included on line 1. If you have deductible points, see the separate instructions	5	6,333
6	Divide the amount on line 4 by the amount on line 1 and enter the result as a decimal (to two places)	6	.96
7	Multiply the amount on line 5 by the decimal amount on line 6 and enter the result. Also, enter this amount on Schedule A (Form 1040), line 9a or 9b, as applicable, as **home mortgage interest**	7	6,080
8	Subtract the amount on line 7 from the amount on line 5, and enter the result. Also, enter this amount on Schedule A (Form 1040), line 12a, as **personal interest**	8	253

For Paperwork Reduction Act Notice, see separate instructions.

Form **8598** (1987)

415

Form **8606**	**Nondeductible IRA Contributions,**	OMB No. 1545-1007
Department of the Treasury Internal Revenue Service	**IRA Basis, and Nontaxable IRA Distributions** ▶ Please see Recordkeeping Requirements on back. ▶ Attach to Form 1040, Form 1040A, or Form 1040NR.	**1987** Attachment Sequence No. 86

Purpose of Form

The Tax Reform Act of 1986 allows you to make nondeductible contributions to your IRA. You may wish to do this, for example, if all or part of your contributions are no longer deductible because of the new income limitations for IRAs.

If you choose to make nondeductible contributions to your IRA, you must report the amount of the contributions that you choose to be nondeductible. Line 3 of Form 8606 is used for this purpose. First figure the amount of your deductible contributions using the Instructions for Form 1040 or Form 1040A, whichever applies to you. You should then report on Form 8606 the amount you choose to be nondeductible.

When you receive distributions (withdrawals) from your IRA, the part attributable to nondeductible contributions will not be taxable. Form 8606 is used to figure an amount called "basis" (which includes the part of your IRA that is from nondeductible contributions). The form is also used to figure the nontaxable part of any distributions you receive. If you received any distributions in 1987, line 12 will show the amount that is not taxable.

Line 13 of the form reflects the "basis" in your IRA as of 12/31/87. This amount will be used on Form 8606 in future years if you make nondeductible IRA contributions or receive distributions in those years.

Name (If married, file a separate Form 8606 for each spouse. See instructions.)
TERRY A. JONES

Your social security number
111 22 3333

Present home address (number and street) (or P.O. Box number if mail is not delivered to street address)
1234 STEEL AVE.

City, town or post office, state, and ZIP code
PITTSBURGH, PA 15219

1	Enter name of trustee and value of all your IRAs (attach list if more than three)— Name of trustee (bank, credit union, mutual fund, etc.)		Value on 12/31/87
a	**FIRST NATIONAL BANK**	1a	**7437**
b		1b	
c		1c	
2	Total value of all IRAs. Add lines 1a through 1c	2	**7437**
3	Enter your IRA contributions for 1987 that you choose to be nondeductible. (Include those made during 1/1/88–4/15/88 that were for 1987.) (See instructions.)	3	**1730**
4	Enter only those contributions included on line 3 that were made during 1/1/88–4/15/88. (See instructions.)	4	
5	Subtract line 4 from line 3 and enter the result. (The result may be zero if all of your nondeductible contributions for 1987 were made in 1988 by 4/15/88. Please continue.)	5	**1730**
6	Adjustments. (See instructions.)	6	
7	Combine lines 5 and 6 and enter the result. If you did not receive any IRA distributions (withdrawals) in 1987, skip lines 8 through 12 and enter the amount (or zero, if applicable) from line 7 on line 13 . .	7	**1730**
8	Enter the value of all your IRAs as of 12/31/87 (from line 2). Include any outstanding rollovers. (See instructions.)	8	
9	Enter total IRA distributions received during 1987. Do not include amounts rolled over before 1/1/88. (See instructions.)	9	
10	Add lines 8 and 9 and enter the total	10	
11	Divide line 7 by line 10 and enter the result as a decimal (to two places) .	11	.
12	Multiply line 9 by the decimal amount on line 11 and enter the result. This is the amount of your nontaxable distributions for 1987. (See instructions.) . . . . ▶	12	
13	Subtract line 12 from line 7 and enter the result. This is the basis in your IRA(s) as of 12/31/87 . ▶	13	**1730**

Please Sign Here Under penalties of perjury, I declare that I have examined this form, including accompanying attachments, and to the best of my knowledge and belief, it is true, correct, and complete.

▶ *Terry A. Jones*   ▶ **4/9/88**
  Your signature   Date

General Instructions

Paperwork Reduction Act Notice.—We ask for this information to carry out the Internal Revenue laws of the United States. We need it to ensure that taxpayers are complying with these laws and to allow us to figure and collect the right amount of tax. You are required to give us this information.

Who Must File.—You must file Form 8606 for 1987 if you make nondeductible contributions to your IRA(s). If you and your spouse each choose to make nondeductible IRA contributions, you each must file a Form 8606.

Report your deductible contributions on Form 1040, Form 1040A, or Form 1040NR and not on Form 8606.

When and Where To File.—Attach Form 8606 to your 1987 Form 1040, Form 1040A, or Form 1040NR.

If you do not have to file an income tax return because you do not meet the requirements for filing a return, you still have to file a Form 8606 with the Internal Revenue Service at the time and place you would normally be required to file Form 1040, Form 1040A, or Form 1040NR.

Form **8606** (1987)

Form 8615 — Computation of Tax for Children Under Age 14 Who Have Investment Income of More Than $1,000

Department of the Treasury
Internal Revenue Service

OMB No. 1545-0998
1987
Attachment Sequence No. 33

▶ See Instructions below and on back.
▶ Attach ONLY to the Child's Form 1040, Form 1040A, or Form 1040NR.

General Instructions

Purpose of Form. Before 1987, the tax law allowed income-producing property to be given to children so that the investment income from the property could be taxed at the children's lower tax rate. The law was changed for 1987 and later years so that, for children under age 14, investment income (such as taxable interest and dividends) over $1,000 will be taxed at the parent's rate if higher than the child's rate.

Do not use this form if the child's investment income is $1,000 or less. Instead, figure the tax in the normal manner on the child's income tax return. For example, if the child had $900 of taxable interest income and $200 of income from wages, Form 8615 is not required to be completed and the child's tax should be figured on Form 1040A using the Tax Table.

If the child's investment income is more than $1,000, use this form to see if any of the child's investment income is taxed at the parent's rate and, if so, to figure the child's tax. For example, if the child had $1,100 of taxable interest income and $200 of income from wages, Form 8615 should be completed and attached to the child's Form 1040A.

Investment Income. As used on this form, "investment income" includes all taxable income other than earned income as defined on page 2. It includes income such as taxable interest, dividends, capital gains, rents, royalties, etc. It also includes pension and annuity income and income (other than earned income) received as the beneficiary of a trust.

Who Must File. Generally, **Form 8615** must be filed for any child who was under age 14 on December 31, 1987, and who had more than $1,000 of investment income. However, if neither parent was alive on December 31, do not use Form 8615. Instead, figure the child's tax based on his or her own rate.

Additional Information. For more information about the tax on investment income of children, please get **Publication 929**, Tax Rules for Children and Dependents.
(Instructions continue on back.)

Child's name as shown on return: **SUSAN C. JONES**
Child's social security number: **123 45 6789**

Parent's name (first, initial, and last). (Caution: See Instructions on back before completing.): **TERRY A. JONES**
Parent's social security number: **111 22 3333**

Parent's filing status (check one): ☐ Single, ☒ Married filing jointly, ☐ Married filing separately, ☐ Head of household, or ☐ Qualifying widow(er)

Step 1 — Figure child's net investment income

1	Enter the child's investment income, such as taxable interest and dividend income (see Instructions). (If this amount is $1,000 or less, stop here; do not file this form.)	1,200
2	If the child DID NOT itemize deductions on Schedule A (Form 1040 or Form 1040NR), enter $1,000. If the child ITEMIZED deductions, see the Instructions.	1,000
3	Subtract the amount on line 2 from the amount on line 1. Enter the result. (If zero or less, stop here; do not complete the rest of this form but ATTACH it to the child's return.)	200
4	Enter the child's **taxable** income (from Form 1040, line 36; Form 1040A, line 17; or Form 1040NR, line 35)	700
5	Compare the amounts on lines 3 and 4. Enter the **smaller** of the two amounts ▶	200

Step 2 — Figure tentative tax based on the tax rate of the parent listed above

6	Enter the parent's **taxable** income (from Form 1040, line 36; Form 1040A, line 17; Form 1040EZ, line 7; or Form 1040NR, line 35)	19,467
7	Enter the total, if any, of the net investment income from Forms 8615, line 5, of ALL OTHER children of the parent. (Do not include the amount on line 5 above.)	0
8	Add the amounts on lines 5, 6, and 7. Enter the total	19,667
9	Tax on the amount on line 8 based on the **parent's** filing status (see Instructions). Check if from ☒ Tax Table, ☐ Tax Rate Schedules, or ☐ Schedule D	2,831
10	Enter the parent's tax (from Form 1040, line 37; Form 1040A, line 18; Form 1040EZ, line 9; or Form 1040NR, line 36). Check if from ☒ Tax Table, ☐ Tax Rate Schedules, or ☐ Schedule D	2,801
11	Subtract the amount on line 10 from the amount on line 9. Enter the result. (If no amount is entered on line 7, enter the amount from line 11 on line 13; skip lines 12a and 12b.)	30
12a	Add the amounts on lines 5 and 7. Enter the total	12a
b	Divide the amount on line 5 by the amount on line 12a. Enter the result as a decimal (to two places)	12b x
13	Multiply the amount on line 11 by the decimal amount on line 12b. Enter the result ▶	30

Step 3 — Figure child's tax

Note: If the amounts on lines 4 and 5 are the same, skip to line 16.

14	Subtract the amount on line 5 from the amount on line 4. Enter the result. 14	500
15	Tax on the amount on line 14 based on the **child's** filing status (see Instructions). Check if from ☒ Tax Table, ☐ Tax Rate Schedule X, or ☐ Schedule D	56
16	Add the amounts on lines 13 and 15. Enter the total.	86
17	Tax on the amount on line 4 based on the **child's** filing status. Check if from ☒ Tax Table, ☐ Tax Rate Schedule X, or ☐ Schedule D	78
18	Compare the amounts on lines 16 and 17. Enter the **larger** of the two amounts here and on Form 1040, line 37; Form 1040A, line 18; or Form 1040NR, line 36. Be sure to check the box for "Form 8615" ▶	86

For Paperwork Reduction Act Notice, see back of form.

Form **8615** (1987)

SUPPLEMENT # 1

CONTRIBUTIONS OTHER THAN CASH (SCHEDULE A, LINE 16)

Telephone expenses as solicitor for Heart Fund . $ 32

Teaching Sunday School
  Auto transportation: 324 miles @ 12 cents/mile   39

Clothing donated to Salvation Army on 7/14/87 ... 47

Foreign exchange student living in home.......... 162

YMCA Board Member meetings
  Auto transportation: 210 miles @ 12 cents/mile   25

Transportation for Boy Scouts
  340 miles @ 12 cents/mile   41

Transportation to Church Choir rehearsal
  405 miles @ 12 cents/mile   49

Church Choir robes   76

        TOTAL $471

SUPPLEMENT # 2

JOB-RELATED TRAVEL EXPENSES AWAY FROM HOME OVERNIGHT
(FORM 2106, PART I, LINES 3 AND 5)

1. Sabbatical at University of Arizona to do research: Feb.1-April 30

Meals		$1,135
Round-trip airplane fare	$ 406	
Lodging	1,412	
Cleaning and laundry	146	
Daily bus fares between temporary home and school	170	

2. Trip to attend meeting of American Physics Society: Oct. 10-Oct. 16 in Los Angeles, Cal.

Meals and Entertainment		213
Round-trip airplane fare	458	
Lodging	341	
Taxi fares	35	

3. Trip to interview for new job in same line of work: Jan.7-Jan.9 in Miami, Fla.

Meals		68
Round-trip airplane fare	356	
Lodging	126	
Airport Limousine	15	

TOTAL OTHER THAN MEALS & ENTERTAINMENT
(FORM 2106, PART I, LINE 3) $3,465

   TOTAL MEALS & ENTERTAINMENT
   (FORM 2106, PART I, LINE 5) $1,416

SUPPLEMENT # 3

JOB-RELATED EXPENSES-OTHER THAN FOR TRAVEL, MEALS, & ENTERTAINMENT (FORM 2106, PART I, LINE 4)

A. Books & Equipment:

  Listed Property (Form 4562, Part III, Section A)

  1. Video Recorder purchased 6/12/83 for $900 used 40% for job-related purposes:

    Depreciation deduction using 5-year regular table percentage (21%) for item in fifth year of use and 95% basis reduction factor for 5-year items (which applies to such items on which the investment tax credit was claimed prior to 1986):
    Basis for Depreciation:
    $900 x 40% x 95% = $342
    Deduction for 1987: $342 x 21%. . . . $ 72

  2. Camera, required by employer, purchased 9/24/84 for $483 used 45% for job-related purposes:
    Depreciation deduction using 12-year listed property table percentage (9%) for item in fourth year of use:
    Basis for Depreciation:
    $483 x 45% = $217
    Deduction for 1987: $217 x 9% . . .   20

  Non-listed Property Purchased in 1987

  1. Books $382
  2. Calculator   36
  3. Typewriter   287

    Expensing Deduction
    (Form 4562, Part I, Line 1).   705

  Non-Listed Property Purchased before 1987

    Depreciation on Books & Equipment:
    (Included on Form 4562, Part I, Line 8)..   391
TOTAL DEDUCTION FOR
  JOB-RELATED BOOKS & EQUIPMENT $1188

SUPPLEMENT # 3 (continued)

B. Educational Expenses:

Expenses connected with attending seminar in Advanced Mechanics at University of Pittsburgh to learn new material for use in job-related research. (This seminar was not needed to meet the minimum requirements for holding my job nor was it part of a program qualifying for a new job.):

Tuition.	$240
Textbook	35
Supplies	10
Laboratory Fee	20
TOTAL EDUCATIONAL EXPENSES	$305

C. Other Expenses:

Dues to National Education Association . . .	$ 40
Dues to A.A.U.P.	60
Dues to American Physics Society	25
Subscriptions to professional journals . . .	90
Supplies used in teaching—paper, pens, record book, etc.	146
Laboratory apparel (including cleaning) . . .	75
Laboratory equipment	57
Required physical exam	40
Payment to substitute teacher	165
Bond posted to go on Sabbatical	50
Employment agency fee to obtain job	150
TOTAL "OTHER EXPENSES"	$898

GRAND TOTAL (FORM 2106, PART I, LINE 4) . . .	$2,391

SUPPLEMENT # 4

SCHEDULE C DEDUCTIONS

1. Home Office (1 room of 6 room house)

    Home Expenses:
    Mortgage interest $7600
    Property taxes 1125
    Gas for heating   751
    Electricity for light and air
       conditioning 814
    Fire insurance   156
    Cleaning person   775
    Repair of furnace   128

    $11,349

    Home expenses attributable to office:
    1/6 x $11,349 . . . . $1892
    Plus: Painting the office   147
          *Depreciation   745

    TOTAL HOME OFFICE DEDUCTION
    (SCHEDULE C, LINE 20) $2784

    *Depreciation Calculation:
       Purchase price of house (excluding land): $63,830
       Date of purchase: 1/18/83
       Basis of home office: 1/6 x $63,830 = $10,638
       Depreciation deduction for 1987 (using prescribed
          method for 15-year property in fifth full year
          of use): 7% x $10,638 = $745

    (Depreciation included on Form 4562, Part I, Line 8)

2. Home computer (including peripherals) used exclusively in home office only for business-related research, purchased in 1987:
    Purchase price: $3362
    Date of Purchase: 5/16/87
    EXPENSING DEDUCTION:
       (SCHEDULE C, LINE 12) $3362

    (Expensing included on Form 4562, Part I, Line 1)

SUPPLEMENT # 5

JOB-RELATED AUTO MILEAGE (FORM 2106, PART II, LINE 3)

1. Travel between two different jobs:
   18 miles per week for 20 weeks . . .   360 miles

2. Travel to temporary job away from
   home in city 51 miles from home:
   2 weeks x 3 days/week x 102 miles .   612

3. Travel to attend seminar on Advanced
   Mechanics   514

4. Travel to libraries to do research . .   282

5. Travel to pick up official visitors
   at airport   120

   TOTAL . . . .   1888 miles

INDEX

(Boldface indicates primary reference)

Abortions 86
Accelerated depreciation method 67-70, 72-73
Accident
   insurance 339
   loss from 334 340
Acupuncture 85, 92
Adjusted gross income 15-16
Adjustments to income 11, **15-17,** 24, 133, 154, 158, 194, 215, 228, 230, 275
Air cleaner 88-89
Air conditioners 76
   medical deduction for 88-89
Airplanes 276, 279
Alcoholics Anonymous 92
Alimony 15, 24, **156-161**
   IRAs based on 200
Allergies 88
Alternative minimum tax 399-400
Amending tax returns **18-19,** 324
Annuities
   retirement 253-255, 259-262
   tax sheltered 13-14, 32, 208-209, **215-225,** 254, 258-262
   3-year rule 13
   withholding on 274
Apartment buildings 63, 73-77
Appliances 127
Appraisal fees 234
Artistic activities 341
   loss-producing 356-359
Aspirin 84, 86
Assessments 119-120
Athletic wear 38
Audit 317-333
   of auto travel 322
Authors 48-50, 52-53, 58, 209-217, 275-276, 295, 341, **344-349,** 356-359, 361-364
Automobile **133-145,** 231, 276-277
   accident 334
   charitable use 95, 317-318
   deduction for child's 187-188
   depreciation 12, 63-73, 137-145
   expensing option 138-144
   garage rent 138, 142

   insurance 89-90, 142, 339
   interest 12, 79, 82, 138-139
   license 142, 144-145, 146, 318
   loans 12
   logs, mileage 134-137
   luxury 139
   medical use 87, 90
   mileage rate 23, 87, 90, 95, 133, 137-138, 142-144, 153, 280, 302, 318
   operating expenses 138, 142-145
   parking fees 133, 137-138, 143-144
   record keeping 134-137
   registration fee 144-145, 146, 318
   reimbursable expenses 133
   rental 280
   repairs 138, 142, 145
   sampling techniques for expenses .. 135-136
   taxes 144-145, 146, 318
   towing expenses 138
   trading in 145
   used for moving 152-153
   washing 142
Averaging, income (see Income averaging)
Awards 367
Babysitting expenses 24, 95, **101-108**
Banquets 278
Basic rules **15-33**
Basis 75-76, 123-125
Bedroom used as home office 45-46
Birth control pills and devices 86
Boats 78
   as second home 109-110
Bonds
   interest on 81
   mutual funds 176-178
   required to go on sabbatical 232
   savings 184
   tax-free municipal 168-169, 173, 176-178, 182
   transfer tax 147
   trusts 177-178
Books 11-12, 34, **36-37,** 249, 351, 395
   depreciation 34, 63-73
   donated to charity 99-100
   expensing 34, 63-67

Index

Brackets, tax 9-10
Briefcases 36
Broker, reports to IRS.............164-165
Burglar alarm 232-233
Business, outside 52-54, **341-359**, 397-398
   losses from...................356-359
Business expenses...**21-22**, 24, 32, 227-234, 351
Business interest 78, 80, 114
Business school (see MBA expenses)
Calculators 39, 55, 63-73
Camera 34-36, 39, 64-65, 69-73
Camp, summer 102-103
Capital gains tax..............12, 28, 147, 160-161, **162-166**
   effect of casualty deduction on........340
   on home..................62, 121-126
   on mutual funds................172-175
   on sale of stocks or bonds 81
Capitalizing expenses 346-347
Cash management accounts 179-182
Casualty losses 15-17, 29, **334-340**
Certificate fees 232
Chairs 39
Charity
   contributions to.......11, 23, 29, **93-100**, 313, 316, 318
   deduction for non-itemizers 11
   recordkeeping 96-98
   travel for 23, 94-95, 317-318
Check, payment by 82-83
Checking accounts
   fees............................179
   interest-paying 178-182
Child
   custody 159
   deduction for purchases by 187-188
   dependent....10-11, 14, 17, 20-22, 25-27, 159-160
   income received by............14, 25-27
   loans to.......................187-188
   lowering your tax 183-188
   paying for assistance ...185-186, 353-356, 396
   shifting income to 14, **183-188**, 348-349, 353-356
   social security number for........11, 264
   support...................157-160, 184-185
   tax-return of............14, 20-21, **25-27**
   trips taken by 102-104
Child care tax credit ...24, **101-108**, 354-355
Childbirth classes 88
Church, contributions to...........93-100
Cigarette tax 146
Cleaning (also see Laundry) 55

Clifford trust.....................14, 185
Clothing 38
   given to charity 98-99
Cohabitation....................18, 356
Cohan rule 29
College, contributions to 93-100
College education
   deduction for 235-252
   loans for 14, 79
Collision insurance...................339
Commissions, real estate 121-122, 153
Commuting 275-277, 289-301
   to school....................249-250
Computation of tax 15-16
Computers 34-36, **39-43**, 63-73
   deduction for child's 187-188
Condominium (see Home)
Consulting 52-54, 59-61, 80, 209-217, 230-231, 275-276, **341-359**
Consumer loans (see Personal interest)
Contributions
   charitable............11, 23, 29, **93-100**, 313, 316, 317-318
   deduction for non-itemizers 11
   political 11
Conventions 275-276, 279-280, 302
Corporations 342-344, 349-353
Cosmetic surgery 91-92
Cost-plus amount of home.....111-112, 115
Credential fee 232
Credit cards.........................12
   interest..........................79
   payment by 32
Credits (see Tax Credits)
CREF (see TIAA/CREF)
Crutches 86
Date of payment 32
Day care 95, **101-108**
Debt-ceiling on home 110-115
Decorating.......................55-56
Deductions..................15-17, 20-21
   accelerating to save taxes 31-32
   average claimed by taxpayers.....322-323
Deferred compensation plans.....14, **225-226**
Defined-Benefit Keogh plans ..189, **212-213**, 350
Dental expenses 85
Dentures 86
Dependent.....10-11, 14, 17-18, 20-22, 159
   parent 22
   tax return of...................25-27
Depreciation 12, **63-67**
   5-year recovery class 63-73
   7-year recovery class 63-73
   accelerated method 67-70, 72-73
   apartment building 63, 73-77

Index

automobile 63-73, 137-145
basis 75-76
books 63-73
calculators 63-73
camera 64-65, 69-73
computers 42, 63-73
entertainment items 64-65, 69-73
equipment. 63-73
  expensing option 63-67, 138-144
  40%-rule 72-73
  furniture 63-69, 72-73, 127-128
  home 55, 57-61, 63, 73-77, 127-131
  items purchased late in the year 72-73
  items used part of the year 72-73, 75
  listed property 64-65, 69-73
  prescribed (PRE) method 67-70, 72-73
  real estate class 63, 73-77
  rental property 73-77
  research items 63-73
  straight-line method. 67-75
  typewriters 63-73
  video equipment. 64-65, 69-73
Desk 39
Diet program .88, 91
Dinner meetings 11, 265-270
  80%-rule 267
Disability, payroll deductions for 147
Disability income 17, 92
Dissertation expenses 232, 242, 249
Dividend reinvestment plan 186
Dividends 81
  exclusion from tax 12
  reporting on tax return 15-20
  shifting tax on 183-188
  withholding on. 272-273
Divorce 85, 108, **156-161**
Doctor bills 84-85
Donations (see Contributions)
Driver's license. 146
Drought, damage from. 335
Drugs. 86-87
Dues to unions or professional societies . .232
Earned income credit 20-21, 376
Educational expenses 78-79, 82, 86, 90-91, 104-105, 114-115, 231, **235-252**, 275, 299-300, 308, 317, 351
Educational materials, miscellaneous 44
Educational reimbursements
  from employer. 235-236
  80%-rule for meal expenses 228-230, 267, **277-278**, 283, 291-293
Electricity (see Utilities)
Employee business expenses 11

Employee, definition of 341-342
Employment agency fees 231
Entertainment expenses 11, 228-231, **265-270**
  80%-rule 228-230, 267
Entertainment items 64-65, 69-73
Equipment 11-12, 34-36, 39, 55, 63-73, 231, 351, 379, 387-388, 395
  medical .88-89, 91
Estate tax. 125, **310-316**
Estimated tax. 273-274
Exemptions 10-11, 15-18, 25
Exercise. 91
  equipment. .88-89
Expensing option 12, **63-67**
  items converted to personal use 67
Extension of time to file 19-20
Exterminators. 57
Extracurricular activities 232
Eyeglasses. 86
Face lifts 91-92
Family members, hiring. 353-356, 396
Fees. 20, 200
Fellowships . . .11-12, 251, 299-300, **366-392**
Film. 36
Fire, damage from 334
Fiscal year. 352
Flood, damage from. 334
Food. 228-231
  at business meetings 11, 265-270
  banquet meals .278
  80%-rule 228-230, 267, **277-278**, 283, 291-293
  per diem rate 282-283
  special diet 88, 91
  while away from home 11, 152-153, 276-283, 291-306, 394-395
Foreign income 345-346, **360-365**, 378
  moving expenses. 154
Forms (also see Sample Tax Forms at end of book)
  Form 843. 391
  Form 942. 108
  Form 1040-ES. 273
  Form 1040X 18, 206
  Form 1099. . . . . .164-165, 173
  Form 1099-G. 149-150
  Form 2106. . . . . .22, 133, 136-137, **228-230**, 248, 251, 270, 275, 278, 299, 300, 396
  Form 2119. 124
  Form 2120. 17
  Form 2210. 273
  Form 2350. 365
  Form 2440. 92

Index

Form 2441.........................108
Form 2555.........................364
Form 2688..........................19
Form 3903.........................154
Form 4506..........................19
Form 4562..........34, 36, 44, 64, 66,
                    69, 134, 136-137
Form 4684.........................340
Form 4868.....................19, 364
Form 5500-EZ......................212
Form 6765.........................398
Form 7004 PC......................264
Form 8283..........................98
Form 8332....................156, 159
Form 8582.........................168
Form 8598....................110-115
Form 8606.........................195
Form 8615.......................26-27
Form IO-673.......................364
Form W-2................318, 370, 389
Form W-4.....................271-274
Form W-4A....................271-274
401(k) plans................14, 225-226
40%-rule for depreciation...........72-73
Freeze, damage from.............334-335
Furniture............12, 34, 39, 55, 57,
                       63-67, 127-128
Gambling losses................227, 234
Gas (see Utilities)
Gasoline.......................138, 142
Gasoline tax........................146
Gifts................33, 183-184, 367
  tax on...................125, **310-316**
Gold coins, IRA purchase of.......203-204
Graduate assistants...243, 366-376, 389-392
Graduate school education........242-245,
                                  247-249
Grants, tax-free.......11-12, 251, 299-300,
                                  366-392
  awarded after August 16, 1986...367-370,
                                  389-392
  awarded before August 17, 1986..370-392
  National Endowment for the
    Humanities..................379-381
  NSF..........................381-386
  new rules....................367-370
  non-degree candidates 11-12, 366, 368-370,
                                  376-392
  received outside the U.S.........378
  reporting on your return.....389-390
  sabbatical..........381-382, 386-389
  social security tax on..366, 368, 370, 390-
                                  392
  summer............380-381, 384-389
Hair, removal and transplants......91-92

Handicapped, aids for the...........91
Handicapped workers, expenses of .227, 234
Head of household...........22, 27, 156
Health spas.........................91
Hearing aids........................86
Hiring a child or spouse........185-186
Hobby.........................356-359
Home
  adjusted sales price.........122-123
  capital gains on sale........62, 121-126
  cost-plus amount..........110-111, 115
  debt ceiling on..............110-115
  depreciation............55, 57-61, 63,
                     73-77, 127-131
  equity loans......12-13, 78-79, **109-115**
  fix-up costs before sale.....122-123
  improvements..........30, 76, 121-122
  insurance...............57-61, 127-128
  interest, mortgage 12-13, 57-61, 78-79, 82,
                  109-118, 127-131, 399
  joint ownership........124-126, 312-313
  mobile...................78-79, 109
  owner's expenses.............109-132
  passive interest.........78, 80, 82, 114
  recordkeeping.....................30
  refinancing of..........110-116, 399
  renting to others........73-77, 126-132,
                                  166-168
  renting to relatives.............132
  repairs............57-61, 76, 121-123
  sale of..............62, **120-126,** 318
  second..............78-79, 82, **109-110**
  settlement charges...............121
  taxes......57-61, 109, **118-126,** 127-132
  transfer taxes..............121, 147
Home computers............34-36, **39-43,**
                                  63-73
  deduction for child's........187-188
Home office.......**45-62,** 64, 231, 351, 395
  carryover of losses...........60-61
  depreciation...........55, 57-61, 73-77
  items used in.....................55
  losses on.......................58-61
  research, used for.......45-46, 48-52
  travel to and from................56
  used by 2 persons..............51-52
Homeowner's expenses............**109-132**
  Form 8598....................110-115
Honorariums................209-215, 349
Hotel (see Lodging)
House (see Home)
Household services, tax
  credit for.........24, **101-108,** 354-355
Housekeeper, tax credit for........101-108
Housing, free or low rent..........33

Index

Humidifier..........................88-89
Hurricane, damage from..............334
Ice, damage from....................334
Improvements on house.....30, 76, 121-122
Imputed interest....................187-188
Income
    foreign....................345-346, 378
    received by child..................25-27
    unearned..........................183
Income averaging.....................10
    for lump-sum distributions..212, 214-215, 226, **253-255**
Income forecast method............346-347
Income shifting..............14, **183-188**, 348-349, 353-355
Income tax, state and local...23-24, 146-150
Incorporation............342-344, 349-353
Individual retirement account (see IRAs)
Inherited property....125-126, 165, 310-316
Insects, damage from.................335
Installment sale...............165-166, 400
Insulin..........................84, 86
Insurance............................43
    automobile..................88-89, 339
    home....................57-61, 127-128
    life..............................312
    medical....................84-85, 88-89
Interest........................**78-83**, 399
    automobile.............12, 138-139
    business..........................114
    child's, taxed to parent..............14
    consumer (see personal)
    home-equity loan...12-13, 78-79, **109-115**
    imputed.........................187-188
    investment...........13, 78, **81-83**, 114
    late payment charge..................23
    margin......................13, 81-83
    mortgage on home...12-13, 57-61, 78-79, 82, **109-118**, 127-131
    on checking accounts............178-182
    on credit cards......................79
    on loans to relatives.........80, 187-188
    on passive activities..78, 80, 82, 114, 166-168
    on portfolio income....13, 78, **81-83**, 114
    on rental property 78, 80, 82, 114, 166-168
    on stock purchases................81-82
    paid to relative.....................80
    passive........78, 80, 82, 114, 166-168
    personal......**78-80**, 82-83, 114-115, 130
    phase-in rules.................79-81, 399
    reporting on tax return..............20
    shifting tax on..................183-188
    tax-free......168-169, 173, 176-178, 182
    tax-sheltered..........183-188, 189-226

trade or business....................80
withholding....................272-273
Interest-free loans................187-188
Interns............................376
Investing your money............162-182
Investment expenses..............232-234
Investment income, shifting
    tax on........................183-188
Investment interest.......13, 78, **81-83**, 114
Investment plan, stock................186
Investments....................162-182
IRAs...................13, 159, **190-209**, 215, 218-219, 234, 254, 354
    beneficiary........................207
    bonus, hidden.....................200
    borrowing....................204-206
    distributions from..............196-200
    dividing contributions between
        spouses............191-195, 197-198
    early withdrawal...............199-200
    fees..............................200
    non-deductible
        contributions to.......13, 191, 194-199
    rollovers into..........207-209, 218-219
    spousal................191-195, 197-198
    taxation of withdrawals.........196-200
    withdrawal before age $59^{1}/_{2}$......199-200
IRS (see Audit)
IRS private rulings..............330-333
Itemized deductions, average.......322-323
Itemizing deductions................15-17
Jewelry, deduction for child's.......187-188
Job-hunting expenses.........231-232, 301
Job-related expenses..............227-232
Joint ownership..........124-126, 312-313
Joint return.................23-24, **27-29**
Joint tenancy................124-126, 313
Journal subscriptions...............36-37
Keogh plans............32, **209-215**, 234, 254, 344-345, 349, 354
    defined-benefit........189, 212-213, 350
Laboratory clothing.............38, 396
Lamps..............................39
Land............................63, 74
Late payment charges..........23, 79, 109
Laundry while away
    from home.......276, 278, 280, 291-296 394-395
Law school........................246
Leave of absence................288-301
    rental of home during..........126-132
    to obtain education............246-249
Lecturing fees......................349
Legal expenses..........121-122, 127-128, 153, 161, 233, 317

Index

Libraries, travel to 133, 284-285
Licenses 142, 144-145, 146, 318
Life insurance 312-313
Limited partnerships 78, 80, 82, 166-168
Listed property 29, **34-36,** 44,
　　　　　　　　　　　　64-65, 69-73, 143-144
Loans (see Interest)
Lodging 11, 152-153, 276-280,
　　　　　　　　　　　291-306, 394-395
　discounts for teachers 308-309
Log 35
Loss, passive 166-168
Loss produced by outside activity ... 356-359
Lump-sum distributions from
　retirement plans 207-209, 212,
　　　　　　　　　　214-215, 218-219, 226,
　　　　　　　　　　　　253-255, 313
Lunch, business-related 11, 231-232, 265-270
　80%-rule 228-230
MBA expenses 248-249
Magazines 36-37, 233
Maid, tax credit for 101-108
Mailing in your tax return 18
Management fees on mutual funds .. 11, 173,
　　　　　　　　　　　　　　　　　　233
Maps 36
Margin interest 13
Marriage deduction 10
Married couples
　deduction for working 10
　filing joint returns 23-24, 27-29
　filing separate returns 23-24, 27-29
　joint ownership by 124-126, 312-313
　living apart 294-295
Meals (see Food)
Medical expenses 11, 15-17, 23,
　　　　　　　　　　28, 78, 82, **84-92,** 114,
　　　　　　　　　　160, 200, 216, 232,
　　　　　　　　　　249, 350-351, 355
　getting around 7.5% floor ... 30-31, 84-85,
　　　　　　　　　　213, 350-351, 355
　loans for 12, 114
Medical reimbursement plan ... 350-351, 355
Medicine 84, 86-87
Mileage rate for auto travel 23, 87,
　　　　　　　　　　　90, 95, 133,
　　　　　　　　　　137-138, 142-144, 153,
　　　　　　　　　　280, 302, 318
Minimum tax 399-400
Miscellaneous
　deductions 11, 15, 28-29, 43-44,
　　　　　　　　　　61, 64, 133, 165,
　　　　　　　　　　173, 200, **227-234,**
　　　　　　　　　　251, 270, 275, 351, 396, 399
　educational materials 44, 249

supplies 44
2% floor on deductions ... 11, 31, 227-231
Mistakes commonly made 22-24
Mobile home 78-79, 109
Money-market accounts 178-182
　fees on 233
Money-market funds .. 11, 173, **181-182,** 233
Mortgage payments
　interest portion 12-13, 57-61, 78-79,
　　　　　　　　　　82, **109-118,** 127-131, 399
　late payment charge 23
Motels (see Lodging)
Motor club membership 142
Moving expenses 15,61, **151-155,** 365
Multiple support agreement 17
Municipal bond 168-169
　funds 173, 176-178, 182
　trusts 177-178
Municipal taxes (see state and local taxes)
Mutual funds 20, **170-178**
　directory of no-load 170
　fees 170-171, 173, 233
　hidden fees 170-171
　high-yield corporate bond 178
　management fees 11, 173, 233
　money-market 11, 181-182
　phantom income 173, 233
　reports to IRS 164-165
　tax-free 176-178, 182
　taxes on 172-175
　12b-1 funds 170-171
National Science Foundation 381-386
Necessary business expense 21
Negative income tax 20-21
Negligence penalty, appeal of 329
New trade or business, education
　to qualify for 235, 244-246
Newspapers 37, 233
1986 Tax Reform Act **9-14**
NOW accounts 179, 182
Nursery school 101-102, 105
Nursing services 85
Office at home (see Home Office)
Ombudsman 19
Ordinary expense 21
Orthopedic shoes 86
Outside business activity 52-54, 209-215,
　　　　　　　　　　　　341-359, 397-398
Painting 57
Paper 36
Parent
　shifting income to 348-349
　support of 17
　tax return of dependent 25-27
Parking fees 133, 137-138, 143-144

Index

Partnerships 342
Passive activities ...78, 80, 82, 114, 166-168
Passive losses 13, **166-168**
Passport fee........................146
Payroll taxes 147, 390-392
Penalty 23, 79, 118
Pencils............................36
Pens...............................36
Pension plans (see Retirement plans)
Pensions, withholding on.............274
Per diem travel rate...............282-283
Periodicals 34, 36-37, 233
Personal interest .**78-80**, 82-83, 114-115, 130
Personal property tax 10
Phantom income.................173, 233
Phase-out
   of exemptions for dependents..........10
   of 15% tax bracket 9-10
   of interest deduction 12-13, 79-81, 399
   of passive loss deductions.....13, 166-168
Photography 34-36, 39, 341, 356-359
Physical examinations 85, 232
Physical therapy 85
Pictures............................55
Plants...........................55-56
   damage to 334-335, 337
Podiatrists..........................85
Points charged on loan ...109, **115-116**, 121, 153
Political contributions..................11
Portfolio interest 13, 78, **81-83**, 114
Postage 233
Prepayment penalty on loan............118
Prescribed (PRE) depreciation
   method 67-70, 72-73
Private contractor 341-342
Private IRS rulings 330-333
Private school 90-91, 104-105
Prizes.............................367
Problems Resolution Officer 19
Professional society dues 232
Profit-sharing plans 350
Projectors 39
Property taxes 11, 57-61, 109, **118-121**, 127-132, 145, 146, 149
Psychologist fees 85
Publication costs 395-396
Radios 39
Rainstorm, damage from 334
Real estate
   commissions 121-122, 153
   passive investment in 80, 166-168
   transfer tax on.....................147
Recordation tax, real estate........121, 153
Record books 36

Recordkeeping..........29-30, 35-36, 72, 76-77, 96-98, 134-137, 251-252, 270, 279-283, 339
Records, phonograph 36
Recovery exclusion...............147-149
Reduction-in-salary agreements 215-216, 221-225, 258-259
Refereeing...........52-54, 209-215, 341
Refinancing of home..........110-116, 399
Refund of state taxes..............147-150
Reimbursable expenses .21-22, 133, 227-230
Reimbursement for educational
   expenses......................235-236
Religious orders, members of 33
Religious organizations,
   contributions to 93-100
Rent................................57
Rental of home 12, 54, 73-77, 126-132, 167-168
Repairs..............57-61, 76, 121-123, 138, 142, 145
Research assistants **366-376**, 389-392
Research done at home 45-46, 48-52
Research expenses.............63-73, 133, 231, 249, 284-285, 308, 346, 377, 387-388, **393-398**
   special ruling for college
   teachers.....................393-394
Research grants 366-393
Research tax credit 397-398
Residents..........................376
Retired persons 308-309
Retirement home fees..................86
Retirement plans 253-264
   deferred compensation 225-226
   defined-benefit.............212-213, 350
   individual retirement
     account (IRA).........13, **190-209**, 215, 218-219, 254, 354
   Keogh plans...........**209-215**, 345, 354
   lump-sum distributions
     from 207-209, 212, 214-215, 218-219, 226, **253-255**, 313
   penalty for early distribution from.....255
   rollovers into IRAs..............207-209, 218-219, 254
   tax-sheltered annuities .13-14, 32, 208-209, **215-225**, 254, 258-262
   3-year rule........................13
Reviewing...........52-54, 209-215, 341
Ring, damage to 335-336
Rollovers into IRAs..............207-209, 218-219, 254
Roundoff...........................19

Index

Royalties........183-188, 209-215, 344-349, 363-364
  shifting to child or parent........348-349
Rulings, private IRS...............330-333
Sabbatical..............**288-301,** 381-382, 386-389, 394-395
  foreign......................361-363
  rental of home during..........126-132
Safe deposit box..................232-233
Safety equipment.....................38
Sales tax........................10, 146
Sampling technique.....35-36, 38, 135-136
Savings, investing your....162-182, 189-226
Savings bond........................184
Savings plans, tax-free.............189-226
Schedules
  A................11, 15, 43, 57, 59-61, 64, 66, 81, 84, 94, 110, 114, 118, 130-131, 133, 145, 147, 154, 173, 200, 227-231, 233, 251, 270, 275, 317-318, 340, 351, 396
  B....................20, 81, 173, 233
  C.........16, 22, 24, 43, 60-61, 64, 80, 133-134, 215, 230-231, 233, 251, 270, 275-276, 342, 345-346, 351-352, 394, 396
  D......................81, 164-166
  E....................127, 132, 345
  SE.....................342, 345
Scholarships.............11-12, 17, 251, 299-300, **366-376,** 389-392
School
  contributions to.................93-100
  expenses of attending..........86, 90-91, 104-105, **235-252,** 299-300, 317
School-related trips...............102-104
Scout trips.......................102-104
Second home.....................109-110
Self-employed persons........16, 24, 52-54, 209-215, 275-276, **341-359,** 397-398
Seminars, travel to....................284
Senior citizens...................308-309
SEP...............................211
Separate tax returns.......10, 23-24, **27-29**
Separated couples............108, **156-161**
Sheet music........................36
Shoes, orthopedic.....................86
Sick pay............................92
Silver coins, IRA purchase of......203-204
Simplified Employee Pension (SEP).....211
Single tax return.....................27
Slides.............................36
Small case tax court...............329-330
Smog, damage from................334

Snowstorm, damage from............334
Social lubrication test................269
Social security..........**262-264,** 342, 355
  checking your account..............264
  excess withheld....................15
  household workers.............107-108
  income tax on.................263-264
  number of spouse..................23
  number for child...............11, 264
  overpayment of....................15
  tax on grants......366, 368, 370, **390-392**
  tax on tax sheltered annuities.........221
Software......................39, 42
Sole proprietorship...................342
Spousal remainder trust............14, 185
Spouse
  paying for assistance...185-186, 353-356, 396
  retirement plan for......191-195, 197-198
Standard deduction....10, 15-16, **24-25,** 26, 31-32, 194, 351
Staples.............................36
State and local taxes 10, 23-24, **146-150,** 318, 322
  interest paid on....................79
  penalty paid on....................79
Stereo, deduction for child's........187-188
Stock investment plan..................186
Stock market crash...............165, 174
Stock options.......................399
Stockbroker..................164-165, 233
Stocks
  bought on margin..............13, 81-82
  interest paid on..................81-82
  transfer tax on.....................147
Storm, damage from.................334
Straight-line depreciation
  method.........................67-75
Students............20-21, 235-252, 272
  living expenses at summer job........296
  loans to.................12, 79-81, 114
Subleasing home....................132
Substitute teacher, payment to..........232
Summer camp.....................102-104
Summer jobs.......................272
Super-NOW accounts (see NOW accounts)
Supplemental retirement
  annuity (SRA).................219-220
Supplies....................11-12, 34, 36, 55, 231, 233, 249, 351, 395
Support, legal definition of..........17, 185
Support of child......17, 157-160, 184-185
Supreme Court unisex decision.........220
Swimming pools...............88-89, 91
Tape.............................36

Index

Tape recorders 39
Tax brackets....................... 9-10
Tax court, small case 329-330
Tax credits 15, 24
   child care 101-108, 354-355
   earned income............... 20-21, 376
   elderly 15
   foreign income tax 365
   household services...... 101-108, 354-355
   political contributions............... 11
   private school.................. 104-105
   research 397-398
   social security overwithholding 15
Tax deferral......... 189-226, 349-350, 352
Tax guides..................... 233, 351
Tax home 276-277, **288-301**, 360-362
Tax rates 9-10
Tax Reform Act of 1986.............. **9-14**
Tax returns, obtaining from IRS 19
Tax-sheltered annuities .. 13-14, 32, 208-209,
                  215-225, 254, 258-262
   withdrawals from....... 208-209, 216-220
Tax-sheltered plans 13-14, 32, **189-226**
Tax shelters 166-169, 183-188,
                    253, 350-353, 400
Tax tables 9-10, 15-16, 22
Taxable income 9-10, 15-16
Taxes
   automobile 144-145, 146, 318
   capital gains on home 121-126
   disability 147
   estate 125, 310-316
   estimated 273-274
   Federal......................... 318
   gift 125, 310-316
   income, state and local 146-150
   interest paid on 79
   payroll 147, 390-392
   property 10, 57-61, 109,
                  118-121, 127-132,
                  145, 146, 149
   recordation, real estate.......... 121, 318
   refunds.................... 19, 147-150
   sales....................... 10, 146
   state and local ...10, 23-24, **146-150**, 318,
                    322, 399
   transfer, bond 147
   transfer, real estate 121, 147,
                    153, 318
   transfer, stocks 147
   utility 318
Taxi fares................... 276-277, 279
Teaching assistants ...243, **366-376**, 389-392
Technical service specialists............ 344
Telephone 38-39, 55, 61, 232-233,
                  276, 279, 396

Temporary job 275, 288-301
   moving to.................... 154-155
   rental of home during 126-132
Tenancy-by-the-entireties............. 313
Tenancy-in-common 312-313
Tenancy, joint 124-126, 313
Termites, damage from 57, 335
Theft losses........................ 336
Thesis, expenses of writing ... 232, 242, 249
TIAA/CREF
   retirement system 261-262
   tax-sheltered annuities............ 218-220
Tips 276, 279-280
Title fees 121
Tolls............... 133, 137-138, 143-144
Towing expenses.................... 138
Trade or business interest.............. 80
Transfer taxes....... 121, 146-147, 153, 318
Transportation (see Travel)
Travel..................... **275-309**, 351
   airplane fares 276, 279
   automobile.......... 87, 90, 95, **133-145**,
                  276-277, 280, 302
   away from home overnight...11, 250-251,
                  275-283, 288-309
   between job locations 275, **283-288**
   charitable............ 23, 94-95, 317-318
   children's 102-104
   combining business
      with pleasure 302-307
   commuting 249-250, 275-277,
                  289-301
   convention....... 275-276, 279-280, 302
   deduction without receipts 280-282
   difference between travel
      and transportation 275
   education-related 242, 249-251,
                275, 299-300, 308
   extracurricular activities............. 232
   foreign 302-307
   funds from grants 377, 387-390
   home office 56
   hotel discounts for teachers....... 308-309
   leave of absence............... 288-301
   log 279-282
   medical-related......... 23, 84, 87-88, 90
   miscellaneous.................. 283-285
   moving 151-155
   per-diem rate 282-283
   recordkeeping 29, 279-283
   reimbursement 280, 283
   reporting requirements 279-283
   retired persons 308-309
   sabbatical 288-291
   senior citizens 308-309
   spouse, expenses of 278, 302

Index

taxi fares 276-277, 279
temporary job 275, 288-301
to do research 133, 284-285, 393-395
to libraries................133, 284-285
to look for a house 153
to look for a job 231, 301
to pick up visitors 284
to seminars 284
to stock brokers...................233
train fares 276
vacation 102-104, 302-308
Trees, damage to 334-335, 337-338
Trips taken by child...............102-104
Trucks, depreciation of..............63-73
Trusts 14, 184-185, 315-316, 349
Tuberculosis test....................232
Tuition 82, 90-91, 102, 104-105, 249
  free for faculty dependents...........236
  medical portion of.............86, 90-91
  remission plans 236
Tutoring 52-54, 209-215, 249, 341
Two-earner marriage
  deduction 10
Typewriter 39, 55, 63-73
Typing........................249, 341
Unallowable items.................317-318
Unearned income 183
  of dependent....................25-27
Unemployment compensation 376
Unemployment fund, contribution to 147
Underpayment penalty 79

Uniform Gifts to Minors Act...183-184, 315
Uniforms 38, 94
Union dues 232
Unisex mortality tables 220, 261-262
University, contributions to 93-100
Utilities...................55, 57-61, 127
  late payment fee 79
Utility taxes........................318
Vacation trips............102-104, 302-308
Vacuum cleaners.....................57
Vandalism, loss from 334
Vasectomies.........................86
Video recorders........34-36, 64-65, 69-73
Vitamin pills........................86
W-2 Form......................318, 389
W-4 Form......................271-274
W-4A Form.....................271-273
Wages 15, 389-390
Water (see Utilities)
Weight reduction program 91
Wheelchair......................86, 91
Whiskey 88
Wills 314-315
Withholding...................271-274
  on grants 370, 389-392
  state and local tax 147-149
Work-related expenses 227-233
Workers' Compensation................92
Yearend strategies 30-33
Zero bracket amount (see Standard
  deduction)